Opera in America

Opera in America

A Cultural History

John Dizikes

Yale University Press   New Haven and London

This publication has been supported by a grant from the National Endowment for the Humanities, an independent federal agency. The publishers also gratefully acknowledge the assistance of James M. Kemper, Jr., and Robert F. Kalman.

The publishers acknowledge permission to reprint excerpts from the following:

"Metalogue to *The Magic Flute,*" from W. H. Auden, *Collected Poems,* ed. Edward Mendelson. Copyright 1955 by W. H. Auden. Reprinted by permission of Random House, Inc., and Faber and Faber, Ltd.

"The Idea of Order at Key West," from *Collected Poems by Wallace Stevens.* Copyright 1936 by Wallace Stevens and renewed 1964 by Holly Stevens. Reprinted by permission of Alfred A. Knopf, Inc., and Faber and Faber, Ltd.

The Cradle Will Rock by Marc Blitzstein. Reprinted by permission of the Estate of Marc Blitzstein.

Designed by Sonia L. Scanlon.
Set in Berkeley type by Keystone Typesetting, Inc., Orwigsburg, Pennsylvania.
Printed in the United States of America by Vail-Ballou Press, Binghamton, New York.

Library of Congress Cataloging-in-Publication Data

Dizikes, John, 1932–
    Opera in America : a cultural history / John Dizikes.
      p. cm.
    Includes bibliographical references and index.
    ISBN 0-300-05496-3
    1. Opera—United States.   I. Title.
  ML1711.D6   1993
  782.1'0973—dc20   92-39971
                CIP
                MN
                Rev.

A catalogue record for this book is available from the British Library.
The paper in this book meets the guidelines for permanence and durability of the Committee on Production Guidelines for Book Longevity of the Council on Library Resources.

10 9 8 7 6 5 4 3 2 1

For Helen and Peter

Now, what is music? This question occupied me for hours before I fell asleep last night. Music is a strange thing. I would almost say it is a miracle. For it stands halfway between thought and phenomenon, between spirit and matter, a sort of nebulous mediator, like and unlike each of the things it mediates, spirit that requires manifestation in time and matter that can do without space.

We do not know what music is.

—*Heinrich Heine,* **Letters on the French Stage**

Contents

Preface

This book must sing for itself. Although "I think of it as it should have been, with its prolixities docked, its dullnesses enlivened, its fads eliminated, its truths multiplied," no words of mine, here, can alter its limitations or conceal its imperfections. Even so, a brief explanation may avoid misunderstandings about what I have tried, and not tried, to do. My subject is the American cultural environment into which English and European opera came and within which Americans composed operas of their own. My definition of opera is that of its Italian originators, drama by means of music, a broader one than what is usually associated with the terms *opera* and *grand opera,* allowing me to include operetta, the musical, and musical comedy in my story. My original subtitle, abandoned for the brevity and familiarity of the term *cultural history,* perhaps gave a better idea of my emphasis: "Scenes and Stories, People and Places."

There is no general American operatic history, though there are many excellent books on many aspects of it. My attempt at such a general history is written for literate common readers, not for specialists. Its scope is national and its narrative stretches in time from the early eighteenth century (and earlier) to recent times. It includes a great deal about audiences and their response to what they heard and saw onstage, about the buildings in which they responded, and about the people who have sung, conducted, performed, and produced opera. I have written a narrative, not an encyclopedia.

Long as my story is, I hope readers will understand it as an essay, a first provisional effort. I touch on most of the major places, events, people, and institutions in American operatic history, but much of importance is left out. I welcome corrections, additions, revisions, suggestions for improvement, especially about touring companies and small-town opera. When *their* stories are better known, we will approach a truly national history. Some people think any general history an impossibility. Obviously I disagree, believing that there are no impossible subjects, only inadequate historians.

N o w , to the pleasantest part of my work—thanking the many people who have helped me, an indebtedness stretching over half a century, beginning with my mother, who took me to hear the San Carlo Opera Company; with the Saturday afternoon Metropolitan Opera radio broadcasts; and with my teachers Mary Anton Thurman and David Dollinger. The superb staff of the McHenry Library, University of California at Santa Cruz, has been ever resourceful. Without the assistance of the Interlibrary Loan Department, past and present, headed by Joan Hodgson, Betty Rentz, Alice Morrow, and Judy Steen, this book could not have been written. Janet Pumphrey, of the Microfilm Department, assisted greatly, as did the Photography Laboratory and the typists in the Word Processing Center, Judy Burton, Rebecca Fuson, Rebekah Levy, Peg McCray, Zoe Sodja, Heidi Swillinger, Jodi Tannheimer, Cheryl Van de Veer, Valerie Wells. But, of course, I owe most of all to the thousands of musicians who have edified and entertained me over the years.

Many institutions, and the people who give them life and direction (though I cannot acknowledge them individually), have helped: the Bancroft Library and the Music Library of the University of California at Berkeley; the Cambridge University Library; the Center for Cuban Studies of New York City; the Central City Opera; the Civic Library of Trieste, Italy; the Dallas Opera; the Department of the Interior Museum, Washington, D.C.; the Harvard Theatre Collection; the Historic New Orleans Collection; the Historical Society of Pennsylvania; the Houston Grand Opera; Indiana University School of Music; the Library and Museum of the Performing Arts of the New York Public Library at Lincoln Center; the Metropolitan Opera Guild; New York University Archives; Opera Theater of St. Louis; the Philadelphia Free Library; the San Francisco Opera; the San Francisco Performing Arts Library and Museum; the Santa Cruz Opera Society; the Santa Fe Opera; the Seattle Opera; the Performing Arts Center of the State University of New York at Purchase. The fifty state historical societies all responded to my request for information about local opera houses. And I am grateful to the University of California at Santa Cruz for assistance with photocopying, translating, and travel.

In Santa Cruz and elsewhere I have been the beneficiary of friends and colleagues: Rex Beckham, Gabriel and Arlette Berns, Sara Boutelle, Michael Cowan, John de Lancie, Dean and Marilyn Dizikes, Miriam Ellis, Keith Hardman, Dallett Hemphill, Irene Herrmann, Happy Hunter, Pamela Lawson, Tom Lehrer, Hervé Le Mansec, Todd and Louise Newberry, Dick Painter, Alan Ritch, Esther K. Schultz, Buchanan Sharp, Page and Eloise Smith, Byron and Lee Stookey, John Stookey, Mary Takayanagi, Marion Taylor, Judy Yung. A few words of thanks are little enough to give in return for the support of many students over many years, especially those of Cowell College, and of my colleagues in American studies and history.

I am particularly indebted to Jonathan Beecher and Richard Bienvenu, who read part of my manuscript at any early stage and encouraged me to continue; and to Helen and Christopher Morris and Forrest Robinson who later read all of it with meticulous care and heartening approval. Robert Durling translated Lorenzo Da Ponte's unpublished story of the Montresor company. Yale University Press blessed me doubly, with two editors, Edward Tripp and Harry Haskell. Sadly, three friends didn't live to see this book: Bruce Anderson and David Marlowe, who both delighted in opera; and Ann Thimann, whose love and knowledge of music remain a perpetual inspiration. Margaret Sowers has been a virtually full-time assistant, as indefatigable as generous. And behind it all, my wife, endlessly diverting, who has shown me what it is to make beautiful things. My fondest hopes for this book will be realized if it provokes others to do a better job than I have been able to do, inspires readers to support opera in the present, and pleases the two individuals to whom it is dedicated.

a c t   o n e

Origins, 1735–1836

An opera! Fine thing! As usual it will be a semi-serious play, a long, melancholy, boring, poetic rigmarole. In the worst taste! What a corrupt age!

—*Dr. Bartolo in* **The Barber of Seville**

The entire pleasure of music consists in creating illusions, and common-sense rationality is the greatest enemy of musical appreciation.

—*Stendhal*

c h a p t e r   o n e

The Garcías at the Park

At last. Twenty minutes late, the orchestra launched into the overture. Then the curtain rose and the audience found itself transported to a square in Seville. As the music surged and sighed along, in came Fiorello, with his lantern, followed by Count Almaviva, with his musicians, the appearance of each being greeted by bursts of applause. Facing the balcony of Dr. Bartolo's house, Almaviva began his serenade:

> In the smiling sky
> The lovely dawn was breaking . . . .

But what the audience actually heard was:

> Ecco, ridente in cielo
> Spunta la bella aurora . . . .

For a detached observer nothing was perhaps more startling than this: that an audience was gathered to spend three and a half hours listening to songs only the merest handful would understand.

In a few moments Figaro would appear to sing uproariously about the tribulations of a barber's life, then Rosina would step out on the balcony to sing of her unknown lover, and then. . . . But before we reach the conclusion of this performance of Rossini's *The Barber of Seville,* let's pause to find out more about the singers who were performing it, and what brought them to the Park Theatre, and to New York City, on Tuesday night, November 29, 1825.

They were (mostly) the García family. Its head, Manuel—García senior, as Americans came to call him—was born in Seville on January 21, 1775. Revealing musical ability as a boy, he became a chorister in the cathedral school and embarked on a musical career. By the end of the century he had established himself throughout Spain as a singer and composer. Ambitious for European musical fame, García went to Paris in 1807, where he made his debut in Italian opera, and to Naples in 1811. There, his clear tenor voice attracted the attention of Gioachino Rossini, who wrote for him the roles of Leicester in *Elizabeth, Queen of England* (*Elisabetta, Regina d'Inghilterra,* 1815) and of Almaviva in *The Barber of Seville* (*Il Barbiere di Siviglia,* 1816). His fame as a singer rested on his mastery of florid music. A contemporary observer's description of his singing—"The progress of the melody would sometimes be rendered scarcely perceptible through the dust of Signor Garcia's gambols"—reflected the contemporary taste for ornate extravagance. His acting was equally admired. "I love the Andalusian frenzy of the man," a French singer said. "He puts life into everything."[1] García went to London in 1818, singing Rossinian roles with great success then and in 1819 and 1823. Wherever he lived and sang, he composed operas, seventeen in Spanish, eighteen in Italian, eight in French.

Manuel's second wife, Joaquina, was an accomplished singer who devoted most of her time to raising three children. Manuel junior, born in 1805, whose high baritone voice matured slowly, had not yet sung opera in public when the family came to New York. His precocious sister, Maria Felicia, by contrast, had already made her operatic debut, age seventeen, in London in 1825, just before sailing for America. The third child, Pauline, also destined for a musical career, was still a baby.

Naturally, Manuel García took an intense interest in the musical education of his children, showing unusual restraint in not pushing the development of their voices beyond what was sensible. Although he was an exacting disciplinarian, Pauline insisted that he treated her with "angelic kindness." Only once did he strike her, in exasperation because she wouldn't concentrate on a piano piece he had given her to practice, and then she remembered most vividly his anguished reproach: "You should have spared both of us—yourself the physical pain of receiving a cuff, and me the moral pain of giving you one." Maria was the center of conflict. The father's unyielding exactions and the daughter's obdurate will produced fireworks. But according to Pauline, Maria once said: "If father had not been so severe with me, I would never have accomplished anything. I was always lazy and indolent."[2]

W h a t brought the Garcías and their company to New York in the fall of 1825? At fifty, García senior's singing career was almost over. America would be an excellent place to test and refine the talents of the two older children. Above all, it offered the hope of making a lot of money. Even so, given the dangers and difficulties of the month-long Atlantic crossing, the simple conditions of performance, and the uncertainty of their reception, the audacity of the Garcías' undertaking can hardly be exaggerated. Culturally, America seemed to Europeans the other side of the moon. In Stendhal's *The Charterhouse of Parma* (1838), Fabrizio del Dongo, the hero, threatens to go to New York and become an American citizen. "What a mistake that would be," the Duchess of Sanseverina tells him; Americans know only "the cult of the god Dollar." She contemptuously dismisses life in the United States, a life "without smartness, without music, without love affairs." And, she adds with crushing finality, "they have no opera!"[3]

On the American side, the Garcías' journey was the result of the efforts of three men. Lorenzo Da Ponte, Mozart's erstwhile librettist, now living in New York, used London friends to persuade García that he would make his fortune in the United States. Stephen Price, manager of the Park Theatre in New York and at one time manager of London's Drury Lane Theatre, worked out the performance arrangements. Dominick Lynch, one of those opera-mad characters who will dot these pages, provided financial guarantees.

There was no publicity campaign to drum up interest in the García visit, only an announcement by the Park Theatre that a "double-band" would be added later in the year to its regular season of opera in English. Knowledge of the García company's

Maria García as Desdemona and Manuel García as Othello in Rossini's Otello. *The portrait of Maria is by W. Sharp, that of Manuel by an anonymous French lithographer. From George C. D. Odell,* Annals of the New York Stage *(New York, 1927–49), vol. 3.*

arrival on November 7 spread by word of mouth in a town which, for all its aspiration to be regarded as the metropolis of North America, still seemed smaller than its population of 150,000. In 1825 the Battery was a genteel promenade. Greenwich and Bleecker streets were the center of wealthy residences. Beyond 14th Street there were only farms and a straggle of houses. Washington Square was a potter's field, Union Square a sandhill. Far to the north was the country hamlet of Harlem.

John W. Francis, medical doctor, historian, opera enthusiast, but typical of his time and place in assuming that European musicians were likely to be dissolute and lazy, met the Garcías and was reassured by their habits and energy. "The troupe had not crossed the Atlantic twenty-four hours ere they were at their notes and their instruments." They lived quietly, ate simply, drank moderately. "A taste of claret, a glass of lemonade, sugar water, were all the drinks tolerated."[4] Besides the Garcías, the company included Félix Angrisani, a once well known basso—he had sung in the first performance of Mozart's *The Magic Flute* (*Die Zauberflöte*) in 1791—who had come out of retirement for this adventure; Paulo Rosich, who specialized in buffo roles and also wrote music and librettos; Madame Barbieri, a young, inexperienced soprano; and Giovanni Crivelli, a young tenor, son of a leading Neapolitan singer. Hardly some of "the first artists of Europe," as a New York newspaper later described them. The young were untested, the experienced well past their prime.

The Garcías had a great deal to do in a very short time. On November 17 local newspapers announced that *Il Barbiere di Siviglia* was in rehearsal and would be given soon, though no specific date was set. In so small an ensemble, singers often had to double their roles. Members of the company helped to build and paint scenery. Crivelli drilled the chorus, most of whom were recruited from immigrant English factory workers who had sung in church choirs and could read music. The company had brought some costumes with them; others had to be made on the spot, with members of the chorus doing the sewing.

An orchestra had to be assembled. Instruments of high quality had been produced in America for years. But bassoons, trumpets, and kettledrums were hardly represented in American orchestras, and it is uncertain if there was an oboist in all North America. Scores were difficult to procure. García brought most of what he needed. The orchestra was local, with a nucleus from the recently formed Philharmonic Society. Denis Etienne conducted from the piano.

The general quality of orchestral performance in the early 1800s is difficult to establish with confidence. Even the orchestras in the leading Italian opera houses left a good deal to be desired, if we can trust the scathing descriptions by Berlioz, Mendelssohn, and Stendhal. The resident orchestra at the Park Theatre, which played regularly in English opera and during the interludes in dramatic productions, was thought the best in the city. Yet Joe Cowell, a visiting English actor of wide experience, reported that one night the conductor, apparently under the influence of drink, lost his balance and fell into the orchestra, carrying with him the second violin, his stool, and a music stand, to the amusement of the audience, which seemingly took such things for granted. "This efficient conductor with six or eight other professors, form a very wretched orchestra," Cowell wrote, but "even so many, and of such a quality, could only be obtained at a very high price." A visiting German musician reported that in a performance he heard there were serious breakdowns in execution, but "the players think 'this is only of passing importance,' provided the music rattles away again afterwards."[5]

The heart of the matter, for Manuel García, was that, whether or not American orchestral players were equal to the demands previously put to them, Rossini's music was new and daring and difficult, called for a larger orchestra and presented it with formidable demands. Rattling away would certainly not do. Additional players were recruited, making twenty-four in all: seven violins, two violas, three cellos, two basses, two flutes, two clarinets, one bassoon, two horns, two trumpets, drums. Monsieur Etienne rehearsed them for five or more hours a day. Finally, they were ready.

S o we return to the Park Theatre, to that square in Seville, and to Rosina, leaning out of the balcony, peering at the audience. What kind of an audience was it? Well-to-do, certainly: a box cost $2.00, up from the usual $1.50 or $1.00; a seat in the pit was $1.00, 25¢ for the gallery. There were "numerous and elegantly dressed" women, "decked in native curls, or embellished with wreaths of flowers, or tasteful turbans." The curtain time was the fashionable European 8 o'clock rather than the conventional New York 7 or 7:30. At the same time it was an uncertain and apprehensive audience, encountering something exotic and new. People wrote to newspapers to inquire "how they should dress for the opera 'in the European manner' and what was the correct

The Park Theatre attracted a cross-section of New York society. This audience is watching a performance of the farce Monsieur Tonson *in 1822. Note the courtesans in the upper balcony. Watercolor by John Searle. New-York Historical Society.*

etiquette during performances." And so that night began a new chapter in American social history, a chapter sometimes amusing, often dismaying, frequently crass.

The Park Theatre held over two thousand people and was well filled with a fair representation of the social classes of the city. In the gallery and the two upper tiers were the artisans and shopkeepers who set the bourgeois tone of the town, in the pit a contingent of European immigrants. In the lower tier of boxes were some of the town's leading citizens, among them James Kent, jurist and author of famous commentaries on the federal constitution that earned him the honorary title of "Chancellor." There were prosperous city merchants, Ward, Prime and Company being represented by the Ward family, father and mother, children Julia and Sam. There were newer entrepreneurs, outsiders pushing their way forward, like James Gordon Bennett, Sr., the journalist. There was even a king, or an ex-king (of Spain), Joseph Bonaparte, Napoleon Bonaparte's brother, living in exile in the wilds of New Jersey. The arts and letters were represented too. Seated next to Joseph Bonaparte was the poet and essayist Fitz-Greene Halleck, and next to him James Fenimore Cooper, whose novel *The Last of the Mohicans* was to be published within a week.

But now Rosina approached the footlights with exquisite grace to sing the most familiar song from the opera, "A voice heard a little while ago" ("Una voce poco fa"). Familiar to some in the audience from piano and band performances, it was greeted with "the most unbounded applause" and was encored. And so the story moved on its boisterous, comic way. Well after 11:30, when the curtain finally fell, witnesses recalled the shouts of "Bravo," the French and Italian gentlemen in the pit "almost melted into tears," the lobby ringing with enthusiasm, the city "reverberating with acclamation."[6]

' ' I n what language shall we speak of an entertainment so novel in this country?" asked one writer after the Garcías' appearance.[7] American theater and music criticism was in its infancy. There were no regular reviews or reviewers. Reporters, writing anonymously or sometimes using pseudonyms, covered special events, their notices mixed in the stream of daily news of commerce, crime, politics, foreign affairs. Most papers carried a theater column listing forthcoming performances, and occasionally a letter to the editor would take issue with a previous writer or amplify a report. Many performances were never mentioned at all and the monthly or quarterly journals, which sometimes had longer articles, often appeared weeks or months after the event. Theatrical and musical reports were essentially part of the news of the day. They were social in their emphasis and point of view, as much about the audience as about the performance.

These tentative efforts at operatic criticism were dominated by a tone of wonder and puzzlement. So pervasive was the literal, prosaic spirit of American culture that many observers were surprised to find that music drama could generate such powerful emotions. "Until [opera] is seen it will never be believed that a play can be conducted in recitative or singing and yet appear nearly as natural as the ordinary drama." The singers were unexpectedly convincing, even though their acting style "differs widely from any to which we have been accustomed." Twenty years later Walt

Whitman struggled to describe the power of an art in which the story was told through singing.

> You listen to this music, and the songs, and choruses—all of the highest range of composition known to the world of melody. It is novel, of course, being far, very far different from what you were used to, the church choir, or the songs and playing on the piano, or the songs, or any performance of the Ethiopian minstrels. A new world—a liquid world—rushes like a torrent through you. If you have the true musical feeling in you, from this night you date a new era in your development, and, for the first time, receive your ideas of what the divine art of music really is.

One aspect of this new operatic art was reassuring. There was in the actors' style "a remarkable chasteness and propriety; never violating good taste and exceeding the strictest bounds of female decorum."[8] Yankee moral anxieties about the theater could be put to rest, although they would arise again in the future.

Journalists also commented on the singers' technical skill and personality. They applauded Angrisani for his acting, despite his declining vocal powers. Rosich, as Don Basilio, was in such bad voice that his chief aria was simply omitted. Manuel García junior disappointed as Figaro, but his father was a forceful Almaviva, even if his "slightly overwrought" gestures distressed some. The evening belonged to Maria as Rosina, "the magnet who attracted all eyes and won all hearts." Her contralto voice poured forth "a rich stream of over-flowing and almost over-powering melody." Yet such was her "science and skill" that she could "touch any two notes however distinct, in rapid succession, either from low to high or high to low without one false note." Her person, her movements, her manner were enchanting. "About middle height, with luxuriously formed chest and shoulders; her face is beautiful, her eyes dark, arch and expressive, and a playful smile is almost constantly the companion of her lips." All this at seventeen years of age! Samuel Ward fifty years later recalled "the shiver of delight" that swept over him when Maria sang "Una voce poco fa." The irascible James Gordon Bennett remembered it too: "I never applaud or make noise at theaters. I leave that for loafers and block-head critics to perpetrate; but at that moment I could hardly resist the contagion." For both, Maria's performance was a "divine revelation of what music might be."[9]

Not everyone agreed. No sooner had Almaviva launched into his first-act serenade than Chancellor Kent rose to his feet, shouted, "It's an insult to human nature," and strode out of the theater.[10] Here was a premonitory event: the confrontation between the eighteenth and nineteenth centuries, between the traditional and the modern. We will encounter it over and over again in the pages that follow.

T h e r e were several more performances of *Il Barbiere*. The enthusiasm for Maria increased. "The least glimpse of her is greeted with repeated cheerings from box, pit and gallery." However, even Rossini's delightful music and the presence of "the Signorina" couldn't justify going on with only one opera. Some novelty was required. In the middle of December the Garcías offered their second production, *The Cunning Lover* (*L'Amante astuto*), a family affair: music by García senior, sung by the four

Garcías, along with Rosich, who wrote the libretto. It failed. Repeated once and then dropped, its music was flat after Rossinian champagne.[11]

On December 31 the company presented the "Grand Serious Opera" of Rossini's *Tancredi.* García doubted that a serious subject would please New Yorkers, but a good house dispelled some of his misgivings and Maria disposed of the rest. That evening, by the animated intelligence of her conception of the title role and by the boldness of her dramatization, Maria changed from being a "youthful favorite," full of high spirits and charm, to a singing actress to be measured against "the Pastas and Catalanis of Europe." When in the first act Maria launched into "So many emotions, so much pain" ("Di tanti palpiti, di tante pene"), the aria which proved to be Rossini's passport to fame, "sung by duchess and dishwasher, whistled and hummed to distraction all over the Continent," New Yorkers were in the presence of something marvelous.[12]

In February 1826 there was another "long-looked for" Rossini opera, *Otello.* "Surpassing in effect and cost any of the previous operas of the company," the production was a great success. García senior had scored his greatest triumph in Europe as the Moor of Venice; the role suited his vehement style of acting and singing. Edmund Kean, the great English Shakespearian actor, newly arrived in New York and performing *Othello* on alternate nights at the Park, was in the audience for the opera's first performance and came backstage to congratulate the elder García. As Desdemona, Maria induced an ecstatic response. "The most fastidious criticism would say that she was faultless, and a generous admirer might be permitted to pronounce that she was almost perfection." *Otello* combined passion and pathos in a way Americans had rarely experienced in the theater.[13] In the dawn of American romanticism, in the countryside soon to be made famous by the Hudson River painters, this music drama touched deep feelings of the terrible and the sublime.

P e o p l e came from other cities to see and hear the Garcías. There was talk of the company going on tour to Boston and Philadelphia, and some opera lovers, in the early stages of their enthusiasm, proposed building an opera house in New York if the Garcías agreed to stay permanently. During the severe New York winter, however, the company often played to many empty seats. To stimulate interest they put on four more operas. Neither *Giulietta e Romeo* by Niccolò Zingarelli (1752–1837) nor García's own *The Daughter of Song (La Figlia dell'aria)* drew well. So the company went back to the seemingly inexhaustible Rossinian well for *Cinderella (La Cenerentola)* and *The Turk in Italy (Il Turco in Italia)*; but by then the limits of New York's appetite for Rossini had been reached.[14] A number of performances were canceled. Influenza took its toll of singers and audiences. On July 4 the deaths of John Adams and Thomas Jefferson closed the Park Theatre. The season sputtered into the scorching summer. The Garcías began to organize their departure. But their visit had a memorable finale.

A newspaper notice on May 23 announced it matter-of-factly: "This evening for the first time in America, there will be performed the semi-serious Italian opera of *Il Don Giovanni.*" Thirty-nine years had passed since its world premiere. It had taken thirty years for *Don Giovanni* to get to London. Could the Garcías bring it off? The requirement for so many first-rate vocalists would cruelly show up the limitations of the company. Nevertheless, influential citizens urged García to make the effort. García senior would be the Don; Maria, Zerlina; Madame García, Donna Elvira; Madame Barbieri, Donna Anna. Thereafter casting problems multiplied. Angrisani would double as the Commendatore and Masetto. García junior would sing Leporello, though the role was unsuited to his voice. To sing Don Ottavio, a local tenor named Milon was pressed into service, but failed utterly. At the end of the first act the performance threatened to fall to pieces. "Manuel Garcia, with sword in hand, rushed to the footlights, stopped the performance, and ordered the conductor to recommence the finale."[15] With this second effort the act, and eventually the entire opera, was brought to a more or less harmonious close.

Mozart opera in America, at last. Contemporaries, of course, didn't think of it as a momentous event. There don't seem to have been any newspaper reports of the performance. The first-night audience, while appreciative of its good fortune, didn't bother much with what history would (or wouldn't) say and instead delighted in the ravishing music. A letter signed by "One of Many," addressed to García senior, appeared in a newspaper, pleading for another performance of "this beautiful opera, their favorite." García yielded. *Don Giovanni* was given nine more times.[16]

The season ended as it began, with *Il Barbiere di Siviglia.* In nine months the company had given seventy-nine performances of nine different operas. Gross receipts were $56,685, ranging from $1,962 on the best night to $25 on the worst; not the golden harvest Manuel García had dreamed of, but not a disaster either. The family had made enough money to stake them to another audacious adventure. They would go next to Mexico City for a season of opera, all but the Signorina.

T h e n and later people disagreed about the significance of the Garcías' visit. For some, New Yorkers' enthusiastic reception of Italian opera was a sufficient indication of success. Others argued that the season should be considered a failure, as it had not led to the immediate establishment of a permanent opera company. The debate had political implications, in terms of class and geography, though it was not argued in explicitly political terms. If opera was the most aristocratic of the arts, then its success or failure in America would depend on whether American society developed in a more or less democratic way. A South Carolina writer insisted that opera must inevitably fail in New York (and in other northern cities) because urban values were commercial, not the traditional values associated with land. New York, in this view, had "accomplished as much as could have been expected," since northern culture was "in closer connection with the counting house" than with enduring values. What was really needed everywhere was an American aristocracy, but that would require "the lapse of centuries."[17]

The counterview was that opera had definitely found a home in America and that the people of the nation would "never hereafter dispense with it." The mixed democratic-commercial nature of urban society—by implication, the model of the future social order of the nation as a whole—would permit opera to free itself of aristocratic associations and to become a popular entertainment. This "strange art" and its "stranger artists" would become "fashionable," if fashionable was understood in a new way: the result of commercial desires. One of the journals reported a story which exemplified the idea of bourgeois fashion. A merchant had imported some beautiful silk shawls which didn't sell, despite vigorous advertising. "Then Signor Garcia and the Italian Company set themselves down among us and began una voce-ing and poco fa-ing until everyone's head was turned." The next day the merchant advertised "opera cloaks, a brand new importation" and sold his entire stock in a few hours.[18]

Would bourgeois democratic America adopt opera by seeking to turn it into an exclusive privilege, as the European aristocracy had done? Or would opera genuinely become an art form for the common man and woman? Manuel García was not one to reflect on such philosophical questions. He most likely thought in more personal terms, of himself as a pathfinder, an operatic Columbus, bringing "a new experience, an unimagined delight" from the Old World to the New. Less grandly, we might think of him as Almaviva in the first scene of *Il Barbiere,* singing of the dawn that drives away the gloom of night, a dawn heralding the end of the long American night without opera.

England and Italy

But wait. The story of Manuel García as an operatic Columbus is a tall tale. There had been opera in North America before the Garcías, before the Park Theatre, before the United States existed at all. That opera was English opera, composed by English men, sung in English by English women and men. In the eighteenth century North America was an English operatic colony. Therefore, if we're to do justice to the history of opera in America, we must recover the story of English opera. Even that, however, is only half of a still larger story. At the very time that North America was becoming an English operatic colony, England was becoming an Italian one. What happened in England, interesting as a premonition of what would occur in America after the Garcías, is most significant because it introduces into our story the development that shaped operatic history everywhere—cultural nationalism.

O p e r a is one of the most successful reform movements in European history. The idea of staged drama unfolding in integrally combined words and music was conceived in Florence about 1600, the achievement of two groups of Florentine intellectuals, one circle or group (*camerata*) centered around Giovanni di Bardi, Vincenzo Galilei, and Giulio Caccini, and another around Jacopo Corsi and Jacopo Peri. Both groups were intrigued by classical Greek drama, convinced that music had played an important role in it. Both wished to use Greek drama as a model for reforming and re-fashioning a purer kind of contemporary drama. The problem was that no one knew, or could ever know, just how the Greeks had combined words, music, and dance, since only the words had survived. The fruit of three decades of talk and experimentation was the first lyric drama, Peri's *Daphne* (*La Dafne*) of 1597. But *La Dafne* and its successors were not the re-creation of an old form. They were a new one.

Words and music. What combination of these would most effectively tell a dramatic story? What was the proper balance between them? The Florentine answer to these questions was an experiment, not a formula, a reform forever in a state of revision. However, certain primary characteristics were firmly established. The story was a verse play, a little book (*libretto*), an original work or an adaptation by a poet of some earlier story or legend, to which a composer set music. Opera was a collaboration between writer and composer. But this was not a story with incidental music. The drama would be *entirely* sung. The singing took two forms: songs (*arias*), which allowed characters in the story to express personal emotions and states of mind; and choruses, which made possible outside comment on the action. Singing was accompanied by an orchestra, which enriched the drama without obscuring the words, all this heightened dramatically by dance, costume, and scenery.

Here a difficulty arose. The forward movement of the story often required the swiftness of dialogue or comment, whether for ordinary statements or for moments of passionate significance, both of which cried out for a kind of expression not possible with the slower rhythmical intricacies of songs and choruses. The Florentine originators solved this difficulty by evolving sung recitation (*recitativo*). The singer's voice floated on top of an accompanying musical base supplied by a single instrument or group of instruments, in such a way that every word could be heard and understood. In this kind of sung speech, words conveyed their semantic meanings and their sonorous ones simultaneously. This remarkable achievement lies at the heart of the idea of opera, and it was, and remains, the feature people find most odd. "Recitative is not nature; it is a convention for suggesting nature by unnatural contrivance."[1]

A new and audacious art form, opera spread with astonishing speed throughout the Italian states, and beyond. It was greeted with enthusiasm, and more; the combination of words, action, and music moved audiences to tears. What so affected audiences was first known as *dramma per musica,* drama through (by means of) music, a broad and accurate description of almost infinite possibilities, any kind of drama, any kind of music. However, in time the name evolved in a surprising way. These dramas by means of music were thought of in the general sense of a work or body of work produced as the result of laborious effort. The Italian word for such a work was *opus,* plural *opera.* It was commonly applied at the time to literature and to painting. (We continue in our day to use the term *work of art.*) However, as the seventeenth century wore on, so exciting was this new art and so great its prestige that the word *opera* came to be associated outside Italy with one kind of artwork, Italian music drama. The individual works came to be called operas. The triumph of the name paralleled the triumph of the art, one of Italy's most noteworthy conquests, more enduring than military glory. And this was important not as a curiosity of terminology but because people associated the art form with its Italian version. For two centuries, opera meant Italian opera.

T h e birth of opera coincided with a Golden Age of English music. No one thought the English were in any way less musical than other Europeans. English composers were welcomed everywhere on the Continent. The English court patronized music and foreign musicians were welcome at it. Much of this music was theater music, as a prelude to performance, accompanying stage action, between the acts of plays, songs within plays. The English evolved a form in which music and drama were combined, the masque, mythological and classical stories in verse, with an emphasis on dance, with songs and speeches intermixed, and with rich costuming and lavish scenic effects. An orchestra and sometimes a choir played and sang, and some of the greatest poets, among them Ben Jonson and John Milton, wrote verse for masques. Despite these similarities, the masque was not opera. The verse text was not sung throughout; it was episodic and not shaped as a dramatic whole.

This great age of English musical history came to an end in the middle of the seventeenth century. The English Civil War (1642–1651) cut across it and marked its end, though whether the war caused its termination or only coincided with it is difficult to say. (The effect of war on opera will concern us several times in our story.) In any event, theaters in England were closed in 1642 and the lot of theatrical musicians became a precarious one. The establishment of the Puritan Commonwealth (1649–1660) has frequently been cited as more devastating for art than the war, but this too is more complex than it seems. The Puritans were not opposed to music and were often very musical people. They disapproved of liturgical music because they disapproved of the liturgy; and though they enjoyed certain kinds of music, they loathed the immorality they identified with theatrical life; so a theatrical musical form like opera was unacceptable on moral grounds.

Nevertheless, certain elements of operatic music entered English musical culture in these years. As early as 1617 the composer Nicholas Lanier introduced recitative into the English masque, and though English composers seem to have felt some awkwardness in handling recitative, they were familiar with it. The lament "Ah! Let me die" ("Lasciatemi morire") from the opera *Arianna* (1608) by the first great master of opera, Claudio Monteverdi (1567–1643), was widely performed throughout Europe and had been set to English words. English composers and poets frequently discussed whether the English language could be set to music as well as Italian, and how an English recitative, "recitative musick" or "recitative song," could be achieved. By the 1630s the recitative style was well enough known for audiences to appreciate a "Recitative Burlesque" that made fun of it. And though there seems to have been a deep general cultural dislike of recitative, it continued to be slowly assimilated. During the Commonwealth, Sir William Davenant, the poet laureate, produced the first English opera, *The Siege of Rhodes,* privately performed in 1656, with music by five different composers. It was sung throughout, "being Recitative, and therefore unpractis'd here; though of great reputation amongst other Nations, the very attempt of it is an obligation to our own."[2] The composition of English opera by English composers, along Italian lines, proceeded without any familiarity with the original source. No Italian opera had yet been seen or heard in England. And when opera came, it was French and not Italian opera which crossed the Channel. Thus artistic nationalism, which played a pivotal role in the subsequent history of opera in Europe and in the United States, bursts into our story.

In Paris a clash of nationalities became a clash of cultures and was fought out in political terms. The central figure was the Italian Giulio Mazarini, minister to French kings. As Cardinal Jules Mazarin, he was regent for the boy-king Louis XIV. For political purposes—to strengthen the power of the monarchy by distracting the nobility—Mazarin imported Italian opera. This provoked a powerful anti-Italian, anti-Mazarin reaction, also politically inspired, emphasizing Mazarin's extravagance and opera's foreignness. "Avoid these excesses," said Boileau. "Leave to Italy all this false brilliance and foolish glitter."[3] Eventually, after Mazarin's death in 1661, Louis XIV banished Italian musicians from France and a nationalistic counterreformation began.

The cry was for opera, in French, based on French esthetic principles. And behold! Jean-Baptiste Lully appeared, the first in a long line of cosmopolitan operatic composers. The founder of French opera, born Giacomo Lulli in Florence in 1632, was the son of an Italian miller. At age fourteen he went to France as a boy-page in a nobleman's retinue, working for a time as a cook's boy in the royal kitchens. His musical precocity attracted attention. By his early twenties he was an important figure in the court's music; by thirty he had been granted French nationality and changed the spelling of his name.

Aware of the royal desire for a national opera, Lully, who initially didn't think the French language adaptable to opera, jumped on the bandwagon. He gained invaluable theatrical experience collaborating with Molière in composing comic ballets, and he found an ideal librettist, Philippe Quinault. He discerned that in the France of his day opera must serve as a means of glorifying the court. "Flattery was an essential ingredient; grandeur was a necessary condition." Lully understood also that he must base French opera on the literary culture of his time; the drama of Racine, Corneille, Molière, must aim for neoclassic qualities of balance, clarity, and stateliness. He perfected a kind of musical declamation that suited contemporary taste because it fitted the language perfectly. His recitative was lengthy; many found it monotonous. Lully's operas struck foreigners as too formal, stiff; yet they moved his French audiences by the directness of their feeling. "There are some spots in the music which have already made me cry," Madame de Sevigné said, and added: "I am not the only one who cannot withhold tears." Lully's operas marked the victory of "our poetry and our music over a foreign language, poetry, and music,"[4] and by 1687, when he died, they had been performed in Brussels, Amsterdam, Hamburg, and even Rome. The Italian monopoly was broken.

L u l l y ' s operas had also been performed in London, without success. Anti-French feeling in the last part of the century may have played a role in their failure, just as patriotic feeling may have nourished the emergence of two different kinds of English opera in these years. One kind was represented by Matthew Locke (1630–1677), who composed in a mixed operatic style, part drama, part music, with songs and choruses but with spoken dialogue in place of sung recitative. "Drammatick opera," Locke called his work. An example of the other kind was *Venus and Adonis* (1682), the only work for the stage by John Blow (1649–1708). Entirely sung, its "passages of recitative . . . have a boldness and brilliance that show how supple and sensitive the English language could be in the hands of a master composer."[5]

Henry Purcell (1659–1695), the towering genius whose appearance seemed as providential for English opera as Lully's had for French opera, worked in both forms. *Dido and Aeneas,* about 1690, is the first unquestioned English operatic masterpiece, an opera as English in spirit as it is in language, sung throughout, with moving recitative. The other Purcell operas, *King Arthur, The Prophetess, The Faery Queen,* belonged to the mixed form Locke had initiated: music, dancing, spoken dialogue, no recitative. Purcell might have returned to the form of *Dido and Aeneas* and developed it in various ways, but he died at age thirty-six.

Into this void, in the early years of the eighteenth century, Italian musicians at last brought Italian opera to England. Initially, these Italian operas were sung in English and adapted to English tastes in various ways. The first big hit was *Il Trionfo di Camilla* by Marc Antonio Bononcini (1677–1726), part of whose cast sang in Italian, part in English. Even so, there was much hostility to the Italian form, sung in Italian, and there was no reason to think that Italian operatic influence would be more long-lasting than had been the French twenty-five years before. But Italian opera swept to popularity, and the reason for it was the arrival in England of George Friedrich Handel (1685–1759), whose appearance, as unpredictable as Purcell's disappearance, fundamentally altered the balance in English musical life between Italian and English opera. Handel, a German, Italianized English music drama, beginning in 1711 with *Rinaldo,* the first opera he composed in England. Although many operas by other Italian composers were also performed in London in these years, Italian opera owed its supremacy to Handel alone.[6] However, the exotic quality of this imported art, the exaggeration of its supporters' admiration, produced a fierce revulsion against foreign forms and styles, against foreign language, against Italian opera. Audiences wanted something indigenous and their desire found expression in a new English operatic form: ballad opera.

Ballad opera was a prose play with songs interspersed throughout.[7] There was no recitative. The story moved forward by means of spoken dialogue only. The songs, though selected to express the mood and sentiments of the characters, were not integral to the drama. They were not original compositions but were borrowed from the large body of tunes and ballads of the common people, old and familiar melodies used with new words. Italian serious opera treated noble mythical or historical themes with recondite literary references, in formal and ornate verse. Ballad opera emphasized the disreputable aspects of contemporary life. Its characters were neither gods nor heroes but rebellious children, intriguing servants, stupid rustics, drunken squires, as well as highwaymen, prostitutes, pimps, rakes. This world was neither pleasant nor moral, though ballad operas usually concluded on a conventional moral note. And English opera's demotic and racy prose contrasted with the elevated literary verse of Italian opera.

Although ballad opera was not necessarily comic, it tended toward satire and parody. *The Beggar's Opera* of 1728, a robustious celebration of lower-class life, satirized the political ministry then in power and, to a lesser extent, Italian opera. It ran for an unprecedented sixty-two nights in London, quickly spread to all the larger provincial towns, then to Ireland, and eventually across the seas. Handel rose to its challenge, composing some of his greatest operas after 1728. The English operatic world was divided in half. And it was the ballad opera half that crossed the Atlantic.

S o unremarkable a part of common culture was ballad opera that we cannot be certain when or where the first American operatic performance took place.[8] The first we have a trustworthy record of was in Charleston, South Carolina, in 1735, Colley Cibber's ballad farce *Flora, or Hob in the Well.* A century and more had intervened between it and the first English settlements in Virginia. What had happened in between? Operatically, little or nothing. North America proved exceptionally stony ground for operatic sowing. Material resources were scarce. The population was scattered. There was little time for entertainment. There were few musical instruments, even fewer musicians. But the chief obstacle to opera was puritanism. Implacable opposition to theater was the dominating fact of the first century of settlement. The consequences of this attitude remained long after formal prohibition of theater disappeared, a prevailing sense of awkwardness about singing and acting, an embarrassment in the presence of the public display of emotion, suspicion of pleasure.

The southern settlements proved to be the weakest links in the chain of hostility. Southern planters thought of themselves as British men and women who happened to live in places remote from Britain. Their remoteness only re-emphasized their Britishness. When William Byrd I, of Westover Plantation in Virginia, heard Italian opera in London, he reacted like any other English squire and scorned "the whelping of the foreign syrens, who charmed with felonious intent to devour us."[9] When in England, frequenting the theater was a way for these Southerners to reaffirm their cosmopolitanism, especially by comparison with the dour New Englanders. They brought back printed plays for their libraries and for performance, in which they often assumed leading roles, but listing themselves anonymously in the playbills. However, their theatrical or operatic efforts were always hindered by the fact that theater is an urban amusement and there were so few cities in the South.

In this first period of American theatrical history (1720–1750), opera played only a small part. Itinerant amateur actors began to appear in the middle colonies as well as in the South. These wanderers were often respectable citizens, tradesmen, indentured servants, artisans and their wives. Women played women's roles, though actresses' names were not given in the playbills. The emergence of a public theatrical audience can conveniently be marked by the first known performance in the colonies of a Shakespeare play, *Romeo and Juliet,* in New York in 1730. In the second period (1750–1776), the first professional acting companies appeared, traveling groups of professional actors supplemented by locally recruited amateurs. They were mostly English, usually family groups, and they made no distinction between sung and spoken drama. The Hallam Company's advertisements announced grandly that they had been "perfected in all the best plays, Operas, Farces, and Pantomimes, that have been exhibited in any of the Theatres for these ten years."[10] With many false starts and postponements, and in the teeth of bitter opposition, these companies performed in Philadelphia and New York, in Baltimore and Annapolis, and in numerous smaller towns where no theatrical performance had been seen before.

Touring companies moved from south to north, usually originating in Jamaica or Cuba, where the passion for music and theater was intense. A few operatic milestones stand out: the first American performance of *The Beggar's Opera,* in New York in 1750; the first opera performance in which singers were accompanied by an orchestra, in Upper Marlborough, Maryland (again *The Beggar's Opera*). This performance was sponsored by the Ancient and Honourable Society of Free and Accepted Masons, "with instrumental Music to Each Air Given by a Set of Private Gentlemen."[11] *The Beggar's Opera* made its way almost everywhere: Annapolis in 1752, Philadelphia in 1759. Well before 1800 it had been given in Boston, Providence, Newport, Baltimore,

Richmond, Williamsburg, Norfolk, Charleston. Anti-opera sentiment remained powerful, however. In 1750 the Massachusetts legislature passed by a large majority a law prohibiting any theatrical performance. The very fact that a law was needed suggests that informal opposition was no longer sufficient to suppress theatrical activity.

Printed music became more generally available. Local printers, booksellers, and music shops began to carry sheet music and American collections of English songs. By the 1760s every colonial capital offered for sale music by Arne, Vivaldi, Corelli, and Handel (his oratorios, not his operas). Violins, guitars, harps, harpsichords, and organs were being manufactured. American composers began to publish their songs. There was a notable rise in the level of singing and in the vocal music sung in churches. Religious sects which had forbidden instrumental music in church now allowed it, believing that instruments would help the congregations sing their psalms. New collections of vocal music introduced more complex British hymns and anthems. Hymns, set to non-Biblical texts or to texts drawn from parts of the Bible other than the Psalms, became popular, those of Isaac Watt and the Wesley brothers especially so. The latter introduced new texts and a vocal style which included trills and elaborate variations. Equally important were anthems for several voices, singing sustained for several minutes. The most important collection of anthems, James Lyons's *Urania,* was published in Philadelphia in 1761. Hymn singing became more specialized. Formerly, the entire congregation had sung together. Now, more expert members gathered in the front of the church, forming a kind of choir. The way was being opened for more complex, more highly stylized music.

In the South, though the planters still depended largely on local resources, the level of musical cultivation was rising. Much of the music on plantations was supplied by African American slaves who, when given a chance, became proficient on many instruments, and the quality of whose singing voices was often admired. But slaves and masters could not form a common audience, a curse which dogged southern musical culture for two centuries. The planters found their entertainment where they could. William Byrd II, traveling across remote stretches of the Virginia backcountry, spent a week with the Randolphs at Tuckahoe, where the company passed time and "triumphed over the bad weather" by reading *The Beggar's Opera* aloud.[12] In Charleston, the Saint Cecilia Society, founded in 1763, numbering 120 members with many others clamoring to join, hired musicians on long-term contracts to give public concerts.

There were other indications of the maturing of operatic culture in these years. The first critical notice of an opera, *Love in a Village* by Thomas Arne (1710–1778), appeared in the January 1767 issue of the *Pennsylvania Gazette.* A few singers became popular favorites. Maria Storer, a soprano, especially admired as Lucy in *The Beggar's Opera* as well as in popular concerts, was honored by a volume of music published in Virginia in 1772 called *The Storer, or The American Syren.* Beautiful and talented, jealous and capricious, she may lay claim to the title of the first American prima donna. The most popular male singer for many years was an Irish actor named John Henry, a large, engaging man who kept a carriage and lived grandly.

In the 1760s and after, opera played a much larger part in the theatrical repertory offered by touring companies and became a lively element in popular culture, "comic operas being printed in American editions, sold at the theatre, sung at home, and used as settings for patriotic songs." New operas came across the Atlantic with remarkable quickness. Arne's *Thomas and Sally* and *Love in a Village,* produced in London in 1760 and 1762, respectively, were being performed regularly in America by 1768. *Lionel and Clarissa,* by Charles Dibdin (1745–1814), first performed in London in 1768, reached America by 1772. His *The Padlock,* brought out at Drury Lane in October 1768, was given in New York by May 1769. The Douglass Company, in Charleston for the 1763–1764 season, stressed the freshness of its repertory as well as the proficiency of its actors "in the Singing Way, so that English COMIC OPERA, a species of entertainment that has never yet appeared properly on this side of the water, is likely to be performed here this winter to advantage." These comic operas also continued the ballad opera tradition of social satire, showing the possibility of love triumphing over social class and including sharp thrusts at the upper classes. "Such works

To the Printers of the PENNSYLVANIA GAZETTE.

AS the Practice prevails in our Mother Country, I hope you will have no Objections against inserting in your Papers, the Observations that any Gentleman may decently make concerning the Actors on our little Theatre here.

I do not rely wholly upon my own Delicacy of Judgment in the following Remarks, for I have gathered and compared the Sentiments of many others, who have had good Opportunities of improving their Taste of both Plays and Players. The Practice of altering the Author's Expressions is universally condemned by all Men of Sense, and leaves no Excuse for the Vanity or Neglect of the Actor; and I hope this little Hint will be sufficient to guard our Actors against any Thing of the like Nature for the future; for they ought to consider, that one indecent, ungarded, ill judged Expression, will do them inconceivable Mischief in this Country, and that no one Advantage can arise from taking such a Liberty, but if they clearly avoid this Rock, and are prudent in the Choice of Plays, the rational Entertainment must, and will, succeed, agreeable to the highest Wishes of those who are concerned in it.

I am sorry Mr. *Hallam,* who is genteel in his Person and Action, could not take Copy from the inimitable *Garrick,* and speak plain English, whenever he assumes a Character that may be supposed to understand the Language. There is no Necessity of destroying the least articulate Beauty of Language, thro' Fury, Eagerness or Passion; Miss *Cheer* never loses the sweetest Accent, or falters in the Clearness of Expression, from any or all those Causes, though I believe she is equally delicate, and capable of feeling the Force of Passion.

I am not alone, when I pronounce her one of the best Players in the Empire; she appears to me, from that Ease of Behaviour which always shines through every Action, to have been much among People of Fashion, for she well fits the highest Character she ever assumes.

I must beg Leave to inform the Public, that the pleasing *Love in a Village* is done here beyond Expectation, and must give real Delight to every Person void of Ill-nature.---Miss *Wainwright* is a very good Singer, and her Action exceeds the famous Miss *Brent.* Mr. *Hallam* exceeds every Thing in the Character of Hodge; and Mr. *Woolls* almost equals *Beard* in Hauthorn. Miss *Hallam* deserves universal Applause and Encouragement. I could wish to see the House better filled whenever this justly applauded Entertainment is exhibited.

A review of Thomas Arne's Love in a Village, *the first known notice of an opera in an American newspaper. From the Pennsylvania Gazette, Jan. 22, 1767. Sterling Memorial Library, Yale University.*

perhaps shaped the political perceptions of Americans who did not read Locke or Cato's Letters but who did frequent the theater," and may have played a role in the growing political discontent of the time.[13] In these years the colonists began to think of themselves as something other than English women and men, as Americans. Reflecting this nationalist sentiment, English operas were often modified to suit American tastes and values, in plot, subject matter, language, use of local reference.

It is in this context that there appeared the work of the first American operatic composer. He called himself Andrew Barton, but that was probably a pseudonym and it's not certain who he was—perhaps Thomas Forrest, a Philadelphia businessman and legislator. The circumstances of the composition and appearance of his opera are

THE

DISAPPOINTMENT:

OR, THE

FORCE OF CREDULITY.

A NEW

American COMIC-OPERA,

Of Two ACTS.

By ANDREW BARTON, Efq;

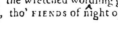

Enchanting gold! thou doth confpire to blind
Man's erring judgment, and mifguide the mind;
In fearch of thee, the wretched worldling goes;
Nor dangers fear, tho' FIENDS of night oppofe.

NEW-YORK:
Printed in the Year, M,DCC,LXVII,

The title page of Andrew Barton's The Disappointment, or The Force of Credulity, *the first opera by an American composer. Although the libretto was published in 1767, the performance was canceled: Philadelphians apparently took umbrage at Barton's bawdy satire.*

uncertain. The Douglass Company, perhaps hoping to placate Quaker opposition to the theater by promoting works by Americans, announced a performance of *The Disappointment, or The Force of Credulity* for April 1767. In two acts, with twenty or more songs, its story was typical ballad opera, satirizing greed and national types, the Irish and Scots, local businessmen, African Americans, all of them involved in the hunt for buried treasure left by Blackbeard the pirate somewhere on the banks of the Delaware. It was untypical in that much of its satire was aimed downward. The lower-class characters cheat and trick each other. One scene takes place in a brothel run by Moll Placket, the chief female character, whose lover is Raccoon, a dandified African American who sings a risqué song to a melody that would come to be known as "Yankee Doodle."

The Disappointment was announced but never performed. It is said that local businessmen, the objects of some of its satire, forced Douglass to cancel by threatening legal action. Then, too, the story was bawdy to the point of scandal. Although the music for *The Disappointment* subsequently disappeared, the story was published in New York in 1767 and in a revised version in Philadelphia in 1796. Still trying to capitalize on patriotic feeling, Douglass, in place of Barton's opera, produced the first spoken drama written by an American author, Thomas Godfrey's *The Prince of*

Raccoon and Washball in Treasure Hunt, a 1930s Federal Theater version of The Disappointment. *Library of Congress Federal Theater Project Collection at George Mason University, Fairfax, Va.*

Parthia. There were no Parthians around to threaten libel suits. So ended the first effort to compose an American opera.

T h e n came the Revolution. The anti-English sentiments unleashed by war had disastrous consequences for the English theatrical companies. Douglass's broke up. His leading actors returned to England and he took what remained of his group to Jamaica. Like many subsequent revolutionary movements, this one was accompanied by an intense desire to purify social life, as in the Resolves of the Continental Congress: "We will, in our several stations encourage frugality, economy and industry . . . and will discountenance and discourage every species of extravagance and dissipation, especially all horse-racing, and all kinds of gaming, cock-fighting, exhibition of shows, play, and other expensive diversions and entertainments." While the Congress preached austerity, British soldiers brought with them entertainments such as dancing, plays, operas, concerts. They reopened theaters recently closed and, in New Hampshire, New Jersey, Pennsylvania, Virginia, and Georgia, built new ones. Generals Clinton, Burgoyne, and Howe were patrons of the arts. Burgoyne was a playwright and wit, Clinton a violinist who took several musical instruments with him on his campaigns and whose "principal activity, to judge from his account books, was not military but musical."[14]

British troops brought theater to Boston, the intellectual capital of New England puritanism. Soldiers had been stationed there since 1768 to protect customs officials from harassment. Under British law, the local antitheater regulations of 1750 were discarded. *The Beggar's Opera* and *Love in a Village* were immediately performed. Many Bostonians regarded these performances as deliberately hostile acts. Both sides understood the symbolism involved. The British performed *The Beggar's Opera* only three weeks after British troops had fired on local citizens in what the Americans called the Boston "massacre," and once war broke out, the British converted Faneuil Hall, a meeting place for local radicals, into a playhouse.

When American officers emulated the British example and put on plays and operas for the amusement of their troops, the Second Continental Congress sternly warned that "Play Houses and theatrical entertainments have a fatal tendency to divert the minds of the people from a due attention to the means necessary for the defence of their country and the preservation of their liberties," and threatened participating officers and troops with dismissal from the service.[15] Despite such fulminations and threats, American soldiers continued to amuse themselves theatrically. George Washington firmly believed that theatrical performances improved army morale. At Valley Forge, the low point of American fortunes, officers and their ladies, accompanied by a military band, sang *The Padlock* to an overflow house. Civilians shared in the growing enthusiasm. There was so much theater at Yale College that President Ezra Stiles commented caustically that the college should be renamed Drury Lane.

When British troops came to the colonies in the 1750s to fight the French, they brought their bands with them. Copying the British example, Americans added bands to their militias. An inspector of bands and a superintendent of music were appointed. The American bands played at all kinds of occasions, parades, assemblies, college commencements, victory celebrations, hangings. They became the finest musical ensembles most Americans had ever heard. "The varied sounds of the flute, of the clarinet, of the hunting horns, and the bassoon" introduced citizens to marches from Handel operas and to other operatic tunes. Innumerable people must have shared the experience of a young English boy who, with some companions, heard an army band playing a tune. "So ravishing was the piece" that they "imitated the sounds of oboes and clarinets." This was the beginning of Leigh Hunt's life-long passion for opera, though it wasn't until later that he learned that the song "You'll roam no more," ("Non più andrai") came from an opera called *The Marriage of Figaro* and that its composer was named Mozart.[16]

New Orleans

English opera and army bands playing Italian operatic tunes weren't the entire story. In exploring the origins of opera in America, we have to look elsewhere as well. And this time we'll go outside the national boundaries of the new United States, to the town of New Orleans, in the French-speaking, Spanish-governed province of Louisiana.

Opera in New Orleans had its own legendary founding, involving a García-like troupe. In 1792 a group of traveling singers were supposed to have put on an opera in the theater on St. Peter's Street. But while musicians did move back and forth on a triangular path between the Caribbean islands, France, and Louisiana, no single troupe can be credited with bringing opera to New Orleans. A taste for opera came with the settlers and flourished in the rich local soil. By 1796 operatic dates can be securely established. There were performances of operas by André Grétry (1741–1813), Nicolas Dalayrac (1753–1809), and Nicolas Dezède (174?–1792), remarkable in a town which, in the 1790s, numbered about twelve thousand people, half white, half African American slaves. New Orleans had a colorful atmosphere, more Mediterranean than North American, and opera was one of the elements—along with its brick-and-stucco houses with massive fronts, arched doorways, and elaborate iron-work balconies, its streets lighted by oil lamps hung at the intersections on ropes suspended from the corners of houses—which marked it as a foreign place. The theater on St. Peter's Street was small, its productions modest but impressively numerous. No sharp distinction was drawn between actors and singers or between spoken and musical drama. "The gentlemen of the [town] often perform in the orchestra at the theatre," a visitor noted; "in fact, there is no other music there but such as they obtain in this voluntary way."[1] Yet these local nonprofessional inhabitants had sufficient skill to perform contemporary French opera, music more demanding than the simple songs and accompaniments of English ballad opera.

Around 1800 this community began to break up. Louisiana had been Spanish since 1762, when it was ceded to Spain by France. The Spanish government thought the province a liability, costly to maintain and difficult to defend against the menacingly expansive Yankee colossus to the north. Since 1795 rumors had circulated that the Spanish government was seeking some way to free itself from its burden. In fact, between 1800 and 1802 secret agreements were arrived at by which Spain ceded Louisiana back to France. Soon after knowledge of this reached New Orleans, there came the news of the United States' purchase of the province from France. Spanish and French citizens accepted the inevitability of Yankee occupation and political domination, but resisted the idea of American cultural hegemony. Creole disdain for the barbarous Americans fueled a concerted effort to maintain cultural distinctiveness.

The history of opera in New Orleans was shaped by this attitude. For the French, the crucial thing was to preserve their language—not an easy thing to do as the number of Americans increased and as spoken and printed English became the official language of the province-become-territory. Yet to give French opera in English was as unthinkable in New Orleans as in Paris. Opera was a rallying point for intensified French self-awareness. And a very successful one. Between 1803 and 1815 the St. Peter's Street theater was outgrown and replaced by one on St. Philip Street, until this was also outgrown and replaced by a larger theater.[2]

The extent of Creole operatic activity was remarkable. In these years there were over 700 performances of about 150 different operas by fifty composers. Most of the contemporary French operatic repertory was given. Audiences were drawn from all elements of the population, including African American slaves, who were, however, restricted to one section of the gallery. Prices were modest: box seats cost a dollar; orchestra floor (the "pit") and balcony seventy-five cents; children and slaves fifty cents. Along with popular trifles, enduring and difficult operas were performed: *Joseph* by Etienne-Nicolas Méhul (1763–1817), with an all-male cast; *The Water Carrier* (*Les Deux Journées*) by Luigi Cherubini (1760–1842). The city's appetite for entertainment was insatiable and the opera drew on the numerous up-country residents who visited the city during the winter. It was a tolerant audience, taking in its stride *The Sisters of the Visitation* (*Les Visitandines*), a scandalous anticlerical opera by François Devienne (1759–1803). Local talent was given a chance. Philip Laroque, a New Orleans composer, had two of his operas produced, one of them being performed three times. Hyacinthe Laclotte, engineer and architect, designed sets.

After 1815 an operatic decline set in. The war of 1812–1814, and especially the Battle of New Orleans which concluded it, stimulated the American presence, bringing new people and new money into the city. Other forms of entertainment drew people away from opera and theatergoing dwindled. Only five new operas were put on between 1815 and 1820. The old cohesive French audience was being submerged in the new larger American one. The extinction of French opera in New Orleans seemed irreversible. The future took a different course, however, largely because of two unusual men whose intertwined lives form the backbone of the New Orleans operatic story for the twenty years after 1820.

B o r n in Paris in 1773, John Davis emigrated to Santo Domingo as a young man, was driven from there in the early 1790s by revolutionary turmoil, moved on to Cuba, ended up in New Orleans in 1809. He made money as a gambler and in the hotel business, fought in the Battle of New Orleans, and achieved local celebrity because of his services to Andrew Jackson. A shrewd businessman, Davis had "somewhere and somehow obtained a fine musical education and had learned all that was to be learned about the exacting business of directing an opera house." He decided to use this skill

The Camp Street (American) Theatre in New Orleans around 1830, when it was the center for English-language musical theater. Historic New Orleans Collection, acc. no. 1945.11.

in reviving French opera. As a start, he erected a group of buildings including a hotel, a ballroom, and a theater named the Orleans, which opened in 1819.

James Henry Caldwell was born in England about 1793, became an actor, emigrated to the United States in 1816, performed widely throughout the middle Atlantic states and the South, brought his Virginia Company to New Orleans early in 1820. His was not the first American theatrical troupe to perform English drama in English in New Orleans; but his company, able to perform English music and opera as well as spoken drama, was the first to challenge French music and drama in a significant way. Caldwell moved into the Orleans Theater, alternating performances with Davis's company. This was a temporary measure only. The Americans needed their own theater and in 1824 Caldwell moved to the Camp Street Theatre, a brick structure seating eleven hundred which became the center of American (and English) drama and music.[3]

In the 1820s the two managers experimented in order to find a firm basis for the kind of theatrical culture each represented. Davis believed he must expand French opera beyond its local base and resources. Beginning in 1822 he went to France to recruit singers and dancers. Ballet was an essential part of French opera. He brought back the first real ballet group to dance in America, as well as Rossini's *Il Barbiere di Siviglia*, performed in New Orleans two and a half years before the Garcías presented it in New York. Rossini was not immediately popular. It took time for Italian opera to win the affection of French Louisianians. Davis tried other things as well. He elaborately redecorated the Orleans Theater. He understood the importance of finding a star, which he did with Madame Alexandre. A dancer and singer, she became a popular favorite. He also got a real operatic hit, a result of the craze for musical adaptations of Walter Scott's novels which swept Europe in the 1820s and 1830s, in *The White Lady* (*La Dame blanche*) of Adrien Boieldieu (1775–1834). Performed in New Orleans only one year after its Paris premiere in 1825, *La Dame blanche* played for three nights in a row, an unprecedented run, and eleven times that season. Davis's company also introduced the operas of Daniel Auber (1782–1871), tuneful and elegant works which became the mainstay of the French repertory in these years, and, in a more innovative enterprise, organized a handsome production of Carl Maria von Weber's *The Freeshooter* (*Der Freischütz*), but in French of course, as *Robin des bois*.

The expansion of the repertory to include Italian and German opera, and the increased scale of the productions, changed the nature of New Orleans opera. The previous system—simple productions, low costs—had been essentially local. While popular works were repeated, new ones could be tried out, even if they were given only two or three times. Now every production was a gamble, with larger stakes, and the consequent temptation was to play safe by repeating proven favorites. The cost of maintaining an opera troupe of the kind Davis now assembled was about fifty thousand dollars per year. Something had to be done to increase revenue.

But what? Davis could emphasize season subscriptions, which allowed greater flexibility in planning. His unwavering policy, however, had been to keep prices low and to attract support beyond the season subscribers, so there didn't seem to be much hope along that line. He could lengthen the season, since it made little sense to pay the costs of travel for foreign artists for a New Orleans season limited to the winter and spring. However, the enervating Louisiana summers ruled that out. Davis solved this problem, and in so doing became a figure of importance in the history of American opera beyond New Orleans: he decided to take his French company on the road. His first attempt was a visit to Havana in 1824. Then he turned to the big cities of the American Northeast. Fancy going to Philadelphia and New York City and Boston because of their temperate summers! But that was the scheme: showing off French opera, "the pride and hope of the generation raised on the ruins of the old French regime."[4]

In June 1827 Davis's troupe sailed for New York. The obstacles facing them were only a little less formidable than those Manuel García had confronted two years earlier. Shipping singers, musicians, and scenery north was complicated and dangerous. The voyage was a long one and Davis had no financial guarantees. Still, there were some things working in favor of his enterprise. All the competing theaters would be closed for the summer. There was a substantial foreign population in New York and French opera would be "a favorite resort to those studying the language." And, of course, "something must be allowed for fashion." And novelty. They opened with *La Dame blanche,* followed by *Les Deux Journées* and Auber's *The Mason* (*Le Maçon*), among other works. The company stayed two months and gave forty performances, but there was an air of disappointment about the visit. Perhaps the repertory was a bit heavy for a summer season. Ironically, the scorching New York summer was partly to blame, for only ardent opera lovers could endure "the suffocation of a play house." Unaccountably, French opera was not a social success and some of the New York newspapers were condescending: "The company is so much better than could have been hoped for, that it would be ungenerous to quarrel with it for not being as good as we could desire."[5]

In September Davis's company moved on to Philadelphia, where they generated tremendous enthusiasm, musical and social. The French population of the city came out in droves and "the American proportion of the audience was more considerable than expected." Philadelphians liked *Cinderella (Cendrillon)* and *Joconde* by Niccolò Isouard (1775–1818), Auber's *Solitaire,* and Boieldieu's *The Red Hood (Le Petit Chaperon rouge).* And they seem to have understood and enjoyed those very French afterpieces, the vaudevilles, such as *My Aunt Aurore, The Tassel and the Tailor,* and *Werther,* a parody of the Goethe story. All were done with "precision, spirit and care," and gave Philadelphians "a true and most engaging picture of the tone, customs and feelings of Parisian life."[6] Gratifying as such success was, and whatever the reasons for it, the unpredictability of taste and the largely incalculable role of chance and fashion demonstrated how precarious was the career of an opera manager.

Between 1827 and 1833 New Orleans provided northern cities with almost the only European opera they were to hear. For half a decade the arrogant, querulous, somewhat ungrateful states of the Northeast were operatic colonies of the South. Davis's group made five more tours. In 1828 Philadelphia was again the center of attention, with a visit also to Boston. That second year the French company gave Philadelphia its most serious and formidable works, but it was the company's orchestra which received the most attention in the press. "Not a single fault was committed by the instrumental performers and this in itself furnished a great treat to those who, like us, have generally been obliged to make great allowances, even for the best orchestra we could assemble." In Boston, the operas were criticized as "too Frenchified," their language "gabble and perfect nonsense to the spectators," which provoked a New Orleans newspaper to sneer that "a cockfight would be more to the taste of Bostonians than French opera."[7]

In 1829 Baltimore replaced Boston on the tour. French opera was beginning to seem familiar. *La Dame blanche* was now referred to as an old stand-by, "one of those compositions which confirms the opinion that music is not conveyed in so captivating a manner by any other process as by opera." The French introduced two Rossini operas never before performed in the North: *The Lady of the Lake (La Donna del lago)* and *The Thieving Magpie (La Gazza ladra).* Rossini's music still seemed technically formidable, *La Gazza ladra* "very difficult, generally obstreperous, and, to us, less delightful than several of [his] other compositions."[8] In 1830 and 1831 the tours, though short, were long enough to introduce one more Rossini, *Count Ory (Le Comte Ory).* Cholera swept the eastern seaboard in 1832 and there was no northern tour. The last visit north was in 1833, with appearances in Philadelphia, New York, Baltimore, and Boston.

Meanwhile, at the Camp Street Theatre, James Caldwell labored to establish opera in English, to bring to his theater an American population not familiar with opera while also attracting the operatically more sophisticated French speakers. This was especially difficult because a large proportion of Caldwell's prospective American audience consisted of frontiersmen whose rowdy chauvinism—"They average about six rows in the course of an evening's entertainment and have a gouging match by way of interludes"—typified what was most repugnant about American popular culture to the Creoles. The experience of the actor Noah Ludlow vividly illustrated this. On his first appearance at the Camp Street, Ludlow, instead of conventional French theatrical garb, came onstage dressed in buckskins and moccasins, with a slouched hat on his head and a rifle on his shoulder. A roar of approval greeted him from the river men, many of them dressed just like him. (Minus the rifles?) The roar increased when Ludlow launched into "The Hunters of Kentucky," an adaptation of a song from the old ballad opera *Love Laughs at Locksmiths.* As Ludlow sang, stamping feet and prolonged whoops and howls accompanied him, and when he finished, "shouts and yells came from the pit and tremendous applause from the other portions of the house." Ludlow recalled, "I had to sing the song three times that night before they would let me off."[9]

Throughout the 1820s Caldwell resourcefully struggled to create a new audience out of discordant elements. He gave his frontiersmen a steady diet of English opera and musical farces, and altered well-known operas to suit unsophisticated tastes. Madame Feron, a mainstay of Caldwell's company and later a popular singer in English opera in Philadelphia and New York, appeared in *Il Barbiere di Siviglia,* interpolating English ballads such as "The Arab Steed" and "The Old Man Would Be Wooing." Yet Caldwell also gave them *The Marriage of Figaro* (*Le Nozze di Figaro*), though much adapted, a revival of *The Beggar's Opera,* Rossini's *Cinderella* (*La Cenerentola*), and Auber's *Fra Diavolo.* In 1826 he presented Weber's *Der Freischütz,* in English, using all his theater's resources to emphasize the magical effects the story calls for. "The [frontiersmen] expressed their satisfaction with a hurrah which made the walls tremble," and it was given four more times in a month, a much better run than this powerful but difficult opera usually achieved elsewhere.[10] Caldwell's audience was volatile. Failures were frequent, so were successes. Little was predictable.

The volatility was connected with the city's transformation from the small French American town into a large American city with a lingering French influence. The fifty thousand people of 1830 became a hundred thousand by 1840, a population half again as large in the winter. New Orleans unabashedly amused itself and theater was the focus for its play: opera, drama, farces and burlesques, circuses and balls. New Orleans was dance-mad. Social life was institutionalized public gaiety. Stimulated by this, the two impresarios embarked on more ambitious efforts.

T h e half-dozen years beginning in 1835 marked not only a brilliant phase in New Orleans opera but also one of the most noteworthy in the history of opera in America, with two established companies, important productions, loyal audiences. Four milestones marked the period.

The first involved a direct confrontation between the two theaters. Both Davis and Caldwell wanted to produce a work by the reigning operatic composer of the day, Giacomo Meyerbeer (1791–1864). One of the major operatic internationalists, Meyerbeer created with remarkable facility in three national styles. A German who began by writing German operas, he fell under Rossini's spell and composed Italian operas which became popular in Italy, then went to Paris, where he became the principal figure in the creation of the most important kind of nineteenth-century opera, grand opera. His fame rose steadily in the 1830s and 1840s and reached its apogee at mid-century. As no operatic reputation has declined more disastrously than Meyerbeer's, one must emphasize the prevailing (but by no means unanimous) admiration for his operas at the time, though less for their music than for their dramatic spectacle.

No wonder New Orleans was eager to see *Robert the Devil* (*Robert le diable*), the opera which made Meyerbeer's name. Both companies raced to be first with *Robert*. Caldwell spent ten thousand dollars on his production, beefed up his forces, employed better singers, surrounded them with elaborate scenery, and profited from the advice of a basso named Reynolson, who had seen the work as directed by Meyerbeer in Paris in 1831. Davis's company also worked strenuously. The Americans won the race. Caldwell's show opened on March 30, 1835. Nervous at his own audacity, Caldwell hedged his bet by putting Thomas Dartmouth Rice, the creator of the minstrel figure Jim Crow, on his program as a separate act. Meyerbeer plus "Jump Jim Crow" packed the theater, playing for five successive nights, then three more later in April. The Davis company put on its first performance on May 12, precipitating a furious debate as to the relative merits of the two productions. The French, who found it impossible to admit that the Americans might do French opera as well as they, had an edge in their chorus and orchestra and in authenticity of style. Their version proved more popular in the long run, but Caldwell had taken a bold step.

His next was even bolder. Eager to escape the cramped confines of the Camp Street Theatre and to demonstrate how much his artistic aspirations had outgrown his old audience, Caldwell built the St. Charles Theatre, the largest and grandest in the United States up to this time. He poured an estimated $350,000 into creating a theater for opera on a Meyerbeerian scale. Borrowing a page from Davis's libretto, Caldwell also took his company on the road, to the upper Mississippi Valley, to St. Louis, Memphis, Natchez, where opera had not been before. The prolonged season helped balance his books but it wasn't enough.

And so, the third of the period's milestones, Caldwell imported two Italian companies. The first was the Montresor Company from Havana, in March 1836. Giacomo Montresor brought an opera new to New Orleans, *The Pirate* (*Il Pirata*) by Vincenzo Bellini (1801–1835). A few complained that there was "too much noise and instrumentation" in Bellini's score,[11] as some had a few years earlier about Rossini's music; however, this time Italian opera captivated New Orleans. It turned into a Bellini season. *The Stranger* (*La Straniera*) was more popular than *Il Pirata*, and *Norma* was most popular of all. There was an affinity between the sensuous elegance of the music and the style of the city. The following year Caldwell brought the Antonio de Rosa Company, a group with strong soloists and chorus. They opened with more Bellini, *The Capulets and the Montagues* (*I Capuleti ed i Montecchi*), adding fuel to the Bellinian blazes raging in the city. Little noticed at the time, New Orleans also made the acquaintance of an opera by Gaetano Donizetti (1797–1848) that would become one of the irreplaceable favorites of American audiences, *Lucia di Lammermoor*. The success of these visitors resolved Caldwell's immediate financial problems but had far-reaching consequences beyond anything he could have imagined. The lighter French operas seemed thin and artificial compared with the passionate lyricism and irre-pressible vigor of the Italian. Italian opera broke forever the French monopoly of non-English opera in the city, reducing its importance in sustaining French cultural identity.

The last of our four operatic milestones returns us to John Davis and to Meyerbeer. Competition with Caldwell brought Davis to the brink of bankruptcy, and he had saved the Orleans Theater only by "some very clever and rather questionable financ-ing."[12] His company was able to make one final effort. On April 30, 1839, Meyerbeer's *Les Huguenots,* the grandest opera of its day, received its first American performance in the grandest production in the city's history. It was given eight times in five weeks and solidified Meyerbeer in the city's esteem. This was a splendid capstone to an astonishing period of operatic activity. Between 1836 and 1841 at the Orleans Theater there were 364 performances of sixty-five operas by twenty-seven different compos-ers. Sixteen of the operas were given for the first time in America. Caldwell at the St. Charles presented half as many operas but of a very wide range, including many English operas. In number of performances and of new works and in seriousness of purpose, it was a tremendous achievement for both.

Davis didn't live to see this flowering continue into the 1840s. He died on June 13, 1839, living just long enough to witness *Les Huguenots* on stage. A "large concourse of citizens" turned out for his lavish funeral. Some remembered him for his role in aiding Gen. Andrew Jackson at the Battle of New Orleans; most recalled his raising French theater and music "from a wretched condition to prosperity and excellence." A special requiem, composed for the occasion by the French émigré composer and conductor Eugène Prévost, was sung by the Orleans Theater company.[13] Caldwell lived on. His 1839–1840 season broke new ground, with half a dozen operas, given in English, all of them based on stories by Scott, then and long after an immense favorite in the South. Caldwell's efforts were abruptly cut short in 1842 when the St. Charles Theatre burned down. It was rebuilt, and opened in 1843.

Interesting in its own right, New Orleans's early operatic history illustrated the central importance of the audience in the evolution of opera in America. Given the absence of state patronage, opera in America had to compete within the capitalist entertainment marketplace for its audience. An opera audience could not be assumed but had to be continually created. Moreover, as New Orleans also revealed, the opera audience in America was closely tied to the fluctuating degree to which European immigrants thought of opera as either a means of assimilating to American society or of maintaining a separate ethnic identity. To explore more fully the differences between the European and American situations, we must return to Italy and consider the origins of opera's audiences and of the buildings that housed them.

chapter four

Buildings and Audiences

In 1821 New York's Park Theatre was extensively remodeled. The artisans employed on the job, proud of their country and of what they believed to be the originality of their work, attributed their success to the fact that "the Architect, Painters, Masons, and Carpenters, are Americans, who never have been abroad or seen a foreign theatre."[1] If we smile at the naïveté of the notion that people are influenced only by those things they have experienced themselves, we should remember that this view, minimizing the power of ideas and discounting the influence of history, is as common today as it was in 1821. Nevertheless, ideas are real, traditions do exist, history does shape how people live and what they think. The idea of the Italian opera house, for example, had crossed the Atlantic long before the Park Theatre was built and rebuilt, and with it had come a bundle of ideas associated with the word *opera*—ideas about manners, class, money, about morals, religion, politics. Ideas about operatic performance had worked on the minds and feelings of Americans whether or not they had seen an opera or an opera house, and they were the more potent for often being unrecognized.

Originating in the courts of Renaissance Italy, operatic performance evolved within the context of political absolutism. Opera began as a court monopoly, the personal amusement of the sovereign who personified the state. The court audience was not an audience at all in the modern sense; or, strictly speaking, it was an audience of one: what pleased or displeased the monarch pleased or displeased the court. Because Gluck's *Alceste* had captured one emperor's fancy, no other opera was performed at that court for two years. One king removed an aria from an opera because he disliked it. Another removed a composer: the king of Prussia banished Carl Maria von Weber because his operas displeased him—the same Weber whom all Germans would later cherish as a cultural treasure. At many courts no performance could begin until royalty appeared. What was sung, how it was sung, what was danced, what costumes were worn—such things were often decided by royal decree. Obviously, much depended upon the monarch's discernment, or lack of it. But no matter how individually enlightened and how respected the artist, musicians ranked as servants and were often treated with casual contempt.

Opera was not an end in itself but a means toward other ends, political and social. Its objective was the glorification of the monarch's reign and realm. It was a form of flattery to amuse the idle, to elevate the king above all others; but it was only one of several forms of the celebration of royalty. "Feasts and banquets; welcomes and farewells; processions and progresses; disguises and tourneys; births and birthdays; weddings and funerals; visits and victories—if it could be celebrated with any touch of the dramatic, celebrated it was; and if it was celebrated, then it was celebrated with music."[2] Courtiers seeking power and preferment put up with the tedium that accompanied such a life in the same spirit that power-seekers in the twentieth century attend committee meetings. One consequence of this is the astonishingly persistent feeling, of three hundred years' duration, that going to an opera is a form of duty.

Festivities at court were always elaborate, often protracted. A famous example was Pietro Cesti's *The Golden Apple* (*Il Pomo d'oro*), an opera of 1667 composed for the wedding of the Hapsburg Leopold I. Fantastically lavish, costing an immense sum, its performance spread out over two years! *Il Pomo d'oro* had five acts, sixty-seven scenes, twenty-three changes of scenery, fifty soloists, and a cast of thousands. The opera-ballet *Hercules in Love* (*Ercole amante*), put on to celebrate the marriage of Louis XIV, took three years to prepare and lasted six hours. Each of its five acts terminated with a spectacular ballet. It cost 88,000 livres at a time when Jean-Baptiste Lully worked as a cook's boy in the royal kitchens for 150 livres a year. Such magnificence and splendor appeared as if by magic, at the king's command. But it was not magic which paid for them. The power to tax was the power to produce opera. Everything came from taxes extracted from the king's subjects, almost none of whom would ever see this product of their labor. The image of a tiny elite amusing itself at the expense of a dejected and downtrodden populace had a firm historical basis. Opera would be indelibly associated with rapacious privilege. Small wonder, then, that in later days the entire system of royal and aristocratic patronage would come to seem an abomination and disgrace.

Opera's buildings were another form of extravagance. Special theaters were built for special occasions and then were torn down. What more visible symbol that the monarch need not be bound by prudence or common sense? Actually, most courts could not act in this way, or not often. There were limits to their resources. The common thing was to adapt already existing rooms to operatic purposes. As most rooms were rectangular, this was the prevailing shape of the court theater. It was an all-purpose hall suitable for various court functions. There was a stage at one end, connected to the main floor by steps, or by a ramp, but not sharply separated from auditorium or audience. In processions or in dance, the performers came down into the audience's space. Members of the court often participated, along with the professional performers. Louis XIV, a famous dancer, took part in his own court ballets. The audience was very small. Seating, installed only as required, was removed for some events. The orchestra didn't yet have one clearly marked place. It might be in the wings, along the sides of the hall, or in the gallery, if there was one. Generally, important personages sat in the center of the hall, with lesser folk ranged around them. There was no need for reserved places or distinctions as to the kind of seats. In the court everyone knew everyone and everyone's clearly understood social place. Seating didn't establish order. It reflected an order already there.

Meanwhile, a different kind of theater came into existence. In time, this specialized auditorium swept away the all-purpose theater and became fixed in people's minds as *the* operatic theater. In Venice, on March 6, 1637, a performance of Francesco Manelli's *Andromeda* was given at the Theater of San Cassiano. Opera and composer have long been forgotten. The original building has disappeared. But its importance in the history of opera would be difficult to overestimate. It was the first public opera house to which one gained admission by paying money. It signified a different social order and a new kind of audience.

V e n i c e was a commercial republic whose prosperity was based upon trade, with a vigorous middle class not overawed by the aristocracy. Yet its patrician elite, as ancient and as self-conscious of its privileges as any in Europe, set the tone of the city's life and was resourceful in maintaining its position and power.[3] Since there was no court and no court-sponsored entertainment, the city combined private and public efforts. The public opera house evolved from this tradition. The palaces of the Venetian patricians (San Cassiano had been the home of the Tron family) often had theaters in them, used for numerous private theatrical performances. Now, Venetian noblemen formed companies to build and manage opera houses, drawing audiences from the entire community and not just one class. An eyewitness noted that the

One of the classic Italian opera houses, the Teatro San Carlo in Naples (opened in 1737), as it appeared in the late 1700s. Traditionally associated with aristocratic privilege, opera houses—like opera itself—increasingly drew audiences from all social classes.

Venetians competed to give these "as they say, works in music, ample and exquisite form." Opera became a popular entertainment, "the industry of the people, the wealth of the country itself," entertainment specially suited to a city which, with its open, sunny piazzas, was like "one vast dwelling-place where the inhabitants could conduct their lives in the open, just as if they were at home, rich and poor united as it were in the bond of a common existence."[4] The Venetian opera house was truly revolutionary. Money, more than class, determined who could attend.

No wonder musicians like Claudio Monteverdi, Piero Cavalli, and Pietro Cesti flocked to the city. Venice created its own style of opera, combining high drama and bawdy farce and emphasizing spectacular stage effects. Its theaters had the most sophisticated stage machinery in Europe. The English traveler John Evelyn was impressed by the "variety of scenes painted and contrived with no less art of perspective, and machines for flying in the air, and other wonderful notions." The aria became a more integral part of the musical drama and the role of the orchestra was also expanded, using carefully selected instruments to give dramatic color to the music. The place of the orchestra in the theater was fixed, in front of the stage, and its members became regularly employed professional musicians. Another significant innovation followed from the increased emphasis given to songs: singers began to play a more independent role. Written contracts for performers, simple agreements to appear at a certain theater for a given fee, date from this period. Along with star singers, Venice also produced the first touring companies.[5]

Tracts of open land were not readily available. It was therefore important to pack as many people as possible into the available space, so Venetian opera houses expanded vertically and eventually became much larger than court theaters. The San Moïse Theater, opened in 1640, seated eight hundred and came to be thought small by Venetian standards. In the interior the Venetians introduced another of their fusions of the public and the private—the opera box. San Cassiano was built in the form of a U. Around the perimeter of the auditorium were installed rings of walled-off, self-contained compartments, or boxes, tiers of these rising one above the other to as many as seven levels. At the back of each box was a "withdrawing" room, sometimes equipped with a fireplace, in which food and drink were served. Everyone paid a fee for entering the opera house for each performance. In addition, boxholders paid annual rent for their boxes, which provided a substantial part of the operating income of the companies which built the theaters.

Financially, in terms of use of space, the opera box was inefficient. Open galleries would have held more people. But that was beside the point. The Venetian opera theater was a second house for citizens, the box another room in that house. If Saint Mark's Square was "the drawing room of Europe," a box at the opera was the boudoir adjoining it, where politics and fashion (and sometimes music) were discussed. Possession of a box was thought of in familial, not individual, terms. The box became part of a family's hereditary rights, belonging to it so long as the rent was paid; at the death of a tenant, it passed, like all entailed property, to the heirs. The city took responsibility for maintaining public order in the boxes, and the Doge himself allocated them to the heads of foreign diplomatic missions. A resident English diplomat frankly explained that "he did not care for music, esteem poetry or understand the stage, but merely desired [a box] for the honour of his office."⁶

The invention of the opera house as a public social institution had far-reaching consequences that are still being worked out in our day. It altered the relationship of members of the audience to the music drama on the stage and to each other. The stage performance was now separated from the audience both by the proscenium arch, which framed the action, and by the orchestra. The occupants of the boxes faced one another across the auditorium as well as the stage. To see and be seen was as much identified with the function of the opera house as to see and hear what took place on stage. This encouraged a free-and-easy approach to the stage performance. English and American visitors to Italy were routinely shocked at the casual ways of the boxholders, at the little attention they seemed to pay to the opera. There was incessant talk in the boxes, banging of doors, a restless in-and-out, to-and-fro.

Public display was only half the story. The box at the opera was a private place as well. In Venice, carnival was an opera season and its carnal pleasures were symbolized by the mask and the masked ball, by role playing and deception—both characteristic of "this permanent masked ball which is called Venice." The public nature of the city's social life was balanced by a passion for disguise. Much of its political activity was conducted in secrecy. Masks were universally worn during carnival, attracting even the crowned heads of Europe, who could play there incognito. The Venetian opera box was the equivalent of the mask. With its door shut, with shutters pulled across the front, the box became a place of intimate privacy, redolent of the furtive and the illicit, associations which still linger about it in our time.

Venice contributed enormously to the expansion and enrichment of opera as a musical form. Its achievement in the social sphere was equally impressive: the creation of an informed and critical musical public, the basis of musical culture as we have come to know it. Venetians didn't feel that they had to choose between esthetic and social values. For them, opera consisted inseparably of both. In Venice, Walter Pater wrote, "life itself was conceived as a kind of listening."⁷

O p e r a spread quickly throughout Italy, from Florence to Mantua and Parma and Venice and beyond. In Rome the first public theater was built in the 1670s by Queen Christina of Sweden, living there in exile. It was subsequently closed by papal decree, but private theaters were gradually opened to the public by the early eighteenth century. In Naples, opera was first given in a pavilion in the royal park previously used for games of pelota. Later, a theater was built specially for opera, limited to the use of the court, but a public theater was opened by the end of the seventeenth century. More astonishing was the rapidity of opera's diffusion throughout Europe and the enthusiasm of its reception. Within a century it covered the continent, from London to Lisbon, Stockholm to St. Petersburg. Attending the opera, like speaking French, was one of the things the governing class shared as Europeans, in the face of the hostile nationalisms, religions, and rivalries which distracted and divided them. Opera was Italy's principal export for the next two hundred years. Everywhere, people competed for Italian composers to create and singers to perform it, stage designers to build the machinery for its production, architects to build their opera houses.

Transplanted opera, behind its uniform Italian facade, grew increasingly diverse. Initially, opera was taken up from court to court, but as it could not be maintained as the exclusive possession of one interest or class, and as an audience came into being which could not be commanded to appear but did so of its own free will, exclusive possession was replaced by different forms of patronage. The court, the aristocracy, and the middle class, each influenced by differences in local circumstance, social structure, economic resources, religion, musical tradition, shared in supporting opera. And a group of independent figures emerged, entrepreneurs or impresarios (from the Italian *impresa,* undertaking) who undertook to organize performances for them. The social history of opera involved a series of continually varying answers to three questions—Who would pay? Who would attend? In what language would it be heard?—as Americans would discover in their turn.

Royal patronage took many forms. Vienna, with its long-standing involvement in the political affairs of Italy and its intimate familiarity with Italian music, was an Italian operatic colony. Given exclusively in Italian, opera was a means by which the court distanced itself from its polyglot cultural surroundings. Pietro Metastasio (1698–1782), the Italian-born court poet and most famous librettist of the eighteenth century, after living in Vienna for fifty years, didn't speak a word of German. The emperors Leopold I and Charles VI had eagerly subsidized splendid operatic productions for the court and this support was continued in the eighteenth century, when two court theaters were leased to various impresarios who, with a court subsidy, guaranteed an opera season. As the century wore on, Metastasian Italian opera would be challenged by German-language opera, even in Vienna, where the first German-language operatic masterwork, Mozart's *The Abduction from the Seraglio (Die Ent-führung aus dem Serail)*, was first performed in 1782.[8] Court opera's atmosphere retained something of its initial intimacy in places, as in Prussia at the end of the seventeenth century, where Italian opera was introduced in the theater of the Charlottenburg Palace, sponsored by Queen Sophie Charlotte, who sometimes accompanied performances on the harpsichord or, with her tutor, the philosopher Leibnitz, joined the guests in singing. Or in the surroundings of the opera house built at Drottning-holm, outside Stockholm, in 1766 by Queen Marie Louisa. The oldest extant European opera house, it still has its original stage sets and machinery.

Berlin, under Frederick the Great of Prussia, was anything but intimate and informal. Determined that his court equal any rival dynasty in splendor, Frederick erected a State Theater, a monumental, free-standing opera house in 1742. There was no admission charge, since one went there only as the king's guest. Occupants of each tier of boxes were placed strictly according to rank and importance in the affairs of state. Army officers regularly attended, at the command of the king, and sat in a specially designated section. Occasionally, properly dressed citizens were also admitted. For all his nationalistic pride, Frederick docilely accepted the supremacy of Italian opera, in Italian.

France was the supreme example of royal patronage, of art intertwined with the interests of the state, indelibly impressed upon the consciousness of all Europe and of the Americas. Music was put in the service of the state by means of an ambitious and coherent program of national patronage, an expression of the prevailing economic idea of the time, mercantilism, the use of economic means to achieve national ends. In the esthetic as in the economic sphere, France would free herself from dependence on foreign influences. National academies were created to train artists who would enhance national glory: the Academy of Dance, 1661; Painting and Sculpture, 1663; Science, 1666; Music, 1669; Architecture, 1671. Each of these academies had a teaching faculty, appointed by the king, who were given a yearly stipend and certain perquisites. Students were recruited from all over France and were exempted from military service. There were no entrance fees. Exams weeded out the lazy or untalented. Prizes and scholarships rewarded the ablest, rich and poor alike. There were even pension systems for singers and dancers, and medical benefits "for those crippled in the service of the opera."[9]

The Royal Academy of Music was charged with the "producing and singing of public operas and performances in music and French verse." Only work by French composers, in French, could be given there. In 1671 the academy was made a personal monopoly of Jean-Baptiste Lully. No opera could be given without his permission. He was assigned all rights to publish his own music, to set admission prices (even for persons of title and officers of the royal household), and to sell his librettos. Lully showed no part of his operas to anyone until the king had seen it. The king also had the first opportunity to see a performance. Yet Lully's music drama depended on the aristocracy. On the day of a performance, the street outside the Royal Palace would be lined with the carriages of the nobility. The price of seats was double that of other entertainments. The middle class also appeared frequently and in increasing numbers. A description of the Parisian audience by the Abbé du Guet was not empty bombast: "Does [opera] not attract all the estates, and do the workers not leave their shops, the men of war their camp, the merchants their companies, the magistrates their benches? Do not the seigneurs leave the court and the king his throne in order to come and hear?"[10]

The setting of the performances clearly revealed the growing social diversity. From 1674 on opera was given in the rectangular Great Hall of the Royal Palace, a room holding two thousand, with two tiers of boxes along each side, an open gallery above the boxes, and an open space at the back of the ground floor called the amphitheater. The gallery was filled with military officers, clerks, shopkeepers, artisans. Prostitutes mixed freely with the people there and sexual byplay was blatant. Although the boxholders behaved with the traditional indifference to the stage performance, the rest of the audience, gallery and amphitheater, volubly demonstrated its approval by fervent applause and its disapproval by whistling and hooting, a response so tumultuous that a French observer slyly said that the audience "resembled the English Parliament."[11]

If Paris was increasingly out of the court's control, Versailles, the greatest of royal palaces, revealed the absolutist face of the old order. Opera had been given at Versailles in the royal riding school, the royal apartments, out-of-doors as well as in specially built temporary structures. But no permanent court theater had ever been built. In the 1760s the royal treasury, acutely aware of the large number of royal children who would soon be married, and fearful of having to build monstrously expensive temporary theaters to house the wedding celebrations, urged that the court architect build a permanent theater. The result was the elegant, intimate theater designed by Jacques-Ange Gabriel, ready in the nick of time for the wedding of the future Louis XVI to Marie-Antoinette on May 16, 1770. That evening the royal family sat down to a splendid banquet on the theater's main floor, which could be leveled by special machinery underneath, while 180 musicians played on the stage and the courtiers applauded from the boxes. The next night the floor was restored to its raked angle and Lully's *Perseus* (*Persée*) performed, a final flicker of the excess of the old regime in the improbable guise of an economy measure.

Throughout Europe, a network of rich and powerful aristocratic families increasingly assumed the patronage of opera. In Rome, among many, there was the Barberini family, in the garden of whose palace opera was given in the summer, and in the palace theater in other seasons. In Vienna it was the Lichnowskys and Rasoumovskys who had come to the capital and supported music in their city palaces and mansions. The scale of such patronage was often monarchical, as is suggested by the arrangements at the castle of the Esterházy family in Hungary: an opera house seating four hundred, a marionette theater, a concert hall, and a music house, where members of the resident orchestra lived and visiting opera singers stayed. In addition, the Esterházys had the good fortune and good taste, for the better part of twenty-five years, to have a genius as resident composer. Joseph Haydn composed symphonies for the concert hall, operas for the opera house, and puppet operas for the marionette theater.

The diverse character of the evolving patronage system was strikingly evident in the German states, principalities, and municipalities. In general, the court theaters insisted on Italian opera, while the municipalities were more favorably disposed to German-language performances. In Hamburg, middle-class patronage and municipal subsidy were combined. The first Hamburg opera house, a tax-supported civic enterprise, opened in 1678 to a ticket-buying public. The Protestant clergy accepted opera, provided it was morally uplifting. The city commissioned operas by Handel and Telemann. From the first, opera was largely given in German, though sometimes, as with some of Handel's early operas, the arias were sung in Italian and the recitatives in German. Interest in opera declined in the late eighteenth century and municipal sponsorship came to an end until the early nineteenth century, when a new opera house was built as a municipal enterprise. The city's middle-class atmosphere permeated the opera house, as an American visitor discovered. Impressed by the size of the house and by the showy dress of the audience, Henry Wikoff was surprised to find so many boxes empty. The reason? Once every ten days the mail was sent to England. The night Wikoff attended the opera was mail night. The boxholding burgers were home writing their business letters.[12]

As audiences became more diverse, another kind of opera grew up, different from the original Florentine and Venetian opera seria in style and in social and musical origins: comic opera. In its own right, and as America's contribution to world opera would be a form of comic opera, its story is important.

Italian comic opera (*opera buffa*) had two sources. The first was the very ancient form of popular theater called the *commedia dell'arte,* impromptu plays, with no written texts, dependent on the inspiration of the moment and the interests of the day, performed wherever people gathered. A large number of stock characters and situations from this kind of theater were taken over by comic opera—the lecherous old man who lusts after his ward; the clever servant who outwits her master; the comic foreigner who is foiled in his plots. The second source relates to two of the formal arts of the seventeenth century: short comic scenes that often ended the acts of operas, giving comic relief and contrasting crude, everyday life with that of the gods and goddesses of the main opera; and the interlude (*intermezzo*), a brief musical entertainment which was sometimes a contrasting part of a spoken drama, sometimes a self-contained part of an opera. These scenes and interludes were gradually combined until they became independent operas in their own right. This development was largely associated with Naples, but comic opera was not simply a Neapolitan achievement. French *opéra comique* originated in the popular songs, horseplay, farce, bawdiness offered at late medieval fairs. Gradually, these entertainments achieved order and form. Composers began composing special music for them, then entire works. A wide range of characters appeared—virtuous peasants and bourgeoisie, frivolous and lecherous aristocrats. The distinctive element in French comic opera was spoken dialogue. By 1715 the French began performing opéra comique in a separate theater from that for opera seria, and soon French composers turned this rough and popular form into subtler, beautifully balanced art.

In the eighteenth century French and Italian comic opera—as well as such lesser variants as English ballad opera and German *Singspiel*—became immensely popular. Everywhere audiences clamored for it. Yet despite its success, comic opera—which was not always comic and could be sentimental and sugary—remained fundamentally subversive, irreverent, no respecter of rank, power, and respectability. (Witness Mozart's comic masterpieces *Le Nozze di Figaro* and *Così fan tutte,* as well as his tragicomedy *Don Giovanni.*) In Berlin, Frederick the Great had a small theater built, in the royal palace, where comic opera was given by traveling companies, but prudently kept this dynamite out of the hands of the populace by reserving the theater exclusively for royalty and the aristocracy. Comic opera also lent itself to the expression of nationalist sentiments. If opera seria was a formidable imperial power, comic opera allowed the conquered to give voice to their aspirations for independence.

I m m e d i a t e l y after the Revolution of 1688, the British court played only a modest role as patron of the arts, but William and Mary, Anne, and the Hanoverians supported artists with pensions, subsidies, and sinecures. George I and George II both adored opera. George I had a considerable familiarity with it as the former elector of Hanover. George II, as much as anyone, was responsible for bringing Handel to England and encouraging him to stay. German in culture, neither took any notice of English opera, so the Hanoverian court was no rallying point for a nationalist school of opera.

The center of British musical life was London. Musicians were better paid there than anywhere else in Europe, and as a result foreign musicians crossed the Channel in large numbers. The aristocracy supported Italian opera, the middle class—much of it at least—was opposed or indifferent. The strong evangelical elements in middle-class culture were trouble by opera's foreignness, especially its association with Catholic culture. As late as 1745 the King's Theatre, where Italian opera was performed, shut down for a time during the Jacobite (that is, Catholic Stuart) rebellion in Scotland, which provoked a wave of popular prejudice against Roman Catholic performers. Few opportunities were missed to express contempt for Italians, Spanish, and especially "those Pope-ridden, frog-eating, puny, wooden-shoed slaves, the French."[13]

In Britain, dislike of opera drew on other things besides class feeling and xenophobia. There was a long-standing opposition between spoken and musical drama. Something in sung drama embarrassed and disgusted British audiences, especially the awkwardness felt about recitative, about ordinary acts and comments being set to music. Note the revealing way in which only spoken drama was commonly referred to as "legitimate." Another factor may have been the growing emphasis in these years on a fact-centered and literal way of understanding the world, as opposed to a poetic and imaginative one. In 1667 appeared "the supreme example of anti-poetic rationalism," Bishop Spratt's *History of the Royal Society*. "Poetry," wrote Spratt, "is the parent of superstition." All works of the poetic imagination were seductive falsities. "Even ornaments of speech are a form of deceit."[14] Given this view of the life of the mind, opera had to seem one of the more contemptible forms of poetic superstition.

The hostility to Italian opera also centrally concerned the question of language. We've seen that after the early years of translating it into English, the custom became fixed that Italian opera would be given in Italian only. The fact that many people would *not* understand appealed to those who wished to keep opera exclusive. No aspect of Italian opera performance was more discussed than this. Advocates of opera in Italian argued that Italian was especially suited to being sung, that translation altered musical values and that translation was esthetically wrong. The poet John Dryden claimed that Italian seemed "to have been invented for the sake of Poetry and Music" and that, conversely, English was especially unsuited to singing. Despite Dryden's arguments, English writers, among them almost all the most famous of the time, led the assault on opera in Italian as being inherently absurd. Richard Steele and Joseph Addison ridiculed Italian opera in their essays, Alexander Pope lashed out at the "affected airs" of this "harlot form." Jonathan Swift derided the "unnatural taste for Italian music which is wholly unsuitable to our northern climate, and the genius of the people whereby we are over-run with Italian effeminacy and Italian nonsense."

The words *unnatural* and *effeminate* referred to another aspect of Italian opera, familiar to everyone at the time but now long forgotten: the castratos.[15] Castrated specifically for the sake of their voices, subjected to the finest vocal training available in Italy, these half-men, on reaching maturity, became the leading singers of Italian opera, capable of amazing vocal agility, with voices of unearthly purity and sweetness. The castratos were almost identical with Italian opera—and both they and their art were loathed by many. Their appearance was dictated by the requirements of opera seria singing, combined with certain aspects of Christian belief. High voices capable of unusual dexterity were required for singing church music. Women could not supply those voices because of St. Paul's injunction against women singing in church. The necessary voices were supplied by boys, falsettists, or eunuchs. Boys' voices were sweet, but they didn't command the skill required and could not gain it because their voices broke at puberty. Falsettists' voices, shrill and thin, never proved attractive and were not capable of reaching the necessary top range of notes. Eunuchs had none of these disadvantages. They had long been familiar figures in European culture and in the fifteenth and sixteenth centuries were in demand to sing the increasingly complex vocal music used in churches and in royal chapels, though everyone pretended that they were not castratos.

Opera immensely increased the work available to castratos, and for this Christianity was again an important cause. The disapproval of women performing in public on the stage—they were thought the equivalent of prostitutes—was not limited to the European continent. Shakespearean and Japanese Noh drama adapted to this situation, but opera could not do so. This art, so highly stylized and so dependent on the acceptance of conventions contrary to mundane reality, was in this regard insistent on the literal. There was something absurd about a tenor or bass with a clearly masculine voice singing a woman's role. So the castratos took the women's roles. This put the Catholic church in an anomalous position. By discouraging women from the stage because of moral considerations, it implicitly encouraged castration. Pope Clement XIV fulminated against castratos but did nothing to prevent their appearing on stage, and while anyone connected with a castration operation was liable to excommunication, castratos were not forbidden to sing in church or in opera. Every church in Italy, including the pope's private chapel, had such men on its roster. As long as the rewards, financial and otherwise, were so great, the availability of castratos was certain. Seventy percent of male opera singers in the eighteenth century were castratos. It was also said at the time that castratos were necessary because the natural male voice could not be trained to sing the fantastically florid passages composers wrote, but the real reason seems to have been that that epoch found the natural male voice too coarse. The church's prohibition against women on the stage was adhered to in the papal states, in some of the German states, and for a time in Vienna. Elsewhere it was either rejected or simply ignored. The papal ban stood until 1798. In most of the rest of Europe, women were singing on stage by the beginning of the eighteenth century, and the disappearance of the castratos, peacock-like in their vanity and pride, led to the emergence of a certain kind of singer who took their place—the diva.

Echoes of the assault by Swift, Pope, and other writers on opera in Italian and on the castratos lingered in Britain sixty years later. Samuel Johnson famously described Italian opera as "an exotick and irrational entertainment," but went on to say something about it few remember: that opera "has always been combated and always has prevailed." Why, despite the ridicule and hatred, *did* it prevail with British audiences? One reason was Handel's genius. Audiences, after all, didn't hear some abstraction called opera. They heard *Rinaldo, Giulio Cesare, Ariodante,* and the rest, works of "majesty, grandeur, force, fire and invention."[16] Italian opera also prevailed because the aristocracy supported it as a way to distinguish the superior from the hoi polloi.

Aristocratic support for opera was embodied in the King's Theatre. Built in 1705 by Sir John Vanbrugh, architect and playwright, the scene of the premiere of *Rinaldo* in 1711 and later of performances of works by Cimarosa, Mozart, and Rossini, the theater was explicitly "for those of the first rank, so disposed that they who choose may be divided into separate companies" (boxes), as contrasted with the common theater, which afforded "accommodations for every class of people." In the late eighteenth century, when a day's wages for a clerk or skilled laborer were about three shillings and the price of admission to other London theaters was also three shillings, a seat in the pit at the King's cost ten shillings, a seat in the first gallery five, and in the second gallery three. Nor was expense the only obstacle to attendance by the lower orders. Full evening dress was required for entrance, except to the second gallery, "so miserably situated as to prevent that part of the public from visiting the opera who could not afford the first price."[17] For the English-speaking world, the King's Theatre was the model of exclusiveness.

T h e Italian opera house was as widely accepted as Italian opera. It was "the general guide for similar structures in other parts; and they have the credit of having arrived the nearest to perfection."[18] But it didn't go unchallenged. The most important reform—open galleries instead of enclosed boxes—came from France, where Enlightenment thinkers insisted that music, like all the arts, should be available to the people. The French Revolution generated a wave of egalitarianism. In Paris, the opera house, so obviously a symbol of privilege, was closed down by a hostile crowd two days *before* the fall of the Bastille. At La Scala in Milan, with the (temporary) overthrow of the hated Austrian tyranny, the royal box was divided into six small boxes for "liberated people."[19] Eventually, with the end of the Napoleonic Wars, the Congress of Vienna heralded a restoration of the old order. The old Italian opera house reappeared, and with it the opera box.

At much the same time in the United States, with its national commitment to democracy and the abolition of privilege, people began to confront the difficult question of what it would mean to be culturally as well as politically independent. Where better to consider questions about opera, language, types of patronage, buildings, and audiences than in the first capital of the new nation, Philadelphia?

c h a p t e r   f i v e

Philadelphia

In Europe, opera was intimately connected with the centers of power: the patronage of the court, the authority of the state. In America, there was no court, no metropolitan hub, no capital sun around which the provincial planets circled—no center at all. For its first twenty-five years the new nation experimented with government on tour, affairs of state conducted in many different places. Finally, the site for a permanent national capital was chosen, a place so distant and barren that it proved of no importance in the cultural life of the nation for another century and a quarter. The five largest cities, Boston, Charleston, New Orleans, New York, and Philadelphia, competed for cultural predominance. Each had distinctive traditions. Each denied the claims of its rivals. In regard to theater, however, no one disputed the characterization of Philadelphia and New York as "rival monarchs . . . dividing the United States between them."[1] In music, Philadelphia stood alone.

Philadelphia: its trim, well-kept, red-brick houses fronting on tree-lined cobblestone streets, crisscrossing each other with regular rectangularity, exuded an impression of order. From Washington Irving's New York City perspective, the pattern of Philadelphia's streets shaped the character of its inhabitants: "They are an honest, worthy, square, good-looking, well-meaning, regular, uniform, straight-forward, clock-work, clear-headed, one-like-another, salubrious, up-right kind of people, who always go to work methodically, never turn but in right angles."[2] Philadelphia had established its reputation in the eighteenth century as the most progressive city in the Americas. But as cool rationalism gave way to the hot turbulence of romanticism, as growth, not order, became the hallmark of urban progress, Philadelphia began to seem dull, a place where "public amusements are nothing, the fine arts little considered" and "questions of mere speculation in literature or philosophy would be looked upon as a waste of time."[3] Actually, Philadelphia hadn't changed. What had changed was the idea of an environment favorable to artistic inspiration.

From the first, the city combined a tradition of conventional respectability with one of intellectual dissent, of openness to foreign ideas. The Society of Friends, tolerant in other things, was hostile to the public performance of music, and in the colony's early years it had the support in this of Baptists, Presbyterians, and Methodists. However, the Quakers' musical prejudice was undercut by their religious tolerance, which attracted to Pennsylvania Anglicans, Roman Catholics, and Lutherans for

45

whom music was an important part of religious observance. As a result, by the middle of the eighteenth century a diverse musical life existed in Philadelphia and the surrounding countryside; numerous musicians resided and performed there, and music was printed on the city's presses.

Important social changes affected the city's musical development for the next half-century. The Quakers withdrew from political leadership. The Germans concentrated in towns away from Philadelphia. The ensuing vacuum was filled by English music and musicians, whose dominance lasted for seventy-five years. Philadelphia bubbled with creators and inventors. It was the home of lively activity in publishing, architecture, painting. It was the home of speculative science in the persons of David Rittenhouse, Benjamin Rush, and Joseph Priestley. It was the home of the American Philosophical Society. Music flourished. There, the first American piano was manufactured in 1775, the upright piano invented in 1800.

Philadelphia's greatest musical distinction was as the home of American opera composers. Francis Hopkinson (1737–1791) embodied the city's multifaceted activity. Franklin-like in his versatility as politician, signer of the Declaration of Independence, member of the Constitutional Convention of 1787, judge, Secretary of the Navy, he was also a composer of chamber music, of songs, and of opera. *The Temple of Minerva,* which Hopkinson called an "oratorical entertainment," was entirely sung, with no spoken dialogue. It was performed for the French minister on December 11, 1781, before a select company, including General and Mrs. George Washington.

Alexander Reinagle (1756–1809)—English, despite his German-sounding name—was raised in a theatrical, musical family in Scotland. He came to America in 1786 and settled in Philadelphia, where for the next seventeen years he composed piano pieces, arranged and published collections of songs, taught, gave public concerts of the music of Haydn, Grétry, Bach, and Mozart. His own important work was theatrical. Reinagle and his partner, the English actor Thomas Wignell, built the Chestnut Street Theatre in Philadelphia and the Holliday Street Theatre in Baltimore, presenting musical drama at both. Reinagle directed the theater orchestra from the piano (he was the first American musician to replace harpsichord with piano in the orchestra pit) and composed works for its stage: operas, melodramas, pantomimes, farces, comedies. Among the operas were *Robin Hood* (1794), *The Spanish Barbers* (1794), *The Volunteers* (1795), *Auld Robin Gray* (1795), *The Travellers* (1807). Twenty-nine works for the theater are attributed to him, and he took part in several hundred productions. Unfortunately, few of his musical scores remain. Only a few were published in his lifetime, and all the manuscript material was destroyed when the Chestnut Street Theatre burned down in 1820.

Benjamin Carr (1768–1831) was also English, a student of the opera composer Samuel Arnold. He emigrated to the United States in 1793 and launched a career in Philadelphia of impressive activity and diversity, as organist, pianist, conductor, music publisher, collector and editor of sacred music, singer. Carr arranged numerous works of other composers and composed two operas of his own. The better known, *The Archers* (1796), on the subject of William Tell, which Rossini made famous thirty years later, was performed in Boston, New York, and Philadelphia in

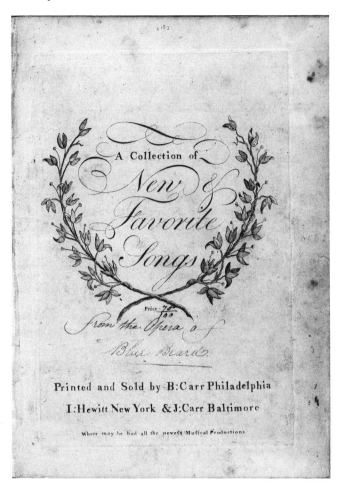

The title page of Benjamin Carr's New and Favorite Songs, *a collection of arias from the opera* Blue Beard. *Carr composed his own operas and provided additional music for ballad operas by other composers. John Herrick Jackson Music Library, Yale University.*

1796 and 1797. Raynor Taylor (1747–1825), trained in England as a choir singer, organist, and leader of a theatrical orchestra, came to the United States in 1792 and ended up in Philadelphia. He was a prolific composer of songs and of a number of operas, including *Buxom Joan* (1801), *May Day* (1815), and *The Rose of Aragon* (1822).

I n the first third of the nineteenth century, Philadelphia's operatic history fell into two clearly marked periods. The first, from 1800 to 1827, was characterized by the dominance of English opera and opera in English. After the War of 1812, English opera became so popular that Lorenzo Da Ponte, who lived there between 1811 and 1818 and dreamed of introducing Italian opera to the city, bewailed the unwillingness of Philadelphians to take an interest in any other kind of opera. The records of the Chestnut Street Theatre from 1810 to 1835 show that fifty-five operas were performed, among them the most popular English operas—Thomas Arne's *Artaxerxes* and *Love in a Village,* Samuel Arnold's *The Castle of Andalusia,* Charles Dibdin's *Lionel and Clarissa,* Thomas Linley's *The Duenna,* William Shield's *Robin Hood, The Farmer,* and *The Poor Soldier,* Stephen Storace's *The Haunted Tower.*

The well-known English opera singers who came to America exemplified the two kinds of operatic singing of the day. The first, deriving from Italian opera, was the "ornate," which required the technical skill to sing elaborate embellishments. It was commonly described as "scientific" singing and, if overdone, the singer was said to have "too much science." The other was the "simple," deriving from ballad opera. In this, technical demands were few but a premium was placed on communicating feeling and on the personality of the singer. Charles Incledon (1763–1826), a tenor, was the most famous exponent of the simple style. Incledon had been a sailor in his youth, turned to singing, made his London debut in *The Castle of Andalusia* in 1790, and remained a popular favorite for the next thirty years. He could manage the ornate style as well—he sang in the first English performance of Haydn's *The Creation* in 1790—but it was his nautical and patriotic ballads which gained him the affection of his audiences. He came to Philadelphia in 1817–1818. His acting was "slovenly and ineffective," but his listeners didn't seem to mind. His personality, his John Bull attitudes, his evocation of old-time English life touched responsive chords. The most famous exponents of the ornate school were Mrs. Joseph Wood and John Braham. Mrs. Wood and her company of well-trained English singers gave twenty different operas in a long season in 1833, all in English. Arne's *Artaxerxes* gave American audiences a chance to become familiar with English opera on the Italian model. Braham (1777–1856), the most renowned English tenor of the early nineteenth century, came to North America in 1840–1842. He was in his sixties by the time he arrived, and his voice was in tatters. Braham's appearance inaugurated a phenomenon that would become familiar to opera-loving Americans—extreme anticipation giving way to intense disappointment: "at last," followed by "too late."[4]

Slowly, Philadelphia's English character was changing in the 1820s. Refugees, many of them French and many of them musicians, fleeing political repression, came to the city. Eventually, there were several thousand French families in the city, with their own newspapers, printing press, and bookshop. "Philadelphia boarding houses swarmed with these emigrés, few of whom knew any English and they supplied the theatres with admirable orchestras and modified the manners of the town." Nevertheless, the city's prevailing sobriety remained intact. The actress Fanny Kemble thought Philadelphians over-solemn: "immovable, very sticks and stones. The most unapplausive I ever acted to." Another visitor recalled that "the greatest quiet reigned in the streets contiguous to the theatre, strongly contrasted with the like neighborhoods in England, or even in New York." But Frances Trollope had heard so much about the city's "decorum of demeanor" that she was shocked to see a man in the lower tier of boxes at the Chestnut Street "deliberately take off his coat that he might enjoy the refreshing coolness of shirt sleeves." That was bad enough. Worse followed: "All the gentlemen wore their hats, and the spitting was unceasing."[5]

In the late summer of 1827, John Davis's New Orleans company introduced Philadelphia to Weber's *Robin des bois,* the French version of *Der Freischütz.* This relatively recent (1821) example of German romantic sensibility seized the attention of Phila-

"Box at the Theatre," from Frances Trollope's Domestic Manners of the Americans (1832). *Mrs. Trollope's criticism of democratic manners infuriated Americans. Beinecke Rare Book and Manuscript Library, Yale University.*

delphia audiences. "Nearly all were in their places before the overture was begun," one writer observed with surprise, "so that this admirable composition was both executed and enjoyed without interruption or alloy." The Hunters' Chorus, listened to with "deep emotion," conveyed powerfully Weber's "wild but splendid genius." The work aroused feelings of terror in the "more sensitive and quick-nerved spectators."[6]

The company also introduced Philadelphia to a unified style of acting and singing—"It is in the ensemble . . . that superiority of the performance over what we have known must be acknowledged." In the resident English companies there were always "some bunglers so awkward and so far misplaced as to throw a shade of burlesque or grotesque over the whole business of the stage." But in the French company, "all the parts are judiciously cast: All understand their several parts and their combined action." The orchestra, "the ablest body of musicians ever collected in the same place," was part of this combined action. Its leader—the term *conductor* was not yet in use— Monsieur Paradol, a musician of "talent and exactness," firmly controlled the instrumentalists and singers and "imparted additional animation to both orchestra and stage, beyond anything seen before at the Chestnut Street Theater."[7]

The French company also brought opera as a special social occasion. Newspapers described the events and the city's social elite in the most extravagant terms: "numerous and dazzling," "elegantly dressed without gaudiness," "uncommonly brilliant assemblages." The glamor of the exotic French opera contrasted with the succession of homely, familiar English operas. Women were the focus. "Very beautiful or very well dressed ladies take much delight in showing off their charms." This was largely an upper-class show, as was made clear by one writer's suggestion that future performances begin earlier because "heads of families do not choose to be kept out until midnight, nor to keep their servants from their beds in waiting for them."[8]

The visit of the New Orleans company inaugurated the second period in nineteenth-century Philadelphia opera history. It was one of a multilingual repertory, English, French, and, by the early 1830s, Italian. Operas were performed in the language of the singers available. *La Cenerentola* and *Fra Diavolo* alternated with *Love in a Village* or *The Young Hussar*. *Il Barbiere di Siviglia* played at one theater, *The Barber of Seville* at another. Operas were combined in what would seem to us incongruous double-bills—Beethoven's *Fidelio* playing with Dibdin's ballad opera *The Waterman*—but perhaps audiences could readily shift from Florestan's peril to Tom Tug's foolery. Singers switched from English to a foreign language in the same week or even in the same opera in one evening. The predominance of English opera was imperiled, but it wasn't clear which school of opera—if any—would win out. Whatever kind of operatic audience was being formed, it would reflect the characteristics of the larger theatergoing audience, members of which brought assumptions, values, and prejudices with them which observers, and especially foreign travelers, had long commented on. In this respect Philadelphia represented the nation.

A b o u t one thing almost all observers agreed—American audiences were "different" from European ones.

One difference was immediately visible: women of all social classes felt freer to sit where they wished. Modest ticket prices meant that middle-class women of no social standing could afford box seats. Even the "pit," the area immediately in front of the orchestra, heretofore a masculine preserve, had been invaded by women. The sight of "several females of respectability comfortably seated" there suggested that this "innovation [would] become universal."[9] Prostitutes had traditionally been restricted to the upper galleries, but observers detected women of the "Cyprian profession" sitting everywhere. Anyway, distinctions of social rank based upon dress were increasingly difficult to detect as cheaper, standardized, ready-made clothing became more common.

Opera in America showed signs of becoming an art consumed by women. Men composed operas, organized their production, staged them, and played in their orchestras. Women sang in them and filled their audiences. "Why does not opera attract a more considerable body of gentlemen?" was asked early and frequently.[10] The answer is that men turned all of art over to women. Art and the home were women's concerns, business and politics were men's. Men felt awkward in the presence of art. Men made war and money. Art was for dilettantes or amateurs. Aristocrats felt easy about being connoisseurs—good taste was one of the things that marked them as aristocrats—but middle-class men in a middle-class culture? For them there was something unmanly about art. There was certainly something unmanly about opera and ballet. They were excessive, emotional, unconstrained.

Conversely, women were temperamentally suited to opera because it demanded emotional response and women were more emotional, more capable of "higher" feelings than men. And women were also suited to opera and opera to them because it was as much a social occasion as it was an art. Max Maretzek (1821–1897), composer, conductor, and impresario, ruminated on the extraordinary importance of women in American artistic affairs. His analysis, while spasmodic and nervously facetious in tone, gives us a deeply informed and often sympathetic description of women's cultural situation.

That situation was hopelessly contradictory, Maretzek believed, because it was rooted in the inability of society to give women a proper active outlet for their talents. The American woman's life was a "concentration of passions, virtues, ambitions, jealousies, loves, mysteries, flirtations, hates, disappointments, and pleasures. These produce a sort of poetic confusion in her own conscience, and render her not only a problem to others, but an enigma, even to herself." After "years of internal struggles, worn out by the doubt which has proved itself unable to afford her a solution for the intricated and Gordian-like riddle of her own existence, in nine cases out of ten she becomes religious, and in the tenth instance sinks into literature." The American woman took up art. Here, too, she did so in conditions severely limited by her culture's definition of art. To the American man, "the most important matter, after money, is fashion." In a bourgeois culture like America, art was a commodity whose value was dictated by the market's demand. Fashion, the expression of that demand, was the domain of women, "originated, kept up, quitted, resumed, revolutionized, restored, put out of the way, found again rebaptized by the ladies!" But the American woman had two supreme qualities which rescued her from the triviality of her social condition—common sense and appreciation for "the really grand and beautiful."

America was indebted to its women for "whatever has been done in this country for artistic cultivation and progress, or refinement of life." "It is the ladies alone that patronize and love the Arts. These, alone, know anything about them."[11]

Another important characteristic of American audiences was that they seemed less clearly distinguished by class. They mirrored the larger society, whose mixed condition was a byword throughout Europe. The main reason for this was the greater abundance of material means and the greater diffusion of those means throughout society. "Elsewhere luxury is only to be found in the upper ranks of society," but in America it was everywhere. It had penetrated "to the cottage of the workingman and the country laborer," so that in the United States there was no distinction in dress. "The maid is dressed like the mistress, and the poorest workingman like the First Magistrate."[12]

As a result, American audiences were a "strange medley of manners and deportment." There was no coherent style, "no such thing as conformity of dress, behavior, or appearance." Even the first tier of boxes in any theater or opera house, the most socially desirable, "exhibits all sorts of apparel: cloaks, overcoats, frock-coats, yellow, black and parti coloured cravats; a perfect chaos of garments and colours." The European opera house, clearly marked and ordered, was being replaced in America by a theater of social uncertainty. The extended comment of one English traveler brings

NEW OPERA COSTUME.

The early American opera house was preeminently a woman's realm. Despite the blurring of social distinctions, fashion-consciousness never waned. Godey's Ladies Book *published this design in 1850. Sterling Memorial Library, Yale University.*

together a number of these observations. He visited a theater and bought a ticket. So far, so good.

> I went to the pit, concluding that, with an allowance for the difference in country, it would resemble the same department in an English establishment; but found it consisted of none in dress, manners, appearance, or habits above the order of our Irish brick-layers; a strong fact this to prove the good payment of labour. Here were men that, if in London, would hardly buy a pint of porter—and should they ever think of seeing a play, must take up their abode among the gods in the upper gallery; yet, in America, they can pay three-quarters of a dollar—free of care, and without feeling, on the following morning, that they must compensate, by deprivation or extra-ordinary labour, for their extravagance.[13]

Audiences were prudish. They associated art with the erotic and licentious, especially theater and dance, painting and sculpture. Any worldly American took for granted the prudery of his native land, "where a nude statue flushed the cheek of innocence, and where the unadorned nymphs of a Rubens or a Titian would have been stigmatised as indecent." Joseph Bonaparte (present at that first performance by the Garcías) had settled in the United States at "Point Breeze," near Bordentown, New Jersey. He had classical statuary in his house and garden. When American visitors came, he assumed that they would be embarrassed by what they saw, so out of deference to them he covered his statues with cloth.[14]

Opera was less directly troubling because it was often incomprehensible. An American visitor in Paris, profoundly disgusted by Victor Hugo's play *Lucrecia Borgia,* the prominent feature of which was the incestuous love of a brother for a sister, was disconcerted a few years later, back in the United States, to find that, converted into an opera, "with the plot disguised in Italian and embellished with exquisite melody of Donizetti, it had become one of the most popular of lyric dramas." Some operatic customs made people uneasy—"trouser" roles, for example (women dressed as men). Occasionally, an operatic scene was unmistakably disturbing. It usually turned out to be French. Auber's *Fra Diavolo* contained "the peculiar scene of a lady retiring for the night and going through the ceremony of attiring herself for that purpose." Right on stage! Shocking in 1833, it was also a portent. Most operas were set in a vague and very distant past, which gave the goings-on an air of unreality. Even so, drama had enormous power, "as we are more apt to imitate the actions and passions of men when we see them represented than when we merely read or hear them." Therefore, the "greatest care" had to be taken to banish the immoral or obscene from the stage. Yet frequently in the theater, not least in English drama, things were done and said "which caused the females present to conceal their faces in their handkerchiefs and to turn away their heads in disgust."[15] *Fra Diavolo* was almost contemporary in its setting. What would be the reaction of audiences if operas someday dealt in franker terms with the contemporary world?

Dance was the most erotically charged dramatic art for Americans, and the least familiar. In October 1815, a Spanish vessel headed for Cuba was forced by storms at sea to seek refuge in Baltimore. Aboard was Signora Aira, a dancer engaged to perform in Havana. While the ship was being repaired, the Spanish consul in Baltimore arranged for two performances by her. The audience was startled by the "peculiarity" of the bolero, a wholly unfamiliar dance. At the end of the first evening, "so divided were the audience as to the decency of the exhibition . . . that a strong remonstrance was forwarded to the manager against a repetition of her performance." A strong counterremonstrance also circulated, and Signora Aira danced again. The manager noted ruefully, however, that "the number of ladies on the second night was unusually small."[16]

A decade or so later, the manager of New York's Bowery Theatre audaciously introduced Madame Francisquy Hutin, "from the Opera House, Paris," who gave that audience their "first glimpse of 'modern' French dancing." The house was crowded. When she came on stage, "her light and scanty drapery floating in air, her symmetrical proportions liberally displayed by the force of a bewildering pirouette," an anxious look of "curiosity and expectation dwelt on every face." Accounts of that evening were contradictory. For some it was so shocking that "the cheeks of the greater portion of the audience were crimsoned with shame, and every lady in the lower tier of boxes immediately left the house." Others responded calmly. "Such a thing was as novel and startling as the performance of Italian opera had been a year ago." But fears about the "liberal style of European dancing" proved groundless. Madame Hutin's performance was "triumphant." "The rapidity of her movements is only to be equalled by their precision, ease and beauty." And, reassuringly: "She is besides a very fine woman."[17]

American audiences were undiscriminating, susceptible to slogans. "They heave and bellow at every allusion to Liberty, Freedom, or other Republican pass-words." They succumbed to superficial theatrical effects.

> Showy scenery and new dresses, which may be admired without any learning or effort of thought, come in for a large proportion of praise: and a speech, which has cost perhaps some hours of labor is eclipsed by a handsome moon, an old bridge in the background. A grocer's sign, in the farce, will set the house in a roar, when Falstaff's wit has failed; the supernumeraries hitting each other on the head with wooden javelins, make the house tremble to the foundations [while the speeches of Hamlet] are listened to with a sort of patient resignation.[18]

Was this simply another aspect of that European image of the New World as essentially, perhaps permanently, uncivilized—and, added to it now, the pervasive European fear of the leveling effects of American democracy?

American audiences were prevailingly materialist. This, to put it plainly, meant that Americans cared only about money. "Gain is the aim of the education—the morals, the politics, the theology . . . of all ages and classes of Americans. It is the centre of their system, from which they derive both light and heat."[19] This was the most persistent and familiar charge brought against American culture. How could theater audiences have escaped it? It wasn't only foreigners who said it. Americans said it of each other. The South said it of the North. The East believed it of the West. And everyone understood about the South where, beneath the thin glaze of gentility, human beings were sold for money.

In any event, numerous commentators believed that the charge of money-madness was a superficial one. A deeper American value was utility. Whether one made money or not was not the primary issue. Opera and theater suffered because material prosperity produced in Americans a disdain for leisure, not an increased appetite for it. It was a basically utilitarian frame of mind which led Americans to regard business and science as rational, because practical, while art was irrational, because useless. Added to this was the literal-minded, fact-centered quality of American education. American republicanism appealed "to the reason of men, and ignored their imagination." So it was that "the very advantages of America turn against the arts," because excellence in art, "to be rightly judged, must be powerfully felt," whereas Americans were taught that "logical analysis, to think correctly on all subjects, is to feel strongly on none." Scientific detachment was cool, artistic inspiration hot. Americans could discover "no practical benefits of which [art] is productive. In their eyes, it is a mere appanage of aristocracy."[20]

Aristocracy! In these early years of American republicanism, when some citizens did more than merely pay lip service to the idea of equality, when Americans called each other "citizen" and newspapers announced marriages between Citizen Jones and Citizenness Smith, when foreign titles such as "ambassador" were abandoned for the purity of the designation "minister," and when the first citizen of the land was called simply "mister," few words carried more unfavorable connotations than "aristocracy." Much of what was brutal, exploitative, and decadent in European culture was, for Americans, symbolized by the image of the arrogant, licentious, rapacious aristocrat. Opera had been intimately associated with aristocratic patronage, which was identified with exclusive privilege. Why not free art from the patronage of corrupt aristocrats and kings? There *was* an alternative. Many years earlier John Adams had ruminated: "Is it possible to enlist the fine arts on the side of truth, of virtue, of piety or even of honor? From the dawn of history they have been prostituted to the services of superstition and despotism."[21] Let America free itself from the dead hand of this past. Let America lead the way, in this as in other things, by developing public sponsorship of art, patronage by a democratic state. Let the *people* be patrons!

T h e 1820s mark the beginning of a decisive shift *away* from the mercantilist ideas which had dominated political thought, in America as well as in Europe, for a century and a half. In place of the idea that the state should intervene intimately in the affairs of the community in order to achieve agreed-upon public goals, the United States was moving toward opposition to state intervention. In this view, the ultimate goals of the community would emerge unplanned, as the sum of individual values, by means of a competitive marketplace. This philosophy went directly contrary to the idea that Alexander Hamilton had fostered in the early years of the new nation, in which government subsidy and direction would serve as the engine for development and growth: a state-run national bank; subsidies for manufacturing; a tariff to protect infant industries. As late as the presidential administration of John Quincy Adams (1825–1829), this mercantilist idea retained its coherence and some power. Adams extended it beyond business activities and proposed a system of national astronomical observatories.

But the tide was beginning to run strongly in the opposite direction. Adams was for this, and for other reasons, swept out of office in 1828. Andrew Jackson swept in. Such planning and patronage was seen by Jackson as "aristocratic" and "undemocratic." The existing national bank was abolished, national turnpikes were struck down, proposals for a national university and national observatories were rejected with contempt. America turned from mercantilism to laissez-faire.

There still were "public" enterprises—docks, railroads, warehouses, customhouses, jails, bridges—but these were state or local in sponsorship and they were mostly connected with commerce and profit-making activities. The imagination and energy with which Americans pursued such public projects was impressive. Frances Trollope, the English observer who infuriated Americans by her caustic comments about their uncouth social behavior, shrewdly and vividly celebrated their achievements in this other realm of action:

> There is no point in the national character of the Americans which commands so much respect as the boldness and energy with which public works are undertaken and carried through. Nothing stops them if a profitable result can be fairly hoped for. It is this which has made cities spring up amidst the forests with such inconceivable rapidity; and could they once be thoroughly persuaded that any point of the ocean had a hoard of dollars beneath it, I have not the slightest doubt that in about eighteen months we should see a snug-covered railroad leading direct to the spot.[22]

Few aspects of American culture seemed odder to Europeans than this new attitude toward the state. It also meant that artists were free from the rules and regulations, the licenses and petty exactions of the artistic bureaucracy. As Lorenzo Da Ponte wrote to an Italian impresario who had inquired about the role of the state in musical affairs: "As for a license from the government and the assurance of being able to sing without tax or fees, set your mind completely at ease. The government does not interfere in such matters at all. It has no theater that it owns, it does not pay and asks no payment from the entertainments of the citizens. As long as order, decency, observance of the laws, and the peace are preserved, everyone can do as he pleases."[23] Do as you please! William Dunlap, the playwright, saluted the fortunate America of the 1830s: "that thrice happy country where the man of virtue and talents is the only acknowledged superior, where the artist needs no protector and acknowledges no patron."[24]

There was another side to this "freedom" from the state, however—the negation of public patronage for the arts. The consequences of applying laissez-faire principles to public art patronage were made clear by an early incident in Philadelphia. The city had built waterworks, designed by Benjamin Latrobe, in Fairmount Park. Latrobe had also been commissioned to design a fountain for the park, to be built with public funds. The fountain provoked vehement opposition. The waterworks justified themselves. But a fountain? Who really *needed* it? One might well have asked, Who needed the park? The answer was, of course, that the citizens of Philadelphia needed the park, just as they needed the waterworks, and needed the fountain too—to enhance their lives in their community in regard to things which could have nothing to do with making a profit. After much clamor and commotion, the fountain was built and placed in a handsomely planted square, the *first* public fountain erected in the United States. It became one of the city's most popular meeting places. No appreciable harm befell the city.[25] That was as far as Philadelphia was prepared to go in sponsoring art in 1809, and for many years afterward, but the fountain, in its modest way, raised important issues in the history of all the arts in America.

Three American Theaters

Markets and warehouses, taverns and tobacco sheds, the local court-house—these were the first homes of opera in North America. Like the court theaters of Europe, they were all-purpose places adapted to theater. Unlike them, they were the scene of ordinary public business that had nothing to do with the splendor of the state, everything to do with day-to-day commerce.

The first specially built theaters came in the 1740s, small wooden affairs, customarily painted red: on Dock Street in Charleston, South Carolina; near the capital building in Williamsburg, Virginia; on Nassau Street in New York. These were soon replaced by more substantial structures, privately financed by the manager of a touring theatrical company which needed a semipermanent base for its jaunts through the countryside. Such were the two theaters built in New York in the 1760s or the brick theater in Annapolis, Maryland. The most notable was the Southwark, built in Philadelphia in 1766. Ugly, ramshackle, the largest theater of its day, it was also the first American theater to be called an opera house. The provisional character of these colonial buildings was summed up in the words on the stage curtain of the log theater built by British troops in Staunton, Virginia, during the Revolutionary War—"Who would have expected this here?"[1]

They were English theaters, in an English country, but in a cruder form than their prototypes across the Atlantic. In some theaters, sharpened metal spikes separated the boxes from the rest of the seats, and the function of the boxes was unclear. In Royall Tyler's play *The Contrast,* of 1787, Jonathan goes to a playhouse: "So I went right in, and they shewed me away, clear up to the garret, just like meeting-house gallery. And so I saw a power of topping folks, all sitting around in little cabins, just like father's corn-cribs."

Time and new conditions turned these theaters into something different, though people tried mightily to reconstruct the old forms, as we see in John Esten Cooke's nineteenth-century historical novel *The Virginia Comedians,* which describes the visit of the Hallam Company to "the old theatre near the Capitol in Williamsburg," the velvet-cushioned and flower-decorated boxes glistening "like a line of foam around the semi-circle of the theater," the pit occupied by "well dressed men of the lower class," the gallery folk still speaking "the unforgotten slang of London," the young gallants of the day behaving as their peers did in London theaters, clustering in the wings, flirting with the actresses.[2]

In the first decade of national independence, there was a burst of theater construction—the Charleston Theatre and the Chestnut Street Theatre in Philadelphia, both 1792; the Federal Theatre in Boston, 1794; and the Park Theatre in New York, 1798. Although they were built on English models and managed on English principles, they were being transformed into something American. The parquette, the seating adjacent to the stage or orchestra pit, in America came to be called the orchestra. The section at the rear of the parquette, a fashionable location, came to be called the dress circle. The balcony was called the gallery in England. And the opera season, which in England meant from May through July, in America would come to mean anything—a few days or weeks or months at almost any time of the year.

American theaters were in many ways crude and uncomfortable places, unbearably hot in summer, frigid in winter. Cumbersome efforts were made to heat them. Stoves were placed under the stage and in the lobby, with pipes carrying the heat into the auditorium. Lobbies often had a fireplace, sometimes one at each end. Prudent people came warmly dressed and brought their own foot-warmers. So cold were the winters that when, in the 1820s, oil replaced wood, the oil sometimes froze. Severe snowstorms frequently closed theaters. Other arrangements were equally rough. There were no facilities for dining other than benches along the walls of the lobbies, where people sat to eat the fruit, pies, and custards sold there. Theaters had no toilets. The Bowery Theatre's management built a privy in the grounds outside the building. But there *were* bars or saloons where members of the audience drank brandy, gin, or whiskey. Their liberal patronage by theatergoers led to so many fights that the maintenance of a special police force, paid by the management, was necessary. In San Francisco and New Orleans, gambling rooms were adjacent to, or actually part of, the theater.

Theaters were as dark as they were uncomfortable. Chandeliers furnished most of the light, whether a large central one or a series of smaller ones. They ranged from elaborate and expensive works of art to simple arrangements in which candles were fitted into holders or were jammed onto nails. In any case, dripping was a serious problem. A man was usually employed by the theater as stove and chandelier watcher. With so many exposed flames or fires, with the prevailing wooden construction and with flammable decorative materials, no wonder theatergoing was haunted by the awareness that fire was a likelihood, not just a possibility. This was true in Europe as well as in America. In the century from 1797 to 1897 there were eleven hundred auditorium fires in Europe and America. The average life of a theater or public hall was estimated to be eighteen years. Early fire insurance companies refused to cover theaters on actuarial, not moral, grounds.

Lighting the theater's auditorium was a great problem even beyond the fire danger. If the main chandelier was over the apron of the stage, the balcony was well lighted and so was the stage. However, the view of the stage from the balcony was obstructed, while the pit and boxes could see the stage but were themselves plunged in gloom. If chandeliers were placed to light the pit and boxes, visibility from the upper tiers was impeded. Lighting the stage properly was also difficult, so performers tended to move to the front where they could be seen. Lowering the lights in the auditorium was done in full view of the audience by a stagehand or by someone employed specially for that job, if possible while the scenery was being shifted and accompanied by music. Lowering the lights on stage was sometimes done by a performer, who might interrupt speech or song. The only way the footlights could be diminished was by literally lowering them. They were generally a row of candles, often without covering glass, attached to a board or piece of metal. This was lowered below the level of the stage. Everything changed in the gaslight era, beginning in the 1830s and 1840s. Then it was possible to turn the lights down at once for the entire house by reducing the amount of gas from one central location.

The eighteenth-century American theaters were very small, perhaps eighty by forty feet, seating only a few hundred. The theaters of the 1790s and the early 1800s were considerably larger, comparable in size to large Italian opera houses, seating as many as two thousand people. The typical stage was small and shallow, even as the rest of the theater increased in size. However, as the nineteenth century developed a taste for more elaborate productions and the means to gratify it, the size of the stage also increased. The orchestra pit was lowered. The stage was hidden from the eyes of the audience by a green curtain, behind which were several other curtains. Painted on these might be a landscape, a famous historical scene, an allegorical painting, or some local associations. The complex process by which the audience was involved in the performance began with the raising of the green curtain. With its lowering, as the comments of that inveterate theatergoer Washington Irving make clear, "we might ascertain the termination of a piece." Otherwise, "one had to await the polite bows of the actors for this pleasing information."[3] For many country folk, a visit to a theater was a new and remarkable event, whose conventions were learned slowly.

The means for creating illusions to beguile audiences were not as sophisticated as the machinery the Venetians and French had developed long before. There were four types of scenery for opera: wings, flats, flies, drop curtain. Three to five parallel grooves were cut in the stage and the wings and flats were pushed along in these by hand. Backdrops, used to represent interiors and exteriors, were mounted on rollers and could be fastened to frames and lifted above the stage—these were the flies. Everything was painted on canvas. A few standard pieces of scenery were used for all opera productions, whatever the subject or historical period. In the early nineteenth century a change began to take place. There developed a desire for greater authenticity, scenery designed for particular works and suited to individual productions. This made productions more complex and expensive. The need to accommodate more elaborate scenery was one of the reasons for enlarging the stage and backstage, and the need to meet the increased costs for this was a factor in enlarging the theater. American theaters had depended upon scenery designed in England, though painted in America. Among the émigrés of the 1790s were a considerable number of French and Italian scenery designers whose presence raised the level of design, and thereafter Americans designed their own sets. A new means for creating special effects was also developed: dioramic, or moving, scenery. In these ways American theaters were better able to respond to the increasingly complex demands of nineteenth-century opera.

Architecture was a new profession in the United States in these years and only a handful of men practiced it, but among them were a number of talented individuals who devoted considerable time to building theaters: Charles Bullfinch in Boston, Ithiel Town and Alexander Jackson Davis in New York, Benjamin Henry Latrobe and William Strickland in Philadelphia. The surge in theatrical construction provided them with an exciting opportunity to work out their ambivalent feelings about England and about the idea of equality, as a closer look at three theaters will show.

T h e first theater on the site, on Chestnut Street, near Sixth, built in 1791–1794 by those two Philadelphia musical-theatrical men, Thomas Wignell and Alexander Reinagle, was too small for the growing town by 1801, its lobbies and entrances cramped, its gabled brick exterior "old-fashioned." Latrobe remodeled it as one of the first Greek revival buildings, an effort by Americans to connect their democracy with Athens and disconnect it from Great Britain. Some of the first American public sculpture—Comedy and Tragedy, carved in wood by William Rush—adorned its facade.

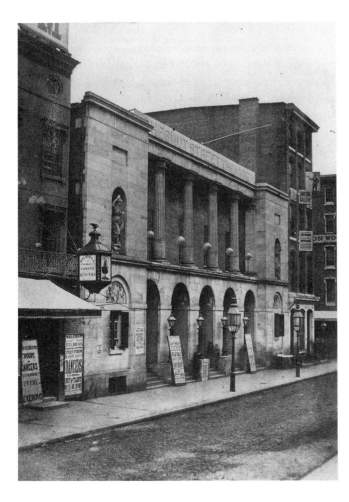

The staid neoclassical facade of Philadelphia's Chestnut Street Theatre, photographed in 1870, belied the diversity of its clientele. Note the saloon next door. Library of Congress.

61

In 1820 the theater burned to the ground and was quickly rebuilt by Strickland, a pupil of Latrobe's and a native Philadelphian. He retained its old configuration and the Rush sculptures, and made it even more neoclassical. Contemporary accounts emphasized "spacious lobbies warmed by fireproof furnaces" and a handsome saloon and coffee room, but the Chestnut Street retained much of its staid, somewhat stiff angularity.

Philadelphians called it "Old Drury," but its audiences were enthusiastically patriotic, which in these years meant a mixture of admiration and hostility for things British. In 1798 "Hail Columbia" was first sung on its stage, received with rapture, repeated eight times. The ninth time "the whole audience stood up and joined the chorus." Yet the Chestnut Street was also identified with an elite sympathetic to Britain and British culture. During the war of 1812–1814 it was the scene of several disturbances in which class feelings and patriotic emotions were involved. In one incident, otherwise unexplained, the theater's manager "maligned the mechanics of the town." In another, members of the Congress called for patriotic tunes from the theater orchestra, which refused to comply. "Some words and a blow passed," and the congressmen, "heated with wine," pelted the orchestra with nuts and apples.[4]

Whatever the anglophile sympathies of its management, the Chestnut Street attracted a mixed audience. It aimed at a family trade. Prices were modest, with a portion of the gallery "appropriate to persons of color." Reconciling British traditions with emerging democratic values was difficult, as the Anne Bingham affair made clear. Anne Willing Bingham lived in Europe with her wealthy husband in the 1780s, enjoying the social life of the royal courts of Paris, London, and The Hague. Rich, intelligent, ambitious, on her return to the United States she conceived the idea of presiding over a salon, like those which had become familiar to her in Paris and London, where she could bring together the fragmented pieces of American social, political, and artistic life. She was forthright about her social aims. Two of her daughters married into the English financial house of Baring Brothers, and she frequently entertained aristocratic French and English visitors. At the same time, she wanted somehow to come to terms with American democratic culture. That posed problems. Thomas Jefferson was a friend, and often in her house. But his followers disliked what she represented and they didn't meet her standards of elegance and sophistication. The failure of Anne Bingham and the Jeffersonians to find a common ground was a portent. She wanted to introduce in Philadelphia the kind of privileges she had enjoyed in Europe, which Jeffersonianism opposed, and the Chestnut Street Theatre played an important part in her plans.

Anne Bingham proposed that she purchase a box at the theater, to be furnished and decorated at her expense, on the condition that the key to it be kept by herself and that only she determine admission to it. From Thomas Wignell's point of view there were obvious practical considerations in favor of this proposal. Mrs. Bingham's patronage would serve as a powerful social encouragement to others like her. Offending her would damage the theater's prospects. However, looking at the matter in its "more comprehensive and philosophic regards," he explained why he refused her offer. "The theatre in a country like ours must depend entirely for permanent success, not upon individuals, however powerful, not upon clubs, cliques, factions, or parties, but upon THE PUBLIC alone. In a country where the spirit of liberty is so fierce as in ours, such a privilege would excite from an immense class a feeling of positive hostility."[5] Wignell staked his theatrical future on the belief that hatred of privilege would predominate in the United States. That seemed possible in the early 1800s. A quarter of a century after Anne Bingham's offer, for example, the disposition of box seats still remained a source of contention. Another manager of the Chestnut Street Theatre dealt with the same issue in a different way. He designated six boxes which, for an hour after the box-office sale of tickets opened, would be reserved for anyone who wished to take an entire box. After that, the seats would be sold on an individual basis. Even this excited opposition because it seemed to be yielding to the taint of privilege.

As late as the 1830s, William Woods, a Baltimore theater manager, took the same position as Wignell. A man who loved the drama proposed to Woods that he buy a box for the season, in order to be certain of seats for his family. He expressly stipulated that he did not want a fashionable box and that by noon of each day he would indicate whether the box would be used by his family. If not, the manager would have the key and could dispose of the box as he wished, augmenting the theater's income. Even this proposition had to be opposed. "Private boxes and a system of exclusive privileges have always been hankered for by a small class," wrote Woods, sometimes because of a genuine desire for privacy, but mostly because of "the love of ostentatious exhibition." No matter what the motivation, "every wise manager in America will set his face like a flint against it."[6]

Not so. Mrs. Bingham didn't get her personal box, nor did the anonymous Baltimorean. But boxes remained a feature of American theaters and the subscription system, in which boxes were bought for the season, to be used or not used as the subscriber wished, became the prevailing American system. This was a form of privilege, based on money, not social standing. It was the logical outcome of middle-class patronage—patronage by a plutocracy. Were the privileges associated with money not privileges?

This was the specter haunting the egalitarian imaginings of Jeffersonians and Jacksonians—not privilege from above but privilege from within. Did the middle class want to abolish social distinctions associated with privileged status or simply to inherit them from the disinherited aristocracy? Thomas Wignell and William Woods insisted that blatant forms of privilege like an exclusive opera box would be unacceptable in a country where "the spirit of liberty is so fierce as in ours." Was the spirit of liberty really so fierce? Wignell made the mistake of identifying it with the spirit of equality. What if its object was not equality but freedom—the freedom to be superior to others by being richer than others? Was wealth a form of privilege? An observer at the time noted how Americans treated Mrs. Robert Morris of Philadelphia: "As she is the richest woman in the city, and all ranks here being equal, men follow their natural bent, by giving preference to riches." Wignell suspected the worst and was forthright in his condemnation. Plutocracy was "the most despicable and poorest of all grounds of distinction."[7]

By the 1820s and 1830s, few Americans agreed with him in practice. Since there was no public sponsorship by city, state, or national government, and no court or aristocracy, what alternative was there to sponsorship of the arts by the wealthy—if they could be persuaded to sponsor them? Wignell wasn't consistent about this. Scathing as he was about plutocracy, he also argued that any theater manager must operate his theater on the assumption that it was open freely and equally to all—"all men free to come into his house and equal while they continued to be there and behave themselves in it." Free meant free to afford the price of admission, while equal meant . . . what? Women were not entirely free there, though freer than they had been. And what of those African Americans for whom only the twenty-five-cent gallery was available? Ticket buying was democratic but not egalitarian.

L i k e the public schools of later days, theaters were a kind of social laboratory where people mixed together. Given the volatility of the elements combined one can understand why, from time to time, these theatrical melting pots boiled over.

The Bowery Theatre in New York: "Americanism inside a Greek temple." From Frank Leslie's Illustrated Newspaper, *Sept. 13, 1856. Library of Congress.*

The Bowery was a theater of contrasts and paradoxes, Americanism inside a Greek temple. Visitors praised its architecture: "the boldest execution of the Doric order in the United States," a "tour-de-force of early New York classicism," the "finest building in New York City." The first Bowery Theatre (properly the New York Theatre, commonly the Bowery, which eventually became its official name: the people had their way) opened in 1826, burned down in 1828, and was rebuilt and reopened eighty-five days after the fire. Seven marble steps led up to the porch on which rested six massive columns (of newly invented stucco, imitating marble), between which five large doors led into the interior. The auditorium, seating two thousand, was a horseshoe, somewhat flattened at the center so that the boxes along each side had a better-than-usual view of the large, deep stage projecting out into the seats and creating a feeling of intimate involvement between audience and performers.

The interior was blue and crimson. The boxes were painted gold and ornamented with griffins, harps, and wreaths. The back of each box was painted apple-blossom color because that showed off the occupants best. The blue-and-gold dome revealed a figure scattering flowers on the audience below. Sumptuous crimson stage curtains opened and closed with an upward diagonal movement. The Bowery was unusually well lighted. Cut-glass lamps, in the shape of antique vases, each vase holding three large illuminated globes, were attached to all the tier fronts by brass scrolls. "As pretty a theater as I ever entered, perfect as to size and proportion, elegantly decorated," reported Mrs. Trollope; "scenery and machinery equal to any in the land. But it is not the fashion."[8] Walt Whitman recalled it "packed from ceiling to pit with full-blooded young and middle-aged men, the best average of American-born mechanics—the emotional nature of the whole mass . . . bursting forth in one of those long-kept-up tempests of hand-clapping peculiar to the Bowery, no dainty kid-glove business, but electric force and muscle from perhaps two thousand full-sinewed men."[9]

That audience evolved slowly, the result of chance, mischance, and policy. Charles Antonio Gilfert, the Bowery's first manager, a musician who had eventually become leader of the orchestra at the Park Theatre, had always wanted to be the impresario of an American opera house and bring opera to American audiences. He set about doing this by offering all tickets at the same price, making them available as much as three days in advance, with no reserved seats. He made the orchestra the best in the city. But he also set out to bring in the fashionable and sophisticated audiences. He imported French dancers, a new kind of play, *Life in New York, or Fire-Men on Duty,* characters and events from ordinary life familiar to his audience. He emphasized English opera, *Native Land, Guy Mannering, Rob Roy,* and Italian singers too. He induced a young American actor, Edwin Forrest, to come over from the Park Theatre, where he had made his debut. The Bowery flourished, but Gilfert did not live to discover if he had found a way to fuse his working-class and middle-class audience into one. He died, suddenly, in 1829.

Thomas Hamblin took over and headed the Bowery in a very different direction. He wanted to foster native talent and make the Bowery the preeminent American theater, to identify it with the interests and amusements of its neighborhood. Germans and Irish were moving into that neighborhood. At the same time, a strong anti-Catholic, anti-foreign sentiment was developing there. Patriotism bound these different people together. On a typical Fourth of July, "determined that the Bostonians [should] not alone enjoy the festivities of the joyous anniversary," Hamblin decked the theater with flags and banners, a North Carolina band "enlivened the scene by discoursing sweet music in the balcony,"[10] and army and naval officers "honored the theatre with their presence."

Patriotism easily slipped over into xenophobia, and Hamblin soon found it difficult to control what he had unleashed. He was accused of managing in a way that was "despotic and aristocratic and unprincipled and uncongenial to the feelings of American citizens." Greater trouble followed. Hamblin's stage manager, an Englishman named Farren, was alleged to have "cussed the Yankees, called them jackasses and said he would gull them whenever he could."[11] In July 1834, a benefit performance for Farren was scheduled at the Bowery. Coincidentally, that night a group of nativists gathered to break up a meeting of abolitionists. When the nativist mob got to the meeting place, they found no one there. If they couldn't have an abolitionist, why not an Englishman? The nativists marched on the Bowery, broke in on the middle of the performance, and drove the actors from the stage. Hamblin appeared waving an American flag and asked for quiet. The mob refused to be distracted and started throwing things. Hamblin surrendered and announced that Farren would be dismissed. As the afterpiece to their night's amusements, the rowdies went to the nearby house of Lewis Tappan, a wealthy merchant and abolitionist sympathizer, smashed windows and made a bonfire of his furniture. Then they went home. This storm quickly blew away and was soon forgotten (though not perhaps by Farren or by Tappan). Hamblin was forgiven. Perhaps it was as a signal of reconciliation that he soon after put on a production of *The Beggar's Opera*.

A contemporary writer emphasized the nativist element in the Bowery Theatre's success: "Not English money, not English patronage, for its attractions, name and money are all American; not English talent, for it has profited wholly by the native genius of our soil. It is a proud, a glorious feeling, that it is *our country*, that it is fostering America, which enables genius and industry to win success."[12] The implications of such sentiments would have seemed severely to restrict the role that opera might play in the Bowery audience's amusements. But opera was closely identified with nationalist feelings. On American subjects, in English, it might have become popular, as Edwin Forrest had popularized Shakespeare.

Forrest's initial appeal was an alternative to those who disliked the leading English actors of the day, whose accent, manner, and pretensions to cultural superiority were repugnant to many Americans. Forrest showed that Shakespeare and the classic stage literature need not be an exclusive English domain. Forrest translated Shakespeare into American. In doing so he created an American audience for Shakespeare that had not before been interested in those plays. These workers and shopkeepers, in turn, supported Forrest in his rivalry with contemporary actors. Forrest was much more than a popular actor, he genuinely was a hero to his followers. What a combination they made—the volcanic, flamboyant Forrest and the men of the Bowery, with their hair close-cropped in front, long in the back, curled and greased, wearing high beaver hats, black coats, full pantaloons stuffed into their boots. Forrest made Shakespeare manly and his audiences—mainly men—roared their approval, of Forrest and of America. His most popular role was in *Metamora,* an American play about the tragic and inevitable destruction of an Indian chief and his people. Romantic drama and romantic opera touched many of the same chords. Where was the operatic *Metamora?*

In some things Americans did together they were casual and informal. They made a lot of noise at their sporting events, raised an uproar in their religious revivals. In the presence of traditional culture they were subdued. The Bowery was an exception. Perhaps they inhabited their land without entirely belonging to it, gained possession of high culture from Europe as an act of will, not as a birthright. It would take time to be at ease in this democratic Zion.

I n its day the largest theater for opera in the United States, and intended to rival the splendor of European houses, James Caldwell's St. Charles Theatre opened in New Orleans in November 1835. Caldwell and his fellow citizens took great pride in its extravagant cost, $350,000.

For his money Caldwell got a large building, 132 feet across the front, 175 feet deep, four stories high. The exterior was a rather awkward two and a half stories of Corinthian columns supporting a level of Doric columns, with a pediment capping it all. There were windows at every level and the nine muses peered down from the pediment. The interior achieved the desired magnificence. Five doorways led into a huge columned hall flanked by stairways to the upper floors. The auditorium was an elongated semicircle with four tiers of boxes. The first tier had forty-seven boxes. Each sold for a thousand dollars per season and had a retiring room behind it, closed off from the main corridor by mahogany doors. The boxes were curtained in front and separated from each other by latticework grills. The second tier was like the first but without retiring rooms for the boxes and with an open gallery in the center section instead of boxes, with cushioned seats for its three hundred occupants. The grand promenade salon of the house, 129 feet long and 26 feet wide, carpeted and statued, opened off this second level. The third tier was a copy of the second, without the promenade salon, and the fourth tier was an entirely open gallery, entered by a separate stairway off the downstairs entrance hall, and with its own reception room.

The boxes were gold and ivory, with red-and-blue draperies. Heavy Doric columns with gilded capitals separated the boxes of the first tier and supported the second. Double Corinthian columns flanked the proscenium arch. The stage was conventional in width but immensely deep, 86 feet. The sunken orchestra pit ran across the full width of the stage. Caldwell emphasized the quality of his orchestra. It was large, included some of the leading instrumentalists of the day among its members and Americans as its leaders. Most nights during the season it played an overture or various other pieces as people were being seated. The St. Charles's crowning splendor was its chandelier. Made in London, weighing two tons, twelve feet high, fourteen feet in diameter, thirty-six feet in circumference, it cost nine thousand dollars and contained 175 gas burners whose light diffused and glittered and glowed through twenty-three thousand prisms of glass. The theater had its critics—which opera

The St. Charles Theatre in New Orleans burned down in 1842 and was rebuilt the following year. This 1845 playbill shows that the repertoire had changed little since James Caldwell's day. Crawford Theater Collection, Manuscripts and Archives, Yale University Library.

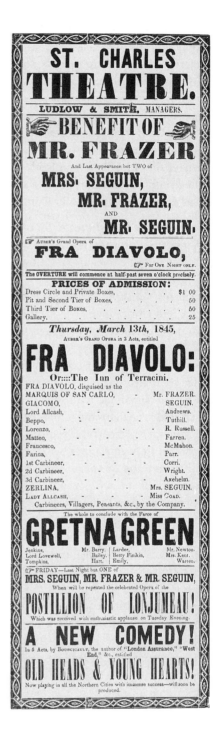

house didn't? The sound was uneven, the atmosphere cold, the latticework distracting. No one disputed its splendor.

The next task was to find an audience which lived up to the building and matched the image of that elegant and aristocratic European opera audience always in the mind of every socially conscious American. That was a formidable task. Since Caldwell could not assume or inherit such an audience, he had to make it up. The people in the boxes could be presumed to be fashionable. The fourth-tier gallery was for a "mixed" audience in the special Southern sense—countrymen and their countrywomen; women of "a certain type"; free men and women of color; slaves who had their masters' permission to be there. With its separate entrance and reception room, this didn't diminish the effect of the glamor below. What of the rest? Caldwell was the first American impresario to regulate dress. He reserved a section of seats immediately in front of the first tier of boxes for men only, where everyone was required to be dressed in black coats and dress shirts. The opera house may have been Italian, but Caldwell's audience derived from the King's Theatre in London.

The other thing Caldwell did was to dictate how the St. Charles audience behaved. He made clear, in notices in his theater programs, what was permissible, what was not. No hats were to be worn during a performance. No smoking was permitted in the boxes or lobbies. No talking aloud. No knocking on the floor with canes or walking sticks. He waged war on vulgarity and on the notion that the market would send him people who felt free to do what they wished to do. A note in the program for the opening of the theater made his views clear: "The Proprietor is determined to keep strict order in the establishment; to put down, at every risk, every attempt to disturb the quiet and attention which ought always to be ascendant in a public assembly, but which is too often violated by ignorant, at other times by disorderly persons, who think because they pay their money and because it is a theatre, they may make as much noise as they please."[13]

Was James Caldwell fighting the wrong battle? The prevailing tone of the American theater was as much poker-faced reticence as boisterous vulgarity. People sat in utter silence, giving nothing away as to their state of mind, and then turned up again the next night for another performance. An observer at a comedy reported that "the fun occasionally verged rather on buffoonery, and I laughed a good deal; but the faces of the stolid audiences seemed immovable. I hardly heard or saw a laugh the whole evening." A traveler arrived in Pittsburgh, where a touring dramatic company headed by a Mr. Hutton had just given *Hamlet,* followed immediately by another company which gave a performance of a burlesque of the play. In this farce, a Mr. Entwhistle played Hamlet in the broadest possible way. The audience remained solemnly unresponsive. Ophelia appeared in the mad scene decked not in rosemary and violets but in a large supply of carrots and turnips. The audience didn't move a muscle, "except for those who reached for handkerchiefs out of sympathy for the love-sick maiden." So it went the entire evening. The following morning a well-traveled Pittsburgh lawyer said: "I was at the play last night, Sir, and do not think Mr. Entwhistle acted Hamlet quite so well as Mr. Hutton."[14]

The most common explanation for this stolidity was Americans' historical inheri-

tance—something of the Indian's stolidness, something of the Puritan's bilious melancholy. In addition there was a contemporary element, the serious, self-controlled
demeanor of the middle class. The English opera audience had startled Henry Wikoff
by its "cold repose," its "rigid dignity." They were attentive and applause was frequently hearty, but there was about them "an imperturbability quite chilling after the
vivacity of the French and the geniality of the Italians." It was the habitual manner of
the aristocracy, "and it had spread through all classes."[15] Caldwell, who after all was
English, wished to reproduce that manner if he could. His dream of the proper
audience for his splendid theater was one of grave order. The Venetians would not
have understood it.

A Columbia Professor

On stage, the Garcías were giving *Don Giovanni* for the first time. In the audience was a white-haired, hawk-nosed, loose-limbed old man, an Italian immigrant who had come to the United States in 1805. Poet, scholar, and teacher, with musical interests as well, he had arrived with a violin, a trunk of books, and little else. He quickly found that there was no living to be made as poet or scholar in Jeffersonian America, so he improvised. He established an Academy of Young Gentlemen in Manhattan, teaching Italian geography and putting on amateur theatricals. He opened a grocery store, operated a delivery wagon, set up as a milliner, manufactured artificial flowers, ran a boarding house. He lived in New Jersey and in Pennsylvania for a while, then moved back to New York City in 1819 and thereafter concentrated his energies on teaching university-age students in Italian and Italian literature, on lecturing, writing book reviews, translating Dante into English and Byron into Italian, buying and selling books. In 1823 he published his memoirs—in Italian. (Had more Americans read them, they might have formed a different impression of the scholarly old gentleman.) Columbia University made him a professor (unpaid) of Italian in 1825, the same year that Harvard University established a chair of Italian literature.

The arrival of authentic Italian opera made 1825 a noteworthy year in the history of Italian culture in the United States. This alone would have explained the professor's presence at the Park Theatre. But in fact he had more reason for being there than his passionate advocacy of Italian culture and his support of the Garcías. His connection with *Don Giovanni* was personal, intimate, historic. It was partly his opera. It was wholly his libretto. The professor's name was Lorenzo Da Ponte.

I t is a long and tangled way from the Jewish ghetto of Ceneda, in the Venetian state, where Emilio Conigliano was born in 1749, through the boy's conversion to Christianity, baptism into the Roman Catholic church, adoption of the name of his patron, the bishop, the taking of holy orders, and the pursuit of a career as poet and teacher of rhetoric, interspersed with incessant and turbulent movement—to Venice, Dresden, Vienna, Trieste, Paris, London. His life in all those places, a bewildering mixture of brashness, struggle, and achievement, had two recurring themes: a chronic shortness of money and a superfluity of scandal. He was exiled from two of those cities and departed the last, London, in utmost haste, leaving a large body of poems, pamphlets, criticism, drama, which posterity relegated to the care of specialists in Italian literature. He also bequeathed the librettos for three operatic masterpieces—*Le Nozze di Figaro* (1786), *Don Giovanni* (1787), and *Così fan tutte* (1790)—though it has disagreed about Da Ponte's proper share in them. Did he help or hinder Mozart's genius? Da Ponte's and Mozart's contemporaries assumed that the librettist deserved equal credit with the composer, but the verdict of later generations was mixed. George Bernard Shaw thought Da Ponte's libretto for *Don Giovanni* "coarse and trivial," whereas the poet-librettist W. H. Auden wrote: "The verbal text of an opera is to be judged not by the literary quality or lack of it which it may have when read but by its success or failure in exciting the musical imagination of the composer."[1] By that standard Da Ponte did his work superlatively well.

Manuel García shared the favorable view. It is said that on first meeting Da Ponte in New York, he embraced him with fervor, did a little dance of joy, and, as a token of his respect, sang the drinking song from *Don Giovanni*. For his part, Da Ponte indefatigably promoted García's opera performances, insisted that his students attend, translated his libretto into English and sold it in the lobby of the Park Theatre, located a suitable boarding house where the Garcías stayed, and even personally supervised the preparation of their food. This early scene in the history of opera in America must surely delight anyone with an eye for the incongruities and ironies of life. Picture this worldly old man, this puzzling combination of roguery and talent, this heir to the librettist's crown of Metastasio and former poet to the imperial Hapsburg court, in the bare glaring light of bourgeois America, selling hats in Elizabethtown, New Jersey,

Lorenzo Da Ponte, Mozart's librettist turned impresario, championed Italian opera in New York in the 1830s. This portrait was made late in his life.

peddling sausages from "L. da Ponty's Wagon," and supervising boarding-house cooking.

A f t e r the departure of the Garcías, one might have expected Da Ponte to sink into a reverie about times past, but he was not sentimental and was incapable of inactivity. The visits of the French company from New Orleans provoked him to familiar Italian mockery of French opera, and to punning on *gatti* (cats) and *Galli* (Gauls): "Every year a company of Cats, I mean Gauls (my pen slipped), comes from New Orleans and after a tour of two or three months goes back with their pockets full of silver and with the applause of all those who love French yelling and the meowing of cats in time." The success of the French reinforced his conviction that there was a great deal of money to be made in Italian opera. True, García had not made much, but Da Ponte was undeterred. "A good and well-regulated company of Italian singers will make a fortune in America."[2] He planned an Italian counterattack.

In 1829, a mere eighty years of age, Da Ponte opened negotiations with Giacomo Montresor, tenor and impresario in Bologna, who agreed to come with an opera company to America. They exchanged letters. Da Ponte's give an invaluable picture of conditions as reflected in the equipment and materials Montresor should bring: a scene painter, "since those that are here charge sixty times what they ought"; adequate scores, because copying them in America was also expensive, "six times what it costs in Italy"; strings for instruments and a provision of pigments for makeup. As for performers and instrumentalists: "a good first violin, a good oboist, a good harpsichordist, and a prompter." Choristers? There were many in America and they sang well, "but when they sing our words they flay the hearers' ears." Finally, some dancers: "I actually think the novelty would have a fine effect here in a country that has never seen one." But the crucial thing was the singers: this must be "a very good, a stupendous, an excellent company." Recalling Maria García's popularity, Da Ponte asked whether an extra three or four thousand dollars might be enough to persuade Giuditta Pasta, the reigning diva of the 1820s, to come to America. "I have some reason to think that it would." He was wrong.[3]

Da Ponte set about signing up subscribers, raising between four and five thousand dollars in New York and another thousand in Philadelphia. But the inducements to artists must be more than monetary. "The disturbances in Europe and the peace we enjoy in America could be a very strong spur to come here," Da Ponte wrote, contrasting "the Earthly Paradise of America" with the "tragic, distressed condition of Italy." Then he would revert to money. There was gold in America. It justified the risks. It was the familiar siren song for immigrants, who would "accumulate enough to return in better times to enjoy it in Italy." Still, Montresor must recognize that in America the entire European operatic system—state subsidies, aristocratic patrons to make up deficits—was missing. Americans were money-conscious and costs must be kept strictly under control. "The Americans are almost all merchants; they make a business of everything, even entertainment. Come; do your best to please; awaken in some the enthusiasm born of pleasure, in others the hope of profit, and then dare all, hope all."[4] Hope all—the necessary motto of all impresarios!

E v e r y t h i n g went wrong at first. Delays at the Italian end prevented Montresor and his group from reaching New York until midsummer of 1832, a time of year when theater was always in the doldrums. Worse, their arrival coincided with a severe outbreak of cholera, so that the singers "must waste their sweetness on the desert air until the destroying angel has sheathed his sword and our citizens have returned to their homes."[5] Since none of the regular New York theaters was available, they used the old residence of Aaron Burr, recently converted and called the Richmond Hill Theatre. Small as it was, Richmond Hill did not have good sound. Moreover, seat prices were higher than usual: boxes and parterre were $1.50, the pit and gallery $1.00.

Da Ponte had urged Montresor to perform Rossini—"without fail the most favored composer in America"—as well as Mozart. "I am of the opinion that many of the operas by past composers will please greatly here." He advised a repertory of the previous half-century: Paisiello, Sarti, Martini, Cimarosa, Salieri. It was true that almost no operas by these composers had ever been given in America, and also true, as Da Ponte admitted, that even in Italy audiences "have all gone to sleep; but here they will not sleep not let anyone in the theater sleep." Taste had declined, anyway, as the neglect of "the great Mozart" proved.[6]

Instead, Montresor presented a contemporary repertory. He began, on October 6, 1832, with Rossini's *La Cenerentola.* The orchestra was a strong one and impressed New Yorkers as that of the French company had impressed Philadelphians: it set a new standard of performance. The scenery and costumes excited admiration, especially compared to the "worn and dirty finery at the Park" used for English opera. Some of the singers were excellent and New York audiences discovered what is, for some, one of opera's delights—drawing comparisons between singers and performers. Luciano Fornasari, the bass, was especially admired, and so was Montresor, whose voice was superior to García senior's and whose technique was free of the excessive ornamentation "with which García sometimes disguised the inability to sustain his voice." Much to Da Ponte's consternation, the company numbered fifty-three people instead of the twenty he had anticipated, and there wasn't a passable soprano among them. Edelaide Pedrotti was hurriedly brought from Havana. She was handsome. "Her features, as is the case with most dark women, light up well before the lamps." She sang with power and though her technical execution left much to be desired, her acting was effective. (However, it was absurd of Da Ponte to write, "We sigh no more for Malibran!") Montresor's second opera was *Elisa e Claudio* (1821) by Saverio Mercadante (1795–1870), and with Pedrotti leading the way it was a success. But Rossini's *The Italian Girl in Algiers* (*L' Italiana in Algieri*) was a distinct failure. *Il Pirata,* by Bellini, was most successful. One critic was divided as to its merits, finding it a work "of uncommon genius" but also "deficient in melody."[7] The company gave thirty-five performances in New York and then twenty-four in Philadelphia at the Chestnut Street.

An unmistakable sense of anticlimax and disappointment hung over Montresor's visit. The novelty of Italian opera had worn off. The New Orleans summer seasons had intervened between García and Montresor. New Yorkers and Philadelphians had more knowledge and higher standards by which to judge what they heard and saw. The first rapturous moments of discovering something wonderful could not be repeated. From Da Ponte's and Montresor's point of view, the season was a financial failure. As a result, their collaboration ended in acrimony. Montresor went to Havana. Da Ponte went to his desk to write *An Incredible Story But a True One,* an essay filled with amusing and sarcastic asides, shrewd comments, and lamentations about how badly he had been treated: "I dreamed of roses and laurels; but of the roses I have had only the thorns, and of the laurel the bitterness! SUCH IS THE WAY OF THE WORLD."[8] I wish we had Montresor's side of that story. Roses and laurels were all very well, but one thing was indisputable: Italian opera had brought gold into no one's hands.

N e v e r mind. Vigorous and resilient at eighty-five, Da Ponte insisted that the chief problem had been the absence of a proper theater. Italian opera presupposed an Italian opera house. So once again the old man went to work. He brought together a group of people who subscribed $150,000 for a plot of land and an opera house. In extraordinarily rapid order, a site was selected and an opera house designed and built in time to open a season in November 1833.

The Italian Opera House, white stone facing over brick, approached by a flight of a half-dozen steps, its entrance flanked by six tall square columns, was the first building in the United States designed exclusively for opera. One observer described the exterior as "very plain and unpretending," adding that "the subscribers' money has

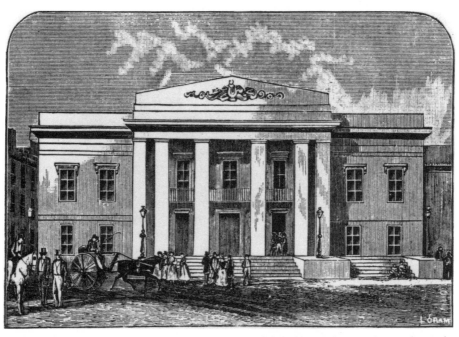

New York's Italian Opera House, opened in 1833, was the first building in the United States designed exclusively for opera. From Henry Krehbiel, Chapters of Opera *(New York, 1908).*

not been spent to please the eyes of non-subscribers." By contrast, the interior was sumptuous. It was lighted by gas, entirely carpeted, and had individual upholstered seats in the pit instead of the usual benches "soiled, worn and begrimed by the Goths and Vandals who remorselessly stand upon them at the theaters." It was a small house, with two tiers of boxes circling the auditorium, topped by a dome from which hung a large central chandelier. The prevailing colors were white, blue, and gold, with crimson-and-gold panels dividing the boxes. The drop curtain depicted an Italian cottage-dotted landscape with peasants dancing the tarantella. The act curtain— "splendid beyond example" and applauded by the audience on opening night— showed famous Italian palaces with a Roman charioteer in front. The most luxurious feature was the boxes, all of which had sofa seats covered in blue damask. The first tier of boxes was available to the general public, but the entire second tier was the exclusive domain of the shareholding subscribers. Individuals could decorate their own boxes as they wished.[9]

New York had its opera house. But who would sing in it and what would be sung? The subscribers chose as their manager the Chevalier Rivafinoli. To augment the members of the Montresor company who had stayed in America, Rivafinoli made a recruiting trip to Europe, from where, in the summer of 1833, publicity puffs appeared in New York newspapers about the marvelous singers being signed up "alike for their talent, beauty and irreproachable conduct." In the end, the group contained no famous names and "made no mark on American musical experience."[10] Two singers gained popularity during the first season: Clementina Fanti, who took most of the important roles, and Luigia Bordogni, only seventeen years old and with just one year's operatic experience, whose shyness and freshness made her Rosina seem "not unworthy of *the Garcia.*" The orchestra, of twenty players, was locally recruited, as was the chorus. Ticket prices were high—$2.00 for one of those sofa seats in the lower tier of boxes, parquette $1.50, pit $1.00, gallery 75¢.

There were two seasons of opera at the Italian Opera House. The first one, under Rivafinoli, of forty performances, was virtually all Rossini. It opened with *La Gazza ladra,* followed by *Il Barbiere,* of course, then *La Donna del lago, Il Turco in Italia,* and *Matilde di Shabran.* Only *La Donna del lago* was a success. *Matilde,* while it had "melodies and passages of uncommon beauty scattered throughout," was "one of the feeblest of Rossini's productions in originality and conception." Non-Rossinian comic opera fell flat. Cimarosa's *Il Matrimonio segreto* contained some of "the most perfect and enchanting" music "ever imagined by the human mind," but its story was of a "domestic and uninteresting nature." Meanwhile, an opera by Giovanni Pacini (1796– 1867), *The Arabs in Gaul (Gli Arabi nelle Gallie),* played to packed houses, "not from the excellence of its music" but because of "beautiful scenery, magnificent dresses, and interesting stage incidents." "Our taste for music is comparatively in its infancy, and we all know that a little gold leaf on the surface of the gingerbread enhances its value."[11]

New York audiences were beginning to feel more at home with opera. They applauded enthusiastically and often called for encores. When a singer refused to comply, one writer reprimanded her: "In this country it is the custom." They threw bouquets of flowers at the singers. "At first the American portion of the audience laughed at it as a piece of foreign harmless foppery, and so it passed; but it has become a positive nuisance." Expectations were rising. Audiences assumed a higher level of orchestral performance than in earlier years, so a poor night's work by the opera house orchestra, "playing out of time and embarrassing the singer," was firmly criticized. "This ought not to be, and the leader should enforce attention." Despite these positive signs, attendance lagged. One observer believed he could identify regular attenders as "consisting of about three hundred of the very elite of our city" and estimated that, besides the regulars, "scarcely two hundred strangers" were present at one performance of *La Gazza ladra*.[12] The end of the season left a substantial deficit to be met by the manager, and Rivafinoli responded by skipping town.

Da Ponte took pen in hand and retold aspects of the season in verse, excoriating Rivafinoli and lamenting that so little had come of his own efforts. *A Squib to Make You Laugh,* he called it, but the laughter was mixed with tears. He concluded with a prose exhortation "to those Americans who love the fine arts," hoping to rouse them from lethargy and to save the operatic enterprise "for which I have so long and ardently labored, so calculated to shed luster on the nation, and so honorable in its commencement, ruined by those who have nor means, nor knowledge, nor experience." There was only one thing to be done: send to Italy for a new company to "redeem the fortunes of your disorganized, betrayed, dishonored establishment." "For God's sake let the past become a beacon light to save you from the perils of the future. Do not destroy the most splendid ornament of your city."[13]

There was a second season, of fifty-seven performances, though a new company was not imported and Da Ponte played no role in it. The singers on the spot formed a cooperative. The season opened in November 1834, with Bellini's *La Straniera*. Attendance was disappointing. The company stopped performing for a month at Christmastime, then took up again, bringing forward more Rossini in the hope that his magic might save the day—the first American performances of *Le Siège de Corinthe,* in February, and of a much shortened version of *Semiramide* in April. The season lasted until May, but once again there was no one to assume the deficit or to guarantee another year. The subscribers had had enough. No opera was given the following year. In 1836 the opera house was sold to new owners and all its scenery and stage props disposed of at auction.

W h a t to make of the "failure" of the two seasons at the Italian Opera House? Contemporaries interpreted it in various, often contradictory, ways. Some regarded it as a trivial incident and took refuge in unwavering optimism: "The spirit of the public in favour of this charming and rational amusement is beginning to awaken, and the success of Italian music here is no longer problematical." Pessimists were equally certain: "A century must elapse before even New York can sustain a permanent operatic establishment." Philip Hone, one-time mayor of the city, diarist, and opera-house subscriber, gave two reasons for the failure: "The first is that we want to understand the language; we cannot endure to sit by and see the performers splitting their sides with laughter, and we not take the joke." The other had to do with the private boxes, which formed "a sort of aristocratical distinction. . . . I like this spirit of independence which refuses its countenance to anything exclusive."[14]

The misfortunes of the Italian Opera House shed light on middle-class patronage in America. The opera house symbolized the yearning of some Americans quickly to appropriate prestigious cultural emblems. Organizing an opera company and producing opera were more difficult and less immediately gratifying than erecting a building. At this point, "establishing" opera meant importing it from abroad on a regular basis. That kind of trade imbalance caused no alarm.

Initially, the Italian Opera House had seemed a "brilliant—quite overpowering" social success.[15] New Yorkers had done what they wanted to do—emulate the glitter of European operatic audiences. But the social transplanting of opera was more complicated than it seemed. As opera's novelty wore off, it lost its hold on the fashionable set. They were consumers, not patrons. Attendance at the opera had somehow to become part of the structure and ritual of social life in a deeper sense, had to be expected, not merely hoped for. European opera existed in an old and complex web of larger customs and institutions. Such a society was not created at will or overnight. Was American culture dense and rich enough to nourish such a social life? The English novelist Thomas Love Peacock at this very time, 1831, described its chief characteristics as precisely the opposite of such denseness. One of Peacock's characters, writing home to his daughter from America, wittily caricatured the blankness of the American social tablets:

> Here are no rents, no taxes, no poor-rates, no tithes, no church-establishment, no routs, no clubs, no rotten boroughs, no operas, no concerts, no theatres, no beggars, no thieves, no king, no lords, no ladies, and only one gentleman, your loving father,
>   Timothy Touchandgo

Half a century later, pondering the items of high civilization that were absent from the social life of Jacksonian America, Henry James concluded: "The moral is that the flower of art blossoms only where the soil is deep."[16]

Was the soil deep enough for opera—European opera, with all its associations and connotations? The aristocratic style—grand, confident, reckless—was so different from that of these New York burgers—cautious, conventional, restrained. They were incorporators who believed in limited investments. They carefully restricted their obligations to the manager/impresario they employed to furnish their entertainment. The impresario paid rent to the subscribers for the use of their house. From the box-office proceeds and the annual fees for their boxes, the impresario had to pay his performers and all the expenses of production and maintenance of the opera house. A prescient writer warned against subscribers "encumbering themselves with expenses for the mere site," so that the enterprise "starts with an overwhelming responsibility for rent, which clogs its operations and insures its ultimate bankruptcy." Some capital must be reserved, he warned, "to be devoted to the science [of music] and its professors."[17] None was.

Art patronage would be measured, like everything else, by the yardstick of profit and loss in the marketplace. The Italian Opera House was a failure because it lost money. Did patronage mean paying the impresario's debts? Middle-class patrons wanted to behave like aristocrats without spending money as aristocrats were expected to do. No wonder these prudent New Yorkers drew back and closed out their investment.

T h e closing of the opera house was too much even for the indomitable Da Ponte. "If fate had led me to France instead of America I would not now fear that my remains might become food for the dogs." He was bitter about the indignities heaped on him, "I, the inspiration of Salieri, of Weigl, of Martin, of Winter, and of Mozart." What had possessed him to try to educate the Americans? "I do not know whether a good or evil genius inspired me to bring music here also. I had hoped that in doing so my name might become immortal. It was just the opposite. My name was given instead to scorn, calumny, indigence and oblivion! I sunk in this enterprise all I had saved for my decrepit days, and I was rewarded with ingratitude by EVERYBODY!"[18] Old students rallied round—Julia Ward Howe, Clement Clark Moore, Fitz-Greene Halleck. Moore, later author of "The Eve of St. Nicholas," sent him a check and Da Ponte gave up the thought of returning to Italy to die.

At age eighty-nine, he was finally failing. Dr. John Francis attended him at his house, 91 Spring Street, and in gratitude and with a flash of the old spirit, Da Ponte wrote two sonnets for him hours before he died, on the evening of August 17, 1838. His last moments made an affecting scene. The old poet's magnificent head lay on a pile of pillows, his eyes still clear and shining brightly. The women of the family, the doctor, Italian countrymen, a few members of the Montresor company, all knelt for a farewell blessing. Why shouldn't we imagine that as he slipped into the final darkness and as the curtains that hide the past from us were lifted one after the other, Lorenzo Da Ponte thought of the Garcías and their performance of *Don Giovanni* and then New York dissolved and Maria García and Carlo Angrisani and Manuel senior disappeared too and in their place were Luigi Bassi and Teresa Bondini and Giuseppe Lolli and the rest of them and he was in Prague for the world premiere and in the pit was the diminutive pop-eyed man who had composed the music?

A good many people turned out for the funeral three days later. Allegri's "Miserere" was sung and Da Ponte was interred in the Catholic cemetery on Third Avenue. A contemporary account stated that "it is the intention of his countrymen to erect a monument in memory of their poet. On the completion of this a discourse is to be pronounced." People forget. The monument was not erected until almost 150 years later.[19]

H a v i n g looked backwards several times in this brief story, let's look forward half a century, to 1887. The principal cities of Europe competed to celebrate the one hundredth anniversary of the first performance of *Don Giovanni*. In Paris, the manuscript score of the opera, owned by Pauline Viardot-García, was reverently displayed in the foyer of the Opéra. In Dresden, citizens restored the grave of Luigi Bassi, the first Don. Few Americans of that time would have remembered Da Ponte's efforts on behalf of opera in the United States. Still, his fame as Mozart's librettist inspired a few to do him honor. Those who sought out the old Catholic cemetery found it had been paved over long before and all its records lost. Lorenzo Da Ponte's remains had disappeared forever. Once again fate had contrived to unite sublimity and farce, and once again Da Ponte was linked to Mozart, who lay buried in an unmarked plot in Vienna, both "triumphant over all chaotic earthliness."[20]

Maria Malibran

The first act is almost over. But before we move on to the expansive operatic years ahead, let's pick up some threads from the past, ending, as we began, with the remarkable García family.

After they left New York at the end of the summer of 1826, Manuel senior, Joaquina, Manuel junior, and Pauline went to Mexico City, where they remained for two apparently successful years. When the family began their return journey to Europe in 1820, they had with them seventeen thousand dollars in gold. Then disaster struck, in the form of highway robbers who took everything they had—gold, jewels, clothes. Pauline, age eight, remembered her father's response to the loss of his fortune: "natural and infectious bursts of laughter during the night."[1] Eventually the Garcías made it back to Paris, where Manuel senior, finished as a singer, resumed teaching. He died in Paris in 1832. Joaquina died in Brussels in 1854.

The story of the Garcías now becomes the story of the three children. Manuel junior, realizing that he had no future as a singer, established himself in Paris, in the 1830s, as a teacher of singing and a scientific student of the voice. He wrote treatises and invented the laryngoscope, the "little mirror," an instrument with which to observe the structure and function of the vocal organs. His success was finally proved to the world by the success of his students, several of whom had fine careers, so that Manuel came commonly to be described as the greatest singing master in the world.

Those students are all forgotten now, except one. In 1841 a young woman came to Manuel in despair. Having sung with some early success, she was, at twenty-one, losing her voice. Convinced that García, and only García, could save her, she sang some scales for him, then an aria. His verdict was terrible: "It would be useless to teach you, Mademoiselle. You no longer have a voice." She begged for another chance. He relented. She must go away and not sing, or even speak, for six weeks, and then return for another test. She did as he said. Her second attempt gave García some slight reason to go on with her, provided she started over as a singer: lessons twice a week, scales, and only scales, over and over. He had never met anyone who worked so hard, and she never made the same mistake twice. She kept it up for one year, laying the foundations for a faultless technique. Amazingly, her voice came back. She had an extraordinary sense of pitch: "I never heard her sing a hair's breadth out of tune, so perfect was her natural ear."[2] When there was no more he could do for her, she left, for she loathed Paris. Returning to Stockholm, she made a second debut and then, unlikely as it seems, a second career. The next decade was one of glory for Jenny Lind.

Manuel García later moved to London, where he taught for many years. Spry and clear-minded, he lived to the age of 101—García the centenarian, he came to be called, able to recount first-hand the horrors of the Napoleonic occupation of Spain and to lament the war between Spain and the United States ninety years later, witnessing in his youth scenes painted by Goya, and living to be painted in 1905 by John Singer Sargent.

Pauline also lived into the twentieth century. She studied voice with her brother and mother and then piano with Franz Liszt. She made her first success in Paris as Desdemona in Rossini's *Otello,* married soon after, and under the name of Viardot-García sang all the important mezzo-soprano roles, creating several of them. Her voice was uneven, often harsh. It was the intelligence and conviction of her interpretations which gained her fame. More than a remarkable vocalist, she was one of the most discriminating musicians of the nineteenth century. She sang in a famous revival in Paris of Gluck's *Orfeo ed Euridice* which brought that opera back into the European repertory. She encouraged composers, helping the young Charles Gounod get *Sapho* staged in Paris, performing excerpts from Berlioz's *The Trojans (Les Troyens)* in an effort to gain acceptance for it, singing Isolde in a private performance of *Tristan und Isolde,* with Wagner singing Tristan. And when this "great and admirable artist" (Liszt's words) retired as a singer, she composed operettas, painted, wrote poetry and plays, was the center of a musical-literary circle, admired by Charles Dickens and many other writers, and the long-time intimate friend of Ivan Turgenev. She died in Paris at age eighty-nine, in 1910, her life spanning Italian opera's history from Rossini to Puccini. Although she encouraged new composers and new works, her heart remained with that Italian tradition that was the family's inheritance and its glory. As she was dying, her last word, pronounced clearly (as always), was "Norma."[3]

F i n a l l y , what of the Signorina? Maria Felicia García became the most famous of all the Garcías, renowned beyond the wildest imaginings of her American admirers, by common consent one of the handful of most celebrated singers of the entire nineteenth century. Yet Maria García would be unknown to all but a few historians of music, for her greatness came to her under a different name.

On March 23, 1826, in New York, the night before her eighteenth birthday, she surprised everyone and disheartened many by marrying a middle-aged French merchant—a man more than twice her age, an obscure character named François Eugène Malibran, an émigré who had lived in the city for some years and amassed a substantial fortune, or so it was believed. Why in the world did she do it? She may have loved the man. It may also have been a means of escape from the harsh domination of her father. Or she may have been rebounding from a forbidden love affair. Manuel junior's biographer, decades after the event, repeated stories, presumably coming from his subject, according to which Maria had wished to marry Fitz-Greene Halleck, the young American poet. We have some lines Halleck wrote under the influence of Maria:

Maria Malibran, the consummate romantic diva, as Desdemona in Rossini's Otello. In her left hand she holds five flowers, the initials of which form the name Carlo, for her second husband, Charles de Bériot. Luigi Pedrazzi painted her portrait in 1834.

And when, that grass is green above me,
And those, who bless me now and love me,
     Are sleeping by my side,
Will it avail me aught that men
Tell to the world with lip and pen
     That once I lived and died?

No! if a Garland for my brow
Is growing, let me have it now,
     While I'm alive to wear it;
And if, in whispering my name,
There's music in the voice of fame
     Like Garcia's let me hear it.

Neither memorable poetry nor conclusive evidence of anything except a romantic sensibility that Maria may have found attractive. Supposedly, García senior intervened and "sternly refused to allow things to go farther."[4] Was it likely that the father, a worldly man with lofty ambitions for his immensely talented daughter, would allow her to throw herself away on a poet—and an *American* poet at that? Malibran's wealth also may have played a role in this drama, even if one doesn't accept another story, current at the time, that the brutal and avaricious father received fifty thousand dollars for forcing Maria to marry. Whatever the truth, the Signorina was now Madame Malibran. It was as if Rosina had, after all, married Dr. Bartolo!

That was why she stayed behind when the rest of the family went to Mexico. Maria occupied herself singing in occasional concerts. She made a trip to Philadelphia, to sing in the newly opened Musical Fund Hall, and we have a description of her, in youthful high spirits, delighted with the hall's acoustics in rehearsal, extemporizing songs while walking up and down the aisles. She soon learned that Malibran's fortune was a sham and that he was heavily in debt. Maria turned over everything that was hers in the marriage settlement to her husband's creditors, "a noble act, which gave rise to strong manifestations of favor and approbation on the part of the American public."[5] Is it any wonder Americans loved her? She had talent, charm, beauty—and a respect for the sanctity of contract!

In January 1827 Maria Malibran returned to the stage. The Bowery Theatre engaged her for a series of performances of English opera. (She had learned to speak English while the Garcías lived in London.) The Bowery raised its prices for her five appearances. All were sold out. She sang Count Belino in *The Devil's Bridge* and Rosetta in *Love in a Village*. "Were the Signorina an actress only, without the power of melody, she would be charming." But she was a good deal more, rescuing shabby productions in which scenes were omitted and two of the Bowery's stock company players "scarcely knew a word of their parts." No wonder English opera so often began to seem unprofessional and makeshift by comparison with its Italian and French rivals. One reviewer observed tartly that "it was to the credit of the Signorina (foreigner as she is) and to the rebuke of the other performers that she not only knew her own part perfectly, but prompted the others, and directed the whole stage arrangement." She wasn't above stunts of her own. She took a song, "Home, Sweet Home," from the American composer John Howard Payne's opera of 1823 *Clari, Maid of Orleans,* and interpolated it into the lesson scene of *Il Barbiere.* Her Bowery audience loved it. (Other singers took this up and, fifty years later, it was especially identified with Adelina Patti.) So great was the enthusiasm that she agreed to another engagement at the Bowery, at the unprecedented salary of six hundred dollars a performance. This second time she appeared again in *The Devil's Bridge* and *Love in a Village,* as well as in *Don Giovanni,* in English, one of the ramshackle Mozart adaptations common to English and American theater at the time. Maria was no doubt delightful as Zerlina, but the production's virtues began and ended with her. The actor who played the Don didn't even attempt to sing and the Spanish peasants danced a Scottish reel. So fed up with all this was the Bowery audience that when Maria sang the aria "My true heart," she was urged to encore it by shouts of "Vedrai carino."[6] So she repeated it in Italian, to wild applause.

In October 1827, Maria let it be known that she was returning to Europe the next month. The Bowery immediately scheduled a series of farewell performances. Several "eminent artists" were to be engaged to back her up and "every exertion made to offer a powerful and effective orchestra." She sang in English operas, in a full *Barbiere,* and in programs made up of complete acts, of scenes, and of songs from various operas. Her final appearance concluded with songs by Gluck, Boieldieu, Weber, and Rossini, sung in French, German, and Italian, the very last being Rosina's "Una voce poco fa," recalling those first magical moments at the Park Theatre almost two years before. As the applause died away, she advanced alone to the front of the stage, sat down at a harp placed close to the footlights, and prepared to accompany herself in "Farewell," a song written especially at her request—words by Arthur Keene, music by Maria Malibran. The Bowery audience was perfectly still. There was a long pause. It seemed as if the Signorina could not go on. At that moment Monsieur Etienne (he, too, had stayed in America), seated at his piano in the orchestra, played some chords as an improvised prelude to her song, giving Maria the moments she needed to recompose herself. "With trembling voice and agitated frame," she sang:

> Away, o'er the blue waves of ocean
>   I go to my own native shores;
> Yet this bosom will glow with devotion
>   To the clime and the scenes it adores.
> Round memory's shrine fondly lingers
>   The joy that has twined here a spell;
> And the harp that vibrates to these fingers,
>   Sighs in sadness the tones of farewell!
>   Farewell! Farewell!
> Sighs in sadness the tones of farewell.
>
> Where Italy's bright skies are shining,
>   And France, sunny France, spreads her bloom,
> This heart will look back with repining,

> And its pleasure be saddened with gloom.
> Deep thrilling emotions are breaking,
>   While my thoughts on remembrances dwell;
> And my voice, as these visions are waking,
>   Breathes in sadness the notes of Farewell!
>   Farewell! Farewell!
> Breathes in sadness the notes of farewell!

"In the buoyancy of youth and hope," a talented young woman was preparing to go away for a while—no more than that. Yet her "increasing agitation" as she sang, the earnestness with which she conveyed the words, the slow and measured accompaniment, created a powerful sense of foreboding.[7]

T h e Garcías began the process of connecting the United States with Italian opera and with its international network of singers, composers, and impresarios, whose careers intertwined as they moved from one opera house to another. Maria García Malibran gave Americans their first experience of the most remarkable aspect of that system, the diva, the goddess.

The emergence of the diva was the result of several things. First, it was the expression of an inherent division in opera, as in any other collective form of performance, between the desire for unity, in which the individual elements—singing, acting, production—are subordinated to the whole, and the desire to emphasize one or more of the elements at the cost of ensemble. Second, the diva's emergence was closely connected with the evolution of opera as a form of business. Singers, orchestra players, architects, designers of stage machinery (highly prized in the seventeenth and eighteenth centuries, just as conductors have been in the twentieth)—all made money according to the demand for their services. The scope of this demand was vastly increased when opera spread throughout Europe, with numerous opera houses, large and small, subsidized by the great wealth of courts and aristocracies, competing with one another to attract eminent artists.

A third factor in the diva's ascendance was historical: the disappearance from Europe's operatic stages of the castratos, those extraordinary men who dominated opera from its beginnings through the eighteenth century. The divas of their day, they left a legacy of their behavior, their style of life, which was adopted by the women who took their place. Everything about that style and manner—the absurd flattery, the endless indulgence, the gratification of every whim—was extravagant. But how did such extravagance persist even when opera was being absorbed within the prudent, restrained atmosphere and values of the middle-class society of the nineteenth century? It was because the flattery of the operatic goddess had a special twist.

The diva had power. Her tantrums and caprices were fearful to those of lower station or lesser prestige, and especially to her fellow singers and musicians, because her presence was thought indispensable and theirs was not. Another aspect of her power was the erotic desires, the intense longings she inspired in patrons and audiences. She was an object to be pursued. (This was a bisexual longing, as became clear later in the nineteenth century when the male counterpart of the diva, the

leading tenor, emerged as an object of desire for opera audiences increasingly dominated by women.) Yet, powerful as she was, the diva was closely associated with the
courtesan. She was bought. She was a prize. And this is the clue to the special
treatment the female deity received. For men, the diva's extravagant behavior was part
of her appeal, because it was seen as something essentially childish and ridiculous.
Goddess as she was, she was also a bit of a joke. She fulfilled the archetypal male
image of the emotional and hysterical woman who was never to be taken seriously.
Her patron possessors didn't fear her. Possessing her who frightened others only
proved the patrons' own masculine power. The singing goddess must never forget the
image which defined the limits of her power: she was a nightingale singing in her
master's cage.

The supreme instance of the caged songbird comes from castrato days. It is the
story of Carlo Broschi, known as Farinelli (1705–1782), a singer of prodigious talent
and equally prodigious fame. King Philip V of Spain suffered from incurable melan-
cholia, and Farinelli was invited to Madrid to soothe the king's sick mind with his
singing. He was given a huge sum of money and many perquisites and favors, but on
one absolute condition, which he accepted: that he sing for the king and only for the
king—who allowed "none but his most intimate entourage to hear the miraculous
voice"—and that he sing only the same four songs, chosen by the king, every night for
as long as the king wished. Farinelli's hold over Philip V extended to his successor,
Ferdinand VI. His political and social influence lasted for more than twenty years,
something that would have been impossible for a woman, however talented.

Something else haunted the diva (and all other singers, male and female): the
shadow of their own demise. This is an inescapable part of the fascination of opera,
and Maria Malibran's career made Americans aware of it for the first time. The
mystery of the diva's voice is connected with the mystery of its existence. It comes to
her unbidden and might be taken away just as arbitrarily as it was given. It is a gift,
oddly lodged in the larynx, not entirely within the control of its seeming possessor.
The bird sings and sings until it dies, unmindful that its song must cease. The diva
knows her song will end, in old age or in the very prime of her life and career. In either
case, the preciousness of the gift of song is equaled always by its precariousness. The
singer's art is filled with the possibility of disaster and the imminence of death.

O n November 1, 1827, Maria Malibran, not yet twenty years of age, traveling alone,
sailed for France. Within two months she made her Parisian operatic debut and began
the dizzying climb to fame. Success in London soon followed. For the next four years
she moved back and forth between the two capitals. Her admirers began the custom
of bringing or throwing wreaths and bouquets of flowers to her on stage. Crowds
followed her and stood outside her house "as if they were under the influence of
magnetism." Composers asked to write for her. Poets offered their verses. Americans
could keep track of her through occasional notes in their newspapers, stories about
her challenging and surpassing the fabled singers of the day—Pasta, Pisaroni, Sontag.

Malibran had the inexhaustible energy and the versatility of her father. "Her talents
were as multiple as her character was many-sided. She was a splendid swimmer, a
daring horsewoman, and a talented artist—she left, for example, a charming portrait

of her friend, the composer Bellini." She thought intelligently about her art. She happily sang English operas, and other operas translated into English, paying scrupulous attention to the words and their pronunciation, helped by her fluency in the major operatic languages. She was the first Amina, in Bellini's *The Sleepwalker* (*La Sonnambula*), to wear realistic peasant dress. Though she lacked conventionally beautiful features, she was immensely attractive to men, with a brilliant smile, dark, lustrous eyes. Contemporaries analyzed her remarkable voice, which ranged from contralto to high soprano, and the way she artfully concealed the break between registers. But even these things did not account for the "fascinating radiation" which captivated people. It was more than her art, and her beauty, and her voice.[8]

Malibran was the incarnation of romantic *feeling*. Her interpretations of roles were marked by passionate intensity and by a willful impetuosity which sometimes verged on frantic exaggeration. She conveyed to audiences a sense of recklessness, of rebellion, of audacity. In her personal life she typified the artist who defied social conventions. She fell in love with a Belgian violinist, Charles de Bériot, and while still married to Eugène Malibran lived with Bériot and bore him children. (She eventually got a divorce and married him.) Chopin, Alfred de Musset, Lamartine, and many others were right to feel that she captured the spirit of their epoch. George Sand saw her as Desdemona in *Otello,* "as beautiful as one of Raphael's Virgins," but with the ability, not associated with virginity, to suggest the release of overpowering emotion. "She made me weep, shudder, in a word—suffer, as if I had been witnessing a real-life scene." She was simply "the foremost genius of Europe."[9]

In 1832 Malibran toured Italy. Wild enthusiasm was the order of the day. In Bologna, a public subscription raised money to put a bust of her in the opera house. The Venetians were "thrown into ecstasy with her marvelous voice," and a theater (still standing, but now a cinema) was named for her. She was paid more money than any singer before her. "Soon a city will be the price offered for a cavatina, and for a single rondo an entire province."[10] James Caldwell tried to bring her back to America, to New Orleans. But one day in September 1836, while riding horseback in the countryside outside Liverpool, England, Malibran was thrown and injured her head. She was in excruciating pain for days but concealed it and went on with her singing engagements until she collapsed. Her condition worsened, became critical. She lingered for nine days, singing snatches of her favorite songs as she drifted in and out of consciousness.

Maria Malibran died on September 23. All musical Europe mourned her: writers, painters, poets as much as musicians. "Probably never has the death of an opera singer so shaken the cultured world." Rossini, with whose music her life and that of her family was so identified, was asked near the end of *his* life many years later to name the greatest woman singer of the earlier years of the century: "The most remarkable was Madame Pasta; Madame Colbran was the foremost; but Madame Malibran was unique." That uniqueness was her embodiment of the spirit of romanticism, in her death as in her life. At the height of her brilliance, in the glory of youth, she was cut down, "consumed by the fire of her own genius."[11] She was twenty-eight.

Expansion, 1836–1863

I hear the chorus, it is a grand opera,
Ah this indeed is music—this suits me.

— *Walt Whitman*

I thought the time had come to say something for American Art; that the
applause of Philadelphia is quite as good as that of Vienna—each for its
"native Art" and that of the two I prefer that of Philadelphia.

— *William Henry Fry*

In America every business or undertaking, whether an Opera or slaugh-
terhouse, a soap-factory or a public library, a railway or a monument to
Daniel Webster, is a private speculation. The success of an enterprise
depends upon one of two features—the general utility of the work, or the
amount it realizes.

— *Max Maretzek*

The Bohemian Girl

The second period of opera in America cut across four decades and divided itself into two fairly distinct phases. In the first, from 1835 to mid-century, the operatic situation remained much as it had been, with English opera at the center of theatrical life and French and Italian opera sporadically available. In the second phase, expansion became the dominant note, the California gold rush its symbol and partial cause. Famous European singers visited the United States, opulent opera houses were built, prices rose, and Italian opera, in Italian, displaced English-language opera.

The first years of this second period opened inauspiciously. The financial panic of 1837 and the protracted depression that followed it devastated American theatrical life. "The play houses suffered frightfully." Wages were sharply cut. The spoken drama was hardest hit and many smaller theaters, between 1839 and 1843, shut their doors for a time. Musical entertainments flourished in the midst of this misery. These were "ultra operatic days." The public wanted opera and the public got what it wanted.[1] Familiar English operas dotted programs at all the theaters— *Love in a Village, The Castle of Andalusia, Guy Mannering, No Song, No Supper;* and there was even a revival of *The Beggar's Opera* in 1840, with women in men's roles and men in women's. Italian and French operas were just a part of this repertory, the most frequently performed being Bellini's "inexhaustible" *Sonnambula.* Among Rossini operas, *La Cenerentola* and *La Gazza ladra* gradually gained favor, the new Donizetti opera was *The Elixir of Love,* sometimes called *The Love Potion* (*L'Elisir d'amore*), and of French operas Auber's *Fra Diavolo* and Adam's *Le Postillion de Longjumeau* were frequently done. There was a revival of an older opera, Boieldieu's *Jean de Paris.*

Operas were performed in a casual, slapdash manner, cut, adapted, and modified without a second thought. This was due partly to the absence of a later age's reverence for authenticity, partly to the limitations of the theatrical stock companies. English opera depended on visiting English singers and on American theatrical companies. Foreign singers were not yet prepared to learn English. Many actors simply couldn't sing at all. In one production of Weber's *Der Freischütz,* given with "unusual splendour," the part of Bertram, because there was no competent bass, was converted into a nonsinging role and Alice, requiring a first-rate vocalist, "was played by Mrs. Sharpe, who does not throughout the whole piece sing a single note." However, things concluded in a cheery way: "Though the present version differs somewhat from the original, its interest is increased by the change, and by the addition of several choice productions from the works of Rossini and Bellini."[2] Operatic double-bills were still conceived in an entirely uninhibited manner, with no attention paid to national origin or compatibility of style. As everything was always cut drastically, two full-length operas could be performed in one night.

Nevertheless, more difficult operas were also tackled, Meyerbeer's *Robert le diable* one year, Fromental Halévy's (1799–1862) *The Jewess* (*La Juive*) another. In 1838 *Le Nozze di Figaro,* with the strongest cast of English singers yet assembled in America, ran for several nights. Beethoven's *Fidelio* received its American premiere in 1839. Although some people assumed that "Beethoven's music was beyond the ability of its audience to appreciate or understand," and although the production was uneven musically, there were fourteen performances in a row, "an achievement far beyond anything the Metropolitan Opera House could dream of a century later."[3] And it was repeated the following year.

What about singers? *Fidelio, Guillaume Tell, Robert le diable* required vocalists well beyond the scope of the average theatrical stock company. New York and Philadelphia and Boston "heard some beautiful singing in the autumn of 1840," from intelligent and conscientious artists of respectable ability but no special fame. They were mostly English singers, the best groups yet assembled in the United States in quality, though later forgotten. Between 1833 and 1840 the most eminent and admired was Mrs. Joseph Wood (the English convention was to give a woman singer her husband's name). Born and trained in England, where she had gained considerable experience, she came to America with her husband in 1835 to stay for a number of years. She possessed that rare gift, "the utter absence of apparent effort," and as an actress "the lamented MALIBRAN in her best days could not give more pleasure in this branch of art to an English audience than can Mrs. Wood."[4] Her husband was a competent tenor, though not as popular as his wife, nor as talented. The other men were able, W. F. Brough, Charles Manvers, John Wilson, the latter the possessor of a sweet voice and finished technique, much admired in *L'Elisir d'amore.* Another wave of English singers came over at the end of the 1830s, centering on the one singer of all these whose career later historians have recalled. This was Anne Seguin (1814–1888), who had sung sufficiently in England to establish herself there as a respected performer and who, with her husband, Arthur Seguin (1809–1852), a bass who sang at Covent Garden and Drury Lane in English and Italian opera, came to America in 1838. Once in the United States, Arthur Seguin organized the Seguin Opera Company, the earliest of the innumerable English-language opera companies which would play a vital role in opera in America in the next half-century. There were two other lively and popular English sopranos, Jane Shireff and Miss Poole, as well as two well-established non-English operatic Europeans: Marie Caradori-Allan (1800–1865), Alsatian-born, English-trained, who came to America in 1837 and stayed for some years; and Giuseppe de Begnis (1793–1849), a leading comic singer, who crossed the Atlantic in 1838 and stayed until his death.

English composers showed signs of renewed vitality. Charles E. Horn, born into a musical family in London in 1786, was trained as singer, composer, and conductor, writing a number of ballad operas as well as *Circe,* an all-sung opera. In 1823 he emigrated to America, where he spent his early years as a singer at the Park and other New York theaters. Active in Boston in the 1840s, he died there in 1849. In the 1830s Horn composed several operas, most notably *The Maid of Saxony* and *Ahmed al Kamel, or The Pilgrim of Love,* based on Washington Irving's *The Alhambra,* which received eight performances. The popular hit of the time was *Amilie, or The Love Test,* a Donizetti-inspired work by William Michael Rooke (1794–1847), an Irish-English composer, the only work of his to gain popularity. The first night of *Amilie* in New York, in 1838, offered the American debuts of Arthur Seguin, Jane Shireff, and John Wilson. It ran nightly for some time and was frequently revived in the next few years. *Amilie* seemed a portent of a creative upsurge in England and Ireland, at just which point an even more popular opera flashed across the horizon and the Atlantic, Michael William Balfe's *The Bohemian Girl.*

T h e opening night at the Park Theatre on November 25, 1844, was different from any other comparable event that had preceded it in the American operatic experience. Considerable publicity had made New Yorkers aware of the composer and of the opera, which less than a year before had achieved a sensational London success. *The Bohemian Girl* had generated such anticipation that even on Thanksgiving weekend the Park Theatre was filled. Leading members of the resident acting company took roles as supernumeraries. The production, in careful preparation and lavishness, invited comparison with the grandest of French or Italian opera productions seen in the city. The chorus, sixteen men and eight women, was well rehearsed. Four leading dancers and sixteen supporting ones had been specially recruited, the "exceedingly beautiful" scenery was matched by picturesque costumes. As for the singers, all were able and experienced, and Anne Seguin, as Arline, was repeating the role she had created in London. *The Bohemian Girl* was a roaring success. Bursts of applause punctuated the performance, demands for encores of the most popular numbers were frequent. Anne Seguin was in her best form, in control of her voice, all her embellishments in good taste, acting with confidence and freedom of movement. If the music seemed unoriginal—"several of the arias are mere adaptations from favorite operas"—the audience didn't mind. Remarkably, the opera seemed both fresh and familiar.[5]

Despite terrible weather in December and virtually impassable streets all around it, the Park Theatre was continually jammed. *The Bohemian Girl* ran until the middle of the month, when previously scheduled Christmas engagements forced its withdrawal. "The English opera at the Park is beginning to lose its attractiveness," the *New York Herald* rashly, and rather sourly, predicted. "The processions and dances and all that are becoming tiresome to the multitude." Far from it. In January the Seguins brought it back to the Park for twenty-two consecutive performances, far more than any other opera had received. In February the Bowery Theatre, refurbished for the occasion, produced its version of the opera, and though the Bowery's singers were so feeble that Balfe's uncomplicated music had to be rearranged and simplified to suit them, the opera ran all through February and into March. The Chatham Theatre did it in September and the Park again at Christmas of 1845. Boston and Baltimore saw it soon after New York. Then *The Bohemian Girl* headed west. It had a sensational opening-night success in Philadelphia, where it remained a great favorite. By the end of the century it had been given 376 times there, 100 more than its nearest competitor for popularity, Verdi's *The Troubador (Il Trovatore)*.[6]

Within five days of the first American performance, a music publisher announced that "already four of the gems [of the opera] were issued and several of the duets, marches, songs, would be soon forthcoming." Piano versions of its songs and choruses came pouring off the presses: the Arline gallop, the Bohemian quickstep, the Arline waltz. There were collections of its songs called *The Beauties of "The Bohemian Girl," Bouquet of Melodies, Gems from "The Bohemian Girl."*[7]

Michael Balfe's name was one to be reckoned with. Born in Dublin in 1808, he gave evidence at an early age of unusual musical ability. Help from friends enabled him to pursue his studies in Italy, where he eventually made his operatic singing debut, as Figaro in *Il Barbiere di Siviglia,* under Rossini's approving eye and ear. By age twenty he appeared at the Italian Theater in Paris, sang with Malibran and later with Pauline Viardot-García. In 1841 he was Papageno in the first English-language production of *Die Zauberflöte* in London.

Balfe was that rarity, a singer-composer. While in Italy he composed several operas in the Italian style. In England, in the 1830s, he began composing in English, *The Siege of Rochelle* in 1835, *The Maid of Artois,* written expressly for Malibran but not produced until 1837, the year after her death. He had three operas produced in Paris, one of them the first commission given to a British composer by the Opéra. Adept in several styles and languages, Balfe finally settled on English opera as his proper form. The ballad was his strength and an ampler version of ballad opera the congenial way to express himself. His friend Hector Berlioz wrote: "There are people who are amazed that an Englishman could have written this pretty music, but . . . why should not an Englishman make good music? There are plenty of Italians, French and Germans who make very bad music; M. Balfe's music . . . is expressive and dramatic and only needs occasionally a little more originality."[8] Balfe belonged to English musical culture, but by reason of his Irishness and his cosmopolitan travel, he was also detached from it. He made this tension fruitful by grafting onto ballad opera a special quality of fancifulness.

In 1842 he saw a ballet in Paris entitled *The Gypsy,* involving abductions, concealed identities, a wicked queen, and an artful gypsy leader. He sensed that it was an ideal subject for him. Despite a wretched libretto, the subject released in him a genuine flow of melody. Balfe conducted the first performance of his opera at Her Majesty's Theatre (formerly the King's Theatre) in London on November 27, 1843. It concluded with scenes of wild enthusiasm. Within a year *The Bohemian Girl* achieved a hundred performances in London and moved out across Britain and, as we know, across the Atlantic. On the Continent it received a welcome unprecedented for an English opera. In Berlin the composer was invited to be present at the first performance. In St. Petersburg the imperial family all came to hear it. In Vienna it had been heard three hundred times by 1853, the year it reached Italy. Only the French proved stubbornly resistant to its charms.

O n c e familiar, *The Bohemian Girl* is virtually unknown today, so a brief summary of its plot is necessary if we are to understand its special quality. Set vaguely in central Europe, in the mid-eighteenth century, the story concerns Thaddeus, a Pole unjustly exiled from his homeland, who is living, in disguise, with a band of gypsies. They, persecuted by the Austrian governor, had years before abducted the governor's daughter, Arline (whose life, years before *that,* Thaddeus had saved when she was attacked by a wild boar). Arline lives with the gypsies but is unaware of her true identity. False charges are brought against her by the queen of the gypsies, who loves Thaddeus and is jealous of Arline. Vindicated at a trial, Arline sees her identity revealed; the queen of the gypsies attempts to kill her but is herself accidentally killed. Thaddeus is revealed to be a Polish nobleman, and he and Arline are united.

What was appealing about this seeming nonsense? One answer was clear to everyone: *The Bohemian Girl* was filled with attractive melodies. "Its songs beat upon the ear night and day like the waves of the restless ocean."[9] This tunefulness put it among a handful of operas that have gained a special kind of popularity. Their distinguishing feature is an immediate, contagious singableness. This is closely connected to rhythmic energy, song translated into dance. People are swept off their feet. *Le Nozze di Figaro* was the first such opera. Prague went mad, *Figaro's* music being converted into dance tunes played at the balls of the nobility, in the wine and beer cellars of the lower classes, arranged for piano, wind instruments, for chamber groups of all sizes and combinations. Bands played *Figaro* in the public gardens. Even the wandering harpist at the tavern door was obliged to strum out one of its songs if he wished to gain any audience at all. Rossini's *Il Barbiere* had such melodies, so had Verdi's *Il Trovatore* and *Rigoletto,* several of Jacques Offenbach's operas, and a few others. One man recalled of *The Bohemian Girl* that "the charming melodies heard for the first time the night before came back, now in fragments, now completely to recollection, haunting the memory."[10] This haunting quality was almost obsessive. At the height of *Der Freischütz's* appeal in Germany a gentleman advertised in the papers for a servant who was *not* able to whistle its songs.

This instant popularity is so familiar an aspect of music in our day that we forget it has not always been so. It seems to date from the eighteenth century and is connected with the evolution of a widespread general audience and with the multiplication of means to reach that audience: through bands, transcriptions of the music for other instruments, especially those great popularizers, the barrel organ, the accordion, and, above all, the piano. In these forms music went out to the people. Most who heard these tunes didn't go to the opera. It was, and is still to some extent, an art existing in pieces, in selections, in highlights. The farther away one was from a theater, the more likely it was that opera existed only in this way. The songs came first, long before the complete operas, and were domesticated for many purposes, a part of common cultural life. Weddings, funerals, academic processions were inseparable from the music of Wagner or Handel or Verdi, even for people who had no idea what they were hearing. The ability to write such melodies has rightly been seen as a rare gift and as conferring a special kind of power. Edgar Allan Poe insisted he would rather have written the best song of a nation than its noblest epic poem, and the folk humorist Artemus Ward observed: "Let me write the songs of a nashun and I don't care a cuss who goes to the legislater."[11]

If *The Bohemian Girl*'s tunefulness was the basis for its success, it was tunefulness of a very familiar kind. Balfe's opera made no new or demanding claims on its audiences. It connected easily with the kind of opera they were already familiar with, only *The Bohemian Girl*'s ballads were newer, fresher, more elaborate and energetic. For countless Americans, both those already familiar with opera as well as those for whom it was new, *The Bohemian Girl* represented just what an opera was.

At the same time it told a story. To educated and sophisticated people that story seemed implausible and absurd, but to many others *The Bohemian Girl* conveyed a particular American attitude toward Europe and Europe's history. There was quaint old Austria, with soldiers in colorful uniforms, with castles and strange customs, titles of nobility, national rivalries. The story involved conflict and the possibility of injustice. There were some disagreeable characters, and of course wretched old Europe was as usual bedeviled by class feelings. There was even a killing onstage. And yet *The Bohemian Girl* had a happy ending and left its audiences joyful and delighted. Everything worked out for the best. Love triumphed. Issues of class were evaded. History turned out to be make-believe, fantasy. The silliness of the story was part of its attitude toward history. It represented the absurdity of that European history many American immigrants had escaped from. This was the appeal of the gypsies, with their rousing choruses, feckless hedonism (and rather casual kidnappings). Exotic, strange and mysterious, free and irresponsible, they too represented an escape from the reality of history. So were the gypsies in *Il Trovatore,* that tuneful near contemporary of Balfe's opera, also supposedly handicapped by an incomprehensible plot. Both operas, without an intentionally satiric note in music or libretto, worked for American audiences (English too) as parody.

Balfe's opera is an important link between ballad opera and the other forms of opera Americans became familiar with in the later nineteenth and then twentieth centuries—"operetta," "light opera," "musical." *The Bohemian Girl* is a bridge from *Love in a Village* to *H.M.S. Pinafore.* Equally, but less obviously, it is also the link to forms of European opera—to French comic opera, Offenbach, Audran and Lecocq; and to Viennese opera, Strauss, von Suppé, and Lehár. And beyond that *The Bohemian Girl* prepared the way for the Americanized versions of Continental works, for the operas of John Philip Sousa, Reginald De Koven, and Victor Herbert.

"Operetta" was the opera of the unsophisticated. Where *The Bohemian Girl* became popular was as revealing as why. It became one of the staples of the touring English-language opera companies. There was an old adage among traveling opera companies: "When business is bad, give *The Bohemian Girl* and fill your purse."[12] As it lost its appeal in the metropolitan centers, it fixed itself in small-town culture, a local property, suitable to amateurs. It was for a long time the opera of middle-western,

Rocky Mountain, southern America, insular, Anglo-American, reinforcing their ideas about how odd "abroad" was.

From 1846 Michael Balfe worked energetically to establish English opera in England. In 1847 he singlehandedly sponsored a season of English opera that failed disastrously, "terminating for the nine hundred and ninety-ninth time its temporary existence," as one of the participants in the venture wrote. Of his other operas, only *The Rose of Castille* (1857) gained any popularity. Much of the initial enthusiasm about *The Bohemian Girl* arose because after two centuries of ostensible "failure," English opera had apparently raised its head among the national operas of Europe. That turned out not to be the case. When Balfe died in 1870, the fortunes of English opera were still as low as if he hadn't lived at all. At the time Giuseppe Verdi wrote to a friend about English music: "How nice it would be if that nation that never has been musical should now join hands with us."[13]

William Fry and the American Muse

William Henry Fry was fourteen when the New Orleans company first visited Philadelphia. Other troupes—Montresor and Rivafinoli—followed. We can imagine the impression made upon a young boy who had begun writing music in his teens by the presentation of composers living and creating at that moment—Rossini, Auber, Bellini. Those visits fixed his determination. He would join their company! And he did. If Fry is remembered now, it is as the composer of "the first grand opera in America," a description that does scant justice to his achievement and to the heartache he experienced as an artist.

He was born in Philadelphia on August 10, 1813, the second of five sons of William Fry, publisher of the respected *National Gazette.* Descended from ministers and Revolutionary patriots, the Fry children grew up intensely proud of the United States and of the possibilities of its democratic culture. The Frys were Roman Catholics, educated at Catholic schools with a tradition of fine singing. Another musical influence was that of Robert Walsh, a Baltimorean, well traveled in Europe, who became music editor of the *National Gazette* and emphasized music at a time when most American newspapers barely mentioned it.

Although not rich, the Fry family was sufficiently well off to allow William Henry to concentrate on composition without any worry about supporting himself. The first of his works performed in public was an overture, identified modestly as "by an amateur of this city," included in a program along with overtures by Auber and Rossini for a concert by the Montresor Company at the end of its 1833 visit. His composing was encouraged by Leopold Meignen, a member of the Philadelphia French community, a conductor and teacher of composition who had been trained at the Paris Conservatory, emigrated to America, and played an important role in the city's musical life. Fry composed another overture, for an opera called *Cristiani e pagani (The Christians and the Pagans),* and then began work on an opera entitled *Aurelia the Vestal.* In 1836 Walsh retired from the newspaper to live permanently in Paris, and William Henry began writing music criticism in his place, joining the editorial staff of the paper full-time in 1839. Unfortunately, the effects of the depression of 1837 forced the *National Gazette* to suspend publication in 1841, so Fry took a position with the *New York Tribune,* a paper he would be associated with for the rest of his life. In that same year he finished *Aurelia.* It had an original libretto by his brother Joseph and dealt with the rise of Christianity and the clash of rival religions in the time of Constantine the Great. He didn't even try to have it performed in America, but instead gave it to a singer friend who took it to London to show around. No one there was interested. William Fry swallowed his disappointment and began work on another opera, *Leonora*.[1]

The greatest musical influence on Fry was Bellini, especially *Norma*. In the decade since its first performance, *Norma* had gained a position on every important operatic stage in Europe as one of the undisputed masterpieces of the age. The Frys wished to produce *Norma* in a way that would demonstrate to Americans what classic Italian opera was. Robert Walsh sent a complete score from Paris, and though this and the text were modified somewhat, in now indeterminate ways, the overriding aim was authenticity. Subsidized by the Fry family and by well-known Philadelphians such as Nicholas Biddle and Henry Carey, the production was lavish and painstakingly organized. The orchestra, led by a Mr. Cline, the resident conductor of the Chestnut Street Theatre, was the largest yet assembled for an American operatic production. The scenery was painted by Russell Smith, the leading American scenery painter of the next thirty years. The singers were the best available without looking to Europe.

Norma was a great success, repeated a dozen times. People came from Boston and New York to see and hear it. Two things stand out about it, from our perspective. The

William Henry Fry, composer and critic, was a tireless advocate of American music. Although he sought to infuse his operas and concert music with indigenous elements, one critic complained that he was "neither a patriot nor a cosmopolitan."

99

first is that it was given in English. Gradually, in the 1840s, Fry had apparently come to the conclusion that the dramatic effect of opera could be communicated fully only if operas were given in English. The second was that this production was the first in American history supported by financial guarantees given ahead of time—the old European model of aristocratic patronage adapted to America. But the precedent was followed by no one else. Two years later the Frys mounted another production, this time showing off another of the recent works of Italian genius, Donizetti's *Anne Boleyn* (*Anna Bolena*). This, too, was in English, translated by Joseph Fry. The Seguins sang the principal parts. While all this was going on, William Fry continued working on *Leonora,* whose libretto had been adapted by Joseph Fry from a very popular play of the time, *The Lady of Lyons,* by the English writer Edward Bulwer-Lytton.

I n the "Prefatory Remarks" to the vocal score of *Leonora* published in Philadelphia in 1845, Fry explained his ideas about opera. In his own work he saw himself as going back to the origins of opera in Florence and reconstructing the "high, complete, and classic form" of opera, "every word being sung throughout, and accompanied by the orchestra." He was opposed to the "mixed speaking style" of English opera, believing that spoken dialogue destroyed "proper uniformity of style." The words of the text were as important as the music, and it was for that reason that they had to be comprehensible to the audience. Fry admitted that recitative seemed strange to Americans. The reason was that England, "to which Americans should naturally look for such a union of [music] and literature," had handed over a deeply flawed inheritance. There was only one example of English classic opera in Fry's view, Thomas Arne's *Artaxerxes.* Still, a receptive American audience was being created, one that would be "as much interested in a prolonged English dialogue in recitative, as in any melody exhibiting the vocal skill of the performer." The Fry family productions of *Norma* and of *Anna Bolena* were part of the effort to educate Americans along these lines. Opera must be clearly separated from spoken drama. There was no more reason why a "tragic and serious singer should be required to speak than a tragic actor to sing."

An operatic libretto should be judged by the same high standards one would apply to spoken drama. It was fatal to imagine that "feebleness, obscurity, or nonsense in the drama, will be overlooked because it is connected with music." The history of opera demonstrated conclusively that wretched stories prevented the success of operas "whose music deserved a better fate." And, of course, he denied flatly that English was not suited to sung drama. He had "too much admiration for the resources of the English language, to admit of the supposition that it is excluded, by its nature, from the highest form of opera."

Words and music. As the Fry brothers pondered this eternal subject of operatic concern, William recognized that a successful libretto was difficult to achieve because, in addition to other important attributes, such as a plausible plot, developed characters, and interesting incidents, the operatic text had to have one special quality. It had to allow, or better yet to foster, melody, "the genius of melody as a universal dialect, which claims, indeed, supremacy over words." The greatest operatic composers had been melodists. That was what Fry found so compelling in Bellini's operas.

There were many kinds of melody, of course. *Fidelio* had a "true melodiousness," but not of a kind to make it popular. He also knew that some people equated melody-dominated opera as "light" music, a synonym for "trivial" or "cheap." He thought this simply snobbery. Were Weber and Bellini and Mozart "trivial"?[2]

These ideas were put to the test on the night of June 4, 1845, at the Chestnut Street Theatre. The first performance of *Leonora* is a long-forgotten opening night in American operatic history but nonetheless one of the most interesting, and, because it raised issues which would confront American composers in the years ahead, one of the most significant. There was enthusiastic applause that night, not surprising from a hometown audience filled with family and friends, and there were laudatory comments in the newspapers. There were sixteen more performances, followed by a concert version and, in December 1846, four more performances at the Walnut Street Theatre. At first, *Leonora* seemed a success. Not for the first time, however, initial response, favorable or unfavorable, proved misleading. A decade later there was a New York City production. That was not successful. *Leonora* did not capture an audience and it was soon forgotten.

Leonora failed because its music didn't please, and it didn't please because it was derivative. Fry couldn't get out from under the shadow of Bellini and Donizetti. "It is full of reminiscences." "It constantly recalls the *Sonnambula* and *Norma.*" Or more harshly: "Almost everything in *Leonora* is poorly shaped and put together, and what is worse, worked closely after the most common pattern." Fry had failed his own test: he had created no "melodies of that indescribable and ethereal cast" one found in the great operatic masters, and out of the depths of his own frustration he cried out: "Critics forget that the ability to create gems of melody is the rarest of gifts."[3] He wasn't alone in his failure. Throughout Europe in these years innumerable operas were composed by talented but second- and third-rate composers who had mastered the style of their romantic predecessors, but not their genius.

Fry couldn't be Bellini, but he wouldn't be Balfe. He turned his back on the idea of English comic opera, musically or dramatically. As we've seen, Fry was opposed to any spoken dialogue. Furthermore, the dramatic power of the Italian opera Fry had learned to admire made English opera, as he knew it, seem trivial by comparison. He no doubt agreed with a contemporary critic who wrote: "We all know that nothing is more tedious than a so-called ballad opera," because "modern opera writing means a strong dramatic accentuation, much coloring, and a strong contrast."[4]

Joseph Fry's libretto for *Leonora* was a triangular love story set in vaguely distant historical past, about Julio, a peasant, who loves Leonora, a lady of rank. A rival for Leonora's love tricks them into marriage, thinking that such a union will not be tolerated and the two will be separated forever, but Leonora returns to her family and Julio goes away to make a fortune and become worthy of Leonora. Three years later, the possessor of great wealth, he returns and triumphantly reclaims his bride.

Leonora is a contemporary comedy of social manners, about class and money, two subjects of perennial interest to American audiences, but disguised as a historical drama. Julio is a familiar figure, Horatio Alger disguised as a Spanish peasant, who understands that money can undermine the structure of social privilege. He accepts

A page from the score of Fry's Leonora (1845): echoes of Bellini and Donizetti. John Herrick Jackson Music Library, Yale University.

the rules of his society and wins out by means of them: there are no grounds for thwarting him once he has got enough money. The Frys had seen this same story enacted all around them in Philadelphia, New York, and everywhere else. It was very much in keeping with the traditions of ballad opera, where the underprivileged and marginal often turned the tables on their supposed superiors. Yet William Fry and his brother buried this comedy under the deadening paraphernalia of a conventional costume drama by transferring the original story "to a more distant and hence romantic era," to a time "before nations." Comic opera in English couldn't serve as a foundation for him to build on. He accepted the García view, writing that, until the advent of Italian opera, "operatic music had no existence in this country."[5]

F r y ' s European experience helped him understand the historical situation of the American artist. Europeans had one incalculable advantage over Americans: that there were established musical institutions within which musical talent could be nourished. The United States, lacking such institutional arrangements, needed academies of music, competent teachers, a rigorous system of instruction. "We have no standard, no polar star. Not 12 persons in the 24 millions in the United States could read an orchestral score." Nor could American composers make themselves heard in their own country. "A composer may as well burn his compositions for any opportunity he has for making himself heard." American artists lived at the level of provincial beggars, Fry declared. His homeland's emphasis on practical utility was devastating to art. Americans had somehow to learn that music could rejuvenate "the desert of trade and politics."[6] There was no reason to despair. In 1852 Fry returned from abroad to live in New York, where he took the job of musical editor for Horace Greeley's *Tribune,* the most influential newspaper in the nation, and prepared to take up a second career, as a propagandist for American music.

In November he rented Metropolitan Hall for a series of public lectures, "teaching the elegancies of music to the millions." His title was "The Science and Art of Music— a historical, esthetical, scientific, and critical review of music in 10 lectures." It was an "imperial prospectus." And an imperial presentation: an orchestra of eighty, a chorus of one hundred, a corps of vocalists, and a military band of fifty. The lectures cost the general public five dollars for the series, and they cost Fry ten thousand dollars.

The middle of the nineteenth century was the great age of American lecturing and lecturers, but even so these lectures stood out as one of "the remarkable events of the season" because of the novelty of the subject matter and the scale of organization. They were widely reported in the press, and Metropolitan Hall was "thronged every Tuesday," the first and last lectures attended by three thousand people. Fry put on a lively performance. There was a touch of the Bohemian and of the dandy in his dress, as befitted someone who had lived five years in Paris: dark coat with vest buttoned up to the throat, loose pantaloons, and kid gloves. He used no notes or podium but paced back and forth across the stage, only occasionally referring to scribblings on an old card he kept in his waistcoat. "For two hours and a half he talked brilliantly, quaintly, convulsingly, learnedly, button-holedly, prophetically, half-inspiredly, whimsically, conceitedly, bravely, truly, about everything—and music."

These lectures constituted the first music appreciation course in American history.

An admiring observer believed that they left a "marked and permanent impression upon the public mind." But as Fry had spoken spontaneously and didn't subsequently transcribe his thoughts to paper, we have no record of what he said. It was a great loss, not just because the lectures were an "unequivocal success" by conventional standards of popularity, but because Fry had it within him to "write such a history of Music as has not yet been attempted."[7]

As a composer, he took his own admonitions to heart and sought to infuse his music with specifically American elements. He wrote only orchestral pieces during the 1850s. He experimented with programmatic music, including in it the sounds of mundane aspects of American life. His *Santa Claus: Christmas Symphony* conjured up snowstorms, the sounds of trotting horses, sleigh bells, and the cracking of whips. He composed a *Niagara* symphony. These efforts delighted and amused some but puzzled and disgusted many others. The middle of the decade was marked by numerous acrimonious exchanges between Fry and his allies and the defenders of traditional forms.

He didn't fight alone. An ally emerged in the person of George Frederick Bristow (1825–1898). A New Yorker, son of a composer and conductor, Bristow had a professional career of forty years as a violinist and conductor and wrote several books about the teaching of music. In the 1850s he battled, along with Fry, to establish a national school of music. At one point he resigned for a year from the Philharmonic Society of New York because of its unwillingness to play the music of American composers.

Bristow was a prolific composer in a wide range of musical forms, and although his music was conventional in form and structure, he chose American subjects, as reflected in titles such as *The Great Republic, Ode to the American Union, Niagara Symphony, The Pioneer,* and others. Keenly interested in vocal music, in 1850 he played the violin in the orchestra that accompanied Jenny Lind on her tour of America. Stimulated by hearing her sing "much choice vocal music," he began sketching an opera and worked away at it from 1852 to 1855. Jonathan Howard Wainwright prepared a libretto for him based on Washington Irving's *Rip Van Winkle,* in three acts, with spoken dialogue, departing sharply in this from Fry's ideas. It was first performed on September 17, 1855, at Niblo's Garden, "jammed to the doors" for the occasion. The singers were members of the Pyne-Harrison English-language opera company and the production was highly praised, with Catskill scenes based on the drawings by the American painter and caricaturist F. O. C. Darley. Bristow's music was light and cheerful, the orchestration an unusual mixture of brass and woodwinds. The great criticism of the libretto was of the second act, a love story, not in Irving's original, for some secondary characters during Rip's twenty-year sleep. *Rip Van Winkle* received seventeen performances in September and October and was a reasonable box-office success, but no impresario took it up for production elsewhere until the Richings English Opera Company gave it in Philadelphia in November 1870. After that, *Rip* joined *Leonora* in operatic limbo. Bristow left another opera, *King of the Mountains,* half completed at his death.[8]

I n Europe, powerful nationalist operatic movements arose at this time. Smetana,

Dvořák, Borodin, Musorgsky are among the innumerable musicians who took part in an effort to create national opera, based on indigenous folk materials—Smetana's *The Bartered Bride* is the classic instance—so that people who could not achieve political independence might at least free themselves from the imperial operatic sway of the Italians, French, and Germans. To some extent, cultural nationalism may have served as a substitute for political nationalism. Nothing like this happened in the United States. The eruption of the Civil War at mid-century, absorbing vast national energies, south and north, may have played a role in dissipating the emergence of nationalist folk culture. But the heart of the problem remained the daunting prestige of European musical art: "If we continue to stand tip-toe along the Atlantic shore endeavoring to catch the last word from Europe, nothing great will surely be done," warned Samuel F. B. Morse, painter and inventor. A more crucial factor was the absence of the folk materials for a native tradition to be built on. Fry believed that was his problem. "The actions of an opera laid in this country could not be illustrated with national music," he wrote, "since the original type is wanting."[9]

Was it "wanting," or was it that American folk culture was divided by an element absent in Europe—race? African American music played an incalculable subterranean role in American musical culture, but most white Americans, whether native-born or immigrants, would have been shocked by the candid comment of a contemporary observer that "an army" of American composers had failed to add anything of value to the world's musical literature, producing instead only "feeble imitations of foreign models." The observer concluded morosely: "Mortifying as the fact may be to our vanity, it must be acknowledged that the little music we have that possesses really distinctive American characteristics takes its inspiration from the negroes."[10] The idea that African American music might be a generative influence in the evolution of American opera would have seemed fantastic to contemporaries; and yet it was so, as was suggested by the appearance of a kind of popular opera, minstrel shows, and by the songs of Stephen Foster.

In the early 1840s, minstrel shows exploded into tremendous popularity, a vogue which lasted for the next half-century. Theatrical sketches imitating African Americans had been popular, in England and America, since the late eighteenth century, and entertainers, performing with circuses, had frequently appeared in blackface (burnt cork). The most influential of these was Thomas Dartmouth Rice (1808–1860), who sang an African American tune while he did a curious shuffle dance, the chorus of the song being marked by a jump with his heels clicking together. "Jump Jim Crow" became a sensation, reached London by 1836 and fueled the desire for more of these "Ethiopian" songs, which in the next few years became the nucleus of shows made up of various elements. In 1842 and 1843 E. P. Christy and Dan Emmett turned individual performances into performance by a group. Four or more men sang minstrel songs, danced, told jokes, accompanied by minstrel instruments, some of which derived from African originals—banjo, bone castanets, tambourine. Minstrel shows were white men's shows (though African Americans developed their own minstrel companies in the 1850s). Even while they perpetrated crude stereotypes of African American behavior and attempted to reconcile white Americans to the culture of slavery by suggesting that the life of slaves was an enviable one, these white minstrel performers closely imitated African American culture. "Early minstrels used Afro-American dances and dance-steps, reproduced individual Negro songs and routine intact, absorbed Afro-American syncopated rhythms into their music and employed characteristically Afro-American folk elements and forms. Black and white Americans influenced each other."[11]

By the 1850s minstrel opera had evolved into the form which endured for four decades. There were three acts. In the first, the entire company appeared in a semicircle. An Interlocutor, seated in the center, acted as master of ceremonies, his unruffled dignity and decorum contrasting with the jokes and banter and high jinks of the rest of the performers, especially the two men at either end of the semicircle, the end men, Tambo and Bones, named for their instruments. They were the heart of the irreverent and boisterous quality of the performance, mocking the gravity of the Interlocutor. The musical star of act 1 was a tenor who sang sentimental songs and romantic ballads. Act 2 was a variety show, featuring acrobats, songs, people playing exotic instruments, and concluding with a parody of a stump speech of the day. Act 3 brought the entire company back on stage, in bright costumes. It consisted of a sketch or a play, perhaps about plantation life or a parody of a popular drama or opera, or it might be an original Ethiopian farce opera, *Long Island Juba, The Black Cupid, Bone Squash Diavolo*. The Kneass Opera Troupe, a prominent minstrel company, specialized in parodies of well-known operas. The third act concluded with a vigorous dance, the "walk-around," and indeed perhaps the most striking aspect of these minstrel operas was their great emphasis on dancing. African American dance was already celebrated. William Henry Lane, "Master Juba," the greatest African American dancer of the day, seen and much admired by Charles Dickens on his visit to America, combined European dance with African elements to produce something unmatched by anyone else. And "Jump Jim Crow" was only the first of many African American dances to become a world-wide success. The "soft shoe" and the "buck and wing" dances emerged from the later stages of minstrelsy onto European and American stages, to be taken up by white performers. Naturally, the success of minstrel shows meant that a vast number of song writers sprang up to meet the voracious demand. Among them was Stephen Collins Foster.

Born near Pittsburgh, on the Fourth of July, 1826, he grew up in a family of considerable musical cultivation, though very modest means. The boy was encouraged to play the clarinet, guitar, flageolet and piano and began composing songs in his teens. He fell in love with minstrel shows and music. At nineteen he wrote his first important song, in the Ethiopian vein, "Old Uncle Ned," and met Thomas Rice, who encouraged him to compose for minstrel shows. In the mid-1840s Foster moved to Cincinnati, where he worked as a bookkeeper in his brother's office. In 1847 he composed and published the song that first made him famous—"Oh! Susanna." The 1850s were the great period for him. Memorable melodies of a distinctive cast and quality poured out in a flood—"Camptown Races," "My Old Kentucky Home," "Old Dog Tray," "Jeannie with the Light Brown Hair." Foster did what Mozart and Rossini and a handful of other song writers were able to do: write a song which was "on

50 VERSES.

The only Correct Copy of the

EXTRAVAGANZA OF

JIM   CROW

As sung by Mr. Rice.

A nineteenth-century broadside advertising the "Jim Crow" lyrics of Thomas Dartmouth Rice, the most influential of the early black-face minstrels. Beinecke Rare Book and Manuscript Library, Yale University.

everybody's tongue, and consequently in everybody's mouth. . . . Pianos and guitars groan with it, night and day; sentimental young ladies sing it; sentimental young gentlemen warble it in midnight serenades; volatile young 'bucks' hum it in the midst of their business and pleasures; boatmen roar it out stentorially at all times; all the bands play it; amateur flute blowers agonize over it at every spare moment; the street organs grind it out at every hour; the singing stars carol it on the theatrical boards, and at concerts; the chamber maid sweeps and dusts to the measured cadence of 'Old Folks at Home.' "[12]

Foster married and moved to New York. In the 1860s his life took a sudden, irreversible downward turn. His marriage failed. He drank heavily, sank into poverty and died, alone, on January 13, 1864.

As a composer, Foster combined the popular and the cultivated traditions. In Europe, born into the same circumstances, he might well have had the chance for formal musical training, in a church school or a royal chapel or a state-sponsored academy of music. As it was, he had to educate himself as best he could. Prolific as he was—he wrote more than two hundred songs—he was not an untutored natural warbler. In Cincinnati he had become familiar with opera. His brother described him, studying the music of operatic composers, copying out parts of opera scores, attending opera when it was available from touring companies. And of course in New York there was much opera in the 1860s. In 1854 Foster published *The Social Orchestra,* a collection of some of his songs and of popular operatic pieces, duets, trios, quartets, arranged to be performed at home on the piano and guitar—music by Bellini, Donizetti, Boieldieu, Mozart, Schubert, Johann Strauss, Weber. More than that, he composed operatically. H. Wiley Hitchcock has illuminated Foster's relationship to operatic song by means of "Come Where My Love Lies Dreaming," which "has whole chunks of opera in it. It's difficult for us to hear it that way because we know it as a 'Stephen Foster song,' and we have to make an abrupt turn to try to think of it as an Italian operatic song. But if we quite carefully identify the stylistic traits of Italian opera—its melodic style, its treatment of the voice, and other things—and then look at certain Foster songs and find the same traits; we begin to see Foster in a different perspective from the one that has been presented to us."[13] Foster never attempted an opera and the ability to compose beautiful songs is no guarantee of the ability to compose musical drama, as the career of Franz Schubert reminds us. But his work suggests what American ballad opera could have sounded like—as the twentieth century would show.

E a r l y in the 1860s William Fry learned that he had tuberculosis. Time was pressing, so he took up an opera he had been working at, off and on, for a dozen years. Once more, Joseph prepared a libretto, based on a popular novel of the day, Victor Hugo's *The Hunchback of Notre Dame*. William finished the music by the end of 1863 and on May 6, 1864, *Notre Dame de Paris* received its first performance, in Phila-delphia, in one of those generously financed and carefully rehearsed Fry family productions, with well-drilled singers and chorus and a large orchestra led by Theodore Thomas, one of the new generation of German conductors taking com-mand of American music.

Critics, acknowledging the composer's industry, once again heard Bellini and Donizetti in the background, but the derivativeness of the music was no longer the main point of criticism. The primary objection to *Notre Dame,* by the 1860s, was not that it was second-hand but that it was old-fashioned. Why was it that Fry still yearned for that Italian "mock Eden"? One critic wrote: "A composer must be either a nationalist, tilling a small but distinctive plot, or an internationalist, transcending his origins in the achievement of universal forms. But Mr. Fry is neither a patriot nor a cosmopolitan." As a writer and popularizer he had been tireless in his advocacy of a national music. Horace Greeley, who employed him, was caustic about this. He had once sent a political column to his own paper only to find that the editor had "crowded out what little I did say to make room for Fry's eleven columns of argu-ments as to the feasibility of sustaining opera in N.Y." With studied asperity Greeley asked the editor: "What would it cost to burn the opera house? If the price is reasonable, have it done and send me the bill."[14]

William Fry did much for his country and for the life of its people. A sympathetic colleague argued that *Notre Dame* showed "a constructive power and mastery of the resources of opera" that promised "with encouragement and time to produce some-thing of which musical Americans might have been proud."[15] Fry wasn't given that time. He had gone to Santa Cruz, West Indies, for relief from his illness, and died there on December 21, 1864. As a composer his labors came to nothing. As an advocate of American music his ideas were soon forgotten. Never mind. It was a life we can recall with gratitude and pride.

chapter ten

Gold Rush

West they came to El Dorado, "ghostknockers and fakers, Don Quixotes, pick-pockets, orators and hawkers, ballet dancers and virtuosi." One of that fantastic horde was a musician named Miska Hauser, whose sprightly letters depicted the San Francisco of 1850: a chaotic shantytown without adequate water, plumbing or lighting, with people living in tents and improvised shacks, a sea of mud in the rain and a cloud of dust in the dry summer. "Murder is an every day occurrence," Hauser wrote. "Anyone who intends to stay here for any length of time would do well to contemplate the heavens at night from the windows of his hotel room."[1] Few gold rush Californians followed such advice. Their lives were intensely public, their contemplations unheavenly. For all of its makeshift squalor, entertainment was more important to the city's inhabitants than anything besides gold. San Francisco boasted handsome gambling saloons and theaters. Theater brought this rootless, familyless population together and gave it a few hours of respectable sociability.

Opera came early to El Dorado in the form of the Pellegrini troupe, a handful of Italian, German, and French singers, a couple of instrumentalists, some costumes, but no scenery or chorus. On January 24, 1851, the Pellegrinis presented scenes and selections from *La Sonnambula*. Two weeks later was its first complete performance. Just how complete is uncertain, but we know that the chorus included no women, and that they sang in English while the soloists sang in Italian. An audience packed with adventurers and desperadoes, flannel-shirted miners down from the mountains and linen-shirted city gamblers, loved that pastoral tale of innocence and virtue rewarded. *La Sonnambula* was repeated four times. Then, in February, *Norma;* in April, Verdi's *Ernani*.

Italian opera wasn't the only operatic show. In October 1852, a Cantonese dramatic troupe, 123 members, including an orchestra, arrived in the city to perform at the American Theatre. They opened with a program of jugglers, acrobats, and conjurers and then, on October 18, using simple props and scenery, performed an opera, *The Eight Genii, Offering Their Congratulations to the High Ruler, Yuk Hwang, on His Birthday.* So successful were the performances which followed that the company stayed for six months and also traveled to the mining towns where thousands of Chinese were working. They brought with them the framework of a theater, which was erected and opened in December, "a pagoda-looking edifice," decorated with ornamental paintings and lanterns, with seats for one thousand, an inclined floor, and an orchestra pit accommodating forty

In the late 1800s, as many as four Chinese opera companies appeared simultaneously in San Francisco. This view of a Chinese theater is from F. E. Shearer, ed., The Pacific Tourist *(1879). Beinecke Rare Book and Manuscript Library, Yale University.*

musicians. In March, their season over, the theater was auctioned off for $1,150 and the company sailed for New York.

Despite intense local prejudice and legal discrimination against them, the Chinese population grew in numbers and their theater survived, sinking deep roots among the local populace. Successive troupes came from China, part of a well-organized circuit that included Canton, Hong Kong, San Francisco, Mexico City, and Havana and eastern American cities. Like Englishmen in the early eighteenth century who first encountered Italian opera, the response of Americans to Chinese opera was often a mixture of harsh derision and total incomprehension; the highly stylized conventions of Chinese opera, scenic and acting, men playing women's roles, much pantomime, were baffling. Listeners responded even more harshly to the music: "screams, gobblings, brayings, barkings," likening it to "the mingled midnight music of forty cats." Nevertheless, in the 1860s and 1870s Chinese opera became popular with American audiences and San Francisco had as many as four opera companies playing at the same time. Charles Nordhoff, American journalist and traveler, visited the "China Theatre" in 1872. He found an "interested and decorous" audience, who did not applaud, cheer or give "noisy manifestations of displeasure or delight." Women were strictly segregated from the men in the audience, in a special section of the gallery. While the music seemed "only a horrible discord," Nordhoff understood that "there was evidently a method in it; the leader, whose instrument consisted of two ivory sticks, with which he beat time on a block of iron, had his shirt-sleeved orchestra under full control; and the singers and the players all kept admirable time." He thought it the "strangest sight San Francisco has to show," but one no visitor should miss.[2]

B y contrast, Americans depended haphazardly on wanderers to bring them their

European opera, mostly marginal artists, failures elsewhere, given a second chance in the land of golden promise. Elisa Biscaccianti came first. Born Elisa Ostinelli in Boston, of a music-teaching father, she was perhaps the first significant native-born American operatic singer, though her dainty, birdlike coloratura soprano gained her little success in the East. The winter of 1852 found her in San Francisco, where her concerts, of Bellini, Meyerbeer, and Donizetti, plus English ballads, made her the city's first vocal sensation. The day after her initial performance, even "the most sober minded and judicial" citizens went about in a "daze of delight." Biscaccianti traveled throughout northern California, gave seventy-one concerts, and made a lot of money, but as soon as she encountered her first operatic rival, she left hastily for South America. When she came back, in 1859, she had been forgotten, took to drink, sank to singing in dance halls and brothels, somehow found the strength to break away, and returned to Peru.

The rival who drove Elisa Biscaccianti out of the state was a more accomplished singer, "the swan of Erin." Catherine Hayes, born in Ireland, studied with Manuel García in Paris, made her debut there in 1845, and sang with success in Italy, Austria, and England. She came to America in 1851, expecting, but failing, to cash in on Jenny Lind's success. That was forgotten in the clamor of her San Francisco reception, which had more to do with her Irishness than with her voice or pretty features. Tickets were auctioned for her appearances. At the peak of Hayes mania, $50 per seat was not an unusual price. Irish volunteer firemen were especially ardent and vocal supporters. The Empire Fire Engine Company paid $1,150 for seats for one concert, and in Sacramento someone paid $1,200 for a single ticket. Audiences were so noisily demonstrative—hats and money raining down on the stage—that it was often difficult to hear her sing.

In the early winter of 1853, Kate Hayes went mining in the Sierras: "That is, after the miners had dug and washed the precious ore, she, with characteristic shrewdness, picked out the big lumps." She didn't ever appear in opera. Instead, she gave costume recitals, no chorus or scenery, sometimes an orchestra, sometimes only a piano. In the spring of 1853 she, too, went to South America, then returned for three more months in 1854. She made more than thirty thousand dollars in California and retired to England, where she died at age thirty-eight in 1861.

Between Kate Hayes's two California visits, San Franciscans once again saw some opera, a French company headed by Anna Thillon. English by birth, Anna Hunt studied in France, married a French music teacher, and became well known for her interpretation of Auber's operas. She sang with success in London, Paris, and New York. In San Francisco she did Italian and English, as well as French, opera: *The Bohemian Girl, La Cenerentola, La Fille du régiment,* and *The Crown Diamonds* (*Les Diamants de la couronne*). This was the first San Francisco opera season of a professional character and it gave Anna Thillon, too, the means to retire, which she did the following year on her return to London.

Anna Bishop arrived in 1854. She had force and theatrical presence, though her voice was pretty well gone. People always differed about her, some finding her showy but appealing, others dismissing her as a vulgarizer. After beginning with concerts, in

April she appeared in *Norma*, followed by the fullest season of opera yet: *La Sonnam-bula, Don Pasquale, Martha, Lucrezia Borgia, Lucia di Lammermoor,* and *La Favorite*. She stayed for eighteen months, giving concerts as well as forty opera performances. Anna Bishop drew a large number of foreign-born people to her audiences, but no fire companies turned out. In late 1855 she left for Australia.[3]

San Francisco's musical life had become more systematic. The major force behind this transition was one of the most unlikely operatic impresarios in all the varied chapters of the history of opera in America.

T o m Maguire was born sometime in the early 1820s in New York City and grew up in the streets, drove a hack, operated a livery stable, booked prizefight bets, and managed a saloon frequented by Tammany Hall nabobs. The most important place in his life was none of these. It was the Park Theatre. There, he operated the bars on the second and third tiers and gained experience of theatrical management. There, in the lobby, he won his woman, "Little Em," fighting another Bowery rowdy for her. (Eventually he married her. She had brains and business sense.) And there, too, in the by then shabby, run-down, out-of-fashion Park, his heart and mind were seized by the

The flamboyant Tom Maguire made and lost a fortune promoting opera and other entertain-ments in California. Bancroft Library, Univer-sity of California, Berkeley.

desire to own and manage a theater and produce classic drama and opera. He never expressed this desire in writing—for one thing, he was illiterate; he simply acted it out with all his considerable energy. In pursuit of those dreams, Tom Maguire and Little Em became 49ers.[4]

He went to find gold in entertainment, not to dig it out of the ground. He opened a saloon and a gambling room and, as soon as he could, built a small theater, seating five hundred. He gave it the most glamorous name he knew—Jenny Lind (whom he never saw). Fire wiped Tom Maguire out five times between 1849 and 1851. Each time he rebuilt on a larger scale. There were three Jenny Lind theaters, light, airy, with white woodwork and lots of gilt. He was his own architect. Jenny Lind Theater III, of yellow Australian sandstone, seated two thousand. Maguire aimed for quality and expected his patrons to pay for it: a box seat sold for $3.00, a seat in the parquet $2.00. Building the last Jenny Lind bankrupted him. His Tammany experience showed him the way out. He persuaded the city to buy the theater from him for $200,000 and use it as the City Hall.

Through all his theater building, Maguire had kept his saloon and gambling room, "The Diana" and "The Snug," so that by the mid-1850s when San Francisco grew more respectable—gambling was prohibited by state law in 1855—he had made a fortune. From then on he concentrated on his theatrical operations. In 1856 he opened Maguire's New Opera House. However, he didn't put on opera—yet. He imported minstrel shows, trapeze artists, novelty programs, and vaudeville. He guaranteed engagements, paid top prices for talent, and changed the bill of fare frequently. "Above all he was deeply impressed by the instability of public fancy and believed in a complete change of program at frequent intervals."[5] He expanded to other northern California cities, building theaters in Sacramento and Marysville, and sent a touring company to remote southern California. (It failed.) For a few years he owned, controlled, or operated most of the important theaters in the state. He sent talent scouts to Europe and Asia, and at one time had three dramatic companies, an opera troupe, and a minstrel company operating at the same time. Burlesques of opera were especially popular in San Francisco, where things respectable, politics, art, and government, were subjected to withering irreverence.

Tom Maguire operated in a wholly informal way. He had secretaries do all his writing while, faultlessly attired, swinging a cane, diamonds flashing from hands and scarves, he conducted his business standing on the curb in front of his opera house: meeting would-be employees, fixing agreements, and hearing petitioners. "You might as well have tried to get him inside a church as to enter an office for his business." He remained hot-tempered and combative and had numerous public brawls. When he battered a certain Mr. MacDougal, Mark Twain wrote:

> Tom Maguire
> Rouse to ire,
> Lighted on MacDougal;
> Tore his coat
> Clutched his throat,
> And split him in the bugle.

> For shame! Oh, fie!
> Maguire, why
> Will you thus skyugle?
> Why curse and swear
> And rip and tear,
> The innocent MacDougal?

Maguire took it in good humor and suggested to Twain that he should do more of it. It was at Maguire's Academy of Music that Mark Twain began his lecturing career.[6]

By the end of the 1850s he had added a fortune made in the theater to his gambling one and estimated he was worth a million dollars. It was time to start spending it. In the spring of 1859 he brought an opera company headed by Eugenio and Giovanna Bianchi to California for performances at popular prices—$1.00 and 50¢. Their association soon dissolved in a furious argument. Maguire replaced them with the traveling Lyster English Opera Company, although he didn't like English opera or opera in English. Nevertheless, in 1860 the Lyster troupe gave an extensive opera season for him—sixty-five performances, more than was offered in any one season in New York, Philadelphia, or New Orleans. Performances were well attended. This gave him confidence to expand his operations, which inevitably meant building more theaters.

In Virginia City he put up a replica of Maguire's Opera House. And in the spring of 1864, in San Francisco, he built his grandest house, Maguire's Academy of Music. It had an Italianate marble front of four stories with a balustrade and pediment. There were three tiers of boxes, and everything was in the Maguire white and gold. Sixty ventilators in the walls drew in fresh air. There was a large chandelier and lights on each tier of boxes. A painting, known as *The Age of Gold,* was reproduced on the act curtain, and the seats were covered in red plush. It was his greatest achievement as a theater, but it was ill-fated. Little Em had opposed its being built.

Maguire's Academy was intended for opera, and the late 1860s in San Francisco were not a congenial time for operatic productions. There was labor unrest and increased theatrical competition. Most of all, audience tastes were changing, and Tom Maguire didn't want to change with them. He didn't approve of the growing vogue for French comic opera. He was prudish, and he was a traditionalist. He wanted the best of the past. Just when he should have been retrenching, he had a chance to bring something special to San Francisco. His advertisements glowed with pride: "Mr. T. Maguire takes pleasure in informing the patrons of HIGH ART in San Francisco that while in the Atlantic states he succeeded, at an ENORMOUS EXPENSE, IN EFFECTING AN ENGAGEMENT WITH THE GREAT LYRIC ARTISTE, MADAME PAREPA ROSA."[7] Euphrosyne Parepa-Rosa, body like a barrel, voice like an angel, a Scottish-born soprano, daughter of a singer, had sung in England and toured the United States. Later she married Carl Rosa and became the principal singer of the Carl Rosa Company, one of the most influential groups in late nineteenth-century opera in England and America. Parepa-Rosa came to San Francisco for two brilliant months. She opened in *Il Trovatore* and went on from one success to another. But expenses were very high, and, although receipts for Parepa-Rosa's visit reached $50,000, Maguire lost money. He had to sell the Academy. In the 1860s he calculated he lost $120,000 on opera.

The opening of the transcontinental railroad marked the end of gold-rush California, of California as a perpetual carnival of the flamboyant bizarre. Much of its appeal had been its remoteness. Tom Maguire went on in the old ways. Little Em died in 1870. With her restraining hand gone, his obsession with opera grew. He remarried, and in 1878 traveled to Europe. In London he saw a new opera, *Carmen:* "Just the hit of the century," he predicted. He went to Italy hoping to sign prominent singers to contracts, but in the late seventies the silver mines failed and the California stock market collapsed. Maguire splurged what he had left on two extravagant gambles—a combined opera house and hotel, built with Lucky Baldwin, the southern California speculator and sportsman, and the Maurice Strakosch Opera Company, with Marie Roze and Annie Louise Cary, as fine singers as any he had ever sponsored. That was a spectacular failure. By 1880 he was bankrupt.

Why had he done it? What had opera meant to Tom Maguire? He admired those who were themselves the objects of admiration. Actors and singers personified a kind of magical, limitless power. When Edwin Forrest was playing for him in 1866, Maguire hailed a friend in the street, on the day of Forrest's appearance in *Coriolanus.*

"Say, coming to see the old man tonight?" Maguire asked.

"I don't know. What's the play?"

"Corrylanus. It's first-rate. One of his own."

"Do you mean to say Forrest wrote it?"

"Of course he did. He kin do anything that man kin."

Artists were *somebody.* And he had been nobody. They moved in and out of the great world. In a kind of reverie, Maguire once spoke to a friend about Charles Kean, musing aloud about the great English actor's life as well as his art. "Not much of a figure of a man is he? Not much of a man to look at. And he's not rich. Well, I'd give all the money I ever made, all I have got and all I expect to make, if I could take his place. I don't mean as an actor; as a man in the world." Maguire's friend pressed a bit, trying to find out more about what Kean represented to him. "He is invited to see the Queen of England, he is; goes and comes at all the palaces, just as he pleases. Queen talked to him, familiar like; and there ain't many she does that to, I can tell you. He hasn't much money; but money's nothing compared to treatment like that." That old image of the court—the court of unparalleled splendor and authentic exclusiveness—how it still haunted American dreams!

About to lose his last theater, Maguire turned to his young assistant, David Belasco, for help. Belasco could not or would not help. (But he will reappear in our story.) So Tom Maguire lost his theater, left San Francisco, and after thirty-three years returned to the city where he had begun. His second wife eventually went mad and was committed to an asylum, but not before she had squandered what was left of his money on real estate speculations. A benefit was held for him at the Metropolitan Opera House on May 10, 1894. An imposing list of theatrical and musical people took part, but the proceeds were very modest. Tom Maguire meant little to New York. He died alone in a rooming house in 1896, but his zest for opera, not the pathos of his

San Franciscans flocked to burlesques of opera such as Ill Treated Il Trovatore, *presented in 1880 as a benefit for the now bankrupt Tom Maguire. Library of Congress.*

FAREWELL APPEARANCES
in San Francisco of the Famous
COLVILLE
OPERA BURLESQUE COMPANY.
Musical and Stage Director, Mr. JESSE WILLIAMS. Stage Manager, Mr. WM. FORRESTER.

TUESDAY EVENING, January 27th,

WEDNESDAY MATINEE, January 28th,

—ALSO ON—

THURSDAY EVENING, January 29th, 1880,

FOR THE BENEFIT OF THE TREASURER,

MR. J. T. MAGUIRE;

Will be presented, an original Burlesque, in 2 acts, founded on a
famous though somewhat confusing Opera,

Ill Treated Il Trovatore,
Or, The Mother, The Maiden and The Musicianer.

CHARACTERS.

MANRICO, (a wandering Minstrel, a real good fellow, tho' a *true-bad-doer*)
....Miss EME ROSEAU
COUNT DI LUNA, (a Count di Magistrate)..............Mr. ROBT. GRAHAM
FERRANDO, (his creature)..........................Miss KATE EVERLEIGH
FIRST GUARD...Mr. AMBERG
SECOND GUARD..Mr. FRAIL
THIRD GUARD...Mr. ADAIR
FOURTH GUARD..Mr. DE SMITH
KINCHEN, (a Gypsy thief, lent for the occasion from "The Flowers of the
Forest")..Mr. ED. CHAPMAN
COSPETTO, (a dizzy and dizipated Romaney).........Mr. A. MAFLIN
RUIZ, (not half a bad sort of fella, don't you know) .....Miss ADA LEE
LEONORA, (a ward of di Luna's evidentually awarded to Manrico,)
....Miss ELLA CHAPMAN
AZUCENA, (an elderly Gypsy party with a great deal on her mind)
....Mr. ROLAND REED

MIRA ANTOINETTA WILKINS		Miss CARRIE McHENRY
PAQUITA MERCEDES ALDABELLA	School Girls at	...Miss ANNIE DEACON
ISABELLA	the Finishing	..Miss BESSIE TEMPLE
FRASQUITA..............	Academy of Madame	... .Miss LORING
BRIGLIA......................	"Catalina	...Miss T. LAMBOURNE
PARTHIA	Grimalkina."	......Miss ELSIE DEAN
PRISCILLA		...........Miss CARSON
DORCAS.........................		....Miss JONES

ANNETTA LISA...............................Miss ALICE WRIGHT
MADAME CATALINA GRIMALKINA, (Governess)......Miss FANNY WRIGHT
INEZ, (Leonora's confidential, and very tired, tire woman)Miss ROSE LEIGHTON
Gypsies, Guards and Attendants.

NOTICE

THE 100th PERFORMANCE in San Francisco will transpire on SATURDAY EVENING,
January 31st, and will be celebrated as a GALA NIGHT, when a

TESTIMONIAL BENEFIT

will be tendered by the management to

MISS EME ROSEAU.

THE SECOND AND LAST SERIES OF THE

WILHELMJ GRAND CONCERTS,

will take place

WEDNESDAY EVENING, January 28th,

THURSDAY MATINEE, January 29th,

FRIDAY EVENING, January 30th.

OBSERVE THE

THURSDAY WILHELMJ CONCERT,

At the usual Matinee Prices.

French Mixed Candies, Photographs of Celebrities, Soda Water and Opera
Glasses. Umbrellas and Overcoats checked at the Opera Glass Stand. M. Peyser Prop.

end, is what should be remembered—that feeling he expressed at the end of a season when he said; "I lost $30,000; but didn't I give them opera—eh?"[8]

I n 1879, the year that Tom Maguire promoted his final season of San Francisco opera, Walt Whitman went west on the last long journey of his life. Sometime during that trip there came into his mind the image of an army band in an outpost on the desolate Dakota plains playing operatic selections. Whitman never went to the Dakotas and didn't visit an army post, though he may well have heard an army band playing opera. The sources of that particular image can't be disentangled from the mystery of poetic inspiration. No matter. The important thing is what Whitman did with that image, not where it came from.

He brooded on it, gave it poetic form, and in 1881 added "Italian Music in Dakota" to a new edition of *Leaves of Grass.*

> Through the soft evening air enwinding all,
> Rocks, woods, fort, cannon, pacing sentries, endless wilds,
> In dulcet streams, in flutes' and cornets' notes,
> Electric, pensive, turbulent, artificial,
> (Yet strangely fitting even here, meanings unknown before,
> Subtler than ever, more harmony, as if born here, related here,
> Not to the city's fresco'd rooms, not to the audience of the opera house,
> Sounds, echoes, wandering strains, as really here at home,
> *Sonnambula's* innocent love, trios with *Norma's* anguish,
> And thy ecstatic chorus *Poliuto;*)
> Ray'd in the limpid yellow slanting sundown,
> Music, Italian music in Dakota.
>
> While Nature, sovereign of this gnarl'd realm,
> Lurking in hidden barbaric grim recesses,
> Acknowledging rapport however far remov'd,
> (As some old root or soil of earth its last-born flower or fruit,)
> Listens well pleas'd.

Opera was a metaphor for art. Between nature and opera there was "a strangely fitting" harmony. Song was the most natural form of human expression, and it is delightful to think of Nature listening "well pleas'd" to the earliest human society conducting its business entirely through recitative. Reflecting on Italian opera, of all the arts the one his countrymen thought most *un*natural, Whitman discerned in it "meanings unknown before," among them this long-forgotten notion that opera was closer to nature ("as if born there") than to civilization ("the city's fresco'd rooms").

The American artist was greatest when most natural. Consider the acting of Edwin Forrest, whose style was operatic. Everyone agreed that there was something peculiarly American in Forrest. It was the rude force of pioneer America in his vigor and his commonness, so that for Bowery Boys and for "rough-fisted Westerners" alike Forrest was the "natural antagonist of Old-World elegance, cultivation, and caste." A traveler described him as the doomed Indian chief in *Metamora.*

I freely acknowledge that, for power of destructive energy, I never heard any thing on the stage so tremendous in its sustained CRESCENDO swell, and crashing force of utterance, as his defiance of the Council, in that play. His voice surged and roared like the angry sea, lashed into fury by a storm; till, as it reached its boiling, seething climax, in which the serpent hiss of hate was heard, at intervals amidst its louder, deeper, hoarser tones, it was like the falls of Niagara, in its tremendous down-sweeping cadence: it was a whirlwind, a tornado, a cataract of illimitable rage![9]

Consider the affinity between opera and the oratory of the time: the high-flown, hours-long performances of Benton and Clay and Webster, lyrical flights alternating with purple patches, effect piled on effect, moving audiences to tears and to frenzy; between opera and painting: the swirling clouds and tempestuous storms, the gorgeous colors and outlandish effects of Bierstadt and Church; between opera and vernacular decoration: the riotous embellishment of Mississippi steamboats and California gambling halls and brothels. In all these, an unbound release of emotion, a protest against the literal, the fact-bound, the prosaic. How naturally, excessively, sublimely "operatic."

At the same time there was a completely opposed view of the relationship of nature and the arts of civilization. In this view, nature was not the inspiration of art but freedom from it. In popular American thought, the return to nature was identified with the frontier West, an El Dorado of the American mind and spirit more bewitching even than the prospect of infinite gold, absolute freedom. From Natty Bumpo, in Fenimore Cooper's *The Pioneer,* dying with his eyes set toward the unsettled and open West, through Huck Finn, lighting out for the territories to get away from the dreadfulness of being civilized, the West and the frontier have, down to the present, represented a flight from society and the state, from artifice and history.

That was the mythic West of fantasy, with the power of pure poetry. The historical West, the West of Tom Maguire and Kate Hayes and her admiring firemen and all the rest, was a different matter. Countless people testified to the fact that the people of the frontier could not free themselves from the burden of history, and didn't try to. Sam Ward heard the first performance of *Il Barbiere di Siviglia* in New York in November 1825 and heard *Norma* in San Francisco in 1854. It was his conviction that the San Francisco audience, "from pit to paradise," had been the more worldly one. Louis Gottschalk, the American pianist, played before an audience of miners in Dayton, Nevada: "They listened attentively, and their decent and tranquil manner would cause shame to many audiences that pretend to the refinements of civilization." Everywhere along the moving frontier the experience had been the same in this respect: opera and the frontier were "strangely fitting." Cincinnati in the 1830s, when Harriet Martineau visited it, had only lately been a "canebrake echoing with the bellow and growl of wild beasts," but people gathered unostentatiously to listen to Mozart.[10]

Opera and the historical West were in harmony, but it was different from what Whitman meant by harmony. The explosive energy, the massed choral power, and the soaring individual voices of opera corresponded to the infinitely mixed voices of the American people, to their feeling of immense movement and release after the Mexican War, freed from previous constraints: free as the Mississippi rushing to the Gulf, free as the plains stretching endlessly over the horizon. Italian opera and the West mirrored each other in passion and terror. The duels, murders, poisonings, and assassinations on the operatic stage spoke directly to the western audience's experience of its own history—its Indian massacres, vigilante floggings and lynchings. True: the imaginary madness of opera paled beside the actual madness of "bleeding Kansas," the fury of operatic villains was mild beside the rage of secessionist fire-eaters, the cruelty of slave drivers, and the ravings of Indian killers. But in the audience and on the stage one sensed people out of their own control, driven fatally toward some obscure destiny. Thus the blood of Ernani mingled with that of Sitting Bull and John Brown, the madness of Lucia invoked the spirits of those innumerable women maddened by the isolation of the plains and mountains. The heartbeat of western history was violence, a timpani beat of inexorable fatality. Verdi amid the redwoods. Donizetti in the Sierras. Music, Italian music, in Dakota.

New Orleans and Havana

Two visiting companies challenged the predominance of English opera in the large cities of the Northeast in the 1840s.

In 1843, with economic conditions improving at last, the French company from the Orleans Theatre came again to New York, to Niblo's indoor theater. Ten years had passed since their last visit, and their appearance was eagerly anticipated as "a great treat for the New York public." The first works given were unfamiliar vaudevilles and comic operas—*The Outrageous Night, In God's Hands, Polchinelli,* and *Memories of the Devil*—light, amusing pieces in which the company's perfection of ensemble and unity of style were shown off to advantage. No one singer was singled out for notice. The orchestra, a marvel of discipline, earned "rapturous plaudits." The costumes were elegant, the scenery handsome. It was the strength of the company as a whole that impressed everyone. "All the company, stars no less than the smaller lights, are compelled to come upon the stage, so that the choruses are well done." They rehearsed one of their operas an unprecedented eight times. Instead of repeating the same opera several times in succession, their program was changed each night. Observers were astonished that "pieces of such magnitude could be produced in such rapid order." Because all the performers were familiar with all the operas, productions could be alternated as quickly as the scenery could be changed.

Imagine the surprise, then, at the unexpected appearance of a star, Julie Calvé, a soprano with a fresh and sweet voice, technique equal to any demands. She appeared first in Auber's *The Ambassadress (L'Ambassadrice).* The opera was new to New York. Its overture was "a gem of the first water," "sweet in the opening and sprightly in the principal movements," its harmonies "original and delicious." Calvé managed all its "graceful and exquisite *roulades* without any apparent effort," and "at once took captive the hearts and minds of her auditors," two-thirds of whom were women. More Auber followed. *The Black Domino (Le Domino noir),* a "pleasant compound of light, festive, and serious music," struck listeners as more effective than *L'Ambassadrice,* "which is according the *Domino* the highest praise." Then came the "long-expected" *Diamants de la couronne,* "filled with some most beautiful airs," more dramatic than the other operas heard so far, and "pronounced by European and New Orleans journals as the best opera of Auber." The orchestra played superbly. Calvé sang with "a precision, grace, and flexible finish, that has perfectly astonished many who have hitherto been but slightly interested in French music," and "the Americans as well as the French seemed to rival each other in applauding" everything.

Two more new operas followed, *Lightning (L'Eclair)* and *The Clerks' Meadow (Le Pré aux clercs)* by Ferdinand Hérold (1791–1833). *Le Pré aux clercs* was new but not unfamiliar, its music having been "before the public in every possible shape of selection at concerts, ballrooms, and theatres." It was a "beautiful opera," more powerful than the "glittering and somewhat tinsel compositions for which Auber is remarkable." Calvé's singing was "chaste in style, clear in tone," and put to rest any lingering doubts as to whether she had enough voice and appropriate manner for "a grand style of music."

In July the company moved into Niblo's open-air garden and branched out into the Italian repertory. They began on the 19th with an important first performance— Gaetano Donizetti's *La Fille du régiment.* Only one opera by him, *L'Elisir d'amore,* had been done previously in the East. "Donizetti is a composer but little known in America from any immediate knowledge of his works, but his fame in Europe is only excelled in the grand operas by Meyerbeer." The "dashing spirited style of the music" matched the lively execution. Calvé "marched and countermarched with all the precision and confidence of a drill Sergeant" across the stage, delighting her audiences. This success topped everything else, and had *La Fille* come earlier in the season, it could have been given a dozen times and drawn capacity audiences. One more Donizetti opera ended the visit: *Anna Bolena,* which the Frys gave at about this time in Philadelphia as an outstanding example of Italian dramatic opera. Observers in New York were struck by how difficult and complex the opera was, "Italian opera music with French *paroles.*" "The whole piece consists of singing," and it mounted in the third act, in Donizetti's most "sublime passages," to "absolute tragedy." Calvé proved in this role that she was truly a prima donna "equal to anything she undertakes." The season ended on that triumphal note.[1]

The French returned in 1845. Taking up where they had left off, drawing on their well-established strengths of balance and ensemble and orchestra, they gave a season of "towering ambition." They began with their repertory of light comic works, then brought out another new Donizetti opera, *La Favorite.* "We can positively assert," wrote the *New York Herald,* "that there has never been brought out in New York an opera of that magnitude with such remarkable *ensemble.*" The heart of the season was "grand opera" in the contemporary French mode: *Guillaume Tell,* which began the genre; Meyerbeer's *Robert le diable; La Juive,* "heavy and hard to give, made impressive the hot nights of July." The audacity of the French became even more apparent as the season advanced, presenting Auber's grandest opera, *The Mute Girl of Portici (La Muette de Portici)* and Meyerbeer's *Les Huguenots.*[2]

Their accomplishments were impressive. They performed at a level well beyond that of English companies such as the Seguins, and they kept alive the taste for French comic opera (which would become the rage in the post–Civil War years). And they did these things at very cheap prices. All seats at Niblo's cost fifty cents, with no effort made to court fashionable society or wealthy subscribers. Most of all, the French presented a persuasive example of what it was to create a genuine "company," performers who stayed together, shared a common style, and worked toward an artistic ideal. But as the prevailing conditions of American operatic life outside New Orleans remained hostile to the existence of a resident company stressing *ensemble,* the influence of the French was fleeting. Another company would reintroduce the concept.

H a v a n a was a musical crossroads. Its Catholic culture, sympathetic to theater and to dance, had long made it attractive for actors and singers, who used it as a jumping-off place for going north. By the late eighteenth century, two developments established its musical importance in its own right. It had grown to be a large city, population fifty thousand, and it had become a cathedral city. The creation of the Diocese of Havana in 1787 meant that, like Mexico City, Lima, and La Plata, it had a choir school and musical archive connected to the cathedral, where native-born musicians had a chance for musical training. The first Havana playhouse, the Teatro Coliseo, had opened in 1776, and thereafter some of the important works of the contemporary operatic repertory were given there.[3]

The operatic life of the city also gained strength from the evolution of a Spanish form of musical theater, the *tonadilla.* This was a very short opera with spoken dialogue, songs, and sometimes choruses, usually on contemporary subjects, and mostly dealing with lower-class life. Originating as interludes between acts of a serious play, like Italian *intermezzos,* tonadillas took on an independent form of their own, were widespread by the middle of the eighteenth century, and flourished for another century. Hundreds were composed, and, as with ballad opera and comic opera and *singspiel,* they were an important way of bringing lower-class culture into the theaters.

Given this stimulus, a second theater for opera opened in Havana in 1801, and between 1811 and 1832 there was a local opera company established with government support. Singers came to it from Italy and France, and the company gave some eighty performances annually, including operas by most of the important contemporary composers: Paisiello, Cimarosa, Grétry, Spontini, and Rossini. On November 3, 1818, seven and a half years before the Garcías' production, *Don Giovanni* received its first Havana performance. The theater orchestra included eighteen players and was led by a black musician named Ulpiano Estrada. In November 1846 a new theater, the Teatro de Tacón, was inaugurated, a new opera company formed, and the most splendid period in Havana operatic history got under way. The impresario of the company, Francisco Marty y Torens, brought Luigi Arditi, a young, promising Italian conductor, to organize a permanent company, which he guaranteed to subsidize handsomely.

Havana had had a specific indirect influence on American operatic life in 1843, when a group of Italian singers on their way to perform there made arrangements for brief visits to New York, Philadelphia, and New Orleans. Arriving in New York only days after the French company's departure, they capitalized on the excitement it had left behind. They offered their operas at Niblo's Garden at fifty cents a seat and drew large audiences. This group included one exceptional singer, Cirillo Antognini, a tenor who was the despair and delight of impresarios and music lovers because of his splendid voice and irresponsible behavior. The tenor as prima donna. The Italians gave *Norma* ("full of sweet and enchanting airs") to an audience "crowded to suffocation," with so many turned away a second performance was given. After that came Donizetti's *Gemma di Vergy,* and then *Lucia di Lammermoor,* known to New Orleans but new to the East. Antognini's Edgar was sung "with such consummate skill that it stamped him at once as a perfect artiste" and "drew tears from many a fair brow." *Lucia* became very much a woman's-audience opera. The crucial thing about the visit of these Italians was that, though the singers, other than Antognini, were quite ordinary, any comparison of them with the typical English opera company was ominous for the future of opera in English. After the performance of *Norma* one writer summed up: "While English Artists have rendered us familiar with the [stories] they have given us a faint idea of the beauties of Bellini's music. It was left as a right to the Italian company to convey to one's heart the pathos of these exquisite melodies of their countryman."[4]

In 1847 the Havana company made its first appearance. "The most finished and excellent company that has ever visited this city," the *New York Herald* admiringly asserted, "the largest and most completely appointed and equipped." There was an orchestra of thirty-two and the company as a whole, seventy to eighty persons, was a veritable "army to travel with." The costumes alone, it was said, were worth thirty thousand dollars. The visit, however, was badly and hastily conceived, actually an attempt to keep the company together and perhaps pick up some Yankee dollars when it could not perform in the enervating heat of the Havana summer. There was no advance publicity and the schedule was a mess, two performances in New York, a short season in Boston, then a return to New York, an expedition to Philadelphia, and yet another visit to New York, in mid-August, for a month's performance at Castle Garden. Despite everything, the Habañeros succeeded. Word of mouth and delighted comments in the newspapers did their work. A soprano, Fortunata Tedesco, was the most notable of the singers. The rest were no more than competent. The first Havana company's effect wasn't dependent on its leading singers. Like the French, its work was marked by overall balance, confident leadership.

The Havana company also introduced new opera: another Donizetti, *Linda di Chamounix.* But the real novelty was the first opera by Giuseppe Verdi (1812–1901) heard in the United States. The day after they got off the boat, they performed *Ernani.* "Its style is full of original melodies and abounds in expressions of genius." Its overture was imposing, one cavatina ("*Ernani involami*") was "a perfect gem." The scene in which Ernani hears the fatal horn was "written by Verdi with genius and care. The trombone and horn solo produces a terrifying impression." In June the company gave their second Verdi premiere—*The Two Foscaris* (*I Due Foscari*). This, too, had its adherents, who admired the new young composer for going beyond the "old style" of Rossini and Bellini. Verdi's orchestration was "more scientific, his recitative less monotonous." Still, many commentators disliked Verdi's music very much. It was thought noisy, harsh, and cheap. There were too many drums and trumpets. It was complex and brutal. "It is a pity such singing and such splendid appointments should be lavished on such bad music."[5] More would be heard on this subject.

I n its second, well-planned visit of 1850, the Havana company revealed all its previous strengths, but amplified. Far from being an anticlimax, as some feared, the second visit had an even greater impact. The repertory was largely divided between Donizetti and Verdi, the immensely popular operas of the former (*Lucrezia Borgia, La Favorite, L'Elisir d'amore*) and four operas of the younger man: *Ernani* and *I Due Foscari,* little known but gaining favor, and two new ones, *Macbeth* and *Attila.* "The most triumphant" of its three New York sojourns was the "long-famed" late summer season at Castle Garden. Rude comments about Verdi were common in these years. "*Macbeth* is the absurd attempt to marry Northern legend to modern Italian music." Verdi's "supernatural music in this opera is especially comical. The unfortunate man is incapable of real melody—his airs are such as a man born deaf would compose." Yet many people liked what they heard, were moved by it, and intrigued to hear more. And so the operas drew excellent houses. At the same time, and from the first, that audience was more sharply divided than audiences for the operas of other composers: a favorable majority apparently made up of ordinary operagoers, and a hostile minority, among whom were many of the more discriminating listeners and musicians of the day.[6]

The new feature of the group that bowled over American audiences was its cluster of superior singers, America's introduction to star singers on a large scale. Everything else yielded to the excitement kindled by their presence. For the first time, some of the men were first-rate. Lorenzo Salvi, a tenor, was the creator of two Verdi roles in Milan. He sang in London with great success and, though no longer young, "his voice was perfectly preserved, a mingling of manliness and tenderness, of human sympathy and seraphic loftiness, which we call divine." The bass was Ignazio Marini, who established himself throughout Italy as a Verdian interpreter, introducing a number of Verdi roles in many European capitals. "A semi-giant," he had a "stunning voice, which rattles out like a discharge of ordnance." The leading soprano was Balbina Steffanone, whose Norma was wildly applauded: "We say again, at last we have the grand Italian opera in New York, and no, no, no mistake." Another: "At last New York has a real, true, undoubted prima donna, equal to the best artists we have ever seen."[7] This enthusiasm cooled as Steffanone showed herself to be a very uneven performer, but she was always exciting. The most dazzling star was a surprise, to everyone. Angiolina Bosio, made her debut in Milan in 1846 and went to Havana the same year. Not classed among the principal singers, she was hardly mentioned when the company came to America, but it was in New York that she came fully into her powers. Neither slender nor tall, with luminous eyes, she carried herself with unmistakable elegance. Her voice was pure, silvery, delicate, and her phrasing was incomparably fine. "Whether the music was grave or gay," a Philadelphian wrote, "she always sang it with the proper expression, and with exquisite delicacy and finish." She didn't immerse herself in her roles. "She was always Angiolina Bosio and appeared on the stage like a lady performing admirably in private theatricals." Middle-class audiences wanted excitement but preferred that it come in persons of bearing and breeding. Wherever Bosio appeared, audiences packed the theaters to see and hear her.[8]

The Havana company came again in 1851 for the last time, adding Bellini's *The Puritans* (*I Puritani*) and Donizetti's *Don Pasquale,* operas they hadn't given before. Of the performance of *Don Pasquale,* a Philadelphia historian wrote: "This was the most perfect performance I ever witnessed. Each part was admirably filled. The artists in this opera were probably but little inferior to the great quartette for whom it was written." This sense of overall strength and balance left an indelible impression, as did Italian opera performed at this level: "this sustained style, intensely dramatic situations, grand finales, and concerted pieces; altogether it was a new experience for us."[9] The company vastly increased the prestige of Italian singers. And they helped fix the American predilection for stars, a galaxy, a cluster, to light up the heavens. They prepared the way for the appearance in the 1850s of such celebrities, the most famous of whom came just three days after the Havana songbirds had vacated Castle Garden at the end of their memorable season. Already well trained in stargazing at Italian singers, Americans now turned their eyes to the horizon to observe a Swedish nightingale from the north.

The Song of the Nightingale

Thirty thousand New Yorkers climbed the spars and rigging of nearby ships, packed the piers and bulkheads, jammed into the windows and onto the roofs of neighboring buildings at the foot of Canal Street when the steamship *Atlantic* docked on Sunday morning, September 1, 1850. They were there to catch a glimpse of a Swedish soprano who was about to begin a concert tour of the United States. It's true that she was not simply any Swedish soprano. She was Jenny Lind, a singer who had made a sensational London operatic debut in the spring of 1847 and in the intervening years had become the best-known vocalist in Europe. The excitement about her there was extraordinary. Perhaps it was contagious and had spread to the United States. Even so, it was difficult to explain why thirty thousand people, few of whom had ever heard the name Jenny Lind six months—or six weeks—before, would turn out to *look* at a singer. Was it that new democratic disease, publicity?

In that case, the explanation was to be found in the person of one of the two men, bouquets in hand, hurrying up the gangplank to greet Jenny Lind, who was waiting for them, wearing a silver-grey dress and blue bonnet, with a lap dog (a present from Queen Victoria) in her arms. The first man was the president of the Collins Steamship line, whose ship had brought her safely across the still fearsome ocean and who, handing over his flowers, withdraws from our scene. The second, never one to withdraw himself from sight, was the celebrated, the notorious Phineas Taylor Barnum, who had thought up the concert tour and whose guile, courage, and dollars ($187,000 of them, on deposit at Baring Brothers, London) had brought it about. But even the wizard of publicity may not have been responsible for the mass of humanity at Canal Street that morning. The size of the crowd was certainly a great surprise to him. Now, down the gangplank she came, arm in arm with Barnum, through archways of flowers, past massed flags, struggling toward a carriage surrounded by the swirling throng.

I t was a portent of things to come. Everywhere that Jenny went the crowds were sure to follow, calling out to her. "The street around the Irving House [her hotel] was blocked up with a mob night and day." If Barnum had created the crowd he hadn't generated its emotions. And no one had yet heard her sing a note! George Templeton Strong, lawyer and music lover, analyzed this clamor in his diary. "Jenny Lind has arrived, and was received with such a spontaneous outbreak of rushing, and crowding, and hurrahing, and serenading as this city has never seen

"Coronation of Jenny the First—Queen of the Americans": a common European view of the Jenny Lind–P. T. Barnum tour. Presumably, the Uncle Sam / Yankee figure crowning Lind is Barnum. From Punch, January–June 1850.

before." Shrewd and observant, Strong was puzzled. Here was a "good amiable, benevolent woman, fully equal, I dare say, to the average of our New York girls," endowed with "a larynx so delicately organized that she can go up to A in alt with brilliancy, and precision, and sing with more effect than any other living performer," which explained—what? "If the greatest man that has lived for the last ten centuries were here in her place," Strong wrote, "the uproar and excitement could not be much greater and would probably be much less." He concluded his diary entry as he began it, in puzzlement: "Really, it's very strange."[1]

So it began: with strangeness and frenzy in the air. The first concert was at Castle Garden, only three days after the Havana company of stars had concluded their memorable and wildly applauded appearances. The audience which packed that vast hall, waiting with breathless expectancy for the first sound of Lind's voice, showed little interest in the overture or the baritone's song which opened the program. She, and she alone, was the focus of a feeling that something would be experienced which could occur only once in a lifetime. She came on stage, at last. The waiting was unbearable. Finally, the orchestra began the "Casta diva," the invocation to the chaste moon goddess from *Norma*. Jenny Lind began to sing. She was visibly nervous and her voice a little unsteady, but she quickly mastered her nerves and exquisite sounds floated out to all parts of the auditorium. There was a burst of applause when the song was over, an explosion of nervous relief, gradually replaced by something more familiar and reassuring—the excitement of an artistic conquest. At the end, when she sang folksongs, accompanying herself on the guitar, the audience surrendered unconditionally.

In city after city the moment when Jenny Lind came forward to sing marked some kind of turning point in people's lives, though they would have been hard pressed to say just what turning point. Someone said: "The Age of Music had come to America." In city after city the crowds gathered at the railroad stations or the boat landings,

Castle Garden was thronged for Lind's American debut in 1850. This illustration appeared in the recital program. Sterling Memorial Library, Yale University.

clustered in front of hotels and theaters. People named things for her—a trotting horse, a clipper ship, a theater, tobacco, even a cigar. (She hated cigars.) Innumerable objects were sold with her name or picture put on them: bonnets, coats, gloves, hats, opera glasses, wreaths, sheet music, greeting cards, parasols, combs, bric-a-brac, jewelry. There were songs, waltzes, and polkas; pancakes, sausages, and tea kettles, "which, being filled with water, commenced to sing." Her portrait was in shop windows. Chambermaids sold hairs from her hairbrush.

Originally, Barnum proposed 150 concerts stretching over a year and a half. He agreed to pay Lind a thousand dollars per performance, to cover all her traveling expenses, from Europe to the United States and within the U.S., to furnish her with a male servant and a maid, a secretary, a conductor, and her choice of baritone, and to put a carriage and horses at her disposal. After nine months and ninety-five concerts, the Lind-Barnum association was dissolved. She stayed in America for another year, giving concerts under her own management. The Jenny Lind tour people remember

To drum up excitement (and income) for Lind's tour, Barnum held public ticket auctions in major cities. This nineteenth-century sheet music cover shows the impresario introducing Lind to Ossian E. Dodge, a singer who gained notoriety by paying $625 to attend her first concert in Boston. John Herrick Jackson Music Library, Yale University.

was the one sponsored by Barnum. For it he outdid all his previous publicizing exploits. "A reputation was manufactured for her, by wholesale. It was not merely made by the inch, but was prepared by the cart-load."[2] He invented new devices to sell his warbler, among which auctioning of tickets was the most important. In each city the first ticket for the concert was publicly auctioned. The next few tickets were also sold for whatever price they would bring above the fixed price. Then the remainder of the tickets were made available, at between $3 and $7. The auction in New York for the first ticket brought $225. That was a good start. New Orleans boosted the price to $240. In Boston the first ticket brought $625. Philadelphia matched that. Providence topped everyplace, with $650. Ticket auctioning became the subject of much discussion and debate. It was one of the aspects of Barnum's promotion Jenny Lind most disliked.

Barnum got cities to compete against each other. The major cities were to be the sites of several concerts, but beyond that the identity of the cities to be visited was uncertain. It suited Barnum to generate suspense, which served his promotional skills. Cities pleaded to be included and Barnum allowed them to bid for this privilege, provided only that they had a theater or a hall or a church large enough to meet the minimum receipts necessary. Several church congregations refused to cooperate as they wished to have nothing to do with an opera singer, even so respectable a one as Jenny Lind. Barnum never forced her to sing in circus tents or stockyards, as Europeans believed. The days between performances allowed Barnum time to get his newspaper publicity machinery into action. The Barnum-Lind tour included nineteen cities, from Boston to New Orleans (and Havana) and as far west as St. Louis and Madison, Wisconsin. Lindomaniac symptoms were evident everywhere, but two-thirds of the concerts took place in four cities: seven in Boston, eight in Philadelphia, twelve in New Orleans, and thirty-five in New York, showing how far New York had now outstripped all its old competitors as a musical market.

J e n n y Lind's visit to America remains—a century and a half later—one of the best-known events in the nation's entire operatic history, even though she never sang in a single opera. So associated is it with opera that people are surprised to learn that she sang only in concerts. The effect of her visit was felt in a number of ways. The tour established the importance of publicity as a means of success in the arts. Everyone agreed on the effectiveness of Barnum's efforts. He flooded the newspapers with portraits, sketches, letters, stories, many fictitious. "He exaggerated her virtues; he proclaimed her a ventriloquist, romanced about Victoria's adoration of her excellences, and fabricated charities by the bushel-ful." The American press cooperated with a readiness compounded of gullibility, cynicism, and self-interest. "Everywhere, the curiosity to see her was stronger than the enthusiasm after hearing her," Max Maretzek wrote, "and great as her merit most unquestionably was the 'humbug' of her manager was by far the most powerful attraction to her concerts." Maretzek was biased: his opera company at the Astor Place Opera House was devastated by the Lind competition. But many shared his view. Publicity changed the nature of the tour itself. As it went on, its success came more and more to be fixed in box-office terms. This had been prefigured in that scene of Lind's arrival. When Barnum put Jenny Lind inside the carriage for the drive to her hotel, he climbed up to the outside seat next to the driver, as much a star to be gawked at as the diva. "I took that seat as a legitimate advertisement."[3]

The aspect of Barnum's methods that most intrigued the public at the time was whether Lind approved or disapproved of them. Her conductor, Julius Benedict, insisted that "Jenny Lind never recovered from her horror of this exploitation of the woman as well as of the artist and its effect was to intensify the dislike of public life which eventuated in her premature retirement." There is no doubt that, when it was all over, she felt resentment, even rage about it. An American woman who talked to her in 1866 was surprised by Lind's bitterness. "She abhorred the very name of Barnum, who, she said, 'exhibited me just as he did the big giant and any other of his monstrosities. I was nothing more than a show in the showman's hands; I can never forget that.'"[4]

That was the European view. Barnum's capers and contrivances reinforced the deeply cherished belief that Americans cared solely about money, with an overlay of Yankee hypocrisy. A Parisian caricature showed a Philadelphia Quaker going to the theater to hear Jenny Lind and paying for his ticket with several African American slaves labeled $1,000 apiece. In another, congressmen turned themselves into horses to draw the nightingale's carriage, and in another, the notes from Lind's voice curled upward like wreaths of smoke, while crowds knocked each other down trying to seize, bottle, and sell them. It wasn't only Europeans who felt this way. Louis Gottschalk, the American pianist, was approached by Barnum, who "wanted to engage me for a year, offering me twenty thousand dollars and expenses paid, but my father had prejudices (unjust) against Barnum, whom he obstinately insisted in seeing only as a showman of learned beasts."[5]

The central feature of Barnum's promotion was the emphasis he placed on Jenny Lind's personal character and morals. He cast her as the heroine in a drama larger than the tour or opera, a drama about the relationship of art and morality. Again, many Europeans shared the admiration for her character. "What a great, heaven-inspired being she is! What a pure, true artist soul!" Clara Schumann said. And Hans Christian Andersen was inspired by her to write "The Ugly Duckling," "The Angel," and "The Emperor's Nightingale": "She showed me art in its sanctity—I have seen one of its Vestal Virgins." Such excessive language led Heinrich Heine to mock Lind's "air of saintliness" and deride the notion of the "prima donna immaculata."[6] Still, there wasn't anything unusual in all this. Artists had their admirers and detractors. Sophisticated Europeans assumed a distinction between an artist's personality and character and his or her art. They were less likely to confuse a singer's roles with that singer's private life and personal values.

The difference was that in America the emphasis was persistently personal. While she was "a lady whose vocal powers have never been approached by any other human being," it was more who she was than what she did that mattered. In March 1850, with her arrival still five months away, Nathaniel Parker Willis, journalist, poet, and sometime music critic, took careful aim at his largely feminine public in the *New York Home Journal*, stressing that Lind's talents were much more than merely vocal: "Humility, tender-heartedness, and sensibility . . . a heart still free from world stains, and the uninterrupted habit of a daily observance of her religious duties." "Even in the most scintillating of her arias," Americans would overhear "the beating of a pure and gentle heart." Other writers took up the theme: "Her magnificent voice, always true and firm, seems like the audible beauty of her nature and character." Or: "She is to us the Artist Woman. Her true voice is the audible vibration of her true soul."[7]

Barnum saw to it that everyone was aware of her generous gifts to charities. She dressed simply in white or grey or pale blue and carried flowers when she sang. "She seemed transformed into a kindly angel." She refused to sing or to travel on the

Lind's widely publicized gifts to charities enhanced her saintly image. Merchants like Genin Hatter in New York basked in her reflected glory. Library of Congress.

Sabbath. "All these things conspire to give Mlle. Lind a place in the affections and confidence of the good, such as no other foreign artiste—if we may apply the term to her—has ever enjoyed."[8] What a triumph such a sentence was for Barnum! In the person of Jenny Lind, art was familiar, unthreatening. She was neither foreign nor even that odd thing, an artist. She was simply Jenny.

People searched her appearance and especially her face for clues to that inner person. She was small, an innocent country girl who had somehow wandered onto the stage by chance. She would begin hesitantly, nervously, and then: her talent would come to the rescue, her voice, almost as though it existed independently of the body which contained it, would gush out in crystalline splendor and convert a precarious moment into an ecstatic one. A few people kept their heads. George Templeton Strong put it simply: "She is not pretty nor handsome, nor exactly fine-looking, but there's an air about her of dignity, self-possession, modesty and goodness that is extremely attractive." That was certainly too matter-of-fact for many. Engravings and drawings failed to capture her "honest greatness, sublimely simple and unconscious." Writers resorted to rhapsody: "The truth is that God never yet lit the flame of a great soul in a dark lantern; and, though the divine lamp burning within Jenny Lind may not be translucent to all, yet, it is, to others, perfectly visible through the simple windows of her honest face."[9]

I n n o c e n c e and simple morality implied simple art. The cultural significance of Jenny Lind's tour of America is inseparable from the programs she gave. A typical Lind program consisted of two parts. Part 1 opened with an operatic overture, then an operatic aria by Giovanni Belletti, the baritone who accompanied her throughout the tour, then an instrumental solo, followed by a folksong by Lind. Part 2 began with another overture, an operatic aria by Lind, an aria by Belletti, then a song by Lind, a song by Belletti, and then a concluding song by Lind. On a handful of occasions some orchestral music by George Frederick Bristow was played, and a few American soloists performed with her, among them William Henry Fry. The heart of the programs was in the "folksongs," by which was meant both anonymous folk ballads and art songs, by well-known composers, of a simple and folkish sort: "The Gypsy Song," "The Last Rose of Summer," "Home, Sweet Home." Lind gave her audiences what was easiest to take and what they wanted. One observer noted that "audiences sat relatively unmoved during the exercise of her matchless powers in the scientific productions of Mozart, Bellini, etc.," while the folksongs moved them to thunders of applause. Whatever may be the range of Jenny's power as an artist, a Philadelphia writer noted, "there is little doubt that her popularity is mainly founded on her execution of those less legitimate melodies."[10]

Nobody today would think of those songs as "less legitimate" than any others. But Jenny Lind was an opera singer. The conventional wisdom has long been that she did much to "elevate" the standards of American musical taste. Much of that was easy self-congratulation. Americans had heard Jenny Lind, this argument ran, they had heard the best and they now knew the best. But best of what? Unquestionably, Jenny Lind exemplified technical proficiency at its highest contemporary level. But she did not "elevate" taste. She fixed it at a certain mediocre level, the level of respectable and fashionable taste. She didn't in the least challenge contemporary taste. One could hardly expect her to do in America what she had not done in Europe, because it was outside her artistic imagination. The last thing Barnum wanted was for her to appeal to any exclusive group or taste. One critic frankly yearned for an evening, just one evening, devoted to the finest, most demanding music Jenny Lind knew. "At no one of her previous concerts was all the music worthy of the genius of the singer. This yielding to the demands of the uncultivated and artificial taste was, doubtless, under the circumstances, politic as well as kindly; but now . . . let us have one concert which, from the opening overture to the final section, shall be unimpeachably good—in keeping with the eminence of the giver of the entertainment."[11]

Jenny Lind represents an important point in the graph of middle-class taste. "True to the instinctive love of homelike, simple things," someone wrote in defense of her taste, she "continued to give her audiences the best of both worlds." But she represented only the one world of middle-class respectability. She much preferred concerts to opera. It has always been said that this was because she loathed backstage intrigues and immorality, present in opera and not on the concert platform. William Henry Fry pointed out a deeper reason. Concerts were a matter of fact, an opera was a matter of imagination. The middle class had long played a role in the operatic culture of Europe, but it had been a role balanced by that of the aristocracy and the courts. In the nineteenth century that balance was finally tipped toward bourgeois dominance: in comprising the audiences for opera, in supplying the resources for it, in beginning to shape the nature of opera as an art. Lind's role in Europe was ambiguous. "She is as great an artist as ever lived," wrote Felix Mendelssohn, who knew her well and admired her exceedingly, "and the greatest I have known. But she sings bad music the best."[12] Americans would have said that what *she* sang best *was* the best.

Not surprisingly, Jenny Lind and P. T. Barnum made an immense amount of money. Nothing in the previous history of American music or entertainment came near it. The Barnum-sponsored ninety-five concerts averaged seventy-five hundred dollars each. Barnum grossed five hundred thousand dollars for his part and, even allowing for the considerable expenses, his profit must have been very great. For her entire visit, Jenny Lind cleared two hundred thousand dollars. It was another gold rush. It had the same effect on Europe's musical economy. It is the beginning of a long period in which American money devastated the Italian operatic system in particular, the Italians finding it harder and harder to compete with the growing American market. So there began a steady drain of Italian musicians to the Americas.

The consequences for American musicians were destructive. Established Europeans—as we'll soon see—moved quickly to capitalize on the Lind bonanza. How this affected American performers we can follow in the career of Louis Moreau Gottschalk. Certainly the most talented American musician of the first three quarters of the nineteenth century, he was born in New Orleans in 1829, grew up and revealed his pianistic precocity there. His parents sent him to study and prepare himself for a musical career in France, where he made a reputation as a dazzling virtuoso and as a composer who was among the first to draw on Caribbean African themes and melodies for his piano pieces. These enjoyed a terrific vogue in France. Gottschalk returned to America, where he wished to live and to make his career, in 1853, immediately after the Lind furor. His first concert was a critical success, but he made little money. His next concert was a financial failure. He was now competing against European pianists no more talented than he but who had one great advantage over him, one they didn't have in Europe but that was becoming crucial in America: they were Europeans. Jenny Lind's success had the effect of stamping almost anything European in music with the label "best."

The uncritical admiration of European art in American culture, rooted in the lack of self-confidence of the American middle class in the middle of the nineteenth century, was now revealed with startling clarity. The more the American middle class made money, the less confidence it revealed in itself and its own taste, especially for home-grown things. Nowhere was this more true than in music and dance. Americans didn't care for Gottschalk's "American" compositions, for example. What they wanted from him was the European classics. And to make matters worse for American musicians, the prospect of returning to Europe or of beginning and making a reputation there was also made more difficult. "It would be painful to confess," Gottschalk wrote, "that I had not succeeded in my own country, America, which at this time was the El Dorado, the dream of artists, especially as the exaggerated accounts of the money that Jenny Lind had made there rendered my ill success more striking."[13] American musicians struggled with this paradoxical situation for a century—are struggling with it still.

Frenzy about a singer was neither a new phenomenon nor one unique to America. Prima donnas had produced public excitement since the eighteenth century, and by the nineteenth it had crystallized into conventions and ritual: men pulling the diva's carriage through the streets, showering her with gifts and adulation, attention and propositions. It is true that the Lind phenomenon took Europeans by surprise and seemed excessive by any standards. Yet in Copenhagen, Berlin, and London too people responded with a kind of frenzy. Gentlemen and ladies pushed and shoved and fought for places to hear her. Hector Berlioz wrote to a friend: "I shall not go to London this season. The Lind fever makes all musical enterprises impossible."[14] For all its wildness, however, Lindomania fit into a comprehensible European context. The sudden appearance of a new star in the operatic firmament meant that the first house to hear her, or him, spread the word quickly through a well-established musical and social network, in which personal oral communication played a more important part than newspaper comment or reviews.

The contrast with the situation in the United States is instructive. The Lind hysteria in America had unusual aspects. The range of people involved, so far as observers could tell, extended well beyond sophisticated people familiar with operatic events. Many women took part. It was not primarily an audience reaction, though audiences shared in it, nor was it an audience-inspired reaction that spilled out into the streets. The Lind fever in America began in the streets, often well away from the opera house. Furthermore, there was little established social context or operatic system to contain or support it. The network of connected opera houses or theaters existed only in a rudimentary form. Here one crosses Barnum's path and influence. Advertising was necessary to supply the link between the few who understood about things operatic and the many who knew nothing and cared little. Barnum could not wait for the social network to work, to ensure some future appearance for Jenny Lind. He had to create the audience out of virtually nothing, and he had to create it immediately. Hence the evolution of a new form of newspaper reportage, the interview (real or supposed) with an artist. This did several things at once. It increased—often created—familiarity with a performer otherwise unknown. It reduced the distance between the reader and the great star. It created an appetite. The thrust of Barnum's publicity was always to make the unknown or exotic familiar.

Lindomania in America drew on some specially powerful American sources. Lind's power belonged to the realm of nature at a time when that word was particularly potent. Jenny Lind was a goddess of nature, associated with flowers, with the birds of the air. Her tones died away "as soaring skylark fades from the sight into the deep blue coping of the serene and tranquil heaven." Her power was grounded in the natural union of beauty and morality. She was "a bright bird cutting through the buxom air while the sun plays on its plumage . . . the guiding soul which inflames the tones to a heavenly warmth and places one in the region of ecstasy." The comparisons were usually high-flown, but occasionally direct. "Jenny Lind is kindred with Niagara, and with every vigorous and decided power of nature, and the effects which she produces resemble this." She moved at both a natural and a spiritual level. Her appeal "is partly owing to a simplicity and naturalness of manner which appears to be simple and natural beyond any other which was ever seen or heard of," but it was also due to her possessing a natural force "which amounts to absolute fascination, and almost to witchery in the primitive sense of the word." It was a quality, this observer thought, beyond sexual attraction, for as she sang she seemed "like one possessed, as if some spirit more than human inspired her."[15]

Jenny Lind as natural songbird bore an interesting relationship to her much admired technical skill. That technique, that "science" was most dazzlingly displayed in coloratura arias from opera, where her effortless trills and runs, embellishments and cascades of notes took people's breath away. It was her art at its most exotic. We have seen how deeply engrained was the Anglo-American view that such singing was irrational and unnatural. A few years after this, an American singer appeared at the White House, to entertain Abe Lincoln, and was warned by an aide to the president: "None of your foreign fireworks." She replied tartly: "Shall I sing 'Three Little Kittens'? I think that is the least fireworky of my repertoire."[16] Lind somehow persuaded her audiences that her singing of pieces of pyrotechnic display was part of her homely naturalness. As an American writer explained, "I never weary of such singing, not that I usually relish Italian airs and Italian music, for in fact, I have ever preferred simple English ballads to all this gingerbread work of embellished science. But Jenny Lind gives this ornate style new beauty. She seems to simplify and fit it for the heart."[17]

The power of the human heart and passions. Jenny Lind was also an immensely powerful erotic symbol, drawing here too on a special source. She was a Nordic nature goddess, a Nordic enchantress and temptress. Her appeal was heightened by her coolness and remoteness, by that blondness which yet inflamed and impassioned people into near frenzy. "The God who made the people of the pine lands as well as the people of the olives fashioned her," wrote Ik Marvel, the American cracker-barrel humorist. "Her voice," wrote another, "could never be fed on anything warmer than cold air. . . . Her organization is suited to please the people of our cold climate. She will have triumphs here that would never attend her progress through France or Italy."[18] Her three Havana concerts were the least financially successful of all her appearances.

At the time, Jenny Lind's sexual appeal could only be hinted at—in the reiteration that she was not married and presumably a virgin. Most of the discussion of her artistic divinity drew on the assumption of her chastity: *Casta diva!* And then, in the spring of 1852, near the end of her visit, she married. Now the chaste goddess had, in the language of the time, become fully a woman. There was an unmistakable glumness in the newspaper accounts, as there had been about Maria García's marriage. People were miffed that it had been kept secret, a member of the family neglecting to tell the other members of the family. Even more disillusioning was the identity of Jenny Lind's choice. No man could have lived up to this fantasy-enshrouded semi-divinity, and certainly not Otto von Goldschmidt, her accompanist: several years younger than she, not a dashing or glamorous figure in his own right, not a celebrity—and a Jew!

A throb and thrill went out of her subsequent appearances. "The world which has so cherished Jenny, as a bridge of its own," a *Harper's Magazine* editor wrote, "will not give up its claim without a spark of jealousy. . . . Matrimony dulled the edge of triumph. . . . Why is Madame Goldschmidt so much less than Jenny Lind? Simply in this way: she who has conquered the world by song and goodness, has herself been conquered: and the conqueror, if rumor tells a fair story, is no better, or worthier, or stronger than the average of men. The conclusion, then, is inevitable, that she, having yielded, is, in some qualities of head or heart even less than he; and so reduced to the standard of our dull every-day morality. . . . Poor Jenny—that she should have gone the way of the world" and succumbed to "the weaknesses of human attachments." It was as if she had died and not simply got married. "The nightingale has cut her wings, the ANGEL has become a woman, the divinity has descended from her pedestal. The prestige has disappeared. Will the popularity vanish like the prestige?"[19]

The answer to that was no. Lindomania died away, replaced by a continuing, but calmer, respect and admiration. Jenny Lind touched a deep and responsive chord in the women in her audience, for many of whom, perhaps, coming down off a pedestal transferred her to a sphere of life they could understand as few could that of the life of the prima donna nightingale. Her appearance coincided with the movement gathering force in the United States and which had announced itself only two years before in the women's rights convention in Seneca Falls, New York. A larger public role was possible for women in the theater than in almost any other field of endeavor, and especially in opera. Middle-class, Protestant American women had before their eyes an example of a woman, on her own, who had struggled and disciplined herself and made decisions and won through to fame and fortune—and perhaps even to a fuller married life of her own choosing. With very little to depend on but her own talent and courage and determination, she had suddenly emerged and entered the affections and consciousness of the women who listened so raptly to her song.

L e t P. T. Barnum have the last word, as he usually did. "It is a mistake to say that the fame of Jenny Lind rests solely upon her ability to sing," he wrote in 1890. "She was a woman who would have been adored if she had had the voice of a crow."[20] Looking back at that first moment, in September 1850, when Jenny Lind arrived in America, we see how complex and powerful were the elements available for her adoration. We see, too, how much was involved in bringing those thousands to Canal Street, more than Barnum's skills, more than Lind's talent. Down the gangplank she came and into American operatic history: nature-mother, enterpriser, Protestant, nightingale, saint, goddess, embryonic suffragette.

Mario and Three Divas

Gold fever lasted long after the gold rush, and Jenny Goldschmidt's departure for England didn't end the American interest in celebrated singers. "The very call-boys in the theatres were ambitious of becoming Barnums. Not a hungry teacher of the piano, not a theatrical check-taker, but had a longing to try his hand at the great game of sowing nothing and reaping dollars. There was not a dealer in concert-tickets but would have given the hair from his head to gather money by the speculation in opera stars." Steamships made travel safer and faster. The telegraph allowed impresarios to spot opportunities from far off. Then, too, the image of America changed significantly. Instead of a country inhabited by a "set of savages, barbarians and Red Republicans, who eat raw meat, chew tobacco and drink unheard of quantities of whiskey," it was now "El Dorado, filled with silver and gold," a land "populated exclusively by railroad speculators and land promoters."[1] The fabulously rich American appeared for the first time in European literature. Sure enough, four of the greatest European singers came to America to try their luck.

T h e first to arrive was Marietta Alboni, "in the full maturity of her marvelous powers." Few who heard her sing disagreed with Adelina Patti's estimate of her voice—"the most beautiful contralto that the world has ever known." And she possessed the technique and musicianship to match. Maria Anna Marzia Alboni was born in Città di Castello in 1823, in very humble circumstances, studied music from an early age, came to the attention of Rossini, who taught her the contralto roles in his operas. She studied assiduously, made her debut in Bologna in 1844, and moved steadily on from there, with engagements in Vienna, St. Petersburg, and Dresden. "Everywhere she appeared unheralded and everywhere she triumphed." Her first appearance in London was in 1847, as Arsace in Rossini's *Semiramide,* with Giulia Grisi in the title. Such was her success that she took her place among the top rank of singers and, though not a soprano, was promoted as a rival to Jenny Lind.[2]

That rare combination, an artist wholly confident and entirely modest, Alboni could sing anything. In Covent Garden's first performance of Verdi's *Ernani,* she sang the baritone role when two men refused to do so. Yet for all her talent, she wasn't a typical diva, was very superstitious and nervous before singing, but not difficult. She was earthy, direct, with a laugh that infected those around her (though there was sadness in her life). Her face was handsome and charming in its expressions. However, she conveyed little sexual attraction, wasn't at all glamorous. Marietta

Alboni was very fat, her figure composed of "a connected system of globes and ellipses," which provoked the simple-minded to simple-minded jokes. In *La Fille du régiment,* dressed in short petticoats, she was as close to Falstaff as to Marie. As Amina, in *La Sonnambula,* her bulk added suspense to her somnambulistic trance on the treadmill. Whatever else, she was not at all the kind of fetching young woman— Maria García, Julie Calvé, Jenny Lind—who had captured the hearts of Americans.

She arrived in New York in June 1852, in her usual unheralded way, and at the worst possible time, since the opera season was over and the summer outdoors season hadn't yet begun. "Nothing had been done to get up an excitement." She had no publicist, no manager. Her decision to visit the United States was an impetuous one, and she made the trip entirely at her own risk, with no engagements or arrangements fixed ahead of time. In her own words, "America was a magic word for artists. They believed that in the New World the larks fell from the skies already roasted. It was a true fever; every artist wanted to go to America. I too had this craze."[3] Undaunted by the hurdles before her, she wasted no time, secured Luigi Arditi, formerly of the Havana company, as her conductor, and gave her first concert at Metropolitan Hall on June 23. By the time she got through the first line of her first aria, from *Semiramide,* "the quality of her voice was revealed to the evident delight of her whole audience, who, at the end of the second line, could no longer restrain their impulse to give expression to their feelings and shouted *bravo, bravo* in the most impassioned manner." At the concert's end the audience was standing and waving their hats and handkerchiefs, "while she laughed all the time as if she was enjoying a good joke."[4]

Marietta Alboni, of whom Walt Whitman wrote: "All persons appreciated Alboni—the common crowd quite as well as the connoisseurs." Historical Sound Recordings Collection, Yale University Library.

No Albonimania swept the eastern seaboard. Perhaps Jenny Lind had depleted the reserves of public hysteria. Or was it the absence of a Barnum? Everywhere Alboni's magnificent nature, irresistibly genial, full of life and gaiety of soul, produced delight. Her singing produced great enthusiasm inside the halls where she sang. But far from igniting frenzies, its sense of absolute mastery created a contrary feeling, of calm, repose, tranquillity. She gave concerts successfully in most of the eastern cities through the summer and into the fall. Nevertheless, there were lots of empty seats. She made "hardly enough money to buy wine with."

People were ravished by the "cool lusciousness" of her tones. Richard Grant White, the most astute newspaper critic of the day, confessed himself tempted "to go and kneel down before her and do something abject in grateful acknowledgement of this manifestation of supreme musical divinity." She sang with a playful, almost disdainful, ease of execution, a kind of "unconscious carelessness," as if "an infant sought a moment's sport in unstringing and scattering priceless pearls."[5] But it wasn't enough. There was no novelty to it, or so people felt. Plans were made for an opera season when the news arrived that Marietta Alboni wouldn't have the field all to herself. Another, and a very different, artist was on her way across the Atlantic.

G l a m o r enveloped Henriette Sontag, the glamor of a life lived among European kings and queens. Born in Koblenz, Germany, in 1806, Henriette Gertrud Walpurgis Sontag was the daughter of actors who lived the nomadic, dissolute life of the profession. She studied at the Prague Conservatory and sang in Vienna at sixteen. Carl Maria von Weber's support set in motion a series of events which connected her career with famous incidents in European musical history. In 1823 she sang in the world premiere of Weber's *Euryanthe,* a milestone in the development of German music drama. In 1824 she sang the soprano part in the first performance of Beethoven's Ninth, the "Choral" Symphony, in the presence of the composer. At the conclusion, when Beethoven, who had sat with the orchestra, stood with his back to the audience, so deaf that he couldn't hear its ovation, it was Sontag who touched the great man on the shoulder and turned him to face the cheering crowd.

She was one of the first German singers to attain international celebrity. The Germans went mad about the "divine child," and she inspired a frenzy rivaling that for Jenny Lind twenty years later. All classes shared in it. Students at the university in Göttingen, where a Royal Mail coach had been put at her disposal, pushed it into the river, explaining that "having been used by such a divinity no other mortal was fit to ride in it." The king of Prussia admired and pursued her, and she deftly contrived to stay in his favor but out of his bed. Between 1828 and 1830 Sontag sang on equal terms in London and Paris with Giuditta Pasta and Maria Malibran, and put the final seal on her European reputation. Her style was neither grand like Pasta's nor intense like Malibran's, but exceptionally polished and finished, with a soft, refined quality in her voice. Exceedingly pretty, almost beautiful, with large pale eyes, fair complexion, auburn hair, she acted in a reserved, ladylike manner.[6]

In 1830 she did the one thing remaining that could add to the celebrity of her career—and that was to abandon it. She fell in love with Carlo de Rossi, a young nobleman and diplomat at the court of King Carlo Felice of Sardinia. Although the social gulf between them was immense, the idea of marriage was not impossible unless Rossi wished to continue his career. The diplomatic service was still socially exclusive and no European court would receive the husband of a paid performer. Rossi refused to give up his career. The prudent thing would have been for Sontag to become his mistress, but she wouldn't agree to this and insisted on marriage. Eventually a compromise was worked out. King Wilhelm of Prussia conferred on her a patent of nobility, making her the Countess Lauenstein, so that she was eligible for presentation at court in her own right. Carlo Felice thereupon allowed the marriage and his court accepted Sontag as the wife of an ambassador. In return for all this—Henriette Sontag retired from the stage.

Instead of singing in opera, she became the subject of one. These much discussed events inspired Auber to compose *L'Ambassadrice* (1836), about a great singer who, on the point of becoming the wife of a nobleman, is so disgusted at the obstacles thrown in the way of her marriage that she impulsively gives everything up and returns to the stage. One wonders what Sontag thought of the Ambassadress's choice. Anyway, she had made hers and stuck with, had several children, and was a devoted mother. Within a few years her fame and name was almost forgotten. Her heartache at what she had lost never disappeared. Sam Ward, that most remarkable American man-of-the-world, connoisseur, lobbyist, and acquaintance of the great, who in his ubiquitous way has several times popped up in our story—in the Park Theatre in 1825, in the California gold rush in the 1850s—met the Countess Rossi at dinner and asked the unaskable: Was she happier now than she had been as a performer? "I,

Henriette Sontag, from an engraving by G. Zabel after a painting by A. Salome. "To hear Sontag sing is to be in good society," a contemporary wrote. From Odell, Annals, vol. 6.

happy? I would give all the crowns in the world, and the Holy Father's tiara, for one hour behind the footlights and in front of the pit!"[7]

And then the revolutions of 1848 rocked Europe, "ruined what there was to ruin in Count Rossi," brought his diplomatic career to an end, and cost him his fortune. A second romantic chapter in Henriette Sontag's life began: after eighteen years she returned to the stage. Once again she was a sacrificial heroine, working to preserve her family's name and fortune. Her technical skill enabled her, at forty-two, to surmount vocal difficulties. She first sang again in London and was warmly received. Her appearance unleashed a great outpouring of sympathy, especially among women. What more likely, propelled by financial necessity, than for her to think about America?

L e Grand Smith, a former Barnum employee, wishing to branch out on his own, approached her. He would promote her as a "singing countess." At first she said no. She thought Jenny Lind had been subjected to indignities, and after all, she *was* a countess. Still, given her circumstances, how could she resist the possibility of a bonanza? Arrangements were made: Carl Eckert as her conductor, a guaranteed sum of money plus a percentage of the profits. Smith set the publicity going so that, in September 1852 when Henriette Sontag got to New York, her arrival produced all the by-now customary trappings which Alboni had lacked: a crowd, banners, and inter-views, a tumultuous serenade which turned into a near riot (the Rossi coat of arms on the doors of her coach was a nice touch). Sontag's worst fears were confirmed. Her dignity and Smith's publicity didn't mix. Eventually Smith withdrew or was forced out.

In the fall of 1852 Alboni and Sontag opposed each other in direct concert-hall rivalry, often singing in the same cities at the same time. Vocally, the advantage was all Alboni's. While the first response to Sontag's voice was enthusiastic—"less power than Jenny Lind's but, if such a thing be possible, sweeter"—it was soon evident that "the bloom and richness are gone, and the fame of Sontag is historical." John Sullivan Dwight, the Boston critic, who admired Sontag greatly, thought it "absurd and toadyish to pretend to find all perfect, where in the nature of things it cannot be."[8] Other things favored Sontag: a better orchestra and more popular programs, shrewdly modeled on Lind's mixture, while Alboni's were entirely operatic. The box-office verdict was indisputable—Sontag. This had less to do with quality of voice or programs than with publicity, or its absence. Alboni had "only carelessly and lightly employed the genius of advertising, and of various other means of catching the public eye," reported *Putnam's Magazine.* "Men like Barnum do not live in vain." Advertising needed to fasten on something, usually something external to the art or the artist, and with Alboni there seemed to be nothing to catch hold of beyond that glorious voice.

With Henriette Sontag it was her title. The long-suppressed Yankee fascination with titles, with nobility, with aristocracy—those discredited blotches on high Euro-pean culture—swelled the attendance at Sontag's concerts. She personified the diva as great lady, great beyond her musical gifts: "The Countess Rossi, singing as count-esses should sing." There was nothing about her of country-girl simplicity, or of Nordic purity. Sontag appeared in magnificent gowns that cost fabulous sums, wore glittering diamond necklaces and gold bracelets. "To hear Sontag sing is to be in good society."[9]

Alboni and Sontag. The two divas were rivals in a social comedy of manners which reveals a lot about what underlay the materialist expansiveness of these post–gold rush days. One writer mocked the kind of talk that one heard: "It was a 'nice thing' to assist at an entertainment where a 'real lady' performed. Had we not met her at dinner? Was not her fate romantic? Was she not the most perfect singer, actress, countess that ever was known?" Occasionally, there were protests against this snobbery. *Harper's Magazine* pointed out the irony that a member of the "great feudal brotherhood which has so long wrung the entrails of central Europe for its sustenance, should now come singing songs to our healthful young democracy—for money!"[10] A few people complained or mocked. Many more bought tickets. Then, too, there was a straightforward empathy for Sontag's odyssey in search of dollars. It was a kind of romance Americans could understand. They were searching for the same thing themselves.

In the winter of 1853 the contest switched to opera and Alboni evened the balance of success somewhat. For a while, in New York, she and Sontag sang night after night, in direct competition with each other, often singing the same operas. "Glory descended on both houses." Alboni's acting was intelligent. She was especially effective in the great comic roles, in *Il Barbiere di Siviglia, La Fille du régiment, La Cenerentola, Don Pasquale.* Here she found the right outlet for her inextinguishable amiability, and while the productions had little sense of overall coherence, especially given the pickup nature of the casts, "she sings away with her great, rich, rollicking voice, and smiles in the thunders of applause that follows." Sontag's chief strength was that she had a clearer sense, which she imparted to some extent to her colleagues, of the opera as a whole. Her intelligence and the individual finish of her interpretation were very fine. But her concert strengths were operatic weaknesses. She lacked dramatic power. In comic roles she was too artificial. She "sometimes looked like a middle-aged woman playing young."[11]

There was one unforgettable moment for Marietta Alboni. Recognizing that she would not triumph in America as she had hoped or get rich as she had dreamed, she gave herself a present, which she would have denied herself in Europe. She sang Norma in *Norma,* then regarded as the grandest tragic role in all opera. The high soprano of the part was unfitted to her voice. The music had to be transposed down, and the tragic solemnity and force of the role were unlikely for her. But the queen of contraltos had her way and satisfied a deep yearning. "Ah, one must scream a little to sing Norma, and I do not yet know how to scream," she said. She sang it twice, with unexpected fervor and passion. "*Norma-ly,*" Richard Grant White, who heard both performances, wrote, "it was open to objection." But "she must have brooded over the part until it took complete possession of her. . . . In its own way it was a very great performance."[12]

Intertwined for a while, these two dramatically contrasted lives and careers unwound themselves in 1853. In May of that year Alboni returned to Europe and resumed her great career. For all her appearance of mastery, singing was nervous agony for her and she longed for retirement—so that she could indulge her appetite for macaroni, she said. She was able to quit the stage in the mid-1860s. But before that she sprang a surprise. She married—a count. Marietta Alboni became Countess Pepoli. Undoubtedly a most amiable one. Her husband, alas, showed signs of madness and she had continually to watch over him. He died in 1867 and in that year she retired for good, being coaxed out of her peaceful ways a few times only, for charities or on very special occasions, one of which we'll note later on.[13]

Americans had heard one of the world's great voices in its prime, in opera, but Alboni shared the common estimate: her visit had been a failure. "I neither conquered the New World nor accumulated many dollars. [To do so] it would have been necessary to put myself in the hands of a Barnum and this was not my way of practising my art." Still, those who heard her sing were not likely to associate the glory of her art with failure. Richard Grant White put his own estimate memorably: "That which is perfectly beautiful in its kind seems the more beautiful the more its beauties are scanned; and whatever may be the relative rank which aesthetic criticism may hereafter assign to the style of Madame Alboni, there can be no doubt, we think, in the mind of any gifted with the ability to judge, that in her style, her singing is as surely and absolutely beautiful as it is possible for anything earthly to be."[14]

Henriette Sontag stayed on in the United States, making a long tour of the South and West in the fall of 1853 and winter of 1854. She ended up in New Orleans in the spring. There, she decided to push on to Mexico City, although warned about an outbreak of cholera. She arrived in June 1854. After just one performance she came down with a fever and died on the 17th.

The visits of these celebrated divas inspired two writers, both unknown then. The first, a young Boston woman, Louisa May Alcott, published her first story, "The Rival Prima Donnas," under the pseudonym of Flora Fairfield, and having this melodramatic tale of jealousy and murder out of her system, found a voice of a very different sort. The second, responding intensely to Alboni's genius, attended every one of her operatic performances, "enraptured by the melody gurgling and gushing up from her lips." For Walt Whitman, opera was crucial to the kind of poetry he was struggling to write, and we shall soon see how it was that Marietta Alboni's voice helped *his* song take flight.[15]

S o n t a g and Alboni didn't exhaust the limits of European fame and glamor. There was a royal couple of opera then reigning, a special pair of singers, wife and husband, soprano and tenor: "Europe found no words of admiration too strong to express the merits of Mario and Grisi." They were Giovanni Mario (1810–1883) and Giulia Grisi (1811–1869). Performers who are husband and wife hold a special interest for many people, and in the case of Mario and Grisi, romance with a touch of scandal added to the interest.

Born Giovanni Matteo, Cavaliere di Candia, Mario in early life had nothing to do with music. In his mid-twenties he eloped with a ballerina to Paris where, to support them, he began studying singing. It turned out that he had a magnificent voice and, after a successful debut at age twenty-eight, he quickly became tremendously popular. "His voice was considered one of the most beautiful ever heard, and he sang with

Giovanni Mario as Arturo in I Puritani *and Giulia Grisi as Anne Boleyn in Donizetti's* Anna Bolena. *They were one of opera's great husband-and-wife teams. Music Division, New York Public Library for the Performing Arts.*

elegance and style." Even more, however, his handsome looks, dashing bearing, and suave manner on stage made him the greatest male idol of the middle third of the nineteenth century. Giulia Grisi was born into a musical and artistic family in Milan. She studied with her elder sister, Giuditta, also a fine singer. (Their cousin was the famous ballerina Carlotta Grisi.) Giulia Grisi's career moved forward quickly and she made her debut in Milan in 1828. She created the role of Adalgisa in the first *Norma* of 1831. However, unhappy at restrictions on her career in Italy, she broke her contract at La Scala and fled to Paris, reestablishing her career there and in London. She created the role of Elvira in Bellini's *I Puritani* in 1835 and of Norina in Donizetti's *Don Pasquale* in 1843. Mario also sang in the latter. "Her voice was rich, beautiful and flexible," and with much hard work and study she became an actress of uncommon power, presence, and passion. With the death of Malibran and the retirements of Pasta and Sontag, Giulia Grisi became the leading soprano of the 1840s until the appearance of Jenny Lind at the end of that decade. Mario was unrivaled after the retirement of Giovanni Rubini in the early 1840s. Grisi had married early in her career but was by then divorced. In 1844 they married and began their joint reign over European opera.[16]

I n the early 1850s, James H. Hackett, a popular comedian and theatrical manager, opened negotiations with Mario and Grisi to induce them to come to America. After protracted dickering, it was announced, in the late spring of 1854, that they would come to New York in September to inaugurate the new opera house being built there. Hackett guaranteed them eighty-five thousand dollars for five months, plus many of their expenses. By the end of summer, excitement was building: "The steamer *Baltic* swiftly approaches, bearing two gifted artists, destined to delight a nation." When the singers reached New York they found that the Academy of Music wasn't ready, so, like Jenny Lind, they made their first appearances at Castle Garden. (When Mario first saw it, he mistook it for a circus and asked where the horses were.) Tickets were very expensive—five dollars for a box, three for a seat in the parquet. Their first opera was Donizetti's *Lucrezia Borgia.* The applause at their entrance was deafening and long. Mario was subdued, so casual in manner as to seem almost indifferent, but his voice was smooth and sweet, a refined contrast to the usual noisy, straining tenors Americans had heard. Grisi's Lucrezia was "exquisite in finish and dramatic coloring." Applause at the end of the opera was faint. It wasn't a remarkable performance. There was a pervasive sense of anticlimax. Next came *Norma* which, over the years, became her most famous role. "Her poses are majestic, her carriage stately, her walk Juno-like." She was "beyond all comparison the greatest Norma we have ever had." And yet here too there was a sense of anticlimax, as though something were missing. Mario didn't make much of the role of Pollione. As Norma, Grisi looked a "beautiful fury," but the lightning and rage appropriate to the role were intermittent. Her voice was worn.[17]

In October the Academy of Music was ready and "the very high priests of the art were present to aid in the rites of inauguration." The first opera done was again *Lucrezia Borgia.* Perhaps it was a Borgia curse, but the opening was also a disappointment. "Never before was an opera house opened more inauspiciously." There were "whole banks of vacant seats." In the second tier, which held 700, there were only 30 or 40 people present. Once again the price had been set much too high—three dollars for boxes and parquet, down to fifty cents for the gallery. Grisi and Mario visited Boston, Philadelphia, Baltimore, and Washington in the months that followed. In the winter they sang at Metropolitan Hall in New York. Mario, in *I Puritani,* dressed splendidly as a cavalier, produced the kind of romantic sparks that people had expected. Attentive listeners also understood the reasons for Grisi's towering reputation. "More than any other lyric actress whom we have heard," one noted, "she possesses the power of fusing the dramatic and the vocal elements of her part." She made her music "the fitting and natural expression of the idea" she was trying to communicate. She showed her versatility. In *Don Pasquale* she was superbly comic: "Humanity has no phases which are not mirrored in her representations of character." "Every bar of the music was illustrated with consummate skill."[18] They made a great deal of money, but both singers were happy to leave in March 1855.

What had gone wrong? One observer thought that Grisi and Mario "labored under the disadvantage of not being Barnumised." The reverse is closer to the truth. They weren't undermanaged, they were overpublicized. Someone said: "Perhaps we expected too much." An indication of exaggerated expectation was the statement of one writer that in the news of their arrival "there was more to quicken the pulse of any opera lover than in any operatic announcement ever before made to the public." People saw the problem. "The very intensity of interest excited was a danger to their success."[19]

Hackett was inventive in promoting their interests at the box office. In Philadelphia, librettos on sale in the theater lobby were autographed by Mario and Grisi, perhaps the first instance of this in American operatic life. One unstated difficulty was that Mario's sexual appeal, in those more inhibited days, could not be openly marketed. There were discreet stories, however, about an "infatuated" woman who went to every performance and followed him about. Polite society was initially interested in them and the singers agreed to give lessons to a select few, who would come "from that class of the community the members of which behave well, and dress better."[20] But Mario and Grisi kept to themselves, didn't need or seek social approval. For them, after all, the visit to America was primarily a business venture. If, for their audiences, the visit was much more than that, it finally came back to art, and art took time. "Even Niagara is a source of almost universally confessed disappointment at first glance."[21]

Boston

Words or music. Thought or emotion. These were the opposed terms that shaped Boston's response to opera, and not simply the actual and supposed puritan antipathy to it. The need to study the word of God through his biblical texts resulted in that supremacy of the word, written and spoken, which remained an inescapable fact of New England culture. At the same moment the Venetians invented San Cassiano, the first public opera house, Massachusetts was founding Harvard College to train its sons to be ministers. Education was New England's pride, books were its sacred icon. And when, after two centuries, the period of unquestioned Calvinist ascendancy in religious belief and practice had ended, puritanism lingered, transformed but pervasive, as a cluster of attitudes hardened by history into conventional stereotypes: dislike of the theater, suspicion of art that was not useful, fear of art that emphasized feeling and unrestrained emotion. Literature and oratory were the respected arts.

Boston's institutions reflected the stress placed upon reading, speaking, and analysis. The American Academy of Arts and Sciences of 1780 was followed by the Massachusetts Medical Society, 1781; the Boston Library Society, 1794; the Massachusetts Historical Society, 1797; and the Antiquarian Society, 1812. Musical institutions were slower to develop. That didn't mean that music was not cultivated, only that it was best left to individual effort, most appropriate as a private accomplishment not as a public enterprise. New Englanders sang a good deal, and dancing was also widely enjoyed in family gatherings. Women played keyboard instruments. Men played the flute, clarinet, and occasionally the violin, though this instrument had "foreign associations" which had to be overcome. There had been an organ in the Brattle Street Church since 1745. By 1815 there was an organ factory, and five other Boston churches had organs. Those congregations which disliked organs as ostentatious used the clarinet or bass violin to accompany singing.

In 1800 Boston was a town of about twenty-five thousand. Federalist culture was extremely insular and sceptical of the values of the rest of the country, let alone the world beyond it. It hated Jeffersonianism for many reasons, its cosmopolitanism not the least of them. "As a specimen of continental degeneracy, Jefferson was condemned," Patrick Henry said, "because he kept a French cook and liked French dishes—'abjuring his native victuals.'" But as the eighteenth century gave way to the nineteenth, and the new nation grew, Boston had more interchange with places other than northern Europe—China and the Mediterranean—and its horizons widened. At the same time, Boston's self-absorption, kept intact its concern with ethical behavior. The rest of the country ridiculed this, but it was one of the things that made Boston great.

The most acrimonious public struggle between "official conscience and public desire" was about theater. The colonial prohibition against theater was a subject of furious and protracted debate after the Revolution. It was finally revoked in 1793. Quickly, then, the Federal Theatre was built and opened in 1794, the Haymarket Theater in 1797. The Federal Theatre was a substantial brick building; its audiences were cosmopolitan and sympathetic to French culture. However, it also had strict regulation of conduct. The manager was responsible for everything from enlarging the orchestra when needed, to requiring women to remove their hats, to prohibiting requests for encores or for tunes which would "destroy the arrangements," that is, the previously planned program. The Federal Theatre burned down in 1798. A new theater, designed by Charles Bullfinch, replaced it, remaining a Boston landmark until 1852. The Haymarket was in the hands of Federalists, its programs and atmosphere very pro-English.

The didactic tradition in Boston revealed itself in a pamphlet, written in 1792 by a William Haliburton, entitled *Effects of the stage on the manners of a people, and the propriety of encouraging and establishing a virtuous theater.* Haliburton proposed a huge theater seating sixty-two hundred people, a quarter of the population of the city, because he envisaged the theater as a central community institution, one in which everyone would learn proper values. Music played a large role in establishing those values, "lending its divine aid, softening the savage heart, and lifting the rapt soul to God." The interludes between acts and scenes would have music which "praised the virtue of heroic souls." What kind of music? Along with a premonition of Transcendentalism in the desire for "the deep-felt voice of nature, in harmonic sounds, vocal and instrumental united," there is an echo of that old English tradition of dislike for opera in Haliburton's emphatic description of the kind of music he *didn't* want: "all unintelligible Italian airs, trills, affected squeaks and quavers."[1]

In the first third of the nineteenth century, Boston entered its most creative literary period. It was also a golden age for the spoken word, in church sermons and in public lectures. The sung word was encouraged, too. Singing had always been more common in New England than other forms of music. By the early nineteenth century there were numerous singing schools, primarily to train women and men to sing in church choirs, and they raised the general level of performance. Singing masters and professional organists were employed in some churches. Orchestral playing lagged behind because there were few theaters and theater orchestras, and a career in music as an orchestral player seemed unremunerative. "The clear-eyed Yankee knows this very well."[2]

The chief institution of Boston musical life in the first half of the nineteenth century was neither a theater nor an orchestra. It was the Handel and Haydn Society, founded in 1815 to promote the cause of sacred music. It depended entirely upon voluntary community support. No salaries were paid to those who ran it. The society tried to attract a wide audience, presenting its concerts with a uniform admission price of fifty cents. The range of works it performed went well beyond Handel and Haydn—Beethoven's *Christ on the Mount of Olives,* Mozart's *Mass in C,* Neukomm's *David* (a great favorite in Boston), and Mendelssohn's *Elijah*. Its fortunes certainly fluctuated, but the Handel and Haydn Society remained for a long time the focus of the city's musical energy.

M u s i c a l education was a second characteristic Boston and New England achievement, along with sacred music. The most important figure in this was one of those New Englanders who combined the visionary and the practical in equal parts, William C. Woodbridge (1794–1845). A teacher, Woodbridge suffered a nervous breakdown in the 1830s and traveled to Europe to recuperate. His attitude toward Europe and Europe's music is instructive. He admitted that he had always looked upon the cultivation of music with distrust, regarding it as "suited only to professional musicians or to females; and, in our sex, as a mark of a trifling or of a feminine mind." At the same time Woodbridge regarded the idea that music had power over people as "the dream of poetry as opposed to the sober and practical conclusions of philosophy." (What a conception of philosophy!) A trip to Europe showed him how wrong he had been to think this. There he felt music's power, in the "heart-swelling music of the bands, in the fascinating but corrupt strains of the opera, and in the over-powering chants of the Vatican." This discovery left him in a quandary. The true power of music had been used for degraded purposes, "to cover the point of a song whose sentiments would not be tolerated in any other form," or by placing "noble and solemn" ideas "in the mouths of those who never felt a corresponding emotion." Performers should *be* moral as well as sing moral songs.

Woodbridge found the way out of his dilemma in Germany, where he discovered the method of musical instruction based on the theories and work of Johann Heinrich Pestalozzi (1746–1827), a Swiss reformer who emphasized the direct experience of music by young people. Hearing music's "animating strains echoing from the walls of a schoolroom" moved Woodbridge deeply and persuaded him that there was in the Pestalozzian method something especially pertinent for America. Taught this way, music was not exclusive. It was "the property of the people, cheering their hours of labor, elevating their hearts above the objects of sense, which are so prone to absorb them, and filling the period of rest and amusement with social and moral song in place of noise, riot, and gambling."[3]

On his return to America, Woodbridge enrolled Lowell Mason (1792–1872) in his cause. A musician and teacher, Mason became the foremost proponent of musical education in the public schools, and his tireless work to put Woodbridge's ideas into practice eventually resulted in the establishment of the Boston Academy of Music, an institution to train teachers of music. Proper musical instruction in the schools was to follow in two steps: first vocal music would be established as a branch of ordinary study, and then instrumental music. The Boston School Committee was reluctant to approve Mason's scheme until he offered a year's trial run free of charge. He would do all the instruction himself. Thriftily, the committee accepted the offer. At the end of a year its evaluation was favorable, and the program was expanded. One common objection to Mason's program was that it opened the door for all kinds of non-academic subjects. Why instruction in music, for example, and not in dance? Mason's answer? "Because music has an intellectual character, which dancing has not; and, above all, because music has its moral purposes, which dancing has not."[4]

How was opera to establish its moral claim to be heard? No wonder it came later to Boston than to any other major city. However, once English opera had gained a toehold in the turbulent revolutionary days, and when finally the colonial antitheater ordinance was rescinded, opera spread rapidly, by means of touring English opera groups, to the small cities and the towns. Yet English opera was not more strongly entrenched in New England than foreign-language opera. New England was ambivalent about British culture, prickly at the slightest hint of British condescension. British actors had as much trouble in Boston as anywhere else. It wasn't until after the Civil War that Boston would more or less come to terms with British culture.

As early as 1797, Boston had a taste of French opera, given in English, Grétry's *Richard the Lion Heart* (*Richard Coeur-de-lion*), John Quincy Adams's favorite opera. There were also English-language performances of operas by Philidor and Rousseau. Performance of French and Italian opera in their original languages was infrequent until the late 1840s. The New Orleans French company visited Boston, but the Garcías did not, nor did the Montresor Company or Rivafinoli's troupe. The introduction of foreign-language opera really put Bostonians in a difficult position, divided between scepticism about art that was incomprehensible and a desire for what was authentic, which meant opera in the original language. This was important because Boston viewed itself as a bastion of integrity in a culture increasingly given over to vulgarity and crass pursuit of money. Those qualities characterized New York, in Boston's view, and caustic comments about New York were a persistent theme: "The business of art has come to resemble all other kinds of business in New York. It is a business of humbug, of deception, of gambling."[5] The purest expression of the city's musical views and values was *Dwight's Journal of Music*. The first number appeared in April 1852 and for thirty years, though the number of its subscribers probably never exceeded fifteen hundred, it was the most serious and respected musical journal in the country. Boston had done nothing of importance in American opera. Now it would make its presence felt, appropriately enough, by means of the printed word.

J o h n Sullivan Dwight was born in Boston on May 13, 1813, an exact contemporary of William Henry Fry. Dwight's inclination was theological. He attended Harvard College, graduating in 1832, and then Harvard Divinity School. He was a member of the movement toward liberal Unitarian reform of Calvinism centered around Channing, Alcott, and Emerson; but even unitarianism was too restrictive for him, and his experience as a minister was deeply unsatisfactory. He joined Brook Farm, the famous utopian community later satirized by Nathaniel Hawthorne in *The Blithedale Romance*. There he found the outlet for his literary and musical interests, writing for the *Harbinger,* a utopian socialist periodical. He received no formal musical training, though he apparently learned to play the flute and piano moderately well. In music he found the subject which absorbed his passionate reflections about the meaning of life; and in the 1840s, as he wrote increasingly on music for various ephemeral journals, lectured on musical subjects in public, and discussed music with a small circle of

Transcendentalist friends, he recognized that what he had so revealingly described first as a "truant occupation" was the occupation of a lifetime. A fervent love of music (he was in the truest sense an amateur), dogmatic certainty, high standards, and a passionate desire to teach, to unite an interest in the best music with the highest ethical aspirations of the community—these were the impulses expressed in *Dwight's Journal of Music.*

At the center of Dwight's thought was the desire to understand the true nature of music, something which had an existence in and of itself and was not dependent on the response of an individual auditor or audience. The function of musical criticism, which was a kind of "natural history of music," was to explore aspects of this essential core of music. In terms of historical significance, Beethoven was the most important of composers because it was he who began the self-conscious composition of this kind of music, "pure" music. It was not connected with any other art essentially but had its own separate existence. It followed from this definition that, for Dwight, instrumental music was much more important than opera, which, obviously, was composite, impure, a mixture of arts. However exalted the operatic achievement—Mozart's *Don Giovanni,* for example—it was still inferior to pure instrumental work. Opera moved the feelings, not the mind. Opera was analogous to virtuoso instrumental playing, which Dwight regarded as a contemporary corruption of true music, hence his notorious denigration of Louis Gottschalk as a pianist. Opera, with its "appeal to easy sympathies which demand no great culture, powers of thought, or depth of character," played an important transitional role in the evolution of music toward its instrumental culmination. It made "whole multitudes musical who were not before." The highest ideal of vocal music was the songs of Schubert: "We cannot possess too many, and yet one of them is more than we can exhaust in a life-time."[6]

Germany was the home of pure music. There music was somehow natural, organic. "In Germany, songs grow. Italian Opera airs are full of melody and sweetness, but one is too much like another; it is an endless regalvanizing into life of a vein of sentiment and melody long since exhausted." Therefore, Dwight's evaluation of the achievement of Italian composers was an effort to find Germanic qualities in their music. He ranked Rossini highest among the Italians, with *Semiramide* his masterpiece. Rossini had carried opera's transitional nature as far as it could go. He had done more than any composer who ever lived "to popularize music, to educate the ear." But he had done so by melodramatic, "effect" music, which played on external emotions, not deeper thoughts, and by so doing Rossini had also created a "false and dangerous" school of music. Bellini wrote superb melodies, but of a "sweet and sickly" sort. The effect of Bellinian melody on the listener was to make him sad, passive, "softened, melted, but not roused, not strengthened." One longed for "a good cold north wind to sweep away the mild, vague haziness that hangs about your senses, and breathe a bracing atmosphere, feel your spirit and your nerves invigorated, and see things by the clear, literal light of day." Donizetti seemed of little consequence, his music "sugary and feeble," though capable of dramatic power.[7] Dwight had considerable respect for Verdi, who, whatever else, had little in common with his predecessors. Verdi was trying to deepen Italian music with German ideas, but he was crude, lacked discipline, above all, lacked the philosophically grounded musical culture necessary for his task. Verdi's operas of the 1850s didn't seem a step forward. However, Dwight was prepared to wait and see, as he was also about the newest German composer whose theories he found troubling but whose music he hardly knew, Richard Wagner.

Many of the central musical cultural issues of the 1850s came vividly to life in the contrasting views of Dwight and Fry, who commented on each other's ideas in print throughout the decade. The claims of nationalism versus cosmopolitanism were the primary point of contention. Fry, as we've seen, advocated the nurturing of music by American composers, while Dwight scorned the "boastful, shallow patriotic, 'manifest destiny,' all annexing, Yankee Doodle way." They also differed about democracy and art, Fry championing American opinion while Dwight was sceptical about the "clapping masses." A third issue was whether there was progress in art. Dwight believed in the superiority of certain perennial esthetic forms; Fry insisted on "an inflexible rule in the philosophy of art, that it must assume new forms, or if the old ones are adhered to, they must be improved." A contemporary scholar has characterized their "debate" as no less than the effort to determine "which of these antagonists deserves to be called 'the Emerson of American music.'"[8]

O n e other New Englander deserves mention here, for though his work was not associated with opera, his achievement was a remarkable one in the history of American music and representative of many aspects of Bostonian culture in these years. Alexander Wheelock Thayer was born in South Natick, Massachusetts, in 1817 and educated at Harvard. After many years of indecision about a career, he got a law degree in 1848 but never practiced law. Instead, he became a musicologist. He wrote on American psalmody in the seventeenth and eighteenth centuries, and in 1849 he went to Germany to prepare a corrected translation of Anton Schindler's biography of Beethoven. In the next few years, Thayer decided to expand his labors beyond translation and to write a full-scale biography of Beethoven free of the inaccuracies and myth making which had gathered round the great man's life. He devoted the rest of his life to this project. He traveled several times to Europe, supporting himself partly by writing numerous articles for *Dwight's Journal* on many subjects, but especially on Beethoven, his views and information largely shaping Dwight's ideas. In 1866 Thayer was appointed American consul at Trieste, where he worked until 1882, all the time collecting materials, interviewing people who had known Beethoven, and struggling heroically to get the story straight.

The first volume of Thayer's *Life of Beethoven* came out in 1866, another volume followed in 1872, and a third in 1879. All were translated into German and established themselves as the standard scholarly source and a mine to be quarried by subsequent scholars, some acknowledging their debt to Thayer, others not. On he labored. There was so much to master and so much still to do. Thayer died in Trieste in 1897, the *Life* unfinished. It wasn't translated into English until 1921. Thayer wrote interestingly on other American musical subjects and events, but his life was essentially Beethoven's life, a mighty subject seriously addressed. Very Boston, too, in its passion for accuracy, its stern, unbending, high standards, its commitment to truth and to having the final word.

c h a p t e r   f i f t e e n

Gardens and Academies

From its earliest years, opera had been given out of doors, in the gardens and parks of the court or aristocracy. English public pleasure gardens were very different—informal, inexpensive, amusement for the masses. Vauxhall, Ranelegh Gardens, and Sadler's Wells were the prototypes imitated by Americans as early as Charleston's "New Vauxhall" of 1767. Over the years imitation gave way to places more distinctly American but still dedicated to the belief that opera could be domesticated, could be rooted deeply in the soil of popular culture.

N i b l o ' s Garden was on lower Broadway. One end of the site had been a circus arena, remodeled into a hall suitable for year-round use, the other end a banqueting room and summer theater. In between was "the charmed ground" of the actual garden, with tubs of orange and lemon trees, pots of flowers, and intersecting walks sprinkled with chairs and tables, covered with arbors. The aim was to create a magical and mysterious effect with "wild, fantastic scenery." Chinese lanterns hung from the arbors, multicolored gaslights lighted the columns supporting a covered promenade. There was an illuminated wheel, constantly in motion, at one end of the garden, a huge mirror multiplying all the effects at the other. "Niblo certainly possesses Aladdin's Lamp and exercises the skill of a necromancer." In the evenings people strolled and lolled, ate delicious ices, and forgot the scorching temperatures and the heat of commerce.

William Niblo was born in 1789 in Ireland, came to New York at an early age. Jovial, kind-hearted, wanting to make public entertainment his business, he opened his first Niblo's on July 4, 1828. He wished to make people feel at home in his garden and delighted in surprising them with new things. He had an almost unfailing intuition about popular taste. For three decades he guessed what would be star attractions—in the 1830s it was singing groups like the Ravel family; in the 1840s, minstrel shows; in the 1850s, military bands—and he guessed correctly. Niblo neither pandered to popular taste nor felt contemptuous of it. He tried to improve it by making the best things of their kind available as cheaply as possible. Price of admission to the garden was fifty cents, no reserved seats.

Opera, orchestral, and singing concerts alternated with spoken drama and a wide variety of shows. Niblo had opened the garden with operatic selections and pieces from Handel's *Messiah,* and for years there were concerts of sacred music every Sunday evening. Opera was often given in English, and lots of English singers appeared there. At the same time Niblo brought the New Orleans company to sing in Italian. He aimed at

Niblo's Theatre: opera (in English) and ice cream in the gardens of New York. From Ballou's Pictorial Drawing-Room Companion, *Feb. 24, 1855. Library of Congress.*

"innocent, thoughtless, side-shaking, brain-clearing mirth," but that didn't rule out Handel, Donizetti, a German opera company in later years. Great artists appeared there—Marietta Alboni, Julie Calvé—but Niblo didn't depend on big names. And it wasn't only the garden. There was entertainment the year round in the enclosed theater. New York changed enormously between the time Niblo opened and the time he left the business, but Niblo's approach changed very little. He survived a fire in 1846. In 1858 his lease expired and was not renewed. He retired from theater and never set foot in the garden again. He died in 1878.

Niblo's: opera and ice cream in the gardens of New York. It was "a great institution, perhaps the greatest New York has ever known."[1]

N e i t h e r a garden nor a castle, Fort Clinton, built between 1807 and 1811 for the protection of New York City and its harbor, was a stark, dark, seven-sided, red-stone pile built out in the water, just off the Battery, connected to land by a long, wooden, covered gangplank. No shots were ever fired from its cannons. In 1824, no longer needed for military purposes, it was converted into a place of amusement where food and drink were available and even dancing was permitted (with the mayor's approval). It quickly became a popular gathering place. The interior was planted with shrubs and flowers and a fountain built in the open central area, and that is how it gained its informal but lasting name.

In 1844 the architect Calvin Pollard turned this garden fort into a concert hall and theater. With imagination and good taste, he converted the outside terraces to walkways and covered over the open space with a brightly colored, elaborately decorated dome supported by seven iron columns. Seats filled the main floor beneath the dome. A stage was added, with adjoining platforms for scenery, so that dramatic productions were possible. It was a large place, seating five thousand people, many of whom had to look past the columns to the stage, only partially visible from the extreme sides of the main floor. Even with these drawbacks, however, most people thought Castle Garden attractive, with surprisingly good sound. Its great glory was its enchanting view of the splendid harbor.

All kinds of things took place there—fireworks, balloon ascensions, the greeting of visiting dignitaries, fairs, theatrical performances, orchestral concerts (it was the site of the first American performance of Beethoven's Ninth Symphony), as well as some of the most memorable moments in New York's operatic history: Mario and Grisi's first performance, Henriette Sontag's last. Most exciting of all were August and September 1850, when the Havana company gave its triumphant season, followed immediately by Jenny Lind. Not everyone liked the place. "It is as much a garden as it is an opera house, and partakes more of the character of a circus than either," one

Castle Garden, a converted fort in New York harbor, seated five thousand beneath its brightly colored dome. Whitman recalled "the cool sea-breezes, the unsurpassed vocalism." From Odell, Annals, *vol. 6.*

observer said sourly. But Walt Whitman recalled "the cool sea-breezes, the unsur-passed vocalism. What tales those old trees and walks and sea-walls could tell!" And then, abruptly, in 1855, this "cool house of sweet memories," was converted into an immigration reception station.[2]

The nation's largest city, New York also became its entertainment capital in the 1850s, though Boston and Philadelphia still disputed this. The city's vigorous theatri-cal life was reflected in the number and variety of its theaters and music halls, general stores of amusement, all-purpose places built in response to the needs of the market. When the market changed, these theaters changed (or disappeared). Their names told little about what went on. Apollo Hall, where French and German opera and drama were put on, became the People's Opera House but didn't change its program—or attract the multitude—while Hooley's Opera House in Brooklyn kept its name, though opera was never given there. There was even a movable opera house, or at least a floating one. The Temple of the Muses was an old steamship converted into a theater, with a small horseshoe-shaped stage, an orchestra pit holding nine musi-cians, and one tier of boxes circling the auditorium. Intended as a home for opera in English, for the "around the town" aristocracy, it attracted some attention, few patrons, moved from dock to dock—and then disappeared, perhaps sailing, "via the Hudson River, to Mt. Parnassus." Little was expected of Tripler Hall, renamed Metro-politan Hall, hastily built in 1850 to cash in on the Jenny Lind excitements, yet it turned out to be a handsome, spacious, fine-proportioned hall, with magnificent sound, "unsurpassed, if equalled, by any other hall in the world."[3] Fire destroyed it in 1854, and there was no adequate replacement until Steinway and Carnegie halls were built many years later. The theaters intended specifically for opera also varied in their fortunes.

A m o n g some unobtrusive commercial buildings in a "quiet and respectable neigh-borhood" on Chambers Street in lower Manhattan was a three-story building which had housed Stoppani's Arcade Baths. (Bathtubs were still a rarity in private houses and were mostly found in public establishments.) In 1843 Ferdinand Palmo, who had made some money in the restaurant business, converted it into an opera house. Modest exterior remodeling produced a rusticated stone facade, in the first story of which, directly off the sidewalk, were three romanesque arches, the center one leading to the theater. A sunbeam design filled the arch above this main entrance, and over this were two stories of windows divided by Ionic pilasters, capped by a simple cornice. Inside, the auditorium was horseshoe-shaped, with boxes along one side, and with an open gallery above the main floor. The prevailing feeling was one of plainness, borne out by the seating accommodations: benches in the gallery and in the pit, with wooden, shoulder-high slats for support. Those who wished softer seats had to bring their own cushions.

This simplicity was the result of Palmo's modest financial means and of his objective—to make opera available to people with little money. There was nothing fashionable about his enterprise. Prices were reasonable and, because Palmo wanted to attract families, every seat was reserved and arrangements were made for horse-drawn cars, heated in winter, to run to the theater from various sections of the city.

Once there, everyone could see and hear everything—Palmo's seated eight hundred. "Rarely, if ever, has there been a keener enjoyment of Italian opera in New York than in this humble lyric shrine."

The first season opened in February 1844, with Bellini's *I Puritani,* given six times in a row, followed by *Lucia di Lammermoor* and a new Bellini opera, *Beatrice di Tenda,* "the crowning triumph of the whole season." Palmo's singers were mediocre. Each of his two sopranos gained a small but fervent group of supporters, and New York was treated to its first operatic war between rival prima donnas, newspapers treating it as rather a joke. Palmo's first season was also his last, for he lost whatever money he had. Other directors took over the opera house for the 1845–1846 season, putting on Italian opera, *The Bohemian Girl, Der Freischütz,* Swiss bell ringers, and minstrel shows. A different group tried a season in 1847, Italian opera, including two new operas, Donizetti's *Linda di Chamounix* and Verdi's *The Lombards (I Lombardi alla prima crociata).* They failed too.

What had gone wrong? Palmo, and his successors, never found a popular woman singer. Palmo had been unlucky, since the singer who might have saved his season came to America only weeks after he had shut his doors. Laure Cinti-Damoreau, a French soprano who had sung Rossini operas with great success in Paris and had appeared there in the world premieres of Auber and Meyerbeer operas, aroused enthusiasm during her brief American stay. But Palmo's means were so modest that a foreign star might have been out of the question, and anyway, his aim was opera without stars. The audience Palmo counted on was that of foreign-born immigrants already familiar with opera. He was trying to do, on a more diverse ethnic basis, what John Davis had done in New Orleans: use opera to reinforce a non-American cultural identity. He succeeded to some extent, if one can go by the description of one of his audiences as made up of "Italians, Spanish, French, English, Germans, Dutch, Russians, Poles, Turks, and Mexicans alike sympathizing with the divine creations of Italian genius." Palmo was premature in his attempt. There were not enough immigrants who cared about opera. Or was it that opera worked differently in New York in the 1840s than it had in New Orleans in the early 1800s, that in New York many of those immigrants wanted to assimilate to American culture, and opera worked against that desire? So Palmo added his name to the honor role of those ruined by opera—ruined but not embittered. In later years he was often seen about the Academy of Music. "Italian opera was his delight to the last."[4]

E v e n as Palmo's faltered, a very different sort of operatic endeavor got under way. After a decade of inactivity, those members of New York's upper class who were interested in opera mobilized their energies and resources with meetings, proposals, and committees, "for the permanent establishment of Italian opera." The upshot, two years later, was the Astor Place Opera Association, fifty gentlemen who paid a thousand dollars each for stock, a shareholder being entitled to one free ticket for seventy-five performances of opera per year, for five years. The site chosen, at Astor Place and Eighth Street, one of the city's commanding locations, and a lease signed, things then moved rapidly forward. Ground was broken in March, and by November 1848 the Astor Place Opera House was ready.

The exterior was classical, three stories of Doric piers and pilasters. The prevailing atmosphere of the white-and-gold interior was intimate, a "small but comfortably arranged bon-bonière." The house's eighteen hundred red plush-covered seats were distributed as follows: five hundred on the main floor, six hundred in two tiers of single and double boxes (with iron trelliswork in front) for four and eight people, seven hundred in the entirely open third-tier amphitheater. Instead of the usual plaster, the walls were wood paneling covered with canvas, a factor in Astor Place's remarkably good sound. Every seat gave an unobstructed view of the stage, which was narrow but deep. There was a central chandelier with sixty lights.

Opening night was November 22, 1847. The opera was Verdi's *Ernani,* in many ways a surprising choice. Although the Havana company had given it the preceding spring and summer, a new and unfamiliar opera was not usually chosen for opening night. The season was almost entirely Donizetti and Bellini, with another new Verdi opera making its way, *Nebuchadnezzar (Nabucco).* The company included no singer capable of exciting much enthusiasm. They visited Philadelphia in the winter and then returned; but attendance fell off badly, and by April the management abruptly declared insolvency.

Under the direction of Edward Fry, another of William Henry Fry's brothers, a second season opened on November 1, 1848, with Donizetti's *Linda di Chamounix.* Fry was an exceedingly high-minded and serious director, but he had had no previous experience in running an opera company. He strengthened the orchestra—it now numbered forty-five instrumentalists, double the size of the García days. Very little Rossini was done any longer, some Verdi, somewhat more Bellini. The season was virtually all-Donizetti: the 1840s were the Donizetti decade, in fact. But *Norma* retained its popularity; *Ernani,* alone of the Verdi operas, established itself. Fry changed the program frequently, but the second season ended as had the first. He gave up in March 1849. If that was disheartening, fate was preparing a much harsher blow.[5]

The background of the event that made the Astor Place Opera House notorious in its day was that anti-British feeling frequently encountered in American theatrical affairs. The parties involved were Edwin Forrest and William Macready. In the two decades since his early Bowery Theatre days, Forrest had become the most popular of American actors and a special favorite of New Yorkers. His visits to England had embroiled him in acrimonious encounters with Macready, his chief acting rival and his opposite in style, temperament, and values. Forrest was bombastic, powerful, democratic, intuitive. Macready was taciturn, introspective, antidemocratic, intellectual. Forrest's supporters believed Macready had incited a hostile response to their hero in England. They wanted revenge.

Their chance came in 1848 when Macready toured America. He appeared at Astor Place in *Macbeth* on May 7 at the end of his tour and was greeted with a storm of catcalls. Refuse was thrown at him on stage. He canceled the rest of his performances and prepared to return to England. Leading citizens published an appeal in the newspapers urging him to try again. Reluctantly, Macready agreed to one more appearance, on the night of the 10th. Meanwhile, this theatrical row took on a different political and cultural character. Rumors circulated that British sailors were ready to come ashore to defend Macready and that the New York militia would be called out to support him and his patrons. The morning of the 10th, posters appeared throughout New York City calling for action of some kind.[6]

WORKING MEN

shall

AMERICANS

or

ENGLISH RULE

in this city?

The crew of the British steamship have
Threatened all Americans who shall dare
To express their opinion this night at the
English ARISTOCRATIC opera house!
We advocate no violence, but a free expression
of opinion to all public men.
WORKINGMEN! FREEMEN!

stand by your

LAWFUL RIGHTS

That evening large crowds gathered outside the opera house. Barricades were erected in some of the streets around it. The militia appeared. When Macready came on stage, fighting broke out inside the theater and spread to the crowds outside. Macready fled. After much uncertainty and confusion, finding itself involved in a series of battles with the local Bowery B'Hoys, the militia fired, whether at the gangs or randomly into the crowd is not clear. A squabble between two actors and their friends ended in horror. Twenty-two people were killed.

Everyone blamed everyone else. Some believed that the city's leaders conspired to find an excuse to fire on the Bowery gangs, others that riot and civil war, in the contagious atmosphere of the European revolutions of 1848, were about to erupt in America. Although it was chance that Macready appeared at Astor Place and not at another theater, there was something appropriate about the opera house being the scene of cultural and class hostilities. The Astor Place Opera House was built to demonstrate the wealth and power of New York's social elite. The Bowery B'Hoys didn't have to attend opera there to know what it meant in cultural terms for them and for their antagonists. Opera was foreign and upper-class. "The 'native' organs are very savage against theatrical entertainment," a reporter commented in 1844. "The opera—the ballet—the acted drama—are all abominations maintained by foreigners, and imported into this country by 'foreigners.'"[7]

Max Maretzek, the impresario there, discerned xenophobic and class elements in the conflict. "That portion of the public who were called the 'Upper Ten,'" he wrote, "declared that they would have whatever amusement they chose to pay for, whether it might consist of English actors, or of Italian Opera." At the same time, "the 'Lower Class,' declared that they would permit *no* English actor, *no* Italian Opera, and *no*

The riot at the Astor Place Opera House in 1848. "The Temple of Harmony was transformed into a Morgue for the dead and a hospital for the dying," lamented Max Maretzek. From the Illustrated London News, *June 2, 1849. Library of Congress.*

aristocratic theatre in New York, they being a free and enlightened people." The opera house was the innocent victim. "The Temple of Harmony was transformed into a Morgue for the dead and a hospital for the dying."[8]

Then, and later, people argued that the riot destroyed Astor Place as an opera house. Associated with bloodshed and class hatred, it ceased to be fashionable, attendance declined. But so general a view left out important aspects of its situation before and after the riot. Astor Place's social function was clear enough. Philip Hone, a proprietor of the Da Ponte Italian Opera House fifteen years earlier, explained it from an insider's perspective: a "charming place in which our young ladies, the flower of New York society, are planted to expand in a congenial soil, under the sunshine of admiration." Max Maretzek put it simply. "Everybody could see, and what is of infinitely greater consequence, could be seen. Never, perhaps, was any theatre built that afforded a better opportunity for the display of dress." It was an outpost of old New York, serving a restricted clientele, what remained, as the city grew rapidly, of a once coherent elite. It was not the house of new money. It aimed at refinement not grandeur, believing that "public exhibition of superior wealth is not in good taste." Among the people who occupied its modestly price boxes and main floor—a dollar, fifty cents for the amphitheater—"there was a certain degree of congruity and coherence," "friends and acquaintances, and those who, although not acquainted, were yet familiar with one another's faces."[9]

The purpose of the opera house was the amusement of the subscribers and the social education of their children. Given this, attendance by the general public shouldn't have been the primary issue. Labor was so cheap that opera on this scale was not an extravagant form of entertainment. Even by the frugal standards of those who built and owned the opera house, the cost of membership in the Astor Place Association, a thousand dollars per year, was a considerable but not excessive sum. The riot diminished the appeal of the place, but empty seats had been a fact almost from the first night. Small as it was, Astor Place was rarely filled. Well before the riot, fashionable people abandoned it. It lacked the excitement of star singers. It didn't make an effort to attract the foreign-born musically knowledgeable immigrants. Its patrons wanted what it represented but were unwilling to pay much for it. Aristocratic gestures in building an opera house were ill suited to bourgeois calculation in supporting it.[10] Opera was given there for three years after the riot, and then the building was sold and converted into a library.

I n the 1850s people in Boston, Philadelphia, and New York proposed to build opera houses of unprecedented size and grandeur. Each of the three buildings had features associated with the culture of its city, but the three also had a good deal in common, seeming to point to a new direction in the evolution of American patronage.

As early as 1840 Philadelphians had been thinking about an opera house which would "eclipse the San Carlo, the Scala, or the King's Theatre in London." That project collapsed, however, as did four others during that decade. In 1851 another effort got under way, for a popular opera house with large seating capacity, low prices, and offering opera in English. It was based on the premise that "the opera house must support itself." This would be accomplished by increasing the size of the house (5,000 or more) and by broadening the social composition of the audience. There would be opera of all kinds, for all classes, "those with limited means and large families," as well as several kinds of boxes for the rich. The opera house would be financed by $250,000 of stock, of two kinds, selling at $100 per share: one entitled the holder of five or more shares to a seat for each performance, and the other, strictly an investment, would yield a 7 percent return.

Two aspects of this 1851 proposal were new. Opera was explicitly thought of as a commercial enterprise of value to Philadelphia "merchants, hotel keepers and businessmen generally," by helping to attract out-of-town visitors. And, for the first time, Americans addressed the issue of the supply of opera as well as the demand for it. Plucking the chords of memory associated with the academies of Louis XIV two centuries earlier, the opera house would provide for "the establishment of a school of vocal and instrumental music, and for the organization of a corps of competent Professors." Its pupils would prove "useful members of the orchestra and choruses." Someday there might be American-born, American-trained singers.

The proposal moved forward slowly. A site at Broad and Locust streets was bought and a competition held for the best design. The winner was a local architectural partnership whose chief figure was Napoleon Eugene Le Brun (1821–1901), son of a French émigré who had come to America in Jeffersonian times. Le Brun received his architectural training in Philadelphia in the office of Thomas U. Walter (designer of the national capitol) and designed the city's Catholic cathedral at age twenty-eight,

The Philadelphia Academy of Music, photographed about 1857, is the oldest continuously functioning opera house in the country. Free Library of Philadelphia, Print and Picture Department.

the Academy of Music at thirty-three. This design differed in important respects from the original proposal. He reduced the house to a capacity of about twenty-eight hundred and, as one of the economies necessitated by the $250,000 budget given him, emphasized the auditorium and produced an austere (actually unfinished) exterior. He took great pains with the sound. The surface of the walls was kept "soft" to absorb sound and resonance pits were introduced beneath the floor and the stage. The result was much admired then and subsequently.

The interior was in the neo-Baroque style coming into vogue with the Second Empire of Louis-Napoléon. Louis Gottschalk thought it "certainly one of the most beautiful [opera houses] in the world," and a contemporary, present at the opening, described it vividly: "The building is very large and admirably arranged—4 tiers of boxes, an immense parquette, wide corridors, with saloons, dressing rooms for ladies, etc., all richly decorated & furnished. The woodwork is white and gold, the seats all covered with crimson velvet and the walls with crimson paper. It is thoroughly heated & brilliantly lighted. The central chandelier is very beautiful, light, airy, of cut glass, with innumerable burners; it looks like a fairy fabric of gleaming crystal & diamonds."[11] The Academy of Music opened on January 26, 1857, with an inaugural ball.

The first opera was given there on February 25, a work new to Philadelphia—Verdi's *Il Trovatore*. The season included two other Verdi operas, *La Traviata* and *Luisa Miller*.

Whatever the Academy of Music did for the commercial life of Philadelphia, it didn't stimulate a revival of the city's creative musical life of earlier decades. The subscribers turned management over to an impresario, and the terms they fixed for him left no room for imagination—they used their seats or received their dividends and the impresario survived (or didn't) on what was left over. The other fruitful aspects of the original conception also disappeared: there would be no music school and no cheap opera for the people. The atmosphere of the Academy was not socially inclusive. The exception was that applications "on behalf of colored people, asking that a part of the amphitheater be set aside for them" was granted, especially as this "could be accomplished without the slightest interference with any other portion of the house, there being a distinct entrance on the south side." In one respect, however, the Philadelphia Academy of Music was successful beyond the dreams of Napoleon Le Brun, the shareholders, or anyone else. It achieved permanence and exists today as a direct connection with the nineteenth-century operatic past, the oldest opera house in continuous existence in the country.

I n Boston, too, the impetus was commercial. At a meeting of businessmen in 1852 the mayor strongly supported the building of an opera house. "Traveling businessmen, who might otherwise neglect to visit Boston," he said, "would be attracted to the city by the dramatic and operatic entertainment such a theatre could provide and would be likely to remain in the city longer for the same reason." A committee was formed, a site selected, an act of incorporation approved, $250,000 worth of stock issued, shares costing $1,000 each, and a local architect, Edward Clark Cabot (1818–1901), who practiced architecture with his brother and had designed the Boston Athenaeum in 1846, was chosen.

Cabot faced a formidable challenge, an irregular site wedged between the small, obscure Mason Street and "narrow, dirty, mean-looking Washington Street." He resolved it by building a three-story Italianate entrance arch on Washington Street and connecting this to the opera house proper, on Mason Street, by means of a narrow hundred-foot-long passageway. As no one approached the building by way of Mason Street, this allowed Bostonian austerity: "All extravagant expenditure on mere external decoration is uncalled for—architectural display will not be aimed at." Expenditure and imagination were concentrated on the auditorium (modeled on the Bordeaux opera house in France), a three-quarters circle, with three balconies, surmounted by a large dome. The most striking feature was that the depth of the auditorium was no greater than the depth of the stage, which meant that all seats had a good view of the stage. There was open seating everywhere, except for eleven family boxes, each holding twelve seats, located at the back of the parquet and of the balcony above it. The interior walls were red, the balconies and proscenium arch white and gold. A two-windowed clock surmounted the proscenium and the fourteen-paneled dome had twelve brightly colored representations of the seasons, plus Shakespeare and Mozart. Single gas burners and a central chandelier lighted the auditorium.

Steam heating came from a separate building. A New York journalist thought it "a charming opera-house, elegant in its decorations, convenient in all its arrangements, admirable in its acoustics, and probably better provided than any other theatre in the world with entrance halls, dressing rooms, supper rooms, and other adjuncts."[12]

The Boston Theatre opened on September 11, 1854, with a performance of Sheridan's *The Rivals*. Auber's *Les Diamants de la couronne* was the first opera to be given there, followed by *Fra Diavolo* and *The Bohemian Girl*. Ticket prices were very reasonable—twenty-five cents for the top gallery, fifty for the rest of the house, except for the parquet and the boxes. Spoken drama dominated for the first few years, and the hard economic times of 1857 and 1858 made it seem unlikely that the theater would survive. In 1860 the name was changed to the Boston Academy of Music, without even the pretense that there would be any kind of musical instruction, but in 1863 the name was changed back. The theater's fortunes picked up during the Civil War. Opera became established as the house's specialty—but opera offered by touring companies.

L o c a t e d at Fourteenth Street and Irving Place, then a very fashionable neighborhood, the New York Academy of Music was proudly declared by New Yorkers to be the largest opera house in the world, seating forty-five hundred. Designed by Alexander Saeltzer (1814–1883), a German who came to America in 1842, opened an architectural practice, and in 1849 designed the Astor Library, the Academy grew out of the desire of a new and larger group of prosperous, ambitious New Yorkers to efface the failure of Astor Place and to make clear New York's predominance in commerce and art. The Academy had one novel feature: the parquet had no aisles. Seats were entered from the side. Otherwise, Saeltzer sedulously followed the Italian horseshoe pattern. The long, narrow auditorium was twice as deep as the stage. The sound was excellent but the sight lines were terrible. One-quarter of the first tier seats, one-third of the second tier, and many of the side seats in the third tier had a severely obstructed view of the stage. Ventilation and lighting were also poor.

The sedate, restrained Italianate exterior, with Corinthian pilasters marking off a central block with three entrance doors and smaller flanking bays, didn't prepare one for the baroque extravagance of the huge interior. The Academy represented "the glorification of gew-gaw," "possibilities of ornamentation which transcend the wild dreams of the Arabian Nights." A restrained white and gold, the interior depended on form, not color, for its effects. Massive pillars supported each tier, and each pillar was faced with ponderous stucco caryatids, gilt lyres, cherubs. There were fluted pilasters with capitals longer than their shafts, grotesquely twisted pillars flanking the proscenium boxes. Ironically, in later years the Academy came to be cherished by many as a reminder of a simpler, less ostentatious New York, but though many of the Academy's patrons had also been associated with Astor Place's modest coziness, this new house reeked of new money. On the whole, the public liked it. "And why not? Steamboats that cost half a million dollars, lie unnoticed at our docks, and why should we permit ourselves to be excited at the opening of a new opera-house which, after all, is but an exaggerated steamboat saloon."[13]

The Academy's financial arrangements were the old, familiar, and cripplingly restrictive ones: the stockholders' seats were taken entirely out of circulation. In addition, stockholders charged their impresario very high rent—twenty to thirty thousand dollars per year. Inevitably, after its opening with Mario and Grisi in October 1854, the Academy suffered through a succession of failed impresarios. And yet, from the capitalist's point of view, the opera house didn't compare favorably with other contemporary forms of investment. "To sew up gold in a bag, and drop it off the Battery would seem to be as promising an investment as opera-house stock."[14]

As it stabilized its operation in the late 1850s and during the Civil War, the Academy signaled the shape of the plutocratic future. No thought was given to its supposed future as a teaching institution. Opera would be given in French or Italian, never in English, and the necessary European stars would be imported. To pay for them, seats were expensive. The Academy's prices were twice those of the Boston Theatre. "O Maecenac New Yorkers, who boast of the golden patronage you accord to art. What are your titles?" asked Louis Gottschalk. "Is it perchance that usurious enterprise which is called the Academy of Music?"[15]

A Letter from Max Maretzek

To Hector Berlioz, Paris

New York, July 25, 1855

"My Dear Berlioz:—When you take up this letter, open it, and turn to the signature, you will in all probability imagine that you are dreaming." So begins Max Maretzek's *Crotchets and Quavers, or Revelations of an Opera Manager in America.* Published in 1855, the same year as P. T. Barnum's autobiography and Walt Whitman's *Leaves of Grass,* blending the disillusioned realism of the one with the democratic idealism of the other, *Crotchets and Quavers* (English terms for quarter and eighth notes) is in the form of seven letters addressed to celebrated European musical figures. Max understood the cash value of famous European names! Witty, effervescent, one-sided, full of shrewd thrusts at the pompous and self-important, Maretzek's book is exceptionally valuable for its behind-the-scenes explanation of the operatic economic and institutional situation in America at mid-century, and for its description, alternating between hilarity and despair, of the day-to-day madness of an opera company, "children of melody without harmony."

What might have seemed a dream to Berlioz often proved a nightmare for Maretzek. For instance, as soon as he arrived in New York in September 1848, Max went to the Astor Place Opera House to meet the orchestra and chorus he would conduct and the administrative staff he would work with, expecting to find something like the "European school of operatic management." Instead he found virtually no institutional organization but lots of slapdash, "go-ahead-style" improvisation. He didn't find the chorus rehearsing in the opera house at all, but in a room in a nearby warehouse where carpenters were banging away at scenery, chorus women were singing minstrel songs while sewing costumes, and the chorus men were intent on a game of cards. That night he saw and heard at a performance of *Il Barbiere di Siviglia* what he had in the way of orchestra. Signor Lietti, the director and first violinist, led his men by playing more loudly than anyone else, stamping on the floor, and making a series of grotesque grimaces. The instrumentalists, playing with "an extra musical ferocity" that suggested "diabolical possession," sounded like

> a series of saw mills in vigorous operation. Everyone got out of time, everyone felt himself individually called upon to restore order, and confusion ensued: squeaks from the piccolo, loud squalls from the woodwinds, a broadside from the trombones—all seeking a place of

reunion: the screech of the trumpet was no use; the kettle drummer's efforts were no use. At last, struggling and worn out, one after the other, a few completely distanced, the overture was terminated. The audience applauded, and Signor Lietti, by three low bows, demonstrated his intense satisfaction.

Management was equally chaotic. That year Astor Place's impresario was Edward Fry, "evidently a well-intentioned man, my dear Berlioz, and what is infinitely rarer, a well-meaning manager." Unfortunately, he had become embroiled in feuds with his singers, which was not particularly unusual, and with James Gordon Bennett, publisher of the *New York Herald,* who was savage and unrelenting in his attacks on Italian opera. Throughout *Crotchets and Quavers* we get a lively and candid depiction of the rambunctious and often disreputable state of New York journalism. Maretzek's sketch of Bennett, part Satan, part Napoleon, is a brilliant one.

The battles between Fry and his singers were public and perfervid. The company began its season with four weeks in Philadelphia. *Norma,* a work beloved of the Fry family, was announced for opening night. Teresa Truffi, with whom Fry was feuding, and who was to sing the druid priestess, alleged that she was not strong enough vocally for the role. Truffi asked Max to intercede and persuade Fry to pick a different opera. Fry was adamant. *Norma* it would be. On opening night the house was full. The overture was played. The tenor sang his aria. Accompanied by her druidical acolytes, the blonde and bewitching Truffi appeared on stage, to a tremendous reception from the audience, which she received with stately grace. She sang a few notes, staggered, and fell in a faint. Druids, callboys, and Roman soldiers rushed to her. Oroveso brought cold water. Adalgisa applied smelling salts. Pollione called on his Roman gods. The male chorus swore in German. The parquet shrieked, the boxes hissed, and the gallery hooted. Max understood what Edward Fry did not. "A cannon ball cannot be shoved back into the cannon with blotting paper. . . . A prima donna will not sing when her mind is made up not to do so." Fry appeared before the curtain to announce the cancellation of the performance because of Madame Truffi's "sudden indisposition." Had some "hideous nightmare taken possession of my sleeping faculties?" Max wondered. No. All around him was "indisputably nothing but fact." Then how had he got into this?[1]

B o r n Maximilian Mareczek in Brno, Moravia, June 28, 1821, he showed musical talents that were early recognized and encouraged. He studied composition (his opera *Hamlet* received its premiere in Brno in 1842) and conducting, in which he gained experience in Croatia and Bavaria. This secured him an invitation to Paris, where he met Berlioz, Meyerbeer, and Liszt, as well as a group of émigré intellectuals, the Young Hegelians, among whom were Karl Marx, Ludwig Feuerbach, and Michael Bakunin. Perhaps discussion with them reaffirmed in him the belief that opera should be brought within the reach of all people, regardless of class or wealth, an idea he never abandoned. He went to London in 1846 to take part as an assistant conductor to Berlioz, under the sponsorship of Michael Balfe, in a season of English opera. That ended in financial disaster. When William Fry approached him with an offer to conduct in New York, he was at loose ends and the prospect of promoting opera in the

SEPTEMBER 18th AND EVERY EVENING AND SATURDAY MATINEE.

Max Maretzek, best known as an impresario and conductor, composed several scores, including the incidental music for John A. Mack's Baba. *It ran for nearly three months at Niblo's Garden in 1876. Billy Rose Theater Collection, New York Public Library for the Performing Arts.*

open and democratic society there was irresistible. So, at age twenty-six, Max abandoned London for the New World.

It turned out to be the commitment of a lifetime. In the fluid conditions of United States musical life, Max Maretzek became an impresario as well as conductor. The Astor Place riot saddened and shocked him, but didn't change his conviction that there was a hopeful future for opera in America. But one had to be nimble and to improvise. Year after year he traveled throughout the East, went to Mexico City and Havana—wherever he found an audience. The New York Academy of Music became his more or less permanent base as a conductor for two decades. He led the first American performances of numerous major works—Meyerbeer's *The African Woman* (*L'Africaine*), *Rigoletto*, *La Traviata*, *Il Trovatore*, Gounod's *Roméo et Juliette*. As an impresario he was no innovator. He had no interest in opera in English or in Wagner's operas. He continued composing—incidental theatrical music of all kinds, and another opera, *Sleepy Hollow, or The Headless Horseman*, based on Washington Irving's story, produced at the Academy of Music in 1879. It was the early years he described so candidly and amusingly in *Crotchets and Quavers*. His sequel, *Sharps and Flats*, written near the end of his life, lacked the sparkle of his early impressions.

One thing in American culture disturbed Maretzek most—the inordinate use of publicity, as represented by Barnum, a figure who crisscrossed Maretzek's path and who exploited the American eagerness for new experiences. Eagerness, so appealing in itself, easily became gullibility and the acceptance of the fraudulent unless there were established standards and traditions. Maretzek defined Barnum's "humbug" for his European readers as "exhibiting a fly through a microscope and passing it off as an elephant to one who pays." The selling of Jenny Lind had been a searing lesson in the exploitation of novelty. Barnum had merchandised Lind as a curiosity, and Maretzek believed it was a matter of indifference to him whether Lind produced enthusiasm as a "songstress, provided she excited curiosity as angel, woman, or demon." Maretzek admitted that he had once copied Barnum's techniques. Faced with the prospect of being wiped out at Astor Place by the success of Lind's tour, Maretzek fought back by bringing over a rival, a fine artist named Teresa Parodi. He went to work in the Barnum manner, which included bogus anecdotes and stories, "published, admired, and listened to." Parodi had sufficient talent to sustain the reputation manufactured for her and Maretzek's season was successful. But his own success in that line was a disturbing phenomenon.[2]

A m o n g the encouraging and long-lasting developments in the operatic 1850s in America, and one in which Maretzek played an important role, was the popular acceptance of Verdi's operas. The response to them was different from that to composers before him. The usual pattern had been one of predictable stages, from contemptuous dismissal to grudging recognition, then to widespread acceptance, and, finally, general admiration. Not so with Verdi. There had been no protracted delay in performing his operas. *Ernani, Il Lombardi, Nabucco, Attila,* and *Macbeth* had all been heard by the late 1840s. They faced no entrenched opposition. Although Verdi's kind of music drama was harshly attacked and only *Ernani* gained a place in the American repertory, Verdi had enthusiastic advocates from the first and, most remarkably of all, quickly was established as the leading Italian operatic composer. Partly this was because the previous generation of established masters had disappeared. Donizetti had died in 1848, Bellini had been dead over a decade, Rossini had not composed an opera for almost twenty years. Verdi's contemporary rivals, Saverio Mercadante and Errico Petrella (1813–1877), never gained a foothold in America, though the former's *Elisa e Claudio* was performed for a time in the 1820s and 1830s, and the latter's *Ione* excited a brief flurry in the late 1850s. "There is no other composer in Europe so to be depended upon for writing a successful opera at this moment."[3] As the hope of Italian opera and as the subject of contemporary scrutiny, by 1850 Verdi already stood alone.

In the early 1850s came that extraordinary flood of masterpieces: *Rigoletto* (1851), *Il Trovatore,* and *La Traviata* (both 1853). They soon reached America, where they excited vehement enthusiasm and fierce disparagement. Popularity and scorn went together to a degree not seen before and from an audience divided in a different way. The general public was receptive and discriminating opera lovers were hostile. *Rigoletto* came first, in January 1855. The response contained many of the elements which would become familiar. It was greeted as "exceedingly pretty," a fresh and new kind of opera, "a relief after having been satiated for months past with old and hacknied works." But at the same time: "It is poor stuff, and fell dead upon the public ear." "One is not so much deafened with the din of brass and the thunder of drums as one might be led to expect from Verdi's well-known predilection for noise." Surprisingly, few observers recognized that its songs were likely to prove very fetching, let alone among the most popular in all opera. Of "Women are fickle" ("La donna e mobile"): "one of those charming little melodies that linger long in the memory." The celebrated quartet was "as original in conception as it is striking in effect" and no more.[4]

Il Trovatore was first given in May 1855. Few people were restrained in their response. There was "real beauty" in the music, which was of "the well-known Verdi type, aiming at striking effects, and seeking rather to intensify the action than to give a melodious or even natural expression to the words." In terms of dramatic effect, it was "superior to any of the master's compositions with which the American public is familiar." For those who loathed it, the music was brassy, noisy, trite, vulgar. The Anvil Chorus was "about equal to a scene of mending a sewer set to music." Contempt was heaped on the opera's story: "beyond human comprehension," "excessively absurd." "We have many stupid plots in English, varying from weakness to the periphery of idiocy—but none incurably idiotic like the *Trovatore.*" "Fit only for hopeless snobs and imbeciles."[5] But audiences didn't seem to care. With every performance *Il Trovatore* gained in popularity.

In December 1856, *La Traviata* added to the Verdian vogue. Those who disliked it failed to hear its melodiousness. "There are but half a dozen grains of melody to an inordinate quantity of chaff." "The few delicious melodies will become staled with repetition." "Verdi reproducing, or rather redigesting, Verdi; his old effects tried over and over again, as if with a nightmare inability to move beyond them." Many admired it. "Some of the simplest outbursts of the piece are the most touching and overpowering." "The music is fluent and easy, filled with sentiment and passion, eminently natural and simple." "An exquisite vein of sentiment pervades the music, and colors it with sadness and feeling."[6]

La Traviata's immorality disgusted people. The Alexandre Dumas play, *The Lady of the Camelias,* on which *La Traviata* was based, had appalled many. Matilda Heron, an American actress, had caused a sensation in it and had been roundly denounced, but to little effect. "Pieces like *Camille,* can do no good, and may easily do harm." And now here was Verdi's opera, "the perfection of this kind of rottenness, its seductive music casting a spell of sickly sweetness over evil." Violetta, frankly and unashamedly a courtesan, openly lived with Alfredo, defying propriety. Queen Victoria refused to attend any performance. One critic suggested that the moral blindness or indifference of audiences was due to the fact that few people actually knew what was going on. No one was persuaded by this. Quite the contrary. Verdi's "improper opera" met with "complete and humiliating success." It was perfectly clear what was going on and perfectly clear, too, that audiences entered into the "wicked spirit of the play with the greatest possible delight." Any moralist, "viewing the spectacle of keen enjoyment" in the opera house, could have "none but the saddest apprehensions for the future moral prosperity of the audience." As late as 1861 the president of the Board of Directors of the Brooklyn Academy of Music made a powerful speech arraigning the opera's lewdness, when it was proposed that it be given there, and there were ceremonies of protest and resolutions testifying to the opera's unsuitableness for a respectable theater. But Brooklyn yielded in 1862 and "every clergyman within traveling distance was in the house," no doubt to denounce the opera.[7]

Wherever Louis Gottschalk traveled, "the ladies took possession of the theater every time the posters announced *Traviata.*" Max Maretzek noticed the same thing. In Philadelphia and Baltimore, Boston and Havana, he conducted *La Traviata* countless times and all before houses crowded with women. One critic derided the notion that women were endangered by Verdi's music and Dumas's story. Was the life of Violetta "so fascinating and full of happiness," he asked, "that most of the young lady listeners in the parquette are likely to be carried away by it into those paths of Parisian profligacy?" His irony was amusing, but the response of audiences wasn't in the least ironic. The opera produced "sobs, transports, ejaculations at each of the different catastrophes of the drama." Women sympathized with Violetta "as if she were a most estimable and praiseworthy young person." And of course they believed she *was*.[8]

These Verdi operas seemed to many a new kind of opera. They were characterized as essentially "realistic" and brutally and sordidly so. There was carnality and murder in *Rigoletto*. Clara Louise Kellogg, a young American soprano, wanted to sing in it in Boston but was told: "Boston would not have *Rigoletto*. It was considered objectionable, particularly the ending." Two New Yorkers brought a legal action against Maretzek to prevent its performance because it was lewd and licentious, "by its singing, its business, and its plot, an exhibition of opera as no respectable member of the fair sex could patronize without sacrificing both taste and modesty." *Il Trovatore* was derided as "burnt babies and etc.," but it touched elemental feelings. "It was the true Italian model, brimful of passion, crime, intrigue, and murder . . . the exponent of all that is atrocious and extravagant upon the lyric stage." One writer discerned very perceptively what Verdi was up to: "The composition of an entire opera—perfect in every part—the music illustrating the story—always classical, always stirring, always exciting. The story and music are worked up together." Another defined the Verdi style of opera as "Trovatopera." "*Trovatore* is almost the only opera; it stands for all."[9]

L i k e everyone else, Max Maretzek was overtaken by greater events. Lincoln was elected president in November 1860, and in December South Carolina seceded from the union. Most musicians paid as little attention as possible, but for those with ears to hear, an ominous thunder rumbled up from the South:

> Beat! beat! drums—blow! bugles! blow!
> Through the window—through doors—burst like a ruthless force,
> Into the solemn church, and scatter the congregation,
> Into the school where the scholar is studying

People went on as they had before. In January 1861 the Brooklyn Academy of Music opened its doors. In April came word of the firing on Fort Sumter. That night Walt Whitman, who had been at the opera, was walking down Broadway in a state of extreme excitement induced by the melodies he had been hearing. The surging hubbub about him awakened him from his ecstatic state and he learned the news of war:

> Beat! beat! drums!—blow! bugles! blow!
> Over the traffic of cities—over the rumble of wheels in the streets;
> Are beds prepared for sleepers at night in the houses? no sleepers must sleep in
>   those beds.

Would the talker be talking? would the singer attempt to sing?
Then rattle quicker, heavier drums—you bugles wilder blow.[10]

Visiting foreign musicians hastily left the country. Music societies broke up as subscribers and performers went off to fight. Impresarios were driven to all kinds of improvisations. One idea combined novelty with patriotism: arrange debuts of American singers. A handful of American-born singers had already sung in opera in the United States, often under foreign-sounding stage names. A Mrs. Coad sang as Emilia Coadi. We have already encountered Elisa Ostinelli, born in Boston of Italian immigrant parents, in California. The first of the Civil War debutantes was Genevra Guerrabella, who as Genevieve Ward had studied opera in Europe, had sung in Paris in 1859, and now got her American chance, as Violetta in *La Traviata.* Laura Harris was unusual because she didn't feel compelled to change her name, but her career proved a brief one. Virginia Whiting Lorini sang with success in *Norma* and *Lucrezia Borgia,* her name change due to an Italian husband. Two singers who were later to have fine careers also got their chance—Jennie Van Zandt and Clara Louise Kellogg. As a gimmick to increase attendance, promoting American singers was a failure, but it was a start at least, and at last.

Impresarios tried other things as well. There were first performances by unknown composers, such as Errico Petrella, and first performances of unknown operas by very well known composers—Donizetti's *Poliuto,* Verdi's *Aroldo.* Max Maretzek alternated Verdi's *Macbeth* with Shakespeare's. Patriotic stunts were common. When President-elect Lincoln visited New York in February 1862, he attended a performance of Verdi's *A Masked Ball (Un Ballo in maschera).* That night both the "Star-Spangled Banner" and "Hail Columbia" were included in the program, the audience standing and roaring its approval. (An ironic glimpse of the future, this opera about the assassination of a ruler.) At the end of an opera at the Philadelphia Academy of Music, an enormous American flag was brought onto the stage, forming the background for a young woman wearing a scarf of red, white, and blue, who led everyone in singing the national anthem to a tempest of applause, waving of handkerchiefs and hats, stamping of feet and pounding of canes.[11]

The one major success in these early years of the war was *Un Ballo in maschera,* first given in 1861. Listeners reacted in familiar ways. While it was "scarcely likely to obtain the popularity of *Trovatore,*" there was "rare originality" in some of its music. "The composer has sought and succeeded in making his music dramatic—means adapted to ends, with the qualification that the melodies are inferior to his earlier works." "The musician will find much that is excellent, and the public a great deal that is really memorable." It was the "most dramatically consistent of all Verdi's operas, notwithstanding its ridiculous plot."[12]

In the middle of the war "the tide turned, a wave of prosperity that submerged war fears now carried the opera to success, and Max Maretzek was in flood tide at last." Everything succeeded. There was a hectic, almost frenzied determination to be amused, a lot of money in evidence. William Fry noticed it in the new informality of dress, "the free-and-easy air of many men present in frock coats, and shooting jackets."[13] It was harder for "fashionable" society to keep these new-moneyed people out. Novelties succeeded whatever they were. Donizetti's *Don Sebastiano* was repeated nine times. People could afford to be generous. Someone recalled Ferdinand Palmo's earlier services to opera, and a benefit for him was held at the Academy of Music. The war ended on this note, and even Lincoln's assassination dampened things only temporarily. There had been nothing like it since the gold rush.

T h e most important operatic event of the war years came right in the middle, the first performance in America of Charles Gounod's *Faust*. First given at the Philadelphia Academy of Music on November 18, 1863, in German, it was conducted by Max Maretzek in Italian at the New York Academy of Music on November 25. Clara Louise Kellogg was Marguerite, a role she made especially her own until the advent of a greater singer, Christine Nilsson, in the 1870s.

Faust became the most popular opera in America for the next half century, as it also was in England and France. It became the staple of New York seasons: "*Faust, Faust, Faust* carried the season very prosperously," and it spread throughout the nation, like the Verdi operas. *Faust*'s melodies became universally familiar in all the common ways, private and public concerts innumerable, civic occasions. The Soldiers' Chorus was played at the Harvard commencement in 1867, and that was only the beginning. Louis Gottschalk's arrangement of *Faust* themes for six pianos was one of his most popular pieces. It is true that some people at first couldn't hear the melody in it. George Templeton Strong: "The opera has its good points but is, on the whole, a bore. Gounod does his best, but he cannot write melodies, and three hours and a half of unmelodic music are severe." William Henry Fry: "It lacks the indispensable vitality of divine melody." "Strange," "odd," people said. Musicians found it hard to play. Luigi Arditi, the conductor, argued with his orchestra about it. "It will seem almost incredible that the music was not looked upon with any degree of favour," he wrote, "the style and orchestration being so new to them." Arditi added: "I begged them to persevere, assuring them that they would be delighted with the music on a more intimate acquaintance." *Faust* was a new style of opera, a milestone on the road to a different kind of music drama. Gounod treated the voice like an orchestral instrument, and, although there is some florid singing in it, the orchestra primarily carried the melody.[14] Nevertheless, the Germans never approved of it, not so much because of its dramatic and musical limitations, but because a Frenchman had the temerity to set its Goethian story to music.

Faust's appearance marked the end of the second period of American operatic history and opened the next. It was the first great challenge to the popular supremacy of Verdi and, even more, the first of what would be a number of challenges to the supremacy of all Italian opera. In the next period the language of opera would be French and German.

M a x Maretzek championed *Faust* as he had Verdi and the earlier great works of Italian and French opera. His eclecticism as an impresario was held against him by some. "He was inclined to seek success by the art of management rather than by the management of his art." Sometimes, under his leadership and under his baton, "there were unseasonable seasons, and disjointed performances of many old operas and

Competition between opera impresarios in the nineteenth century was spirited and often fierce. This cartoon, entitled "Max Maretzek and Max Strakosch Leading Their Armies of Singers to Battle," appeared in the Daily Graphic *on Oct. 8, 1873.*

some new ones, by companies made up of a jumble of all or some of the materials of companies which had gone to pieces." Max did what he thought possible in the circumstances. And who knew better how odd those American circumstances often were? "He merely could not do what was impossible."[15]

His contribution to opera in America was extraordinary. In 1870 a writer in *Dwight's Journal,* describing the first American appearance of the second Swedish nightingale, Christine Nilsson, contrasted the blazing young star with the "heroic Maretzek," her conductor, "grown gray in the service of an exacting public and spoiled prima donnas." He still had a great deal of nervous energy, disguised, as ever, by a "modest and unobtrusive conducting style." The same writer "could not help regarding the veteran dealer in high art with new respect," by contrast with the often cheap and sordid values of the post–Civil War period. "The failures of Max to get rich out of the magnificent material with which he has been enriching the public these twenty years" seemed ever more honorable "by contrast with the times."[16]

Max Maretzek, in the 1860s, wanted no one's sympathy. He was too busy making music. He had come to America with the idea of making opera available to all, and he had always remained loyal to that ideal, though the American economic system had made it almost impossible to achieve. Of course, it had been exhausting. How could it not be, dealing with musicians, "the most quarrel-some set of beings upon the face of God's round earth!" But he went on, cajoling, mocking, scolding, encouraging, "a man of quick wit and ready information, and as honest a manager as ever served the public." He knew that many rewards would be denied him. He knew that he who sows does not invariably reap the harvest. "Certainly, I scattered the seed but it will remain for another hand than mine, or another time than mine, to gather in the crop. A love for music is a thing that cannot bear fruit the same month in which its seeds have been scattered in the ground."[17]

On he went. Able to sign himself off as he had at the end of *Crochets and Quavers*— "grateful to the public for past kindness, hopeful of future favors"—he might well have signed himself, but was too modest to do so, as

Yours indomitably,
Max Maretzek

Sweet Adeline

She was born into opera. Her baby-sitters were Norma and Amina, Lucia and Leonora. Deposited, night after night, in a safe spot in the wings of Palmo's or the Astor Place Opera House, watching while her mother and father and some of her brothers and sisters sang on stage, "she drank in the Italian melodies that were to come to her as naturally as speech." Then, late at night, when the grown-ups' performance was over and she was taken home and put to bed, she would put on her own show, getting up in an excited state of mind, by the light of the lamp in her room, in her nightdress, barefoot, wearing a cloak of her father's, perhaps a hat and some feathers of her mother's, playing again the scenes she had seen and heard a few hours before, imitating the applause and adulation of the audience, throwing herself bouquets made of crumpled newspapers. Tiny diva!

Even this wasn't the beginning of her operatic life. Her mother, Caterina, a fine soprano, admired in Naples and well thought of by the great Donizetti, had married an Italian singing teacher and composer named Barilli and borne him three boys and a girl. Then Barilli died suddenly. Left to struggle entirely on her own, Caterina soon married Salvatore Patti, a tenor from Catania. Three Patti children followed. With so many children to feed, the Barilli-Pattis sang for their supper wherever they could find it. In 1843 the indomitable Caterina went to Madrid for a season of opera. On the night of February 9 she was singing the title role in *Norma* and her condition may have suggested to the audience that Pollione had given the druid priestess yet another cause for revenge, because Caterina was by then nine months pregnant. At the end of the performance, Caterina felt labor pains begin, was taken to the theater's green room to rest and then home, where Adela Juana Maria Patti was born the following day. The baby flourished, the season ended, the Patti family returned to Italy. Then a great change took place. The Barilli-Pattis emigrated to the United States.

Their move across the Atlantic was connected with Ferdinand Palmo's passion for opera. When his opera house failed, it was taken over by a singer named Sanquirico, who in turn asked his old friend Salvatore Patti to come to New York to sing in the company and to help him run the house. Salvatore apparently didn't hesitate. This New World venture might free him and his *bambini* from the incessant labors of provincial operatic life. Salvatore and Caterina could take leading roles, prolonging their careers. Two of the Barilli children were old enough to take parts and the rest of them, all musical to some degree, would be useful and might make careers for themselves. In late 1844 or early 1845 the family arrived in New York. Unfortunately, things didn't work out as hoped. Even the combined Sanquirico and Barilli-Patti forces couldn't save Palmo's. Undaunted, the two took the direction of the new Astor Place Opera House in 1847, but once more they soon ran out of money and the Astor Place directors turned to Edward Fry and Max Maretzek.

So it was that Adelina, between the ages of two and five, found herself backstage. Surrounded by practicing artists whose examples taught her a great deal about voice production, she received some formal instruction in singing and playing the piano from her stepbrother and stepsister. Mostly, however, she learned by imitation, picking up her parts by listening to them played on the piano while she hummed along. She was an exceptional mimic, with a remarkable capacity for reproducing exactly what she saw and heard, especially her father's gestures and movements—he was thought a good actor. This mimetic ability had its disconcerting side. Her sister Amalia had a fine voice but things didn't come easily to her, and she worked hard, for example, in practicing her trill, repeating the two notes over and over. "Why do you do it like that?" Adelina, age five, asked her sister. "Why don't you trill this way?" And the mite then executed a faultless trill. There seems to have been no resistance among the Barilli-Patti children to musical careers. Adelina never wondered what it was she wished to do. She *knew* she was to be a singer.

Adelina's childish concerns weren't only musical. The Pattis lived in New York on East Tenth Street, next door to the Maretzeks, and the girls of the two families found their amusements when and where they could—skipping rope, playing with dolls, throwing snowballs at the boys. They would occasionally drop by Max Maretzek's office at Astor Place and he would interrupt the stream of visitors, lift up the diminutive Adelina so that all could see her, and tell her to sing an aria, or one of the folksongs Jenny Lind had made popular. (She had of course been taken, age seven, to hear Jenny Lind.) And Adelina would sing, in perfect time and tune, in her childish silvery voice. Then she would be rewarded with some coins and, with her friends, dash out of the building to a nearby apple stand or candy store.[1]

The urge to show her off was irresistible. The Barilli-Patti house was one of the centers of New York musical life. A stream of natives and visitors flowed through it. Marietta Alboni and Henriette Sontag came and no doubt got a chance to hear the little wonder. Once, her mother took Adelina to a hotel to display her talents for Luigi Arditi, the conductor. He remembered it vividly. First Adelina chose a comfortable seat for her doll "whom she told to listen to mamma." Then she turned to Arditi in a matter-of-fact way and asked if he would accompany her in a Bellini aria, which she sang "in a well-nigh perfect manner, without the slightest effort or self-consciousness." On another occasion, Richard Grant White called on Madame Caterina at home and observed a bright-eyed little girl in short skirts who ran in and out and in and out of the room, singing and chirping at her mother, who finally told her sharply either to leave the room or to be quiet. The little girl climbed on the stranger's knee, "swinging one red-stockinged leg as she glanced from her mother's face to mine and sang, like a bird, a little Italian air that I did not know and soon ran away on some childish errand."[2]

Adelina Patti, age ten, pointing to a picture of Jenny Lind.

What was to be done with her? The family's financial situation—Salvatore's efforts as an impresario failing and Caterina's career approaching its end—was precarious. The Jenny Lind gold strike was lost on no one. The urge to show Adelina off transformed itself into a plan to exploit her. She moved from exhibitions among friends to performances for paid admissions, from singing like a bird in the family nest to doing her share, and more, to enrich the family larder. The next few years dissolve into a series of scenes from a prodigy's progress. It isn't certain when Adelina first sang for money. Performances may have gone unrecorded. However, we do know that on November 22, 1851, "Little Florinda," a "musical wonder" of eight years and eight months, performed in New York's Tripler Hall. So small she could barely be seen next to the piano, she was lifted up and put on top of a table, from which position she sang Eckert's "Echo Song" and an aria from *La Sonnambula.* Half a century later, a woman recalled "the perfect coolness and equanimity with which that child stood before a staring crowd . . . and sang with astounding ease and grace."[3] Once started on this path, the prodigy was pushed faster and faster. She sang with her mother and with her sister. She sang alone. She sang with pianists and she sang with violinists. She sang with established musicians and she sang with aspiring unknowns. And she sang with other prodigies. In June 1852 Adelina Patti, Hermine Petit, a nine-year-old pianist, and William Henry Marsh, a four-year-old drummer, united their talents in an orgy of infantile precocity. She sang in theaters, halls, and hotels, in churches and at Niblo's Garden. She sang in Musical Fund Hall in Philadelphia, where Malibran had sung twenty-five years before. Occasionally there would be an announcement in the press, a line or two in a critic's report. She sang and sang, and sang some more, until by age ten she was an experienced performer and was taken on an extended western and southern tour. Glaring red-and-yellow billboards announced "Ole Bull and Maurice Strakosch and Mademoiselle ADELINA PATTI AGED ELEVEN YEARS. THE WONDERFUL CHILD PRIMA DONNA!" (She learned early about top billing.) They gave two hundred concerts. In 1855, 1856, and 1857 there were tours with Louis Gottschalk, as far south as Havana and Puerto Rico.[4]

As she was being exploited, Adelina was petted and spoiled, and this combination produced precocious displays of temper. On one of her family's touring performances of *Norma,* she so misbehaved on stage (as one of Norma's children) that Teresa Parodi, the Norma, stormed offstage and Amalia Patti, the Adalgisa, fainted with mortification. The curtain was brought down while the audience shouted its disapproval. Yet audiences played an important part in encouraging her tantrums. Although Adelina could be induced to sing at almost any time by the promise of a box of candy or a doll or a bird in a cage, she showed an obstinate will when too much was being asked of her. "She hated encores bitterly. When they were called for, she would refuse to give them. The insistence of the audience at last would exasperate her, and she would shake her head vigorously. Thereupon the amused audience would redouble its efforts, only ceasing when she began to manifest anger by stamping her little foot."[5]

Even natural wonders have their limits. At thirteen Adelina experienced trouble with her voice, touches of huskiness and strain. For two years she sang no more, and then her voice was again in perfect order. But her career as a child prodigy was over and it was decided that she should make her professional operatic debut, singing with the full company at the Academy of Music, a nonsubscription evening, the Monday after Thanksgiving. On the night of November 24, 1859, when Adelina Patti sang the title role of *Lucia di Lammermoor,* she was appearing for the first time in her life in a complete opera performance. She was sixteen years and eight months of age.

Adelina didn't find anything very unusual in this. Asked if she dreaded her debut, "she looked up in the most unconcerned manner and replied that she did not dread it at all. She had always known she must make a debut and she might as well make it then as any time. She anticipated it with joy, for she knew she would succeed."[6]

She was right. She succeeded—and more. William Henry Fry, for the *New York Tribune,* noted her astonishing technical facility: "She begins where the best singers

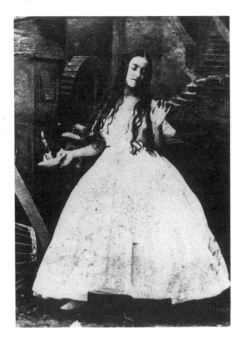

Adelina Patti at sixteen, as Amina in La Sonnambula. *The photograph was taken in 1859, the year of her American operatic debut.*

end. This is saying a good deal, but it is not an over-statement." While overrated singers from Europe, accompanied by "puffs premonitory, puffs contiguous and puffs postcedent," had failed, "Miss Adelina Patti, though an American without a transatlantic puff, though a child brought up in the midst of us, has a positive, unqualified, rich success—because she merited it." Clara Louise Kellogg was unstinting in her praise of what she heard that night: "What a voice! I had never dreamed of anything like. But for that matter, neither had anyone else." Further performances followed, including an unforgettable impression of youthful freshness as Amina in *La Sonnambula.* In Philadelphia the critics hailed the mature artist, not the prodigy, "singing as beautiful as ever fell from mortal lips." At the end of Lucy's mad scene, in *Lucia,* the Academy of Music heard an unequaled shout of enthusiasm. There was less shouting in Boston, but Adelina won that city over, too. John Sullivan Dwight derided New Yorkers for prematurely comparing Patti to Bosio or Lind or Sontag, but agreed that she sang "with an ease, a truthfulness, an artistic finish that astounded and delighted everyone." And in his best Bostonian form, he approvingly noted "the instinct of propriety" which marked her acting.[7]

Adelina Patti dominated the 1860–1861 opera season in Boston, New York, and Philadelphia. Gaining weekly in strength and maturity, as well as in experience, she sang a remarkable number of roles for any young singer, let alone one of seventeen. The Barilli-Pattis were deluged with offers of all sorts. In the winter of 1861 Adelina went to New Orleans, intending to go on from there to Mexico City. Even with war impending, New Orleans audiences exceeded themselves in their enthusiasm. But fear of cholera and the ghost of Henriette Sontag persuaded her to abandon the trip to

Mexico. A splendid beginning had been made, but for anyone aspiring to international fame and to the rewards forthcoming for superlative talent, "abroad" had still to be the plan. As Maria Malibran had realized at the same stage in her career, beginnings were made in America. Reputations were made in Europe.

After her debut in New York, one critic had written that in ten years' time "Adelina Patti will be the greatest of living singers. I wish I was as sure of $10,000 as I am of this fact." Another: "She will go to Europe, where she will undoubtedly receive the honours accorded to Malibran."[8] Dazzling as Adelina's talent was, the road ahead was strewn with pitfalls. London and Paris were crowded with singers her equal in hope, in ambition, in determination. To have an established career in those great capitals in ten years was quite enough. To talk of being the "greatest" seemed Barnumesque humbug. The one certainty was that American operatic life in the 1860s would be much diminished by her departure. Very quietly in March 1861, the young girl, accompanied by her father, sailed for England.

Walt Whitman

Opera's greatest contribution to American culture in the nineteenth century was the poetry of Walt Whitman. "But for Opera," he said, "I could never have written *Leaves of Grass*."[1] Music had awakened Whitman to the true beauty of the world. The music of city life, its rhythm and movement, galvanized his imagination.

> That music always around me, increasing, unbeginning, yet
> long untaught I did not hear

He wanted to immerse himself in living, moving, speaking things. Brooklyn, where he lived, with its immigrants swarming through the neighborhoods, its organ grinders performing in the streets and forming a "profession of street minstrelsy"—Brooklyn was "vocal and instrumental from one end to the other." He found this spirit of movement on unlikely occasions—for instance, interviewing P. T. Barnum. "He told us about his tour through all the capitals of Europe, and his intercourse with the kings, queens, and the big bugs. We asked him if anything he saw there made him love Yankeedom less. His grey eyes flashed: 'My God!' he said, 'no! not a bit of it! Why, sir you can't imagine the difference. There everything is frozen—kings and things—formal, but absolutely *frozen!* Here it is *life*. Here it is freedom, and here are men.'" Whitman concluded: "A whole book might be written on that little speech of Barnum's."[2] One day such a book *was* written—a book of poetry.

The sound of a brass band, "some of the sweetest developments of the divine art," first captured his interest in more formal music. (He couldn't read music and had never received any training.) He liked massed sounds—groups of instruments rather than single ones. Above all, in his early years, he admired the popular vocal groups, the Cheney or the Hutchinson family singers. Their vocal music was fit for "natural man." It was "heart singing," the lusty music of the people, the choral music of democracy.

Opposed to this were the kinds of music he disliked—solo instruments, especially the shallow and tinkling piano, the affectations of the celebrated virtuosos (vocal and instrumental) of the day, with their "art-singing." Walt Whitman (1819–1892) came of age in the crude expansiveness of Jacksonian America, bursting its geographic bonds, conquering Mexico, marching to the Pacific. Art singing was "the stale, second-hand, foreign method, with its flourishes, its ridiculous sentimentality, its anti-republican spirit, and its sycophantic tainting of the young taste of

Brooklyn Daily Eagle.

THE NEW OPERA.—The Italian co. in N. Y. have at last produced their long promised opera of *I Lombardi*, or 'the first crusade,' written by Verdi, and got up theatrically in a very superior manner. Its merits as a spectacle almost equal its qualities as a musical performance—the scenery being very fine, and also superintended by Italian artists, whereat one might imagine some parts of it to be representations of the fair-skied and sunny land. How beautiful, for instance, is that moonlight view in Milan! ..... Beneventano's voice in no previous opera has so fully developed its powers; those powers are indeed wonderful, (there can be but few similar specimens in the world,) and in his bursts of musical furor he seems to possess the ability of drowning the entire orchestra! The music of I Lombardi is written in a substantial manner, and every passing note appears to be governed by a profound knowledge of harmony—the only objection to which is, that it results in something of a heavy style. Rapetti, plays a violin solo in the third act, which alone is worth going from the ninth ward of Brooklyn to hear; and the solo is backed by one of the sweetest songs Barili ever sang. We would advise all who appreciate the inspiration of true music, to go and hear some of the finest chorus-singing, instrumentation, and arias, ever produced in this part of the country.

Walt Whitman in his prime, with one of the opera reviews he wrote for the Brooklyn Daily Eagle *(March 6, 1847). This portrait appeared in the first edition of* Leaves of Grass *(1855), a work infused with Whitman's love of opera. Article courtesy of Cornell University Libraries.*

the nation!" Art singing was old-fashioned, un-American, hindering the growth of something native, hardy. The worst example of this kind of music was florid Italian and French music he heard at Palmo's opera house: "The trills, the agonized squalls, the lackadaisical drawlings, the sharp ear-piercing shrieks, the gurgling death-rattles." He might have been an eighteenth-century Englishman confronted with the Italian opera of Handel's day.[3]

In 1847, the *Brooklyn Daily Eagle* sent him to review opera at Astor Place. He was charmed by the "beautiful instrumentation" of *Il Barbiere di Siviglia* and by the delicacy of some of the musical ideas. He heard *Lucia di Lammermoor* and was moved by the music of the chorus and by the singing of Caterina Barilli-Patti, whose voice reminded him of an "exquisitely played flute, at once dazzling and soothing." He suddenly *felt* Italian opera and he began to revise his views. "Italian opera deserves a good degree of encouragement among us," he wrote, but quickly added, in case anyone suspected he had gone soft, that love of opera need not be "anything to bow down to or servilely imitate." Opera was drama and it touched the understanding as well as feelings. So Whitman heartily approved of its being done in English.

I hear not the volumes of sound merely, I am moved by the exquisite meanings

In the years immediately after his conversion, Whitman heard most of the standard operas of the day—Rossini's *Guillaume Tell* and *La Gazza ladra,* as well as *Il Barbiere,* Bellini's *La Sonnambula, I Puritani, Norma,* Donizetti's *La Fille du régiment, Poliuto, Lucia,* as well as *La Favorite* and *Lucrezia Borgia.* He began to hear "the wild and sweet" melodies of Verdi, first in *I Lombardi* and *Ernani,* then in *Rigoletto* and *Il Trovatore.* And finally Gounod's *Faust.* In these operas the richness of the choral singing moved him. "I listen to the different voices winding in and out, striving, contending with fiery vehemence to excel each other in emotion." He was impressed by the extraordinarily wide range of dynamic effects, from the softest *pianissimo* to the loudest *fortissimo,* achieved with amazing rapidity, as in the Rossinian crescendo. He delighted in the massed power of the orchestra. This quality in Verdi's operas especially delighted him. While others derided Verdi's music as "noisy," Whitman exulted in an almost childlike way in these effects. "And now, a long, tumultuous, crowded *finale* ending with a great crash of all the instruments together, every one, it would seem, making as much noise as it possibly can—an effect which we perceive you don't like at all, but which we privately confess in your ear is one of the greatest treats we obtain from a visit to the opera."[4] It was the "stormy music" of Verdi's "noble" *Ernani* which brought home to him the power of opera to release one's imagination. "With the rise of the curtain you are transported afar—such power has music. You behold the mountains of Aragon and the bandits in their secure retreat, feasting, drinking, gaming, and singing. And such singing and such an instrumental accompaniment! Their wild, rollicking spirits pour themselves out in that opening chorus."[5]

Nothing was lost upon him. In a fever of ecstatic inspiration he drew in the varied influences of the teeming life all about him, politics, literature, music, nature. Everything was absorbed into the great poem fermenting and expanding in his imagination. He was simmering, simmering, he said, and Emerson's essays brought him to the boil. So too was he "fed and bred under the Italian dispensation." And then, "brooding over poems still to come," Walt Whitman was touched by one other influence, "touched and inspired by the glorious, golden, soul-smiting voice of Marietta Alboni."[6]

> The teeming lady comes,
> The lustrous orb, Venus contralto, the blooming mother,
> Sister of loftiest gods, Alboni's self I hear.[7]

In the summer and fall of 1852 and in the winter and spring of 1853, he heard Alboni every time she sang. As the mockingbird's song in "Out of the Cradle Endlessly Rocking" breaks through the boy's reserve and penetrates his innermost soul, mystically firing his imagination, so did the great contralto's song help transform Walter Whitman from the "peaceful child or workaday young journalist he had been before" into a poet.

> The aria sinking,
> All else continuing, the stars shining,

> The winds blowing, the notes of the bird continuous echoing
>
> . . . .
>
> The boy ecstatic, with his bare feet the waves, with his hair
> The atmosphere dallying,
> The love in the heart long pent, now loose, now at last
> Simultaneously bursting[8]

Poetic inspiration is mysterious. The music of the streets or of opera sometimes expressed itself in poems seemingly far removed from the original scenes or sources of inspiration. Sometimes, however, the "recollection of the deep emotion" that had inspired him while he listened to Alboni's singing expressed itself directly. Alboni's singing of Lucia "used to sweep me away as with whirlwinds."

> I see poor crazed Lucia's eyes' unnatural gleam,
> Her hair down her back falls loose and dishevel'd.

Alboni's Norma, that twice-repeated performance never given anywhere else, he remembered for the terrible dramatic power in the scene with the children, "with real tears, like rain, coursing down Alboni's cheeks."

> Across the stage with pallor on her face, yet lurid passion,
> Stalks Norma brandishing the dagger in her hand.[9]

Sometimes, however, nothing came of the original inspiration. Whitman contemplated many projects he never completed: a poem on the power of the human voice, using Joan of Arc and Socrates as examples; a poem about the different kinds of singers' voices, "A Poem of Musicians—tenor—soprano—baritone—basso." Another was a "miniature opera," about western loggers cutting down a tree.[10]

Opera gave Whitman part of his vocabulary. "Music has many good words," he wrote, "of such rich and juicy character that they ought to be taken for common use in writing and speaking." He used these terms—*romanza, cantabile, finale*—in very personal ways, sometimes paralleling their musical meanings, sometimes not. Opera gave him the structure and form of his verse. He confronted that century-long English and American discomfort with musical recitative and arrived at his own mode of combining it with the aria. He called his recitatives "chants." They were his catalogues, his voiced phrases, declamatory passages that conveyed a sense of *movement*. Alternating with this were his songs, long-flowing phrases, lyrical moments of soaring. Whitman's arias have an opening melody, a contrasting section, then a return of the original melody, perhaps somewhat altered. The great challenge was to make these melodies an organic part of the poem. Nature achieved organic wholeness by the infinite replication of patterns. Opera gave him the analogous means—the repetition of melody. Whitman used words like notes. Forty percent of the 10,500 lines of *Leaves of Grass* contain such repetitions. A famous and characteristic example:

I hear America singing, the varied carols I hear,

Those of mechanics, each one singing his as it should be blithe and strong,
The carpenter singing his as he measures his plank or beam,
The mason singing his as he makes ready for work, or leaves off work,
The boatman singing what belongs to him in his boat, the deck-hand singing on
  the steamboatdeck,
The shoemaker singing as he sits on his bench, the hatter singing as he
  stands. . . .[11]

Opera helped Whitman understand the nature of poetry. The poetic act came from
a state of rapture, when the heart had been profoundly touched. Such rapture was
induced in Whitman by the sea, by masses of people, and by the human voice in
opera. In this rapturous state poetry became a universal song, achieving sublime
effects, song surging over the rooftops of the world, understandable by all people, a
rhapsody of brotherhood. It was this that opera represented to him—the possibility
of an art joining, bridging, uniting all things. Opera: the triumph of democracy, the
song of the people.

> O something ecstatic and undemonstrable! O music wild!
> O now I triumph—and you shall also.

T h e most intense and creative period of Whitman's song making ended with the
Civil War. His interest in opera remained keen, however. He kept an open mind about
Verdi's development as a musical dramatist and asked about Richard Wagner's work.
Knowing that these artists must find their own way, as he had found his, he wished
them well. But "it was the old Italian opera which he knew and loved and under-
stood." How grateful he was to singers! Near the end of his life he expressed his
indebtedness. "I should like well if Madame Alboni and the old composer Verdi (and
Bettini the tenor, if he is living) could know how much noble pleasure and happiness
they gave me then, and how deeply I always remember and thank them to this day."
That was 1891. Verdi was just preparing the first performance of *Falstaff,* while
Marietta Alboni was enjoying the placid retirement she had craved. Whitman looked
back at the turbulent, inspiration-filled 1850s with mingled wistfulness and astonish-
ment, those operatic years at Palmo's and Astor Place and the Academy of Music when
he sat, between the acts, writing, altering, adding, expanding his great song. "My
singing years. Oh! those great days! great, great days!"[12]

Monopoly, 1863–1903

On a January evening of the early seventies, Christine Nilsson was singing in *Faust* at the Academy of Music in New York.

Though there was already talk of the erection, in remote metropolitan distances 'above the Forties,' of a new Opera House which should compete in costliness and splendor with those of the great European capitals, the world of fashion was still content to reassemble every winter in the shabby red and gold boxes of the sociable old Academy. Conservatives cherished it for being small and inconvenient, and thus keeping out the 'new people' whom New York was beginning to dread; and the sentimental clung to it for its historic associations, and the musical for its excellent acoustics.

It was Madame Nilsson's first appearance that winter, and what the daily press had already learned to describe as 'an exceptionally brilliant audience' had gathered to hear her singing: "He loves me—he loves me not—*he loves me!*" and sprinkling the falling daisy petals with notes as clear as dew.

She sang, of course, "*M'ama!*" and not "He loves me," since an unalterable and unquestioned law of the musical world required that the German text of French operas sung by Swedish artists should be translated into Italian for the clearer understanding of English-speaking audiences.

—*Edith Wharton*

chapter eighteen

Erie, Eros, and Offenbach

Three developments shaped the history of opera in America in the last third of the nineteenth century: the full flowering of plutocratic patronage of the arts; the rise of popular entertainment; the predominance of German music and musicians. We'll see how these three things twined around each other in the years ahead.

Everywhere the newly rich challenged the older elites for social predominance. There wasn't anything new in this. Though it has been depicted (by the participants as well as by later social historians) as a social drama of epic proportion—the cultivated but exhausted patricians overwhelmed by vigorous barbarians and a tidal wave of dollars—the competing factions in American cities were not fundamentally hostile to each other. They shared basic values: northern European ancestry, Protestantism, a belief in capitalism. The "new" people yearned to be absorbed into the older group; and the "old" money, after some obligatory hesitation and condescension, made alliances and entered into business enterprises with the new. Both groups had come up the same way. In their attitudes toward art, there was little to distinguish new from old. Modest patronage of art authenticated their social position. In this regard the two groups were as one: there were no patricians, only barbarians.

However, some new conditions gave this ceaseless process a special character. The new rich had colossal fortunes, dwarfing those of the past. They were industrialists and bankers, not merchants. They were imbued with a sense of tremendous power, and although they believed in competition and preached its virtues, they also aspired to monopoly. Their children constituted the first leisure class in American national history, revealing new attitudes toward work and art. In Gore Vidal's novel *Lincoln,* Captain Sanford personifies the emerging type: "He hates business. He hates his father. He loves music and when the war is over, he wants to go to Paris and wear a red velvet jacket and compose music." Paris? Music? Red velvet? The captain's prospective father-in-law, puzzled by this trio of terms, couldn't decide "which of the three he liked least— for a young American."[1]

They were blatantly hedonistic and uninhibited in making their pleasures exclusive ones. They built yachts and raced against each other and against the British. They hunted and organized shooting clubs. They played games brought over from Britain—polo, tennis, and golf—on courts and fields and courses reserved for their exclusive use. They bought things: racehorses, pictures, and singers. And they built things which they intended for their exclusive use: racetracks, country clubs, mansions, and opera houses. But public places in a democratic social culture were not easy to keep exclusive, and much of the social history of the time was shaped by these contradictory desires. The younger generation was also freer from sexual restraints than their parents had been. This decline in morals was commonly attributed to the effects of the Civil War. A historian of American music, writing in the 1880s, discerning "the sensuous side of human nature" in contemporary musical culture, blamed the recent war for it and worried that the siren song of the new music would release "the lowest traits of man's animal nature." In America in the 1860s and 1870s, the sirens sang mostly in French.[2]

J a k o b Eberst was born on June 20, 1819, in Cologne, the son of a cantor in the Jewish synagogue. He received some musical training there and, deciding on a musical career, went to Paris, attended the Conservatory, and became an accomplished cellist. All his subsequent musical experience—as cellist and conductor in comic opera—was theatrical. In the 1840s he began composing songs and short pieces for the theater with modest but increasing success, and in 1855 he took over management of a tiny theater on the Champs-Elysées, where he produced farces and one-act and full-length operas. One of these, *Orpheus in the Underworld* (*Orphée aux enfers*), in 1858, made his name familiar throughout Europe. But that name wasn't the one he began with. His father, years before, eager to accommodate to the dominant Christian culture, had changed the family name to that of a nearby German town, and the young man's years in Paris completed the transformation by which Jakob Eberst became Jacques Offenbach.

His operas were like nothing seen or heard before, an extraordinary mixture of cynicism and sentimentality, frivolity, satire, and bawdy sexuality, held together by enchanting melodiousness and the boundless energy of a new dance, the can-can. Incomparable works followed: *Beautiful Helen* (*La Belle Hélène*), 1864; *Parisian Life* (*La Vie parisienne*), 1866; *Blue-Beard* (*Barbe-Bleue*),1866; *The Grand Duchess of Gérolstein,* 1867; *La Périchole,* 1868. All were performed in the musical capitals of the Continent and throughout the provinces. "The Mozart of the *Champs-Elysées,*" Rossini called him, wittily characterizing his cosmopolitanism and his peculiar distinction because, popular everywhere, he was also closely identified with one place and epoch, the Second Empire of Louis Napoléon.

Offenbach's first American audiences, made up of German and French immigrants, heard *The Two Blind Beggars, The Rose of Saint-Fleur,* and his "Chinese" opera, *Ba-ta-clan.* None caused any great stir. More popular were two of his sentimental works: *Marriage by Lantern Light,* given by an excellent cast, including the American soprano Zélie de Lussan, who also sang with Max Maretzek's company at the Academy of Music, and the "tender and expressive," *The Violinist.* German audiences were as receptive as French ones. *Marriage by Lantern Light* had first been done in German, and so had *Orpheus in the Underworld,* which crossed the Atlantic in 1861 as *Orpheux in der Unterwelt.* (It wasn't given in French until 1867.) Almost a decade after he had become the rage in Europe, Offenbach remained a specialized taste and an obscure figure in America.

This all changed in 1867. H. L. Bateman, an American theatrical manager, had gone to Europe in the spring of that year to arrange details for a tour by his actress daughter Kate. While in Paris he saw *The Grand Duchess of Gérolstein,* which had opened in April and become one of the theatrical successes of the century, with Hortense Schneider, as the Duchess, reigning as queen of the European musical stage. Kings and emperors, prime ministers and field marshals, innumerable mere millionaires, musicians, and tourists clamored for tickets. Offenbach's reputation reached its apogee.[3]

Bateman saw the show's possibilities, secured the rights, quickly recruited a strong French touring company, engaged the French Theater in New York City, and sent his company over. They arrived in September. Two weeks later, *The Grand Duchess* made her American debut, five months and two weeks after the Paris premiere, the quickest a European opera had crossed the Atlantic. Opening night was a roaring success, with numerous encores, deafening applause, and bouquets on stage. Even at midnight few people had left their seats. "It sparkles from beginning to end, bubbles over with merriment, carries the audience away by its exhilarating effects and arouses them to enthusiasm." It was quickly reproduced in other forms. "Pianos groan under the digital eulogy of 'Here is my father's sabre,'" and "boarding school misses bawl out 'Tell him,' to their absent sweethearts." Food and clothes were named for it. Grand Duchess waltzes and polkas were danced incessantly, its melodies sung "until the ear was worn to shreds."[4]

The Grand Duchess's mockery of war afforded a release from the memory of the protracted agony of the Civil War. Since the opera's ridicule was safely transferred to a foreign scene in the past, Americans could enjoy the fun while retaining their belief in their Civil War as a sacred struggle. It also released that close-to-the-surface hostility to Europe. In *The Bohemian Girl,* Austria had been a place where the exotic and the silly were combined. But Gérolstein Europe was entirely absurd, its generals and nobility strutting about in a ridiculous manner. Offenbach's mockery of authority of all kinds was very appealing.

The Grand Duchess inaugurated an Offenbach craze. Jacob Grau, a New York impresario, recruited a large company of first-rate French artists, brought them to the United States, and supported them in sumptuous productions of *Blue-Beard, Genevieve of Brabant, Parisian Life.* Between 1868 and 1870 five comic opera companies were performing Offenbach operas at the same time in New York, and there were several in other large cities. New companies, new works, revivals of older works, all followed fast upon each other. "No sooner does some one make a success than a dozen immediately imitate it," an example of "the national vice for running things into the ground." This marked the beginning of a national phenomenon—the rage for comic opera. The other forms of opera and of theater didn't satisfy. When the vogue seemed to be spluttering, a new work or a new singing star reignited it. "Prolonged and heavy feeding" on the music of "the old masters" only made city audiences "long for the fleshpots of Offenbach."[5] *Fleshpots* was the emotive word. His operas became the object of widespread condemnation because of their eroticism. Newspapers and magazines were filled with denunciations in extraordinarily overheated language.

Offenbach was "the half-bestial Pan of Pruriency," the "purveyor of bold, bald indecency." "The mind cannot become familiar with profligacy and indecency without contamination." "The vulgarity of some of the words passes all description." "Grossness which is plainly unfit for the stage." "Insulting to delicate eyes." "Moral filth." "Seduction and passion are not made respectable by the countenance of the Homeric Greeks." "Unfit for the stage." "Effeminate." "The texts are 'filled with indecent innuendoes,' 'the action in places is vile.'" "If an English company should use a literal translation . . . no modest woman could go a second time."[6]

T h e convergence of French filth and "a certain class of new men, suddenly enriched by reckless speculation" was symbolized by the Grand Opera House in New York, a theater specializing in lavish Offenbach production and owned by the most shameless of the new men, "the notorious Railroad Rogue, the wholesale merchant in low art," Jim Fisk. As his carriage came out of his stables on Twenty-fourth Street, drawn by three pairs of perfectly matched black and white horses—in front, two black coachmen in white livery; in the rear, two white coachmen in black livery—there was no mistaking Jim Fisk's checkerboard style or *him,* a smoke-belching cigar in his mouth, rings on his fingers, a huge diamond in his shirtfront, "Jubilee Jim" Fisk, the "modern Henry Hudson," the "Erie King," the "genuine man of the period."[7] His stables cost him ten thousand dollars, and everyone knew it. Nowadays everyone knew what everything cost. That was part of the attraction of things. Jim kept fifteen horses in his stables, as well as six carriages, a phaeton, a barouche, and two clarences (one of them lined with gold cloth). In each horse's stall there was a canary in a cage. In his house he had a caged canary in each corner of every room. Jim Fisk loved canaries. How those birds sang!

He also loved human song and singers. That was how he came to have an opera house. It wasn't originally his. It had been built by another buccaneer, S. N. Pike. He made a lot of money and built it and proudly called it Pike's Opera House, kept it for

Jim Fisk's Grand Opera House in New York, "a huge marble cage filled with canaries," where the spirit of Offenbach reigned supreme. A secret passage led from the auditorium to Fisk's adjoining house, allowing him to go back and forth unobserved.

one financially disastrous season, and then sold it to Fisk, who renamed it the Grand Opera House. A four-story, white-marble palace seating twenty-six hundred, it had a main doorway that opened directly off the street and led into a Pompeian entrance hall with a blue-and-white checkerboard marble floor, walls of highly polished, inlaid black walnut, ceiling of blue, carmine, lilac, and gold, with intertwining green vines, out of which naked cupids and nymphs peeped down at the bust of Shakespeare placed in front of the staircase leading to the auditorium, which was decorated in the same vivid manner. On the ground floor there was a barroom, exclusively for patrons of the opera house, with white marble, mirrors, glittering silver and glass, elaborate frescoes, and gleaming brass. Brass was Jim Fisk's metal.

Behind the opera house were Fisk's stables and a row of houses he owned and in one of which he lived. It had a secret passage connecting it to the opera house so that he could go back and forth unobserved. In one of the other houses Jim installed another of his canaries, Josie Mansfield. Josie was Jim's special woman, but not his only one. At the opera house he surrounded himself with women—actresses, dancers, and singers. Stories circulated: of champagne and pickled oysters from Delmonico's, of naked women cavorting about, of "strange and bizarre scenes," of "the unspeakable realities of the Opera House's off-stage life." Henry Ward Beecher, the most famous preacher of the day, called Jim Fisk "shameless, vicious, criminal, abominable in his lusts." Beecher's words carried weight because he was famous and powerful and because, like other ministers in his day and ours, he knew first-hand about sexual lust.

Jim Fisk made no distinction between business and pleasure. This may have worried his business contemporaries more than anything else about the way he behaved. His peers didn't criticize his sexual immorality much. As to that—who, after all, could throw the first stone? What did disturb some of them was that by mixing together "the ideas of Erie and Grand Opera, of work and amusement, of ballet girls and operatic spectacles, with trains, telegraphs, and time tables," the profitability of the railroad might suffer. It was a bedrock belief that work and play were entirely different things. One Erie stockholder brought suit against Fisk, charging that by debauching women on the premises he was distracting the employees from their business.

Anyway, did the complainant really regard the Erie as primarily a railroad? The Erie! It is a hallowed name in the history of American graft. The Erie: plunder unlimited. It wasn't a railroad; it was a "financial fig tree" to be shaken regularly so that its fruit fell into certain baskets. Jim Fisk was far in advance of his time in many respects. Long before the age of the expense account, he understood the new order of things: work giving way to play, saving to expenditure, scarcity to abundance. Fisk used his opera house as a place for the entertainment of friends, clients, and politicians. Its boxes were shunned by respectable New York society, but they were filled with mayors, councilmen, congressmen, and judges. And more. Ulysses S. Grant, elected president of the United States in 1868, the supreme public hero of the North and West, was entertained by Fisk and Gould when he came to New York. That was Gould's affair more than Fisk's, a part of his astounding effort to corner the gold market. This is not the place to write about the fantastic web Gould, the spider, wove or about what President Grant knew or didn't know. But there, on June 18, 1869, he was, in Fisk's box, watching Offenbach's *La Périchole*. Josie Mansfield sat in her box across the way. Even the brassy Fisk didn't dare take her over and introduce her to the President.

Entertaining the President! What a success story! Jim Fisk left school at twelve, worked in a hotel, and accompanied his father on peddling expeditions throughout New England. At fifteen he worked with a circus, a kind of life he loved. He became a salesman for Jordan Marsh and Company of Boston in 1860 and, guessing correctly that war was coming, persuaded the company to send him to Washington, where he bought blankets and sold them to the Northern government, now prepared to pay almost any price. Fisk the defense contractor: he was bold, he was cunning, and he was sensationally successful. Another battlefield offered greater excitement and re-wards—Wall Street. But there he found himself overmatched. Citizens and civil servants were easy pickings, but "the Street" was crowded with people as unscrupu-lous and clever as he. Jim Fisk lost everything, returned to Boston to borrow money and try Wall Street again, this time joining forces with another New Englander, the experienced, shaggy-browed, piously religious Daniel Drew. Fisk rode Drew's coat-tails from one stock manipulation to another, and this led to Jay Gould and to the Erie.[8]

And to opera. He had a huge marble cage filled with canaries. But what would his songbirds sing? Like so many other self-made impresarios who were not artists themselves, Fisk respected the idea of the "classics." So he subsidized a lavish performance of Shakespeare's *The Tempest* at the opera house. That failed. Then he tried sponsoring a year of opera at the Academy of Music. That failed too. He sent an agent to Europe to bring back a glittering prize—Christine Nilsson. This second Swedish nightingale would enable him to outdo Barnum. Nilsson said no. Anyway, what Jim Fisk really enjoyed about the theater was not abstract prestige but "the organized confusion of the rehearsals, the tantrums and jealousies of the stars. . . . It flattered his ego to be boss over a regiment of performers, stagehands, and musi-cians . . . and to reflect that all this was his."[9] Jim Fisk was not an oddity of his class. He shared its values. Art was a commodity to be owned. In this he was like Cornelius Vanderbilt or Jay Gould, except that he was much more generous with his money than they were with theirs, and he genuinely enjoyed art as they did not. He always wanted the best. If he had Offenbach operas, why not have Offenbach? Fisk, through an intermediary, tried to persuade Offenbach to come to America, but the composer was not (then) interested. Fisk sent Max Maretzek to France to recruit a troupe of French comic opera performers, which was how the Grand Opera House became a center for opéra-comique.

It lasted a very short time. On January 6, 1872, at midday, on the staircase of the Grand Central Hotel, an acquaintance who had quarreled with him about business and about Josie Mansfield, shot Jim Fisk. He died the next day, age thirty-eight. There was a lavish public funeral, which thousands attended. What was it people admired in his life of "half-barbaric prodigality"? Why have people found him interesting enough

Like many another European musician, Jacques Offenbach saw the United States as a land of plenty. This cartoon appeared in the Daily Graphic *on May 11, 1876, the day of his debut at the New York Hippodrome.*

to be the subject of several books? He was genial and generous, admirable qualities at any time, and associated with a lot of money, attractive at all times. Above all, he was no humbug. Many humble citizens, sick of cant, thanked him because he beat rich impostors at their own game, carried on his larcenies without resort to scriptures or hymns, and was free of one prevailing sin—hypocrisy. Those who snubbed him for his vulgarity were quite as vulgar as he. How amused he would have been a decade later when such people built their own opera house, the Metropolitan Opera House, as ostentatious as his but less fun. He expressed an undisguised enjoyment of sensuality in a culture which had severely disapproved of such openness, a cultural transformation at the heart of which was Offenbach's music. Having adored the music, Americans were soon to see the great man himself.

A trip to America? "It's crazy," Offenbach's family and friends all agreed, when he asked their opinion. "What would he *do* there anyway?" His answer: Make money. He had lost a lot of money (more than the family knew) in various theatrical enterprises, and in the 1870s the popularity of his operas was declining. Offenbach felt that such a trip, if details could be satisfactorily arranged, was not crazy at all. It was inescapable. "I would not go to America gladly, but I would go without repugnance." Financed by a rich South American admirer, the tour would include thirty concerts, with a guarantee of a thousand dollars per concert, money deposited in advance in the Bank of France.[10]

So Offenbach found himself, in April 1876, on the *Canada,* sailing west. There were terrible Atlantic storms, and the ship was three days late in reaching New York. He was given an enthusiastic welcome. However, the anxieties he had sailed with wouldn't go away. If anything, the excessiveness of the hoopla about his arrival made them worse. His family had asked the right question. What *would* he do? He was the first famous composer to come to the New World, but Americans already knew his music. He was a conductor. Very well, he could conduct. Wasn't that enough? Clearly these extraordinary people expected something else, something more, something to do with the ideas and feelings his music excited in their hearts and minds, something spectacular and sensational. Offenbach personified certain emotions. Perhaps seeing him would clarify what he represented. Or was it that the Americans didn't themselves know what they expected?

He was in an impossible situation. The first concert made this clear. To accommodate the expected crush of people, it was held in the Hippodrome, a remodeled station of the Harlem Railway. The orchestra was a large one, a hundred instruments, good musicians with an experienced concertmaster named John Philip Sousa. Vast as it was, more than five thousand people filled it, paying a dollar for general admission, five dollars for private boxes. When Offenbach appeared, they all stood and gave him a tremendous ovation. And then? He lifted his baton. There was no puff of smoke. He went briskly to work on the first of twelve numbers on the quite ordinary orchestral program. Disconcertingly, a large number of people left after the first number. Offenbach conducted three more pieces. There were no fireworks. Then he turned the concert over to an assistant conductor. More people left. At the concert's end, only half the audience remained.

Offenbach was crushed. Faced with the repetition of this scene some thirty times, he offered to cancel his guarantee and sail back to France. That was unthinkable. Changes were made. Future programs would be more varied, with soloists brought in to take part. Offenbach would conduct at least half the pieces on the program. Max Maretzek was recruited to conduct the other half. Prices for general admission were sliced in half. The succeeding concerts did well, and they were aided by the publicity generated by a week of comic opera, hastily organized but enthusiastically received, with Offenbach present each evening, bringing in twenty thousand dollars in receipts for the week. Then he went off to Philadelphia to conduct concerts during the Centennial Exhibition. Concluding his visit with a return to New York, for a benefit concert for the musicians' union, Offenbach left in a glow of good will, with not a trace of sulphur in the air.[11]

While in America Offenbach kept a diary, published in France the following year as *Notes d'un musicien en voyage* and in the United States as *Offenbach in America.* It is a shrewd analysis of certain aspects of American culture which intrigued him—technology (he saw Alexander Bell's telephone demonstrated in Philadelphia); food; the tyranny of conventional opinion (a view very like that of his countryman Alexis de Tocqueville); women; manners; the press; the passion for money and for autographs. The book's musical observations, while always polite, made clear his dismay at the artistic barrenness. "So great a people should have every greatness. America should add to its industrial power the glory which the arts alone are capable of giving a nation." He recognized that the entrenched American principle, that "the State should not interfere by giving subventions," was unalterable. Therefore, efforts should be concentrated at the local level, in those voluntary communities which Tocqueville had seen as the glory of American society. "Let private initiative play the protective role in your country which the governments play in Europe." Theaters must be endowed. Academies and conservatories must be established. The best American students should be trained at home. The chief obstacle, as Offenbach saw it, lay in the American craving for immediate gratification. Ten years, perhaps twenty, would be necessary. "But what are twenty years? Twenty years for your students to become masters, twenty years for you to become no longer mere tributaries of European art, twenty years for the theatres of the Old World to come asking you for artists as today you ask them!"[12]

E v e n as Offenbach was visiting America, French comic opera was moving away from the Offenbachian type. The Franco-Prussian War of 1870–1871 ended the irreverent iconoclasm that had been the primary mood of most (but never all) of his operas. Satiric opera gave way to sweeter, sentimental opera, its predominant rhythm languorous rather than vigorous. The waltz displaced the can-can. Offenbach still achieved success that would have been the envy of most composers with *The Perfume Girl* of 1873, *The Creole* of 1875, all the while laboring at his great effort at grand opera, *The Tales of Hoffmann* (*Les Contes d'Hoffmann*), which wasn't performed until months after his death.

New names washed over his. The most important was Charles Lecocq, (1832–1918). His greatest success was *Madame Angot's Daughter* (*La Fille de Madame Angot*), a huge hit in Paris in 1872, quickly exported to the United States, where it succeeded in the big cities and became a staple of touring companies, in the repertory of which it was joined by *Fleur-de-thé,* in an English version called *The Pearl of Pekin.* Other successes followed and established Lecocq as the most popular composer of the 1870s—*Giroflé-Girofla* in 1874, *The Persian Girl* and *The Little Duke* in 1878. At its best Lecocq's music was bright and charming, with a flowing melodic line, united to gentle and untroubled stories. Two contemporary composers loomed very large at the time. Edmond Audran (1842–1901) wrote *The Mascot* (1880), which had many long runs in American cities, as did *Olivette's Marriage* (1879). His operas, too, were pleasantly melodious, emphasizing waltzes and polkas, music of a sweet and sinuous quality. His tunes were easily transferable to the piano, unlike much of Offenbach's music, which was more difficult to play at the right tempo. The single most successful French comic opera came at the end of the decade. This was *The Chimes of Normandy* (*Les Cloches de Corneville*), by Robert Planquette, which ran in Paris for four hundred nights in 1877–1878. Produced in New York within two months of its Paris opening, *The Chimes of Normandy,* often called simply *The Chimes,* did immensely well in New York and other large cities for twenty years, and throughout the country for another forty. "It is doubtful if there was a town of over five hundred people in the entire United States which was not visited between 1880 and 1990 by a touring troupe playing this opera."[13]

The emergence of French comic opera in America should be seen as part of that larger phenomenon, the rise of popular culture. We call it "popular" to distinguish it from the aristocratic art culture, exclusive but refined, and the traditional folk culture, vital but unself-conscious, which had preceded it. Although authorities disagreed about what provoked its appearance and when it appeared—the late eighteenth and early nineteenth centuries seem to be the consensus—there is considerable agreement about the conditions which brought it into being: a greatly increased population (especially an urban one), the spread of literacy, the continuing democratization of social life, the growth of capitalist marketplace values, and the invention of mechanical means for the reproduction of art. And out of popular culture would come the phenomenon of the "mass" culture of the twentieth century.[14]

As opera spread, geographically and socially, it steadily became more popular. But as new social elements were absorbed into the operatic audience, these groups often tried to restrict access to others socially below them or newer than they were. So opera managed to become more popular, while continuing to represent exclusiveness. The middle of the nineteenth century, in America and elsewhere, was a spectacular example of this process. The audience for opera in these years increased enormously. At a time when 30 consecutive performances was remarkable, *The Grand Duchess of Gérolstein* achieved 156. Soon operas and operettas ran for several hundred consecutive performances, and then a thousand or more. The opera audience divided into several specialized ones. The audience for the older kind of opera drew back and responded by trying to make its form of opera more and not less exclusive. The traditional form of opera, much enlarged, became "grand opera," and all the other forms were defined *as simply not opera at all.*

No such term as *grand opera* had been known before the French invented it in the 1830s; or, rather, before it was invented in France by two composers who were Italian and German but who lived in Paris and composed in French—Rossini and Meyerbeer (with Daniel Auber and Fromental Halévy contributing to it as well). Three different but related things, musical and social, were part of it. Structurally, to be a "grand" opera a work had to be in five acts, with an elaborate ballet and with no spoken dialogue—the chief connection with the earlier opera seria. The second feature of grand opera was the romantic desire for the sublime, an aspiration to nobility in tone and treatment and story, producing in the viewer and auditor a sense of moral grandeur. This, in turn, was connected with the third element—grand opera was large in scale, with several leading and numerous supporting roles, a large chorus, a much expanded orchestra, lavish costumes, elaborate scenic effects. Rossini's *Guillaume Tell* established the form and Meyerbeer enlarged it with his massive and spectacular productions, which influenced both Verdi and Wagner in later years.

Grand opera demanded a setting appropriate to its scale and pretensions. The result was the huge opera houses built in the capital cities of Europe and the Americas. The style of singing was adapted to these houses and elaborate rituals of dress and behavior exfoliated to suit them. In the United States, the academies of music were early examples of such operatic palaces, as were Covent Garden, London

(1858), the Vienna Opera (1869), the Metropolitan Opera (1883), and the Chicago Auditorium building (1887). The most famous example, appropriately enough, was French: the Paris Opéra of 1875, which, with its breathtaking grand staircase, its unrelenting elaborateness, and brilliant aura of theatricality, enshrined the idea of grand opera.

Gilbert and Sullivan:

From Gérolstein to Graustark

The fashion for things French was about to come to an end. In the ebb and flow of national musical tides washing over the United States, the next wave originated in England. For the first time since *The Bohemian Girl,* people soon were whistling English tunes, singing English words. The tunes were Arthur Sullivan's, the words William Gilbert's.

William Schwenk Gilbert (1836–1911), the son of a retired naval surgeon, came of a wholly unmusical family. He was educated in an English public school and at the University of London, then worked for a few years as a government clerk and practiced law, but from early on he revealed an inclination for journalism and the theater. He wrote a vast amount of humorous light verse and theater criticism and in 1869 published the *Bab Ballads,* a mixture of satire and nonsense that gained him a modest reputation in the United States. In the 1870s he wrote rhymed theatrical pieces of all kinds—farces, pantomimes, musical sketches, extravaganzas—among the best of them being his parodies of opera and of operatic composers, such as Donizetti in *Dulcamara, or The Little Duck and the Great Quack* and Meyerbeer in *Robert the Devil, or The Nun, the Dun, and the Son of a Gun.* However, Gilbert, contentious, irascible, and counter-suggestible, insisted that his "serious" plays in blank verse were his real claim to theatrical importance.

Arthur Sullivan (1842–1900), by contrast, came from a musical family. His father was a bandmaster. By age eight Arthur could play all the wind instruments in the band and had composed his first piece. He won a scholarship to the Royal Academy of Music and to the Leipzig Conservatory. In England, he supported himself by playing the organ, teaching, composing hymns. He was a man of immense charm. "It was such a relief to find a serious musician who was fond of gambling and horseracing that sporting peers began to feel there must be something in serious music."[1]

In the 1860s Sullivan composed music for two comic operas, to librettos by F. C. Burnand, *The Contrabandista* and *Cox and Box.* The first collaboration with Gilbert came in 1871, a "grotesque opera," *Thespis, or The Gods Grown Old.* It was not a success. So the two men went their separate ways. Then in 1875, Richard D'Oyly Carte, an English impresario, who had seen *Thespis* and discerned that Sullivan's lyrical and vigorous music would be perfectly suited to Gilbert's mordant and equally vigorous lyrics, persuaded them to write a one-act opera to be used by him as an afterpiece to Offenbach's *La Périchole*. In three weeks they produced *Trial by Jury*, an opera without any spoken dialogue, the first successful English opera of that kind since Arne's *Artaxerxes*. It was a decided hit in England but in the United States encountered uncomprehending solemnity. An anonymous reviewer obviously found its subject—a trial for breach of promise of marriage—distasteful and the treatment of the subject even worse, as it presented "a roúe on the bench and a fair plaintiff at the bar, who seems willing to love jury, judge, and everybody else, so that she may secure a verdict." "Without plot or motive," it was "entirely unsuited to a New-York audience of the better class."[2] In 1877 Gilbert and Sullivan produced *The Sorcerer*, which received 175 performances in London but was not sent across the Atlantic. There was thus absolutely no hint of what was to come.

What came next, in 1878, was *H.M.S. Pinafore*. After a slow start, it became a tremendous success in England, and soon numerous unauthorized productions were put on in America. American copyright extended only to work published first in the United States. Otherwise it afforded no protection whatever for foreign authors or composers. A work was available for free-market plunder by anyone who was able to get a copy of the work, and who wished to pirate it. With *Pinafore*, many Americans could and did so. It was first done in Boston in November 1878, a month later in San Francisco, in Philadelphia the first week of January 1879, in New York on the fifteenth of that month.

By the end of 1879, *Pinafore* madness had whizzed from Texas to Montana, from New England to California. The lust to hear and see it was insatiable. New York at this time had twelve major theaters. During the 1879 season each of them played host to a *Pinafore* production. In the spring, three months after its first performance in New York, five theaters in the city (and one in Brooklyn) were performing it at the same time. There were *Pinafore* companies of every kind—English, American, German, black, white, juvenile, professional, amateur. They crisscrossed the country in all directions. What went on in Chicago in 1879 is representative. First given there on January 27, *Pinafore* was performed again by two companies in February, by a visiting company in May, when two local companies also gave it, by two more companies in June, by a German company in July, by the Boston Ideal Opera Company in October and, before the year ended, in the unlikely event that there was someone who had missed it, by two juvenile groups and by two more touring companies.

The popularity of Gilbert and Sullivan's operas was increased by the steady flow of new works from them—as had been true of Italian opera from Rossini to Verdi. Abundance increased appetite. "There is no more reason to fear that the fun and the melody of the authors will fail than that apple-trees will not bear apples." Next came *The Pirates of Penzance*. To forestall the wholesale and high-spirited robbery that had taken place with *Pinafore*, Gilbert and Sullivan decided that the first performance of *The Pirates* should take place in America. They sailed for New York in October 1879. There was a boisterous reception: ships decorated with Union Jacks, bands playing *Pinafore* selections, reporters swarming. The production of *The Pirates* involved unexpected complications. Sullivan carelessly left the score of act 1 behind and rewrote it from memory. The orchestra threatened to strike on the grounds that *The*

Two advertising cards of the 1880s: one for the New York Miniature Opera Company—billed as the "handsomest, youngest, and best juvenile troupe in the world"—in H.M.S. Pinafore, *the other for a brand of spool cotton, using a* Mikado *motif. Sidney Rose Gilbert and Sullivan Collection, John Herrick Jackson Music Library, Yale University.*

Pirates was grand opera and they were entitled to higher pay for playing it! The copying of the score of the overture wasn't finished until the morning of the first performance. Despite everything, *The Pirates of Penzance* was given at the Fifth Avenue Theatre on December 31, 1879, the first world premiere of an opera of importance to take place in the New World. (The first London performance was given on January 1, 1880.)

The audience for *The Pirates* greeted it with "the utmost enthusiasm." The story was "exceedingly droll, full of good points, odd rhymes, and irresistible comic situations." It would have been "impossible for a confirmed misanthrope to refrain from merriment over its incongruous situations, absurd gravity." The chorus of policemen was "the most musically humorous number of the evening." In response to repeated calls from the audience, the author and composer appeared before the curtain. Still, as an early review guessed, it was "doubtful" that *The Pirates* would "be met with *Pinafore*'s reception." After all, what else ever had? In any event, Gilbert and Sullivan had to be alert to protect their property from piratical impresarios. After every performance the music was locked in a safe. Members of the orchestra were offered bribes to lend their scores. Experts in the audience made notes of the melodies. Nevertheless, for a time, Gilbert and Sullivan were successful in foiling the

The Mikado, *first seen in America in 1885, inspired a rage for Japanese art, as well as parodies such as a minstrel show called* The Micky-Doo (1886). *Sidney Rose Gilbert and Sullivan Collection, John Herrick Jackson Music Library, Yale University.*

pirates. They trained and rehearsed three touring companies in addition to the New York one, a lot of work but the source of a great deal of money for them before they sailed back to England in March 1880. In addition, they introduced Americans to the authentic Gilbert and Sullivan tradition, "consistent stylization and artfully conceived stage pictures," something desperately lacking in America, where the innumerable companies took liberties with text and music that would have made "Sullivan weep and given Gilbert apoplexy."[3]

Two years later came *Patience,* a parody of the cult of estheticism associated with Oscar Wilde. Its American production coincided with Wilde's much publicized tour of America, and it was rapturously received among the now considerable body of Gilbert and Sullivan fans, though it was not wildly popular nationally. Gilbert and Sullivan's fortunes reached another climax with *The Mikado* of 1885. While one especially unscrupulous producer had managed to get hold of its piano and vocal score and mount productions in Chicago and New York, these were known to be very faulty, and within a few weeks "a company trained in London to copy with absolute precision the English representation" and with "stage attire of faultless accuracy and uncommon brilliancy" opened in New York. *The Mikado's* exotic locale received much attention, as did the thoroughness of its production, "the unceasing reproduction, by choruses as well as principals, of every known and unknown Japanese gesture and attitude." The "number and splendor" of the Japanese costumes was especially noted. One critic believed the "excellences of the libretto" showed up "the comparative weakness of the music." But if *The Mikado* didn't excite frenzy in its audiences, its success was if anything steadier, more long-lasting even than that of *Pinafore*. It ran for 250 consecutive performances in New York and it produced a rage for Japanese art and for Japanese things throughout Canada and the United States, preparing the way for operas set in Asia—for *Madama Butterfly,* for *Iris,* and for *Turandot*.[4]

Given such success, there was great excitement at the prospect of the first performance of *The Yeoman of the Guard,* October 17, 1887, at the Casino Theatre in New York. Rudolph Aronson, the impresario there, combined resolute efforts to forestall piracy with very effective publicity. With considerable fanfare the score was sent over in bits and pieces—the finale of the second act came first and was put into rehearsal, then part of the first act, then another number from the second, with the manager alone in a position to fit all the pieces of the puzzle together at the end. Perhaps all this raised expectations too high. The yeomen weren't nearly as popular as their predecessors. It may also have been that Gilbert and Sullivan were reaching for something more serious, more complex, than their earlier works. Aronson blamed the comparative failure of *The Yeoman* on its "rather gruesome libretto." After ten years, the fashionable craze exhausted itself with *The Gondoliers* in 1889. If anything, though, Gilbert and Sullivan's general popularity expanded. Their operas reached a wider audience in the moderate-sized cities and small towns of the country, where amateur companies and small touring groups kept them alive for the next quarter of a century and beyond. But the days of national delirium were over.[5]

T h e success of the Gilbert and Sullivan operas was due to a combination of ingredients: witty lyrics, amusingly constructed stories full of twists and surprises, catching melodies, a joyous atmosphere of absurd fun. As always, there were social and cultural factors. Here were operas in a language Americans could understand, no translation, no explanation needed, that also shared in an Anglo-American tradition at least as old as *The Beggar's Opera,* enjoying opera and making fun of it at the same time. Gilbert's librettos showed how "a playwright may begin by making burlesque of opera and end by making opera of burlesque."[6] They also shared attributes that had helped to make ballad opera a popular form. Their scale was modest. A small orchestra sufficed. Vocally, the music was not difficult. Anyone could perform the operas, or at least *try* to. The "patter songs" were popular bits. Operas so effortless and amusing didn't seem like opera at all.

Furthermore, "one of the pleasant facts about the great success of *Pinafore,*" an observer noted with evident relief, is that "success does not depend upon anything doubtful or repulsive." The operas' satire was genial, though cutting, "simple and innocent pleasantry" compared with French comic opera. Everything (almost) turned out happily, the proprieties restored. They were wholly free of erotic suggestion. "The most rigid moralist could no more condemn them—if his scheme of life admitted of any amusement whatever—than he could condemn children at play."[7]

Gilbert and Sullivan were perceived as quintessentially English. In the 1880s and 1890s and after, the unquestioned dominance of Anglo-American culture was challenged by a tremendous influx of immigrants from eastern and southern Europe. The response on the part of the Anglo-American population was a deep longing for things English—English ways, English antecedents, English institutions, English styles. The ancient ambivalence about England, dating from the Revolution—admiration mingled with dislike—now turned into a desire to identify with the "real," the "original" homeland. American colleges were modeled on Cambridge and Oxford. English ancestry became a source of great pride. American literature was once more seen as largely part of an English tradition. No wonder the Gilbert and Sullivan operas struck deep roots in small-town and rural American culture, now itself beginning to feel beleaguered by industrialization and its immigrant labor force, the combination of which threatened the old ways. "Perhaps [*Pinafore*] has just a little higher flavor for us because it is a gay hit at our cousin Bull." The exuberant patriotism of *Pinafore*'s concluding scene was now enjoyed by "the most uncompromising Yankee almost as much as if he had been an Englishman himself," a sentiment unimaginable to Andrew Jackson or William Henry Fry.[8]

> He is an Englishman
>   For he himself has said it;
>   And it's greatly to his credit
> That he is an Englishman:
> For he might have been a Roosian,
> A French, or Turk, or Proosian,
> Or perhaps I-tal-i-an
> Or perhaps I-tal-i-an
>   But in spite of all temptations
>   To belong to other nations,
> He remains an Englishman.

It was all in the family. American and British patriotism were almost interchangeable. An American impresario proposed to Gilbert that he rewrite *Pinafore* as an American opera by changing its location, references, symbols. This would earn a fortune. Gilbert suggested the following.

> He is American!
>   Though he himself has said it
>   'Tis not much to his credit,
> That he is American!
> For he might have been a Dutchman,
> An Irish, Scotch, or such man,
> Or perhaps an Englishman!
>   But in spite of hanky-panky
>   He remains a true-born Yankee,
> A cute American!

Gilbert was assured that New York would go mad over it, but he had seen enough American madness. The "insanity might take unwelcome forms," he responded, and dismissed the project.[9]

T h e r e was a third wave of popular musical theater, coinciding with Gilbert and Sullivan's operas and partially concealed by them. This was central European operetta, "little opera." It provoked neither scandal, *à la* Offenbach, nor frenzy, in the Gilbert and Sullivan mode. Its successes were quiet but its influence, especially on American composers, was enduring. Its most distinctive musical form was an old and familiar one, the waltz. Its language was German and its homeland a city which now displaced Paris, London, and Milan as the supreme musical city of Europe in the American consciousness: Vienna.

The first of these operettas was *Fatinitza* by Franz von Suppé (1819–1895), first performed in America in 1879, followed by *The Queen's Lace Handkerchief* by Johann Strauss (1825–1899) in 1882, *The Beggar Student* by Karl Millöcker (1842–1899), and more Strauss operettas, *The Merry War* and *The Gypsy Baron*. It wasn't until May 1886, however, that Viennese opera established itself emphatically. *Erminie,* music by Edward Jakobowsky, ran in New York for five months, toured throughout the country, and by the end of the century had achieved 1,256 performances. Two other popular successes—*Nanon* by Richard Genee (1823–1895) and *Falka* by François Chassaigne (1850–?)—also turned America in a Viennese direction. Offenbach, Gilbert and Sullivan, were inimitable. Not so Viennese opera. Numerous American composers tried to copy it—*The First Life Guards at Brighton* by J. S. Crossey of Philadelphia; *Deseret* by Dudley Buck of New York; *Elfins and Mermaids* by Charles Brown of Albany; *L'Afrique* by Wayman C. McCreary of St. Louis. All were feeble. Willard Spencer's *The Little Tycoon* of 1886, for which he did book, lyrics, and music, eked out a modest success, and so did Julius Lyons's adaptation of a tremendously popular short story by Frank R. Stockton, "The Lady or the Tiger?"

One American composer succeeded. Reginald De Koven was born in Connecticut in 1859, was sent to school in Germany, and received an Oxford undergraduate degree in 1879. He then studied composition and singing in Stuttgart and Florence, and was a pupil of Richard Genée and Franz von Suppé in Vienna. In 1882 De Koven returned to America, supported himself by writing criticism and composed operas. He attempted to cash in on the interest in the Orient generated by *The Mikado* with a "Hindoo Comic opera," *The Begum* (1887). This failed. But *Robin Hood,* in 1890, was the most successful opera composed by an American up to that point. It was done in the major cities and then taken up by traveling opera companies for several decades. One of its songs, "O Promise Me," for years kept a "vise-like grip" upon the affections of the American people.[10]

T h e career of Rudolph Aronson (1856–1919), the leading impresario of Viennese opera in America, sheds light on its audience. He was born in New York of German immigrant parents, who encouraged his musical interests and sent him to study in Paris. When he returned to the United States, he decided on a career as an impresario and, after several years of observation, gave concrete form to his ideas about new trends in urban amusement in a theater he built on Broadway in 1882.

A new audience, Aronson believed, wanted the glamor associated with opera and opera houses but in a more modest and less inhibiting atmosphere: no tiers of boxes and no millionaire subscribers. And no *cognoscenti* in the galleries. Aronson was after people who were just becoming familiar with operetta, not those who already knew it. His audiences wouldn't see their names printed in the newspapers on opening night in the way the Chicago and New York newspapers printed the names of opera boxholders. All the same, theater going must seem a special event. Aronson named his theater the Casino, after the Newport Casino, then the most fashionable place of its kind in America. He wanted a building that was unusual, perhaps exotic. His architect, George B. Post, gave him a four-story Moorish palace seating three thousand, with a tower on one corner and elaborate "authentic" Moorish decorations on the inside. The theater's most noteworthy feature wasn't its architectural style but its garden. As land was much too expensive for Aronson to build horizontally, the garden was put on the roof of his theater, with tropical plants and colored lights, "a fairy bower with no other roof than the cool starry sky." Another Niblo's. He added another feature. Dining out, a burgeoning part of popular middle-class culture, something no longer reserved for the rich, could be made part of a glamorous evening, so he included a restaurant in his theater. Aronson's Casino marks the beginning of the change in the next few decades from the idea of "society" to that of "cafe society." His audience cared a good deal about dressing stylishly but would not submit to the regimentation of evening dress at the opera. On the other hand, it was distinguishable from an audience at variety or minstrel shows.

Too much formality, too much exclusiveness would have been fatal to Aronson's prospects. The Casino had to be glamorous and up-to-date but affordable for large numbers. Its success depended on the volume of its business. Aronson set the price of orchestra seats at $1.50, the cost of gallery seats at the Metropolitan Opera, and the rest of the seats were scaled down from there. The Casino's uncomplicated program didn't put people off. Productions had long runs so that audiences could get to them at some time or another. Tickets were almost always available. But there was some variety, three or four different productions during a season. In the ten years from 1882 to 1892, the Casino put on thirty-five different operas; 4,305 performances were seen by three and a half million people.

Opera mattered at the Casino, music mattered, singing mattered, but production mattered most of all. Viennese opera, as Aronson understood it anyway, lent itself to elaborate productions and the Casino became famous for the sumptuousness of its presentations. Opulence marked every aspect and the productions were heavily publicized in that regard. Once again, though, Aronson had to steer a careful course between the grand opera house and the lower-class theaters, where spectacular effects were also emphasized. He did so by stressing the authenticity of every detail of Casino productions. This had nothing to do with the authenticity of the text or of carrying out the composer's intentions. Aronson was ruthless in altering librettos to bring them into line with his audience's expectations and wishes. Much that was done at the Casino would strike us now as hopelessly vulgar. For example, the second act of *Erminie,* described as the most ravishing stage spectacle of the 1880s, was a ballroom scene done entirely in pink. The Casino's productions were a kind of fashion show, a way for audiences to learn about the latest styles. This often meant that the production had little to do with the original historical setting of the opera. When Lillian

Lillian Russell, the "ultimate Saxon prima donna," as Offenbach's Grand Duchess of Gérolstein, 1890. Library of Congress.

Russell appeared in a revival of *The Grand Duchess of Gérolstein,* her first appearance on stage was in a scene that Offenbach wouldn't have recognized. The first act was set in winter so that Russell, wearing a magnificent ermine cloak, could come on stage in a sleigh and descend from a hill toward the footlights through falling snow.

Eroticism played a large part in all of this. There was lots of displaying of the female figure at the Casino. Aronson recruited a chorus of young, lithesome American girls. The stories of many of the Viennese operettas often centered on love affairs and all sorts of romantic liaisons, but the eroticism was merely suggestive. Proprieties were maintained, or at least restored by the end of the play. Sexuality might be pervasive but it wasn't scandalous; and sexual love wasn't mocked, as in Offenbach. Even so, a contemporary writer was surely right to wonder "just why the same prudes who railed so vociferously against opera bouffe held their peace with regard to these German efforts." The answer was, no doubt, that twenty years had passed since Offenbach's subversive ridicule of sexual mores burst upon American audiences and that, at the Casino, everything was carefully calculated so that sexuality was part of the theater's aura of worldly sophistication.[11]

As a symbol of desire, no one was comparable to the first great diva of operetta in America, Lillian Russell. The daughter of an editor and of a militant woman suffragist, she was born in Cleveland in 1861. Extraordinary beauty marked her from child-hood. Her parents were quickly aware of it and Lillian's mother, despite her dislike of the exploitation of physical beauty in women, thought her daughter's so remarkable that it was her duty as a mother to raise Lillian with "a full appreciation of her loveliness and a sense of her duty to protect it." Lillian Russell came to regard her beauty as somehow apart from herself, something external and not to be regarded with personal vanity.

She had a lovely voice, a "clear, fully lyric soprano of beautiful quality, but entirely without warmth or variety of color," and in the early 1880s she received voice training from Leopold Damrosch. Nellie Melba, the reigning prima donna of the European operatic world in the 1890s, who much admired Russell, was the prototype of this kind of singer, utterly cool, technically masterful, and this kind of voice, creamy as a violin. After an appearance in *Princess Nicotine,* of 1893, in which Russell sang eight high C's at each performance, seven times a week, Melba went backstage to remon-strate with her: "No prima donna sings fifty-six high C's a week." Russell didn't mind. What a fuss people made about beauty and about art, she seemed to suggest. But it wasn't just her voice and her beauty which people admired. She was without argu-ment the best-dressed woman on the American stage. She took seriously her respon-sibility to be always unblemished in appearance. At rehearsals, she wore substitute gowns of cheaper fabric but identical color so as to suggest the picture she would produce on stage without risking the pristine state of the gowns used in an actual performance.[12]

Lillian Russell was the personification of her audience's dreams, the ultimate Saxon prima donna, matter-of-fact, a no-nonsense performer, who drained the temperament and passion from opera and who served as the object of her audience's desire, a perfect and priceless object.

A s the nineteenth century drew to an end, the popularity of European operetta in America coincided with a tremendous vogue for romantic stories set in exotic foreign lands. The most influential of this kind of novel was English, Anthony Hope's *The Prisoner of Zenda* (1894), a tale set in the mythical kingdom of Ruritania, in which the English commoner, Rudolf Rassendyl, outwits the treacherous Black Michael, who has imprisoned the legitimate king in the castle of Zenda. *The Prisoner of Zenda* unloosed an avalanche of Ruritanian romances in America, written by Americans— Richard Harding Davis's *The Princess Aline*, 1895; Agnes and Egerton Castle's *The Pride of Jennico*, 1898; H. B. M. Davis's *Princess Xenia*, 1899. "Dozens of Danubian principalities, relics of feudal ways, were discovered to lie in the general area of Europe vaguely described as two days distant from London or Paris." The stories, with slight variation, were about a beautiful princess—"a Gibson girl with a crown"— whose rule over her kingdom was threatened by a villainous nobleman and who was rescued by someone who had been "catapulted by some peculiar chance right into the midst of an intrigue." These stories always included scenes set in wild mountain passes and gorges, suitable for horseback chases, and drew on colorful stage props from European history—dungeons and moats, masked balls and quaint Alpine inns. The ending was always a happy one: order restored, the princess on her rightful throne.[13]

In 1901 the United States contributed its variant to the genre, *Graustark* by George Barr McCutcheon (1866–1928), an Indiana farmboy turned newspaper editor. In the first nine months after publication *Graustark* sold 150,000 copies, an enormous sale for the time. McCutcheon had sold his rights outright for five hundred dollars, but profits were so great that his publishers voluntarily paid him 15 percent royalties instead and secured the right to a sequel, *Beverly of Graustark*, which followed soon after. Readers paid McCutcheon the tribute of writing to him to ask directions to the wonderful realm of Graustark.

McCutcheon's twist was to make his hero an American, of an ordinary sort, fresh, clean, young, a believer in democracy and a go-getter, whose modern ideas and energetic ways won out over the plots of decadent, feudal-minded Graustarkians. Also, McCutcheon's hero *married* the princess. Why not? "For is he not an American and is not every American boy a potential ruler, a future President of the world's greatest nation?" And the hero's friend Harry married the princess's lady-in-waiting! George McCutcheon "supplied happiness for many college boys, kitchen maids and daughters of millionaires," which no doubt accounted for the immediate popularity of his novels, but their reflection of certain values in American culture went deeper than that.

We come back, as so often, to the emergence to cultural dominance of the plutocracy of the post–Civil War period. These Graustarkian stories were a way for Americans to come to terms with European culture. They were closely related to, but also different from, the familiar historical novel—such as Charles Major's *When Knighthood Was in Flower* of 1898, set in sixteenth-century England, a bestseller of the time. The Graustark story, while rich in historical props, almost littered with them, was a *contemporary* story. These stories were a way of possessing European culture, and they were, on the surface, admiring pictures of the glamorous artifacts of the European past. But they were, beneath the surface, a highly critical depiction, a way of mocking Graustark, of displacing it—that is, Europe—from its position of inherited superiority. The Graustarkians/Europeans are portrayed as a hopeless lot—corrupt, inefficient, undemocratic, unprogressive, their society on the verge of chaos (dread word for Americans) and ruin. The American hero not only saves the princess but saves the kingdom as well, by reorganizing it. He triumphs over decadent foreign values, over foreignness itself, and over the mortifying hand of the past, over history. A complex and ambiguous version of this story had come some years before, with Mark Twain's *A Connecticut Yankee at King Arthur's Court* (1889), where Merlin, magic, Catholicism, feudalism, and chivalry are all shown up as bogus frauds by the modernizing Yankee, Hank Morgan. Twain's vision was a despairing one. History can't be evaded, it must be blown to pieces, and the end of *A Connecticut Yankee* is catastrophe. But Twain's novel was tragic opera and *Graustark* was operetta.

The readers of these novels of never-never-land were part of the larger audience for popular culture of all kinds, analogous to the larger theatrical audience growing up for minstrel shows, vaudeville, revues, musical comedies, and operetta. This was obviously connected with the increase in literacy and education. Public school pupils multiplied from nine and a half million in 1878 to fifteen million in 1898; public high schools from eight hundred to fifty-five hundred. Public libraries proliferated, too; by 1900 there were more than seventeen hundred. Varied as it was, this reading and theatrical audience shared a great uneasiness about formal "high" culture. Its spiritual spokesman was Andrew Carnegie, the pauper immigrant boy who piled up a colossal fortune, bought a castle in his native Scotland, and built scores of libraries for those like him who wished to enter into this newly accessible world of art, refinement. Celebrating nationalism, Carnegie said: "The sixty-five million Americans of today could buy up the one hundred and forty millions of Russians, Austrians, and Spaniards; or, after purchasing wealthy France, would have pocket money to acquire Denmark, Norway, Switzerland, and Greece." Money would be the means to gain foreign culture. "Once, it was said, admission to society depended on two questions—'Who was your grandfather?' and 'How much do you know?' Now both were replaced by 'How much are you worth?'" But for all its bravado, this audience behaved with the predictable timidity of the nouveau riche. That desire to buy and defy Europe, and at the same time to imitate and defer to it, would shape the future development of American musical theater.

chapter twenty

The Building of the Metropolitan Opera House

A box at the opera. It was the apple of discord thrown among New York plutocrats. It inspired a social comedy of supply and demand. It provoked the building of New York's fifth opera house, a sequence of events that would seem properly to belong to the realm of Gilbert and Sullivan and not to that of historical fact. "A millionairess did not receive the box in which she intended to shine because another woman anticipated her." As a result, "the husband of the former took prompt action and caused the Metropolitan Opera House to rise." As Alexander Pope had observed: "Mighty contests rise from trivial things." Trivial or not, the consequences for opera in America would be momentous.[1]

All through the 1870s operatic affairs at the New York Academy of Music went on much as they had for two decades. Impresarios came and went, nomadic groups of singers appeared on its stage for a few weeks and then returned to wherever they had come from. Despite the fact that no school of music had ever been established to legitimate the Academy's pretensions, occasional American singers, trained abroad, sang on its stage. A fire in 1866 had gutted the auditorium, which was rebuilt on a smaller scale. The years had softened its white-and-gold interior but had done nothing to improve its productions: the scenery and costumes were shabby, the chorus lamentable, the orchestra, despite Max Maretzek's efforts, indifferent.

Nor had the repertory altered much. The once controversial Verdi operas of the 1850s had become the ever-repeated staples of the place, along with a shrinking selection of operas by Rossini, Bellini, and Donizetti, now commonly felt to be hackneyed and threadbare. In 1874 the latest, and it was widely assumed the last, Verdi opera (the Maestro, after all, was sixty-four) was heard for the first time. *Aida* seemed more of what had been heard before, though on a larger scale. Its melodies and opportunities for scenic display were admired but, oddly enough, repeated sporadically over the next decade, it did not gain a stronghold on the audience's fancy. *Faust,* along with an occasional revival of a Meyerbeer opera, alone challenged the Italian hegemony until, in October 1878, Americans saw an opera very different from anything they had seen before on an operatic stage. Georges Bizet's *Carmen* made a powerful impression. Harsh, brutal, shocking—contemporaries were correct in sensing its importance, for it marked the end of operatic romanticism and the appearance of an epoch-making kind of realism on the operatic stage. There was no historical romance about Carmen and none in the impersonation of the role by Minnie Hauk (1851–1929), American-born, who had gone to Europe to learn her trade and had been the first Carmen that London and Brussels had heard. Hauk's voice was small, but she disconcerted audiences with the power of her acting and singing. American audiences, once they got over their shock, responded to the opera's melodic sensuality. Rudolph Aronson, a music student in Paris when he first heard it, thought the melodies "original and characteristic of the Spanish," the fourth act "full of pathos and genuine dramatic power," and rightly predicted a great success for *Carmen* in the United States. By the 1880s it had joined *Faust* as the most popular of modern operas.

Everywhere Italian opera had become so familiar as to begin to seem stale. In American conditions, where many performances were routine and perfunctory, it had almost ceased to exist as music drama and had become an occasion for vocal display when, from time to time, a remarkable singing star appeared, to rouse audiences from this soporific routine. Such was Christine Nilsson (1843–1921), a beautiful woman with a lovely voice and winning manner. Established as a great diva in Europe in the 1860s, she sang first at the Academy in New York in 1870 and quickly established herself there and in Philadelphia and Boston as the undisputed queen of the American

Christine Nilsson as Marguerite in Faust, *1871: the second "Swedish Nightingale." Jahant Collection, Music Division, Library of Congress.*

operatic stage. Marguerite in *Faust* was her most celebrated role. For many she seemed a reincarnation of Jenny Lind, with something of the same cool quality and technical brilliance. But there was nothing of the innocent about Christine Nilsson. It was her glamor that appealed to American audiences in the 1870s, not her simplicity.

Then in 1877 a new and energetic force introduced itself into American operatic life. Col. James Henry Mapleson, an extraordinary character and impresario, brought over a touring company of operatic stars and became the lessee of the Academy of Music. This inaugurated a quarter-century of close connection between London and New York opera. Mapleson's stars excited considerable interest. Increased vigor at the Academy paralleled the astonishing growth of New York. The amalgamation of the various communities into five boroughs in 1869 produced in a stroke a city which, while still less populous than Paris and overshadowed by London, was larger than Berlin, twice the size of Vienna. Manhattan's population alone rose to well over 1.2 million, among them Astors, Belmonts, Vanderbilts, Morgans, Goulds. The possessors of great fortunes, they pushed themselves forward to claim the social rewards their money entitled them to.[2] Their attention focused on the Academy of Music, venerable by New York standards, a symbol of cultural refinement and social standing. The Academy was the hub of the social season and opera boxes were the center of the hub. The Academy had thirty boxes—a substantial number, but if, as Americans unquestioningly believed, growth meant progress, it suffered from the almost irremediable handicap that opera houses are inelastic structures. The Academy boxholders grumbled annually about the cost of their boxes, but the boxes rarely changed hands, and then only within a very limited social circle. New York's plutocracy therefore found itself in an odd position. Musically, it barely supported one opera house. Socially, it needed two.

In the late 1870s, Mrs. William K. Vanderbilt applied for a box at the Academy—and was turned down. When the founder of the fortune, the Commodore, died, he left almost a hundred million dollars to his two sons. Within a decade that had doubled. A vast fortune is not likely to imbue its possessor with so mundane a virtue as patience. It was intolerable to Mrs. Vanderbilt that she could not get what she wanted, so she determined not to tolerate it. Nor was she alone in her frustration. In 1880 a representative of the boxless met with the boxholders of the Academy to make clear their needs and desires. The Academy directors offered a compromise: remodeling the Academy to make twenty-six new boxes available. On reflection the dissidents decided that wasn't enough. For one thing, more than twenty-six boxes were needed to satisfy all the newly rich who craved an opera box, if not opera. And for another, the new boxes wouldn't be in the best location and their occupants would remain a minority.

Bolder steps were called for. Why share someone else's opera house when one might have one's own? Thereupon "a group of Iselins, Goelets, Astors, Morgans and two Roosevelts," and Vanderbilts too, set to work. A site was found uptown, fifty-five gentlemen subscribed ten thousand dollars each, and in April 1880 the Metropolitan Opera and Realty Company was incorporated. A competition was held to select an architect. After the inevitable delays, which led some shareholders to propose abandoning the whole thing, at a meeting in March 1882 the stockholders voted to continue. Slowly the building began to rise.[3]

The winner of the design competition was Josiah Cleveland Cady, who had made his reputation as a builder of Gothic churches, two city hospitals, the main building of the Museum of Natural History, and numerous college buildings. Operatically, his qualifications seemed largely negative. At a time when European architectural training was highly prized, Cady had none. In fact, he had never been to Europe. He had never built a theater. He had never attended an opera. He did, however, play the organ and teach Sunday school. Cady actually drew heavily on the talents of one of the junior architects in his firm, who *had* studied in Europe. Having won the competition, he went to England to look at Covent Garden.

The interest, social as well as musical, of the Metropolitan's owners was concentrated on the interior. The auditorium, seating three thousand people, was enormous, larger than the Paris Opéra or Covent Garden or the Vienna Opera House, a scale proportionate to the money behind it. There was a colossal proscenium arch, flanked by two large paintings, by the American Francis Maynard, called *The Chorus* and *The*

The Metropolitan Opera House in New York, about 1890. Architect Josiah Cady gave the shareholders what they wanted: a "semi-circle of boxes with an opera house built around them." Library of Congress.

Ballet. The waffle-grid ceiling and sunburst central chandelier, elaborately carved gold-leaf box fronts, and wine-colored upholstery exuded an atmosphere of richness, heightened by contrast with the nondescript exterior, "as if one had entered through a labyrinth of narrow tunnels that opened on a sumptuous palazzo." The building's most notable engineering feature was invisible, the exceptional effort to make it fireproof. Its deficiencies were obvious. The sight lines were dreadful. Robert Goelet, whose family were founding stockholders, later wrote that "from the uppermost rows, known as the 'peanut gallery' in common jargon, only one quarter of the seats had a view of the stage." Less visible deficiencies were also serious—a crippling lack of rehearsal space, primitive facilities for singers. So much was unsatisfactory that from the time of the Metropolitan's opening there was recurrent talk about tearing it down. The positive feature was its sound, suited to a powerful ringing voice, though unfair to fine but smaller voices. In any event, such criticisms were of little concern to the subscribers, who didn't sit in the gallery or move scenery.

The Metropolitan Opera House of 1883 was essentially a "semi-circle of boxes with an opera house built around them, a private club to which the general public was somewhat grudgingly admitted." Josiah Cady had given the shareholders precisely what they wanted. There were 122 boxes, seating about 750 persons. By the standards of the late nineteenth century, the proportion of boxes was extraordinary. The opera house built in Toronto, Canada, in 1880, seated 2,000 people and had eight private boxes. The Metropolitan had four tiers of boxes. On the ground floor there were twelve huge boxes, derisively known as *bagnoir* (bathing) boxes, because they resembled immense bathtubs. Above these was the first tier of thirty-eight boxes, the most prized location in the house, reserved exclusively for stockholders. The next tier had thirty-six boxes, also reserved for stockholders. Above this was a fourth tier of thirty-six boxes, most of which were available for yearly rent by nonstockholders.[4]

T h e public response to the building of the Metropolitan affords a revealing glimpse into American social ideals of the time. Back in the 1850s the merchant elites that built the large opera houses in Philadelphia, New York, and Boston were still uneasy about the privilege they claimed, and so they emphasized the extent to which these buildings were intended for the use of the entire community. Whether the stockholders really believed this or were only paying lip service to it, they recognized the power of the older American ideal of social equality and were still fearful of political repercussions if their class interest was too blatantly displayed. But by the 1880s money was thought a rightful basis on which to claim privilege. The builders of the Metropolitan were entirely undeterred by any feelings of guilt or apprehension. They forthrightly reflected the temper of their time and their society, for the general public manifested an extraordinary interest in the actions and values of the plutocracy and apparently approved of its ideals.

In the spring of 1883, the Metropolitan's stockholders and their wives met in the lobby of the still unfinished building to draw lots to determine occupancy of the boxes. Seventy boxes were drawn for, five by members of the Vanderbilt clan. There were detailed and excited accounts in the newspapers, identifying who was present, how the lottery was conducted, and who had won, the entire meeting reported as though it were an important public event, a game, with newspapermen keeping score. And so in a way it was. The justification for plutocratic exclusiveness, frequently made and widely accepted, was that money was ultimately democratic. It was a leveling force, affording access to previously exclusive places for its possessors, a certain means of breaking down class barriers. Yet the Metropolitan Opera House was an entirely private affair, whose members neutralized the power of money they disapproved of. The Metropolitan's bylaws held that "no transfer of stock shall be made except to a person or persons previously approved by the directorate." So far had America progressed from those early nineteenth-century days when theater managers worried about the antidemocratic implications of a few private theater boxes.

In the summer the Metropolitan directors chose Henry Abbey (1846–1896) as their impresario. Abbey was from Ohio, with a varied theatrical background. His chief claim to reputation was his management of the first American tour of Sarah Bernhardt, and he was known for his opulent theatrical productions. It was late to be organizing an opera company, but Abbey set to work with great energy and ambition, if little prudence. His main objective was to find famous singers, and to do this he spared little effort and no money, raiding Mapleson's Royal Italian Opera Company. The great prize—Adelina Patti, the most famous singer of her time—was already under contract to Mapleson, who apparently matched Abbey's offer of an enormous salary if she would leave him and join the Metropolitan.

Abbey got the other reigning diva, Christine Nilsson, and added three very well known singers, Italo Campanini, Sofia Scalchi, Giuseppe del Puente, as well as a young and promising soprano, Marcella Sembrich. His conductor was Augusto Vianesi. Mapleson countered with a company which, in addition to Patti, included three well-known singers: Ernest Nicolini, tenor, Antonio Gallassi, baritone, and a Hungarian soprano who had become a great favorite in America since 1877, Etelka Gerster. His conductor was Luigi Arditi, whose American career went back to the days of the Havana company.

So the battle of the rival companies moved to its climax. On the night of October 22, 1883, while Etelka Gerster sang Amina in *La Sonnambula* at the Academy, Christine Nilsson inaugurated the Metropolitan as Marguerite in *Faust*. People lined the sidewalks to gape at the packed rows of carriages and their glittering occupants. Society was divided in its loyalties. Some decided to stick with the Cuttings and Beekmans and Belmonts, others gave their allegiance to the Vanderbilts, Goelets, and Morgans. Those unwilling or unable to decide were represented by Mrs. Paran Stevens, one of the most energetic social figures of the time, unusual because she actually cared about music, and well known for her "thrifty musicales," who breathlessly divided her evening between boxes at *both* houses.[5]

Nilsson and Campanini were the very ideal of what the Metropolitan subscribers had in mind as opera, but the critics were restrained in their enthusiasm. Nilsson was now well past her prime and Campanini's voice sadly worn. Scalchi sang brilliantly, the production satisfied, bouquets rained down on Nilsson. Gerster was enthusiastically received at the Academy, but her supporting cast was weak. The next night the Metropolitan witnessed the first brilliant debut in its history when Sembrich sang Rosina in *Il Barbiere di Siviglia.* Mapleson's drawing card came later when Patti finally appeared, stealing the limelight for the Academy. Among the operas done at the Metropolitan were *Rigoletto, I Puritani, La Traviata, La Sonnambula, Lucia di Lammermoor, Don Giovanni, Carmen,* and *Lohengrin,* the last two done in Italian. The Academy's offerings were not very different: *Martha, L'Elisir d'amore, Aida, Les Huguenots* (in Italian), *Rigoletto, Faust.* The Metropolitan introduced a novelty, *La Gioconda* by Amilcare Ponchielli (1834–1886), but otherwise it was the same Italian opera New York had known for two decades.

Anticlimax and disaster followed. For the first time in its operatic history New York now had two opera houses and two opera companies, but it became clear within a few weeks that the shareholders of both houses had little idea of what to do with their toys other than to repeat what had always been done. Despite their wealth, the Metropolitan patrons were prepared to support opera only within certain limits: beyond a modest annual assessment to keep their real estate investment in good order, there would be no subsidy on top of their subscriptions.

Unaccountably, Henry Abbey lost sight of these limits. It's true that he found himself in a difficult situation, having to hire an orchestra, chorus, stagehands, scenery designers—all this inventory reverting to the opera house—as well as to pay for the upkeep, which was far more expensive than he imagined it would be. But costs were magnified by Abbey's extravagance. It was said at the time that all the costumes, "every shoe and stocking," came from Worth of Paris. Not so, but they cost a great deal nonetheless. In order to meet his expenses, Abbey set a top price of seven dollars for a parquet seat, with other seats scaled down from there. This made the Metropolitan more expensive than the Academy and far more expensive than opera had been before. Also, pressed for time and desperate to attract stars, Abbey had, in the words of the *New York Times,* "signed all the famous singers in the world for the gratification of the stockholders of the Metropolitan." Musicians realized immediately that they could exploit this competition, in salary and in perquisites. Singers' fees rose dramatically in the next few years. And it wasn't only the singers. The Metropolitan orchestra was hastily recruited from the opera houses in Venice, Naples, and Leipzig, and instrumentalists were paid well by the standards of the time. Abbey was not solely responsible, of course, but he gave a great impetus to a tendency which "demoralized" the prevailing system. The effect was especially felt in Italy.[6]

After the opening-night excitement, attendance dropped off significantly at both houses. Both companies went on tour, to recoup their losses, the rivals crisscrossing each other's paths in other cities, sometimes performing the same operas. Even with Patti, Mapleson suffered serious losses. Because of his greater expenses, Abbey suffered more. By February 1884 he intimated that he would not continue for another season. "The Metropolitan Opera-house season has been financially a disastrous failure," one newspaper reported, pointing out that it would have required sold-out houses for Abbey to make a profit. "But the house is never full and never can be, because there is such a large part of it in which no one can see or hear." Abbey's losses totaled six hundred thousand dollars.[7]

T h e conclusion of this story is as bizarre as its beginning, and quite as comical, though not to Abbey. He was understandably bitter, but put a good face on things. "Naturally, he turned to the stockholders to assist him in his difficulties," one report had it. "It is customary for the stockholders of opera-houses to 'back up' their impresarios." Not so in America, as Abbey surely knew but perhaps couldn't bring himself to believe. The likelihood that the Metropolitan's stockholders would help him out may be judged from the comments one of them made to the press. "Of course we have never pried into [Abbey's] business affairs and we have never asked him how much he has lost or how much he has made out of the opera house. . . . I do not see, however, under the very liberal treatment he has received at the hands of the Directors, how he could have lost much in the opera-house."[8]

The directors spent their time talking about matters which seemed more pressing. They assessed themselves $245,000 as a body to complete the payment for the building and to renegotiate the mortgage. They mulled over whether to repaint the interior (no); whether to carpet the corridors (yes); whether to furnish the ballroom (yes); and what to do about the Thirty-ninth and Fortieth street entrances, which were very windy for people awaiting their carriages (they put in glass doors). Nothing was done about the gallery seating. All through the spring, even after Abbey formally announced his withdrawal as impresario, the directors were loftily unconcerned with a replacement. As compared with the opera house, opera was a relatively minor matter. "Impresarios are as thick as mosquitoes on Sandy Hook."[9]

Despite his own losses, Colonel Mapleson, with characteristic bravado, vowed to continue to battle the Metropolitan "till he was laid beneath the sod." Actually, he had his hands full with a series of acrimonious disputes with the Academy directors. Eventually he worked out arrangements for the 1884–1885 season at the Academy and prepared for battle if faced with a rival.

By early summer the Metropolitan was more or less back to where it had been the year before, with an opera house but no director and no company. Its directors had few choices. One was to rehire Abbey, but they wouldn't accept his new terms and the old ones were poisonous for him. Another was to keep both houses open for use by one company on alternate nights. No one liked this. A third choice was the reverse of what the Academy had proposed in 1880—to combine the two groups and use one house, the Metropolitan. For Academy shareholders, this always broke down on the matter of boxes. An Academy stockholder put it clearly: "What can the Metropolitan Opera house people offer us? They have all the good boxes in the house and . . . do you suppose that they are going to give up those boxes and submit to a new distribution just to oblige us? I don't. . . . It has even been suggested that we might double up and share boxes with them. But every one knows that the dissatisfaction on the first night of a new opera would be so great as to create a split at once. The whole thing is absurd on its face."[10] The Metropolitan directors finally agreed to hire a new impresario.

In one sense, there didn't seem to many shareholders to be a crisis. How could there be when the value of their property was appreciating? The original price of a box was fifteen thousand dollars. After the first year, with the death and withdrawal of some boxholders and the transfer of those boxes to new (and approved) owners, the price of a box had risen to twenty-two thousand dollars. The additional assessment for improvements came to eighteen hundred dollars. Given the sixty-six–performance season, this figured at thirty dollars per box per performance. Even that wasn't what it seemed. One stockholder explained: "I have had no trouble in renting my box for $60.00 a night when I have not wanted to use it myself." Still, it seemed unlikely that the Metropolitan Opera House would last as long as the Academy of Music, and the ghosts of Astor Place and of the Italian Opera House gibbered in the background muttering—*fiasco.*

chapter twenty-one

The Queen of Song

Out of her Welsh castle she came, the most famous singer of the last half of the nineteenth century, perhaps the most famous singer ever. Only Enrico Caruso, of a later day, rivaled her fame. She was coming to sing in the United States for the last time. She had said farewell before—several times before. She may have caught the farewell habit from Ole Bull, the old Norwegian violin virtuoso, with whom she had performed as a child, fifty years before—Ole Bull, who gave "farewells, plain farewells, grand farewells, last farewells, absolutely last farewells and positively last farewells," only to return for another season. As someone said: "He had a retiring disposition."[1] She was now old, old and imperious and hard. She had had a half-century of frantic applause, of bouquets innumerable, of adulation inestimable: but she wanted more. She had made more money than any singer in all the history of European song: but she wanted more. Her acquisitiveness was perhaps rooted in her childhood, when she had been put to work to support her family, singing, singing, singing. She had sung all her life. It was all she knew how to do. Now her voice was an echo of itself, her once effortless breathing laborious, her once faultless intonation wavering. Those who, in her years of glory, had heard that rose-colored, once-in-a-century voice of creamy opulence, grieved at its disappearance; she didn't care. Why did people still flock to hear her, then? She was more than a voice, her appearance more than a musical event. To hear her was a historical obligation, participation in the experiencing of a marvel never to be experienced again. A few people remained who had heard her in the earliest days of her career, and for them perhaps the greater marvel was not what she was now but what she had been. Little Florinda, sweet Adeline, had been transformed into Adelina Patti, the Queen of Song.

When Adelina Patti sailed to England that distant day in 1861, her family's reputation and connections gained her a contract to sing with Frederick Gye's Italian opera company at Covent Garden. London's was notoriously a cold audience and Yankees, even Italo-Yankees, were unknown as singers. Though the chance given her was as likely to produce failure as success, Gye risked little. Adelina's name didn't appear in announcements until four days before her debut. There was no advertising. Nonetheless, spurred by reports of the rehearsals, excitement mounted as the day approached. Gye shared in it. On the morning of May 14, he urged a friend to come that night. "A little girl is to sing Amina [in *La Sonnambula*], and I shall not be surprised if she makes a big hit."[2] In all the storied history of nineteenth-century operatic debuts, that chain of triumphs and sensations, nothing was more dazzling than that night, a growing wave of electricity ending in vociferous applause and recalls. By the afternoon of the next day, all seats for Adelina's second performance had been sold.

Adelina Patti appeared at just the right moment. The torch of genius was passed on. When, later that season, she sang Zerlina in *Don Giovanni,* she appeared with Giulia Grisi, whose last opera season this was after twenty-seven years. When she sang Rosina, in *Il Barbiere,* Mario sang Almaviva. Within two years she captivated Paris and her London appearances had become "Patti Nights," when the fashionable world came to pay her tribute. And pay it they did. Prices were raised on those nights. Despite the presence of numerous other singers of great ability, the era was the Reign of Patti. Her preeminence can be glimpsed in one memorable scene. In November 1868, Rossini died in Paris. His funeral was a solemn tribute of respect. Selected to sing at it were Marietta Alboni and Adelina Patti. Standing hand in hand, they blended their two marvelous voices together, moving this congregation of the famous and worldly to tears.

Patti's Italian visit in the 1870s provoked comparisons with Malibran. People came from all over, packed the hotels, slept in the streets and public places, paid exorbitant prices to stand in corridors and lobbies to listen even when they couldn't see her. But nothing compared to Russia. "It is worth ten years of one's life to be a favorite for one night in St. Petersburg."[3] She remembered evenings when she was brought back so frequently for curtain calls that she had no strength left and was obliged to sit on a chair on stage while the audience went on roaring.

R e p o r t s of all of this came across the Atlantic, in newspapers and journals, excited word-of-mouth descriptions from the favored few who could hear her in Europe.[4] Twenty-one years Americans waited. It seemed unlikely that she would ever return to where she began. And then, with almost no warning, in 1881, she came on a concert tour, suddenly dropping down goddesslike out of the clouds. Patti in America. At last. And that was followed by her operatic season with Mapleson at the Academy in 1883–1884, the first of her nationwide tours, as though inspecting her realm in its entirety, the diva traveling in a regal style appropriate to her majesty.

Across the countryside she swept, her railroad car emblazoned with large letters on its side. The walls of her suite were of embossed leather and cloth of gold, her monogram interspersed among the decorative flowers and musical figures. The saloon of her car was furnished in pale blue plush. Her bedroom was of inlaid satinwood with mirrors, a bath, electric lights, a piano. She was accompanied by a maid and chef. In Cheyenne, Wyoming, the legislature adjourned and chartered a special car to meet the Patti party sixty miles outside the city and escort her into town, where an army regiment in full dress greeted her. In Salt Lake City she had lunch with Brigham Young and was invited to sing in the Tabernacle, never used for such a purpose before. In Burlington, Iowa, hundreds of citizens came to the railroad yards to see the train. In such out-of-the way places, when the company put on a performance, Patti didn't sing—it wasn't in her contract—but people could at least catch a glimpse of the royal presence. In Texas, she noted that "the natives turned out of their huts to stare."[5]

On to exotic Mexico, people in picturesque sombreros and striped blankets, women with roses in their dusky hair, warm balmy nights, orange trees and palms. In Mexico City the reception was overwhelming. People pawned jewelry to buy the outrageously expensive seats. Audiences were sophisticated, critical. Patti was adored. President Diaz gave her a solid gold crown and ruby-and-diamond earrings. California was "radiantly green and lovely," Los Angeles a delightful surprise, "a little town of such beauty almost impossible to describe." The "Patti epidemic" reached frenzied levels in San Francisco. Crowds stood through the night to buy tickets and thousands were turned away, despite the best efforts of Colonel Mapleson, who packed so many people into passageways and aisles that he was cited by the fire marshall and fined seventy-five dollars. When Mapleson paid, the judge, "evidently a lover of music," accepted payment in the form of tickets.[6]

In 1887 her farewell tours began. In 1888 she embarked on her most far-reaching expedition, through South America and then back to the United States. After that she didn't come back to the U.S. again until 1894, and then one genuinely final goodbye in 1903–04, at age sixty-one. She left from where she had begun, New York. A few friends assembled to see her off, back to her castle in Wales. Adelina Patti's voice, in

Adelina Patti, caricatured by Puck as "The Everlasting Prima Donna." Her farewell tours were legion. Music Division, New York Public Library for the Performing Arts.

quality and durability, was one of the most extraordinary in the history of song. There has never been a singing career of more unbroken success over an extended period of time, especially remarkable when one recalls that she began as an infant prodigy, with all the risks that entailed. Her European career deserves closer study. In it one can trace important institutional changes between the 1850s and the end of the century.

She began in the old atmosphere of court opera. Kings and emperors vied to show her favor. For almost twenty consecutive years, Victoria commanded her presence at state concerts. Napoléon III and Empress Eugénie attended her performances, led the applause, bestowed those signs of personal favor she preferred to anything else—diamonds and emeralds. Emperor Franz Joseph took care not to miss a Patti performance in Vienna, while Kaiser Wilhelm I in Berlin, anxious not to be outdone, congratulated her in person each time he heard her sing. And then there was the special friendship of the imperial family in St. Petersburg. "Do you remember how the dear old Empress used to make tea for me between the acts? God bless her! and that grand old gentleman, the Czar, who used to let me call him 'papa.' Ah, me! How I shall miss them both. They were so dignified, and yet so gentle with little me."[7] Little me indeed.

In other ways, however, her career was a very contemporary one, that of a modern-day figure, a calculating goddess of song. Money was part of her appeal, part of the fabulous aura encircling her. The more money she made, the more she was admired. How much she made became common knowledge, printed in the newspapers, a badge of distinction more comprehensible to many than the older honors and rewards of royalty. When Christine Nilsson led the way in the 1870s by raising her fee to a thousand dollars a performance, Patti insisted on being paid more, even if only slightly more. The Italian tour shattered previous standards. Patti doubled her fee, then tripled it. Impresarios readily, if not happily, met her demands. She was a money-making machine. She was the first prima donna to be interviewed by newsmen, an American innovation unknown in Europe until then. Fee inflation also meant that those bonanza lands, the Americas, had to be mined much more systematically.

One can trace these changes in Adelina's personal life. In the late 1870s she separated from her French husband, the marquis de Caux, who had taken a dim view of the vulgar commercialism of the middle class and saw the court as the sole remaining refuge against it. (He had been an equerry to Napoléon III.) Adelina united her fortunes with Ernest Nicolini, a French tenor, who took a very different view of these things. Nicolini moved Patti beyond the court circles of London and St. Petersburg. Had it not been for him, she might never have returned to America. Nicolini hired a business manager to handle Patti's affairs. The marquis had thought the United States the barbarous America of European tradition. Nicolini didn't care about that. He knew how much money was to be made. He must also have sensed that the enormously larger audience represented by operetta and comic opera could be reached, not in the opera house but in the concert hall. Adelina Patti virtually invented the concert tour for singers.

Her conquest of that market, however, was neither untroubled nor easy. Season subscribers often were philistines who didn't care about opera, but they were dependable. The box-office public was whimsical and capricious. It couldn't be commanded into the concert hall but had to be coaxed and enticed. Patti was suppliant as well as diva. Thus her first return to America, in the spring of 1881, was a clumsy and ill-prepared foray. It wasn't clear to her and Nicolini that they *must* prepare the way. It was a concert tour, without publicity. The seats for the first concert had a ten-dollar top price—and this was resented. Receipts from it were only three thousand dollars. The next concert took in only a thousand. Patti was faced with a wholly unfamiliar situation—failure. There was a change of strategy. Prices were cut. She sang a concert for charity (Americans liked that). More important, she and Nicolini realized that a concert tour was premature. For all her fame, Patti had to establish her operatic presence in America first. A hastily improvised, brief season of opera was put on. The level of support and production was so shabby as to be laughable. Patti returned to England unhappy and frustrated.[8]

She came back in the fall of 1882, in the hands of Colonel Mapleson, who had waited a long time to have Patti's name and reputation in his opera company, and was prepared to make the most of his chance. When the steamship *Servia* sailed past Fire Island in October, the necessary reception was ready: boats, fireworks, military bands, midnight serenades outside her hotel, reams of publicity. This was Patti's *real* return. Mapleson presented her in opera, and with first-rate singers to back her up. One memorable performance of Rossini's *Semiramide* drew fourteen thousand dollars. Success was contagious. Patti sang at the Cincinnati choral festival, which immensely boosted her midwestern operatic tour. Mapleson and she had now found the key, and they emptied the vaults.[9]

This was the background to Mapleson's battle against the Metropolitan in 1883 and 1884. He publicized the fact that he was paying Patti five thousand dollars per performance. That alone proved her worth as compared with Nilsson, and it helped solidify her position as the reigning American singer and not just someone with a European reputation, however grand. While critics were frank in pointing out that her voice had lost some of its incomparable qualities, American audiences were madly enthusiastic. A young girl remembered her in *Martha.* "Her birdlike trills evoked scenes of wild enthusiasm, and mountains of bouquets were heaped round her diminutive form."[10]

Now the ground was prepared for her "farewell" concert tours. The programs got shorter as her prices went up. Everything was spelled out in the contract she presented to her sponsoring impresarios. She would appear twice on a program and only twice. She would deliver one encore after the first section and one only; two encores after the second section, and two only. Her programs were printed with the encores included. And her fee had to be paid in cash, and to be in her hands before she would appear.

Colonel Mapleson recounted the diva's implacable ways. In Boston she was to appear in *La Traviata.* Her agent called to collect the five thousand dollars due her. The Colonel, "in low water" just then, inquired at the box office, found that he was a thousand dollars short, and offered four thousand to the agent, who declined the money and announced that the contract was now broken. (This left the colonel to reflect that though he no longer had Patti, he did have four thousand dollars.) Two hours later the agent reappeared in Mapleson's office. An uncharacteristic concession from the Queen? Not exactly. Patti had decided not to break the contract. She would appear at the theater on time, in costume, and ready to go on—except for her shoes. When the balance of the money came in, she would put on her shoes and sing. Mapleson, abandoning the tempting dream of giving up all this nonsense, handed over the four thousand dollars. That evening things went as proposed. Patti arrived at the theater. The box office opened. Eight hundred dollars came in. Mapleson sent it to the diva. She put on one of her shoes. It was now curtain time. Another two hundred dollars came in. Mapleson sent it on. Patti put on her other shoe, went on stage, and, "her face radiant with benign smiles," sang brilliantly—as always.[11]

These rewards were achieved at an extraordinary price. "Such a life! Everything divided off carefully according to regime:—so much to eat, so far to walk, so long to sleep, just such and such things to do and no others! And above all, she allowed herself few emotions. Every singer knows that emotions are what exhaust and injure the voice. She never acted; and she never, never, felt."[12] Clara Kellogg was incorrect in saying Patti never "felt," but she had little feeling left over for others and she was utterly without sentimentality. She separated herself from all her numerous family, left her mother behind in America when she went to England and never brought her over. Her father, who accompanied her to England, opposed her first marriage and was thereafter cut out of her life. She was indifferent to her siblings.

J u s t as Adelina Patti represented the prima donna as a monster of egotism, so too, musically, she symbolized the contemporary system of Italian opera in its most trivial and intellectually contemptible form. She symbolized singer's opera, the operatic production as a vehicle for individual proficiency at the expense of dramatic coherence. Certainly the young Patti accepted that view, because it was the only one she knew. Once, in the early 1860s, she was invited to sing at one of Rossini's celebrated musicales. With youthful bravado she sang Rosina's "Una voce poco fa" for the maestro, embellishing it with so many interpolations of her own that even the imperturbable Rossini grew sarcastic: "By whom is this aria that you have let us hear? I know perfectly well that my arias must be embroidered; they were made for that. But not to leave a note of what I composed, even in the recitatives—really, that is too much!"[13] Her talents were best revealed in comic opera, where her natural sense of impudence and her gift for mimicry often gave dramatic life to the character she was playing. Even those impersonations were self-contained creations. She had little concern for visual or dramatic ensemble. The prima donna seized center stage and did everything in her power to rivet the audience's attention on her alone. She dressed in the most splendid gowns, whatever anyone else wore. In her last appearance in *La Traviata* she had many of her vast array of diamonds dismounted and embedded in a corsage which gave off a blaze of light rivaling the Covent Garden chandelier.

Well, one might say, those were the prevailing notions of the time. Patti was no worse than others. True. But she was more important because she had the power, and the talent, to have been better, to have been other. And she understood very well that other ideas were current and gaining strength. After all, her career actually falls entirely within the period of the mature Wagner and Verdi, of Bizet, when Patti opera was already recognized as anachronistic. She performed into the time when conductors were taking into their hands the power to subdue errant tenors and sopranos and to introduce dramatic sense and order. No wonder the kind and pliant Luigi Arditi remained her favorite conductor. He represented the old order as she had known it since childhood. And at its worst, at its most petulant and egotistic, her attitude was destructive because so influential. From early on she either refused to rehearse with other singers or, if she did so, hurried negligently through her part. Quickly established as a major personage, she stipulated in her contracts that she would not rehearse unless she wished to do so. She often sent her manager or agent to walk through her part. And of course there were lots of people who encouraged her, flattered her, thought such behavior proper for a diva.

We have a brilliant and amusing commentary on, and counterpoint to, the Patti years in the wonderful music criticism of George Bernard Shaw. A famous proponent of Wagnerian music, Shaw for a quarter of a century explained and expostulated, mocked and scorned "the miserable decay and extinction of the old operatic regime" under the sway of prima donnas such as Patti. Shaw's aim, he insisted, was not to kill Italian opera, "for it was dead already," but "to lay its ghost." Patti had never sung any of Wagner's music, though she had been tempted by the role of Elsa in *Lohengrin,* and she insisted that Wagner had written Kundry in *Parsifal* with her in mind. But she would not sing Wagner and called it "too much screeching," just the sort of thing anti-Wagnerians loved to hear. It endeared her to them, but swelled the contempt Wagnerians and a younger generation of modernists felt for her.

So imagine the amazement of all when, in 1894, Shaw described what it was like to see Wagner's name cropping up on a Patti program, "like a modest crocus among those of a Mozart, Rossini and other contemporaries of Madame Patti's grandmother." There it was: "Madame Patti—Adelina Patti—the Patti—the lady who used to appear and reappear as Rosina in *Il Barbiere* at Covent Garden until the old regime died of it," singing Wagner. She sang Elsa's prayer from *Lohengrin* and one of Wagner's songs. And she sang both beautifully, not because of her fabled voice, for by this time, in her early fifties, little remained of that, but because she was capable of intelligent musicianship, bringing to Wagner the great tradition of Italian bel canto. Shaw and others were more exasperated than amused, however. The lesson that Wagner's music was as singable as Rossini's came twenty years too late—for Wagner, and for Patti. One could only lament the singer Patti might have been, "though the world has been at such pains and expense to spoil her for the last thirty-five years."[14]

Against this view there is another, the view, surprisingly, of Verdi, who had first heard Patti in her second season in London, in 1862, in the glorious freshness of voice of those first years of her fame. He was charmed by her. "Dear little Adelina," he wrote, or, occasionally, "naughty little devil"—for he saw at once her failings, and no one had more ferociously attacked singer's opera than he. But Verdi *heard* something else. He heard a singer capable of coloring her voice to convey dramatic mood and feeling, to reduce her audiences to tears by voice alone, since her acting gestures and movements were conventional. Verdi expounded Patti's virtues to his acquaintances for years before Patti sang in Italy, and said "I told you so" for years afterwards. In the words of Vincent Sheean: "The Verdi soprano, that passionate but lyrical heroine of everything he wrote in maturity, owes something to Patti: at least, after he heard Patti, he realized that the kind of artist he had in mind really did exist." Might it be that in playing the role of the imperious Queen of Song, Adelina Patti extinguished a greater artist, one equal to that fabulous voice itself?[15]

Adelina Patti was as international as opera, as cosmopolitan as her exact contemporary, Henry James. She spoke English with no trace of an American accent but occasionally used American idioms. Born Italian, claimed by the Spanish, she loved France best of all, lived most of her life in England, married two Frenchmen and a Swede. What did America mean to her? Identified though it was with a life of toil, exploitation even, "it was of the early days in America that she liked best to speak," of Tripler Hall, of Astor Place, the many vanished places of her extraordinary childhood where her parents planted opera in a strange land.[16]

Famous. Rich. Was she content? Her first marriage had been a miserable one. The dozen years of her second were the happiest of her adult life. In 1898, after Nicolini's death, she remarried—a Swede, Baron Rolf Cederstrom. She was fifty-six, he in his thirties. He forced Patti to separate from many of her former friends. She spent most of her time in the Welsh castle. A small theater had been built for her there, and in it she found pleasure. But everything performed in it was mimed. After sixty years of song, it was a relief for the nightingale to end her life in silence.

Leopold Damrosch and the Triumph of Wagner

German musicians had been important in American musical life from colonial times, and by the early nineteenth century the German music teacher was a familiar figure everywhere. The first operatic stirrings came in the 1840s, in the shape of "loosely formed, often leaderless companies of men and women, usually amateurs, who possessed at best a certain amount of talent and good will, but who had, as a rule, little experience, little money."[1] In New York, one such group took over the Franklin Theater, put on Weber's *Preciosa* and also introduced America to the works of Johann Nepomuk Nestroy (1801–1862), whose tuneful music and parodies of Rossini, Meyerbeer, and Wagner were very popular in Germany. Their crowning achievement was that symbol of cultural nationalism, *Der Freischütz,* in German, with an orchestra of thirty and local singers. Like the French efforts in New Orleans, these performances were an attempt to strengthen German community identity, so seats were cheap, fifty cents, to attract as large an audience as possible. By 1855 there was enough support to put on a German season at Niblo's—with the "aristocratic" idea of season subscriptions, of which there were three hundred—but there was no reason to suppose that this pattern of modest growth would change.

Events in Europe soon transformed the American situation. Growing discontent with authoritarian governments throughout Europe exploded in the revolutions of 1848. The German states were the center of the turmoil. In the harsh repression which followed, liberalism was crushed. The bloodshed and fighting and the desire for political freedom led thousands of Germans to flee their homelands. Between 1846 and 1855 more than one million Protestant and Catholic Germans came to the United States. They settled everywhere, especially in the cities of the East Coast and the Midwest, Louisville, Cincinnati, St. Louis, Milwaukee. And this was only the beginning. Between 1830 and 1920 six million Germans, 50 percent of all German emigrants, came to the United States. Until well into the twentieth century Germans constituted the largest ethnic group in the country.

The social composition of this vast migration was as important as its size. A large number of them were middle-class, journalists, scholars, shopkeepers, artists, lawyers, doctors. All shared in a rich cultural heritage, which included an interest in literature and the arts, a lively ability to argue, and an urban orientation. Therefore, they quickly made their presence felt. Some entered state and national politics (a good number taking up the cause of the antislavery Republican party of the 1850s). Many went into business. Pride in their language—"the German language in its purity and nobility"—and a desire to introduce it to Americans ran through all their efforts. They published newspapers, magazines, books, and pamphlets in German and established a chair of German languages and literature at Columbia University. They founded German-language schools, benevolent societies, athletic clubs. In New York they founded a German hospital, a German orphan asylum. They opened an art gallery and, in 1855–1856, held one of the first important American shows of European paintings.

In response to all this the Germans were met with fear, bigotry, and hostility. This was the common pattern of the history of immigration to America, though it differs appreciably from what one might call the Statue-of-Liberty notion, now so widely disseminated, which insists that immigrants, on stepping ashore, found brotherhood, liberty, and a warm welcome from the natives. In fact, the relationship of ethnic groups to one another in American cities was always tangled and complex, and frequently explosive. The Germans had to deal with outbursts of violence as well as innumerable routine unpleasant incidents in schools and at work. Religion and economic exploitation played an important part in this. The Germans immediately came into conflict with the Irish, into whose neighborhoods they commonly first moved and who were the backbone of some of the xenophobic groups which mushroomed in the fetid atmosphere of national politics in the 1850s. Racist feelings were also an element in this fearful brew. The Germans were singled out because they often identified themselves with the abolition of slavery, again enraging the Irish, who were antiblack and proslavery. The Germans also attracted hostility because they were so forthright in the pride they took in their cultural traditions and because they asserted themselves without deferring to the established groups and ways. As early as 1840, for instance, some thugs attacked a group of Germans who were serenading Fanny Elssler outside her hotel. And as though this weren't enough, the Germans looked with undisguised scorn on the prevailing prohibitions against public amusement and entertainment. As a German woman in Philadelphia said: "They do not love music, oh no! and they never amuse themselves—no! and they have no ease, no forgetfulness of business and of care—no, not for a moment."[2] The Germans favored Sunday performances, combined theater and concert going with beer drinking, and opposed blue laws. So they managed to affront a powerful coalition—Protestants, Puritans, prohibitionists, and philistines.

Their numbers, their confidence, their success in business and politics carried them through the difficult 1850s, a critical decade for German-Americans. Germans inundated American musical life. They organized singing groups and choral societies, orchestras and quartets. Within two decades at least one hundred German singing societies were dispersed throughout the country, thirteen of them in New York. This tidal wave angered and frightened other musicians. Hearing a military band in 1863, Louis Gottschalk sourly asked: "Is it necessary to say that it is composed of Germans (all musicians in the United States are German)?"[3] The Germans steadily took over orchestras and bands. The three leading orchestras—in Boston, New York, and

"Fanny Ellsler's [sic] Last Serenade." Lithograph by H. R. Robinson (1840). This attack on the dancer's admirers by a nativist gang was symptomatic of the anti-German feeling of the time. Library of Congress.

Chicago—were dominated by German musicians, so too the orchestras in Philadelphia, Pittsburgh, Baltimore, Cincinnati, Washington, Buffalo, St. Louis, Indianapolis, Cleveland, Kansas City, San Francisco, usually conducted by Germans or by Americans of German descent.

By the time of the Civil War, German operatic culture was solidly established within the German-speaking community. In 1854 the Bowery amphitheater had been converted into a place appropriate for sung and spoken drama. It was called the Stadt- (City) Theater, and there the Germans "presented as well as they could a replica of what took place in the theatres of the fatherland." In 1864 a new Stadt-Theater was built. "Simply but tastefully decorated," it seated thirty-five hundred. In April 1859 Carl Bergmann conducted *Tannhäuser* there, and *Lohengrin* followed in August. The demands of these works far outstripped the resources available to him. The performances were hardly noticed at the time outside German circles and were subsequently forgotten, Bergmann receiving no credit for his pioneering vision. In 1862 a company under the direction of Karl Anschutz (1818–1870) gave a remarkable season of opera in German. Chorus and orchestra were local, the singers came from Germany. There were no stars among them, but they were serious artists with considerable operatic experience. Business arrangements were secondary to musical ones. The conductor, not the impresario, assumed the leading role, one of the first American instances of this slowly evolving idea. Anschutz's conducting and direction of the company were a revelation, *Fidelio* and *Der Freischütz* performed in an atmosphere authentically German, "almost as if assembled in Vienna, Berlin or Dresden," said William Fry, who was there.

Another notable feature of this season was the performance of four Mozart operas. No American opera company had attempted this, and a later historian wrote with impressive understatement: "We must look far in our history to find so wholesouled a devotion."[4] The Stadt-Theater's audiences heard *Le Nozze di Figaro, Don Giovanni, Die Zauberflöte,* and the first American performance, on October 10, 1862, of *Die Entführung aus dem Serail.* The following year this company took over the Academy of Music for a season, further evidence of their growing support and confidence, adding Otto Nicolai's *The Merry Wives of Windsor* and Friedrich Flotow's *Stradella* to the repertory. The regular stockholders and subscribers at the Academy were not likely to have been troubled by this challenge to their prevailing notions about opera or to conventionally performed Italian opera, since German audiences played no role in fashionable society. Even more interesting is that no one understood the significance of Carl Bergmann's efforts, in 1859, to awaken audiences to the crucial importance of the emergence of the operas of Richard Wagner.

W a g n e r ' s operas entered American life through the concert hall and bandstand. In 1848 a group of twenty-five young orchestral musicians from Berlin, calling themselves the Germania Musical Society, came to the United States "to further in the hearts of this politically free people the love of the fine art of music." They gave concerts up and down the East Coast and eventually settled in Boston, where they supported themselves by touring and by accompanying famous visiting soloists such as Jenny Lind, Ole Bull, Henriette Sontag. By the time they disbanded in 1854, they had given more than nine hundred concerts. One member of the Germania was Carl Bergmann, the first important champion of Wagnerian music in America. Born in Saxony in 1821, he had originally intended to be a schoolmaster, but decided instead on a professional musical career. His political views brought him to the United States, and once here he limited himself to conducting. He had a fine ear, was intelligent and discriminating. His gestures as conductor were graceful, without affectation. "He beat time for his band and not for the audience."[5]

Bergmann championed the music of his generation, of Robert Schumann (1803–1856), Franz Liszt (1811–1886), Hector Berlioz (1803–1869), and Richard Wagner (1813–1883), as much as that of the composers of the generation or two before, Haydn, Mozart, Beethoven, whose music was now coming to be thought of as belonging to the "classical" tradition. Bergmann's insistence on giving new music a hearing was complicated because in Europe Beethoven was recognized as the culmination of this tradition, but in America his music was only beginning to become familiar. New music would have had a difficult time anyway, but in this situation emphasis was understandably given to establishing the central tradition. Yet here were younger composers insistently knocking on the doors of concert halls demanding admittance.[6] It would be misleading to pick out Wagner's music and emphasize its reception apart from that of the other "modernists." John Sullivan Dwight reflected the prevailing view in attacking Bergmann for forcing upon audiences "the mad musical monstrosities of Berlioz, Liszt, and Wagner." Such criticism didn't deter Bergmann. When told that people in his audiences didn't like Wagner, he replied: "Den dey must hear him till dey do."[7] And hear him they did. Bergmann led the Germania in a performance of the overture to *Tannhäuser* in Boston in 1853, played it in New York in December of that year, adding to the program vocal selections from *Lohengrin,* arranged for orchestra, and the overture to *Rienzi,* Wagner's third opera.

Despite the proselytism of Carl Bergmann and other German émigrés, many Americans regarded Wagner's music as bombastic and lacking in melody. This parody of "the Music of the Future" appeared in the Daily Graphic, *Feb. 16, 1876.*

Nor did Bergmann work alone. Theodor Eisfelt, German-born and -trained, who came to the United States in 1848 and eventually became the New York Philharmonic's first full-time conductor, also introduced some of this new music.

The most common response, initially, to Wagner's music was to complain of its difficulty and melodic barrenness. A Cincinnatian denigrated the *Rienzi* overture as "very much like the performance of a brigade of bedlamites in a rolling mill with a nail factory attachment." More common was the characterization of the *Tannhäuser* overture, when the New York Philharmonic first played it in 1855, as interesting "more in the difficulties presented, than in those qualities which awaken interest or sympathy." Henry Timm, an émigré German musician, recalled the first American performance of the *Tannhäuser* overture he played in: "Some of the violin-players complained bitterly of the fatiguing accompaniment of the Pilgrim Chorus theme. They thought it more than human nature could stand." When William Fry first heard a complete performance of *Tannhäuser,* he objected to its "commonplace" libretto and "stupid and crazy" plot, then listened carefully to the tenor's song to the Morning Star and the Pilgrims' Chorus, and denounced them as unmelodious. Wagner's operatic efforts were doomed to failure. "The composer who is not able to scatter with prodigal hand melody, melody, melody, had better not essay opera."[8]

Wagner entered America via the printing press as well as the concert hall—an intense and protracted battle of words about his operatic ideas. It was a curious situation. As early as 1853, *Putnam's Magazine* had detected the important role words would play in the Wagnerian debate. "Herr Wagner, the musical revolutionist in Germany," it reported, was trying to establish the idea that "the words are as essential to an opera as the music."[9] In America, the argument wasn't focused on the librettos of the operas, since they weren't available in translation for many years, but then the operas weren't being performed anyway. The argument centered on Wagner's words *about* opera, in his prose books, among them *The Work of Art of the Future* (1849), *Opera and Drama* (1851), and *A Message to My Friends* (1851). Not that many Americans had actually read the books. In 1875 a selection of his writing was published in New York entitled *Art, Life and Theories of Richard Wagner,* but it wasn't until 1892–1900 that William Ashton Ellis translated and published, in London, all the major Wagnerian works, in seven volumes. The first English biography had appeared in 1872, the first American one, Henry T. Finck's *Wagner and His Works,* two volumes, in 1893. By then the war was over, though skirmishing went on for years. The source of the battle of words about Wagnerian music drama, for Americans, was all second-hand—English and French reports of German events, extracts from journal articles, bits and pieces of gossip, musicians' comments, word of mouth.

For thirty years, critics on both sides of the Wagnerian firing lines blasted away. The consequences of this curious warfare were important in shaping the American response. Wagner's name was associated with a philosophical debate about ideas. Confused and puzzling and ignorant as that discussion often was, Wagner was identified with something *profound*. Who had ever associated Italian opera with ideas or with a philosophy of art? But the primacy of words before music wasn't just a consequence of a lag in translation and in operatic performance. It was also a consequence of Wagner's way of proceeding. He spelled out his ideas in his books and pamphlets before his music dramas were performed, before they had even been composed. Though *Tannhäuser* and *Lohengrin* and *The Flying Dutchman* (*Der fliegende Holländer*) included elements of his theories, they were traditional in form. The revolutionary nature of the music drama of the future was to be revealed in the Wagnerian works yet uncomposed. What presumption! And yet, from *Tristan und Isolde* (1859), through the four operas of *The Ring of the Nibelungs* (*Der Ring des Nibelungen*), composed over a twenty-year period, he did it. He produced a body of work which, if it didn't entirely realize his theories and abolish the opera of the past, revolutionized the European musical consciousness.

What did Wagner mean by music drama? Like the Florentine inventors of opera, Wagner went back to classical Greece to find the sources of Greek drama's power so as to purify the musical theater of his day. Greek drama, Wagner believed, gained its power from the fact that it was religious art, drawing on myth while celebrating human life. Furthermore, it combined several of the arts—poetry, music, dance, song—in such a way that the entire community took part. However, that Greek dramatic synthesis had disintegrated. The arts had become specialized and separate from each other. The religious consensus had dissolved. Historical and not mythological subjects became the basis of opera, and the community audience was divided along social lines. By the nineteenth century, in Wagner's view, opera had reached its nadir. It had become what a later critic characterized as "the most frivolous, vulgar, socially exclusive and contentless of all theatrical forms. . . . Its conventions were grotesque, its plots ridiculous, its libretti fatuous."[10] Yet, opera was reformable. It could be restored to its rightful power, drawing on resources the Greeks and operatic Florentines didn't have at their command. How was this to be done?

The answer? Wagnerian music drama. It and it alone would reintegrate the arts, present mythological subjects of such power as to rise far above mere entertainment. It would become a new religion. Drawing on the example of Beethoven, who had developed music's capacity to express the inner human experience, music drama would explore the minds and psyches of people, the only true drama. Music and words combined indissolubly. No more songs, duets, quartets breaking up the drama. No more virtuosic display. Drama: unbroken exposition, unbroken melody, not contemptible mere tunes. Singers, scenery, direction—all a seamless fabric, with the orchestra woven into the center.

That was a lot, but not all. As a total art form, music drama required a house appropriate to its special nature. The tiny town of Bayreuth, not far from Munich, gave Wagner land for a theater, and for that site he designed the theater of his dreams, the nerve center from which this new art, this new vision of culture, would radiate out across all of Europe. The exterior was of unprepossessing brick and wood. Rightly so, for in Wagnerian terms the meaning of the festival playhouse was to be found in its interior. This was in the shape of a classical amphitheater, without boxes, austere, seating eighteen hundred people, small enough that all the audience could follow all details of the drama through gesture, facial expression, movement. The Bayreuth theater was notable for two innovations. The stage was built out over the orchestra pit so that the orchestra, concealed from the audience, didn't intervene between audience and drama. The sound rose up *within* the drama, enveloping actors and audience alike. It was a superb place to hear. And to see. The second innovation was to remove the aisles dividing the audience and running down toward the stage. At Bayreuth the audience took its seats from the sides, wrapping itself in an unbroken semicircle around the stage.

If Bayreuth was a nerve center, it was also a shrine, a place of pilgrimage, a site sacred to the new musical order of things. And that new order steadily gained ground and adherents, especially among the young. Even conservatives were coming around. Traditional opera, one wrote, in 1873, "is intellectually a monstrosity, and Wagner, with all his extravagance, is probably right in his onslaught upon it."[11]

T h e most influential Wagnerian advocate of the 1870s was Theodore Thomas (1835–1905). Born in Essen, Germany, he was a musically precocious child, but when the Thomas family came to America in 1845, the boy's formal musical education ended and he was sent out on his own, at age fourteen, to fend for himself as a violinist. He played with any band or orchestra that would employ him, performing with Carl Bergmann in the 1850s and absorbing his enthusiasm for Wagner. Thomas conducted some opera early in his career and in the mid-1880s became a director of the American Opera Company, which toured the country giving opera only in English, but he had at best an ambivalent attitude toward opera: "A symphony orchestra shows the culture of a community, not opera. . . . The master works of instrumental music are the language of the soul and express more than those of any art." Still, he presented summer concerts in the 1870s in New York's Central Park, including many Wagnerian excerpts and occasional all-Wagner programs, a novelty at the time.[12]

Cincinnati was the center for German music in America. As early as 1849 German music lovers had established a music festival there, so Thomas was building on older foundations when he began a May Festival in 1873, performing excerpts from *Tannhäuser.* At the second festival, in 1875, *Lohengrin* excerpts were played, and at the third, for which a 4,400-seat music hall had been built, selections from *Lohengrin, The Mastersingers (Die Meistersinger von Nürnberg),* and *The Twilight of the Gods (Götterdämmerung)* were on the program. In 1880 and 1882 there was more Wagner. Amalia Materna, the most famous Wagnerian soprano of the day, sang excerpts from *The Valkyries (Die Walküre)* "to perfection." Christine Nilsson joined Materna on the program in 1884, and Lilli Lehmann, in 1886, sang a work of "wonderful difficulty," performed for the first time in America—Bach's B minor Mass. (But not a complete performance: six choruses and five solos were given.)

Wagnerian dramatic theory denounced the fragmentation of conventional opera into detachable excerpts, but, ironically, Wagner's music won its way in America mainly by means of bits and pieces. It wasn't until 1870 that Adolph Neuendorff conducted *Tannhäuser,* in German, at the Stadt-Theater in New York, but once again the performances were largely within the German community. A wider audience heard *Lohengrin* at the Academy of Music in 1873, in Italian, with Christine Nilsson and Italo Campanini. *Tristan und Isolde* and *Die Meistersinger* and the four operas of the *Ring* cycle were heard as excepts, the overture to *Die Meistersinger* in 1866 for the first time, the Prelude to *Tristan* that same year, and the final scene in 1872, "The Ride of the Valkyries" in 1872 ("almost laughable . . . and not easy to regard as serious music," John Sullivan Dwight wrote), Wotan's Farewell and the magic music from *Die Walküre* in 1875, act 1 of that same opera in a concert version in 1876, act 3 of *Siegfried* in 1880, the Rhine Journey music from it in 1884. In 1878 Neuendorff performed a heavily cut version of *Die Walküre* in German in New York. Poorly done and leaving a "bitter taste" in people's mouths, it did suggest that the battle of words was over, that the introduction of Wagner through excerpts had outlived its usefulness, and that it was time to hear Wagnerian music drama in the theater.

Nothing happened. The war of words continued. Bayreuth was built and inaugurated with the first complete *Ring* in 1876. It marked an important milestone in the history of American operatic criticism; for several American newspapers sent observers to report on the excitement. Leopold Damrosch wrote for the *New York Sun;* Henry T. Finck for the *New York World;* Frederick W. Schwab, for the *New York Times,* cabled his reports the morning after each of the *Ring* operas, the first time a newspaper in the Western Hemisphere published cabled reports from a music critic; and J. R. G. Hassard, for the *New York Tribune,* wrote "lengthy, enthusiastic" articles later republished in pamphlet form, "the finest of the many American reports."[14] Yet the dominance of Italian opera continued in the cities and in the repertories of touring companies. This anomalous situation was illustrated by a seemingly trivial detail from the history of the Metropolitan Opera House, on the proscenium arch of which were inscribed the names of six composers: Beethoven, Mozart, Gluck, Meyerbeer, Gounod—and Wagner. The most striking thing is the absence of any Italian names; Verdi, Rossini, and Donizetti held the Metropolitan stage but were not honored above it. The case of Wagner is oddly the reverse of this. He was, by 1883, a "classic" in an opera house where his greatest operas had never been heard and were unlikely to be heard, as if the names of Beethoven and Gounod had appeared there without anyone having heard *Fidelio* or *Faust*.

In 1883 Richard Wagner died. Innumerable obituaries recorded the impact his operas had had on European music, but in America he died as he had lived, largely as a name. And then change came. One man, a devoted Wagnerian conductor, stepped forward to preside over the realization of the Wagnerian revolution in America. At last.

L e o p o l d Damrosch was born in Posen, Germany, in 1832. Trained as a medical doctor at the University of Berlin, he instead took up music as a career, studying violin and composition. Franz Liszt gave him a position as violinist in the Weimar court orchestra in 1857, and the next year he went to Breslau, where, in the following thirteen years, he established himself as a conductor. In 1871, feeling that his musical advance was blocked in Germany, he came to New York to head the Arion Men's Chorus, a big risk for a man almost forty years of age. He brought with him the increasing prestige of the new music, which he had absorbed by direct contact with its creators. Wagner was a friend of the Damrosch family. By the mid-1870s Bergmann's career was in decline and he died alone and in poverty in New York's German hospital. To the almost inevitable rivalry between Damrosch and Theodore Thomas was added personal antagonism, and they competed strenuously to introduce new music—Goldmark, Saint-Saëns, Brahms, Tchaikovsky. Through the early 1880s each toured the nation with his own orchestra. Then Damrosch had a brilliant idea, which led him, in August 1884, to make an offer to the directors of the Metropolitan Opera House.

He proposed a season of German-language opera. He would be appointed musical director, at a salary of ten thousand dollars per year and would recruit a group of first-rate German singers, organize and conduct the orchestra, and make all production and business arrangements. The directors would be responsible for the cost of the season beyond his salary. The directors of the Metropolitan agreed, because they had no other choice and because they thus avoided another direct confrontation with the Academy of Music. It was Damrosch or nothing. By the middle of August, Damrosch was crossing the Atlantic in search of singers. The directors were reassured by Damrosch's promise to keep costs strictly under control. German singers were much less expensive than Italian ones, and he could readily recruit a fine orchestra from among German instrumentalists in the eastern cities. Damrosch was brilliantly suc-

Leopold Damrosch (left) and his son, Walter, championed new music, particularly Wagner. Historical Sound Recordings Collection, Yale University Library.

cessful in recruiting singers, among them Amalia Materna (1844–1918), the first Brünnhilde in the first Bayreuth performances of the *Ring* in 1876 and the first Kundry in *Parsifal* at Bayreuth in 1882, Anton Schott, tenor, and Marianne Brandt, contralto.

In October Damrosch, working furiously to organize everything that remained to be done, announced the repertory—fifty-eight evening and matinee performances in thirteen weeks, German opera but also French and Italian. Ticket prices indicated that a general unfashionable audience was aimed at, as they were half those of the previous season: orchestra $3.00, dress circle $2.00, balcony $1.50, and gallery 50¢. If the presence of French and Italian favorites was intended to reassure those for whom the "elaborate and ponderous compositions" of Wagner induced feelings akin to those prompted by "the threatened visit of an epidemic," the great event was unquestionably going to be the scheduled production of *Die Walküre*. The music of the future had become the music of the present.

The first season of German-language opera brought a new audience to the Metropolitan, large numbers of musically knowledgeable, serious listeners. The least popular operas were the French and Italian ones, perhaps because German singers were ill at ease in that repertory. Schott disappointed, but Brandt was a memorable Leonora in *Fidelio. Lohengrin* and *Tannhäuser,* done for the first time both adequately and in their authentic German, were as good as new. The season climaxed on January 30, 1885, with *Die Walküre.* Newspapers had been replete with reports of exhaustive preparations, long rehearsals, the length and complexity of the work. The actual performance—the curtain came down at half past midnight—released long-pent-up excitement in storms of applause. "Defects were so few it may be referred to with fairness as a perfect performance." Materna's portrayal of Brünnhilde, "of world-wide celebrity," justified its fame in its expressiveness and majestic power. Schott's declamation was forceful, but "the largest measure of praise belongs undoubtedly to Dr. Damrosch's orchestra. Their energy never flagged, their proficiency never wavered." It was Damrosch's "crowning achievement." And Wagner's night.[15]

Ten days later a shocking series of events began to unfold. Damrosch had been overworking for months. He had continued to direct the New York Oratorio Society as well as the Symphony Society, in addition to his crushing operatic responsibilities. On the night of February 10, while rehearsing Verdi's Requiem, he felt unwell, suffering from a cold and a chill, and couldn't continue. The following day he was worse. The doctors diagnosed pneumonia, though they remained generally reassuring. Leopold summoned his son, Walter, who served as deputy conductor, and together they went over the score of *Tannhäuser,* which Walter conducted that evening, as well as Meyerbeer's *Le Prophète* two days later. Word began to spread that Leopold Damrosch was seriously ill, but the gravity of his condition was concealed; even the family was perhaps not aware of it. On the 14th his condition seriously worsened. He died during the early hours of February 15. A concert had been scheduled at the Metropolitan Opera House that night, and when people arrived they found a black-bordered notice posted near the box office window. At the Thalia Theatre a performance was interrupted by the manager, who announced the news and dismissed the audience. Damrosch's funeral was held at the Metropolitan, funeral address by Henry Ward Beecher. The Metropolitan Board of Directors attended to pay tribute.[16]

The season was almost over, with only a few performances remaining in New York and on tour in Chicago, Cincinnati, and Boston. Wagner had pulled the Metropolitan out of its dead end of the year before and had greatly enhanced its prestige and popularity. As well, Damrosch's death concealed an interesting development in American operatic patronage. Under the Damrosch arrangements, shareholders had been directly responsible for the cost of the season. This first Wagner year, there was a deficit of about $40,000—$570 for each shareholder—little enough considering the plaudits heaped upon them as imaginative patrons. However, having gone that far, the Metropolitan shareholders drew back. In finding a replacement for Damrosch, they split the duties of the new general manager with those of an executive secretary, Edmund Stanton, selected to look out for the shareholders' interests by taking care to limit their responsibility.

Anton Seidl (1850–1898) was selected as the new musical director and conductor. A member of the second generation of Wagnerian conductors, he had authentic credentials, having assisted Wagner at Bayreuth several years and served as choral director for Hans Richter, the most eminent of Wagnerian conductors. Seidl, exacting, meticulous (he discovered 180 errors in the printed score of *Lohengrin* used at the Metropolitan), had conducted at Leipzig and Bremen, led the first complete *Ring* in London in 1882 and a famous European Wagnerian tour by the Neumann opera company in 1883. He brought new singers with him (Materna didn't return to New York): Max Alvary, a tenor from Weimar, Emil Fischer, a bass from Dresden, and above all, the great soprano Lilli Lehmann.

Meanwhile, the Academy of Music had gone its Italian ways in the season of 1884–1885, with apparent success. Adelina Patti was the great drawing card. Her performances on tour were constantly sold out. But Colonel Mapleson's position was much less secure than it seemed. Patti let it be known she would not return to America the next year. The German season had boosted the Metropolitan's position, gained society's attention, tipped the balance decisively away from the Academy in the rivalry of the two houses. Mapleson's company had done its best business on the road. Its New York support was deteriorating. In the spring of 1885, while the Metropolitan smugly looked ahead to the coming season with Seidl and Lehmann, there were rumors about whether the Academy might not try a German season of its own. Mapleson had no such plans, for he characterized German opera in crude terms, saying, "The sauerkraut opera cannot last. Italian opera is the only opera that can depend upon fashionable support," which inspired German partisans to respond in like fashion, calling Italian opera "ashcan" art. Without Patti, Mapleson's plans remained concealed in the fog of rumor, offhand statement, and bravado that accompanied his efforts.[17]

T h e next six years saw the triumph of Wagner. In 1886, after immense anticipation and arduous preparation, *Die Meistersinger* was given for the first time. The "picturesquely burgherish" Hans Sachs of Emil Fischer captivated the audience, but with an opera that, though much cut, lasted four and a quarter hours and in which the "taking numbers are unfortunately not very abundant," Anton Seidl's conducting carried the day. That same season, after a quarter of a century of waiting, came *Tristan und Isolde,* greeted with frantic enthusiasm. Seidl masterfully conducted a performance considered "better than Bayreuth," with Albert Niemann as Tristan, magnetic despite his fifty-seven years, and Lehmann "beyond praise" as Isolde. *Siegfried,* in 1887, clinched the case for Wagnerian music drama as existing on an entirely different plane from other opera. Its music, "not an enjoyment but a task," was "learned and complex and demands some study; and this militates against its success among those who seek musical performances simply as a mode of entertainment." In 1888, *Götterdämmerung.* What did New York make of this tremendous vision of the overthrow of order? Lehmann, as Brünnhilde, "was a benediction to the memory" and Niemann's death scene, as Siegfried, sent "magnetic shocks through the audience. One could hardly listen to *Götterdämmerung* among throngs of intense young enthusiasts," Henry Adams reported, "without paroxysms of nervous excitement." Last of all, in 1889, was *Das Rheingold,* the first of the four *Ring* operas in the proper sequence of performance, a makeshift production but impressive musically.

"A new world burst forth!" exclaimed the young American music student Sidney Homer on hearing his first *Ring.* His ecstatic words convey wonderfully the spirit of the Wagnerian ascendancy. Here was art of a wholly different kind. "Life would never be the same again, the commonplace was banished from our several lives forever! Music went beyond, where words could not go. The music—the music was truth itself, the unveiling of fundamentals, a revelation of the primitive impulses and sources of all things."[18]

The consequences of these German seasons rippled out in many direction. "It might almost be said that along with building a theater in Bayreuth, Richard Wagner had created the means to keep one open in New York and close another." Colonel Mapleson's 1886 season at the Academy of Music failed. Adelina Patti was absent. Without a star, what was star opera? While the Colonel jauntily insisted that Italian opera was not "dead," the best he could offer was Minnie Hauk, the first American Carmen of a decade before. Her voice was thin and shrill, and *Carmen* on opening night fell flat. He introduced one novelty, *Manon* by Jules Massenet (1842–1912), sung in Italian. It wasn't nearly enough. The Colonel called it quits, leaving America with a famous parting shot at his cross-town rival: "I cannot fight Wall Street." Touring companies used the Academy for the next decade, and then it ceased to be an opera house and was demolished in 1929.[19]

While the box-office audiences at the Metropolitan wanted more and more Wagner, the subscribers were increasingly bored and irritated. For Wagnerian opera the house was plunged in dark for interminable hours, and it was virtually impossible for the boxholders to while away the time looking about the house and at each other. They therefore decreed that the lights not be lowered during performances, whatever the aesthetic consequences—for example, that the dungeon scene in *Fidelio* was done in bright light. Emulating the casual insolence of the European aristocracy in their opera boxes, they made noise, caused commotions coming in and out. Cyrus Field, a boxholder, complained in print about "Hogs and Opera Boxes," only to be admonished in the name of private property: "You can no more hinder a man from conversing in his own opera-box than you can hinder him from snoring in his own pew." And after all, the Metropolitan originated in response to social, not artistic, needs. The stockholders had history on their side. More important, they owned the place. Yet everything was subordinated to Germanic solemnities about art.

Edmund Stanton tried to distract the shareholders from their miseries by offering them novelties—Viktor Nessler's *The Trumpeter of Säckingen,* Gasparo Spontini's *Fernand Cortez,* Peter Cornelius's *The Barber of Bagdad.* The last was much admired by critics and musicians and was "quite within the comprehension of the most fashionable brain," as the *Times* gibed. The stockholders were amused neither by the gibe nor by the opera. Nor did Ignaz Brüll's *The Golden Cross* or Karl Goldmark's *Merlin* make the boxholders forget those days when one went to the opera house for simple pleasure. Stanton's efforts grew desperate, contemporary Italian operas composed under the Wagnerian spell—Albert Franchetti's *Asrael*—opening night!—and Antonio Sareglia's *Il Vassalo de Szigeth*. Neither succeeded. Then came a forty-year-old curiosity, *Diana von Solange* by Ernest II, duke of Saxe-Coburg-Gotha. (Rumor had it that Stanton was influenced by the propensity of the duke to bestow decorations on those who produced his opera.) The critics were outraged by it. "The music is simply rubbish. There is no excuse whatever for the attempt of the Opera House to foist such trash upon the public."[20] A petition signed by three hundred people asked that *Diana* not be given another performance, a signal to return to the German and especially Wagnerian favorites. Instead, the shareholders used it as a pretext for throwing off the shackles of German opera. Within a week the directors announced an end to the German-language seasons and the reintroduction of French and Italian opera. As a manifest of the return to the old order, they brought back an old name—Henry Abbey, this time in partnership with John Schoeffel and Maurice Grau, a triumvirate of impresarios. So much for the individual-performance ticket buyers. So much for Wagner. So much for the Metropolitan as a temple of art.

The German audience saved the season, but they couldn't save the Metropolitan as a House of Wagner. The last performance of the season, *Die Meistersinger*, was Emil Fischer's farewell as Hans Sachs, the occasion for an enormous outpouring of emotion, a tribute to singers, orchestra, and to this remarkable seven-year period in the history of opera in America. One observer noted the "rapt attention which even the occupants of the boxes bestowed upon the performance" and wondered if there might not be regret on the part of those "who have voted to return to the sweetmeats of the past." At the final curtain, there was a half-hour ovation, with flowers and tears for Seidl, Fischer, Walter Damrosch. "I hope it is not the last time I shall sing for you here, on this stage, in German," Fischer said. And Anton Seidl: "Believe me, ladies and gentlemen, I understand the meaning of this great demonstration."[21]

T h e triumph of Wagner was indisputable and final. That was the ineffaceable lesson of these seven years, even as German opera in German gave way to a different ordering of things. Where, eight years before, none of the greatest of Wagner's music dramas had been performed on an American stage, all would now be part of the repertory. More had been involved than simply the Wagner operas. The admiration for them, and for German music in general, was part of a growing admiration for other aspects of German culture—German science, German philosophy, German economic power, German military might. The German most written about in American newspapers and magazines in these years, neither an artist, philosopher, nor scientist, was Prince Otto von Bismarck. Music had for two centuries been identified with Italy. Now, the triumph of Wagner reinforced the supremacy of German musical culture.[22]

And yet: the ascendancy in America of Wagnerian music drama was limited. In the theater, the *Ring* reached a few thousand people in a handful of cities. Philadelphia, Boston, Milwaukee, Chicago, and St. Louis heard it in 1890, San Francisco in 1900. Its complexity and length meant that it would not be performed by the numerous

Albert Pinkham Ryder,
**Siegfried and the Rhine
Maidens** *(1888–91).
Andrew W. Mellon Col-
lection. Copyright Na-
tional Gallery of Art,
Washington.*

small touring companies that brought opera to Americans away from the metropolitan centers. Its dominance at the Metropolitan was short-lived. Nevertheless,
the Metropolitan German seasons had far-reaching consequences, and they remain
(along with the company's radio broadcasts half a century later) one of the Metropolitan's two most important contributions to American operatic culture.

O n e result of the Wagner operas was of a different but enduring kind. Living in New
York in those years was an extraordinary American artist, the visionary painter Albert
Pinkham Ryder (1847–1917). Always shy and quiet, in his later years eccentric and
reclusive, in the 1880s and 1890s Ryder was still sociable, enjoyed music, and went to
the Metropolitan. In 1888 he saw *Götterdämmerung*. Profoundly moved by it, he
wrote: "I had been to hear the opera and went home about twelve o'clock and began
this picture. I worked for forty-eight hours without sleep or food, and the picture was
the result." In fact, Ryder worked on *Siegfried and the Rhine Maidens* for another three
years, completing it in 1891, when it was shown and much praised for its "mystery
and mastery of color."[23]

Ryder's painting depicts the scene in the third act of *Götterdämmerung* in which
Siegfried encounters the three Rhine Maidens, who implore him to return the
accursed ring of the Nibelungs and thus avoid the certain death which awaits its
possessor. There are two puzzling aspects in Ryder's vision. Why has he shown
Siegfried as a knight on horseback? And which moment in the story has he portrayed? Are the maidens imploring Siegfried to give up the ring? Or has he already

refused their plea and determined his fate? Whatever the answers, the focus of the painting is neither Siegfried nor the maidens. It is an enormous tree with wind-whipped, sinuous, writhing branches, behind it a turbulent sky of gold and bronze. Like Walt Whitman, Ryder connected opera with "man as part of the wider rhythms of nature." Wagnerian music drama would also inspire another individualist American artist, Louis Sullivan, architect. And so it is to Chicago we turn next.

chapter twenty-three

Chicago

Chicago was founded in 1833. Its early musical progress was modest—a harmonic society in 1834, a church with a quartet of professional singers by 1836, a brass band by 1841. Its operatic history began in 1850 when, having swollen to a population of twenty-eight thousand, the town attracted a summer touring opera company which spent three days in "conquering the marine hazards" of Lake Michigan and then put on a performance of *La Sonnambula* at J. B. Rice's Chicago Theatre. The company consisted of a handful of singers and a conductor and relied on the local theater orchestra and local singers for the chorus. The opera was a rousing success and was repeated the next night. Just after the beginning of the second act, the theater caught fire from a blaze ignited in a nearby stable and was one of twenty buildings destroyed. The city heard no more opera until 1853, when the ballroom of a hotel was converted into an auditorium and Rosa de Vries appeared there in *La Sonnambula, Norma,* and *Lucia.* Another operatic drought followed, lasting until 1859, when Maurice Strakosch brought Amalia Patti, with a full company, presenting a number of operas, including *Don Giovanni* and the new *Traviata.*

In 1865 Uranus H. Crosby, a Cape Cod distiller who had made a fortune selling liquor during the Civil War, built an opera house. It was an elaborately decorated multistory building, housing an art gallery, offices and artists' studios, and a three-thousand-seat auditorium, with fifty-six private boxes. The visiting Grau Opera Company opened it with *Il Trovatore.* "Carriages lined up for blocks before the theater's entrance" and "fine clothes and splendid jewels were much in evidence." The city's socially aspiring middle class used Crosby's to establish its social and financial authority—opera tickets cost twice the price for spoken drama— and the auditorium was used for various purposes: Ulysses Grant won the Republican nomination for the presidency there in 1868. Over the years there were 433 operatic performances at Crosby's, the most popular operas being *Martha, Il Trovatore, Faust, The Bohemian Girl,* and *Norma,* but from the first the opera house was a shaky financial proposition.

Crosby out-Barnumed Barnum in trying to make a go of it. His most brazen scheme was his opera house lottery. Along with the purchase of engravings of popular paintings, Crosby offered five-dollar lottery tickets for 302 prizes, the grand prize being the opera house! Two hundred thousand tickets were sold. As the day of the drawing approached trains were crowded with people coming to take part. Hotels were filled. Temporary quarters were set up in saloons. The drawing took place on the stage of the grand prize. The "winner" was conveniently not present and it was eventually announced that, not interested in owning an opera house, he had sold his ticket back to Crosby for two hundred thousand dollars. The public did some calculating—almost a million dollars worth of tickets had been sold—and concluded it had been swindled. Crosby "found it expedient to retire to a New England village." The great fire of 1871 ended the Crosby Chicago opera story. "It destroyed every audience-room, disrupted every musical society, laid every music store in ashes, and drove nearly every teacher of music away from the city."[1]

T h e city rebuilt itself and by the 1880s was the railroad hub of the country, a meat packing center, the site of extensive manufacturing and industry. Chicago passed Boston and Baltimore in population and rivaled Philadelphia as the nation's second city. Between 1870 and 1890 Germans comprised the largest number of new immigrants. Stock companies performed plays in German, the German press was lively, German was taught in the public schools. Hans Balatka, one of the pioneer conductors in America, had started a Philharmonic Society orchestra before the fire, and now it and other musical organizations sprang back to life. Theodore Thomas made almost annual visits after 1872. In 1873 Max Maretzek brought an Italian opera company, Christine Nilsson first appeared in the city in 1874, and in 1877 a German company performed Wagner at Hooley's Theater. Two years later Colonel Mapleson brought his company from the New York Academy of Music.

None of this altered the picture of Chicago that had formed itself in the national consciousness: a crude and raw city, energetic, ambitious, boastful, its capitalists the newest of the newly rich. This caricature, the brawny and brawling hog-butcher, so necessary to some Chicagoans even today, was also useful to the plutocrats of other cities as a way of validating *their* social superiority. Ward McAllister summed up eastern snootiness. "The fact that a man has been brought up in the West does not

Crosby's Opera House, Chicago, about 1866. Five years later the great fire put an end to its brief heyday. Library of Congress.

mean that he is not capable of becoming a society man. I could name many men and women who have been forced to spend a large part of their early life in the West, but who have nevertheless established themselves in a good position in Eastern Society."[2] In reality, Chicago's new capitalists were no more crass than most of their contemporaries. If anything, the number of wealthy people in the city involved in public service, in philanthropy, and in support of the arts surpassed the number found elsewhere.

The prevailing image of Chicago was tremendously reinforced by the fire. How could a city that was starting over be anything but crude and unfinished? Raw power, not art, was what it represented. And such preconceptions were confirmed by high jinks such as those of Wilbur F. Storey, the courageous and outrageous editor of the *Chicago Times* who, in the post–Civil War years, established an unsurpassed reputation for journalistic sensationalism. The standing order of his paper was "Telegraph fully all news and when there is no news send rumors." A headline about a hanging read: "JERKED TO JESUS." Nor had the musical world forgotten Storey's response to Offenbach's operas, when they were brought to Chicago by Lydia Thompson and her British Blondes: "BAWDS AT THE OPERA HOUSE: WHERE'S THE POLICE?" Thompson responded in kind, threatening to horsewhip Storey.[3]

The 1880s were a period of increasing vitality in music in Chicago, and they were equally creative in architecture, with the invention of the "tall building," described by the French novelist Paul Bourget as "the first draught of a new sort of art—an art of democracy made by the masses and for the masses." In the fermenting growth of the city, music and architecture came together with startling results.[4]

M a r c h and April 1885 marked the crossroads in Chicago's operatic fortunes. Two visiting opera companies presented the opera of the past and of the future. The first, the German company from the Metropolitan Opera House, performed in the cramped confines of the Columbia Theatre, its stage too small for their scenery. They stayed three weeks, gave twenty-one performances, ten of Italian and French opera, eleven of German, two of *Fidelio,* three each of *Lohengrin* (given before in Chicago but in Italian), *Tannhäuser,* and *Die Walküre,* the last two new to the city. Noting the "marked attention by large audiences," one critic commented on the new conception of opera that Wagner's music dramas represented. "The German idea of a perfect ensemble, rather than a performance in which a star attraction is the leading feature, is a most commendable and truly musicianly plan." Others struggled to convey the power of Wagner's music drama, whose foundation was the leitmotif, a musical theme associated with a character or idea or situation which recurs in the story. Understanding these themes demanded much of the listener. "At a first hearing it would be quite impossible to follow with any completeness or a full understanding of their signification," though some were familiar to Chicagoans because of the work "of Mr. Thomas and his orchestra." The "wonderful charm," of that "great mysterious tone-poem," *Die Walküre,* was its orchestration, in which "the real poetic inspiration of Wagner is made manifest." Nevertheless, certain aspects of Wagner's work remained puzzling. Its mythological subject matter was foreign to the fact-inclined, literal American mind, so it was necessary to remember that Wagner turned to mythology "to reanimate a national love for it among his own people" and because he wished "to lead art back to its primitive poetical state in the great realm of nature." This approach, as one critic circumspectly but honestly noted, raised moral issues. Wagner's genius delighted in "the utmost limits of expression," the "unrestrained play of fancy," "the most intense utterance of unbridled passion," which explained the incestuous love of Siegmund and Sieglinde. "In the mystic hands of the ancient gods and goddesses morality had its own rude forms, which accorded more with the emotional instinct than the intellectual nature." Therefore, these "old legends" had to be viewed "from their poetic side."

Baffling, at times repellent—but enchanting: this new music drama rendered the older classics obsolete. *Fidelio,* "this fine old opera," written "in the early period of the German school, when the influence of Mozart was felt so strongly upon the lyrical stage," had "a limitation about it that might not accord with the general taste of day" after the "larger form which German opera has assumed" with Wagner. When the German company performed *Don Giovanni,* it wasn't even reviewed. Wagner towered over everything.[5]

Three weeks after the Germans left, the second opera company arrived, Colonel Mapleson's Academy of Music company returning from a visit to San Francisco. Its roster included names which were as well known to Americans as those of the German company had been unknown. Furthermore, the contrast in repertory was as striking as that of singers. Mapleson's company announced *Der Freischütz* and *Lohengrin* (in Italian), the ever-familiar *Faust* and one little-known Gounod opera, *Mireille.* *Aida* was the most recently composed opera, but otherwise the fare was standard— *Semiramide, La Sonnambula, I Puritani, Lucia.*

Although the operas were old and the company familiar, the occasion was a special one in Chicago history. This was the first Chicago Grand Opera Festival, sponsored by the Chicago Opera Festival Association, an all-out effort by opera lovers to establish opera permanently in the city. It was advertised as "MUSIC FOR THE PEOPLE!" "The Greatest Musical Event in the History of Chicago." To create a space commensurate with the undertaking involved the sponsors in an extraordinary feat of improvisation. The Interstate Exposition Building in Grant Park, a huge barnlike structure used for fairs and exhibitions, was wholly reconstructed at one end, a temporary wooden structure built within it, with a huge stage, a ground floor of orchestra seats, boxes, dress circle and gallery, holding up to ten thousand people, steam heat, and miles of matting to deaden the noise of footsteps. Here, in the most hard-headed of cities, was extravagance European monarchs would have admired. And all created in six weeks. Tickets were at popular prices, $1, $2, and $2.50, with a reduced rate by the week. Boxes cost $12.

The Italian season was the grandest social occasion in the history of Chicago. "Scarcely a man of any prominence . . . has neglected to provide himself with a box for the season or with season tickets." Familiar operas with famous singers: Adelina Patti, Sofia Scalchi, Emma Nevada. On opening night Patti drew six thousand, and more on succeeding performances. Perhaps ten thousand packed into the hall, sitting and standing, for *Faust.* "A vacant seat was an unknown quantity and persistent females even encroached upon the sacred rights of box-holders." At the conclusion of Do-nizetti's *Linda di Chamounix,* Patti sang "Home, Sweet Home" with the "most perfect purity of voice, and in sweet and plaintive tones, and gave the old song that delicate feeling that seemed to come from the heart." The applause was "overpowering."

Patti and Scalchi sang with lordly command. Nevada (1859–1940), a California soprano trained in Europe and at her best a fine singer of Bellini, played the old-fashioned prima donna to the hilt. Her performance of *Mireille* was not one Gounod would have recognized. "You see in the first part of the opera I hear the birds singing and I want to sing, too, so I have there a beautiful waltz song. Now the end of the opera is very gloomy. I am cut down by a sunstroke and I die in the desert to a mournful and endless recitative—one of those things that make people furl their umbrellas, steal out on tip toe and go home." So: the waltz was removed from the first act and at the end of the opera, "just as people are feeling sad and I am about to gasp my last, I revive, come down to the footlights and sing my waltz song, and send everybody home humming." All this, Nevada recognized, was "crazy so far as the artistic and dramatic values are concerned," but it had "a very happy effect on the public." In two weeks Mapleson's company drew almost a hundred thousand people. If the advocates of Wagnerian music drama proclaimed such apparent success to be the expiring glow of Italian opera, there were still many who thought it not a sunset but a sunrise.[6]

A t the end of the last performance, Ferdinand Peck, president of the Opera Festival, made a speech in which he expressed the hope that the people of Chicago would "look upon this as a stepping stone to a great permanent hall where similar enter-prises would have a home. [Applause.]" He believed there were important reasons why this would, and must, happen. "Magnificent music, at prices within the reach of all would have a tendency to diminish crime and Socialism in our city by educating the masses to higher things. [Applause.]"[7] In a building-besotted city like Chicago, such a hope was not remarkable, but Peck's words did have an exceptional outcome. Within three years an opera house was built, and it turned out to be one of the great accomplishments in the history of American architecture. Unfortunately, the presi-dent's other hopes proved elusive. Robbers didn't abandon housebreaking to take up *Rigoletto,* nor did socialists turn to music drama instead of the class struggle. Ferdi-nand Wythe Peck (1848–1924), a lawyer and visionary, conceived the idea of the opera house, enlisted the support of other capitalists, and took an option on property facing Grant Park. Within weeks he had formed an Auditorium Association and got $750,000 in pledges. Then, at the end of 1886, he made an inspired choice of architects—the local firm of Adler and Sullivan.[8]

Dankmar Adler was born in 1844 in Germany, son of the local cantor and rabbi. His mother died six days after his birth, hence his odd name—*dank,* German for "thanks," and *mar,* Hebrew for "bitter." The infant's father remarried, and in 1854 the family emigrated to the United States, to Detroit, where Liebman Adler was rabbi of the Temple Beth El. In the next few years Dankmar developed an interest in architec-ture, and when the family moved to Chicago in 1861, he found work with the German-born engineer Augustus Bauer. After service in the Union army during the

Civil War, in which he received engineering training, Adler returned to Chicago and in the next fifteen years worked with many architects on a wide range of buildings. Efficient as an administrator, adept at getting clients, he was also an able designer, with a special interest in theaters. In 1879 he went into business for himself and that same year employed Louis Sullivan as a part-time free-lance draftsman.

Louis Henri Sullivan was born in Boston in 1856, the son of an Irish father who had emigrated to America in 1847 and of a mother of French, German, and Swiss ancestry. When his parents moved to Chicago in 1868, Louis stayed on in Boston with his maternal grandparents. He attended the new Massachusetts Institute of Technology in 1872 but, scornful of the conventional curriculum and resentful of authority, left after one year. Restless and impatient, his next eight years were spent in travel and in work of various kinds: half a year in Philadelphia with the architect Frank Furness, half a year in Chicago with the engineer Le Baron Jenney, two years in Europe, including one at the Ecole des Beaux Arts in Paris. He returned to Chicago and in 1881 began full-time work with Adler. By 1883 they were partners.

Ferdinand Peck's choice of Adler and Sullivan was based on the extensive theater work Adler had done, which the partners continued and expanded. Their work on the remodeling of the Exposition Building clinched their selection. Of course, the new opera house—now prospectively called the Auditorium Building—was an enormously more ambitious and complex project than anything the two men had done before, and they received intelligent support and advice from the board of the Auditorium Association, their employer. Peck had concluded that an opera house as a single monumental building wasn't a viable enterprise and that Chicago's opera house would be part of a large commercial structure, including a hotel, revenue from which would underwrite it. And the board made specific recommendations about exterior and interior design, including the "severe simplicity" of its facade, which Adler lamented but later generations have found appealing.

Work went forward through 1887 and into 1888. Complex engineering problems required novel solutions. The supply of Minnesota granite was unpredictable, so the association bought the quarries. Bricklayers and iron men worked at night, under electric lights. By ingeniously "erecting one building inside another," the theater was used for the Republican convention of 1888, "as magnificent a space as any Republican had ever witnessed." Sound and sight were splendid, allowing the Republicans to view with dismay the depredations of the Grover Cleveland–led Democrats and nominate Benjamin Harrison as their candidate. Adler meanwhile traveled to Europe, to visit some of the great European houses, in particular the Budapest Opera House, reopened in 1884 after a fire and equipped with the most up-to-date hydraulic stage equipment in the world. Sullivan stayed in Chicago to complete the interior decoration, for which he required an additional thirty persons, one of whom was a young Wisconsin man named Frank Lloyd Wright. As the building neared completion in the spring of 1889, Cornelius Vanderbilt visited it: "Wonderful! Wonderful!" Senator Chauncey Depew was more expansive: "The most impressive structure in the world." By summer the business space was rented, Italian artisans laid twenty-five thousand feet of marble mosaic, and the hydraulic lifts were installed backstage. In the fall the final copestone was placed in the seventeenth floor of the tower.

Louis Sullivan's Chicago Auditorium, opened in 1889, was Wagnerian in its operatic extravagance. Library of Congress.

It was a true Chicago building—immense in scale and innovative in style. There was a four-hundred-room hotel, a business building with 136 offices in the main block and in the tower, and a forty-two-hundred-seat auditorium. It cost 3.2 million dollars, the most expensive building in the city. Its seventeen-story, 270-foot tower was the tallest building in the city. At 110,000 tons it was the heaviest building in the world. It covered 63,350 square feet. Pride matched its scale. "Biggest thing in the world," boasted one citizen, and recalling his tour of La Scala and of the San Carlo in Naples, asked: "What are they to this? Mere molehills, Europe can't build theatres. Europe has lost the art. Chicago overtops them all."[9]

Everything was secondary to the theater, Sullivan's greatest achievement in conception and decoration, Adler's in the clarity and trueness of its sound. The auditorium was 246 feet long by 118 feet wide. The main floor rose seventeen feet from the front of the orchestra and seated fourteen hundred. A deep elliptical balcony seated sixteen hundred, and above it two galleries held five hundred each. Along the sides of the auditorium were two tiers of open and airy boxes, ten per side, seating two hundred. The stage was 70 by 110 feet, and backstage there was elaborate machinery which enabled stagehands to put one set in place while one was in use. The auditorium was illuminated by five thousand lights, and there were thirty-six fully equipped dressing rooms.

The response to the Auditorium, from critics and from the general public, was overwhelmingly positive from the first. For once, something audacious and icono-clastic was greeted with discerning enthusiasm. The *Chicago Daily Inter-Ocean* ex-ulted: "The new spirit has triumphantly asserted itself in the Auditorium, which is the most splendid tribute to the genius of art on the American continent." A little more coolly, the *American Architect* arrived at the same conclusion: "The sight is one of the most remarkable of its kind in the world. One of the culminating points of American life." Montgomery Schuyler, the leading architectural critic of the day, though he had some criticisms of the block as a whole, had nothing but praise for the auditorium. Its "noble largeness and simplicity" were a "striking and unchallenged" success. This "great and simple" space offered equal hospitality to all, regardless of location or ticket price. In contrast to the "royal" or "imperial" opera houses of Europe, here, Schuyler saw, was "a new kind of art," "the art of democracy."[10]

The grand opening of the Auditorium Building, December 9, 1889, was Chicago's most spectacular event since the fire, outstripping the Opera Festival of four years before. Present were the President and Vice President of the United States, the governor of Illinois, the mayor of Chicago, the Auditorium's financial backers, the city's social elite, and a vast crowd of mere citizens, along with the hero of the hour, Ferdinand Peck. A local poet, Harriet Monroe, recited a dedicatory ode. There were numerous speeches. One orator "sized up the Parthenon, the Pyramids, and the Acropolis with the Auditorium and found them shy."

The celebration of the world's finest auditorium required the presence of the world's most famous singer, so the Auditorium Association engaged Adelina Patti to sing two songs, for five thousand dollars. (The following evening a regular opera performance, Gounod's *Roméo et Juliette,* also with Patti, would take place.) When, at last, the speeches were finally over, but Adelina sang Eckert's "Echo Song" (it had been Jenny Lind's song forty years before) and "Home, Sweet Home." That was it. The audience applauded voluminously, out of appreciation for Patti's artistry and also because an encore was hoped for, but Adelina believed as resolutely as anyone present in the sanctity of contract. The crowd got what it paid for, and not one note more. In all the speechifying and fulsome praise spread about, Adler and Sullivan were never referred to by name.[11]

T h e inspiration for the Auditorium leads us back to Walt Whitman.

In February 1887, as he was immersing himself in this first important expression of the architectural ideas which were fermenting in his mind, Louis Sullivan wrote a letter:

Chicago, Feb. 3rd, 1887

My dear and honored Walt Whitman:

It is less than a year ago that I made your acquaintance, so to speak, quite by accident, searching among the shelves of a book store. I was attracted by the curious title: *Leaves of Grass,* opened the book at random, and my eyes met the lines of "Elemental Drifts." You then and there entered my soul, have not departed, and never will depart.

Be assured that there is at least one (and I hope there are many others) who understand you as you wish to be understood; one, moreover, who has weighed you in the balance of his intuition and finds you the greatest of poets.

To a man who can resolve himself into subtle unison with Nature and Humanity as you have done, who can blend the soul harmoniously with materials, who sees good in all and overflows in sympathy toward all things, enfolding them with his spirit: to such a man I joyfully give the name of Poet—the most precious of all names.

Trusting that it may not be in vain that I hope to hear from you, believe me, noble man, affectionately your distant friend,

Louis H. Sullivan

Sullivan found in Whitman's poetry confirmation of his idea that there was an organic connection between art and nature. The Auditorium Building must reflect the rhythms of nature. "Spontaneous and vital art must come fresh from nature," Sullivan wrote, "and can only thus come." Ornament must reflect the fluidity of nature: "Hard lines flow into graceful curves, angularities disappear in a mystical blending of surfaces." And so the interior of the Auditorium was exuberant with sinuous vines and tendrils, rich and intricate detail which did not, however, distract from the "noble largeness and simplicity" of the essential design. Sullivan paid Whitman the tribute of adopting his prose style in writing, in echoing the expansive freedom of Whitman's language. And he paid explicit tribute to Whitman's rootedness in nature by having designed and installed three large murals, one over the proscenium arch, one on each side of the auditorium. They depicted allegorically the natural themes Sullivan absorbed in reading *Leaves of Grass*.

Further, Sullivan found in Whitman's poetry powerful testimony for the generative and liberating power of new democratic culture. Whitman's vision of democracy had about it openness of form, breadth of vista, and Sullivan responded rapturously. "With me," he wrote, "architecture is not an art but a religion, and that religion but a part of democracy." But Sullivan's idea of democracy was complex, certainly more so than Whitman's. Years later, near the end of his life, he wrote mockingly about Ferdinand Peck, "the dreamer for the populace," "the man of the hour," "who declared himself a citizen, with firm belief in democracy—whatever he meant by that; seemingly he meant the 'peepul.' " The disparaging tone was no doubt due to the depressed state of Sullivan's mind in his last years, but also to his chronic scepticism about democracy if it meant the mass of people. Sullivan had no confidence in *them*. Finally, Whitman inspired in Sullivan a reaffirmation of the belief that art must be indigenous to its contemporary culture, not an eclectic copying of various forms of the past. The American opera house must grow up on native grounds.[12]

T h e Auditorium also leads back to Richard Wagner. As a young boy Louis Sullivan lived for a time with a family who introduced him to music—to oratorios. Like Whitman, Sullivan passionately admired the sound of the human voice in song. Some years later, in Chicago, at age seventeen, Sullivan worked in an architectural firm the foreman of which was a young man, only seven years older than Sullivan, but worldly and sophisticated compared with him, named John Edelmann. Edelmann served as a mentor to Sullivan, introducing him to new ideas, talking for hours with him about politics, philosophy, music. He gave Sullivan an entree to the German culture of Chicago, and together they went to concerts conducted by Hans Balatka where Wagner was played.

Wagner personified for Sullivan the example of the lone artist who by "the stamp of a large and forceful personality" was able to advance art singlehandedly. Sullivan responded to Wagner's power—to the immense Wagnerian attempt to achieve a synthesis of the arts in opera, prefiguring his own desire to recombine the arts in architecture so that designer, builder, sculptor, painter would once again build organically whole buildings. Chicago would be architecture's Bayreuth. Frank Lloyd Wright acutely described Sullivan, at the time of the Auditorium Building, as coming into the fullness of his powers, with a force of self-expression "as complete as Wagner's."

We have Sullivan's own words, written about himself in the third person. "One could see at a glance that this piece [*Lohengrin*] was a work of genius," and later, when he heard *Tristan* and *Die Walküre*:

> Louis needed no interpreter. It was all plain to him. He saw it all. It was all as though addressed to himself alone. And as piece after piece was deployed before his open mind, he saw arise a Mighty Personality—a great Free Spirit, a Poet, a Master Craftsman, striding in power through a vast domain that was his own, that imagination and will had bodied forth out of himself. . . . Here, indeed, had been lifted a great veil, revealing anew, refreshing as dawn, the enormous power of man to build, as a mirage, the fabric of his dreams, and with his wand of toil to make them real.

In its operatic extravagance, the Auditorium was Sullivan's Wagnerian building. Ornament provided a visual equivalent to music. Above the murals, depicting mythic themes, above everything, soared the splendid series of arches rising up out of their piers, spanning the interior space, twinkling with the myriad lights embedded in them, leading the eye down to the music drama on the stage, the source of this "music world of enchantment." The arch and pier symbolized for Sullivan two contrasting rhythms in creation, the rhythm of life in the arch, the rhythm of dissolution in the pier. In creating these magnificent arches, Sullivan echoed one of the great themes of Wagnerian music drama, the transcendence of our mortality, for the arch was also a bridge by which the spirit crossed from this world to a Valhalla fit for heroes.[13]

On Tour

So far as we know, nightingales and larks don't go on tour, but human singers do, and the diffusion of opera has largely been the story of transient groups of singers traveling within Italy, across the Alps, the Atlantic, and to places beyond. Bringing opera to people who had never heard it before typified the first, heroic phase of touring. It was commonly thought of in military terms—territory invaded and conquered, audacious forays, intermittent battles fought against incomprehension and primitive conditions. "To make a victorious tour is for the artist to gain his chevrons," one veteran tourer wrote. "I am tempted to have inscribed at the head of my program: 'Gottschalk has made the tour of the West three times,' as the French legions inscribe 'Arcole Marengo, Austerlitz' on their standards."[1] What such operatic enterprises meant was not subject to any simple calculation. A touring company appeared, an audience gathered, the performers performed, the audience dispersed, the company departed. Opera had been "introduced." But what followed the introduction?

In America, where early conditions were unpropitious, innumerable groups labored anonymously, achieving neither fame nor fortune. In September 1856, signors Morelli and Giannoni, Signorina Aldini, and Miss Vail embarked on a tour of upstate New York and Canada, singing operatic selections, under the management of Mr. Thies, expenses and profits to be equally shared by all members of the company. They began in Albany, where the first performance yielded $159.50, barely enough to meet expenses. Short of cash, manager Thies borrowed twenty dollars from Morelli, "with which he succeeded in keeping his band together and was enabled to lodge them safely" in Troy. The appearance there was "a faultless failure," earning the luckless artists "the enormous sum of twenty six dollars." Once again Thies borrowed money from Morelli, to enable them to get to Syracuse, where the proceeds "fell far short of paying expenses." Morelli, Giannoni, and Aldini gave up and returned to Albany, leaving Thies and Vail behind "to take care of themselves as best they could." Penniless but resourceful, Thies prevented the baggage of the three deserters from being forwarded to them, "which in a day or two had the effect of bringing them back to Syracuse." Somehow, relations were restored. Morelli advanced enough money to enable the party to reach Oswego, where their fourth appearance "again emptied the pockets of Mr. Thies." (Thies's pockets, Morelli's money!) Once again Morelli was appealed to, Thies insisting that if they reached Montreal, "a complete and profitable musical success would inevitably have ensued." Morelli refused. The group broke up. Expenses for the Morelli company totaled eight hundred dollars. Receipts were three hundred dollars. Morelli sued Thies for violating the terms of their contract, but lost.[2]

Morelli's gullibility seems excessive, but without optimism, who would have introduced opera to Troy in the 1850s, San Francisco at that same time, or New York City in the 1820s? Without such hope, who would put up with "bad hotels, snow, mud, railroad accidents, delays, setting out at three o'clock in the morning"? "It requires an iron constitution and a flinty will to succeed in it." The military language of this heroic age often had about it an ironic ring. What was the Morelli conquest, with no enemy vanquished, no land captured, no prisoners taken? Yet even the Morellis may have kindled imaginations. Vincent Sheean pondered this phenomenon. He heard *Carmen* with a mezzo-soprano named Elaine de Sellem. "I have never heard of this artist since, but I thought she was wonderful and I went back again." No doubt the artistic level was pretty low, "but just the same, in these small, traveling companies with their shabby stage settings and their sketchy orchestras, their powerless conductors and their general bad taste, you could get to know the works performed and imagine for yourself, if you had that kind of imagination, what they might be under other circumstances."[3]

A second stage of opera touring emerged gradually. A schedule was arranged ahead of time (but always subject to change!) and places were visited with some regularity. This was the "circuit" stage. The phrase "on tour" entered the English language about 1790, and by the nineteenth century the context for touring had changed. The dissemination of operatic music by other means had greatly increased—"It is wonderful how soon a piano gets into a log hut on the frontier," Emerson said—and the audience was likely to know songs, famous bits. What the touring company brought was opera as musical drama.

Touring influenced the operatic repertory. In the second half of the nineteenth century, perceptive operatic observers noted two related phenomena: the stream of operas composed began to dry up, and the number of operas performed became much smaller than it had been. Opera began to be less a contemporary form of creativity and more a historical exercise in revival. Touring opera was held up as one of the causes of this—impresarios presented only the safest bets to unsophisticated audiences in the hinterlands. But in America, with its large audience distant from metropolitan centers, the repertory was increasing, not decreasing. At the same time, it was more difficult for American audiences to understand how the bits and pieces came together in a dramatic whole, since operas were usually given in incomprehensible foreign languages, and this must have been one of the reasons that audiences increased enormously for the various kinds of "light" opera—Viennese, French, Gilbert and Sullivan—while "grand opera" remained foreign.

Touring made it more difficult to establish a consistent standard of excellence. "Each performance was an event in itself," discrete, not clearly connected with any traditional style. "If the fourth performance was not so good as the second had been, the earlier performance counted for nothing. Each one was judged on its merits as if it were a debut."[4] For performers, conditions were often primitive. Fire was always a hazard. Stages were cramped, scenery was old, shabby. Lighting was makeshift. The orchestra was often doubtful, the chorus equally so. There was little time for rehearsal. Touring was stamped with the brand of accident: lights failed, props disappeared, scenery fell. Theater roofs leaked during rainstorms. And tour audiences behaved surprisingly. The little Adelina Patti sang in Ohio before an audience which indicated its approval by whistling en masse. In Atlanta, all the women in one audience held bouquets of flowers in their laps, turning the auditorium into "an enchanted flower garden." Into Bozeman, Montana, in the fall of 1871, wandered a group of itinerant Italians who were playing the territory wherever they could find a hall. The company, consisting of a few singers, three violins, and two harps, used the opera hall in Bozeman, located above a saloon. They played to a good house, but made little money. Some of the local "boys" had stolen a lawyer's professional cards, similar in appearance to tickets for admission, and the Italians, who understood little English, accepted them. When the fraud was discovered, a "general breakup" ensued. "Several pistols were drawn, and some of the congregation went downstairs like a demoralized whiskey barrel—head first."[5]

No wonder that performers often took liberties, and that touring came to represent

Operatic touring in its imperial phase: Adelina Patti (top row, center) and her entourage in Los Angeles, 1904. Opera News / Metropolitan Opera Guild.

a most mediocre level of performance. Many older performers had no future. Young and ambitious ones had to avoid the trap of carelessness and cynicism. Reputations weren't made in Salt Lake City. There was the Grand Italian Opera Company managed by a Neapolitan named De Vivo, which seems to have specialized in performing operas more rapidly than anyone else. Of course, "certain malevolent spirits might perhaps remark," a writer explained, "that the absence of choruses and of orchestra, of decor and of basso profundo was injurious to the effect." But not being impeded by such accessories, the company's performances "gained in vivacity"—"three operas could sometimes be played in the same evening, with cuts of course, in two hours and a half. And all for 50¢." That was an extreme case. But performances like it were enough to produce a general feeling of contempt among the more sophisticated and among those who disliked opera in any form. Sol Smith, the theatrical impresario, mocked an art which had "no permanent home" but, "broken into fragments, scatters itself into the interior towns and cities where, with scant orchestra and chorus of eight or ten cracked voices, *Il Trovatore, Il Barbiere di Siviglia,* and all the other ils of the Italian repertoire, are given to the worthy citizens of Peoria and Detroit at a dollar admission, children at half price."[6]

Opera was an urban amusement, and much of the criticism of touring opera's low standards reflected the powerful strain of urban-rural hostility which ran through American culture in all periods. Small-town culture deserved what it got. When small-town audiences were unresponsive, they were damned for their ignorance;

Operatic touring in its primitive phase: "Monsieur Matthieu Leading a Small Orchestra." From Sol Smith, Theatrical Management in the West and South for Thirty Years *(1868). Sterling Memorial Library, Yale University.*

when they shouted for more, they were said to be too easily pleased. "A fine quartette and nothing besides may do very well for small towns," the *New York Times* sniffed in 1855, "but something better is wanted here."[7]

T h e operatic history of Charleston, South Carolina, makes clear how much touring companies shaped the operatic culture of even the more important American cities. In the eighteenth century the various English touring companies made Charleston one of their chief bases. In the 1790s it boasted a handsome theater, white and silver inside, seating twelve hundred, with three tiers of boxes. Its culture was very southern and very English. Opera season coincided with the thoroughbred racing season. The rule of the theater was "no admittance for People of Colour in any part of the house." Some bright spots were long remembered—Charles Incledon's singing of English ballads in 1818 and the visit a year later of President James Monroe, who sat in a box decorated with wreaths and roses, an American eagle, and gold letters spelling out "The People's Choice"—but theater fell into the doldrums by the 1820s and 1830s. There was a good deal of religious opposition to it, and only the circus did well.

Things picked up in the 1840s. The value of cotton and slaves rose sharply, and a railroad line connected Charleston to other cities. A new theater was built, a horseshoe-shaped auditorium in Greek revival style, with Ionic columns, tiers of boxes, and a spacious vestibule. W. H. Latham, an Englishman by birth, became the manager. He brought the Seguin English Opera Company, who performed Bellini and Donizetti, Auber and Rossini, *The Bohemian Girl*. A critic who had complained of too much opera changed his mind. Charleston would be "the first to welcome, and the last to part with [opera's] votaries." Anna Bishop's Norma created a sensation. "We scarcely know which to admire most, her singing or her acting." Theodore Thomas conducted there, and so did that "great tactician, and general favorite Max Maretzek."

The two operatic highlights were unquestionably the visits of the Havana company and of Jenny Lind. Though ticket prices were doubled, the Habañeros played to houses that "overflowed." Charlestonians agreed that "this company proved equal to what the most critical taste could demand." They joined wholeheartedly in the Lindomania. One admirer, the haughty daughter of a planter, was so determined to see the singer in private that she "bribed the servants, put on a cap and white apron, and carried in Miss Lind's tea tray." By the late 1850s Charleston had heard *La Traviata* and *Il Trovatore* and, at one time or another, operas by Bellini, Donizetti, Mozart, Adam, Auber, Balfe, Mercadante, and Meyerbeer. The end of the decade was dominated by portents of war. When secession came the theater closed and, in December 1861, with remarkable appropriateness, it burned down.[8]

S o m e singers concentrated on touring, and became famous by doing so. A considerable number of the best-known companies were headed by women. Most of these specialized in opera in English and English opera. These companies kept alive the English operatic tradition in America between *The Bohemian Girl* and *H.M.S. Pinafore*. The Seguins were such a company in the 1840s. The most influential company of the 1850s and 1860s was led by Caroline Richings (1827–1882). Mary Caroline

Reynoldson was born in England and brought to the United States at an early age by her adoptive father, the actor Peter Richings. She began her musical career as a pianist but soon took up singing and made her first opera appearance in Philadelphia in *La Fille du régiment*. Peter Richings formed the Richings Grand Opera Company in 1859, with Caroline as the company's star, and she became its head when her father retired. She was an excellent actress with a serviceable voice and was tireless in championing opera—French, German, Italian—in English. She often translated the librettos herself, not hesitating to edit and adapt the operas to her company's needs.

The greatest singer to take part regularly in touring opera was the remarkable Euphrosyne Parepa de Boyescu (1836–1874). The daughter of the singer Elizabeth Seguin, who taught her music, and of a Romanian father, she made her debut in 1857, sang widely throughout Europe, and in 1865 first came to the United States, joined a concert tour with Theodore Thomas's orchestra, married the violinist Carl Rosa, and took the name by which she endeared herself to multitudes—Euphrosyne Parepa-Rosa. Possessing a powerful and rich voice and an overflowingly generous nature which won the hearts of audiences in a way few singers have ever done, she and her husband formed the Parepa-Rosa English Opera Company, a large (one hundred members) troupe, with fine supporting singers and orchestra, which toured throughout the United States for two years. Parepa-Rosa returned to England where she died, suddenly, much mourned, in 1874.

The most notable of American touring singers was Clara Louise Kellogg (1842–1916). Born in Sumterville, South Carolina, she found enough teaching in America to enable her to make a successful debut at the New York Academy of Music in 1861, in

The soprano Clara Louise Kellogg was one of several women who led touring opera companies in the late 1800s. Historical Sound Recordings Collection, Yale University Library.

Rigoletto, and to sing the first American Marguerite in *Faust.* Only then did she go to Europe, where she sang widely in the 1860s and 1870s and though not achieving stardom, gained the respect of musicians everywhere for the intelligence of her interpretations. Americans got to know her through her years of service to operatic touring, by means of the company she first organized in 1873 and which, in various forms, lasted until 1889. Kellogg traveled everywhere, the first American impresaria to champion opera in English.[9]

Another energetic and successful proponent of opera in English was Emma Juch (1863–1939). Her parents were naturalized American citizens of Austrian descent. Emma was born in Austria while her parents were visiting. She studied with her father, a musician, and made her debut as a singer in London and in New York in 1881. She had a fine voice and her diction was remarkably pure. She sang with the American Opera Company and in 1889 formed her own group, the Juch Opera Company, regularly visiting a large number of towns throughout the United States, Canada and Mexico until 1891. The American Opera Company was organized in 1885 by Jeanette Thurber, to perform opera in English, using unknown American singers. Theodore Thomas was its conductor and musical director. Its repertory— Mozart, Wagner, Verdi, Gluck—was ambitious, and it gave the first American performance of Anton Rubinstein's *Nero.* The first season, 1886, was a six-month tour of the country and was an undoubted artistic success, but a financial failure. Reorganized as the National Opera Company, once more under Thomas's direction, it made another tour in 1887, failed again, and was disbanded.

The history of these touring companies has yet to be written. Until the coming of radio and records, it was by means of these small troupes that a national American audience was created. The Alice Oates Opera Company, the Solomon Opera Company, the Comley-Barton Opera Company, the Emily Melville Comic Opera Company, the Castle Square Light Opera Company—these went wherever railroads would take them after the Civil War. And then there were the regional companies. The Pike Opera Company played in and about San Francisco. The Chicago Church Choir Opera Company covered the Middle West. The Bennett and Moulton Opera Company limited itself to New England.

These touring companies sustained the old tradition of opera performed in English; or perhaps one should reverse it and say that Offenbach and Planquette and Lecocq were so popular because they were done in English. The Hess English Opera Company was one of the important touring groups which translated French comic opera into English and took it to the people. Emily Melville, an arch but amusing performer with a fine voice, was the star of this company, which first did Planquette's *The Chimes of Normandy* in English. Another favorite of the time was Emma Howson, an English singer, for whom Gilbert and Sullivan created the role of Josephine in *Pinafore.* Before that she had spent years in America campaigning with Offenbach's operas. The Howsons were the first professional company to visit the Comstock, where they performed *The Grand Duchess, Orpheus in the Underworld, The Princess of Trebizond.* These companies brought their operas to the provinces with remarkable rapidity. The Howson Company did Lecocq's *Giroflé-Girofla* in the West the same season it received its premiere in New York City. Julia Mathews brought her company from England in 1875 to do French comic opera. Exceptionally appealing, she combined French chic and English jollity. Another English company, led by Emily Soldene, was known for its gorgeous costumes, rich scenery, good singing and acting, and beautiful women.

The longest-lasting of the touring French opera companies of the 1870s was that of Alice Oates, of Nashville, Tennessee, who went north and south and coast to coast throughout the decade. The Oates Company altered its operas at will, introduced contemporary anachronisms into the text, and used local references. Mrs. Oates was "a sprightly and energetic" woman, with a powerful voice, "whose most pleasing quality was its strength." Her acting was full of "snap." New York critics were condescending: "She is admired elsewhere for doing things in a boisterous, rough and angular way . . . a 'rough diamond' which may be often seen on our stage, and which is mostly found in the Western valleys." She gave the first American performance of Lecocq's *The Little Duke* in San Francisco in 1878, where it ran for twenty-two weeks, and she brought it to New York in 1879, achieving popular, if not critical, success.[10]

A n Adelina Patti tour was an imperial progress. Parepa-Rosa brought a European reputation and a large company. Clara Louise Kellogg, Emma Juch, the Richings, the Seguins, and others were part of the general network of operatic culture. They had European experience behind them, English or European prestige. But the kind of touring that reached most small American towns, American operatic culture at its most ordinary, was represented by Emma Abbott, the populist prima donna.[11]

Emma Abbott's life and career embodied many of the folk myths of popular culture. Pluck and luck brought success to Horatio Alger, whose stories were so popular in Abbott's day, and those qualities, plus talent and will, defined her success. She was born on December 9, 1850, in Chicago. Her father, who was in the coal business and earned extra money teaching music, detected signs of unusual talent in his daughter and "spared no pains in its development." She later propagated stories about desperate childhood poverty—wearing rags and walking barefoot—but her family actually lived comfortably, though there wasn't any money for extra musical study. Many people pitched in to help and famous singers encouraged her. Parepa-Rosa heard her sing and was supposed to have discerned "the promise of a great artist." Kellogg gave her a wardrobe for public appearances. She aimed at New York and finally got there, appearing in public with the redoubtable Ole Bull. Study in New York convinced her that she must go to Europe. "She always believed in herself and was determined to make the world believe in her also." At a time when Patti and Nilsson were singing "to crowded houses and immense receipts," Emma daily asked herself: "Why not I?" replying always, "I can and will."

Emma Abbott's time in Europe, however, didn't produce the climb to greatness that had become the archetypal pattern of the career of the ambitious young American prima donna. She didn't like Europe and she didn't approve of it. In London she signed a contract with Colonel Mapleson, who assigned her the role of Violetta in *La Traviata*. Abbott refused to sing it because she believed Violetta was "a wanton who was wicked simply because she loved sin." Mapleson thought this nonsense and was

Emma Abbott, another soprano-impresaria, combined operatic populism and opulence. She is shown here as Donizetti's Anne Boleyn.

caustic: "If you are so good, so very good, you should have taken the veil, and ought to be a Mother Superior in some nunnery instead of trying to acquire a position in opera." But she believed that her stand won her hundreds of supporters in America.

One other incident showed her discordant relationship with Europe and the new idea that singers' performances should be ruled by the intentions of the composer. Singing in Milan, in *La Sonnambula*, she interpolated "Nearer My God to Thee" into one of the scenes and was surprised that the Milanese hissed her. The manager had to come out and apologize for her, and she then appeared before the curtain "bowing and kissing her hands to the ladies present" and singing some Italian songs to placate the irate auditors. What lesson did Abbott learn from this? "Em, you have had a close call; learn from this to be sure your interpolations are suited to the locality in which you sing, even though they fail to accord perfectly with what goes before and comes after."

The defiance of Europe indicated the direction in which her operatic career would go. Emma Abbott became a home-grown diva, presenting opera for Americans in ways they could appreciate. At the time this cost her great anxiety. For weeks after rejecting Mapleson's contract, she suffered attacks of anxiety, insomnia, colds, and paralysis of her vocal chords. "Abbott will sing no more," one reporter concluded. And at this very moment she received news of the death of Horace Greeley, one of her staunchest patrons. "She fell on her knees and prayed for the Greeley family and then in tones as clear as any she ever uttered, she sang once more the old familiar song— 'Auld Lang Syne'—to the memory of that great and good man. And from that hour her voice was restored and her nervous depression cured."

In 1878 Abbott returned from Europe. The next year she formed the Emma Abbott English Opera Company with Charles H. Pratt, whom she had secretly married and who became her business manager. But she really ran the company herself, and she ran it on strict business principles. Touring with Abbott was arduous. The company appeared six or seven times in a week. She insisted that singers could sing that often without impairing their voices. At least, they almost always sang in small opera houses and with a small orchestra. She was grasping and tyrannical. She accepted the dictates of the marketplace without demur, and it would never have crossed her mind to challenge it. No moral improprieties of any sort were tolerated by her. She encouraged marriage among her performers. Nevertheless, the early years were very difficult. "It was certainly up-hill work to gain a foothold and overcome the prejudices of Americans who declared that English opera could not prosper." She had also to contend with religious folk who attacked her because she was a singer and appeared on the stage. A Presbyterian pastor in Nashville, hearing that some members of his congregation had gone to hear Abbott's opera company, used his pulpit to denounce all actors and to remind his parishioners that opera was sinful, "in league with hell and abetting Satan." Abbott, who happened to be in the church that day, stood up and rebuked the minister, saying that theater was a profession "which can be followed with hearts as pure, and lives as irreproachable as may your own." The congregation burst into applause when she finished.

Incidents such as those never shook her optimism about the future, her faith that hard work would achieve anything. She was censorious, dogmatic, but also profoundly naive. "I hope within the next four years to rise to the distinction of the world's greatest singer," she said to an interviewer. "I have already the best, most thoroughly drilled company, fine principals, my wardrobe is the finest ever worn by mortal woman. Why may I not hope by study and the aid of the best instruction Europe affords, to gain that to which I aspire?"

In the early years of the Abbott Company, the repertory consisted of the most popular, established operas—*The Bohemian Girl, La Sonnambula, La Fille du régiment, Martha, La Traviata, The Chimes of Normandy, Roméo et Juliette*. But as she went along, convinced that the repertory had to be kept fresh, she added new operas. Popular songs were interpolated into them. For example, Emma didn't think that *Erminie* was of sufficient merit to be in her repertory, but the "gem" of the opera, the Lullaby Song, was inserted into her company's *Mikado*. Captious critics objected to this incessant interpolating. She introduced various English ballads into *Faust*. She refused to allow aesthetic considerations to outweigh cultural and political ones. "She was the most democratic of women." She sang for the people. During tours of the South, her stage manager reported, "as many as fifty requests would come in on one evening, for the 'Last Rose of Summer,' and she always sang it when thus requested, no matter what opera."

She brought glamor and enchantment to ordinary people's lives. Lavish costumes were the outstanding feature of all her productions. She spent a hundred thousand dollars for Worth costumes alone. Her gowns had virtually nothing to do with the production but were objects of interest in themselves. Nothing was too good for her audiences. Dressing up was a way of bringing joy into humdrum lives. *Martha* was her personal favorite among operas. She sang it when she felt "particularly jolly and wanted a frolic," and one aspect of it touched the deepest level of her imagination: the great lady masquerading as a peasant girl. Transformation scenes epitomized her view of art and of life. The peasant girl turned into a queen, the singer with an ordinary voice—"her voice was not faultless, being at times shrill almost to unpleasantness"— turned into the greatest diva in the world. *Crispino, or King for a Day (Crispino e la Comare)*, by Luigi and Federico Ricci, contained the ultimate in such transformation scenes. Emma, dressed as a drab market woman, stripped off her rags at the climactic moment, revealing a gown of "rose-colored crepe and black velvet with magnificent gems glittering at her throat, wrist, ears, on her fingers, in her hair. She looked every inch the Queen." So could every woman in her audience imagine herself also as Queen for a Day.

Abbott was constantly chosen for a signal honor—to inaugurate new opera houses. Not the operatic palaces of the big cities, the local glories of the small towns. In twelve years in which the Emma Abbott English Opera Company toured, she dedicated twenty-five "temples devoted to music and drama," the first in Springfield, Ohio, in 1880, the last in Ogden, Utah, in 1890. She sang in Gounod's *Roméo et Juliette* in the first, in Balfe's *The Rose of Castille* in the last. She dedicated thirteen houses with *Martha.* Having built a theater they looked upon with pride, citizens selected a star who possessed not only "artistic skill, gracious manner, and comely appearance, but a name known and honored for beauty of character: a name which cannot by any means be associated with reproach."

The sources of Emma Abbott's art were in nature and in the people. "She laid her ear on the breast of nature and caught all the harmonies of humanity." Whitman would have understood how she combined this with her democratic faith. "She sang the songs of the people, and with no more pretention than the thrush that pipes his evening roundelay to ravish the ear of the cottager." She ignored fiercely dismissive criticism of her work. Ordinary people, if not highbrow aesthetes, believed in her and in her people's art. That she didn't succeed outside the United States was a sign of her national virtue. "She was nothing if not American. She never aspired to be anything but what she was." After her death one critic lamented that "only time and increasing intelligence can eradicate Abbott opera." To which a Minneapolis paper replied that "the critics have said that Emma Abbott was not a great singer, as there are roles she could not interpret, and heights to which she might not hope to attain." But she was "a singer of the people." Abbott's reply was much the same: "The people pay their admission fee and thus make my future; the critics deadhead their entrance, to rob me of what the people give."[12]

In the winter of 1890, despite too much travel and work, she insisted on going through with a performance in Salt Lake City. There was a full house she didn't want to disappoint, or lose. She collapsed with a raging fever. When the doctor came to her in her hotel room she sensed that she was dying.

"Doctor, I think I am booked."

"Booked. For where, Miss Abbott?"

"For Paradise, doctor." She sank into a coma but at the very last was heard distinctly to say, "I'm not afraid."[13] She left a fortune estimated at one million dollars.

Touring opera companies brought illusion into mundane reality. They were exotic and all the more magical for that. But like all magic shows, performance was shadowed by an awareness of its own ephemeral nature. Opera touring companies were saturated in the pathos of our mortality. They were transient as life is transient, life which is a kind of tour, a journey from one place to another.

Local Glories

They sprang up all across the land—odeons, academies of music, opera houses—and made the late nineteenth century the great period of American opera house building. Post–Civil War prosperity nourished them; and the increased appetite for popular entertainment overcame much of the lingering rural religious hostility to theater. Railroads and the telegraph made movement faster and more dependable, while the growth of population heightened a sense of impersonality. So townspeople felt the need for a common meeting place which would identify them as a community as well as a town.

Sophisticated urban folk, if they noticed these buildings at all, dismissed them as inconsequential. In the words of the editor of *Musical America:* "I do not call them opera houses in Elmira and Wilmington. . . . We make a distinction between opera houses and opera houses." This paralleled the view that only "grand" opera was opera at all. Theodore Dreiser, who should have known better, was puzzled by the small-town opera house phenomenon. In his novel *The "Genius"* of 1915, he described the fictitious Alexandria, Illinois, a town of ten thousand people, as possessing the symbols of urbanity: a streetcar line, two railroad stations, a public square, and "a theatre—or, rather, an opera house, so-called (why no one might say, for no opera was ever performed there)."[1] Perhaps Dreiser's hatred of small-town life accounted for his being so unperceptive about that "so-called" opera house. Calling it an opera house *was* the point. Carved in stone, lettered in brass or iron, painted on a wooden surface, the words *opera house* were a lifeline to the great world beyond the plains or the mountains, a part of the tradition which stretched from San Cassiano to San Francisco.

Small-town opera houses followed a common plan. As private speculations, they were put on the second or third floor, above commercial space which would pay for the building and its maintenance. A stairway went straight up to the second floor, at the head of which were a small lobby and ticket window, perhaps a cloakroom. Inside, there was a slightly raised stage, framed by a proscenium. A few of the larger houses had a box on either side of the proscenium, but often there wasn't any permanent seating. Folding chairs were brought in when needed. There was no orchestra pit, only a piano off to one side. The average small-town opera house seated about five hundred people. In some of the larger ones, seating one thousand or so, there was a balcony or gallery. (In many small towns, and not just in the South, that was the only place African Americans could sit.) The stage was small and the mechanical arrangements for handling scenery were very simple. Occasionally there would be a dressing room of some sort. Lighting was by gas, though by the 1890s some houses were installing electricity. The interior was undecorated, except for some scrollwork, a fresco painting, or a painted drop curtain. Everyone could hear, since the auditorium was small, but as the floor was only rarely raked, it was difficult to see from the back. Externally, the building was usually indistinguishable from its neighbors except for the occasional more ornate pediment or gable and the crowning glory—the words OPERA HOUSE.

Sometimes these opera houses did stand out from their surroundings, representing virtually every imaginable architectural style. In Buena Vista, Virginia, it was Queen Anne, with a rounded corner tower and twin gables over the front; in Elizabeth City, North Carolina, Richardsonian Romanesque, three stories elaborately plastered. Natchez, Mississippi represented Greek Revival; Sesser, Illinois, California Mission style. The opera house in Cheyenne, brick faced with stone, "combined several styles of architecture," while that in Leesburg, Virginia, resolutely defied categorization, as did the one in Ray, North Dakota, its facade a metal false front stamped to simulate rusticated stone blocks. Four windows ran across the second story, each with a pediment with rosettes and Corinthian brackets.[2]

Anonymous builders, often not professional architects, put up many of these opera houses, sometimes borrowing the plans of one in a neighboring town. However, professional architects designed them as well. J. B. McElfatrick and his company built small-town opera houses throughout the Middle West, a few of them grander than the ordinary ones. Most architects worked within modest limits. The Bismarck, North Dakota, Auditorium, "viewed at the time of its construction as a tangible symbol of the capital city as cultural center," was the work of Arthur Wesley Van Horn, a Bismarck architect with a prolific practice throughout the state. It was a civic enterprise, to be paid for by taxes and by forty-five thousand dollars in city bonds. The plans were originally sent to a St. Paul, Minnesota, firm, whose bid called for an additional forty thousand dollars. This was rejected by the city's voters. The city commissioners then employed Van Horn to build what he could with the original forty-five thousand dollars. What he did the local press hailed as "the most magnificent show house west of the eastern metropolitan centers."[3] It opened with Reginald De Koven's *Robin Hood*.

Opera houses, like everything else, were part of the boom-and-bust nature of American life. Buena Vista, Virginia, founded in 1889, grew rapidly, with local land companies promoting a building boom—a hotel, a college, then an opera house. However, in 1893 the panic and depression abruptly ended expansion. The opera house became a skating rink. Marmarth, North Dakota, founded in 1902, owed its rise to the Chicago, Milwaukee, and St. Paul Railway, which made it a terminal point, with roundhouses and repair shops. Soon it had lumber yards, restaurants, a grain elevator, a bank, and an opera house. Then there was a strike of machinists and carmen. The railroad responded in the familiar crushing fashion of the time. Work was taken elsewhere, striking workers were not rehired, the railroad shops closed. So did the opera house. Marmarth shrank to its population of a decade earlier. Elsewhere

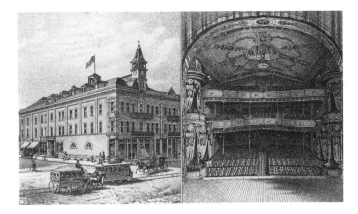

Ragsdale's Opera House and Business Block in Newton, Kansas. Small-town opera houses were often on the second or third floor, above commercial space. From the Kansas Atlas (1887). Library of Congress.

The Opera House in Traer, Iowa. Note the painted drop curtain and side boxes. Library of Congress.

In Littleton, New Hampshire, the Opera House shared quarters with town offices and a fire station. Library of Congress.

the boom was more sustained. In Rushville, Illinois, where most of one side of the city square was destroyed by fire in 1882, the Phoenix Opera House arose from the ruins, giving "notice to the surrounding area that this was no longer a rough frontier settlement, but a center of both commerce and culture." Meridian, Mississippi, grew from four thousand to seventeen thousand in ten years. A five-story brick hotel was built, some businesses were illuminated with incandescent lights, and the town's streets, "though unpaved, were smooth and hard, many of them having a gravel surface." Next came "one of the most needed public institutions," an opera house. "It will add greatly to the attractiveness of the city, not only for the residents but for the country merchants and the travelling man." With its blue, cream, gold, and red interior, the Meridian Opera House was "one of the prettiest in the South, in which any city would take pride."[4]

Politics and ethnic identity were important reasons for building opera houses, and music came in often only when the original purpose had been abandoned. In Red Lodge, Montana, in 1898, the Finnish Rauhan Toivo Society built an opera house, a two-and-a-half-story wooden structure, with a wooden false front that rose above a gabled roof. It served as the center of Finnish social life in the town and surrounding countryside. It housed a library; secret societies met there, as did a local Finnish chorus. The Knights and Ladies of Kaleva staged theatrical performances on its stage. In Rockford, Illinois, the Svea Music Hall was built by the Sveas Soner Singing Society, to promote Swedish unity through song. Built in the heart of "Swedetown," it became the center of many activities besides music for the Swedish population. "In the olden days, you didn't have any place else to go," said one older resident. "We had everything at Sveas Soner." For the Chinese, as we have seen, opera was an important means of preserving their native culture in gold rush California. But after the Chinese Exclusion Act of 1882, which prohibited them from emigrating to the United States, it became crucial. Exclusion made it more difficult to establish families; there was a very high proportion of young single males for whom "opera houses were gathering places, their 'clubs,' their 'community centers.'" Opera achieved its greatest popularity as nativist bigotry intensified. "Even more perhaps than religion," opera "sustained the spirits of beleaguered Chinatown dwellers with its drama of the people's resistance to oppression, their triumphs over wrongdoers, the resilience of heroes and heroines in adversity."[5]

The Opera House built in Oldham, South Dakota, in the 1890s was originally called Socialist Hall, its name proudly chiseled in large block letters across the front. The Socialist party used it for a number of years, but with the waning of its political appeal, the last three letters of its name were removed. The building became neutralized as Social Hall, and then as the Oldham Opera House. The Blue Ribbon Temperance Hall in Galva, Illinois, was built in 1878 by an enterprising temperance leader in the town—888 women and men signed the pledge at its opening—to further the cause of total abstinence. Seven hundred and fifty shares were sold at ten dollars each to finance the "substantial brick edifice on the Square, an ornament to the town and the pride of every member of the club." In 1886, when the initial enthusiasm dwindled, the building became the Galva Opera House, and *The Mikado* and *Olivette's Marriage* took the place of temperance meetings.[6]

The price of tickets at the opera house was usually within the reach of most residents, and its prevailing atmosphere was informal, democratic. Town residents belonged to the same class. But that didn't prevent local elites from using the opera house for social display, local newspapers copying the tone and language of the big-city papers. "One of the largest and most fashionable audiences ever seen" turned out for the once-in-a-lifetime opening of the Meridian Opera House. "I have rarely seen so many beautiful women and so many well-dressed men collected in one place," a local reporter enthused. People crowded around the entrance "to watch the 'first-nighters' dressed in their finery ride up in their carriages." Emma Abbott opened the Burlington, Iowa, Grand Opera House in 1881, "society folk, beautifully dressed, gracing the performance with their presence." "No one thought of attending the theater and sitting in the parquet without white gloves and best gown." When Colonel Mapleson brought his company to Cheyenne, "silks and satins appeared in every fashionable shade and color," proof that the elite of the city "presented an appearance equal in point of intelligence, culture, dress and beauty with any of the metropolitan centers in the east." And in terms of current fashion, everything was up to date in Central City, Colorado. Mrs. J. O. Raynolds wore a black-silk-and-velvet dress and pink hair ornaments; Mrs. Hanington also wore black silk and velvet, *valencienne fissue;* Mrs. Randolph ecru lace, scarlet flowers; Mrs. T. D. Sears, lavender silk, white opera cloak, and blue flowers; Miss Calloway, a pink silk tulle, *à la princesse.*[7]

Wilmington, Delaware, had a long tradition of clerical opposition to theater. In the early nineteenth century, Bishop Francis Asbury, singled it out as a place where "Satan was diverting the people with a play." By 1870, however, the city was tantalized by the prospect of becoming a railroad center, and "in order to fulfill such a prophecy, Wilmington had to look like a big city." An opera house was one of the necessities. The usual pattern was inverted. The Wilmington Masonic Order wanted a place to practice their mysteries and the ground floor was not private enough, so a temple was built to include a theater on the ground floor, with commercial space and the Masonic rooms above. To finance this, five thousand shares were sold to the public at twenty dollars each, an excellent site in the center of town was taken up, and a local man, Thomas Dixon, selected as architect.

The Grand Opera House was a handsome, multistoried building, Second Empire in style. Three of its walls were brick, but the front was of cast iron, painted white. The auditorium seated fifteen hundred—five hundred in the one curved gallery, the rest downstairs, which included a circle of twenty-four boxes. The architect had his own theories about sound. He kept the main floor virtually flat, because he believed this aided hearing. This made seeing difficult downstairs, but the sound *was* excellent. It was a handsome auditorium, with "new style" seats "flying up against the back of the cast iron chairs," to leave more room between the rows. A gilded eagle with out-stretched wings soared over the proscenium arch.[8]

The same kind of opera house was found throughout the South. In North Carolina, twenty counties had towns with such opera houses, though Carolinians referred to them only as theaters. Lexington, Kentucky, proudly called itself "the best one-night stand in the nation." Its opera house, designed by the architect Herman Rose, opened in 1887, with Emma Abbott doing *The Mikado.* In Corinth, Mississippi, one entire side of the city square contained an opera block, bank, museum, cafe, with the opera house, which symbolized "the more leisurely way of life the period stood for," occupying the second, third, and fourth floors. It had been designed by the architect W. McGee, and in it "there was grand opera. It was the real thing." The Henshaw Grand Opera Company presented *Martha* there, and three acts of *Il Trovatore*.[9]

The Ohio Valley and the Plains states were the center of small-town opera-house culture. The region's population included a large number of influential German and central European immigrants, people familiar with opera and with the idea of municipal opera houses. A Wisconsin gazetteer for 1888–1889 listed 134 theaters in the state, of which 50 were called opera houses, the rest being academies of music or merely theaters. Opera house building flourished in Kansas in the late nineteenth century. In Marshall County there were five opera houses in four towns within a twenty mile radius. Western Illinois was once thick with opera houses. A railroad timetable for Nebraska listed dozens of opera houses and academies of music. Many of the Iowa opera houses built in the 1870s and 1880s were financed by the selling of stock and by money donated by civic-minded citizens. They were therefore not built on the two-story plan. Somewhat more elaborate than most, they were at the same time more explicit in revealing social distinctions based on money. "Sometimes a row of enclosed boxes for stockholders separated the parquet from the dress circle," and the balcony or gallery would be correspondingly undecorated. And it wasn't thought incongruous for a local druggist or grocer to put advertising on the drop curtain. A study of ten Kansas opera houses bears out the general pattern, though it was always possible that a more enterprising and imaginative town might come up with something different. The Wamego Opera House brought its ornaments from the Columbian Exposition in Chicago. The proscenium arch was made up of six iron columns used in one of the Exposition buildings, and the house's interior was adorned with six large paintings also bought there. In many places, where the local churches still looked askance at theater, the term *opera* was used as a disguise, to convey respectability. The true nature of spoken drama was concealed by including some music which had no actual connection with the play, or by accompanying a play with a musical variety show. Something too wicked to be spoken might be sung.[10]

In the West, the diversity of buildings was as dramatic as the diversity of terrain. Oregon had a lively theatrical culture in which music played a significant role. The central valley of California was dotted with opera houses. While the bonanza atmosphere of the West produced buildings of surprising lavishness, most communities struggled with more limited resources. The Garcia Opera House in Socorro, New Mexico, dated from the early 1880s. It was a simple one-story rectangular building, its interior walls covered with hand-painted paper floral designs, and simple gas reflectors provided what light there was. In Santa Cruz, California, a wandering, fast-talking promoter from Kentucky named Budd Smith persuaded local businessmen to give him credit to buy land and lumber for an opera house. In November 1877 Santa Cruzans packed the place, sitting on kitchen chairs to watch *The Bohemian Girl*. Later, a local physician bought it, put in red plush seats, set off the stage from the rest of the auditorium with a gold chain, and built two proscenium boxes. Admission was fifty to twenty-five cents.[11]

There was a venerable western tradition of collective action. In the early settlement of Montana, Bozeman included a People's Theatre, a hall over a saloon, where a visiting Boston company put on Dumas' *Camille,* the players being paid in the form of a gold brick valued at $711. In 1880 John Ming built an opera house seating seven hundred. It had an iron roof and dimmable gas jets. In 1894 a combined city hall and opera house was built as a civic enterprise, "an integral part of the American heritage dating back to colonial days and the New England town hall." Over the years, Bozeman's citizens saw a remarkable range of operas and the Bozeman *Chronicle* could say proudly of this initiative: "Its blessings have been many." Salt Lake City in the 1860s was the scene of an extensive public works program: schoolhouses, homes for church leaders, a bath house, the wall around Temple Square, the Tabernacle. And the Salt Lake Theatre. Built in 1861–1862, it was modeled on London's Drury Lane and the craftsmen who worked on its interior were English immigrants. It seated three thousand with a parquet, dress circle, and three balconies—all this at a time when the population of the Salt Lake Valley was probably about twenty thousand people. Its workmen were paid in the form of tickets for future performances, and one cherishes the thought of people bringing potatoes, corn, oats, hams, pigs, honey in exchange for tickets.[12]

T h e West and bonanza went together, as we've seen. When the Colorado Territory became the El Dorado of gold seekers, florid operatic palaces, that once inflamed the civic bosom with pride, sprang up as if by magic. They have disappeared, their local glory gone with the gold dust. But the story of one Colorado opera house was the reverse of notions of fantastic wealth and fabulous luck. It was the work of modest and persistent people who fulfilled their dreams even when prosperity deserted them.

In the Colorado gold rush of 1857–1859, miners poured into the Pike's Peak region, north of Denver, the area that would eventually come to be called Central City. "Hard work and hard whiskey" were the order of the day, but minstrel shows and plays were brought up from the flatlands into the mountains, a theater was built, the miners saw *Uncle Tom's Cabin* and *Hamlet,* heard a brass band and, from time to time, English ballad operas—*Night Hand, Lochinvar,* and a comic afterpiece, *Jenny Lind in the Mountains.* The Howson Company put on *The Grand Duchess of Gérolstein* in 1869 and, as railroads brought the outside world closer to Central City, other opera troupes followed. In 1874 there was a devastating fire. Worse, gold was soon exhausted. Money was less plentiful. People moved away. At which point some townspeople decided that what Central City needed was an opera house.

In 1876 Frank C. Young, a local opera enthusiast, was in Chicago, where he saw Clara Louise Kellogg in *The Bohemian Girl* and was "profoundly touched by its many excellences." He made up his mind to put it on in Central City, and people responded enthusiastically to his proposal. Money was raised, local singers recruited, a German violinist who could serve as conductor, "an old Teutonic citizen who played the cornet," and all the other arrangements taken care of. There were two performances, "a rallying point for the entire community, something that appealed to nearly everyone: miners and bankers, laborers and businessmen, housewives and students." So great was the enthusiasm generated by Balfe's opera that plans were made for a

The imposing front of the Central City Opera House embodied the cultural aspirations of post–gold rush Colorado. Central City Opera photo by Mark Kiryluk.

permanent opera house. R. S. Roeschlaub, from Denver, was chosen as architect. He submitted plans; citizens raised twenty thousand dollars. Construction began in May 1877 and was completed in ten months.

The Central City Opera House, a massive building, French provincial in style, with steep mansard roofs, opened on March 4, 1878. It seated eight hundred people—five hundred in the parquet and dress circle, three hundred in the gallery. Its seating plan was entirely open, with no boxes. Inside there was beautiful fresco work, brought out "by the scintillations of one hundred gas jets." The stage was ample, the sound very good. A special train came from Denver for opening night. "There was the same difficulty about seats that there is in Washington about offices. Finally, however, those who were fortunate got inside and those who were out of luck went home." The opening-night program was a concert of songs and arias, by Weber, Bellini, Rossini, von Suppé, climaxed by the bridal chorus from *Lohengrin,* given "with good precision and marked effect." Everything was sung in English, though there was some grumbling because the program didn't contain American music.

And then? Maintaining the opera house in the face of declining prosperity proved an insurmountable problem. A traveling company put on *Maritana* and *The Chimes of Normandy* in 1880, and later the Caroline Richings Grand Opera Company presented *The Bohemian Girl.* In 1884 the Gilpin County Commissioners bought the opera house for eight thousand dollars, arguing that "a place of amusement is just as necessary for the people as the church or the school house," and explaining to the citizens that "in Europe at the present day, in some of the most educated nations such places are partly, if not wholly, upheld at government expense." After much wrangling, the Opera House passed back into private hands. The town had shrunk to a population of three thousand. In most small towns the opera house would have been torn down or fallen into decay. In Central City no other use was found for it and its granite resisted the ravages of time and weather.[13]

C e n t r a l City was the exception. In most American small towns, while the opera house was a nominal tribute to high culture and to the prestige of opera, it was rarely a place where opera was actually performed. It was kept busy with dances, bazaars, temperance lectures, high-school bands, basketball games, and elocution contests. European opera seemed as foreign to the still predominantly Anglo American small-town culture of the late nineteenth century as it had to England in the eighteenth century. Perhaps the fundamental cultural reason for this had to do with religion. Protestant America remained suspicious of art, and though European immigrants— Catholic, Orthodox, Jewish—were transforming American cities into places more hospitable to art of many kinds, the small towns remained true to the values of the old faith. "Indignant Protestants used to say that [European] churches were like opera houses," Kenneth Clark observed. But it was the other way around: "Opera houses were like churches." Opera houses expressed a "new profane religion," Clark argued, and so for many years, "in Catholic countries, not only in Europe but in South America, the opera house was often the best and largest building in the town." A century earlier, musing on his travels throughout all the Americas, Louis Gottschalk made a related point: "A church and a theater are the two prime necessities of a Spanish-American city." Whereas, "in the United States, when they found a new city, they commence building a hotel, afterward a church, and finally the newspaper office. Given the hotel, church, and political discussions, you have the existence of the Yankee."[14]

It was in these years that American city dwellers and intellectuals increasingly thought of the small town as a cramped and bigoted place, unsympathetic to art and artists. Young people with artistic yearnings fled the towns to go to the cities. This depiction of the small town, at that moment in its history, is one of the themes of the finest American novel about art and the artist, one of the most undervalued of Willa Cather's novels, *The Song of the Lark* (1915). This story of "an artist's awakening and struggle; her floundering escape from a smug, domestic, self-satisfied provincial world of utter ignorance," grew out of Cather's personal experience of small-town life. Born in Virginia in 1873, Cather moved with her family to Red Cloud, Nebraska, when she was nine. Bookish, interested in music as well as literature, she attended the University of Nebraska, became a journalist and editor in Pittsburgh and New York. Her first collection of short stories, *The Troll Garden* (1904), was about art and artists, would-be and authentic artists, spurious and genuine art. One of the stories, "The Sculptor's Funeral," is a withering depiction of Sand City, "this place of hatred and bitter waters," and another, perhaps Cather's best-known short story, "A Wagner Matinee," concerns the price a talented woman musician paid in spending most of her life on the frontier, sacrificing art for her marriage.[15]

A decade later Willa Cather returned to this theme in *The Song of the Lark,* subtly and shrewdly depicting the culture of Moonstone, Colorado, the internal dynamics of the Kronborg family, and the mind and character of Thea Kronborg, a young girl who plays the piano and sings and begins to dream of the almost unimaginably distant East and Europe and the world of art.[16] Cather, who had experienced and learned a great deal about late nineteenth-century American musical history, filled her novel with revealing vignettes about it. There is the Moonstone opera house, its seats wooden

Willa Cather, photographed by Edward Steichen, depicted small-town musical culture in The Song of the Lark. *International Museum of Photography at George Eastman House. Reprinted with permission of Joanna T. Steichen.*

kitchen chairs, numbered and nailed to long planks which held them together, the site of performances by the town's Sunday schools, dramatic society, and orchestra, the latter conducted by Mr. Upping, the jeweler, who had once been a violinist with the Andrews Opera Company, which toured the small towns of Nebraska and Colorado. There is Moonstone itself, divided geographically and socially by Main Street, with the people who were "in society" on one side and "all the humbler citizens, the people who voted but did not run for office," the immigrant Catholics and the residents of Mexican Town, on the other.

Moonstone is also divided about art. Some of the townspeople thought that Thea Kronborg gave herself airs. At the annual Christmas Eve concert in the opera house, Thea played a difficult piano piece which bored the audience. Thea's rival, Lily Fisher, "the angel-child of the Baptists," sang "Rock of Ages" and "Home, Sweet Home" and was enthusiastically applauded. That night Thea first understood how easy it was to fool audiences. "Lily Fisher was pretty, and she was willing to be just as big a fool as people wanted her to be." Thea wasn't. "She would rather be hated than be stupid, any day." There was also respect for Thea's talent in Moonstone, based on practical considerations. She was a good piano teacher, conscientious and not too expensive. "There were ten new pianos shipped in here from Denver in the last year," Thea's father noted approvingly. "People ain't going to let them stand idle; too much money invested."

The Kronborg family was as divided about Thea's musical talent as was the town. Her father, a Methodist preacher, worried about keeping up appearances, didn't really like Thea's artistic ambitions but, so long as she played the organ and led the singing at prayer meeting, was content. Thea's sternest antagonist was her older sister Anna. Conventional in nature, like her father, Anna valued her position as the minister's oldest daughter. She felt that "nothing was decent until it was clothed by the opinion of some authority." What most embarrassed Anna was that Thea practiced her "secular music," even the *Blue Danube* waltz, on Sundays, and that she made friends with many of the foreigners in Moonstone, especially the Mexicans and Herr Wunsch, the disreputable German piano teacher. Thea pretended that she liked the Mexicans because they were fond of music. "But everyone knew that music was nothing very real," Anna said, "and that it did not matter in a girl's relations with people." Thea's great ally in the family, whose support vastly outweighed the opposition of the others, was her mother, strong, practical, who understood the source of Thea's talent: it came from *her* father, who had played the oboe in an orchestra in Sweden—"He had even known Jenny Lind"—before he came to America. Mrs. Kronborg did what was essential: she kept Thea practicing four hours a day and gave her a room of her own, so that the family's clamor would not drown "the voice within herself."

Thea Kronborg had other friends in Moonstone too—Ray Kennedy, a conductor on the railroad; Dr. Archie, who took special care of her when she was sick; Spanish Johnny, who played the mandolin and, with his friends, gave Thea her first experience of an appreciative musical audience; Mr. and Mrs. Kohler, whose garden, with its arbor and grapevine, "full of homesickness and sentiment which the Germans had carried around the world with them," unites the twin magics of nature and art (the relationship of art and nature is one that Cather explores more fully in the second half of the novel).

The most important person for Thea was Herr Wunsch—A. Wunsch, as he signed himself. No one ever knew what the A. stood for, nor when or why he had come to America. "He had taught in music schools in St. Louis and in Kansas City, where the shallowness and complacency of the young misses had maddened him." Thereafter, he encountered bad manners, bad faith, bad luck. "He had played in orchestras that were never paid and wandering opera troupes which disbanded penniless." Wunsch ended up in Moonstone, where the Kohlers took him in. He was based on a character from Cather's Red Cloud childhood.[17] She first heard music in the home of friends whose children took lessons from Professor Shindelmeisser, "an old German who wandered into town from nowhere and who often came to talk about the old country and to practice on their new Chickering. He was a heavy drinker and many people thought he was unfit to teach their children." In the novel, Wunsch is charmingly realized as an individual, but Cather refused to sentimentalize him. After a bout of drinking, he leaves Moonstone and Thea never sees him again. Historically, Wunsch is evoked with unerring accuracy. As we have seen so many times, it was innumerable people like him who, laying the foundations upon which others would build, created an American operatic tradition.

Herr Wunsch's limitations are important. Technically, he does not teach the piano very well. When Thea finally leaves Moonstone, with the help of money from Ray Kennedy and Dr. Archie, she goes to Chicago, finds that she is woefully unprepared as a pianist and can have no career, and then discovers her true gift, as a singer, going on from Chicago to Germany, where she becomes a great Wagnerian soprano. But what Herr Wunsch had given her was an initiation into the world of musical artistry, a determination never to accept the second best. And Cather achieves this in one scene of wonderful novelistic realization, hinting at Thea's future vocal artistry.

One day Wunsch showed Thea an edition of the piano score of Gluck's *Orpheus and Eurydice,* turned to the third act, to Orpheus's great lament for the death of his wife, and played and sang it with great feeling. "That is very fine, eh? There is no such beautiful melody in the world." Only one woman could sing it as it deserved, he tells her. Thea is perplexed. "It is written for alto, you see," Wunsch explains and repeats: "There was only one to sing that good." He answers Thea's question about her: she was Spanish, not German, not beautiful. "She was ugly; big mouth, big teeth, no figure. A pole, a post! But voice—ach! She have something in there behind the eyes." And she is still alive—"Paris, may-be. But old, of course, I hear her when I was a youth."

" 'Was she the greatest singer you ever heard?'

"Wunsch nodded gravely. 'Quite so. She was the most. . . .' " He hunted for an English word, lifted his hand over his head and snapped his fingers noiselessly in the air, enunciating fiercely, "*künst-ler-isch!*" [artistic]. "The word seemed to glitter in his uplifted hand, his voice was so full of emotion." Fingers snapping, voice choked with emotion, there in Moonstone, in a nondescript room in the tumbledown Kohler house, on the edge of operatic nowhere, Wunsch evoked the image of the kind of singer Thea Kronborg might aspire to become and forged a link for her (and for us readers) in the great chain of operatic being, planting in her mind the idea that she might be the heiress of Malibran and Alboni and Lind and of that *künstlerisch* singer, the one with something behind her temples, "the only one to sing that good," Pauline Viardot-García.

I n 1896 a film was for the first time in the United States projected in a theater, and short films were brought into theaters and opera houses throughout the country. It was commonly expected that live entertainment and occasional showings of film would be readily combined. In 1897 the Bayliss Comedy Company appeared in the Beardstown, Illinois, Opera House and in connection with its performances displayed a device by Thomas Edison which reproduced pictures. That same year a kinetoscope amazed audiences in the Stephen Opera House in Watseka, Illinois. By 1900 the Beardstown Opera House was advertising Edison's motion pictures, of fire brigades in action, war scenes, prize fights. In 1910 a motion picture machine was set up in the Phoenix Opera House in Rushville, Illinois, and the same thing was soon happening all over America. Live entertainment was soon imperiled, and within a few years traveling theatrical companies were driven out of business. Opera houses became movie theaters. As such they continued to be important places. But something of their glory had departed.

End of the Century

At century's end, change was the order of the day. The fifteen million Americans of 1825 had become seventy-five million, residing in a continental nation that stretched from the Atlantic to the Pacific and from the Gulf of Mexico to the Arctic Circle, a land mass half again as large as it had been when Manuel García arrived in New York. Rural and agricultural life was giving way to an urban and industrial order. The predominantly British and African population had been transformed by newer arrivals from Asia and everywhere in Europe. The isolated provincial republic was now an imperial power. Three very different end-of-the-century opera houses reflected this diversity and represented the struggle to adapt a traditional art form to new ways of living. One sought to maintain inherited ethnic traditions in an age of assimilation; another, a small-scale enterprise in the age of corporate gigantism, emphasized local talent and audiences; while a third uncompromisingly represented the unbounded aspirations of colossal wealth.

S a n Francisco had become a more settled and orderly place since Tom Maguire's days, but the desire for respectability hadn't entirely wiped away vestiges of its raffish past. It remained hospitable to eccentric diversity at one end of the social scale, and at the other, its Nob Hill mansions reflected the uninhibited vulgarity of the new rich. The possessors of the fortunes which made those mansions rise were uninterested in art and unconcerned as yet with any social standing to be gained by its patronage. The artistic culture of the city depended on a middle class of modest means, who had no art-monopolizing plutocracy to contend with. The city remained passionately theatrical and musical, a taste strengthened by the arrival of a growing number of Italian immigrants late in the nineteenth century. At one time or another in the years between the gold rush and the earthquake, twenty-six different theaters in the city presented opera.

The grandest of these was Wade's Opera House, built by a local dentist, Thomas Wade, and opened in January 1876. A fine example of the Erie architectural impulse, it had a large vestibule, two curving staircases, a lobby resplendent in black-and-white marble floor, ornamental statuary, and vases, and—its great showpiece—a central fountain that showered cologne in a perfumed spray! The large auditorium, in shades of blue and gold, had three tiers of open seats and twelve proscenium boxes. Here many touring opera companies came in the 1870s and 1880s, by which time the name had been changed to the Grand Opera House: Adelina Patti and Emma Nevada in the famous Mapleson season of 1885; Enrico Caruso and Antonio Scotti in *Carmen,* on the night of April 18, 1906. San Franciscans were awakened the next morning by a much greater drama, the earthquake and fire which destroyed the city and the opera house.

More popular, more interesting, was the Tivoli Opera House. It began as a public beer garden in 1875, where patrons drank lager and listened to music. It was established by the Kreling family, father and two sons, who had emigrated from Germany via New York. They brought with them their skill as upholsterers and a delight in music. The Tivoli Gardens was the idea of Joe Kreling, one of the sons, then only twenty years of age. It was successful enough to move, in 1879, to a larger site, where an older building was converted into a theater seating a thousand, with one gallery. This Tivoli opened on July 3, 1879, with a production, in the early days of the national madness, of *H.M.S. Pinafore,* which played to full houses for sixty-three consecutive nights. No Sunday or early closing laws were in force in the city, so the Tivoli was open every night of the week, every week of the year. On the back of the

The Tivoli Opera House in San Francisco was a family business, open every night of the year. Patrons were encouraged to bring beer or wine to their seats. San Francisco Performing Arts Library and Museum.

seats was a wide shelf for glasses of beer or wine. Dining was an important part of the attraction and atmosphere of the Tivoli. Waiters with white aprons also served as ushers. The Tivoli was a family enterprise, the Krelings living on the top floor and family members tending the upstairs and downstairs bars. Joe Kreling worked in the box office, supervised productions, and, in his spare time, translated German, Italian, and French librettos into English. The Tivoli's librettos cost ten cents each, or sometimes were given away free. Although the Tivoli was enlarged to accommodate sixteen hundred people in 1880, it remained intimate. The sound in such a small place posed no problems, and the stage was adequate for the more elaborate Italian and French operas as these were added to the repertory.

The Tivoli was a local company. Its singers were mostly Europeans who had emigrated to San Francisco or come with touring companies and stayed. Productions remained small in scale. Of the several competent conductors, Gustave Hinrichs gained valuable experience at the Tivoli and later went to Philadelphia, where he initiated Tivoli-like popular seasons. The Tivoli orchestra consisted of half a dozen violins, one or two cellos, violas, bass fiddles, flute, oboe, bassoon, clarinet, two French horns, cornet, tympani, drums—adaptable even to the early Wagner operas. After the premature death of Joe Kreling, the Tivoli was run by his widow, Ernestine, who advertised it as "The House of Operatic Performances at Popular Prices." A later writer said: "Perhaps more than any other theater of its day, the Tivoli made opera a democratic art."[1]

The Tivoli hardly ever stopped, closing its doors only forty times in twenty-five years. From 1880 to 1890 it relied on English, French, and Viennese opera. Gilbert and Sullivan (ten different operas) received 691 performances, *Pinafore* and *The Mikado* accounting for 357 of them. Offenbach operas were put on 580 times in that decade—fifteen different works, including *Les Contes d'Hoffmann* seventeen times. Six of Lecocq's operas were performed 550 times; the operas of von Suppé tallied 393 performances. In addition, there were 278 performances of Johann Strauss, 268 of Edmond Audran, 191 of Robert Planquette, 182 of Karl Millöcker, 156 of William Vincent Wallace.

In the 1890s the Tivoli embraced Italian opera, presenting 329 performances of five Verdi operas—*Il Trovatore, Ernani, La Traviata, Rigoletto, Un Ballo in maschera*. Donizetti's operas were heard 147 times, Gounod's 139, almost all of them *Faust*. There were two Mozart operas, *Die Zauberflöte* and *Don Giovanni*, but no Bellini or Rossini. A Tivoli season remained an eclectic mix. In 1898, for example, there were *The Mikado, La Belle Hélène,* and *The Bohemian Girl*, but also *Aida, Fidelio,* and *Lohengrin*. In 1900 audiences heard *Otello, Tannhäuser,* and Halévy's *La Juive*, as well as the familiar favorites. In 1901 the Tivoli's repertory would have done any opera house proud—Boito's *Mefistofele, Falstaff, Samson et Dalila, La Gioconda, Norma, Nabucco, The Force of Destiny* (*La Forza del destino*), and *La Bohème*.

Such was the Tivoli: no stars, limited in its resources, frugal in its productions, but a vital force in the musical culture of the city, "the most faithful music teacher of the West." And then it came abruptly to an end, due not to fire but to the fire chief, who declared the Tivoli a fire trap. In November 1903 it shut its doors, and though it was rebuilt the next year, in a new location, on a grander scale, the real Tivoli had come to an end.[2]

I n the 1890s the Metropolitan Opera emerged in the form, social and musical, which marked it for the next forty years. The snuffing out of the German opera seasons showed clearly what the shareholders didn't want. What they *did* want was still to be worked out, a process speeded up by a fire in 1892 which gutted the auditorium and wiped out the forthcoming season. Some shareholders wished to rebuild, others did not, but as the land on which the opera house stood was now worth alone what the land and building had cost ten years before, a rebuilt house was a good investment and a reorganization in ownership ensued. A new company, the Metropolitan Real Estate and Opera Company, bought out the old and many of the original seventy boxholders took their money and retired from the opera business. Nineteen of the original ones stayed on and sixteen new boxholders were invited in. Each of these was assessed an annual payment for taxes and maintenance of the property. The boxholders elected a board of directors to negotiate their business for them, and they had the final say about what pleased or displeased them on the stage. But essentially they leased their house, its sets, costumes, and equipment, to an impresario who put on a season of opera for which they bore no financial responsibility.

And so was born the Diamond Horseshoe, the thirty-five boxes in the first and most prestigious tier of boxes, the ownership circle constituting, self-proclaimed but unchallenged, the top tier in the social hierarchy of New York City. The Diamond Horseshoe represented an effort at social control within a burgeoning plutocracy. If anybody's money was as good as anybody else's, the vast amount of money and the large number of very rich people congregating in the city endangered polite society as it had been known. "It was this power to scrutinize and reject, to include or exclude, that made opera patrons of non music lovers."[3] If the Academy of Music had symbolized the supremacy of commerce, the new Metropolitan symbolized the clear-cut supremacy of finance capitalism. The movement toward centralized national business control had resulted in the era of the trusts, sugar and petroleum, meat packing and tobacco and banking. The Metropolitan Real Estate and Opera Company was an operatic trust, the opera house of Wall Street.

Among the thirty-five boxholders of 1892 were three dominant groups—the Morgans, the Vanderbilts, and the Knickerbockers (representing older New York)— who accounted for twenty-eight of the boxes. The Vanderbilt group numbered eleven and constituted, directly or by marriage, a family interest. The Knickerbocker group, controlling five boxes, was made up of holdovers from the first Metropolitan and Academy of Music days. Twelve boxes were owned by the Morgan group, whose relationships were business and not familial—partners, former partners, friends of Morgan. The reorganization seemed to have the blessing of Providence. At the drawing for boxes, J. P. Morgan received the first choice. He selected box thirty-five, furthest from the stage but in the center of the Diamond Horseshoe, precisely where the imperial box would have been placed in a European opera house. "Seventeen Vanderbilts at one side or seventeen Astors at the other might have to turn their heads to observe his arrival but from his point of eminence he could survey all without effort."[4] The boxholders were people of inordinate ambition and incessant social aspiration, but the Metropolitan was not the scene of "social wars." In this end-of-the-century microcosm of the American world, the Morgan influence worked for stability, order. No one questioned his claim to preeminence. When important decisions by the directors of the Real Estate Company were to be made, the directors met in the Morgan library to make them.

Morgan's standards of social propriety were commonly held. "The people in his social world were of his own kind, and the bankers and business men with whom he came into contact had, for the most part, the same standards of ethics and point of view that he himself had." There were no Roman Catholics in the Diamond Horseshoe, no Jews, no foreign-born. Where, in earlier decades, the dominant social elite in American cities was defensive about its privileges, still concerned not to offend general public opinion, the members of the Diamond Horseshoe were unabashed about identifying their interests and in defending them. As the actress Maxine Elliott, who knew some of these men well, put it: "Why, you men of Wall Street are like a lot of cannibals. You devour anything that comes along—if it is edible."[5]

Not all the titans of American finance shared Morgan's views about society or art patronage. Andrew Carnegie disapproved of opera on moral grounds, supporting choral and orchestral music instead. And though he put up most of the money for the concert hall named for him (1891), he was unhappy that it didn't pay for itself, always insisting that "the greatest patronage of music should come from a paying public rather than from private endowment." John D. Rockefeller had no use for opera houses, concert halls, or "society." He rejected the new impulses toward conspicuous consumption. "There was no reason why he should not have bought a yacht for himself and begun to train his children for polo and polygamy or joined the society of fox-hounds, opera singers and other such heathen *carnivora*," except the fundamental one that Rockefeller remained steadfast in his Baptist faith, the austere faith of the early nineteenth century.[6]

W o m e n played a special role in this opera house. It was built for them. Any hints of the erotic were frowned upon. There were no curtains, latticework, or shutters on the boxes, which were blatantly public. The boxes were for display and it was women who were displayed. Conventions were rigorously adhered to: evening dress for men and evening gowns for women. Even the ushers wore evening dress, with silver badges to distinguish them from the patrons. Two women always sat in the front row of a box, four men behind. Clothes were a means for the display of jewelry. The Diamond Horseshoe: the gold-and-silver-and-diamond-and-emerald-and-ruby-and-amethyst-and-pearl horseshoe! The repainting of the house's interior after the 1892 fire had been a mistake. The cream-colored walls were a poor background for jewelry. In 1903 it was repainted, in gold and maroon, the Astor colors. The anterooms of the boxes were decorated according to personal taste. Lily Hamersley, later duchess of Marlborough, concealed the dull walls of her box with festoons of orchids.

Behind the scenes, women influenced opera house policy, what was sung, who sang it. No woman served on the board of directors. Art was a woman's sphere, but as consumers, not as managers. Morgan's views about the proper role for women were clear: "to select for our wives those who . . . will ever be ready to make us happy and contented with our homes." People critical of society never understood that serious work went on in the boxes. The opera house was a marriage market, where young men and women met under the eyes of their elders. Many in the audience were "unattached and eligible males, with seats in less exalted parts of the house," who "cruised the boxes until vacancies presented themselves." To be invited into one of the box anterooms was a great step forward for the socially ambitious, while "an appearance as a guest" in one of the Diamond Horseshoe boxes "became as much an accolade of social fitness as kissing the royal hand of Victoria, herself."[7]

Caroline Astor, a member of the Knickerbocker group, was the social leader of Metropolitan society, ruling as supremely in her sphere as J. P. Morgan in his. An unvarying social protocol evolved. Mrs. Astor, resplendent in her much publicized diamond stomacher, always arrived at nine o'clock in box seven, regardless of when the opera began. During intermissions, Mrs. Astor "received" her friends, out-of-town visitors and Europeans, if sufficiently distinguished. After one intermission, perhaps two, Mrs. Astor left. No one left before her. After her departure, others would also drift away. Mrs. Cornelius Vanderbilt presided over box four, humming off-key throughout the opera, and always leaving in the middle of the *finale*. On nights when there was a society ball, the opera posed an inconvenience. Balls always began at ten o'clock and, as nothing could interfere with them, society left the opera in droves. Mrs. Astor's reign ended with her death in 1908. Her successor was Mrs. Cornelius Vanderbilt III, "who had a flair for social intrigue" and all "the other qualities that make a ruler." In the 1920s she played an important role in the destinies of the Metropolitan.[8]

The opera house had a place for "Male Penguins only," from which these "gentlemen rovers" launched their forays into box land. After the fire of 1892, the Vaudeville Club took over some unused assembly rooms and Stanford White, the society architect (son of Richard Grant White, music critic of earlier days), designed a Lilliputian reproduction of a music hall, complete with boxes. In 1899 the Vaudeville incorporated as simply the Opera Club. Although it was an all-male preserve, women occupied the first two rows of the club box on Saturday afternoons. On other, more intimate occasions, women came to the club's rooms to sit and talk with friends, their presence concealed by a large screen in a corner.[9]

W h a t kind of opera house did the boxholders want? Diamonds in the boxes and stars on the stage. Without a doubt the most important singing star, the pivotal figure of the decade, was Jean de Reszke, the greatest tenor of the time, who brought with him his brother, a bass, Edouard. Born in Poland in 1850, originally a baritone, Jean de Reszke was that most unusual kind of tenor, consummate musician and popular idol combined. Suave, charming, "darling Jean," an actor of subtlety and taste, his voice was appealing but not notable for sensuous beauty. He took up tenor roles in 1879, became a celebrated figure by the mid-1880s. French and Italian opera were his specialties until, in the early 1890s, he sang Wagner with immense success. Edouard, a large man with a huge voice and a wide range of roles, was a great favorite in his own right. Between them they shaped the Metropolitan's repertory.

Edouard de Reszke, Nellie Melba, and Jean de Reszke taking a curtain call after a performance of Faust *at the Metropolitan. Gounod's opera was so popular that the building was dubbed the "Faustspielhaus." From* Harper's Weekly, *1895.*

In the next few years the roster of the Metropolitan's singers was filled with the most famous names in the world. Emma Calvé, who came in 1893, sang many roles, but there was one fiery, stage-dominating interpretation that was forever identified with her. "What a night it was, that first Carmen of hers," wrote James G. Huneker. "She chucked tradition to the winds, also her lingerie. Some of the elder critics are still blushing." That same year Nellie Melba sang for the first time at the Metropolitan, Patti's successor as Queen of Song. Nevertheless, the men, led by Jean de Reszke, dominated: Pol Plançon, French bass, at home in French, German, and Italian opera; Victor Maurel, another Frenchman, a baritone, who had created Iago and Falstaff in the world premieres of Verdi's *Otello* and *Falstaff;* Francesco Tamagno, Italian, the first Otello, with a voice of astounding power, "the metallic penetrativeness of an eight inch shell."[10] A little later came Ernestine Schumann-Heink, contralto; Anton Van Rooy, one of the greatest of Wagnerian baritones; two American sopranos, Emma Eames and Lillian Nordica; and many more.

Famous singers, *many* famous singers, singing in the same opera, the "nights of stars." Prices were higher for these "ideal casts." Orchestra seats, normally five dollars, cost seven on star nights. *Les Huguenots* was sung by the de Reszkes, Plançon, Nordica, Scalchi, Melba, and Maurel (one dollar per star). *Le Nozze di Figaro* had Sembrich, Maurel, Eames, Nordica, and Edouard de Reszke. Wagner's fortunes fluctuated in these years, but *Götterdämmerung* had Nordica, the de Reszkes, and Schumann-Heink. *Die Zauberflöte,* with its seven major roles, was the ultimate star vehicle. Given in Italian as *Il Flauto magico,* it had "more than enough [stars] for all ordinary purposes": Sembrich, Eames, Plançon, Zélie de Lussan, Campanari, Andreas Dippel, and Milka Ternina. Not all operas required five or six stars, even when they were available. *Faust* was the most popular opera at the Metropolitan, as it had been since Christine Nilsson's days. It included Jean de Reszke's most famous non-Wagnerian role (Edouard's too, as Mephistopheles), and there was no end of splendid Marguerites. There was *Faust* with the two de Reszkes, Jean-Louis Lassalle, and Melba. *Faust* again, with Emma Eames. *Faust* yet again, with Emma Calvé. *Faust* twelve times in one season. No wonder the newspaper critic W. J. Henderson wrote of a stranger visiting New York and wondering what went on in the great *Festspielhaus* (festival playhouse) on Broadway. He was told it was the *Faustspielhaus.*[11]

A second policy established in these years was that opera would be performed in the language in which it had been composed: French, Italian, and German—everything but English. Lilli Lehmann sang in all three languages in the 1880s, exceptional in this as in everything else. (Russian, outside Russia, was not yet a European operatic language.) The willingness of the great French singers (American singers, too) to master the pronunciation of whatever language they sang in was very influential, making them leaders in the first truly international period of operatic performance.

Star opera had destructive consequences, especially because the Metropolitan fixed itself as the model, for Americans, of what an opera company should be. The boxholders stipulated in their contract with the impresario how many and even which stars would sing on Monday nights (at least two out of a list of six). They stipulated how much Wagner would be done. Even more destructive: production hardly mattered. Compared to productions at the state-subsidized operas of Dresden, Munich, Vienna, and Berlin, the Metropolitan managed by simply "omitting factors usually found" there, "namely, a fine chorus, orchestra, ballet and mise-en-scene."[12] Equally damaging: the cost of star nights was compensated for by offering "off-nights," when ordinary ticket buyers could afford to go. These were frequently dreadful because, though the singers were good, the productions were unrehearsed, with dispirited performers merely going through the motions.

It may have been a golden age of singing, but it was far from a golden age of opera, as critics knew and reported. The subscribers didn't care, and in any case they genuinely believed that what they were hearing was the best in the world. If not, find better singers and employ them. But what of the general public? The star system was admired. "It is not difficult to imagine just what this public desires in the way of opera. It desires all the stars it can get at once." Even among the stars, only certain ones were really worth hearing in certain roles. There was a "Melba part" or a "Calvé part," which led the *New York Times* to ridicule the "silliness of the glorification of individual singers" who were now "almost as famous as prize fighters."[13]

Wall Street opera required Wall Street management. Maurice Grau was the representative impresario of the time. Born in Brunn, Austria, in 1849, the nephew of Jacob Grau, promoter of Offenbach in America, Maurice came to America with his parents at age five. He was educated in New York City public schools and attended Columbia University Law School; but he always knew he wanted to be an impresario, though he was only slightly interested in music and had little musical knowledge. It was the business of opera that intrigued him, and he got his chance when, in 1896, Henry Abbey died and the Metropolitan reorganized its management, requiring a large guarantee to be deposited with the shareholders. Grau raised the money from New York banker friends. Jean de Reszke's influence enabled him to become impresario at Covent Garden as well, giving him a virtual monopoly over the leading singers of the day. Between 1896 and 1903 Grau brought the star system to its highest point.

An American singer characterized him as "a great card player, expert at chess, an inveterate operator on the Stock Exchange [who] viewed the profession of an impresario in the light of a complicated and highly interesting game in which, when his partners did not upset his calculations, he was usually successful." When it suited his purposes, Grau didn't pinch pennies for stars. He put Jean de Reszke and Emma Calvé in *Carmen* and, where other impresarios always stinted, paid Emma Eames eight hundred dollars a performance to sing the secondary role of Micaela. However, he didn't hesitate to break the choristers' strike when they wanted more than fifteen dollars a performance. He knew "where to spend a dollar and where to save a nickel." He spent on stars and saved on everything else. "Grau will give you a good cigar," said Jean de Reszke, "but not the match to light it with." Unflappable, friendly, multilingual—he spoke to most of his singers in their native language—Grau had no illusions about what succeeded at the box office and what didn't. "Encouraging, isn't it?" he commented sarcastically when a new opera played to a half-empty house. He felt at home in America, understood American business, which he admired (though he lived in Europe when he retired). His Wall Street employers trusted his single-minded concentration on money, as when he explained why an artist he admired never sang a certain role for him. "I've never made money with her."[14]

The Diamond Horseshoe presented an image of arrogance based upon immense wealth and power. In matters of business and politics, this was true. But in almost anything to do with art, the boxholders were essentially uncertain and timid. They scrambled in a most unseemly way to marry their daughters to European titles. They ransacked salesrooms and imported European objects wholesale. They modeled their houses on European examples, "producing a comic effect with Fifth Avenue con- verted into a mishmash of Venetian canals, Florentine streets and Parisian boulevards, and New Port emerging as a kind of Madame Tussaud's view of the Renaissance." In no art did they defer more to Europe than in music, not least in opera, where their borrowing took a special form: the importation of Continental music and musicians and the copying of English operatic manners. If Bayreuth had been the musical shrine for the German American audience, Covent Garden was the social one for Anglo Americans. The rage for Gilbert and Sullivan fifteen years earlier among the ordinary folk was paralleled by the need of this American elite to identify itself with the British governing class. A member of the Opera Club likened the Metropolitan Opera House to Buckingham Palace, and the joint directorship of Maurice Grau clinched the transatlantic embrace. The symptoms of turn-of-the-century Anglophilia were every- where. "Most Americans, when they accumulate money, climb the golden rainspout of the nearest Episcopal Church, wherein the crude Yahweh of the backwoods is polished and perfumed, and speaks the vulgate with an English a."[15]

Music, being intangible, was not easy to assimilate to materialist plutocratic cul- ture. The acquisition of paintings was more congenial. Rembrandt, Rubens, and Hals were prestigious, commodities of appreciating value. In buying their paintings, some of the Moguls showed flashes of independent judgment, but the prevailing taste and the height of acquisitive ambition was for "Old Masters." Who could question the authenticity of the Renaissance? In this respect, as in the admiration for things British, John Pierpont Morgan was a representative figure. He considered himself more cultivated and worldly than his contemporaries. Educated at Göttingen, he had lived in London and gradually developed his own taste and a shrewd eye for paint- ings, books, and objects, as the Morgan Library shows. But in music his tastes were conventional beyond simplicity. "He liked the old, familiar, romantic tuneful operas," of which his special favorite was *Il Trovatore*. He always went when it was given and, a hagiographic biographer insisted, was "very discriminating as to how the different numbers were sung." Otherwise, Morgan cared little for opera and didn't go much to hear it—an opening night or for some special occasion, and then "he often took naps in the back of the box."[16]

Wall Street millionaires like to think of themselves as Fifth Avenue Medicis, princely patrons of the arts. The actual extent of their patronage, as opposed to their self-congratulation about it, was niggardly. The annual operatic assessment for *all* thirty-five shareholders was less, for an entire decade, than what Morgan paid for one Old Master. The Breakers, the Vanderbilt palace in Newport, cost $2.5 million in 1895. Mrs. Pembroke Jones set aside $300,000 annually for her Newport summer entertainment. Many dinner parties cost more than the opera's season subscription. Balls and costume parties were fabulously expensive. The Bradley Martin ball of 1897, so extravagant that even the rich were impressed, cost $369,000. By comparison, operatic expenditure was a trifle. "What was necessary to preserve the auditorium as the home for a social circle was invariably done; what was necessary to adapt it to house an artistic endeavor adequately was never done."[17]

Victor Herbert, who grew up and was trained as a musician in Germany before coming to America, had a rich familiarity with both musical worlds. From 1879 to 1881 he performed as a cellist in the orchestra of the Russian-born baron Paul von Derwies, who spent summers at his chateau near Lake Lugano and winters in his villa at Nice. The baron, a true musical amateur, supported his own orchestra and opera company, for both of which he engaged first-rate musicians. His orchestra numbered seventy players and, a good pianist, he sometimes played Mendelssohn and Weber with them. Along with the standard works, he also encouraged them to play pieces by Berlioz, Saint-Saëns, Delibes, Tchaikovsky, and Wagner. (Dvořák dedicated three of his *Slavonic Rhapsodies* to Derwies.) As well, he maintained a mixed choir of forty-eight singers who sang Russian liturgical chants in the private chapels of his two estates. The baron's operatic nights, "staged without regard to cost," were a feature of his life at Nice. It was nothing for him to spend $10,000 to get the right kind of bells needed for Glinka's *A Life for the Czar*. And the movement of this princely court from summer to winter domiciles required three special trains. "That is the way those Russian millionaires do things," Herbert said, many years later, after he had studied the American "aristocracy" up close, adding scathingly: "And our Fifth Avenue hostesses expect the whole country to gape if they engage Caruso and two horn players for a single night."[18]

From a European perspective, as Henry James noted in *The American Scene* of 1907, Wall Street opera had other curious aspects. He was most struck by two things. The first was the tentativeness of the American social effort, "the grope of wealth, in the conquest of amenities." Uncertainty took the form of "the insistence on the opera" as the "great vessel of social salvation," a "comprehensive substitute for all other conceivable vessels." Just as ordinary people were crammed into the cars of the subways or the elevators of skyscrapers—both things new to James—the operatic spectacle seemed strained and forced, producing in him "the oddest sense of hearing it, as an institution, groan and creak, positively almost split and crack, with the extra weight thrown upon it." James's second point was that, in this social scene, men were absent. As a consequence, American women moved in a void. They wore tiaras to the opera, but to no purpose. "For to what male presence of native growth is it thinkable that the wearer of an American tiara should curtsey?" Cause and effect were inverted. "In New York, the tiara had to produce the occasion." For once, James missed the largeness of this symbol. In fact, the desire to wear a tiara had produced more than an "occasion." It had produced an opera house.[19]

The behavior of this American plutocracy paralleled that of the English aristocracy, also new and rich, when it first confronted Italian opera early in the eighteenth century and chose it over native English opera. Formidable in politics and wealth, they too felt themselves inferior to Europe in the arts. "Rich enough to afford to imitate the best," wrote the English historian J. H. Plumb, "eighteenth century England lacked the confidence to create its own standards of taste and culture. Behind the braggart attitude there was an inner uncertainty, a sense of being provincial which ever-growing prosperity could not disguise." As with Rome to Greece, so America to Europe: "too conscious both of its riches and its own rawness." European singers took their huge fees but gaped in incredulity at the audience they sang to: "No one in the entire row of boxes which circled the auditorium ever heard the first act at any evening performance. . . . It was barbarism, pure and simple . . . and the comments were filled with righteous indignation. 'Who are these people? Let us sell the boxes to people who really love music. What! They own the opera house? Is it possible? What do they want of it?' "[20]

Countless Americans also loathed the crassness of this display, regarded it as evidence of a hopelessly corrupt culture. The Populist political movement believed it to be utterly foreign to true American culture, a creature of eastern money and of internationalist bankers. For the urban progressives of the early twentieth century and for the growing Socialist movement, it had less to do with foreignness and more with naked class exploitation. By 1913 the Diamond Horseshoe had to take account of political storms. The secretary of the Metropolitan Opera and Real Estate Company emphasized the need for confidentiality in the sale of opera boxes, "to avoid the newspaper notoriety, as far as possible, which usually depicts the purchaser as a plutocrat with social 'aspirations,' in a thoroughly unwelcome fashion."[21] The mockery this spectacle evoked was probably more damaging than the political anger. It suffused the pages of Thorstein Veblen's mordant prose in *The Theory of the Leisure Class* of 1898. Opera became indistinguishable from its social context. The final legacy of the Diamond Horseshoe was its triviality. Grand opera, for intellectuals, professionals, reformers, the high-minded, became a huge joke. At the same time, many Americans admired what they read about it. Magazines and newspapers chronicled the dress, the marriages, and the money of the rich, just as they do today, and this produced not hatred or ridicule but the desire for emulation. The money earned by the singers was admirable. The money spent on parties was exciting. The Diamond Horseshoe was part of the fable of American democratic society, its possibilities limitless, its obstacles not insuperable, a dream of what life would be like if one were as rich as Rockefeller.

F r o m the grossness of the Diamond Horseshoe to the narcissism of Creole New Orleans, to pick up the story where we left it at the beginning of the 1840s. The death of John Davis and the burning of James Caldwell's St. Charles Opera House prefigured the next three quarters of a century of New Orleans opera. It survived and occasionally flourished, but was marked by terrible disasters as well as a long slow decline. Caldwell retired from opera and died in 1863. Davis's son Pierre became manager of the Orleans Theater after his father's death, but lacked imagination and was succeeded in 1853 by Charles Boudousquie. His plans for the theater were interrupted right at the start by the collapse of one of its galleries, in which many people were

The ostentatious display of wealth at opera performances, epitomized by the Metropolitan's Diamond Horseshoe, inspired both mockery and emulation. From Musical America, *Feb. 16, 1907.*

killed and injured.[22] The Orleans was rebuilt and Boudousquie persevered. In 1859 he determined to build a new opera house. Six months and $118,500 later, the French Opera House, designed by M. J. Gallier, a local figure, and an English emigrant named Esterbrook, arose, seating 2,078. Handsome in its external appearance, it was white inside, the front of the boxes gold, with mirrors on either side of the proscenium, numerous entrances and exits, and fine sound. Orchestra seats cost $1.50, gallery seats 50¢.

Rossini's *Guillaume Tell* opened the house. Boudousquie was a lively and enterprising manager, and the opera again became popular. Adelina Patti charmed New Orleans in a formidable series of roles for one so youthful—*Lucia, Il Trovatore, Robert le diable, Les Huguenots,* and Halévy's *Charles VI,* as well as the American premiere of Meyerbeer's *Dinorah*. Opera continued to be given during the Civil War, but bad luck dogged the theater when the fighting was over. In 1866 Charles Boudousquie died suddenly. The three Alhaiza brothers took over. One of them died in Europe, where he had gone to recruit a new company, and the second was on the steamship *The*

Evening Star which sank in a storm; the entire opera company was among the 278 persons who drowned. As if that were not enough, the old Orleans Theatre burned to the ground that same year.

Despite the disaster, Paul, the surviving brother, opened the opera house in November 1866, with a visiting company in which Amalia Patti, Adelina's sister, sang contralto roles. After that there was a succession of impresarios, among them Max Strakosch, Colonel Henry Mapleson, Henry Savage, who leased the house and put on seasons of varying length and quality. Three months was the standard New Orleans season. The French Opera House remained the center of New Orleans cultural life in many ways. It was the scene of balls, as well as opera, for dancing remained a New Orleans preoccupation. The Creole passion for opera became well known nationwide. Those who were poor went without food in order to save money for tickets. Families sold heirlooms to buy season subscriptions. "For some it seemed as if the opera season was the sole reason for their existence, their attendance at each performance their purpose in life." Their servants (perhaps former slaves) shared it, part of Creole lore being that African Americans were part of the community-building magic created by attendance at the opera. Such was Prosper, a retainer who year after year occupied the same seat, front row center, in the "colored" gallery and rose, whenever any white person he knew entered one of the boxes, to offer a splendid bow of greeting. His judgments about singers were supposedly infallible. Stories like this, sentimental and condescending, were a way of pretending that racial conflict didn't exist.[23]

Nationally, New Orleans opera was much less important after the Civil War than it had been in the first half of the century, but the French Opera House, as a symbol of Creole culture, was better known than the St. Charles or the Orleans had been. The reason for this was literary—the rise of the "local color" movement in American

The French Opera House in New Orleans, photographed in the late 1800s, was a center of Creole culture. Library of Congress.

literature. Creole writers—George Washington Cable and Kate Chopin, Lafcadio Hearn and Grace King—were prominent in it. The exotic locale of New Orleans and its eccentric inhabitants fascinated the rest of the country. The city's most celebrated eccentric was Paul Morphy (1837–1884), the precocious chess master who conquered the European chess world at age twenty-two, returned home, gave up chess, and, walking the city's streets, visiting the opera—for he rarely missed a performance there—gradually went mad.[24] Ghosts haunted Creole culture, which interested people because it was doomed.

The French Opera House was a part of that enveloping fate. Boxes belonged "by right of possession" to the same families for years. People lived all around and about it. Most still walked to the opera. It was part of the routine of everyday life. Although it was a relatively new building, its walls and its interior quickly absorbed the rich aura of nostalgia which permeated its surroundings. It *was* the French Quarter, and its opera still had vitality. Its singers, mostly Belgian and French, were of a decent provincial level. "No doubt to Americans outside of New Orleans, even the names of many of the artists mentioned are quite unknown." Opera in America was increasingly based on the presence of singers whose names had international resonance. And the French Opera Company couldn't possibly compete in this respect, any more than the Tivoli could. However, the French company still toured. As late as 1899 and 1900 there were trips, for one and for three weeks, to Chicago, "the good old days when they could play at the Auditorium at a top price of $1.50 and still feel happy over the intake." And a handful of singers who began their American careers in New Orleans went on to become well known, if not nationally famous: Florencio Constantino, Riccardo Martin, Clotilde Bressler-Gianoli.[25]

Equally, the New Orleans audience was still confident enough of its own taste to be open to new works and not to allow the opera house to become a museum of memories. Proudly, New Orleans claimed the American premieres of Gounod's *The Queen of Sheba* (*La Reine de Saba*) and Saint-Saëns' *Samson et Dalila,* as well as *Sigurd* and *Salammbô* by the French composer Ernest Reyer (1823–1909). Four of Massenet's operas received their American premieres in New Orleans—*Hérodiade, Cinderella* (*Cendrillon*), *Esclarmonde, Don Quichotte,* and the very latest word in operatic fashion, realism—Italian *verismo*—was heard receptively, in the form of *Germania* by Alberto Franchetti (1860–1942).

By the beginning of the twentieth century, New Orleans turned to other forms of entertainment. The French Quarter became less a neighborhood than a tourist area. Jazz, music most Creoles disdained, would in a few years be the only kind of music with which New Orleans was associated. The dwindling audience for opera remained loyal to French culture, with one ironic consequence. "The subscriptions to the opera consumed almost all the money that music lovers cared to spend on music, thus precluding the establishment of a symphony orchestra."[26]

At the end of the 1914–1915 season, the French Opera Company declared bankruptcy. No more opera seasons followed. "The companies of late have been very poor," one person was quoted as saying, and another: "People don't care for opera any more; they'd rather dance"; and another: "We're tired of that old repertory, that shabby chorus, that poor ballet, and that awful scenery." And then, miraculously, it seemed as if all was not lost. A local philanthropist, William Irby, bought the French Opera House and gave it to Tulane University to be restored. French-supported opera might have broadened out and become American-supported, and post–World War I prosperity might have fostered a real revival. But the heritage of catastrophe was inescapable. On the night of December 2, 1919, the French Opera House was reduced to a ruin by fire. A journalist sat on a curb and watched the walls crash down. "Last night the heart of the old French Quarter stopped beating."[27]

Lillian Nordica

Opera came west, to America. American opera singers went east, to Europe. The dogmatic belief that it was immoral for the state to sponsor the arts led to the institutional impoverishment of American musical life. By the late nineteenth century there were some good music teachers in America and a handful of music schools and conservatories run on European lines and with European standards. Even when singers were decently taught and had some financial support, the great handicap was the lack of experience of singing in opera. Content to import their singers from abroad, the large American opera houses were largely closed to natively trained performers. The touring English-language companies, where singers also learned their trade, though they valiantly performed their task of disseminating opera throughout the land, had little prestige. To begin a career there was to end it there.

The only solution to the problem was to go to Europe, learn one's art, and hope to gain a European reputation. And from the middle of the nineteenth century, that is what all aspiring American men and women did. Charles Adams and David Bispham were the best known among the men, Elise Hensler, Clara Louise Kellogg, Minnie Hauk, Emma Nevada, Sybil Sanderson—and many others—among the women. It was a thing fraught with anxiety, difficulties, pain. For every one who succeeded to any extent, dozens failed. And they still faced moral disapproval. Kellogg wrote: "One didn't know stage people; one couldn't speak to them, nor shake hands with them, nor even look at them except from a safe distance across the footlights. There were no 'decent people on the stage'; how often did I hear that foolish thing said!"[1]

When American singers did what had to be done, they still faced special difficulties. American artists always felt they were working against the grain, outside the grooves. Their European contemporaries also faced difficulties and few of them succeeded either, but the grooves had long been cut in which their careers could move. American singers succeeded by an act of will. Even a European reputation meant less than *being* European. A soprano by another name *did* sound sweeter.

I n the spring of 1879 Patrick S. Gilmore, the famous bandmaster, and his band were playing a long engagement at the Gilmore Gardens in New York City. Their programs included operatic overtures and orchestral pieces and an occasional operatic solo. Gilmore happened to be looking for a singer to accompany the band. Bertucca Maretzek, wife of Max, who was teaching singing in New York as well as playing in operatic orchestras, took her prize student, a young American woman of nineteen, to be interviewed by Gilmore.

"Thinks she can sing, eh?" said Gilmore, giving her a quizzical but friendly look. "Come right along now. Step right up here on the stage. Yes, yes. Now, what can you sing?" Lillian Norton suggested some Handel and, with no further preparation, sang it.

"Very good, very good. What next?"

She sang some Bellini. "Very good, very good." Then Gilmore abruptly added: "Now what you want to do is to get some roses in your cheeks and come along and sing for me."[2]

Gilmore's band served as Lillian Norton's opera company. She sang in all kinds of places, at the Gilmore Gardens, the Twenty-second Regimental Armory, Steinway Hall. In Providence she sang at an amusement park with Theodore Thomas and his orchestra. She learned a great deal, about audiences, about how to adjust to different halls, how to stand, walk, dress. Valuable training as a singer, but it wasn't operatic experience, and she dreamed of becoming an opera singer. Then Gilmore said to her one day, "I am going to Europe. London! Paris! Rome! All the big cities. Fine chance. Europeans appreciate good singers. Now, little girl, do you want to come? If you do, you can." She did. Only her Boston music teacher was displeased. "After all my training, my advice, that you should come to this. A whole lifetime of ambition, and years of the hardest study, consumed to fit you to go on the road with a brass band. Pah!"

It was Gilmore's first European tour and the band was enthusiastically received everywhere—Ireland, England, Scotland, Belgium, Holland, Paris. So was Norton. Her voice was powerful and durable, which was just as well since the band gave sixty-five concerts in six weeks. The Parisians were especially pleased with the band's precision and ensemble. Norton saw the splendid new opera house. "I am going to sing there some day." Gilmore agreed. "My dear, you are going to be a great singer. You are going to be crowned in your own country yet. Mark my words, they are going to put diamonds on your brow."

In Paris Lillian Norton took a gamble. This was her chance for an operatic career. She left the band to take language and dramatic lessons, and her brother-in-law sent money to get her to Milan to study with Antonio Sangiovanni, who had sung in America and now taught at the Milan Conservatory. She told Sangiovanni she wished to sing in opera.

"Let me hear you."

She sang an aria from *Lucia.* Sangiovanni looked at her silently. "You wish to sing in grand opera?"

"Yes."

"Well, why don't you?"

"I need training."

"Training? Nonsense. We will attend to that. A few weeks' practice in Italian methods, that is all. You have nothing to unlearn."

He put her to work learning ten operas—hour after hour of work, day after day.

Lillian Norton thrived on hard work. Sangiovanni believed that, having learned these roles and absorbed a sense of Italian style, Norton's voice and her "perfect simplicity" would assure her success. After two months he arranged for a *prova,* a test, a nonpaid engagement in an opera house where impresarios could inspect, listen, and judge. Students paid for the privilege of a *prova.* Norton had no money, but Arthur Scovel, an American singer who was also in Italy trying to break into opera, and married to Cornelia Roosevelt, a cousin of Theodore Roosevelt, put up the money for her. She sang Elvira in *Don Giovanni* in Florence. She was ready. And she was lucky. At the first nerve-wracking rehearsal with cast and orchestra, the other singers gave her helpful hints and encouragement. Even so, her debut had its terrifying aspects. As she was waiting to go on, she heard the voluble audience shouting, "Basta! Basta!" ("Enough! Enough!") at the soprano singing Donna Anna, but they liked *her* and the newspapers "singled her out and praised her voice, method, musical style, sympathetic stage presence." Then she went to Brescia to sing Violetta in *La Traviata.* Scovel was singing with her, and Mrs. Scovel loaned her clothes and jewels to wear on stage. The audience was intrigued at the novelty of two American debuts, and word had been passed along by the orchestra and by other singers that the American woman was something unusual. Her reception that night was all she could have hoped for. She was asked to sing in further performances. Critics came from Milan to hear her.

Success meant not going home to America. There was still a great deal to learn, and Italy was the best place to learn it. In Genoa, Lillian sang Marguerite in *Faust.* Patti and Nilsson had sung it there, and even with such comparisons in their minds, the audience liked her. An Italian conductor paid her a double-edged compliment. "He had never heard any person of English blood sing with such soul and expression." She hired an agent, who took 20 percent of her earnings but knew impresarios, critics. He got her a place with the Imperial Opera in St. Petersburg, where she would sing several secondary roles. But it wasn't Lillian Norton who prepared to go to Russia. Antonio Sangiovanni had given her a lot, including a new name. Norton was unpronounceable in Italian. When Sangiovanni realized it signified north, he insisted that her singing name must be the Italian for that—Nordiga or Nortica or Nordica. Yes, Nordica. Somehow that sounded best. As Lillian meant lily, he added the Italian for that and she now blossomed as that Yankee flower, Giglio Nordica. But she drew the line at that. Giglio would be impossible for northerners. So she became an international compromise—Lillian Nordica.

St. Petersburg, the city of the czars, was still in those days a remote and fabulous place, broad streets, splendid churches, sumptuous palaces, charming gardens, an opera-mad but discriminating audience and a nobility which rewarded success with memorable extravagance. Nordica sang with some of the greatest artists of the day, Sofia Scalchi, Marcella Sembrich. She held her own, and more. She began to be given major roles and heard audiences shouting, "La Nordica!" She was invited to the Winter Palace to meet the Grand Duke Alexis. Countess Tolstoy called on her, and she later went to the Tolstoys' to dine. She returned to Italy to sing, the following year had another season in St. Petersburg, and in the fall of 1882, three years after Patrick Gilmore had brought her to France, she went back to Paris, to sing Marguerite in

Faust. Verdi was there at the time and called on her, for he had heard her sing Gilda in Milan and had approved. Ambroise Thomas rehearsed her in the role of Ophelia in his *Hamlet.* Finally, in 1883, she was able to go back home. Colonel Mapleson signed her to join his forces at the Academy of Music as he prepared to do battle with the Metropolitan Opera House.

Her story should have built to a dramatic, triumphant homecoming. Not so. When Lillian Nordica sang in Paris, an American had shouted out with delight from one of the boxes: "She's there, she's there, she's there." But where was there? She sang *Faust* at the Academy of Music in New York. H. E. Krehbiel thought her admirably trained, a singer with taste and intellect but stiff, lacking in natural gifts and graces. "It cost her a manifest effort to do what she well knew how to do, for she is not a phenomenal vocalist." In Boston, the house was half-filled and the critics were dismissive. "Wednesday night we had *Faust* refrigerated," one critic wrote. "If you had seen the calmness of the lovemaking in the garden scene, you would agree with me in calling it *Faust glacé.*" Very funny. Surely Bostonians should have understood her stiffness. She was one of them—a Yankee.[3]

L i l l i a n Bayard Norton was born on December 12, 1857, in the village of Farmington, Maine, the youngest of six daughters. The fifth girl, named Lillian, had died at age two. When Lillian Bayard was born, she was given the name of her dead sister, a New England custom called "repeating." Lillian's father, Edwin, a farmer, was a loving and kindly man, who played the fiddle. He came of old puritan stock and *his* father had forbidden him to play any music, saying that the fiddle was the devil. So he played in secret. He was a failure at everything he did. Lillian's mother, small, immensely determined, was a different sort. "Give me a spoon and I won't hesitate to dig a tunnel through a mountain." Lillian's father sang in the church choir and her mother played the piano. The children were tutored at home and there was much music in the house, the father and mother playing their instruments while the children danced and sang. In 1864, fed up with the miseries of farming, the family moved to Boston, but Lillian always thought of herself as a child of the Maine land, "the hard and rigorous soil from which she sprang."

Boston was difficult, as everything else had always been. Years of hard, grinding work and a life close to poverty were the family's lot as Edwin failed in one job after another. The mother worked in a department store. They had little time or money for any amusement. However, there was one reason for hope. Wilhelmina, the fourth daughter, had musical prospects. She had a splendid voice and began working toward a professional career. Then, with terrible suddenness, that hope was snatched away. In November 1869 she came down with typhoid fever and died within a few days. Even the formidable mother broke down. Two years of unappeasable grief followed. And then new hope appeared, from an entirely unexpected source, from within the family. Someone began to notice Lillian's voice, always previously taken for granted, heard but not listened to. It startled them with its quality: "Lillian sounded like Willie."

She was fourteen. Her mother took her to the newly founded New England Conservatory of Music, to a teacher, Prof. William O'Neill, who had been one of

Willie's supporters. He sat at the piano and took her up the scale until at the end she hit a sure and brilliant high C. O'Neill shouted with delight and enrolled her in the beginner's class. He was a harsh, demanding teacher, sarcastic, fault-finding, chary with his approval, insisting that Lillian be trained for the world's greatest music and only for that. His plan was to perfect her in secret and then spring her on an unsuspecting world. Perhaps the precocious brilliance of Adelina Patti was in his mind. "It was a fine fancy, but it would not have been possible," Lillian rightly said, for it left out of account that she needed experience and some means of support while getting it. O'Neill ignored such things. He thought of her as an oratorio singer, not an opera singer, but he planted one operatic seed. He once told her that "the world knew nothing yet of what Wagner was attempting, but that he would one day be accepted."

To pay for her study at the conservatory, Lillian worked part-time in a bookshop, an editor's office, sorted mail in the post office. Not having money for lunch, she often walked the streets during lunch hour to amuse herself and keep her poverty from the other clerks. One day she made an important discovery. The New England Conservatory occupied the upper floors of the building which housed the Boston Music Hall. At the top of one of its innumerable stairways, she found a narrow grating through which a thin person could squeeze, affording a view of the stage far below. There she heard her first opera, *Il Trovatore,* with Amalia Patti, Euphrosyne Parepa-Rosa, and Pasquale Brignoli. She was enchanted by it and later was able to reproduce much of the music she had just heard—"tenor, contralto, soprano impartially." That was a passing moment of enjoyment. She mostly remembered these years as "stained with tears and sodden with discouragement," but consoled herself with the reflection that "God didn't give me my chin for nothing."

After two years of study she was allowed her first public appearance, singing an aria from *Il Trovatore* in a student concert, and her first professional engagement, for which she was paid one dollar. Next came the title role in *Martha,* sung in the home of Charles R. Adams, the first American male singer to make a European reputation. In 1876 she graduated from the conservatory, singing from *La Sonnambula* at the commencement exercises. Then came her meeting with Bertucca Maretzek and the fateful audition with Gilmore.

S h e marked time for much of the 1880s. She married an Englishman named Frederick Allen Gower, impulsive, erratic, domineering. The marriage was disastrous. Gower detested art, and music in particular. "It was mawkish and sentimental, and not to be borne." They lived in London in the mid 1880s until Lillian, informally but permanently, left him. In 1886 he was removed from the scene in bizarre circumstances, disappearing during a balloon flight over the English Channel; and she was free to resume her career.

Colonel Mapleson signed her for the last of his American tours. Without Adelina Patti, the Mapleson Company played to half-full houses. German opera at the Metropolitan had caught the public's fancy. All around Nordica, prima donnas refused to sing for trivial reasons. She always sang. She had temperament in abundance, but she rarely missed a scheduled performance. From 1887 Nordica established herself in London, where Sir Augustus Harris proved that there was, in the face of the Wagnerian tide, still a large audience for Italian opera done well. She replaced a soprano in *Aida* and sang it without a rehearsal. She relearned the role of Valentine in *Les Huguenots* in one week—she had studied it with Sangiovanni in Milan a decade before. She began singing with Jean de Reszke. Sir Arthur Sullivan became a supporter, and so too the duke of Edinburgh. She worked and worked. "I feel I must work harder than ever now. I would like to settle in London and go on studying as many new roles as I can master. I know my voice is not yet under entire control." She summed up her attitude in a few words. "A singer should never be satisfied but go on working, working all the time." Her Protestant ancestors would have approved of that, at least. She visited Bayreuth to hear Jean and Edouard de Reszke, who were singing in the first *Meistersinger* given there, and she was immensely impressed by the amount of rehearsal time, the attention to detail, the care taken with every aspect of production, a seriousness natural to her own temperament and approach.

Now she felt herself gradually coming into her own, in Mexico City and in the first season of opera at the Auditorium in Chicago, at state concerts in England. She sang with Anton Seidl in New York, to such effect that he thanked her in front of the audience. She sang at the Metropolitan Opera, but not on one of the subscription nights—she wasn't a "star" yet, and so her audience was filled with women in bonnets and shawls and with sightseers from the country. And then in London, with the great Wagnerian conductor Hans Richter, she did the immolation scene from *Götterdämmerung* "with astonishing power, reaching a plane never before reached by her." Perhaps at Richter's instigation, certainly with his approval, she received an invitation, in the spring of 1893, to sing at Bayreuth.

C o s i m a Wagner, widow-keeper of the Bayreuth shrine, had decided to do *Lohengrin* there for the first time and, with great audacity, settled on Nordica to sing Elsa. Nationalist feeling was especially high in Germany at this time, and Bayreuth and Wagner's opera were a potent symbol of it. The selection of Nordica provoked surprise and anger—she was the first non-German to sing a major role at Bayreuth. She understood that the only way to respond to such criticism was by giving a successful performance on the Bayreuth stage. More immediately challenging to her was the rigorous schedule Cosima set out for her, and the authoritarian spirit of the place. Cosima was the pure source of Wagnerian tradition, or certainly believed herself to be, and Nordica was an eager student. They had many intimate talks, which reassured Cosima about choosing Nordica. Writing to a friend, Cosima praised Nordica as "a very gifted, talented and seriously zealous woman." Each day's activities were organized precisely. Nordica was given a detailed schedule, with an hour-by-hour listing of what was to be done and with whom, including social occasions. The names of people invited for lunch or dinner were included. The first two hours of the morning were devoted to a study of the libretto with Cosima, act by act, scene by scene, word by word, no detail too trivial to be overlooked. Pronunciation was especially important, and they went over words and phrases hundreds of times. Then came two hours of piano rehearsal with a coach. A two-hour break for lunch was followed by two more hours of study and then fittings for costumes. This went on for a month.

Then came rehearsals—twenty-six of them, all conducted in complete silence, in an atmosphere of almost sanctimonious reverence. Every detail of the sets was in place for each rehearsal. The stage was covered with matting to deaden the sound, scene shifters wore felt slippers. At some rehearsals Nordica was required to hold a position for as long as an hour while various lighting effects were tried out. There were difficulties. The celebrated placing of the orchestra beneath the stage was a new experience for Nordica. At the first rehearsal she could not hear the music properly and began to sing only because the conductor signaled to her. With the second and third rehearsals she came to feel the music penetrating the house and to be more clearly aware of the "points that ought to be salient." Even the intensely concentrated routine could not blot out the noisy outside criticism, the persistent sniping in the press. The Festspielhaus, she said, haunted her nights like an ogre. She felt a gnawing fear within herself, and even her indomitable spirit wavered. There was so much at stake. But Cosima was unwavering in her support and her son, Siegfried, was wholly confident of the result. "She will be a most extraordinary German Elsa," he wrote to a critic. "The language already causes her no more trouble. With an artist of her talent and reputation it is really touching to watch with what indefatigable zeal she dedicates herself to the perfection of her role. We are all highly enchanted to have found for the part an artist of the most eminent ability."

By the time of the first performance, July 20, 1893, Nordica was ready. Everything seemed second nature to her. "I was not at all nervous, but kept my mind on my business. I felt that the eye of the musical world was upon me and that the stars and stripes were in my keeping and must be brought forth in victory." The struggles and hopes of a quarter of a century culminated in this moment. At thirty-seven years of age, Lillian Nordica came fully into her artistic inheritance. Wholly in command of her voice, secure in her interpretation, she was radiantly fresh and winning. "Her charming appearance, the expression of her beautiful face and noble and plastic movements vividly picture the young Flemish princess," wrote Engelbert Humperdinck, composer (of *Hänsel und Gretel*) and music critic. "Having enjoyed perfect Italian training, her voice is clear and euphonic, displaying a uniformly developed beauty and an almost classic art." Italian and German art were united. George Bernard Shaw, an impassioned Wagnerite but a cool and discerning critic, had railed for years against the crude singing Germans justified in the name of dramatic art. "It is a great mistake to assume, as these German artists evidently do, that their rough, violent, and inaccurate singing does not matter." The arch-critic of Italian opera and of the excesses of the Patti-style prima donna saw in this performance the reconciliation between the best features of Italian and of German art. "I am really tired of going to the theatre to hear the best music associated with the worst singing, and the best singing with the worst music." Now all of Europe could stake its claim to the Wagnerian inheritance. Shaw was at Bayreuth and wrote back with uncharacteristic enthusiasm.

> P.S. I rejoice to be able to get in a postscript before the mail leaves to announce that the curtain has just fallen on the first act of *Lohengrin* amid a roar of enthusiasm, in which everybody, the bishop included, must have joined in order to swell it to such

thundering volume. This triumph is due primarily, of course, to Wagner, whose stage instructions have been exactly carried out for the first time with quite terrific success . . . but a great deal is due to Nordica. The moment she began, the sound of real singing so enchanted the Germans that it set them all singing too; we all shouted for joy; and I have no doubt the morning star would have joined in if that had been possible at a quarter past six in the evening.[4]

Lohengrin established Nordica in Germany. She followed it with concerts in Leipzig and Munich, was decorated, and appointed court singer to the Duchy of Saxe-Coburg-Gotha. "Will that do?" she asked amusedly of a friend. "Oh, these are great times and when I think back a few years it seems impossible. Still, I always felt it in me." That was Nordica's great accomplishment as an American singer in Europe. Now it was time to return to America. She exchanged the austere and otherworldly atmosphere of Bayreuth for the all-too-worldly and star-struck atmosphere of the Metropolitan, where she set her mind on a greater role than Elsa. She would sing Isolde.

S h e took her time and prepared herself carefully, studying the role in Lucerne, again line by line, with Cosima. In the fall of 1895 she arrived in New York to begin rehearsing with Jean de Reszke and Anton Seidl. In a sense, they were doing for *Tristan und Isolde,* and by extension for all the other Wagnerian masterpieces, what the production of *Lohengrin* had done at Bayreuth—internationalizing Wagner, taking him out of the realm of solely German art, arcane and mysterious and explicable only by Germans. A French Tristan, an American Isolde, a German conductor. "We all felt that we were starting out on this new race side by side, with every nerve and every thought on the alert," Nordica said. Seidl was as exacting as Cosima and spent an enormous amount of time with both his principals, acting out every part, thinking through all details of music and text, of costumes and stage movements. As the great night, November 27, 1895, approached, Seidl was reassuring. "Keep calm. Nothing can happen to you. You know what you have to do, and I am down there in the orchestra." Jean de Reszke shared this Germanic vision of the conductor as commanding all the forces on the field. "If I forget a line, I look at Seidl and read it on his lips." Nordica had other thoughts. "No one can know, no one can tell, what it felt like to lie on that couch [in the first scene of act I] and hear the prelude progressing bar by bar, and the sign for the curtain going up. They were awful moments." Will power pulled her through this, as through everything else. Yankee diva!

Overuse has tarnished the word *triumph.* But that night was truly a triumphant one for everyone concerned. De Reszke stilled any doubts about the adequacy of his voice for Wagner, his acting was suave as ever, his musical intelligence quick and subtle. Seidl sustained his already great stature, and Nordica "simply amazed those who thought they had measured the full limit of her powers." Her declamation was forceful, her singing beautifully controlled, with impeccable intonation and clarity of phrasing. Identifying sympathetically with her role, "the most arduous in operatic literature," she had become not "merely a beautiful singer" but "one of the greatest lyric artists of the day." One critic admonished: "Note ye American prima donnas

Lillian Nordica as Isolde, around the time of her triumphant performances at the Metropolitan. She was the first non-German to sing a major role at Bayreuth. Music Division, New York Public Library for the Performing Arts.

what high ideals and incessant application will lead to. There are greater things to be done than *Faust* and *Traviata.*" Nordica's response? Not content to rest, she thought of the *Ring*. "It is with the keenest pleasure that I look forward to the three Brunnhildes."

She sang the three Brunnhildes, at the Metropolitan and at Covent Garden too. Her career satisfied her in ways nothing else could. She lived through three disastrous marriages. A Hungarian tenor followed her Englishman, an American businessman followed the Hungarian. She was vulnerable to men, needed and surrendered to them when she surrendered to nothing or no one else. "I have been duped, betrayed, deceived and abused," she said of her married lives. "I'm just a poor picker of husbands."

In the last decade of her career she became active in the women's suffrage movement. She had always been a fighter, and now resentment at how women were treated drove her to sing on women's behalf and speak up for them. When most people were bitterly attacking the radicalism of Sylvia Pankhurst, Nordica responded with great spirit: "Smash windows? Yes! When men take the view that to gain an end warlike methods are excusable, they are heroes. A man has fought and gone to prison for his principles, and I think no great reform has been brought about without these. It is all very well for those in power to keep on their way, ignoring us. We have to draw attention to ourselves. If we are to be heard, why, we have to make ourselves obnoxious, perhaps, at times." She also wanted to make opera more available to poor people, charging no fee when she sang with the People's Symphony Orchestra, conducted by F. X. Arens, at concerts for "wage earners and the poorer classes." And she also worked on a plan for an American operatic festival and school for singers, to be located on the Hudson, a kind of American Academy of Music and Bayreuth combined.

She was much admired but never inspired audiences to erupt in paroxysms of adulation. She represented control, not abandon. By the early twentieth century, she had already come to represent a kind of "classic" singing which was rapidly disappearing, a spaciousness and nobility somewhat out of place in an operatic world dominated by realism. She was capable of fiery outbursts and conducted herself with a good deal of prima donna haughtiness, but Yankee down-to-earthness was always close to the surface. Her farewell from the Metropolitan evoked a memorable outpouring of gratitude and respect. Cheered and cheered, she was presented with a diamond tiara. Gilmore's prophecy had come true: she had been crowned in her own country.

Nordica as Columbia in a women's suffrage pageant at the Metropolitan Opera House on May 2, 1912. The stars in her crown represented states in which women had been enfranchised. Nordica Homestead Collection, Farmington, Maine.

Nordica was willing to branch out and try new things. She was grand but not stuffy. One year she toured with the San Carlo Opera Company. In November 1909 she sang the leading role in *La Gioconda* at the opening night of the Boston Opera House. One critic's words that night were familiar. "In her zeal for the occasion," he wrote, "Nordica fairly overcame the physical and vocal limitations inevitable in the years that are ending a long, fruitful and distinguished career and time and time again she recalled her golden prime."[5] In October 1910 she finally achieved Parisian recognition. Under the baton of André Messager she sang in four sold-out performances of *Tristan und Isolde* in French, at the Opéra.

There was no denying her failing powers, however. When she sang Isolde in Chicago, Ernestine Schumann-Heink, whom Nordica had befriended years before in Germany, found her mournful. "My great days are over, all over, Ernestine. You are going up and up, and I am going down and down," and then concluded with pride: "I didn't sing well last night, but I did the best I could." Her last husband, who was supposed to be a prosperous businessman, turned out to be a bankrupt. She had put up her jewels as collateral for a loan he took out and felt threatened by destitution in her old age. Death was on her mind. She confided that at her funeral she wanted a baritone to sing Wotan's farewell, and an orchestra to play the funeral march from *Götterdämmerung*.

In the winter of 1913 she embarked on a world tour, starting in Australia and New Zealand. Throughout it she was haunted by a sense of foreboding. She sailed for Java and on the way came down with a fever. On the deck of her old slow ship, a tent was rigged up to protect her from the intense heat. Eventually the ship reached Thursday Island. She stayed in a tiny tin-roofed hospital hut for three weeks, becoming weaker and weaker but fighting on. She was taken to Java. "Nordica dying in Batavia," newspapers headlined.[6]

The languorous Batavian heat seems an odd atmosphere for Lillian Norton to die in, but it wasn't unsuitable for Lillian Nordica. The Yankee diva didn't belong to Maine any more than to Milan or St. Petersburg or Chicago. Hers was an international life. Even so, just as national values remained in opera, there was an inextinguishable American residue in Nordica's last moments. There was no orchestra, no Wotan, to say farewell. Instead, articulating something in her deeper even than Wagnerian music drama, her final request was that at the end someone would say simply—"She did her damndest."

Modernism, 1903–1921

I understand perfectly when a musician says today: "I hate Wagner, but I can no longer endure any other music." But I'd also understand a philosopher who would declare: "Wagner sums up modernity. There is no way out, one must first become a Wagnerian."

—*Friedrich Nietzsche*

After some years of passionate pilgrimages to Bayreuth, I began to have doubts about the Wagnerian formula, or, rather, it seemed to me that it was of use only in the particular case of Wagner's own genius. He was a great collector of formulae, and these he assembled within a framework that appears uniquely his own only because one is not well enough acquainted with music. And without denying his genius, one could say that he had put the final period after the music of his time, rather as Victor Hugo summed up all the poetry that had gone before. One should therefore try to be "post-Wagner" rather than "after Wagner."

—*Claude Debussy*

The Wagnerian Aftermath

Operatically, the beginning of the twentieth century was an intersection where Wagnerism, realism, and modernism collided.

Wagner had been dead a generation, but Wagnerism still dominated the operatic scene. Henry T. Finck, critic and biographer, in his two-volume study of 1893, *Wagner and His Works,* proclaimed that Wagner had conceived "the plan of a perfect music-drama" and in *Götterdämmerung* had accomplished it. Lawrence Gilman, in *Aspects of Modern Opera* (1908), asserted that "no composer who ever lived influenced so deeply the music that came after him" and that the period from Wagner's death, in 1883, ought to be characterized as "the Wagnerian Aftermath." Against the "confused and amorphous background" of that aftermath, Gilman discerned "three salient figures"—Giacomo Puccini (1858–1924), Claude Debussy (1862–1918), and Richard Strauss (1864–1949). Each had taken "many leaves from [Wagner's] vast book of instruction," but each had escaped the Wagnerian spell. "They have been content with their own eloquence; and it has not betrayed them."[1]

For Americans, the Wagnerian aftermath was not very different in many respects from what had preceded it. Wagner was recognized as a great genius but his work was not popularly familiar. A Boston critic, writing in 1912, mused on the situation. "Wagner is still a stranger to our Franco-Italian opera house," H. T. Parker wrote. "We must hear Wagner's music, when we hear it at all, at concerts, shorn of all the stage conditions for which it was written—as though we were back in the elementary Wagnerian days of the 70s and the early 80s."[2] Wagnerian music drama remained difficult, strange, disturbing. In short: in America, Wagner was a "modernist."

American composers interested in modern music drama had either to study it outside the theater or go to Europe to absorb it. Arguably, American composers at the end of the nineteenth century were more cut off from the sources of prospective operatic work than William Fry and George Bristow had been half a century earlier, because those two had been able to see the most recent opera in the theaters of their day. In 1904 the young American composer Charles T. Griffes wrote a friend in Europe: "I suppose you have heard all the Wagner things several times, but you see I have heard so little of him and almost nothing from the *Ring.* The more I do hear, the crazier I am to hear still more." Daniel Gregory Mason represented the view of anti-Wagnerians, writing in his journal in 1895: "Thank God Wagner is dead, and thank God Brahms is alive. And here's to the great classical revival of the twentieth century in America."[3] Of Mason's generation of composers, only Horatio Parker and John Knowles Paine composed operas. The others avoided the issue of what a "classical revival" might mean for the stage. For them, as for John Sullivan Dwight, "classical" music was orchestral, not operatic.

The hunger for Wagner revealed itself in the furor about *Parsifal*, which, first performed in 1882, had never been given in America. It wasn't that Americans lagged behind. No one else outside Germany had seen it either. *Parsifal* was protected by a thirty-year copyright agreement which made Bayreuth the exclusive site for its performance: the sacred opera at the sacred shrine. However, the United States didn't subscribe to the international copyright agreement, and so Heinrich Conried, the new (1903) impresario at the Metropolitan Opera House, anxious to begin his regime with a bang and untroubled by ethical scruples or any respect for Cosima's wishes, scheduled a performance for December of that year. This provoked excitement, publicity, controversy. For the first performance, orchestra seats were doubled in price to ten dollars. A special train, "The *Parsifal* Limited," was chartered to bring Wagnerians from Chicago. ("Would it not be well to include something from *Parsifal*," asked Mrs. Theodore Roosevelt in discussing what a pianist would play at the White House, "now that the opera is so much talked of?") The lavish production, "the most perfect ever made on the American stage," "better than Bayreuth," received ten repetitions, all sold out, and Henry Savage, an enterprising impresario, sent an English-language version on tour across the country.

This incident revealed the declining prestige of Bayreuth as a symbol of "art absolutely free from corrupt contemporary materialism." Nietzsche sensed it early on: "The whole idle rabble had been brought there." Shaw scoffed at the "poor and pretentious pietism," shutting out "every breath of fresh air from the musical atmosphere." Mark Twain mocked the pseudo-spirituality of the place, while Henry Adams, who had hoped to find in Bayreuth the "out of the world, calm, contemplative, and remote" spirit of the Master, found something very different. "The world had altogether changed, and Wagner had become part of it, as familiar as Shakespeare or Bret Harte."[4]

The second of the components of the Wagnerian aftermath was *verismo*, realism. A newspaper critic explained the aims of realist composers: "They present through the medium of music human life as it is. They refuse to idealize. They scorn heroics. They seek the rhythms of everyday hearts and profess to lay bare to us the tragedies that swell in the experiences of the common people."[5] Of the many composers associated with realism, three Italians and one Frenchman were best known to the American public: Puccini, Ruggero Leoncavallo (1857–1919), Pietro Mascagni (1863–1945), and Gustave Charpentier (1860–1956). Realist opera was introduced to America in Philadelphia. Gustave Hinrichs had gone there from the Tivoli Theatre and put on seasons of opera for popular audiences, introducing Mascagni's *Rustic Chivalry* (*Cavalleria rusticana*) in 1891, Leoncavallo's *The Clowns* (*I Pagliacci*) in 1893. Puccini's American reputation was made by three operas, *The Bohemians* (*La Bohème*), *Tosca*, and *Madama Butterfly*. Two of them entered the country in unlikely places—*La*

Bohème in Los Angeles in 1897, *Madama Butterfly* in Washington, D.C., in 1906. *Tosca* opened at the Metropolitan Opera in 1901, Charpentier's *Louise* at the Manhattan Opera House in 1908. Verismo was actually represented by a very small number of operas which (except for *Louise,* which had its Paris premiere in 1900) crossed the Atlantic quickly. Three of them began in popular theaters.

Modernism, the third and most complex of the three movements, played the dominant role in the arts of the first two-thirds of the twentieth century. Its significance was only dimly perceived in 1900. As a synonym for the new—the way ordinary people used it—modernism had long been a familiar term, and fact, much admired in American culture. When it was used in regard to the arts, however, it aroused very different feelings. Chronically insecure in their judgments about art, Americans clung to the conventional. Change was possible in the arts too, of course. Rossini had been new and shocking in those long-forgotten early days of opera, only to become the standard upheld by those who rejected Verdi's novelties which, in turn, were accepted by the majority. But for this to happen, the new (however odd it was) had to establish itself as an extension of the old. Much of the twentieth-century modernism, however, was a negation of the old. It wasn't clear what operatic modernism, represented by Strauss's *Salome* and *Elektra* and by Debussy's *Pelléas et Mélisande* and all promoted by Oscar Hammerstein in the first decade of the century, really signified—the old in unfamiliar guise or the radically new.

The initial response to these new operas, realist and modernist, was similar. People were shocked and angered by them. *Cavalleria* and *Pagliacci* were particularly disturbing because of their "brutality," "fierceness," "harshness." They were "lurid melodramas," "vehicles of excitement and confusion." The Puccini operas too, though to a lesser extent, struck auditors as "coarse," "harsh," "dissonant," "brutal," "violent," "noisy." By the time they heard *Louise,* people were past being shocked, and while *Pelléas,* could be described as "a morbid and stygian pollution of the drama," the general response was subdued, not anger but bafflement at what, if anything, was going on. The response to Strauss was most fierce. Of *Salome:* "The opera depends wholly upon its nastiness for its appeal; there is nothing alluring in the noises that Strauss calls music," "lawless and inhuman." Of *Elektra:* "GRUESOME ELEKTRA STAGGERS AUDIENCE AT FIRST HEARING," ran one headline; "the most soul and sense shattering music," "the most horrible and wildest passions."[6]

These new operas were the front line in the battle for sexual liberation, challenging still very powerful sexual taboos. In 1915 Sergei Diaghilev's Russian Ballet was to tour the country, and Edward Bernays, its publicist, called on the editor of the *Ladies' Home Journal,* Edward Bok, to gain support for the ballet with a story in his magazine. Bernays proudly showed Bok colored photographs of dancers and of scenes from the ballets. Bok said: "Mr. Bernays, I am afraid my public would not approve of these photographs in which the skirts of the women do not come below the knees. The American woman, our reader, won't permit such pictures in her home." What would such an audience make of *Louise's* final scene, the heroine defying her family and running off to live with her lover? Andrew Carnegie, for one, would have no part of it. "It's a bad, bad story—that girl and her young man. Not for me, thank you." *La*

Richard Strauss as demonic modernist, photographed by Edward Steichen during Strauss's first visit to the United States in 1903. International Museum of Photography at George Eastman House. Reprinted with permission of Joanna T. Steichen.

THE "SALOMÉ" SITUATION IN BOSTON

Strauss's Salome *scandalized American audiences with its explicit eroticism and degeneracy. Mary Garden's performance of the Dance of the Seven Veils aroused indignation in some and fascination in others. This Boston cartoon appeared in* Musical America *on April 10, 1909.*

Bohème's characters were openly licentious, and one critic thundered: "*La Bohème* is foul. . . . Its heroine is a twin sister of the woman of the camellias but Mimi is fouler than Camille, alias Violetta." Tosca was "tragic and repulsive," saturated in sexual lust. *Cavalleria* and *Pagliacci* combined adultery with murder. *Pelléas et Mélisande* was like the rest, a story of infidelity but less shocking because ambiguous, indirect. *Madama Butterfly* was about seduction and rendered more unpleasant because an American naval officer was the seducer-villain.[7]

If these operas produced cloudbursts of protest, *Salome* was a sexual stormfront, a shocking combination of eroticism and degeneracy, its climactic scene being Salome's lascivious fondling of the decapitated head of John the Baptist in her exultant Dance of the Seven Veils. The first American performance took place at the Metropolitan in January 1907. Though the audience was divided in its response, what mattered was that one person was very upset by it. Mrs. Herbert Satterlee, J. P. Morgan's daughter, registered her opinion with her father, who registered his opinion with the directors, who registered their opinion—*Salome* was "objectionable and detrimental to the best interests of the Metropolitan Opera House"—with Heinrich Conried, who canceled further performances. That was that. Twenty-seven years passed before *Salome* was given again at the Metropolitan. In 1909 Oscar Hammerstein produced it at his Manhattan Opera House, with Mary Garden in the title role, to overwhelming acclaim, but when it was taken on tour other cities were less accepting. Philadelphia ministers denounced the "progressive disrobing" of the Dance of the Seven Veils because it "approached realism almost too closely at times." Later, "no account of what Miss Garden did in *Salome* can so much as faintly mirror what *Salome* did to Chicago." The chief of police went to the Auditorium. "It was disgusting," he reported. "Miss Garden wallowed around like a cat in a bed of catnip." The head of Chicago's Law and Order League said that the opera should be "classed as vicious and suppressed along with houses in the red light district. I am a normal man, but I would not trust myself to see a performance of *Salome*." Running no risk, he never saw it. Billy Sunday, the famous evangelist, who was in town and had not seen it either, called *Salome* "a very sinful opera."[8]

There was incest in *Die Walküre,* "yet nobody ever seriously thought of padlocking Wagner or any woman singing Sieglinde." Why did Andrew Carnegie object to *Louise* but not to *Faust,* equally impure by his own standards? "You see, once a work of art is established, it becomes pure." *Louise* was new. *Faust* and *Die Walküre* were "classics." Mary Garden noted that opposition to *Salome* was led by Protestant ministers. "What the men of the pulpit held against *Salome*," she said, "was that it was Biblical." This also explained some of the criticism occasioned by the Metropolitan's *Parsifal*. In it, some Protestant clergymen feared, the person of Jesus Christ was represented directly on stage. Religious and sexual sensitivities were mixed together in the American reception of *Thaïs* by Jules Massenet (1842–1912). It was one of Garden's most famous and provocative roles, her daring costumes and sensual dancing producing a great hubbub. Its story was modernist but its music was conventional, and Europeans were amazed at the American response. Anyway, Massenet's operas were difficult to categorize. *Werther,* first performed in Chicago in 1894, seemed strikingly realistic. There were no "gods, kings, peasants, gypsies, fairies, demons, villains, slaves, soldiers" in it, and not even a chorus. All its people were from "the lower middle classes and were called Schmidt, Johann, Sophie and Katie."[9]

Given all this, it is all the more striking that these operas, realist and modernist, were also enthusiastically received and supported. *Salome* was greeted with intense respect. Audiences listened to this "new music of Strauss's with its crashes, its tremendous climaxes, its terrible dissonances, and its moments of beautiful melody" with a quiet concentration unusual in opera houses. In Boston the audience sat for an unbroken one hour and fifty minutes of *Elektra,* "in a silence so tense that the orchestra seemed at moments the expression of the answering emotions of the audience as well as of the emotions of the drama." At the end, there was "an instant of recovering silence," and then "by spontaneous impulse, the whole audience, high and low, in every corner of the theater, broke into applause so intense that it seemed a new and strange and exciting thing." Audiences responded warmly to *Louise,* its depiction of life in the streets of Paris, its novel scene in the dress-making workshop. They were deeply touched by the last scene. Ten times it was given, with few empty seats.[10] *Pelléas et Mélisande* generated serious and intelligent reflection, often puzzled, more often discerning. "It is not every generation that can witness the emergence of a masterpiece which may truly be called epoch-making." All this suggests that, while the Diamond Horseshoe at the Metropolitan still dominated the social scene, a new and expanding audience, transcending the familiar ethnic boundaries and unconcerned with opera's old hierarchical associations, was coming to opera houses in all the major cities. It was a *musical* audience, and the failure of the Metropolitan Opera to welcome it was one of its major disservices to opera in America. The turning away from opera by a younger generation in the 1920s was connected to it.[11]

Meanwhile, led by the trio of Puccini operas, verismo staged a coup d'état and seized control of opera's commanding heights. So used are we, at the end of the twentieth century, to the central place occupied by Puccini's operas in our opera houses that we must be reminded how rapidly the operatic repertory changed in the first decade of the century. The excitement occasioned by Strauss, Debussy, and Charpentier paled by comparison with the significance of this change. Puccini quickly became the most famous operatic composer in the world. The transformation of the Metropolitan Opera House repertory is representative. In the twenty-two seasons 1900 through 1921, *La Bohème* was performed every year but one (121 performances). *Tosca* never missed a beat, being given every year (112 performances). *Madama Butterfly,* first performed in 1906, made up for its late start by being put on every year, 106 performances in sixteen seasons. Add to this the two other verismo stalwarts, *Cavalleria,* performed every year but two (95 performances), and *Pagliacci,* every year but one (121). Compare these operas with the well-established older favorites. The all-time Metropolitan favorite for this period was *Aida*—triumphal *Aida,* spectacular *Aida,* season-opening *Aida:* 142 performances in twenty-one seasons. But after it came the five realist operas, outstripping all the other standbys. Comparisons by composer in these years are illuminating. Four Mozart operas received 65 performances (half the number of performances of *La Bohème* alone). Ten Verdi operas, 409 performances. Ten Wagner operas, 548. The big three of Puccini received 341 performances by themselves. Add to these the other Puccini operas and the total is 419. Add *Cavalleria* and *Pagliacci,* and verismo totaled 635 performances.

Even figures such as these don't fully reveal Puccini's impact. The Puccini and other realist operas rapidly became staples among the touring companies. *Madama Butterfly* was taken on a national tour in 1907–1908 by the Savage English Grand Opera Company. This *Butterfly* tour was the most comprehensive, for one opera, of any in the history of American operatic touring up to that time. Every region in the country was visited, and there were 300 performances in 112 cities.

Puccini's appeal was closely connected, in the United States, with the nature of the realism found in his operas. Should Puccini be included in the realist category at all? Certainly there is little in his work of the naturalism of *Cavalleria* and *Pagliacci,* and it could be argued that the garrets of Bohemia, Napoleonic Rome, exotic nineteenth-century Japan are as close to the imaginary lands of Graustark as they are to realism. However, American audiences never had any doubt about this matter, and what they found convincingly realistic about Puccini was summed up in that newspaper comment, quoted earlier, about the realist school: that it sought the "rhythms of everyday hearts . . . the experiences of the common people." The writer went on to mock the efforts of the young Italian composers. "Ah, what a boon are those common people. Lo, they do all those things that the lords and ladies did in the old-time dramas and novels and operas, but they wear common clothes and speak in the tongue of the streets, and therefore we find ourselves in a new world."[12]

Precisely. The writer was ironic, but his point was the central one. This was (always excepting *Carmen*) a new operatic world. Puccini's stories were sometimes violent and the treatment melodramatic, but at the heart of his vision was the depiction of the ordinary. He and the other realists democratized operatic experience. The tantrums and quarrels of Puccini's Bohemians are common, their passions pathetic, not grand. They are preoccupied with money and things, and with the absence of money and things. *Tosca's* theatricality heightens the contrast between its surface glitter and the commonness of the power and lust beneath it. And calculations and bargains abound in the operas. Puccini's genius was to raise this mundane world to a pitch of lyrical rapture.

These realistic dramas presented themselves, musically and dramatically, to American audiences in a compact, streamlined, and powerful form of theater. Puccinian opera, as theatrically effective and absorbing as anything on Broadway, was much closer to popular theater than to the older conception of "grand" opera. Here was lyric drama "in the modern sense": "swift, significant, running musical speech in the intervals between lyric and emotional expansion." The orchestra and voices both carried the story, which accounts for the Wagnerian element contemporary critics frequently found in Puccini. Puccini and Wagner: dual pillars of the contemporary repertory. But how different too: there is no mythology behind Puccini, no great weight of history. The stories exist here and now, even when the costume is of an earlier period. People were correct in seeing them as contemporary opera.[13]

Verismo in its various forms resonated with an old and venerable tradition of American culture, the delight in the ordinary, represented most famously by Emerson's vision of the common raised to the level of the remarkable: "I ask not for the great, the remote, the romantic. I embrace the common, I explore and sit at the feet of the familiar, the low. Give me insight into today, and you may have the antique and future worlds." In the late nineteenth century and the beginning of the twentieth, there was a resurgence of this attitude. It was in the "objectivist" painting of John Frederick Peto (1854–1907) and William Harnett (1848–1892), with their lifelike, loving representations of the shabby, worn objects of the material world, and in the paintings of John Sloan, Robert Henri, George Luks, and George Bellows, who were derisively called the "ashcan" school because of their depiction of the backyards, alleys, ordinary aspects of city life.

Believable stories and *melody,* abundant, passionate, singable melody, unforgettable solos, melting and rapturous duets. Quickly published for all the usual means of dissemination, pianos and bands, the Puccini melodies arrived just as recordings arrived. Fantastic as it seems, the very first American newspaper response emphasized not Puccinian melodiousness but the "harshness," "dissonance," the differentness of the music. But different as they were from the melodies of Verdi and Bellini, Puccini's were captivating. And it was in regard to melody that American audiences clarified the distinction between realist opera and modernist opera. Strauss and Debussy were listened to intently and respectfully. Their operas were accepted, but they didn't become popular. Strauss's *Der Rosenkavalier,* first given in America in 1913 and well received by audiences for the next four years, was dropped during World War I and then gained acceptance. But *Der Rosenkavalier* was the exception, and not enough by itself to alter the perception of Strauss as a formidable, nonmelodic composer. That was, as it had been for over a century, the distinction that mattered—whether people could sing or hum individual melodies, or play them on the piano. In this line Puccini was a genius. Who could sing songs from *Pelléas et Mélisande?* Hum the music of *Elektra?*

Conversely, for the musically advanced, that melodic gift branded Puccini's art as hopelessly vulgar. In *Aspects of Modern Opera*, Lawrence Gilman offered an analysis of this issue which summarized the point of view of sophisticated musical opinion for the next half century. Gilman spent several pages expressing his admiration for Puccini's dramatic skill—"sure," "swift," "incisive," capable of building great suspense; and the orchestral accompaniment suitable to this—"spare, lithe, closely-knit, clean-cut." But Puccini had not truly fused his music and his drama. He retained a "lingering devotion to full-blown melodic expression achieved at the expense of dramatic truth, logic, and consistency." Puccini "played upon the insatiable desire of the modern ear for an ardent and elemental kind of melodic effect," and the trouble was that the "Neo-Italians," at their best in the expression of dramatic emotion, were at their worst in voicing purely lyric emotion. Their lyricism was "almost invariably banal, without distinction, without beauty or restraint."

The classic instance of this was in the second act of *Tosca,* where Puccini halts the scene between Scarpia and Tosca, which he has up to this point developed with superb dramatic logic, "in order to placate those who may not over-long be debarred from their lyrical sweetmeats." At this crucial moment, Puccini "interrupts everything" to write "the sentimental and facilely pathetic prayer, 'Vissi d'arte, Vissi d'amore.'" Puccini marked it *dolcissimo con grande sentimento*—"most sweetly, with great sentiment"—and it is "a perfectly superfluous, not to say intrusive, thing dramatically, and a piece of arrant musical vulgarity." Puccini represented truly the composers of his country and of his day. "When the modern Italian music-maker dons his singing-robes he becomes clothed with commonness and vulgarity," becomes "blatant and rhetorical." Puccini, on closer reflection, far from being a modernist, embodied something all too familiar. "We have here, in fact, nothing more nor less respectable than the old-fashioned Italian aria of unsavory fame."[14]

The new opera had its distinctive way of being acted and sung. Realism stressed theatrical effect, "which forbids the separation of singing and acting." With younger singers "the question becomes whether they are singers who act or actresses who sing. Their task is to keep the two offices equally balanced." Roles that had seemed to the earliest critics of Puccini and Leoncavallo and Mascagni to be superficial, merely melodramatic, soon revealed depths of interpretative possibility. Tosca was easily the most popular of these, with the leading sopranos of the time wanting to do her. Mary Garden, Geraldine Farrar, and Feodor Chaliapin became famous exponents of the realist method. Even the older operas were interpreted in this way. Farrar turned *La Traviata* into realist drama. She made Violetta "a personage and not a voice, kept her within the drama, gave her emotions as well as cavatinas and cabalettas and read the letter in the final scene with a Duse-like intensity of longing." Chaliapin's Don Basilio, in *Il Barbiere di Siviglia,* was so realistic as to "transgress the bounds of good taste."[15]

The new realist opera changed the way the older operas were sung, threatening the sensuous beauty of the old style of singing. Verdi's music depended on a long melodic curve and on flowing phrases, while realism required singers to cut everything into shorter declamatory phrases. The emphasis on a big voice, personified by Enrico Caruso and Tita Ruffo, undermined the old-style vocal mastery. There was more applause and money in ringing tones than in subtlety. In this view—and it was widely shared—realism marked the end of bel canto.[16]

In capturing the central place in the American repertory, realist opera extinguished French operas of the first half of the nineteenth century—Adam, Auber, Boieldieu, Spontini. Meyerbeer held on by a thread until World War I, and then went under. Early nineteenth-century Italian operas, if not extinguished like the French, were largely displaced. Puccini and his peers came from within the older tradition, and the impact of their works was devastating. For the next fifty years, Rossini was known only as the composer of *Il Barbiere,* and only the realistic school's lack of a sense of humor spared Donizetti, of whose huge repertory (*Lucia* excepted) *Don Pasquale, L'Elisir d'amore,* and *La Fille du régiment* alone survived.[17] *I Puritani* and *La Sonnambula* were revived very rarely, and even *Norma,* sung at the Metropolitan in 1891, wasn't heard there again for thirty-six years. The name of Vincenzo Bellini was almost forgotten.

Oscar and Goliath

Immigration and opera shaped the life of Oscar Hammerstein. Born in 1847 or 1848, he grew up in Berlin, the eldest son of a middle-class German Jewish family dominated by a harshly authoritarian father. Both his parents were musical. His father, a building contractor, played the violin; his mother, of a French Huguenot family, the piano. Oscar was taught the flute, violin, and piano and at twelve enrolled in the Conservatory, where he learned counterpoint, harmony, and composition. He attended the opera regularly with his family. When he was twelve his mother died. With her protection gone, the long-standing hostility between exacting father and strong-willed son broke out into open battle. At fifteen, after a particularly fierce argument that ended in blows, Oscar pawned his violin and ran away from home forever, going first to England and then, after an eighty-nine-day crossing of the Atlantic in the steerage of a sailing ship, to New York City, where he arrived in the winter of 1863.

He lived in a German boardinghouse, got a job for two dollars a week, and learned two things vital to his future—English and the cigar trade. He married, began a family, became a citizen, prospered in the cigar business, and invented various devices for improving cigar manufacturing, the patent rights providing him with a steady flow of money, the basis for his entertainment speculations. His first great friend in America was Adolf Neuendorff, composer and conductor, who was passionate about opera and who reawakened his musical interests. In the fall of 1871, Neuendorff, Carl Rosa, and Hammerstein (in charge of publicity) put on a season of opera, in German, at the Stadt-Theater. Operatic production got into Hammerstein's blood, and though for the next decade and a half he concentrated on his cigar business and his family, he also wrote plays, songs, and musical sketches and revealed a passion for building theaters. His sons learned to detect the signs and sounds of an oncoming attack of the building virus: their father sat at the piano playing and singing and humming opera.[1]

His first independent venture came in 1889, when he built the Harlem Opera House, an audacious move because it was a long way, geographically and socially, from the city's theatrical district. Hammerstein opened it with a play by David Belasco, but he also wanted to bring opera singers to his theater, so went to see Edmund Stanton, business manager of the Metropolitan, to discuss possible arrangements and there encountered, for the first time, Metropolitan Opera arrogance. "Some people think they can come here and take up my time with the most absurd schemes,"

Stanton told him. "I should think you would have more sense than to come here and talk such nonsense to me." Hammerstein never forgot the snub, and he also learned an important lesson: Go directly to the singer.[2] He approached Lilli Lehmann, well known for scorning "the Vanderbilt view of art." She agreed to sing for him for a week in the spring, when her commitment to the Metropolitan was over. Her admirers flocked to hear her, not in Wagner, but in *Norma*. Hammerstein hired able people to sing with her and got Walter Damrosch to conduct. Still, star opera in a foreign language wasn't, at this point, what Hammerstein had in mind. The next year he presented an English opera company directed by the hard-working and able Gustav Hinrichs, "cheap prices and good singing in our native language." They were good singers all right, but they were foreigners and their English was incomprehensible. "No one could tell what was the purport of the arias." Nor was there enough rehearsal time or enough skill in the chorus and orchestra. Hammerstein kept on cutting corners, hoping to find some quick way to make a name for himself, and to make some money. He built another theater and in 1891 brought the Metropolitan English Opera Company, with Adolf Neuendorff conducting, to its stage, but the repertory was conventional Italian opera and his productions shabby. He took part in the race to be the first to do Mascagni's *Cavalleria rusticana* in New York. Rudolph Aronson beat him to the punch at the Casino, but it gave Hammerstein a taste of successful novelty.

When, in 1892, the Metropolitan was closed due to fire, he considered bringing the French Opera Company from New Orleans, but time and money were short. He put on another season of opera in English, which displeased the critics. "In view of the width and depth of the chasm which yawns between Mr. Hammerstein's promises and his achievements," wrote one, "it is becoming more difficult to take him seriously." The criticisms were just. He recognized that he had to wait until he had the resources to do opera properly. But one decision was final. "I am tired of opera in English and I shall not try it again. The people don't want it."[3]

For the next decade he devoted his energies to popular musical theater. In 1892 he built the Manhattan Theatre, designed by him to express his ideas about theater's social and artistic functions. Seating twenty-six hundred, its auditorium was a flat-tened semicircle, broad but shallow. No one was far from the stage. Its buff-and-blue interior was simple and all fifty-two boxes faced the stage, which was huge and exceptionally well equipped. It dignified popular theater, emphasizing performance. Hammerstein brought in first-class artists, paid high fees, and sent agents to Europe to find interesting acts. He made a lot of money and promptly spent it all on another theater, the Olympia, which had an even more popular emphasis, "to give people what they have never had before," including Isham's Octoroons, the first group of African American singers and dancers to perform in a leading white theater. (He also gave them his own opera, *Santa Maria*, publicized strenuously, lavishly produced. The public wasn't interested.) He overextended himself and in 1898 went bankrupt, losing everything except his cigar machine patents. Borrowing every cent he could, he built another theater, the Victoria, at Times Square, and in so doing largely created Times Square as the city's theatrical district. Once again he tried for a popular mix, prospered, built another theater, the Republic, next door, joined the two at the top and created Paradise Garden, a pastoral refuge, the Petit Trianon of the rooftops. In 1904 he converted the Victoria into a house exclusively for vaudeville. It became the center of Manhattan's popular entertainment. Shows ran from 1:45 to 6 p.m., and from 7:45 to midnight. People came and went. The money poured in. As it did, Oscar Hammerstein spent more and more time at his piano, playing operatic selections, preparing, at almost sixty, for the major enterprise of his life, to challenge the Metropolitan Opera's monopoly.

H o w could he succeed where Mapleson had failed? An iron puddler might as well take on J. P. Morgan's new (1901) behemoth, the United States Steel Company. "Well aware of the history of operatic failures in America," but undiscouraged by them, Hammerstein laid plans for the future based on a thoughtful understanding of the urban experience of the previous forty years. The city he had come to in 1863 had grown to almost five million people, many foreign-born. He had learned how to attract them to his theaters and believed he could bring them to his opera house, if its productions were theatrically compelling, inexpensive. There was also a sophisticated audience, familiar with musical theater, fed up with Diamond Horseshoe opera. The new underground subway system would bring this far-flung audience to him.

Publicity was crucial. His opera plans, opera house, and opera company had to be kept constantly before the public. The numbers of the potential audience were enormous, but he had actually to create them as an opera audience. The story that publicity told and embroidered had to capture that public's sympathy as well as attention. Beginning in 1905, Hammerstein was responsible, as subject or instigator, for a torrent of newspaper articles, interviews, notes of gossip, editorials. He liked being the center of attention and was always ready with a lively quote—accurate, far-fetched, outrageous, shrewd—plans contemplated, plans abandoned, in racy language very different from that of the usual operatic impresario. Operatic populism was his theme—the democrat versus the plutocrats, the mighty mite versus the snooty elite. All true enough. Hammerstein didn't have to invent his story, only to sell it. "I'm the Little Man Who'll Provide Grand Opera for the Masses." One man against massed corporate wealth: one man's money, one man's opera house. His vision wasn't "modernist." He planned on producing the same operas as the Metropolitan, only better. Nor was he opposed to star opera. Stars brought people to the box office. At the same time, his experience of musical theater of all kinds persuaded him that he would have to offer his audiences something new. But what?

In the winter of 1906 Hammerstein began building the Manhattan Opera House, as he proudly called it, on Seventh Avenue, between Thirty-fourth and Thirty-fifth streets, and assembling his company. Heinrich Conried—the two men felt an intense personal antipathy which went back many years—adopted the initial Metropolitan line: lofty condescension. The Metropolitan's only concern was to be "the best opera company in the world, not with any supposed 'rivals.'" In practice, however, it waged war against Hammerstein in defense of its monopoly. It informed managers and singers that dealing with him might endanger their future relationships. Then it played its ace in the hole, getting the Italian publishing house of Ricordi, Puccini's publishers, to give it "exclusive" performing rights to all Puccini operas, though no company anywhere else had been given such rights. Important as Puccini was, even this didn't throttle the Hammerstein enterprise.

Hammerstein made his most important decision by signing as conductor and musical director Cleofonte Campanini, a name from the dim recesses of the American operatic past. He had served for a season as assistant conductor during Abbey's disastrous first Metropolitan year, and in the intervening two decades had become one of the leading operatic conductors at Covent Garden and La Scala, from whose staff he had only recently resigned, "dissatisfied with the artistic standards of that opera house." Hammerstein followed this with other notable, and much publicized, *coups*—Alessandro Bonci, a tenor equal to Caruso in musical stature, who had never sung in America; Charles Dalmorès, a dramatic tenor specializing in French roles; Maurice Renaud, baritone, one of the great singing actors of the day. He also recruited a large chorus of young and fresh-looking students, not the bored routiners and middle-aged stagers so familiar to most opera houses, as well as an experienced stage manager and costume and set designer. He announced a season of twenty weeks of opera, charging four thousand dollars for a season subscription for boxes. Orchestra seats cost $5, dress circle $3, balcony $2.50 down to $1 for the third tier—as expensive as the Metropolitan at the top, but cheaper at the bottom of the scale.

So far so good. But Hammerstein's roster of women singers was thin and he had no great established star. He got one, the most famous woman singer there was—Nellie Melba, who, if a little beyond her best years vocally, remained a singer of ravishing beauty of voice and a powerful draw at the box office. Why would she come to the Manhattan Opera Company? She felt that somehow she had never quite achieved a predominant position at the Metropolitan Opera in the 1890s. In addition to the grand airs and prima donna whims for which she was famous, there was also another side to Melba, love of a good fight (of which she had had many). Proud of her power in the operatic world, she relished the idea of testing it against one of the most powerful opera houses, and not just against other singers. Had she returned to the Metropolitan, she said, "I should have been at their beck and call. My roles would have been dictated for me. I said to myself: I am Melba, I shall sing when and where I like." What Cleofonte Campanini thought of such views is unrecorded.[4]

O s c a r Hammerstein's challenge to the Metropolitan became real on the night of December 3, 1906, when, in an atmosphere of hectic activity and intense excitement and anticipation—"the last carpenter and carpet layer" slipped out the rear door as the first ticket holder swept in the front—the Manhattan Opera House opened. Hundreds of ticket buyers were turned away. Carriages were stacked up waiting to get to the entrance. Streetcar lines were blocked. Those who made it inside found a very large building, 105 feet long, 200 feet wide, 70 feet high, seating three thousand people, twelve hundred in the orchestra and six hundred in each of three tiers. The exterior had a pillared facade, pillasters on the upper stories, the whole capped by a dignified pediment. The auditorium was a large flattened semicircle, light and airy, brightly lighted, with balconies reasonably close to the stage. The red-and-gold interior, supposedly Louis XIV, was not especially ornate. The sound, as in all Hammerstein theaters, was excellent, and every seat in the house had an unob-

Oscar Hammerstein's Manhattan Opera House, unlike the Metropolitan, was not designed for a fashionable high-society audience. Library of Congress.

structed view of the stage. It was the open, modern, democratic opera house, like the Chicago Auditorium, but without Louis Sullivan's soaring imagination. There were forty-two boxes in the front of the first balcony, arranged so that they all faced the stage and not each other. There were no grand entrances to the building, only modest promenade space. The Manhattan Opera House was not intended for a "fashionable" audience. "It is society in the broad sense that I hope to attract and to please," Hammerstein said, "society with a broad sense of music." And like all his theaters, it had been built in a remarkably short period of time.

The opening-night opera was Bellini's *I Puritani,* which hadn't been heard in New

York for twenty years, the same opera with which Ferdinand Palmo had inaugurated his democratic opera house sixty years before. The audience, the kind of musical one Hammerstein had hoped for, "would brook no interruption. The slightest utterance on the part of anyone was silenced immediately with a s-s-sh so imperative that it could not be mistaken. The opera was not to be employed, as society often uses it, as a vehicle for conversation." The audience followed a "go-as-you-please" style of dressing, with some women in the orchestra seats "garbed in ordinary raiment," while others were "gorgeous in evening gowns." The names of the occupants of the boxes were not listed in the program, and Campanini's policy was not to allow encores of anything. Bonci made a great impression. The comparison with Caruso, at the other house, was inevitable. The *New York Tribune* declared, "In nearly all the things which enter into the art of vocalization he is incomparably finer than his rival. His tones are impeccably pure, his command of breath perfect, his enunciation is unrivalled by any singer now before the local public, his phrasing also, his sense of proportion, symmetry, repose, exquisite." The other singers were liked and so too the chorus, "with the freshness and vigor of youth."[5]

The brilliant opening was not sustained. Renaud sang in *Rigoletto* the second night, but he was not well, the performance was indifferent, and attendance was surprisingly disappointing. The third night introduced Dalmorès in *Faust,* with Pauline Donald as Marguerite and Campanini conducting spiritedly, but the house was ominously thin. *Don Giovanni,* with Renaud as the Don incarnate, "every gesture and pose charged with significance appropriate to the part," didn't draw well. For two weeks, despair about the future settled down on the Manhattan Opera House. And then the tide was turned, not by a novelty or forgotten work, but by *Carmen;* or rather, by Clotilde Bressler-Gianoli, "an elemental, utterly frank, physical Carmen, her bodily movements as sinuous as her morals were loose." Bressler-Gianoli had sung with the French Opera Company in New Orleans without exciting much attention, but now she seized New York's attention. *Carmen* received nineteen performances. A sumptuous production of *Aida* was notable for Campanini's galvanic direction. The Metropolitan's *Aida* the same night played to vacant seats, while the Manhattan Opera was filled to overflowing. "Campanini and members of the cast were so elated by this news that they joined hands and danced in triumph about the stage."[6] *Aida* received twelve performances.

Melba came early in January 1907, accompanied by a drumbeat of publicity: about her brilliant singing at Covent Garden; about the costumes in which she would appear in *La Traviata* (it would be the dress of 1848—"the wind blows now for dramatic verisimilitude"); about her jewels, worth 2.5 million dollars and including a five-strand necklace that had belonged to Marie Antoinette. Great diva! As Violetta, her singing was brilliant, her voice luscious as ever. "The enthusiasm of the audience passed all bounds, and for some minutes there was a deafening uproar, during which hundreds of people waved their handkerchiefs, and the younger members of the audience threw their floral button holes at her feet." She sang again in *La Traviata,* then in *Lucia* and *Rigoletto,* with a superlative cast, Bonci and Renaud. Melba sold out the house and society clamored to hear her. One night seven hundred carriages came to the Manhattan, which was "fast becoming a rendezvous of fashion." "It is to be regretted," one writer lamented, "that the house does not possess more boxes."[7]

So ended the first Manhattan season, a profitable one for Hammerstein. The Metropolitan lost money. The rivalry grew more bitter. The Metropolitan hired Bonci away from Hammerstein, who brought in Giovanni Zenatello, a tenor with a powerful, exciting voice, to replace him. Hammerstein made the most, in the press, of this evidence of Metropolitan Opera desperation, but it didn't disguise, from the discerning, the fact that the direction of his own company remained uncertain. He could continue to compete with the Metropolitan in the traditional repertory (minus Puccini), depending on Campanini for vigorous direction and on stars such as Melba for excitement. But a permanent company wasn't built of such materials. Abruptly, Hammerstein moved in a new and different direction. The future of the Manhattan Opera Company would be identified with modern opera. He commissioned works by Victor Herbert and Reginald De Koven, but American opera or opera in English wasn't what Hammerstein really had in mind (and nothing would come of these two commissions). He set his sights on the modernist French and German school, and that modernist road led to Mary Garden.[8]

B o r n in Aberdeen, Scotland, in 1877, Mary emigrated to the United States with her family when she was eight. They lived first in Massachusetts and then in Chicago, where she studied voice. Encouraged by Chicago patrons, she went to Paris. But nothing much came of this and she was about to abandon her studies when, entirely by chance, she was befriended by Sybil Sanderson (1865–1903) of Sacramento, California, another of the many American women who had gone to Europe to make an operatic career. Extraordinarily beautiful, with a voice of unusual range, Sanderson was a great Parisian favorite, whose specialty was captivating French composers. For her Saint-Saëns composed *Phryné* (1893), and Massenet *Esclarmonde* (1889) and *Thaïs* (1894).

With Sanderson's help, Garden came to the attention of Albert Carré, director of the Paris Opéra-Comique, who put her to work studying Charpentier's *Louise,* the world premiere of which had taken place only two months before. Every night *Louise* was performed, Garden sat in the audience absorbing the music and stage business. One night the fantastic happened. The soprano who sang Louise was unable to continue after act 1. Garden, who had never sung on an operatic stage, was summoned backstage, costumed, and in place when the curtain rose for act 2. "What she did is now not only a memorable part of musical history but also a legend." She sang and acted with astounding poise and mastery and captivated a very critical audience, instantly establishing herself as a singing actress. Two years later, in April 1902, she earned her place in French operatic history, creating the role of Mélisande in Debussy's *Pelléas et Mélisande.* Her voice, her manner, her faint but discernible American Scots accent, conveyed unforgettably the ineffable otherworldliness Debussy sought in music and story. Amazed, when rehearsing the part with Garden, by how deeply she seemed already to understand Mélisande, he insisted that he had "nothing, absolutely nothing, to tell her." She was the physical and musical manifestation of the Mélisande of his dreams. In Garden's copy of the score, Debussy wrote: "In the future

*Mary Garden as Méli-
sande in Debussy's op-
era. Oscar Hammer-
stein said: "She knows
she is greater than any
of the others, but she
does not know how
much greater."*

others may sing Mélisande, but you alone will remain the woman and the artist I had
hardly dared hope for."⁹

Garden, the greatest singing actress of the period, delighted in creating new roles.
The quality of her voice was the subject of much controversy. It was not sensuously
beautiful, at times harsh, acidulous. Her admirers argued that her voice should be
judged by its dramatic suitability for each role, not by a generalized standard of vocal
beauty. She put her own view clearly. "I know full well that I have not a great voice. . . .
I am not a Melba or a Calvé and do not expect to be compared with such singers. It is
by an art quite different from that of other opera singers that I have found my way, and
I want to be judged not alone by my singing or my acting or my stage appearance, but
by these combined into one art that is entirely different from all the rest."¹⁰ Hammerstein's money, his appeal as an outsider, his acceptance of all her demands for an

accompanying cast up to her standards, persuaded her, who had never sung in America, to come to New York.

The 1907–1908 Manhattan Opera season was unrivaled for the number and importance of its new works. The season actually began falteringly, with an old war-horse, *La Gioconda,* in which Nordica was in poor voice. Thereafter the company got into its French stride, first with a superb performance of Berlioz's *La Damnation de Faust,* with Maurice Renaud, back with the company for another year, as Mephistoph-eles, and then with a revival of Offenbach's *Les Contes d'Hoffmann,* unperformed for over a quarter of a century. Renaud sang all three baritone roles enchantingly, the production a revelation of *Hoffmann's* musical richness. This was a prelude to Gar-den's first appearance, in the title role of *Thaïs,* "every motion of her sinuous body visible through the thin rose-colored drapery, which clung to limbs and torso," wearing "only the garb of Eve as she moved along the boards with the stride of a tigress and the tortuousness of a snake." Critics disagreed, as always, about what they heard from her throat, but after November 25, 1907, no one disputed her dramatic eminence. "In a field where mediocrity and brainlessness, lack of theatrical instinct and vocal insipidity are fairly the rule," Garden's "unerring search for novelty of expression, the very completeness of her dramatic and vocal pictures, annoyed the philistines, the professors, and the academicians." *Louise* was next, January 3, 1908, "an unequivocal dramatic and musical triumph." The applause after the first and second acts was enthusiastic, after the third, tumultuous, rapturous at the end. "The modernity, humanity, and reality of the characters appealed to many who were unaccustomed to opera plots related to contemporary realism."[11] Another blow for realism was struck at the Manhattan Opera with Franchetti's *Siberia,* capitalizing on "the current taste for violent *verismo* in post-Mascagni vein." A battle already won, *Siberia* didn't prove popular.

These premieres whetted audiences' appetites for *Pelléas et Mélisande* with Garden, but before that took place there burst into this atmosphere of innovation and modernism a kind of singer from the operatic past. Luisa Tetrazzini was in her mid-thirties and had sung for fifteen years in Europe, South America, and Mexico without causing any great stir. In 1904 she sang at the rebuilt Tivoli Theater in San Francisco and was a huge success. Heinrich Conried, at the Metropolitan Opera, heard of this but decided against signing her. After all, what did San Francisco know? Tetrazzini went on to London where, in 1907, she made a once-in-a-generation Covent Garden debut which ranked with Adelina Patti's half a century earlier. That was enough for Hammerstein, who cabled her an offer to come to the Manhattan Opera House as soon as possible.

She did. By January 15, 1908, there was Luisa Tetrazzini singing in *La Traviata,* overwhelming her audience. The effect she produced was cyclonic, bringing tears to the eyes of the people there. "As the history of opera proves, from Lind to Pons, and from Patti to Galli-Curci, there is a kind of aural appetite which nothing satisfies so keenly as the highest notes and the swiftest scales."[12] Tetrazzini's highest notes were incomparably full and brilliant, her scales dazzling in rapidity, in control and even-ness. And she used her voice with unusual dramatic intelligence, coloring her tones to suit each situation. She also proved a delightful person, blowing kisses to her bedazzled auditors, delighted by her own success. But it was the technical virtuosity which sold out the box office every time she sang—twenty-one times in a little over two months.

The true climax of the Manhattan Opera season came on February 19, with *Pelléas et Mélisande.* Listened to with "rather amazed, respectful and intelligent attention," it concluded to restrained applause and mixed opinions. "Deadly dull, monotonous, wearisome," "decadent," some said: "combinations of tones that sting and blister and pain and outrage the ear." Others discerned "page upon page of miraculous, of almost insupportable beauty." "No music written for the stage since the death of Wagner is comparable to this." As Mélisande, Garden converted eminence into supremacy. The other singers, Jeanne Gerville-Réache as Geneviève, Jean Périer as Pelléas, Hector Dufranne as Golaud, all had been in the original Paris production. The Manhattan's finest achievement so far, *Pelléas* was dominated by the "commanding genius" of Campanini, who had plumbed "the innermost secret of this most elusive of all music."[13] Debussy wrote his thanks in letters to Hammerstein and Campanini.

The sensational success of Hammerstein's season had far-reaching consequences. The Manhattan's success alarmed the Metropolitan, whose directors forced Heinrich Conried's resignation and, to replace him for the following season, signed Giulio Gatti-Casazza, director at La Scala. With him they engaged a brilliant conductor in his early forties, Arturo Toscanini. Meanwhile, Hammerstein's subscription list had grown to six times what it had been the first season, a flocking of wealthy patrons worrying to some. "It is to be hoped that society will not become too prominent, as it might tempt the manager from the path of artistic rectitude. So far he has worked for art, and for art alone, regardless of expense." Hammerstein's rectitude wasn't the issue—his ambition was.[14]

A g g r e s s i v e and expansive, like the industrial and financial moguls of the time, Hammerstein decided to extend the battlefield against the Metropolitan to Philadelphia, where the Academy of Music served as an outpost for visiting Metropolitan companies. In the spring of 1908 he took his company there for two performances: *Louise* with Garden and *Lucia* with Tetrazzini. Both were sold out, and there was wild excitement at the end of each. Called onstage, Hammerstein astonished everyone by announcing that he would build a Philadelphia opera house. Cheers greeted his words. He had thought of this for some time and the year before had bought a piece of land at Broad and Poplar streets. Construction began in March and went ahead with the usual Hammersteinian speed: cornerstone laying in June, opening on November 17, 1908. A huge building of cream-colored brick, terra cotta, and marble, handsome in its proportions, it held forty-two hundred people. Every seat had an unobstructed view of the stage and the sound was excellent. There were eighteen hundred seats on the ground floor, the rest in two balconies. The red-and-gold interior, with white fresco work and the arms of the state of Pennsylvania over the proscenium, contained an un-Hammersteinian feature: fifty-six boxes, in two tiers, at the back of the orchestra and suspended from the first balcony.

In building his opera house, Hammerstein was on familiar ground, but in entering a new city and attempting to adapt his operatic enterprise to the local social structure, mores, and taste, he showed himself much less certain about how to proceed. From the beginning he made up his mind that in Philadelphia opera must draw on "society" to succeed. At the same time he insisted that "no opera house I build will be subsidized for the rich." He reconciled these two positions by drawing the old and familiar distinction between the "rich" and the "old families." He knew New York well enough not to make very much of that dubious distinction, but Philadelphia was another matter, and he embroiled himself from the first with society patrons whose presence or control he rejected absolutely in New York. Thus, although he scaled the price of seats down from five dollars top to one dollar in the balcony, to draw the populace and fill all those seats, and although he said that all seats would be available to the ticket buying public, one tier of boxes was reserved for "representative Philadelphia families." Furthermore, he presumed to know how to distinguish the old deserving from the newly rich undeserving—a committee composed of his supporters and of five anonymous society ladies who would pass on all applications for boxes. "This method of selection may cause heart-burnings in certain quarters," he said— presumably among the rich, though it might also have been among his democratic supporters—"but there is nothing else to do." The ghost of the aristocratic Mrs. Bingham, of Philadelphia of a century before, who believed that such social distinctions were both possible and necessary, would have been pleased. In any event, the kind of support Hammerstein desired was slow to show itself, and he had to threaten to pull out before there were enough box subscriptions to go forward in organizing a resident Philadelphia company, with full orchestra and chorus, under the direction of

In Philadelphia, the mayor wanted box seats reserved for city notables at Hammerstein's opera house, to the horror of local blue-bloods. From Musical America, *Jan. 4, 1908.*

Cartoonists delighted in Hammerstein's challenge to the Metropolitan Opera. From Puck, *Nov. 11, 1908.*

Giuseppe Sturani. Hammerstein's stars would shuttle back and forth between the two cities.[15]

The 1908–1909 opera season in Philadelphia and New York was perhaps the most extraordinary in American operatic history, with an array of dazzling names—Mahler and Toscanini, Caruso and Farrar—at the Metropolitan pitted against Campanini and Garden, Melba and Tetrazzini. The Manhattan Opera season alone was enough to have made the reputation of an impresario. Hammerstein had got permission to perform Puccini and *Tosca* opened his New York season, while *Carmen* inaugurated the Philadelphia house. Fashionable society attended both. Tetrazzini was in splendid voice in *Il Barbiere* in both cities. Melba opened in *La Bohème* and finished her Manhattan Company appearances in a new role for her, Desdemona in Verdi's *Otello*.

The first premiere was Massenet's *The Juggler of Our Lady* (*Le Jongleur de Notre Dame*), in which Garden sang the role of a boy, demonstrating her amazing skill in coloring her voice and acting the role—in some ways her favorite—to perfection. That was delightful, but the excitement was provoked by the forthcoming performance of Strauss's *Salome*. Garden had worked on the role all summer in Paris and would dance the Seven Veils herself. (In the first and only Metropolitan performance, a ballerina had performed in place of Olive Fremstad.) There were lavish, and much publicized, preparations, eighteen rehearsals for the orchestra.

On the night of January 28, 1909, Garden "swept on stage trailing a long orange mantle thrown over one bare arm and shoulder," a willful, restless adolescent, depraved and sensuous, crawling across the stage "like a predaceous animal deprived of its victim, a deadly creature . . . implacable, bloodcurdling," smiling only one time, when Herod consented to give her John the Baptist's head, and then rapturously fondling and kissing it. The accounts in the newspapers mirrored the lurid scenes on stage. "She is a fabulous she-thing, playing with love and death—loathsome, mysterious, poisonous, slaking her slimy passion in the blood of her victim." When the curtain fell, the audience sat as if stunned, then broke into applause which gathered and grew for curtain call after curtain call.

The critics admired the performance, were of mixed minds about the music, hated the story. "A sewer is certainly a necessity of our everyday life but the fact of its existence does not also create the necessity for us to bend over its reeking filth to inhale its mephitic vapors." "A hideous nightmare, this wedding of a diseased libretto to a diseased score, in which the gospel of musical ugliness and perverseness is preached almost without interruption." But also: *Salome* was "so monumental in its orchestral features that it must either mark the beginning of a new musical era, or else be one of those sporadic manifestations of sensational and considered eccentricity which will disappear as soon as the novelty has worn off." Garden dominated the reviews. "A conception of incarnate bestiality which has so much power that it is a dreadful thing to contemplate . . . from willful maiden to a human hyena." "There is a terrible intensity in her acting," "absolutely nerve racking to persons susceptible to music." The rest of the cast was first-rate, Campanini unanimously praised. *Salome* received ten performances that season.[16]

When it was taken to Philadelphia, Hammerstein paid the price for the social structure that he had accommodated in his opera house. The announcement that *Salome* would be given produced a demand by six ministerial associations—Episcopalian, Presbyterian, Reformed, Lutheran, Congregational, Methodist—that it be withdrawn because it was "indecent, immoral, demoralizing, a perversion of scripture." "Under the guise of high art [it pandered] to the lowest passions of human nature." Archbishop P. J. Ryan and the Federation of Catholic Societies also opposed it because it would "demoralize the people, especially the youth of the city." The WCTU, the Christian League, the Christian Endeavor Union, and other groups joined in the opposition. Hammerstein went ahead and February 11, 1909, was "the most extraordinary operatic occasion in the history of the city." There were two thousand disappointed ticket seekers. The applause at the end was tumultuous, with fourteen curtain calls. But there was an ominous sign within the house. Four grand tier boxes were empty. *Salome* was given a second and a third time and with the same positive response. Nobody "left the house at crucial moments, no women fainted nor men cried hoarsely 'enough enough!' as the head of the Baptist was handed up from the cistern's depths." But both those nights nine box holders stayed away in protest. Hammerstein yielded and *Salome* was given no more. "I preferred not to take the risk of being the man that taught Philadelphia anything it thinks it ought not to know."[17] Hammerstein also capitulated in Boston, where the company's two-week visit, presenting its Garden and Tetrazzini repertories to huge houses and critical acclaim, was to conclude with *Salome.* But the governor, the mayor of Boston, and dignitaries, civil and ecclesiastical, opposed it.

It had been another immensely successful season, but amid the rejoicing, Hammerstein suffered an irreparable loss. Campanini announced his resignation effective at season's end, the chief reason apparently being his anger that Hammerstein, drained by losses in Philadelphia, had begun to cut rehearsal time. Now the tables were being turned. Hammerstein was feeling the pressure of the elevated Toscanini standards at the Metropolitan.

An innovation began the 1909–1910 season, an "educational" program of operas at popular prices, from two dollars to fifty cents, running from August to October, with good singers, but not stars, a repertory of standard favorites as well as *Louise, Les Contes d'Hoffmann,* and Balfe's *The Bohemian Girl,* subsidized by the opera house. Hammerstein reported that 150,000 people came. "Such a work should of course be undertaken by the municipality of New York, but it appears nauseous to that body. So I am glad to do it." Hammerstein's last great singing discovery was the Irish tenor John McCormack, with a superbly flexible voice, amazing breath control, beautiful enunciation. McCormack and Tetrazzini offered vocal feasts to appreciative audiences.[18] Massenet was becoming as important to the Manhattan as Puccini was to the Metropolitan. His *Hérodiade,* with Lina Cavalieri singing the role of Salome, capitalized on the notoriety of the Judaean princess, though it was dull compared with Strauss's version. Garden appeared in two more Massenet operas new to America, *Sapho* and *Grisélidis,* and Hammerstein also presented comic opera, Lecocq's *La Fille de Madame Angot* and Donizetti's *La Fille du régiment,* revived for Tetrazzini and McCormack.

There was one memorable modernist moment, Strauss's *Elektra.* The orchestra was expanded to 113 members and ten weeks of rehearsal cost fifteen thousand dollars. "Strauss's score is so absolutely foreign to all accepted forms, so revolutionary in treatment," Hammerstein intoned, "that it upsets both my singers and my orchestra." His Elektra was Mariette Mazarin who, it was said, visited a madhouse to gain ideas about her portrayal. A full house showed up on February 1, 1910, "to be electrified, or perchance, Elektracuted." It was an unforgettable night, more powerful than anything previously done at the Manhattan. The roar of applause and shouting at the end was "almost hysterical in quality." Mazarin acted with an intensity she had never displayed before, her voice soaring above and through the Straussian orchestral fabric. The critics were divided, some finding it repellent, some overpowering. There were three performances in Philadelphia, one in Boston.[19]

A s these things were taking place, Hammerstein's son Arthur opened secret negotiations with the Metropolitan to bring the costly rivalry to an end. In mid-April an agreement was reached. Hammerstein sold his Philadelphia Opera House, scenery, costumes, and rights to the operas of Strauss and Massenet to the Metropolitan for 1.25 million dollars. The key clause of the agreement stipulated that for ten years he was prohibited from producing opera of any kind in New York, Boston, Philadelphia, or Chicago—echoes of the Academy of Music war of 1883–1885. Once more Wall Street had won. Frozen out of the United States, Hammerstein took his money to London, where he set himself up as an impresario by building an opera house, a handsome one on the Kingsway, opened in November 1911. London was unreceptive, the season a complete failure. He returned to America, restlessly waiting for 1920 and the expiration of the agreement. But he never entered the operatic field again. Oscar Hammerstein died on August 1, 1919.

He became a well-known American "character," accorded the popular tribute of being known simply as "Oscar." He was a subject for caricature: his top hat, worn indoors and out, his Prince Albert coat. Much of his appeal was as an arch-individualist, who did things by himself without counselors, patrons, a board of directors. He kept no secretary, wrote few letters, worked by means of scribbled notes. Personally neat, he worked in a chaos of old papers, music scores, unanswered bills. His impresario's symbol was the plain kitchen chair he sat on backstage for every performance of every opera he presented, a cigar clamped between his teeth, watching, listening. He had an excellent ear for the human voice and was especially good at working with women,

Hammerstein backstage, with the ever-present cigar. From Musical America, *March 28, 1908.*

arguing with them at times but understanding their talents, special needs. He delighted to read his own words. His speeches at the end of performances or seasons, long, curiously stilted and formal—English wasn't his native tongue—were a way of establishing a conversation with the public, but for all his delight in being in the public eye, there was about him a good deal of the "puzzling, the unreachable, the enigmatic—and the lonely."

He neither pandered to the public taste nor tried to reform it, attempting always to find out what would please it so he could make money and produce opera. Voluble in one mood, he was also laconic, mordant. When he went bankrupt and the mortgage company wrote that they would be repossessing one of his theaters, he replied: "I am in receipt of your letter, which is now before me, and in a few minutes will be behind me." He sometimes made fun of his own shows. A man was thrown out of one of his theaters for being drunk. "I'm not drunk. I paid my money and I want to see the show." "You must be drunk if you want to see this show," Hammerstein replied.

Opera was a different matter. It was "an insatiable appetite," and much of his life was devoted to satisfying that obsessive need. He was quite prepared to sacrifice everything he had for opera, including his family, which they understood. His aesthetic imagination was caught by opera, but so too his moral sense. This worldly, calculating entertainer genuinely believed in the spiritual power of opera. He expressed what he felt with unusual clarity on the occasion of the opening of the ill-fated Philadelphia Opera House. "Grand opera is more than music; it is more than drama; it is more than spectacle; it is more than a social function; it is more than a display of passion, whether subdued or fierce; it is more than a song or a tale of love; it is more than a series of pictures." Others of his contemporaries believed this too, but Hammerstein went on to what was the true source of his energy and audacity. Opera was "all these things and more." And it was that "more" which enabled him to become the greatest impresario in the history of opera in America. His lasting achievement was, on a handful of occasions, to realize his sense of opera at its most exalted: "the awakening of the soul to the sublime and the divine."[20]

c h a p t e r   t w e n t y - n i n e

Whiskey per tutti

Saturday night, December 10, 1910. "The most spectacular event in the history of the Metropolitan Opera." Cars and carriages jammed the streets outside the opera house. Spectators crammed the sidewalks to see the rich and famous enter. Special police had been called out to keep order. Although ticket prices had been doubled, all tickets had been sold and the opera house lobby was packed. To retain the exclusiveness of the occasion, elaborate arrangements had been made to keep tickets out of the hands of scalpers. Season subscribers were required to sign their tickets ahead of time and then to countersign the ticket stubs in the presence of the doormen taking tickets. This took time and caused such a jam that the opening curtain was delayed until 8:23 p.m. Few of the people downstairs minded. They were not known for their punctuality. The Italian and American flags draped over the front of the boxes, the presence of a subscriber wearing a sombrero with his evening clothes, were clues to the nature of the opera. The presence of reporters from European newspapers testified to its importance. What brought everyone was the world premiere of a new opera by Europe's most popular opera composer, Giacomo Puccini. That was much. For Americans there was more. The opera was an "American" one, *The Girl of the Golden West* (*La Fanciulla del West*).

Golden it certainly was. Money hovered over everything. Puccini had been certified by American newspapers as "the most successful of all modern composers from a box-office point of view." "His income averages $15,000 a week during the season," one story explained. In addition he owned three automobiles, three motorboats, and a well-stocked game preserve. The singers were the best the Metropolitan could offer, "which meant that they were the best the world could offer," headed by Enrico Caruso, the most famous vocalist there was and commanding the largest fee per performance. The conductor, also world-famous, was Arturo Toscanini, and the staging was by David Belasco, who, if not world-famous, was at least America's leading dramatist and theatrical producer.

In such a feverish atmosphere, any mere opera might have seemed an anticlimax, and when at last the performance got underway, the audience initially seemed lethargic. The end of each act, however, was accompanied by bursts of applause. Those who counted such things totaled fifty curtain calls all told, including twenty at the opera's end. Puccini and Belasco were called out fourteen times, all the performers were "completely buried in the mass of floral tributes passed over the footlights,"

Enrico Caruso as Dick Johnson and Emmy Destinn as Minnie in The Girl of the Golden West *at the Metropolitan Opera, 1910. Historical Sound Recordings Collection, Yale University.*

and as a concluding gesture Puccini was crowned with a silver wreath decorated with ribbons of the Italian national colors.[1]

T h e connection between Puccini and American literature and theater went back a decade. In 1898 John Luther Long, a Japanophile Philadelphia lawyer, published a story called "Madame Butterfly," which recounted the hopeless love of Cho-Cho-San, a Japanese geisha, for Pinkerton, an American naval officer. David Belasco read the story, at once saw its dramatic possibilities, and in collaboration with Long adapted it for the stage. *Madame Butterfly* opened in New York in March 1900 and was an immediate hit. Seven weeks later Belasco successfully transferred it to London, where Puccini, in town to supervise the production of *Tosca,* his most recent opera, went to see it. Puccini didn't understand the dialogue, but was nonetheless moved by the story. He signed a contract with Belasco and went to work converting the play into an opera. *Madama Butterfly*'s world premiere took place in Milan in February 1904. It was a disaster, but Puccini, undismayed, revised it and soon it was whizzing around the world in triumph.

What could Puccini possibly do next, to follow the astonishing success of *La Bohème, Tosca,* and *Madama Butterfly?* For three troubled and difficult years he rejected story after story. Enter David Belasco, again. In November 1905 he produced one of his own melodramas, *The Girl of the Golden West.* Set in gold rush California, the play was a reimaging of people and scenes Belasco had become familiar with in the years when he worked in California for Tom Maguire. "My youth surged upon me while I worked," Belasco said.[2] Enter Oscar Hammerstein. To combat the Manhattan Opera Company, the Metropolitan invited Puccini to New York in the winter of 1907 for a Puccini "season," including *Manon Lescaut* (1893), as yet unperformed at the Metropolitan. He would be displayed as the exclusive house composer and collect eight thousand dollars, with all expenses paid.

Puccini agreed to this and, like Offenbach thirty years before, immediately regretted his decision: "Why ever did I accept?" Still: he was in the doldrums, he hadn't found his next subject, a change of scene might do him good. He was scheduled to arrive a couple of days before the first performance of *Manon Lescaut.* However, his ship was delayed two days by fog, and it was six o'clock on the afternoon of the performance when he finally disembarked in New York. He was whisked straight to the Metropolitan and taken to the director's box. The performance had already begun. At the end of the first act, when the house lights were raised, the Metropolitan audience, spotting him, burst into applause while the orchestra played a "vociferous fanfare." There followed "extraordinary ovations—I have never seen anything like it."[3]

Many interviews followed. American reporters like Puccini. He was forthright and "used no temperamental or foreign gestures," and, reassuringly, "even his hair is cut." Puccini responded favorably to the hectic pace of the city's life and was fascinated by American machinery and gadgets. Publicly tactful about the Metropolitan's productions, privately he liked that of *Manon Lescaut* but was unhappy with *Madama Butterfly.* "The poetry I put into it" was lacking. "The rehearsals were too hurried and

Geraldine Farrar was not what she ought to have been."[4] He went to the theater a lot and saw three plays by Belasco. Nothing in *The Music Master* or *The Rose of Rancho* appealed to his operatic interests. The third was *The Girl of the Golden West.* Belasco later insisted that in the middle of the first act, when one of the miners sang "Old Dog Tray," Puccini exclaimed, "Ah, there is my theme at last." Certainly the play's subject was different from anything he'd done before. "We've had enough now of *Bohème, Butterfly,* and Co.! Even I am sick of them!" And he wrote to Tito Ricordi: "I find truth and sincerity in the American drama." But he was also acutely aware of the difficulties he'd face in shaping Belasco's play to his own musical dramatic needs. "I have found good ideas in Belasco, but nothing definite, solid, or complete." "The West attracts me as background but in all the plays which I have seen I have found only some scenes here and there that are good." Scenes alone, he knew, didn't make an opera. "It's all a hotchpotch and sometimes in very bad taste and *vieux jeu* [old-fashioned]".

A few weeks later a friend commissioned an Italian translation of *The Girl* for him. By July 1907 he had decided to do it. "I am thinking of it constantly." Carlo Zangarini, who knew English (his mother was American), was chosen to turn the play into a libretto. Then, as was typical with Puccini, a reaction set in, dissatisfaction with his libretto and librettists, fluctuating feelings of elation and despair. The beginning of 1908 found him optimistic: "a really beautiful libretto—it is not fully built, but the foundations have been laid." By midsummer: "*The Girl* is more difficult than I thought. I've lost my way and don't go straight ahead." He insisted on a collaborator for Zangarini. In the summer of 1909 he found his way again. The second act was finished by the fall, but then the third act went slowly: "I'm beginning to be a little fed up with Minnie and her friends." He finished in the summer of 1910. "*The Girl* has come out, in my opinion, the best opera I have written." The title was puzzled over. *La Fanciulla dell'Occidente d'oro* was too elaborate. *La Fanciulla dell'Occidente* meant nothing. Finally the hybrid: *La Fanciulla del West.*[5]

As Puccini was sweating over the revisions, Gatti-Casazza came to Italy to persuade him that New York should be the site of *The Girl*'s world premiere. The Metropolitan would pay handsomely for the privilege, and Toscanini would conduct. Puccini agreed. What more natural than that his "American" opera be given first in America? An energetic publicity campaign was launched with that as the prevailing theme. In the fall, the announcement of the cast produced a flurry. It was stellar: Caruso, Emmy Destinn, and Pasquale Amato; and cosmopolitan: ten Italians, a Bohemian, a Pole, a Spaniard, a Frenchman, two Germans, and one American in the supporting roles. A month before the premiere, Puccini arrived, his regal musical rank reflected in his accommodations (paid for by the Metropolitan), the "stupendous Imperial Suite," on the *George Washington.* Puccini exuded gratitude at his shipboard interview. "Thank you, thank you! Much pleased! Long live Italy." Once again he was portrayed as reassuringly unoperatic. "Puccini would rather talk duck shooting than grand opera." "He looked more like an athlete than a musician." His athletic nature explained "why he had chosen such an open air subject as Belasco's *Girl*" and in so doing had broken "the bonds of European prejudice against America."[6]

At some point the Metropolitan Opera realized that the Americanness of Puccini's opera raised complex difficulties. Despite all the publicity and money being spent on it, and whatever its musical strengths, the opera would have to satisfy audiences' expectations and assumptions about just what, after all, the phrase "American opera" meant. And this would be closely connected to the question of whether the opera reflected audiences' ideas about realism, historical accuracy, and theatrical authenticity. Furthermore, Belasco's play, a long-running popular success, would have been seen by many in this operatic audience. While melodramatic and sentimental in tone, its production was marked by minutely realistic detail, Belasco's trademark as a writer and pride as producer: the Polka Saloon's pine-board interior, bar, gold-dust scales, dice box, safe made out of an empty whiskey keg, poker and faro tables, adobe fireplace. And into the polka, to drink Minnie's whiskey, to whoop and holler and sing songs—Belasco used a good deal of authentic music of the 1850s—came Billy Jack Rabbit, Sonora Slim, Trinidad Joe, types familiar from Belasco's play, but even more from the stories of Bret Harte and Mark Twain. Puccini's opera would be compared, for authenticity, against the limitless archetypal image of the gold rush Wild West.

Rehearsals immediately made clear that some details of Puccini's treatment had to be altered. He had confused his Cloudy Mountain miners with cowboys. Changes in costume rectified that. The cultural susceptibilities of contemporary United States audiences had to be taken into account also. In act 3, Billy Jack Rabbit, an Indian, was to be the man to hang Dick Johnson, the hero. In the United States of 1910, it was unthinkable to allow a red man to hang a white one. So a white miner took Billy Jack's place. Changes of that kind were a familiar part of European operatic history— alterations made to flatter a monarch or satisfy the censor. The central issue was what Puccini had attempted to do and what he had achieved. He said contradictory things. "The music cannot really be called American," he commented, "for music has no nationality—it is either good music or nothing." Having delivered this universalist view, however, he also embraced the particularist position. He had wanted to capture some distinctive American flavor and atmosphere, and so had studied American music of the 1850s and authentic Indian songs as well. "For this drama I have composed music that, I feel sure, reflects the spirit of the American people and particularly the strong, vigorous nature of the West. I have never been west, but I have read so much about it that I know it thoroughly." Belasco echoed that. "Signor Puccini had captured absolutely the California spirit."[7] Toscanini, later famous for his fidelity to the composer's intentions, endorsed the general line but shifted the nature of that authenticity from the music to the story. "The music of the opera is Italian and we can understand that," he said, "but the play is American and not only American but Mr. Belasco's." Besides: "We want every detail to be correct because other theaters in the future must copy this production." So the burden fell on Belasco. And who better to assume it? It was his play, his personal experience. But the libretto was not his, and at this point authenticity became a matter of dramatic style. Belasco had to create unity of style, of gesture and movement, among principals and chorus, who were not American and whose tradition of acting was operatic and Italian. These seemed unlikely conditions and traditions out of which to forge the authentic style of the 1850s American West, whatever that might be. Belasco put it amusingly:

Men and women by the scores and fifties would troop out on the stage, range themselves in rows, and become merely a background for the principals. Then for no clear purpose, they would all begin to shrug their shoulders, grimace, and gesticulate with their hands. I resolved to undo all this at once. I located the ones who shrugged too much and either backed them up against trees and rocks or invented bits of "business" by which they were held by the others. When a chorus-singer became incorrigible in the use of his arms I made him go through entire scenes with his hands in his pockets. Little by little I tamed this wriggling crowd until they themselves began to understand the value of repose.

He was up-beat about the principal singers, insisting that he was "much impressed with the quickness with which Mr. Caruso had acquired an American manner of that place and period." Puccini had reservations about Emmy Destinn—whether she had enough vitality for the role. Lillian Nordica said what she thought. "Mme. Emmy Destinn . . . is a wonderful artist. I cannot but regret, however, that the artist selected is not American."[8]

'' I have no doubt now of its success," a happy Puccini said after the first performance. *La Fanciulla del West* was given eight more times at the Metropolitan that

Realism and make-believe collided in Puccini's operatic evocation of the Wild West. *This cartoon appeared in* **Musical America** *on Jan. 14, 1911, shortly after* **The Girl's** *Chicago premiere.*

DURING A PERFORMANCE OF "THE GIRL OF THE GOLDEN WEST" WITH REAL COWBOYS IN CHICAGO.

season, to very good houses. Cleofonte Campanini conducted the Chicago premiere on December 27, and Boston saw it soon after. It was first given at Covent Garden in May 1911, in the presence of the composer, and in Rome the next month, Toscanini conducting. Everywhere it was well, if not enthusiastically, received. Especially in America, however, once the initial excitement passed away, there was a distinct feeling of disappointment, even of failure. The ironies involved—that Puccini's opera was insufficiently Puccinian; that his American opera didn't seem really American; that a realistic work failed because it wasn't authentic—give us an excellent chance to understand how complex and contradictory were American audiences' ideas about the nature of music drama and its relationship to realism and nationalism.

The simplest explanation was a musical one. Despite the power of Puccini's operas as dramas, most audiences responded primarily to the music. In that respect the inescapable fact about *La Fanciulla* was the absence of melody. "Here and there, in a turn of melody, in a phrase voiced by Minnie, do we hear Puccini of *Butterfly* or *Bohème*. But only here and there." "Nine-tenths of the opera sounds as if it had been written by somebody who was imitating Puccini and was not doing it very well." "The public looked forward with eager anticipation to another *Butterfly*. Instead of which it got an Italianized version of the drama with second-rate Puccini music." Puccini was deeply pained and disappointed by such criticisms. Musically, he had been trying for something different, something broader and deeper. *La Fanciulla* was in many ways his most complex and subtle score, revealing throughout a growing mastery and subtlety and, in his efforts to expand his dramatic scope, the influence of Strauss and of Debussy. There were no arias of the familiar Puccini kind. Dick Johnson's song in act 3, "Tell her I've been set free" ("Ch'ella mi creda"), became a modest concert-hall favorite, but Minnie had nothing memorable. Puccini's attempt to achieve a more integrated dramatic music was marked down as a failure of melodic inspiration. Those who live by the aria die by it.[9]

This explained the disappointment. But *La Fanciulla del West* also provoked criticism, on several grounds. There was nationalist suspicion that it was another European caricature of America. "The polka, the sheriff, the Wells-Fargo agent, the poker games, the heavy whiskey drinking and the ready 'gun' will be gratifying novelties," grumbled one observer, because Europeans would find "all this—especially the lynching—typically American." Others attacked the notion that it was American in any way. "Is it American?" asked W. J. Henderson? "Not in the least. It is an Italian opera on an American story. All that is American in the opera is the work of Belasco. The thematic bases of the musical score belong to the plains of Lombardy, not the Wild West, to the slopes of the maritime Alps, not of the Sierras." Still others insisted that the opera's problems were due to the way it was cast. "Everyone took it for granted that *The Girl* would be sung by Geraldine Farrar, then approaching the zenith of her Metropolitan career, young, slender and beautiful—and an American." Instead, Minnie was "the slavic and none too svelte Emmy Destinn who, whatever her vocal artistry, was visually no glamour-girl," while Caruso as Dick Johnson "suggested a golden-west outlaw about as much as he did the Queen-of-the-Night." Thus, with "a corpulent Minnie, a burly Neapolitan Johnson, caroling away for dear life in Italian," the golden-west atmosphere "melted into thin air."[10]

Behind the varying degrees of criticism, there also lurked that old pervasive Anglo American literalness, a kind of cultural bedrock lying beneath other attitudes and points of view. "The spectacle of a group of unlikely looking miners and cowboys whooping it up" was essentially absurd. Sung speech was unnatural and unreal. One critic said dismissively: "Whiskey *per tutti* and *andiamo* Minnie were not the language of the Wild West."[11] But it wasn't the Wild West on the stage of the Metropolitan, with miners singing, "Whiskey for everyone" or "Let's go, Minnie." It was make-believe. It was art. It was opera.

Virtuoso Conductors

The Hammerstein earthquake, like any seismic movement, produced numerous aftershocks. The most important of these was the introduction of modern operas and the reform of operatic production. The chief instrument of reform was the conductor. In the concert hall, conductors had been gaining power and prestige for several decades, rising from the status of time beaters to that of commanders in chief. In the opera house the leader of the orchestra still largely remained a person "who conducted with as much authority as the singers would allow." Bayreuth pointed in a new direction. In America the decisive change came in the first decade of the twentieth century. A new generation of operatic conductors asserted their mastery over singers and all aspects of performance. They became commanding figures, popular stars of the first magnitude, known for their personalities and individual temperaments as much as for their music, virtuosos of the baton.

The first was Cleofonte Campanini. The "continuous conductor," one critic called him. His control of all his forces, orchestral and vocal, was persistent, unyielding, "always vital, sometimes fervent." While he imparted the quality that was the hallmark of the virtuoso conductor, propulsive energy, Campanini's distinguishing quality was sensitivity, balance. He had a wealth of fine singers to work with and he did so subtly and flexibly, shaping his interpretation to suit the strength—but not the ego—of each. Mary Garden presented a formidable challenge in this regard. Her intensely focused dramatic power threatened to unbalance any performance, though not in the coarse, conventional, prima donna display of whim. The relationship of Garden and Campanini fluctuated, especially because of Garden's insistence upon her prior claims to the French repertory at the Manhattan Opera House, to the exclusion of other singers. But onstage their work together was magnificent, both in New York and, later, in Chicago. Garden's praise was unstinting. "Nobody could touch Campanini, *nobody in the world.* He was the most consummate artist in every way, not only as a conductor. He had faultless taste in choosing operas and in filling the roles with people who were absolutely right for them."

Campanini's repertory was broad. In three years at the Manhattan, he conducted thirty-two different operas, French and Italian. He would have done German opera as well had Hammerstein's original plan for a German wing been carried out, and he conducted German opera very effectively later in Chicago. In breadth of operatic musical culture Campanini was

The conductor as collaborator: Cleofonte Campanini (left) with the tenor Charles Dalmorès, about 1907. Library of Congress.

not surpassed, even by Mahler, and in his championing of modernist opera he was preeminent among conductors in America in his day. Only Stokowski equaled him in later years. In addition to Verdi and Puccini, he also conducted Mozart, Meyerbeer, Rossini, Bellini, Offenbach, Boito, and Saint-Saëns.[1]

The unifying thread of Campanini's three years at the Manhattan was his integration of all elements of production. Capable of angry outbursts, and willing to use the threat of such, he contrived to win the willing cooperation of his artists. In preparing *Pelléas et Mélisande,* with the original Paris cast, he said that he let them teach him the score, a statement unthinkable from Mahler or Toscanini. He was not in the least timid and eagerly engaged the Metropolitan in head-to-head rivalry in the Hammerstein years and when he brought his Chicago company east.

Still, for all his gifts and accomplishments, Campanini was eclipsed in fame by Toscanini. Why? Campanini lacked Toscanini's volcanic power, as conductor and as personality. However, their abilities were more closely matched than the disproportion in their reputations suggests. There are several reasons for this. One conducted in New York, the operatic capital, while the other spent most of his time in Chicago. Campanini didn't have recordings to extend his fame and to perpetuate his work. Above all, Campanini died at age fifty-nine—very early for a conductor. Had he lived through the splendid Chicago seasons of the 1920s and, conversely, had Toscanini died at the end of his Metropolitan period, in 1915, how different their reputations would now be. Campanini was to Toscanini rather as Bonci was to Caruso.

He was the virtuoso as collaborator. He was part of the Manhattan *Company*. At the end of the last performance of the first Manhattan season, after many curtain calls, Oscar Hammerstein gave one of his speeches, outlining his plans for the future. "I am going abroad in a few weeks to engage artists to sing here next year," at which point he was interrupted by a voice from the gallery—"Mr. Campanini!"

"Yes, Mr. Campanini is coming back," Hammerstein responded. "I want him most of all."

That anonymous gallery voice was the authentic voice of the Manhattan and the appropriate tribute to Campanini's work.[2]

W h e n Heinrich Conried took over at the Metropolitan in 1903, he brought Felix Mottl, one of the respected conductors of the day, to revitalize the German wing of the house and to raise the level of its productions. One year was enough for Mottl. The *Titanic* couldn't turn on a dime. Clearly aware that the threat posed by Campanini and company was formidable, Conried in July 1907 announced the appointment of Gustav Mahler (1860–1911) as conductor for the forthcoming season. Famous in our day as a composer, in the early twentieth century Mahler was better known as conductor and as operatic reformer.

Mahler's reputation had been hard won. Resented because he was a difficult person, because he had radical ideas about performance, and because he was a Jew, he gained experience in numerous provincial opera houses. In Prague and Leipzig he served as assistant to Anton Seidl and Arthur Nikisch. In 1888 he became musical director of the Budapest Opera and immediately introduced innovations: all operas were sung in Hungarian, the star system was abolished, and singers with musical intelligence and dramatic ability were sought after. This provoked furious opposition. Mahler left after two years, snatched up by Hamburg, where he worked with growing success for six years. In 1897 he scaled one of the summits of European opera, as conductor and musical director at the Vienna Court Opera.

There Mahler made operatic history. Irascible, energetic, imaginative, dogmatic— "driven by demons, incapable of compromise"—he was ruthless in scraping away the encrusted layers of conventional performance, dismissing singers and orchestral players to bring in fresh talent. He worked in conjunction with Alfred Roller, set designer and producer, who, influenced by contemporary expressionism in painting and the spoken drama, went beyond the realism of the day, using subtle forms of lighting to achieve many of his most striking effects. The key to Mahler's achievement was in fact an old idea, carried to new lengths: rehearsal. Some Vienna productions received thirty to forty rehearsals when, by contrast, at the Metropolitan one rehearsal was common, five remarkable. To attain his goals Mahler stormed and raged. Many members of the orchestras he conducted hated him. Nor were composers' scores untouchable. He cut, rescored, reinterpreted freely. He hated routine. "Tradition is an excuse for slackness," he said. Authenticity, which has since become a crucial twentieth-century performance value, he thought a relative term. Only vigorous but thoughtful reinterpretation could save great works from deadening tradition. Authenticity was an end, not a means. He accepted the same approach to his own music. "What is best in music is not found in the notes." He insisted upon absolute quiet, turning and glaring at offenders. Late-comers were not seated until an act was over. Done in Mahler's spirit, Wagner was a revelation to many who had grown bored with him. Even more, the Mozart operas were rediscovered. *Le Nozze di Figaro* made an immense impression. The raising of the curtain on Mahler's production was momentous: the rococo Mozart giving way to the realist one. Roller's sets

The conductor as reformer: Gustav Mahler caricatured by Caruso. From Musical America, *Jan. 25, 1908.*

depicted Figaro's and Susannah's room as chaotic servants' quarters, with the wash hanging out to dry. A century-long reinterpretation of Mozart began there. Many were shocked, but the young were with Mahler. He swept opposition aside. His success was indisputable. In 1907, after ten tumultuous years, he resigned, and no sooner did he do so than people, many of whom had resisted his innovations, realized that Vienna had lived through a golden decade of opera.[3]

G u s t a v Mahler at the Metropolitan! At last: the irresistible force and the irredeemable institution. Or at least: a conductor to match the voices. What dramatic pictures swirl in the imagination: the injection of this man—"demonic, neurotic, demanding, selfish, noble, emotionally undisciplined, sarcastic, unpleasant, and a genius"—into the temple of singers' opera, the haven of slovenly routine, the play-box of late-arrivers and nonstop talkers! But it wasn't to be quite like that, because at this point in his life and career Mahler didn't want it. "His heart was elsewhere than in the theatre, elsewhere than in conducting. . . . There was always an inner protest, always an almost morbid longing to escape the duties of an executive musician and devote his strength to composition." He would conduct and supervise productions for about three months in the year, and then Metropolitan gold would set him free. "It has all been very carefully thought out," he wrote to a friend. "The most I risk is being rather miserable for three months in the year, to make up for which I shall have earned 300,000 crowns *clear* in four years."[4] What if Gustav Mahler had gone to the Metropolitan in 1897 instead of Maurice Grau? But by 1907 it was too late.

Mahler's first look at Metropolitan productions appalled him: "absolute incompetence," "fraudulent activities," "the situation . . . is bleak." He tried to get the Metropolitan to hire Roller, but no offer was forthcoming. Despite this, and the troubles at the opera house, he was optimistic about America and Americans: "generous, healthy," "tremendously unspoilt," "hungry for novelty, and in the highest degree eager to learn." At times, he got carried away. "Here the dollar does not reign supreme—it's merely easy to earn. Only one thing is respected here: ability and drive." But, as he was not musical director, with final authority, when Gatti-Casazza was brought in, the ground was cut out from under him. The presence of Toscanini also complicated things. Aware that difficulties might arise between the two conductors, Gatti-Casazza called Toscanini in Italy for assurances. "But of course I will have no difficulty at all," he replied. "There is room at the Metropolitan for several conductors and I am very happy to find myself with an artist of Mahler's worth. I hold Mahler in great esteem and would infinitely prefer such a colleague to any mediocrity."[5] Later, Toscanini changed his mind, feeling that Mahler no longer gave enough of himself. In such circumstances, Mahler's accomplishments could only be momentary.

But what magnificent moments they were! One month after his arrival in New York, on January 23, 1908, Mahler led a superb *Don Giovanni,* performing that masterpiece as "what it had almost never been at the Metropolitan: a completely integrated performance." Subtly blending a responsive orchestra and those celebrated voices—Bonci as Ottavio, Scotti as the Don, Chaliapin (held firmly in check) as Leporello, with Eames, Sembrich, and Gadski as Anna, Zerlina, and Elvira—he created a rich texture of sound, the music moving "swiftly, steadily, even relentlessly toward its great climax." Might not a serious reawakened interest in Mozart have followed such a beginning? Not so. The Metropolitan didn't give *Don Giovanni* again for twenty years. There was a celebrated *Fidelio* two months later: massive, brooding sets conveying powerfully a sense of evil and oppression. Mahler succeeded in focusing the audience's attention on the opera as a whole, "not just on how well the soprano sang Leonore." The action moved rapidly under the "breathless intensity" of his direction. On January 13, 1909, Mahler unveiled his second Mozart revival, *Le Nozze di Figaro,* with twenty rehearsals and one of the best casts (not just the most famous singers) assembled in America for Mozart: Eames as the Countess, Sembrich as Susannah, Farrar as Cherubino, Adamo Didur as Figaro, and Scotti as the Count. The sets were grouped around an interior stage to give the illusion of intimacy in the vast Metropolitan spaces, Mahler conjuring up "fine unity of style," as well as "clean, accurate, elastic and transparent" playing and singing. But *Figaro* too went into the Metropolitan's memory hole and wasn't done again until 1916.

The most popular of Mahler's productions was *The Bartered Bride,* the American premiere of the 1866 masterpiece of the Czech composer Bedřich Smetana (1824–1884). Sung in German, as *Die verkaufte Braut,* it had irresistible vivacity. Another premiere was a personal enthusiasm, Tchaikovsky's *The Queen of Spades,* introduced to America on March 5, 1910, again in German, beautifully staged, the orchestra conveying the "singularly insinuating power" of the music with remarkable finish. Performed four times that season, it then disappeared from the Metropolitan's repertory for half a century. On a more personal note, the last *Tristan und Isolde* Mahler ever conducted left him with joyous memories. "A Great Performance," was the heading of the report of W. J. Henderson of the *New York Sun,* who praised Olive Fremstad's Isolde unrestrainedly. "A superb, a queenly, a heroically tragic Isolde," he wrote. "But she was not alone in her glory. Mr. Mahler hurled all petty restraints to the four winds and turned loose such a torrent of vital sound as he had never before let us hear." "The stars were kind," Mahler told his wife that night, when it was over. "I have never known a performance of *Tristan* to equal this."[6]

Mahler turned away from opera to the concert hall and the New York Philharmonic, where his tenure was enshrouded with controversy, opposition from critics, meddling interference from some of the orchestra's directors. "The hostility, prejudice, even hatred . . . of New York newspaper critics" and others, "shattered and killed Mahler," one American journalist wrote later.[7] By the end of his American sojourn he was undoubtedly less sanguine about Americans than he had been in 1907, but it was heart disease, not America, which killed Gustav Mahler, in Vienna, on May 18, 1911. He was the greatest creative musician ever associated directly with the performance of opera in America, the romantic genius, adored and hated, the virtuoso conductor as tragic hero.

A n d then there was Arturo Toscanini. Whether the Metropolitan mainly wanted Gatti-Casazza, and got Toscanini into the bargain, or wanted Toscanini and took Gatti-Casazza as the price to be paid, is not certain. The artistic consequences have been indisputably clear for a long time, however. Toscanini commanded the Metropolitan in its most glorious years of operatic performance. So powerful has been the spell cast by him on Americans, extending well over forty years, that one must distinguish this first of the three distinct careers which make up the Toscanini experience of America and the American experience of Toscanini: the operatic years at the Metropolitan, 1908–1915; the concert-hall career of the 1920s and 1930s; the radio-broadcast career of the 1940s and 1950s.

The forty-one-year-old conductor who came to New York in 1908 had never conducted in the United States or visited it, though he had begun his conducting career while touring Brazil twenty years before. The publicity introducing him to Americans emphasized his six years at La Scala and the prestige that accrued to him from having conducted the world premieres of *La Bohème* and *I Pagliacci*. Few people knew anything of his important role in introducing Wagner to Italy. Nor was there any report of the criticisms of his conducting that had clung to him in Italy: "rigidity of execution, mathematical accuracy and lack of poetry." The press discreetly suggested his salient temperamental characteristic—ferocious determination to have his way. He had left La Scala because he thought it unreformable. Did he believe that the *Metropolitan* was reformable? He knew almost nothing about it and probably didn't care. He knew that in any opera house he would have to fight for his beliefs, and, after all, Gatti-Casazza was there—wasn't he?—to back him up.

"AHA! BUT THERE IS TOSCANINI, THE GREAT CONDUCTOR,"

The conductor as dynamo: Arturo Toscanini caricatured by Caruso. From Musical America, *Dec. 10, 1910.*

Toscanini had no theory of opera as dramatic art, but rather an intuitive desire for what Campanini and Mahler and other reformist conductors wanted: seriousness of musical and dramatic purpose, zeal in pursuit of balanced ensemble, attention to the details of production. He knew what prevented his achieving his goals: opera administrators who skimped on rehearsals, on salaries for choristers and for additional orchestral players, when needed. And prima donna singers, of both sexes. His battles with them were part of the operatic lore of his day. As a conductor he was celebrated as the archapostle of the sanctity of the musical score. Not for him Mahler's excisions and emendations. "The tradition is to be found only in one place—in the music." The difficulty with this position was that different conductors, also defenders of the composer, also seeking to rescue the drama from performers' caprice, read the same notes in different ways. And in practice Toscanini was not consistent about his interpretative literalism. Into his much admired revival of Gluck's *Orfeo ed Euridice,* he introduced music from *Alceste* and from *Echo et Narcisse,* and he modified orchestration. "One is not a machine," he said. "Music must breathe."[8]

In his "insatiable desire for perfection," he snarled, stamped, glowered, shouted, raged, threw things. Caricaturists sought to capture the furious concentration, the glaring, staring eyes. He made the orchestra pit a place of drama. "Since when does Caruso sing on a Sunday night?" asked someone who found a line of ticket buyers encircling the Metropolitan. It wasn't Caruso. It was Toscanini's first appearance as a symphonic conductor in America. So great was the sense of power that radiated from him that even those who saw him conduct didn't always realize how small he was. That he conducted without a score represented more than an unusual feat of memory; it symbolized the intensity of his concentration. He lost himself in the music. No wonder that in a culture which admired mastery, he became an American hero, the virtuoso as dynamo, as personification of will.

Concentration marked his repertory as well. It is true that in his seven Metropolitan seasons Toscanini conducted twenty-nine different operas, a broad repertory. Campanini's was broader. Rightly famous for his interpretation of Wagner, Toscanini concentrated on two operas, *Tristan* and *Die Meistersinger,* and after 1910, only on these two. The *Ring* he treated as a series of excerpts. Puccini and Verdi were the Italian repertory. No Bellini, no Rossini, only one Donizetti, *Don Pasquale.* No Mozart. His response to French opera was interesting. His first attempt at *Carmen* was disappointing. He returned to it in 1914 and achieved a masterful, integrated success. The only Massenet he did was *Manon,* but that was one of his triumphs in balance and elegance. He wanted to do *Louise,* but Gatti-Casazza thought the Campanini/Garden performances were too fresh in New Yorkers' minds to risk comparison. Aside from Paul Dukas' *Ariadne and Blue-Beard* (*Ariane et Barbe-Bleue*), his incursions into the modernist repertory were strictly limited to Italian realists such as Giordano, Franchetti, Montemezzi, as well as Leoncavallo and Mascagni. He never conducted *Pelléas et Mélisande* in America, or any Strauss. He was a revivalist, not an innovator. He brought Gluck to the Metropolitan stage, *Orfeo ed Euridice,* and then *Alceste,* which he insisted upon as an opening-night opera. Weber's *Euryanthe* was a departure from the conventional repertory, and his magnificent performances of *Otello* and *Falstaff,*

Verdi operas then not often performed in the United States, were a premonition of the general Verdi revival in Europe in the 1920s. His most important Metropolitan premiere was *Boris Godunov* by Modest Musorgsky (1839–1881), a "thoughtful, eloquent, well-studied" performance of music which still seemed "rude and un-polished," harsh and difficult, a modernist opera forty-five years old. Toscanini's greatest achievement, however, was based on his brilliant performances of Wagner. He contributed mightily to the internationalizing of opera in America, leveling barriers between German and Italian opera, German and Italian audiences. An un-quenchable dedication to the highest standards of performance knew no national boundaries.[9]

S e v e n years—and it was over. Rumors had circulated for two years that Toscanini had a growing list of complaints. "Is no discipline. With me, yes; but with other conductors, no." He was also involved in an affair with Geraldine Farrar, who may have given him an ultimatum to choose between her and his wife. Divorce for him was inconceivable. One way out was simply to leave. But the primary reason for his departure was discontent with the prevailing indifference to the standards he wished to reach and maintain. The conquest of Oscar Hammerstein aggravated the situation. With its monopoly restored, the Metropolitan began to pile up substantial profits each year. Gatti-Casazza refused to put this back into productions. "The product could be cheapened a bit and still make money. Toscanini . . . thought it could be improved further and had no interest at all in whether it made money." There was no money, for instance, for a stage band in the revival of Verdi's *Un Ballo in maschera.*[10]

Toscanini blamed the directors of the company, in particular Otto Kahn, the most influential member of the board; and for a time absolved Gatti-Casazza of respon-sibility. He urged Gatti-Casazza to join him in quitting, assuming that the Metro-politan leadership would surrender to their joint demands, and it must have come as a blow that Gatti-Casazza wouldn't do that. The climax came with a mediocre perfor-mance of *Carmen* in April 1915. Toscanini was furious. The next night he conducted Mascagni's *Iris,* then canceled the rest of his scheduled performances, with no explanation, and left for Italy. The Metropolitan's explanation was that he had returned home to support Italy's war effort. Later, Toscanini wrote to a friend in America, informing him that a statement could be made public. "I have given up my position at that theatre because my aspirations and artistic ideals were unable to find the fulfillment I had dreamt of reaching when I entered it in 1908. Routine is the ideal and the basis of that theatre. This can suffice for the artisan, not for the artist. 'Renew yourself or die.' *Voilà tout.* This is the only reason which made me leave the Metro-politan. All the others that have circulated in the papers are false and unfounded."

It wasn't until September that a formal announcement was made that Toscanini would not return to the Metropolitan. Kahn and Gatti-Casazza seem to have made serious efforts to change his mind, promising to meet virtually any of his demands, if he would state them. Years later Toscanini spoke "with distaste of much of the Metropolitan audience, reviling the stupid, social elements which, he contended, had no interest in music. That had not changed, he said, over the years." He also spoke bitterly of his former collaborator: "Gatti was Kahn's man." For two decades after that,

Gatti-Casazza and Toscanini never spoke to each other and, though he lived for another half-century, much of it in the United States, Arturo Toscanini never conducted opera again at the Metropolitan.[11]

A fourth star conductor of these years represented the virtuoso as classicist. Felix Weingartner was born in Zara, on the Dalmatian coast, in 1863, studied at the Leipzig Conservatory, where he startled everyone by conducting a performance of Beethoven's Second Symphony from memory, became Hans von Bülow's assistant, and then reacted strongly against Bülow's free-and-easy interpretations, the point of departure for his own ideas. He conducted very widely, but only gradually established himself and his views. In 1908 he succeeded Mahler in Vienna. His great gift was to see a work as a whole and to reveal its structural architecture. He was the Cézanne of interpreters. His classicism expressed itself in a desire for balance, restraint, an avoidance of personalism. He would have agreed with Richard Strauss's wry comment to an orchestra: "Gentlemen, please, not so much emotion. Beethoven wasn't nearly so emotional as our conductors."[12] Even Weingartner's detractors agreed that his Beethoven interpretations were majestic. He was also a man of wide musical culture, an excellent pianist and a composer. The great sadness of his life was that audiences did not admire his compositions.

He was a complex and contradictory person. Undeterred by controversy, he expounded his ideas in articles, pamphlets, and letters, yet he was generous, warm, softspoken, gentle with his musicians. "He was not a dictator, nor the unreasonable school teacher." The conductor's duty, he felt, was to efface his own personality. "His gestures were most simple and unpretentious." He had first visited the United States in 1904, conducting the New York Philharmonic. In 1911 he came to Boston to conduct opera, which he did for part of only three seasons. As a result, his reputation as an operatic conductor in America has been largely overlooked. His years in Boston were tremendously successful, bringing out qualities that the orchestra didn't know it had, sonority without noise, a marvelous, sustained singing quality. The Boston Opera orchestra had greeted his appearance with apprehension as well as eagerness. "They need not have worried. By definition the master was one to get along with his players." In his first season he conducted nine performances in twelve days—*Tristan, Tosca, Faust, Aida, Hänsel und Gretel.* The *Tristan* was a revelation, superior to Mahler's or Toscanini's in the view of Boston critics. He dealt with *Tosca* as intently and seriously as if it had been *Tristan.* "Nowadays conductors in opera interest, stir, hold audiences—when they are conductors of personal weight and great achievement," wrote H. T. Parker. Such was Weingartner. The next season Weingartner helped Boston rediscover the greatness of *Otello,* and then presided over the first Mozart done by the Boston company, *Don Giovanni.* Contemporaries thought it the best Mozart performance ever heard in the city. In his final year Weingartner's time was very limited, but his appearance only confirmed the lesson "that the chiefest need of the Boston Opera House is an eminent, commanding, recreating conductor."[13]

The city and the conductor suited each other in more than simply musical ways. "His appearance proclaimed him a scholar and a gentleman, a combination specially tailored for Boston." There was another kind of appeal as well: "The glamour of youth

*The conductor as classicist: Felix Weingartner,
in a contemporary engraving from* Die Musik.

still lingered about the tall, spare figure." This aspect troubled some, excited others. Weingartner was irresistible to women, and married five times. In 1912 he brought with him to Boston the soprano Lucille Marcel, who at the time was (or perhaps wasn't) "Madame" Weingartner. When she wasn't singing, she went to every performance and greeted him as he entered the orchestra pit by beaming, waving, and blowing kisses at him. "The frankness of it all surprised the reticent New England folk of boxes and parquet."[14]

P o s t s c r i p t —a glance ahead. While this quartet of stars dominated the ten years from 1906 to 1915, other younger virtuosos were coming forward. Of one of these a critic wrote in 1914: "Not one of the younger conductors in America is as individual and temperamental." That was Leopold Stokowski, born in London in 1882, who came to the United States in 1905 as an organist. Cincinnati employed him as its

The conductor as gymnast: one of Giuseppe Creatore's imitators, caricatured in Musical America, *March 14, 1908.*

symphony's musical director in 1909, and he quickly turned the orchestra and the musical life of the city upside-down, introducing "a new kind of glamor, a new set of instrumental standards." He quit, or was fired, amid tremendous uproar in 1912, landing on his feet in Philadelphia, where he introduced the newest of the new music and began a life-long enchantment of Philadelphia (and other) audiences. "Comely and romantic; he conducts with a plentiful fire of gesture and pose," an early observer had written, while another ridiculed any conductor "who clenched his shaking fists, threshed the air with his arms and distorted his body to secure innocuous and unconvincing effects." In glamor, personal notoriety, and publicity, Stokowski out-stripped his contemporaries, the virtuoso as prima donna.[15]

A s the twentieth century opened, Italian bands became the rage in America. Among them was a Neapolitan band led by Giuseppe Creatore, of whose conducting we have a lively description: "Now he leans over the row of music stands, he smiles the smile of a lover—pleading, supplicating, entreating, caressing—with outstretched hand, piercing the air with his baton, like a fencing master. Almost on his knees, he begs, he demands, he whirls around with waving arms. He laughs, he cries, he sings, he hisses through his clenched teeth."[16] *There* was the epitome of the virtuoso conductor!

Boston Renaissance

New England, Indian Summer, the culture of the word dissolving in an atmosphere of "serenity and autumnal splendour, of richness and dangerous ripeness." For most people it wasn't Indian Summer at all. It was a time of beginnings and expansion. The 1880 Boston of 362,000 people had grown to 560,000 by 1900 and 670,000 by 1910, with an equal number living in the suburbs. Many of these people were foreign immigrants, most numerously the Irish. There were other immigrants as well. Some 50,000 people from Sicily and southern Italy came to Boston between 1875 and 1910, and the number of Jews and African Americans increased. By 1900, one-third of Boston's population was foreign-born, over 70 percent of it of foreign parentage.

It was also a time of expansion in the arts—the Boston Museum of Fine Arts was established in 1870—especially in music, where much of this growth took a familiar New England institutional form, the school. In 1867 were founded the Boston Conservatory of Music and the New England Conservatory of Music. Music also intertwined itself with the colleges and universities of which New England was justly proud. Harvard established the first professorship of music and Yale a school of music. Church music remained important. The Handel and Haydn Society continued. A generation of New England composers gained national reputation. One understands the sentiments of the Charleston lady who "never realized before how many good reasons the New Englanders have to think well of themselves."[1]

Boston grew more plutocratic as it grew grander. Unlike New York's, its new men didn't have colossal fortunes. Nevertheless, "with plutocracy came vulgarity, in Boston as elsewhere." In 1869 Boston was the scene of a five-day National Peace Jubilee and Music Festival, which took place in a specially built hall covering three acres and seating fifty thousand. The music was provided by an orchestra of one thousand, organized by the Irish bandmaster Patrick S. Gilmore, with Ole Bull as concertmaster, and a chorus of ten thousand. The prospect of one hundred firemen pounding sledgehammers on one hundred anvils while ten thousand voices roared out the Anvil Chorus from *Il Trovatore,* led John Sullivan Dwight to leave town. He wasn't missed. In 1872 there was another monster celebration—only bigger: orchestra of two thousand, chorus of twenty thousand, with Johann Strauss, the Waltz King, imported to conduct. Along with such grossness was its opposite, equally representative of the city, the Kneisel String Quartet, founded in 1885 and for twenty years the leading chamber music group in the United States. And Boston was frequently cited by foreign musicians as the most musical city in the country, its audiences famous (or notorious) for their cool, undemonstrative, serious attention.[2]

The growth of the city's artistic life and its seemingly placid surface concealed divisions and animosities. By the end of the nineteenth century the Irish immigrants and their children had gained control of Boston's government and made their political presence felt throughout New England. This accounted for a good deal of that sense, among some Yankees, of autumnal decline. "America was swept from our grasp. The future is beyond us," lamented Barrett Wendell in 1893. Socially, the Yankees reacted with a mixture of aggressiveness and defensiveness characteristic of social groups whose power is challenged, closing the chief social institutions to the Irish and other foreigners.[3] This shaped the context within which Boston's artistic life expanded. Could there be *one* audience for art in such circumstances? Ethnic tensions ran like a fault line through everything, the art institutions as well as the social ones. Many of the Irish identified them as Yankee and wanted no part of them. Dublin had a history of enthusiasm for opera, but in Boston it was often perceived as part of a hostile culture.

One thing, at least, united Yankee plutocrats and Irish immigrants: anxiety about the erotic. In 1893 the New York sculptor Frederick Macmonnies offered his *Bacchante,* a beautifully modeled nude fountain sculpture, to the Boston Public Library. A controversy erupted. Boston newspapers representing Irish Catholic readers were "bitter against the sculpture," and they were joined by a committee for the library, among its members the Brahmin aesthete Charles Eliot Norton, which condemned it as "inappropriate for public exhibition." "Banned in Boston" soon became a national symbol of absurd prudery and the expression of a culture deeply uneasy about modernity.[4]

There was a progressive side to Yankee culture as well, personified by the most selfless patron of music Boston ever knew—Henry Lee Higginson (1834–1919). The son of a New York merchant who went broke in the panic of 1837 and then moved back to Boston, Henry hoped to be a pianist and composer and studied music in Vienna for five years. Convinced that he would never be a first-rate musician, he came home in 1860, fought in the Civil War, and after it, having tried various enterprises, formed a stockbrokerage firm with his cousin, married, lived very frugally, prospered. By 1881 he had a fortune of $750,000, not much by Vanderbilt standards, but enough for him to do what he had dreamed of: establish a symphony orchestra that would rank with the finest in Europe. He employed sixty musicians by the year, which gave them security and allowed for proper rehearsal. "It was a god-like act." Though several times close to bankruptcy, he met every deficit until 1914. A public subscription gave the Boston Symphony a home, Symphony Hall (1900), designed by McKim, Mead, and White, seating twenty-six hundred, an oblong brick box, unadorned outside, ornate within, its incomparable acoustics the accomplishment of Wallace Clement Sabine of Harvard. Boston became a symphony city—a German symphony city. The conductors were all German, beginning with George Henschel and including the greatest conductor of the time, Arthur Nikisch, from 1889 to 1893, and Karl

Muck, whose name will reappear in our story. Symphony concerts represented Yankee Boston at its best: they were self-consciously unfashionable (fashion was left to New York), and patrons took their children out of school for Friday matinees and put the Symphony in their wills.[5]

Operatically, Boston lagged far behind this, depending upon visiting companies. Operatic audiences were conventional, the standard Italian repertory with famous stars the prevailing taste. There was a good deal of opera in English. Gilbert and Sullivan remained very popular. German companies came occasionally until the 1890s, but German opera didn't take a strong hold. Bostonians thought opera, that "showy hybrid," a "breathless, exotic, passing excitement," while they took "the pleasures of the concert hall tranquilly, morally, and steadily."[6]

O n to this scene came Eben Jordan, junior (1857–1916), one of the princes of New England commerce. He went to public schools, then to Harvard for one year, eye trouble forcing him to give up his studies. He enjoyed the theater, had a good baritone voice, and was given vocal lessons as a young man. He entered the family business, Jordan Marsh and Company, took over on his father's death. He served on the board of directors of the New England Conservatory (as had his father), was an ardent sportsman, collected American and English paintings. Quiet, prudent in his business dealings (real estate only, never stocks), Eben Jordan, suddenly and surprisingly, transformed Boston's operatic situation.

In early 1908 he announced plans to build an opera house entirely with his own money, on his own site on Huntington Avenue. Unencumbered by a board of directors or stockholders in this enterprise (like Oscar Hammerstein, whose concurrent enterprises in New York and Philadelphia may have had their influence), he selected the Boston architectural firm of Wheelwright and Haven, with Parkman B. Haven taking charge of the project. He and Jordan set off on a tour of European opera houses. Jordan also took steps to organize an opera company, for his aim was to establish a permanent resident Boston company. He proposed that stock be subscribed for $150,000 as operating capital, at $100 a share, which entitled each buyer to one ticket before the public sale, and that the opera house boxes—Haven had proposed a house seating twenty-two hundred, with forty-six boxes—be taken at $2,000 a year for three years. If those conditions were met, Jordan would guarantee the deficit, if any, for three years. The stock was put on sale and a board of seventeen directors organized, with Jordan as president and the composer Frederick Converse as vice president. The response to the stock and box offering was enthusiastic, so the house was enlarged to seat twenty-seven hundred, with fifty-four boxes. Ground was broken in July 1908, and on November 30, "lovers of music, songbirds of the stage, and patrons of the arts" gathered for the laying of the cornerstone.[7]

As director of the company-to-be, Jordan chose Henry Russell (1871–1937), son of a Jewish French songwriter. Russell was raised in London, studied music— his brother became a well-known pianist and conductor under the name Landon Ronald—and taught singing at the Royal Academy of Music. He developed his own method of voice production and attracted some notable pupils, including the great Italian actress Eleanora Duse. In 1903, through her influence, he was chosen as director of an improvised company of Italian singers, loosely connected with the San Carlo Company in Naples, who made a tour of England. Once launched as an impresario, Henry Russell brought his group, which he called the San Carlo Opera Company, to America in 1905. In 1906 they played in Boston and the young critic of the *Boston Post*, Olin Downes, praised them highly as "an aggregation of artists thoroughly at home and in sympathy with each other and understanding the dramatic requirements of opera." Sometime in this period Russell met Jordan. In December 1907 the San Carlo, sponsored by Jordan and with considerable publicity, presented a winter Boston season, opening with *La Gioconda* and lasting three weeks. "All Back Bay turned out," Russell boasted. Jordan entertained Otto Kahn during this San Carlo season, became a member of the Metropolitan's board of directors, and associated himself with Kahn's schemes to combat Oscar Hammerstein.

Henry Russell imported new European and American talent to Boston in an effort to undermine the star system. This is how Caruso, who epitomized that system, saw him.

That visit clinched Jordan's decision to hire Russell, who, in the next few months, tirelessly outlined his operatic objectives. "I wish to have the American people learn to like opera as it is liked in the old country, and not to consider it as a special function, as it is in this country at the moment. I wish to have street boys know opera so well that they will sing and whistle it instead of the wretched stuff that catches the ear for a moment in what is known as musical comedy. This rests largely with the women. They are the ones who cultivate the arts. To them opera looks for the spread of taste. They are the artistic backbone of the country." To do this, American local companies would have to turn away from the star system, fostered in New York and London, "the Metropolitan being the chief offender." Russell amusingly catalogued the extent to which singers dominated operatic production in most houses: "Scenery was modified to suit their taste, light arranged to suit their complexions, tenors chosen to suit their affection and conductors thrown out to gratify their tempers." With characteristic hyperbole, Russell announced that "every stockholder who signed the parchment buried in the Opera House cornerstone may also be said to have signed the death warrant of the star system in America."[8]

Brave words, seriously meant. How to achieve such goals? The educational aspects of opera would be emphasized. A Boston opera school was formed within the New England Conservatory and six scholarships set up. American singers, already trained, would be given a chance. One night each week there would be a "debutante" night, untried singers performing at reduced prices. And the company would follow "modern taste" by seeking younger women and men who were comely. "No longer will the public stand for 'flower maidens' who tip the scale at 250 pounds." Boston would concentrate on "faultless orchestration, well-trained and capable chorus, *mise en scène* beyond criticism, good principals for the essential roles."[9]

The management had thought carefully about how to satisfy the disparate elements of its nascent audience. The subscribers would be pleased with variety, so a long season of twenty weeks was planned, more than twenty operas, a great burden for a medium-sized company. Opera enthusiasts, many of them Italians, in the upper tiers would be attracted by reasonable prices. Experienced singers were recruited—the tenor Florencio Constantino, sopranos Alice Nielsen, Maria Gay, and Lydia Lipkowska, baritone George Baklanoff, bass Jose Mardones, with Arnoldo Conti a serviceable conductor. There were no famous stars among them, so Russell hedged his bets, immediately contradicting his brave words—arranging with the friendly Metropolitan to borrow famous singers from time to time. The ticket prices were modest, $3.00 top, $2.00, $1.50, $1.00. And so the experiment got under way.

The Boston Opera House opened on the night of November 8, 1909. "The wandering tribes have arrived at the banks of the River Jordan." People were pleased by what they saw: an exterior of subdued red brick, gray limestone, white terra cotta, four massive pillars dominating the facade, under the main cornice glazed and colored bas reliefs symbolizing Music, Dancing, Drama, by Bela L. Pratt, a local sculptor. Too fancy a building would have offended sensibilities. "Grand opera itself would provide a brimming measure of the baroque, the rococo, the wildly fantastic." Parkman Haven knew his town. "The opera house was characterized by admirable taste and reticent beauty, rather than prodigal sumptuousness." The first Unitarian opera house.

The "reticent beauty" of the Boston Opera House suited the tastes of a community that was deeply ambivalent about operatic extravagance.

The interior was gray, ivory, dull gold—a little chilly perhaps, though a sky-blue ceiling with white clouds and a glittering chandelier brightened the effect. Not a pillar or post—all three tiers were cantilevered. There was ample lobby space for social promenading, should Bostonians take that up (they did), and on the second tier a smoking room for men and an elaborate soda water and ice cream bar for women. One ring of boxes was slightly elevated behind and above the main floor, and another took up the whole of the second tier. The floors were carpeted throughout, the seats of plain wood, though upholstered. The orchestra pit was sunk well below the level of the first floor. An Italian Renaissance proscenium arch framed a wide and deep stage. The backstage area was ample, lighting system and equipment—including the first revolving stage in an American opera house—were up to date, and there were well-equipped dressing rooms.

La Gioconda served as a homecoming for two divas, Lillian Nordica and Louise Homer, who were not members of the regular company but had New England antecedents and associations. Homer, in the floodtide of her vocal powers, sang with great assurance and opulence of tone. Nordica, now fifty-two, fighting against the ravages of "the inevitable, the exacting years," by "sheer force of will" summoned the "old sweeping amplitudes." A strong supporting cast, a superior ballet, handsome scenery, the excitement of the occasion brought Jordan and Russell forward at the end for hearty applause. That and subsequent Monday nights (the preferred social night, as at the Metropolitan) were also an eagerly seized chance for Boston women to show off and for newspaper reporters to gush about "yellow charmeuse silk that cost seven dollars a yard" and about Mrs. Jack Gardner's fabulous pearls. The men were less cooperative. Opening night, downstairs and in the boxes, they wore evening dress, but thereafter came in their street and business clothes. It was all a little strained, boxholders sitting in their places as though they were pews in a church.[10]

The next opera, *Aida,* brought everyone down to earth with a jolt. The singing was only adequate, the acting atrocious, and, ominously, there were numerous empty seats in the balcony and gallery. The first season showed how difficult it would be to create a loyal audience out of bewilderingly unpredictable social elements. The older traditional repertory—*La Traviata, Faust, Lakmé*—filled the boxes but emptied the upper tiers. The boxes, by contrast, didn't seem interested in modern Italian opera, which packed the gallery and balcony. A "very Italianate assembly" came to *Madama Butterfly. Cavalleria rusticana* produced tumults of enthusiasm upstairs—Josie Ludwig, an American, who sang as Jane Noria, played Santuzza as "a fiery Sicilian peasant in the first flush of vigorous and rather luscious womanhood," raging about the stage in "animal fury,"—but shocked downstairs. The sets were also realistic, showing the village to be a "poor and common place" and (this was pure Boston) "curiously suggestive of the architectural muddle that many centuries and many races have made of Sicily."[11]

Changes were soon made. The second season was shortened. Gambling that the subscribers would remain loyal, the management raised prices for the best seats to $5.00, $4.00, and $3.00, while the balcony and gallery were kept at $1.00, $1.50, and $2.00. The behavior of audiences had been encouraging, boxholders had stayed to the end and were quiet. Though audiences didn't applaud loudly, they came promptly and "floral tributes" were few. Men were present in unusually large numbers—"working men of the working middle class." For the coming season encores were forbidden, as was any acknowledgment of applause by the singers during a performance. Latecomers were not to be seated after an act had begun. New singers were added: the soprano Carmen Mellis, the tenor Giovanni Zenatello, who had sung with Hammerstein, and a new conductor for the Italian repertory, Roberto Moranzoni, only thirty, from Rome, "all youthful energy, even to the tossing hair and extravagant gesture." A new Toscanini, some said.[12]

A more innovative repertory was cautiously embarked on, the second season opening with an opera neither festal nor cheerful, *Mefistofele* by Arrigo Boito (1842–1918). The production was "sumptuous and imaginative spectacle," while the music "hinted now and then at the modern Italian music drama." In addition to the familiar repertory, Boston heard two new French operas, conducted by André Caplet: Debussy's one-act *The Prodigal Infant* (*L'Enfant prodigue*), more a concert in costume than a drama, and *La Habanera* by Raoul Laparra (1876–1943), French verismo, a "sordid, gruesome, fantasmal and bloody tale," which brought "a sprinkling of the musically curious and musically 'advanced,' who seldom come to the opera house." Other new works were Sergei Rachmaninoff's *The Miserly Knight* and two operas by Frederick Converse, *The Pipe of Desire* and *The Sacrifice,* for which audiences were polite but meager. The most discussed premiere was Puccini's *La Fanciulla del West,* two months after New York first heard it. Boston liked it a lot. There were nine performances that season, four the next, and four the season after that. The other highlights had to do with singers—Leo Slezak in *Otello,* Maurice Renaud in *Tosca,* Nordica in *Faust.* Melba came for one performance of *La Bohème,* with John McCormack, a ravishing night of pure vocalism that drew the largest house in the company's two years. "Social elements that for one reason or another have held aloof from [the opera house] were plentiful and obvious." They were there for Melba, not Puccini.

Many didn't arrive until the middle of the first act, knowing that Mimi doesn't appear until then. (They were admitted.)[13] The excitement that evening was extraordinary.

Nevertheless, the 1910–1911 season ended on a worrying note, the deficit larger than Eben Jordan had anticipated. Opera lovers had come faithfully to the balcony and gallery. The subscribers had been there. But where was the middle of the middle class? Where were the fashionable young men of the city? "It was a Boston truism that no play with music could succeed unless it pleased the youth of the colleges, and especially the youth of [Harvard]." Was it the absence of numerous stars? The opera house was not intimidating. One explanation was that the best seats were too expensive for Boston and that, while there were many perfectly respectable seats "occupied, so far as they are occupied at all nowadays, by presentable folk," many people felt that it was degrading "to sit anywhere in an opera house outside the [orchestra]."[14] What in the world could Henry Russell do about that?

T h e answer came early in the third season, and it had nothing to do with singers. Galvanized by the conductor Felix Weingartner and the designer Joseph Urban, the Boston Opera began a two-year period of remarkable achievement and sustained excitement. Moranzoni began the season by conducting a dynamic performance of Saint-Saëns' *Samson et Dalila,* with Zenatello and his wife, Maria Gay; *Tosca,* with Mellis and Maurice Renaud; and *Otello* again, notable as the farewell to opera by Emma Eames as Desdemona. In January, there was *Pelléas et Mélisande,* with Georgette Leblanc overshadowed by a magnificent interpretation of Golaud by Vanni Marcoux, a notable bass-baritone making his American debut.[15]

Weingartner, arriving "like a thunderbolt into Boston's consciousness," dissipated the Debussyan reveries. On February 12, 1912, he conducted a *Tristan und Isolde* that was a revelation. With only four days' rehearsal, "the orchestra played as it has never played before, with beauty and intensity of tone, with eloquent and dramatizing voice, with euphony, with balance," demonstrating to the audience, "the power of a single, guiding, coordinating, commanding and stimulating hand." That audience, "representative of every element in the community upon which the fortunes of the Opera House depend," focused its attention on the slender figure at the podium, "conducting with alert authority, beating time with the right [hand], with the left curving the lines of the music." Furious activity followed—nine performances in twelve days. In *Tosca* Weingartner sensitively searched out the Puccinian feeling. *Faust* was restored to life. *Aida,* done delicately, quietly, emphasized the melodious drama of the last two acts, which rose to an idealizing climax, *Tristan*-like in the transcendence of death. And finally, a charming *Hänsel und Gretel,* and then he was gone. But Boston was promised him again in the following season.[16]

The first half of the fourth season, 1912–1913, was dominated by French opera: *Les Contes d'Hoffmann, Louise,* and *Pelléas.* Moranzoni kept the Italian operas at a lively level and achieved a remarkable success with Wolf-Ferrari's *The Jewels of the Madonna* (*I Gioielli della Madonna*) a "hot, fierce, highly colored musical melodrama," "one more effort of our generation of composers to make opera express the facts of life in an actual environment." Weingartner came at the end of January and began again with *Tristan und Isolde,* with Olive Fremstad and Carl Burrian from the Metropolitan.

Then he turned to Verdi—*Otello* and the shop-worn *Il Trovatore,* with Ernestine Schumann-Heink, conductor and contralto "surpassing the Italians on their own ground."[17]

The major accomplishment of the season was *Don Giovanni.* The cast, Boston and the Metropolitan combined, was excellent: Vanni Marcoux as the Don; Amado Didur, Leporello; Emmy Destinn, Donna Anna; Alice Nielsen, Zerlina. However, even these stellar performers were overshadowed by the supreme vocalization of John McCormack as Don Ottavio, singing with exquisite taste, suavity of phrase, elegance of tone. After "Il mio tesoro" ("My treasure"), Weingartner laid down his baton and "led the applause for this heavenly flight of song." The conducting was supple, energetic but restrained. The sets glowed with color, vibrant as the performance, cleverly conceived to bring the action close to the audience while not impeding its quicksilver movement. This triumphant *Don Giovanni* is an appropriate place to consider the other great achievement of these two Boston years: the sets, costumes, and lighting of Joseph Urban.[18]

T h e r e was little interest in operatic production in nineteenth-century America. Scenery was general enough—a palace, a forest, a city square—to be used in many different operas. Sets were built as cheaply as possible. Extra money went for costumes. Electricity had been introduced into theaters in the 1880s, but lighting was still thought of in gaslight terms. Lack of concern about production was connected to the tyranny of the star singers. Did it matter what they stood and waved their arms in front of when they were warbling?[19]

Reform came in the last years of the century in the form of realism, its source popular musical theater and spoken drama. Everything in David Belasco's productions was as "real" as possible. Opera took this up and the sets used by Hammerstein and Gatti-Casazza aimed for historical accuracy. *Aida* should be archeologically Egyptian, *Otello* incontestably Venetian. Criticism became a contest to spot any anachronisms. This didn't help much with Wagner's mythological subjects, so American Wagnerians contented themselves with coming as close as they could to Bayreuth. Whatever the subject or national school, scenes were crowded, massive in scale. It was grand opera, after all.

The undermining of all this began in the early twentieth century and is associated with the thought of a man then totally unknown in America, Adolphe Appia. Born in 1862, he grew up in Geneva, Switzerland, in a fanatically Calvinist family. Passionate about music, which became for him a "self-contained magic space that at least for hours freed him from the dreary greyness of his parental home," Appia took dreaming refuge in the idea of theater, though he had never been inside one. At last, age nineteen, he saw Gounod's *Faust.* It was a totally disillusioning experience, his feverish expectations betrayed by the gaudy opera house, prosaic costumes, unimaginative sets, accumulation of properties. Everything conspired to *destroy* illusion. So he set himself his life's work, combining his musical and theatrical passions: to reform prevailing ideas of operatic production. He fell under Wagner's spell, read voraciously about the Master, corresponded with his disciples, his "rapturous enthusiasm" leading him to Bayreuth, where he found some of the things he sought—the high-minded artistic dedication, the spirit of collaboration. The actual productions, however, were again bitterly disappointing. Wagner's music was revolutionary, his scenic vision, conventional. But Wagnerian music drama, as the archetype of all music drama, remained the focus of Appia's ideas. In 1895 he published a booklet (only three hundred copies were published) entitled *The Production of Wagnerian Drama* (*La Mise en scène du drame wagnérien*), which he later expanded in a larger work, *Music and Theatrical Production* (*La Musique et la mise en scène*).

Appia rejected theatrical realism entirely—acting, sets, costume, direction. The theater of the future stripped the stage bare. Music, the central element in music drama, existed in time and must be translated into space by determining the means of its own dramatic realization. First one began with a measure-by-measure study of the music, to discern the staging latent within the musical structure. This did *not* mean personal interpretation by the producer. Quite the reverse. "A humble, subservient attitude toward this basic [musical] impulse had to be the guiding principle." Light was the principal means used in realizing this central impulse. Interplay of light and space expressed musical drama without constraining literalism. Light expanded ideas of theatrical space by expanding one's ideas of reality, and the human figure could be coordinated in its movements through this space by an orchestrated set of movements. The audience would see silhouettes, shadows, simple shapes on the subtly lighted stage, but in fact the "bare" space would be filled—by one's imagination.

These ideas frightened most theater directors, and Appia had very few chances to work in a theater. In 1923, with Toscanini's support, he produced *Tristan und Isolde* at La Scala, but he was dissatisfied with the result, having compromised too much with the obstructionist La Scala bureaucracy. His great chance was a complete *Ring* cycle for the Basel Municipal Theater, working with technicians and designers sympathetic to his ideas, but after *Das Rheingold* and *Die Walküre,* powerful opposition forced cancellation of the last half of the cycle. Utterly crushed, Appia talked of emigrating to the United States, "the young, hopeful land." (Imagine him at the Metropolitan Opera!) He died in 1928. His ideas were, of course, not the only source for the new conceptions of production that were emerging in Europe—German expressionist painting and the work of Gordon Craig in England, and of Max Reinhardt in Germany, were also influential. Felix Weingartner was hospitable to new ideas when he succeeded Mahler in Vienna, where Joseph Urban gained his operatic experience and arrived at his own vision, less radical than Appia's, but influenced by him.[20]

Urban was born in Vienna in 1872 and educated at the Art Academy, concentrating on architecture. He established a reputation as a decorator and in 1904 designed the Austrian exhibit at the St. Louis exposition. He made contact with Henry Russell and in 1911 came to Boston. His work surprised Bostonians. He presented recognizable forms and drew on the work of familiar European painters, but his use of color and lighting was like nothing Americans had seen before. He treated color musically. "Certain harmonic effects should be accentuated on the stage; the motive in the orchestra is my cue for the stage." His favorite color—"Urban blue"—became famous, but he also used harsh primary colors or established thematic unity by emphasizing one color in lighting, sets, costumes. He preferred soft, diffused light

Joseph Urban rejected excessive literalism in stage design, preferring to create atmosphere through an innovative use of color and lighting. This is one of his sets for Puccini's Madama Butterfly *at the Boston Opera in 1913. Joseph Urban Papers, Rare Book and Manuscript Library, Columbia University.*

and frequently worked with a stage-within-a-stage or with a series of boxes, reducing the stage space, concentrating (and expanding) illusion. A sympathetic observer explained, "We are told to take the scenery in a new way, not as an actual reproduction of life, as in Belasco," but as a way to get the audience "to feel the emotion expressed in staging." Thus in Weingartner's *Tristan* the first-act ship was represented only by a huge billowing sail that dominated the stage, the family house in *Louise* by irregular rooms which were "the emotional evocation" of poverty. Urban often altered the shape of the stage to give great emphasis to one object dominating the scene—the statue in *Don Giovanni,* a tree in the third act of *Tristan,* a bridge in *Faust.*[21]

The technicians at the opera house had trouble understanding some of Urban's ideas and putting them into effect, and the revolving stage never worked properly, restricting what he could attempt. The interiors for *Pelléas et Mélisande* were rough, damp, dark, with only a few pieces of clumsily shaped furniture, while the walls were striped with primary colors, an attempt to express the mythic as the primitive. People wrote frequently to complain that what to Urban seemed desirably dim was too dark. "They felt depressive if they could not watch this singer's lips or that one's beauty." They had no problem with *Hänsel und Gretel,* a brightly colored fairyland. A huge gold stairway dominated one scene, in which angels, themselves shaped of molten gold, contrasted vividly with a gorgeous blue background.

Some of Urban's best work was in *Les Contes d'Hoffmann,* one of the Boston Opera's greatest successes, with Vanni Marcoux playing the three incarnations of evil superbly, and Edmond Clément, one of the most stylish French tenors of the twentieth century, "shading his words adroitly and subtly" as Hoffmann. Urban's imagination converted "an amusing opera into a graphic music drama," freeing singers from the outworn conventions of operatic acting and finding essential unity in the opera's shifting variety though pictorial and atmospheric illusion. "For the first time in American theatrical history, every element of the stage—scenery, costumes, properties and direction—came from a single hand." It would be pleasant to record that Boston responded to *Hoffmann* with a roar of approval. In fact, the first night's reception was "placid." "To call Urban before the footlights lay quite beyond the imagination of this elegant crowd." But some day, H. T. Parker wrote, "the records may say that a revolution in the setting and lighting of the American stage dates from these innovations at the Boston Opera House. Then how proud we Bostonians will be of ourselves—even though we did not half suspect it while it was actually going forward."[22]

T h e 1913–1914 season, though it lacked the sustained excitement of the previous two, had a number of achievements and high points of its own. There was the American premiere of *Monna Vanna* by Henri Février (1875–1957), which combined the influences of Massenet, Debussy, and Italian realism. It gained from the presence of Vanni Marcoux and Mary Garden and of some of Urban's most imaginative sets, "accomplishing for the drama what Février's music does not do for the ear." New singers joined the company. Russell, like Hammerstein, was resourceful in finding talent: Maggie Teyte, a young, diminutive English soprano of charm and intelligence; the young tenor Giovanni Martinelli; Marguerite D'Alvarez, a sumptuous-voiced contralto. The major production of the season was *Die Meistersinger,* "clear, cumulating and unified design, well-imagined, well-accomplished and illuminating detail."[23]

Weingartner came for a month at the very end of the season and, as ever, inspired renewed interest. He brought two performances of *Die Meistersinger* to life, conducted Scotti, Marcel, and Zenatello in a fiery *Otello,* also *Don Giovanni, Aida, Faust.* His most surprising achievement was *Carmen,* restored to "its true and living self by the vividness and variety of the rhythms." "The music leaped and the music boded." The season ended with a "gala," various scenes from operas. The last was the Dance of the Hours, closing the Boston Opera Company circle as it had begun, with *La Gioconda.* Talk of the forthcoming fall 1914 season centered on a more extensive role for Weingartner, a continuing Boston refrain, and the possibility that André Messager of the Paris Opéra-Comique would conduct the French repertory. Everything was obscured in the spring by a season in Paris, organized by Russell and by Henry Higgins of Covent Garden, including famous singers and famous conductors, having little to do with the Boston Opera except for its financial consequences: it lost money, Boston Opera money.[24] Anyway, opera talk disappeared in the growing concern about war in Europe. Therefore, the sudden announcement that there would be no Boston Opera season in the fall came as a great surprise, as did the reason for it—the company had failed financially. In April 1915, it declared bankruptcy.

Some aspects of the Boston Opera's collapse are clear enough. In the spring of 1912 Eben Jordan reaffirmed that he would not guarantee deficits beyond the three years originally stipulated. Some interesting alternative forms of support were proposed. Mayor John G. ("Honey Fitz") Fitzgerald, seeing the civic value of the opera company, tried to get the Opera House exempted from paying taxes. A Boston legislator introduced a bill to provide money for the city's purchase of the opera house. Neither of these got anywhere. There were votes to be gained by opposing Fitzgerald and identifying him with "elitist" culture, and the old bugaboo about state support for the arts also came into play: support for opera would be a "dangerous precedent." Jordan then circulated a letter proposing new terms for private support. He offered a rebate to the company of its rent, about $60,000. Boxholders were asked to contribute $90,000 and there would be an appeal to the general public for $150,000. The $300,000 would serve as an operating fund for the next three-year period. On this basis Russell was reengaged for another three-year period and went ahead with the fourth and fifth seasons. Apparently, the seventy boxholders (some of the fifty-four boxes were held by two or more people) raised 90 percent of the money asked of them, and about $110,000 was raised from the general public. What remains puzzling is why nothing more was done in the following two years. There was no general campaign. Only "intimate and personal" aid was encouraged. Perhaps a general public undertaking, in our sense, was not yet imaginable. There was a seeming paralysis of will. When the end was in sight, as the opera administration and insiders understood, no notice was given, nothing was done. Perhaps it was all too Boston. A public outcry would have been indecorous.[25]

It was heartbreaking, because the hoped-for growth of a middle group of supporters seems to have been taking place. There was a "significant change" in the "proportions of the audience" in the fifth season. Ticket sales declined among season subscribers. "Above, in balcony and gallery, where sittings are in comfortable reach of moderate and even slender means, more and more [seats] have been taken." It was the subscribers who had become "querulous and restless," for whom opera going was a "boresome obligation rather than a lively pleasure." In terms of Boston's wealth, an extremely modest commitment was required, and it was not forthcoming. Yet that same Boston upper class mocked the vulgarity of New York and of the Metropolitan's Diamond Horseshoe, for whom opera was only "a fad and a fashion." "The passion of the rich, the near rich, and the little brothers of the rich. It does for the owners of jewels and clothes the same office that Madison Square Garden does for horses, automobiles and circuses; it is the showplace of the spenders, the semi-nude and the chatterers; but by-and-by when some other expensive method of exhibiting raw wealth and half-naked women is discovered, New York will flout opera, and only the galleries which love music for music's sake will patronize it."

Were Bostonians really so different? In 1845 Ralph Waldo Emerson wrote: "One would like to see Boston and Massachusetts agitated like a wave with some generosity, and for learning, for music, for philosophy, for association, for freedom, for art; but now it goes like a pedlar with its hand ever in its pocket, cautious, calculating."[26]

So ended the Boston Opera Company and its 516 performances of fifty-one different operas, and so ended the Boston operatic renaissance. At least the opera house remained standing.

The American Muse Again

The early twentieth century was one of those recurrent periods in American history when American art was seen as an important expression of national culture. The ferment of Progressive reform, rapidly growing wealth and population, emergence as a world imperial power—all contributed to the burgeoning sense of national pride. Theodore Roosevelt's New Nationalism applied to more than politics. The extensive publicity about *La Fanciulla del West* may also have helped awaken interest in the question of what was meant by American opera. Organizations to promote American opera were formed, statements of principle issued, articles written, and prizes offered. American composers turned to the composing of operas. They sought an American idiom, searched for American subjects, crossed the boundaries which separated one kind of opera from another.

'' *T o m o r r o w* night is coming to town a young person who has attracted an enormous amount of attention in foreign parts and who is expected to attract as much here," the *New York Times* announced. "Great preparations have been made for her and her wiles are expected to be potent." The young person who arrived, as expected, on October 21, 1907, at the New Amsterdam Theater was Franz Lehár's *The Merry Widow,* whose charm was greater than the *Times* or anyone else had imagined. New York City's opera critics, released from more somber duties at the Manhattan and Metropolitan opera houses, rejoiced in "the supreme musical attraction of the period." W. J. Henderson: "It is the merriest, maddest thing that has come out of the European continent in many a long day." Richard Aldrich: "The applause was almost terrifying in its intensity and there were as many shouts of 'Bravo!' as at a performance of *Pagliacci* when Caruso sings." "The Merry Widow Waltz," "Vilia," "Maxim's," and its other songs promised to keep America "in a state of delicious torment." Henry Savage, its producer, sealed his claim as "a managerial genius." At one point, one hundred companies were giving *The Merry Widow* throughout the world. In America, even the financial panic of 1907, which came just after its opening, couldn't obstruct its path or break its spell.

The Merry Widow was part of the growth of opera in America, in audience, composition, performance. In major cities the number of theaters devoted to opera in all its popular forms increased, as did the number of productions and performances of those productions. New York, the center of production and performance, began to shape the style

Franz Lehár's The Merry Widow *took America by storm in the first decade of the century. It sparked a craze for ballroom dancing and had a far-reaching impact on American musical theater. From* Musical America, *Nov. 2, 1907.*

of the popular opera that was emerging and that one day would achieve a finished form and deserve to be called New York opera.

Musically, Lehár's opera was delicately poised between past and future. It connected traditionalists with earlier days. "The very aged can remember almost thirty years back, when there was a piece called *Pinafore,* and earlier and later they can remember such other things as *The Mikado* and *La Fille de Madame Angot* and *La Belle Hélène,* and *Die Fledermaus* and *The Black Hussar* and *Fatinitza* and *The Mascot,* and others which they would mention if their memories weren't going fast." Lehár's reassuring achievement was the rediscovery of "the long lost trail of melody." Reinvigorating this tradition, it unleashed a torrent of new Viennese operas, Oscar Straus's *The Chocolate Soldier,* Emmerich Kálmán's *The Gay Hussars,* Leo Fall's *The Dollar Princess,* and many more.

Others saw *The Merry Widow* as representing "a new era in musical entertainment." Of course, Graustarkian never-never land hovered over the horizon. Sonia, the sprightly widow, and Danilo, her lover, come from the mythical Balkan province of Marsovia. Nevertheless, the story actually takes place entirely in Paris, in real places such as Maxim's, already known to a few American tourists and soon to become known to all the rest. It also showed a "continuing social leveling," royalty giving way to lower orders, most notably to a heroine of a kind by now familiar, the fabulously wealthy heiress. Lehár's music was technically undemanding. "Listening to Offenbach or [Johann] Strauss with one's eyes closed, one sometimes might have imagined oneself in an opera house; listening to Lehar, one knew one was in a theater or on a dance floor." Dance was the significant new element, and a major part of its appeal. The celebrated waltz, first hummed, then sung, then danced, brought the second act to "an enraptured close." "With this single dance, this single tune, the aging musical theatre recaptured its youth." *The Merry Widow* was one of the primary sources of the rage for ballroom dancing in the 1910s and 1920s, and dance would be an important part of New York opera as it eventually evolved.[2]

The leading roles in Lehár's opera were cast more for acting than for singing ability. In the London production, supervised by Lehár, Joe Coyne, an American song-and-dance man picked as Danilo, had hardly any singing voice at all and delivered his lyrics as a kind of recitative. Donald Brian, the first American Danilo, "light of voice and lighter of feet," began his career in the musicals of George M. Cohan, where acting and personality were more important than voice. "Coyne and Brian established that a leading man need not have an operatic voice to sing in opera."

T h e dual signals flashed by *The Merry Widow,* "gentle waltzing in an age moving to harsher and more rapid tempos," reflected the state of American popular opera, divided between European-based and indigenous American musical theater. Divided —but not unchanging, as the work of two American composers made clear.[3]

Victor Herbert, born in Dublin, Ireland, in 1859, was two when his father died. His mother remarried, and her second husband, a German physician, took the family to Stuttgart when Victor was seven. There Victor Herbert—he kept his father's name— revealed musical talent, on the piano, flute, and especially the cello. He gave up the medical career his parents had hoped for and from age nineteen supported himself as a cellist, composing his first songs. In 1885 he became engaged to Therese Förster, a mezzo-soprano with the Stuttgart Royal Opera. Fate then intervened from across the Atlantic, in the form of the new Metropolitan Opera Company, whose representatives came to Stuttgart for auditions: a tenor failed to please, Therese Förster pleased enough to be given a contract. As an afterthought, her fiancé was engaged as a cellist for the Metropolitan orchestra. They married and spent their honeymoon on a steamer bound for New York.

Therese Förster Herbert's career at the Metropolitan lasted only two years, but her husband's career flourished. He played in chamber music groups, composed a cello concerto, which he performed under Theodore Thomas and Anton Seidl, took part in the American premiere of the Brahms Double Concerto for violin and cello in 1889, conducted the orchestra organized for Tchaikovsky's American tour of 1891, gained experience of the theater on extensive tours with Emma Juch's opera company, and even found time to become conductor of the Gilmore band, after Gilmore's death. In 1900 he became permanent conductor of the Pittsburgh Symphony Orchestra.[4]

Meanwhile, he composed operettas. His first, *Prince Ananias,* did well enough to encourage him to continue. The result was *The Wizard of the Nile* (1895), pure Graustarkian fantasy, with lots of slapstick clowning. By 1900 it had received five hundred performances, played for six consecutive weeks at the Tivoli Theater in San Francisco, and became the first operetta by an American composer to be given in Vienna and Prague. A series of conventional fantasy operettas followed—*The Idol's Eye,* set in India; *The Ameer,* in Afghanistan; *The Tattooed Man,* in Persia; *It Happened in Nordland,* about the adventures of a lady ambassador in a mythical country. Pure fantasy, too, was *Babes in Toyland,* about adults impersonating children in a perpetual fantasy world, a mawkish story linked to charming music.

Herbert wasn't trying to "modernize" light opera. As a serious man of the theater, his imagination and training pushed him beyond its inanities. *Mlle. Modiste* (1905), set in a Paris hat shop, its protagonist Fifi, a stage-struck employee, was a contemporary social comedy, with lyrics of interest and a melodious score. One scene in particular revealed Herbert's growing mastery. In the song "If I Were on the Stage," Fifi conveys three different kinds of music she would sing if given her chance: a gavotte, as a country girl; a polonaise, as a grand French lady; and "Kiss Me Again," a subtle parody of the contemporary romantic song, "emotional and full of soul." (Taken out of its ironic context, sung "straight," it became one of Herbert's greatest hits.) *The Red Mill* (1906) returned to Graustark in Katwykaan-Zee, Holland, but it had rapid rhythms and appealing melodies, including the lively paean "In Old New York."

Naughty Marietta, while an effort to find "romance" in the past, was set in a real place and period, New Orleans at the time of the American takeover, and was Herbert's most ambitious score, an attempt to expand the scale of his work toward "grander" opera. Oscar Hammerstein's first theatrical venture after his surrender to the Metropolitan, it was directed by Jacques Coini, the Manhattan Opera House production manager, and starred two of Hammerstein's opera singers, Orville Harrold, American tenor, and Emma Trentini, Italian soprano. The songs are operatic: a coloratura aria for Trentini, "The Italian Street Song"; a heroic march, "Tramp, Tramp, Tramp"; and Herbert's grandest duet, "Ah, Sweet Mystery of Life."

Younger than Herbert by a generation, content to carry on the Viennese tradition, Rudolf Friml was born in Prague in 1879, educated at the Conservatory, studying composition with Dvořák. He came to America on a concert tour in 1901 and decided to stay. Good luck came to him when, after the success of *Naughty Marietta,* Herbert began composing a new opera for Trentini; they quarreled and Herbert refused to have anything further to do with her or with the opera. Arthur Hammerstein, the show's producer, chose Friml to take over. In one month he composed all the music for *The Firefly,* a fairy tale about an Italian street singer who ends up as a prima donna. World War I cast a pall over Friml's work, but in the 1920s he returned to his old form.[5]

George M. Cohan represented a nativist tradition of opera, one that rejected any foreign musical influence and any association with even the idea of "opera." Born in 1878 to vaudeville parents, he appeared on stage as a toddler, played the violin in a theater orchestra at eight, and spoke his first lines on stage at nine. Within a few years he was writing material—skits, songs, lyrics—for the Four Cohans, his parents, sister, and himself, but he tired of trouping with the family and came to feel that success in the Broadway theater was all he cared for. "Broadway was the only bell I wanted to ring."

In 1904 he rang the bell with *Little Johnny Jones,* the story of an American jockey wrongly accused of throwing a race in England, with Donald Brian as the jockey. This was based on the life and career of Tod Sloan, the greatest American jockey of the day and, in real life, a very different sort of person from the virtuous hero Cohan portrayed. However, Cohan recognized that here, in the guise of the little American snubbed by foreigners, he had his chance to play on his audience's patriotism and to express his own hatred of Britain, which he did with great vigor in "Yankee Doodle Boy" and "Give My Regards to Broadway." So identified did he become with such jingle jingoism that he was challenged by the question, "Think you could write a play without a flag?" and responded with *Forty-five Minutes from Broadway,* a melodrama without a flag and with catchy tunes, of which "Mary's a Grand Old Name" is the most familiar. *George Washington, Jr.* was the story of a rich but patriotic young man so incensed with his father's snobbish Anglomania that he adopted the name of the father of his country and reverted to flag waving—"You're a Grand Old Flag." *The Yankee Prince* (1908) took up the topical practice of American plutocrats marrying their daughters to titled foreigners. "Over There," popularized by Caruso, was the most effective morale song of World War I.

The dramatic integration of songs and stories wasn't Cohan's aim. His was a contemporary American form of ballad opera, current events expressed in often implausible stories on which to hang his songs. His contribution to the form was rhythmical. "The brash, fast-talking Cohan spoke and sang directly to a new world and a new century." "Speed! Speed! And lots of it! That's the idea of the thing," he said, "perpetual motion." It was the motion of New York, the Big Town. A Cohan production was "a great machine shooting out characters, choruses, songs, dances with rapid-fire quickness and precision." Cohan also voiced national and ethnic sentiments. The old resentments of the Bowery B'Hoys smoldered in the urban Irish scorn for the cultural elite who scorned *his* art. Cohan's critics often responded that way. One, using *The Merry Widow* as an unlikely stick to beat Cohan with, predicted "the death knell of the jingle jangle school of comic operatic music" and an end to "kindergarten harmonies." Oddly, some critics were baffled by Cohan's appeal to his audiences. *George Washington, Jr.* was "vulgar, cheap, blatant, ill mannered, flashily dressed, insolent, smart Aleck," but "for some reason unexplainable on any basis of common sense, good taste, or even ordinary decency," it "appeals to the imagination and apparent approval of large American audiences."[6]

Neither side in this battle was comfortable with the breaking down of distinctions and the merging of forms. Each advocated one kind of opera because it *wasn't* the other. There was also another obstacle to the broadening of the idea of what opera was, an obstacle which remains important today: the existence of those palatial places for grand opera, whose size was extremely inhospitable to all modest-sized forms of opera. Crossing over the other way was also very difficult. Theaters lacked the orchestra pit and stage and backstage facilities to handle grand opera. Nevertheless, the movement of twentieth-century opera was against gigantism. (In this regard, *Salome* and *Elektra, Pelléas,* and *Turandot* belonged to the past.) This new climate of opinion produced an imaginative effort to reintegrate the operatic repertory under one roof, an enterprise originating from an unlikely source, the Metropolitan Opera Company, the symbol of the specialized old order.

I t began with Heinrich Conried. His idea was to establish a national repertory theater for both drama and music, a resident company which would present world classics, Shakespeare, Molière, Goethe, Ibsen, Sophocles, and operas not suitable to the Metropolitan's huge space and grand solemnity. Otto Kahn supported the proposal, enlisted Walter Damrosch to assist in the planning, and raised the money to get the project under way. The theater would be dedicated to the highest artistic aims, uninhibited by commercial considerations. It would establish schools for instruction in drama and music, employ actors and singers, set up endowment and pension funds. The operatic company would be drawn from the Metropolitan roster and

The sumptuous interior of New York's New Theater clashed with the founders' stated goals of establishing a popular opera house. Library of Congress.

would include most of its singers. It was to be a second opera house, not a secondary one. In 1905 a site was purchased on Central Park West at Sixty-first Street and architects were invited to submit plans. The winners were the firm of Carrère and Hastings. John Merven Carrère (1858–1911) and Thomas Hastings (1860–1929), both trained at the Paris Ecole des Beaux Arts (where they met), served apprentice-ships with McKim, Mead, and White, and by the 1890s were very fashionable, designing private residences and public buildings inspired by French taste of the seventeenth and eighteenth centuries. Who better to build an American version of the French academies of Louis XIV?

Construction problems after the ground breaking in 1906 were compounded by the contradiction between a modest, all-purpose, innovative theater and the gran-diose vision latent in Conried's scheme, which Carrère and Hastings realized with their well-known ornateness and lavishness. The original plans were "an impresario's dream": a large revolving stage, spacious orchestra pit, adequate storerooms, ballet practice room, three rehearsal halls, dressing rooms. In addition, there were to be a library, restaurant, confection and florist shops, palm garden on the roof, lavish office space. Harley Granville-Barker, English playwright and producer, employed as a consultant, warned that the theater auditorium was much too large. The plans were modified. The theater was reduced in size, some of the extravagant features disap-peared. When the New Theater opened on November 16, 1909, what people found was an extraordinarily sumptuous exterior and interior, with glittering chandeliers, thick carpets, marble and gilt, profuse ornamentation, a disproportionate amount of space in the auditorium devoted to boxes which circled the main floor. "Too palatial, with all that marble. It was something built only for royalty. Common people, for whom it had supposedly been built, looked at those white stairs and trembled with fear." Even worse: the sound was uneven, acceptable for music, impossible for spoken drama.

The dramatic wing of the company faced other problems as well. It was continually the focus of criticism, much of it rooted in professional rivalries and jealousies. The operatic wing, by contrast, got off to a terrific start with Massenet's *Werther,* with Geraldine Farrar, Alma Gluck, and Edmond Clément. The next afternoon Alfred Hertz conducted *The Bartered Bride.* In the following weeks the operatic company presented a number of operas which were marginal at the Metropolitan or had not been given there for decades, breaking down the supposed distinctions between grand opera and all the other kinds of opera—*Il Barbiere di Siviglia* and *Manon* and *La Sonnambula,* but also *Fra Diavolo, Czar and Zimmermann, L'Attaque du moulin, La Fille de Madame Angot.* Nevertheless, the success of the operatic side of things didn't diminish the populist clamor. Henry Miller, Broadway producer: "The New Theatre is un-American and it started with the wrong point of view. Rich people never made the drama anywhere. It had its birth in the hearts of the poor." Blanche Bates, actress: "It is the most un-American institution in America . . . a cross between a Turkish bath and a mausoleum." To counter this, the New Theater directors made cheap seats—ten to fifty cents—available to social and philanthropic agencies: the Society for the Improvement of the Poor, the Rand School, the Women's Socialist Organization, the Women's Trade Union League, the Jewish Women's Trade Union. There were forty thousand applications for seats for Maurice Maeterlinck's play *The Blue Bird.* This program worked well enough to give an idea of what might have been done had a modest and unpretending building been built to fulfill the words of Gov. Charles Evans Hughes of New York at the laying of the cornerstone: "This should be regarded as the people's theatre."

As originally organized, the New Theater lasted only two years. Gatti-Casazza had never approved of it and the Metropolitan withdrew. Renamed the Century, it became a commercial enterprise and was eventually torn down. In the 1920s, reflecting on the venture, Otto Kahn said that "to live and grow" the New Theater "needed air, plain fare and an avoidance of pampering." Instead, "we stifled it with heavy golden raiment; we fed it on a diet seasoned with 'society' ingredients." It has long been forgotten, except as an example of the ostentation of the time and of its builders. Yet with less money and better design, it might have realized the imaginative promise for opera inherent in it and might have been the popular opera house that New York, and the nation, desperately needed in later years.[7]

Among other things, it might have been home to opera by American composers. Its usefulness in that regard was obscured by the unprecedented availability of American opera house stages for such works. How did it happen that the Metropolitan Opera, which in its first quarter-century had never heard a word of English sung on its stage or a single note by an American composer, now hoisted the American flag? Again and again we return to the influence of Oscar Hammerstein and the Manhattan Opera Company. Not personally interested in opera in English, Hammerstein had sensed how the new wind was blowing and had commissioned operas from Reginald De Koven and Victor Herbert. After *Robin Hood,* in 1890, De Koven's career was the sadly familiar one of unrealized promise. He became a tireless advocate of American musical enterprises, as a widely read critic and writer. "Americanism was to him almost a religion, and he always fought any form of foreign aggression, propaganda, or aggrandizement that seemed to limit or shut off opportunities for native composers and their work." Hammerstein was expansive about the significance of his commissions: "I desire to discover something that is more novel than novelty. I want to be an operatic Columbus."[8]

The Metropolitan's situation was more complex. Gatti-Casazza had no interest in American opera, doubted that his board of directors had any, suspected it would prove poison at the box office, spoke no English and would have to depend on others' judgment about librettos. Toscanini was no help. He had little interest in contemporary opera that wasn't Italian and opposed putting Metropolitan resources into productions that would be musically marginal. However, there were other considerations. Gatti-Casazza, a new man in a new position in a new country, and Otto Kahn, chairman of the board of the Metropolitan, an immigrant himself, sensed possible danger. Gatti-Casazza's Metropolitan must not be identified as an American institution run by foreigners for foreign interests. The snobbery which led Americans to favor European names and reputations easily turned into jingoistic xenophobia, and there were those who saw Gatti-Casazza as a stalking horse for the Italian publishing house of Ricordi and its Italian composers.

The result was the emergence of the Metropolitan Opera as a sponsor of American opera. Gatti-Casazza identified the crucial practical point. "No national school of opera has ever developed without the incentive of performance," adding: "The conditions are harder for the [American] composer than in any other country, chiefly because there are so few stages upon which his works can be presented." The Metropolitan announced a contest, open only to American composers, the winner to receive a cash prize of ten thousand dollars and a Metropolitan performance of the work selected. And so, between 1910 and 1920, with reform in the air, and in keeping with the spirit of barriers being removed, the Metropolitan lifted its stage curtain to American composers.[9]

L i k e Herbert and Friml and Cohan, composers of opera intended for the grand houses of Chicago and Philadelphia and New York had to sort out the complex claims of tradition, modernism, and nationalism. Did American opera require an American subject? Some believed so. Others thought that musical treatment, not subject, was what gave a work of art its distinctive American stamp. But if musical treatment was the key, on what distinctive American tradition did one build? Unlike William Fry a half-century earlier, who believed that there was nothing indigenous to use, some American composers of this generation turned to American folk materials, others to native American music. African American composers drew on the abundant legacy of African and American cultures as they intermixed in North America. But some believed that all such nationalist ventures were misguided and that twentieth-century modernism demanded the transcendence of any national tradition.

The career of Frederick Shepherd Converse (1871–1940) was one effort to deal with these various elements. Born into a mercantile Boston family with no musical interests, he began piano lessons at ten, studied harmony with a Wellesley College professor who encouraged his desire to compose, went to John Knowles Paine at

Harvard and on to the Royal Academy in Munich and Josef Rheinberger, the influential teacher of a number of American composers. After his return to America, Converse taught at Harvard and the New England Conservatory, all the while composing, trying to combine the symphonic and the dramatic. The result, in 1905, was *The Pipe of Desire,* a "romantic grand opera" in one act, libretto by George Edward Barton, a Boston architect. Set in a Garden of Eden called the Land of Fancy, *The Pipe of Desire,* filled with symbols of procreation and ecstatic visions, was entirely unhistorical and unnational. Gatti-Casazza chose it as the Metropolitan's first American opera, performed on March 31, 1910, along with two ballets as part of a triple bill. It was sung by American singers at the Metropolitan, Riccardo Martin, Clarence Whitehill, Louise Homer, Herbert Witherspoon. "Pleasant," "hopeless text," a "dubious venture," critics said, and it slipped away after one repetition. Converse tried again with *The Sacrifice,* this time an American subject, California in 1846, a love triangle involving Indians, Mexicans, and Americans, Italianate in style, with songs, duets, choruses, a prayer. Given by the Boston Opera Company (Converse was its vice president) in 1911, it was not a success, though Boston did its best to admire it. Different still were *Sinbad the Sailor,* a fantastic, humorous opera, never performed, and *The Immigrants,* commissioned by the Boston Opera, verismo technique applied to a contemporary subject, but also unperformed when the opera company collapsed.[10]

The winner of the much publicized Metropolitan opera competition was the most respected of American composers, Horatio Parker (1863–1919). Son of a musical Massachusetts mother and architect father, he learned piano and organ from his mother and grew up in a cultivated environment, with every advantage and encouragement. At nineteen he too went to Munich and to Rheinberger, then returned to America to teach and to compose a steady stream of works, of which the greatest was his oratorio *Hora Novissima,* enthusiastically received in America and England. (The University of Cambridge made him a doctor of music in 1902.) In 1894 he joined the faculty of Yale University and later conducted the New Haven Symphony Orchestra.

Primarily a composer of choral works, Parker wrote his prize-winning opera *Mona* at the turn of the century, to a libretto by Brian Hooker, professor of English at Yale. The story about a British revolt against Roman rule and the conflicting claims of love and duty was reminiscent of *Norma.* So was the music—familiar without distinction. Identified as the defender of traditional musical values, Parker was actually quite independent-minded. But his music for *Mona,* long-flowing and angular melodies, was not dramatically powerful. It was given at the Metropolitan on March 14, 1911, with the usual American cast, Martin, Witherspoon, Homer, who did what was to be done with the role of Mona. Parker was the great prize-winner of the time. In 1913 he won a competition sponsored by the National Federation of Music Clubs, with *Fairyland,* dealing with the perplexing problem of historical setting by avoiding specific time or place. Fairyland was a "mountain country" in medieval Europe and the story shifted back and forth from the actual to the fairy world. It was performed once in July 1915 in Los Angeles, but was never given again.[11]

Neither Converse nor Parker had had any theatrical experience. Two conductor-composers who tried their hand at opera had spent many years in the theater. The first, Walter Damrosch, son of Leopold, was deeply involved in American operatic life for many years after his father's death, touring with the Damrosch Opera Company, "everywhere initiating the public into the intricacies, beauties and wonders" of Wagnerian music drama, as well as being director of the New York Symphony Orchestra. "I am an American musician," he often proclaimed, as if to remove any doubt raised by his German birth. In 1894–1895 he ventured his first operatic effort, *The Scarlet Letter,* based not only on Hawthorne's novel but using a libretto by George Parsons Lathrop, Hawthorne's son-in-law. It was first presented in Boston on February 10, 1896, later in New York and Philadelphia. The language of the libretto was English, but the language of the score was German. "Soaring, too soaring," one critic noted, characterizing the orchestra score as "heavy enough to suit the gods of Valhalla rather than a simple pair of Puritans," while Anton Seidl, with gratuitous sarcasm, called it the "New England Nibelung Trilogy." There were moments of beauty in it, but the foreign idiom consorted oddly with the American theme.

Next, Damrosch turned away from nationalism and for his second opera drew on Edmond Rostand's popular play *Cyrano de Bergerac,* with the New York critic W. J. Henderson as his librettist. Damrosch played part of it at a private hearing for Gatti-Casazza, Toscanini, and others. Otto Kahn asked Toscanini if he would like to conduct *Cyrano.* "Thank you, no," said Toscanini, "I don't understand English." What he really didn't understand was why the opera was being considered. The Metropolitan went ahead. On February 27, 1913, with Frances Alda as Roxanne and Pasquale Amato as Cyrano, the first performance had many of the hallmarks of a success, enthusiastic applause, nine curtain calls at the end. Ever eclectic, Damrosch tried for "more Italian and French influence in the music than German," introduced some humor into his score, and achieved a couple of numbers that were later

Horatio Parker's Mona *(1911), one of the Metropolitan's early attempts to encourage American composers and counter its image as a European bastion. The singers are Riccardo Martin (left), Louise Homer, and Herbert Witherspoon. John Herrick Jackson Music Library, Yale University.*

performed occasionally on concert programs. Musical reminiscence couldn't do the trick. After five performances in New York and one in Atlanta, *Cyrano* was never given again at the Metropolitan.[12]

The other conductor-composer had an operatic career that was European as well as American. Henry Kimball Hadley, born in Massachusetts in 1871, the son of a musician, was destined for a musical career. After attending the New England Conservatory, he went for further study in Vienna and for a number of years conducted opera in the municipal theater in Mainz, Germany, where his one-act opera *Safié* (never given in the United States) was performed. He returned to America as a conductor of the Seattle Symphony (1908–1911) and the San Francisco Symphony (1911–1915). His opera about Aztec Mexico, *Azora*, was performed by the Chicago Opera Company in 1917, though it was unsuccessful, and was followed by *Bianca*, another one-act opera, based on a comedy by Goldoni, a modernist work with no set numbers of individual songs. These operas succeeded in bringing Hadley to the attention of Gatti-Casazza, for whom he wrote another opera on a historical, exotic subject—*Cleopatra's Night*. Given at the Metropolitan on January 31, 1920, with Frances Alda, Orville Harrold, Jeanne Gordon, it was performed three times that season and three times the next, with a radio broadcast performance in 1929. Mildly erotic, Alda as Cleopatra exhibited those "unblushing candors of the body which are now practised on the stage."[13]

The search for American subjects inevitably led to Native American culture. Of the many composers who quarried this source the most important was Charles Wakefield Cadman, born in Johnstown, Pennsylvania, in 1881. At age fourteen, seeing De Koven's *Robin Hood* converted him to a career in music. He became interested in the music of Native Americans and in 1909 spent the summer on Omaha and Winnebago reservations, recording tribal songs, publishing four of them that year. "From the Land of Sky-blue Water" was discovered by Lillian Nordica, who sang it throughout the country in her recitals. Cadman's first opera, *Daoma*, was based on material given him by the son of a Native American chief. His major work, *Shanewis, or The Robin Woman*, was the story of a young Native American woman who studies music in New York and whose love for a white man leads to tragedy. First performed at the Metropolitan on March 23, 1918, repeated four times that year and three the next, it was the first opera by an American to be given there in two consecutive seasons. It was also performed in Chicago, Denver, and San Francisco. Although Cadman added modern elements to the score (a jazz band in one scene) and drew on Native American melodies—a Cheyenne song, "Spring Song of the Robin Woman," proved to be the opera's most popular piece—he subordinated everything to the European idiom.[14]

The most publicized operatic effort by an American composer was that of Victor Herbert, who had ridiculed the pretensions of grand opera—"a bastard art which appalled the intelligence of all thinking people"—but also admired its expressive power, "its incredible eloquence in presenting human conflict." Herbert wanted to compose something popular that would go "all over the world as the output of American brain and the inspiration of American surroundings." But his would not be a folk opera. Rather, it would be modernistic, "a continuous logical and well knit stream of orchestral development of the dramatic action, but not the modernist methods of Strauss and Debussy." Herbert turned back to a "modified Wagnerian technique."

His libretto was by a San Francisco lawyer, Joseph Deighn Redding, its story set in the Mission period of California history, its heroine, Natoma, "an absolutely new type" of woman, "mystical and ideal, yet logical and human." Everything would be sung throughout. By the time Herbert completed his work, Oscar Hammerstein, who had commissioned it, had gone out of business and the Metropolitan didn't want it. However, Cleofonte Campanini and the Chicago/Philadelphia company wanted to do it, with Mary Garden as Natoma. "It possesses much melodic charm, and it may please the public," Garden said. And when, after public "rehearsal" performances in Chicago and Philadelphia, *Natoma* was first performed in New York on February 25, 1911, it did seem to please. At least its music did, rhythmically vigorous and richly orchestrated. Oddly, however, Herbert, the experienced man of the theater, had saddled himself with a disastrous libretto: "futile, fatuous, halting, impotent, inane and puerile." Chicago kept *Natoma* in its repertory for several years, and it received thirty performances in various cities.[15]

Unfortunately, the attention lavished on *Natoma* produced something of a backlash, and Herbert's next opera, *Madeleine,* received less notice than it deserved. An intimate, bittersweet, "conversational" one-act work, set in eighteenth-century France, dramatic but unlyrical, it contained his most imaginative and advanced music—melodious, fleeting, varied, short phrases, often repeated. Well sung by Frances Alda, Paul Althouse, and Antonio Pini-Corsi, it was swallowed up in the cavernous Metropolitan, and though it was performed in Philadelphia and Chicago and revived in New York in 1918, it disappeared and awaits some intrepid impresario.

Treemonisha

Song and dance were at the center of African American musical culture in the nineteenth century. "Foreign travellers were poetic in recounting the glories of black singing," especially the singing of the slaves on southern plantations. The nature and significance of that singing was subject to varying interpretations. At the time, and later, it was commonly believed that people collectively—nations, cultures, races—had naturally differing musical endowments. It was a truism among Europeans that Italians and Germans were exceptionally musical, the British exceptionally not. From this "fact" people deduced different things. Some thought that those who were musically talented could not be good at other things: that the Italians, for example, being artistic and imaginative, must necessarily be politically and economically backward. The difficulty with this line of reasoning was that the other musical people, the Germans, were also highly organized, prosperous, and powerful.

African American musicality inspired a similar response. Southern slaveholders were quick to argue that the slaves' propensity for song proved their carefree condition. Even supporters of slavery, however, were not entirely persuaded by this as evidence of the beneficence of slavery. The more familiar line was that, social conditions aside, the African Americans' gift for singing was a racial characteristic which somehow suggested that they were less well adapted than white people to the requirements of advanced society. Many people rejected not only this conclusion but the premise on which it was based: the entire idea of special talent, racial or ethnic. Plantation singing was a social construction. Silence frightened the slave masters, who feared that it concealed the possibility that slaves, despite their supposed happiness, might be plotting rebellion. A silent slave was not liked by master or overseers. "Make a noise, make a noise," was the injunction to slaves when they were silent.[1]

The willingness of Americans to concede special artistic talent to some group or race is comprehensible in the context of their attitude toward art. Singing, for example, was "merely" singing and, like all art, insignificant compared to the importance of nonartistic activities. And yet the idea that art didn't really matter much also went hand in hand with the suspicion that it was fearfully potent. It is no wonder that the slave masters were so confused about the rapturous power of slave song, both as a condemnation of the horrors of slavery and as a jubilant vision of the promised day when the slaves would be unshackled—in heaven, anyway, if not in the United States. Had any slave owner attended a performance of

Beethoven's *Fidelio* in some northern city, seen and heard the ecstatic chorus of prisoners as they climbed out of their dungeons into the light of day and of freedom, and reflected that perhaps he had less to fear from silence than from song?

In any event, the indisputable legacy of these conflicting attitudes was the view that African Americans *were* a very musical people, which heightens the sense of wasted opportunities that haunts this chapter of the American operatic story. It is a northern story, primarily, but north or west or south, during slavery and after it, African Americans were denied their full participation in the evolution of the American operatic audience. Where they were not excluded wholly, they were kept separate. And, equally destructive, their participation was ignored or forgotten. Accounts remain fragmentary, but as they are uncovered and recovered, the picture they give us is of considerable activity on the part of African Americans, as performers and creators, and of considerable influence on the musical taste of the majority. This is especially true of music for the stage.[2]

The African Grove, a garden in lower Manhattan, opened in 1821, suggests a great deal of this vanished world. There African Americans took part in performances of Shakespeare, with contemporary songs interspersed. There Ira Aldridge (1807–1867), one of the first African American actors to achieve an international reputation, appeared with the African Grove players. In New Orleans in the 1840s the "free colored population" of the city opened the Théâtre de la Renaissance, where African American orchestra, director, and singers presented operas, opéras comiques, and French vaudevilles. Francis Johnson led a band much favored by Philadelphia society and commented on approvingly by William Henry Fry.[3] Despite opposition and discouragement, African Americans entered numerous aspects of northern musical life, and in the 1850s the first notable African American professional singers appeared.

E l i z a b e t h Taylor Greenfield, the first African American concert singer, was born in Mississippi in 1809. Adopted by a Quaker family named Greenfield, she was taken to Philadelphia, where she received vocal lessons, and made her professional debut in 1851. She toured the North, appearing before all-white audiences as the "Black Swan," her programs made up of arias by Handel, Bellini, and Donizetti, accompanied by piano and guitar. A promoter took her to Britain in 1853 but abandoned her before her first public appearance. Harriet Beecher Stowe, in London in connection with *Uncle Tom's Cabin,* introduced her to English music lovers, who arranged a concert for her. Stowe reported that Greenfield's voice, "the more touching from occasional rusticities and artistic defects," with its "penetrating vibrant quality," cut its way "like a Damascus blade to the heart." However, there was no future for her in England and no audience for her in America. "The spectacle of a black woman singing virtually the same repertoire as that with which the angelic Jenny Lind had captured the national adoration appeared to have no attraction." The Black Swan retired to Philadelphia, where she became a voice teacher.[4]

Two talented sisters, Ann and Emma Hyers, native Californians, became well-known concert singers in the 1870s, organizing their own touring company. "They are on a par vocally with our better concert-singers," a Boston writer reported, "and a

An 1821 playbill for New York's African Grove, an important center of early African American musical theater.

further hearing may place them in rank with more pretentious vocalists." They produced, and performed in, their own musical shows, and were active as late as the 1890s. In that same decade another singer who attracted attention was Mamie Flowers, the "Bronze Melba." Such a designation, in one way a term of praise, also shows how difficult it was for African Americans to establish identities in their own right, the chief example of this being Sissieretta Jones, whom Mamie Flowers briefly rivaled as the leading African American singer of her day, known everywhere as the "Black Patti."[5]

Sissieretta Joyner Jones was born in Portsmouth, Virginia, in 1869 and raised in

Providence, Rhode Island, where her father was a minister. She received musical training at the Providence Academy of Music and studied voice with well-known teachers in New York. In the 1890s she gained experience in the only way open to her—by touring as a solo performer, singing songs, ballads, and operatic arias. She made a considerable impression, singing for President Benjamin Harrison at the White House in 1892 and appearing in concert at Carnegie Hall. Frustrated by her inability to gain a proper hearing in the concert hall, she reportedly wanted to portray Selika in Meyerbeer's *L'Africaine,* but no white opera company of that day, in the United States, would have even considered such a possibility.

Therefore, in 1896, Sissieretta Jones formed the Black Patti Troubadours, who presented a mixed program that always concluded with an "operatic kaleidoscope"— staged arias from *Lucia, Martha, Il Trovatore,* and John Philip Sousa's *El Capitan* and other operas. Jones's singing, "the marvel of the day," was much admired. The Troubadours concentrated on small towns and medium-size cities and found African American audiences in the South very receptive to their music. One member of the company later recalled the choral support for Jones in her "kaleidoscope": "Nobody in

Sissieretta Jones, known as the "Black Patti," worked to overcome racial stereotypes in musical theater, though she never fulfilled her ambition to perform in European opera. Music Division, New York Public Library for the Performing Arts.

the company had operatic training, but they were told to sing loudly behind Black Patti. We all stood in a row behind her and yelled our heads off, belting out our version of how each opera should go, and I used to think the sound was wonderful."[5]

The Black Patti Troubadours gradually evolved more elaborate playlets or skits in the first part of the program. Near the end of her touring career Jones began to take part in these, while continuing with her operatic conclusion. In 1910 the Troubadours unveiled *A Trip to Africa,* a "three-act musical farce comedy," in which she played the role of an African princess. In 1911 came *In the Jungles,* in which Jones had a speaking as well as singing part, playing the role of a queen. Her next show, *Captain Jaspar* (1912), contained songs by her and by others, ranging from sentimental ballads to ragtime pieces. In her last show, *Lucky Sam from Alabam* (1914), the operatic kaleidoscope was dropped entirely, and the show consisted of twenty-two musical numbers, five of them solos by Jones.

Sissieretta Jones retired in 1916. She became a heroine for many because of her talent, judged by any standards, and because people of all races came to hear her. Her commanding presence, musical intelligence, and natural sense of the dramatic were obvious. "She fought a constant battle on the side of taste and artistic integrity, not only in her singing but also in the entire production of her operatic kaleidoscopes." She retired to Providence and died there in 1933.[6]

T h e Black Patti Troubadours coincided with the emergence of African American musical theater. Its elements were varied. Sam T. Jack opened a theater in Chicago, emphasizing women: first in his "living pictures," pseudo-classical tableaux with women prominently displayed, and then in his Creole Burlesque Show, using aspects of the old minstrel show but with women now in the forefront, singing and dancing: "Silk, Satin, Glitter, Gold." Variety shows, made up of disconnected acts of all kinds, took over the French designation "vaudeville." These white shows increasingly included African American performers and drew mixed audiences to important theaters. Solo dancers played an important role in vaudeville. Early in the nineteenth century African American dancers had impressed white observers. William Henry Lane (1825–1853) seemed to Charles Dickens "the greatest dancer known," dancing the "single shuffle, double shuffle, cut and cross cut, spinning about on his toes and heels like nothing but the man's fingers on the tambourine." Out of the minstrel shows came the first dance of African American origin to be taken up nationally by professional dancers, the Virginia Essence, which was followed by the Soft Shoe, a refined version of the Essence, and then by many many more as the twentieth century opened. Most notably, African American musical theater combined dance and song in remarkable ways.

John W. Isham, the advance man for Sam Jack's Creole Burlesque, organized a group of fifty performers, men and women, Isham's Octoroons, and modified the conventions of the old minstrel show. He introduced more songs and dances before or after a playlet and concluded with a military drill and dance for the entire company. Isham's first show, set in New York, was *A Tenderloin Coon.* His next "musical melodious farce," *John W. Isham's Octoroons at the Blackville Derby,* attempted to achieve unity by means of a lengthy conclusion, "Thirty Minutes around the Operas,"

*African American
singers such as J. Rosa-
mond Johnson and
Sidney Woodward found
an outlet for their tal-
ents in John W. Isham's
interracial Octoroons.
This poster dates from
1896. Library of
Congress.*

selections from *Pinafore, Robin Hood,* and others. *Oriental America,* 1896, featured even more operatic singing by first-class African American singers, J. Rosamond Johnson and Sidney Woodward, their show concluding with a finale of solos and choruses from *Faust, Rigoletto, Carmen, Martha,* and *Il Trovatore* in place of the military drill and cakewalk. Finally, *Oriental America at Mrs. Waldorf's Fifth Anniversary,* retaining the same kind of operatic finale, was notable also as the first African American opera to play on Broadway. It traveled as far as Chicago in one direction, England in the other.

Songwriters were the final and crucial element in the emerging African American musical theater, their fresh rhythms blending in with a familiar song idiom, but retaining a distinctive quality. Sam Lucas (1840–1916), Gussie Davis (1853–1899), and James Bland (1854–1911), among the best-known names, composed many of the most popular songs of the time. Music publishers fostered the "first mass invasion of the amusement world by colored America." Of the seventeen songs which sold over a hundred thousand copies each in 1901, six were composed by African Americans; of the twenty-four in 1902, four. All these songs came from musical comedies. The world of composers was much more integrated than that of performers and audiences. Songwriters, white and black, imitated each other, quoted each other's songs, influenced each other's work. No popular style was separate or isolated. Ragtime, minstrel songs, English and European opera and operetta, the works of Herbert and Cohan—all were drawn upon and mixed together. African American composers brought syncopated song to Broadway and a new kind of rhythmical and metrical flexibility to American stage music that it never lost. They played an important role in creating Tin Pan Alley and popular American song.

New songwriters came to the front. Bob Cole, born in Athens, Georgia, in 1868, went to Atlanta University, then moved to Chicago, where he worked in clubs and attracted notice as a singer, worked for Sam Jack's Creoles. Settled in New York, he toured with the Black Patti Troubadours. J. Rosamond Johnson and his brother, James Weldon, were born in Jacksonville, Florida. J. Rosamond was sent by his parents to study at the New England Conservatory of Music. He toured with Isham's *Oriental America* before returning to Jacksonville to teach. There he and his brother wrote an operetta, *Tolosa*, never produced but enough to persuade them to head for New York.

Will Marion Cook, born in 1869 in Washington, D.C., enjoyed more formal musical training than his contemporaries. His father was dean of the Howard University Law School, his mother a graduate of Oberlin College. Cook followed her there, and his teachers persuaded him to go to Europe. A benefit concert raised money for him to study violin with Joseph Joachim for three years. When he returned to the United States, he found, as so many African Americans before him had, that no career was open to him as a concert artist or orchestral player in the white musical world. So "he threw all these European standards over" in the late 1890s, turned to popular music, taught, stage-managed, composed, organized a touring orchestra, the Southern Syncopated Orchestra, and moved to New York, harsh, crowded, vibrant. The third most numerous category of professional occupations among African Americans in the city was musicians and actors, and a midtown hotel, the Marshall, was a meeting place for those concerned with musical theater. There collaborations were formed, enterprises planned; for suddenly the African American musical stage teemed with life.[7]

B e t w e e n 1898 and 1915 African American composers wrote and produced at least thirty-two operettas. They were a mixture of old and new, the outworn minstrel elements and the art-song traditions of opera vying with contemporary social commentary and syncopated music. Africa played an important background role. It wasn't presented realistically, nor as a place particularly receptive to Americans. But it was civilized. The plots of the operettas abounded in deceit and ruses. Many of the characters were con men, conjurors, tricksters, good-hearted n'er-do-wells. There were plentiful comments about money, social class, education. While many of these satirical thrusts were ostensibly aimed at Africa and African Americans, they applied equally well to contemporary white culture in America. Pompous Johnsing, a character in *Jes Lak White Fo'ks* (1899), observed.

> I want you all to understand I got a plan in regard to di gold. I got social aspirations. You know when white men gets rich dey dont stay hyeah wha everybody knows 'em en knows day ain't much. Dey go to Europe an by n by you readin' de papers en you say: "Huh! hah! Mr. William Vanderbilt Sunflower's daughter married a duke." But I ain't goin' get no bargain counter duke for my daughter, hun-uh, honey. She is going to marry a prince.
>
> She done got huh diploma from Vassar, and I has been engaged in diplomatic negotiations wid an African King. Dis will be a marriage of convenience. I goin' to get Mandy a family tree. Ain't nobody what is anybody keepin' house doubt a family tree. Dey er so cheap in Europe dey use 'em fer kindlin' wood.

So much for the "aristocratic" culture of the Metropolitan Opera's Diamond Horseshoe!

The first of these operettas was *A Trip to Coontown* (1898) by Bob Cole and Billy Johnson. The theatrical syndicates which controlled most theaters refused to stage it, and it found its first audiences in the smallest of small towns, then in Canada, where the syndicates' influence didn't reach. As news of its success drifted back to the States, it was booked into the Third Avenue Theater in New York and became popular enough to end up at the Casino Theater. It was loose in form. The Cole and Johnson songs were altered as the show developed, sometimes using old tunes with new lyrics, ballad-opera fashion. Its importance lay in the fact that as ragtime music was beginning to sweep the country, *A Trip to Coontown* had slight but definite syncopation in its music.

That same year Will Marion Cook presented *Clorindy, or The Origins of the Cake-walk.* "A blackface vaudeville revue," someone dismissively called it. This fairly characterized its structure, a series of unconnected sections, of which "Clorindy" was the concluding one, but failed to do justice to its syncopated vitality and energetic dancing. The Casino agreed to produce it if a first runthrough was satisfactory. Will Cook later described this remarkable scene, a first encounter between conventional white and new African American operetta culture. The Casino orchestra was conducted by an Englishman named John Braham, who ran his group through some of the shorter numbers. When they got to the "Clorindy" section, Cook explained that he had "studied violin under Joachim, a bit of composition under Dvorak," and that "Clorindy" was his, "some new music, a Negro operetta." Braham turned to his orchestra and said: "Gentlemen, a new composer," then held out his hand for the orchestra parts. Cook explained that as he was familiar with the music, the singers might find his beat easier to follow. Generously, Braham turned to his orchestra again: "Gentlemen, a new composer and a new conductor." Cook gestured to the singers gathered on stage and began with the opening chorus. "Twenty-six of the finest Negro voices in America, twenty-six happy gifted Negroes, who saw maybe weeks of work and money before them, singing a new style of music" took his cue. "Like a mighty anthem in rhythm, these voices rang out." The Casino's manager, absent at the beginning, heard them, took in the scene as he came into the auditorium, and shouted to Braham: "No nigger can conduct my orchestra on Broadway!" Braham replied: "Ed, go back to your little cubby-hole and keep quiet! That boy's a genius and has something great." The runthrough removed any objections and Cook remembered the night of the first performance. "My chorus sang like Russians, dancing meanwhile like Negroes, and cake-walking like angels, black angels! When the last note sounded, the audience stood and cheered for at least ten minutes."[8] "Sensational," the *New York Times* called it, but interestingly *Clorindy* was too different for non–New York audiences and didn't do well on tour.

In Dahomey (1903), three acts, with a cast of fifty headed by the comedy team of Bert Williams and George Walker, was more ambitious, a serious effort to achieve dramatic coherence. A story about African colonization, *In Dahomey* had its moments of Graustarkian foolishness, but it also made pointed satirical thrusts at social pretensions, African and American, and the music was varied—syncopated songs, a waltz ballad. "Society," the most extended number, approached operatic dimensions.

It was a trio with three characters responding to each other in song, while the chorus sang behind. After fifty-three New York performances, *In Dahomey* went to London. An English reviewer found it "a new aesthetic thrill," noting "the fascination of the beautiful-uncanny, and a widening of the horizon of the humorous." Here, he wrote, was "*aliquid novi ex Africa*—'something important and new from Africa,' the strangeness of the colored race blended with the strangeness of certain American things." *In Dahomey* later toured the United States, coast to coast, for forty weeks.

Many of these African American operettas didn't move beyond the old minstrel show patterns. *The Southerners*, of 1904, "a study in black and white," was notable socially as an integrated performance, whites and blacks acting and singing together, but aesthetically it was a jumble of separate acts, stereotypes of African Americans matched by stereotypes of Asians. *Abyssinia* (1906) was simple Graustark, about a pair of Kansas con men in Abyssinia, the staging lavish but the dancing conventional. *The Shoo-Fly Regiment*, by Cole and the Johnsons, dealt with the adventures of students of Lincolnville Institute, Alabama, who volunteer to fight in the Spanish-American War and take their girlfriends with them to the Philippines. There was lots of syncopation and in one song, "Li'l Gal," there was "a certain self-conscious modernity: parallel fifths *à la* Debussy in the accompaniment."

The most lavish of these operas was *Bandana Land* of 1908, with Will Cook's songs and starring Bert Williams. It was Williams's greatest success and included his most famous song, "Nobody." "This colored show stands with the foremost of musical entertainments," said the *Dramatic Mirror*. "With all its savor of a minstrel performance the piece comes close to being opera comique. There is a plot and most of the songs relate to it; the comedy is a natural outcome of the story, and the music, some of it at least, is far above the ordinary." There were seventy-five in the cast and twenty in the orchestra, double the usual number that could be mustered. It was the first African American opera to play for a white audience in Washington, D.C. A Cincinnati critic's comments deserve quotation at some length:

> There is just one thing a fair-minded person can say regarding the negroes who participate in *Bandana Land,* and that is, they are natural singers and comedians [and] have a real sense of comedy. They make their points quietly and with restraint. They enjoy it. Every time they speak a line, they do it as if it was new and fresh to them and . . . instead of striving for points, for personal applause, they work to one end, for the thing itself.
>
> As to singing, they are marvels. They tackle the big finales with a vim, a discretion, a judgment as to points and effects which is a revelation. Someone said during the week, "I would like to be blind-folded and hear that chorus and the chorus in the first act finale in *The Merry Widow,* and see which I would like best." It would be hard to decide.[9]

The *Red Moon*, of 1909, capitalized on the popularity of Native American themes and subjects, which African American composers had used in songs like "Navajo," "Rowena," and "Red Wing." With music and lyrics by Cole and Rosamond Johnson, the opera related the improbable kidnapping and rescue of a young girl of mixed parentage, African American mother, Native American father. Clichés abounded in story and music. "Bleeding Moon" was a song about a Native American curse, "Big Red Shawl" a love song, while "Life Is a Game of Checkers" punned about reds and blacks mixing together. There was no pretense at using Native American music.

At the same time, a very different impulse was taking shape, the desire to break free from even the vestiges of European art forms. J. Leubrie Hill, a prolific songwriter and member of the *Red Moon* company, felt that "the real Negro was not on stage." What he heard and saw was "African operetta," and he wanted something else.[10] In 1911 Hill wrote *My Friend from Dixie*, which was first given in Brooklyn. "Performances were poorly advertised and poorly attended, but the show made a favorable impression on a few members of the audience." It had lots of minstrel clichés in it—watermelons, dice games, gin and razors, the most objectionable coon-show stereotypes— but the music was pervasively syncopated, the lyrics and book were colloquial and action-filled, the show was danced as much as sung, and it ended with a genuine ragtime tune. In 1913 Hill revised it as *My Friend from Kentucky*. It ran several hours in its full form, but a reduced version drew audiences in droves to Harlem's Lafayette Theater. The story was a contemporary one, unusual in its frankness. Jim Jackson Lee mortgages his father-in-law's Kentucky plantation to go to Washington to win fame and fortune, and to escape from his wife. But she eventually wins out, brings him back to Kentucky and an orderly life. All the coon-show elements had disappeared and there was a serious love song, the first in an African American opera to be sung not for laughs but in a direct, impassioned manner. The taboo on love making in African American theater was shattered.

The profusion of ragtime numbers made *My Friend from Kentucky* a kind of jazz opera. It was also notable for its dancing. "Hill realized, as none of the directors before him had, that the novel impact of black performers lay in the special ways they could use their bodies and their voices, making the trappings of the nineteenth-century extravaganza or European operettas seem irrelevant." Dances just becoming popular were brought onstage—a moochee slide, a Texas Tommy wiggle, and a tango one-step. The show concluded with a circle dance, a sort of sliding walk, in rhythm. The entire company formed a chain, each with his or her hands on the hips of the person ahead, and danced across the stage and off at one end, then around behind the curtain and back on stage at the other end, circling continuously. The dancing topped "anything Broadway has ever seen," said the *New York World*. Carl Van Vechten, a knowledgeable and sympathetic observer, found the dancing and singing so novel as "to give the spectator who is used to the conventions of musical comedy something of a surprise." Florenz Ziegfeld saw *My Friend from Kentucky* and borrowed its finale for his Follies, where that kind of finish became the hallmark of Ziegfeld shows. Few in his Broadway audiences can have realized its origins.[11]

The culmination of this period of African American opera came unexpectedly in the form of an opera which was produced neither on Broadway, nor in Harlem, nor anywhere else until long after the composer's death. Scott Joplin was more famous than any of these opera composers, yet it would be sixty years before *Treemonisha* was properly placed within the African American operatic tradition and Joplin, the King of Ragtime, was recognized as one of American opera's important figures.

T h e son of a household slave musician, Scott was born in Texarkana, Arkansas, in 1868. When he was three, his father abandoned the family and his mother assumed the formidable task of keeping them together. She taught Scott the banjo and, working as a cleaning lady, saved enough money to buy him an upright piano. He took to it with such passion and skill that friends helped pay for lessons from a local teacher, who introduced him to European art music. At an early age Scott Joplin became an itinerant musician.

In 1888 he settled in St. Louis, a center for African American music. Joplin was in Chicago for the Columbian Exposition of 1893 and went as far east as New York. He began composing songs and a publisher in Syracuse, New York, put out two of his waltzes. In 1897 he settled in Sedalia, Missouri, enrolled in the College for Negroes, played the piano in brothels and saloons and the cornet in a twelve-member African American concert band. Their repertoire consisted of cakewalk numbers and the new ragtime pieces. In December 1897, "Harlem Rag," the first rag by an African American composer to be published, stimulated Joplin to begin publishing his own ragtime

Scott Joplin elevated ragtime music to a new level of sophistication and aspired to compose in more complex forms. This photograph, one of the few extant images of Joplin, was taken around 1908.

pieces. He had sold "Original Rags" to a publisher in 1895, but it remained un-published. In a rare piece of good luck, Joplin encountered John Stark, a piano dealer, who also published music on his hand press as a sideline to promote the sale of his pianos and build local good will. Joplin showed Stark a rag he had been revising for several years, and Stark, immediately discerning its haunting quality, paid Joplin fifty dollars for it—twice his usual price, plus his usual one-cent royalty for each copy sold. Joplin named it "The Maple Leaf," in honor of the men's social club he frequented in Sedalia.

"The Maple Leaf Rag" caught on everywhere. As tens of thousands of orders flowed in, Stark promoted Joplin vigorously and in 1906 brought out a collection entitled *Standard High Class Rags*. Joplin wasn't content to repeat himself. He had strong ideas about rags and how they should properly be played, but he aspired to compose in more complex forms. He studied counterpoint with a German musician in Sedalia and spoke to friends about composing music that would take the public twenty-five years to understand. His rags were different enough. Joplin spoke of their "weird and intoxicating effects" and wrote *School of Ragtime: Six Exercises for Piano.*

Ambitious for a larger stage on which to work, Joplin moved to New York about 1903. He met other African American musicians at the Marshall Hotel and told them that he wanted to compose a grand opera. He had completed one opera, *Guard of Honor,* about which we know little but the title. The manuscript, if ever completed, has disappeared. Now, determined to combine ragtime and grand opera, he set to work writing the libretto, lyrics, and music himself. The flowering of African American comic opera, the Metropolitan and Manhattan opera houses, the operettas of Lehár and Herbert and the musical plays of Cohan and many others—all whetted Joplin's fascination with opera. Throughout the first decade of the century he worked on *Treemonisha*, neglecting his students, composing few rags. Ragtime was waning anyway, superseded by faster dance steps, the turkey trot, grizzly bear, bunny hug. Joplin had remarried before coming to New York and his wife ran a boarding house to support them, along with whatever royalties he collected. He finished his opera by 1911 and printed the piano-vocal score at his own expense.[12]

Treemonisha, in three acts, is in rhyming verse. It contains an overture and twenty-seven separate but connected numbers—solos, choruses, a quartet, one duet, numerous dances. The story is set vaguely in an earlier time in rural America: there are choruses of cotton pickers and corn huskers. Treemonisha, abandoned as a baby at the base of the "sacred tree," was adopted by Monisha and Ned and named for her miraculous appearance. She is kidnapped by a wicked conjuror Zodzetrick, who controls people by selling them "magic powders," but is rescued. The women and men of the neighborhood call on her to be their leader. The only one of her people who can read and write and thus break the spell of ignorance and superstition that allows Zodzetrick and his kind to flourish, Treemonisha agrees, forgiving Zodzetrick and inaugurating a new era of love and harmony, culminating in a stately rag of reconciliation.

Treemonisha drew on many elements of African American operetta: the tricksters, the centrality of the choruses, the dance conclusion. At the same time it was uncan-

Sixty-five years after Joplin's death, the Houston Grand Opera's production of Tree-monisha *belatedly established it as a landmark of American opera. Photograph copyright 1982 by Jim Caldwell.*

nily reminiscent of Bellini's *La Sonnambula,* that idyll of virtue triumphing over suspicion and superstition. *Treemonisha* is an odd, finally compelling opera, fragile in its charm, moving in its appeal, in its naive mingling of old forms and new spirit. Its music, formal and syncopated, has the grave stateliness and classical dignity of a sung ballet.

From 1911 Joplin struggled to produce his opera. Reviewing the published score, the *American Musician* argued that Joplin had "created an entirely new phase of musical art and provided a thoroughly American opera, dealing with an American subject, yet free from all extraneous influence." No one paid attention. No support was forthcoming. In 1915 he arranged a vocal performance, no costumes, scenery or, most crucially, dance, just singers accompanied by Joplin at the piano, in a rented Harlem theater. This "curious alchemical mixture of musical styles and conceptions" baffled and bored its audience. *Treemonisha* had everything going against it. For those who wanted conventional European opera, it wasn't opera at all. For those looking for something entirely African American, it condemned itself by its recollection of European styles. American culture boasted of its eclecticism, but no one wanted this combination of "mid-nineteenth-century European opera, African-American dance forms, and turn-of-the-century American popular idioms."

Joplin was utterly crushed by his failure. He rapidly disintegrated, his piano playing became erratic, and the last of his students left him. It wasn't only depression. Years before he had apparently contracted syphilis, which had lain latent in his system. In 1916 his wife committed him to a mental hospital, and he died there on April 1, 1917. His death was lost in the tumult of the declaration of war that week. Anyway, his fame as a ragtime composer had faded. Told of his death, John Stark said: "A homeless itinerant, he left his mark on American music."[13] For many years it didn't seem as if he had. And yet Scott Joplin's day, and that of his opera, would come again.

Enrico Caruso and Geraldine Farrar

It has been almost a century since Enrico Caruso began singing professionally, more than seventy years since he stopped, yet something of his fame has escaped the obliteration of time. Recordings explain why Jean de Reszke and Mario, Jenny Lind and Adelina Patti, who were in their days fully Caruso's equal in celebrity, are now only names while Caruso is still a voice. But his significance to the history of opera in America extends farther. Although he sang in twenty-three countries in Europe and the Americas, Caruso had a special relationship with the Metropolitan Opera (607 appearances in eighteen years) and with American culture.

The eighteenth child of a mechanic named Marcellino Caruso and his wife, Anna, Enrico was born in Naples on February 27, 1873. All the previous seventeen children died in childbirth or in infancy. Two children followed him, and survived. Enrico adored his mother, who taught him what she could. He had little formal schooling, sang from an early age in the streets, in churches, for private parties, and got some lessons from a variety of teachers. His mother died when he was fifteen, and after that he was pretty much on his own. There was nothing precocious about his early years. On the contrary, his voice was uneven, unpredictable, broke frequently on high notes. One of his teachers said, "Pooh! It's like the gold at the bottom of the Tiber in Rome—not worth going after."[1]

He slogged on, nevertheless, not doubting that he would have an operatic career, that he *must* have one to escape from the Neapolitan slums. Better teaching helped him correct vocal faults, he gained confidence in his voice, and it began to be noticed as rung by rung he moved up the Italian operatic ladder. Puccini's encouragement—he heard Caruso in a private audition—helped him get to Leghorn and Lucca in 1897. He made his first important impression in *La Bohème* and more of one in Giordano's *Fedora.* After that, Caruso sang in St. Petersburg and made the first of several South American visits. By the end of 1900, he was ready for his debut at La Scala. International notice followed when he sang at Monte Carlo with Nellie Melba. This opened the doors of Covent Garden, where he immediately became, and always remained, a great favorite. The British found what the Americans were to find: "the quintessence of the Italian tenor: jovial, well-fed, with a rich, full, sensuous voice, somehow the embodiment of the sunshine of his native land."[2] In London he sang with Lillian Nordica in *Aida,* made a tremendous hit in Donizetti's *L'Elisir d'amore,* absent from London's operatic stage for twenty-five years, and made his first recordings.

Maurice Grau, then director of the Metropolitan, hearing good reports, signed Caruso to a contract for forty performances at the Metropolitan in 1903–1904. When Grau retired in the spring of 1903, the contract lapsed. Heinrich Conried renewed it, cautiously reducing the number of performances to twenty-five. Sometime later, Conried heard a record of Caruso's voice and was impressed enough to offer him opening night for the 1903 season, *Rigoletto,* with Marcella Sembrich and Antonio Scotti, whose presence guaranteed success, whatever the fortunes of the new tenor.

November 23, 1903, is one of the most important dates in the history of the Metropolitan and of opera in America. But it was Sembrich, a superlative musician and vocalist, who dominated the evening. Caruso's debut was favorable but not brilliant, *not* one of the stunning moments of operatic lore. While Caruso had "many of the tiresome Italian vocal affectations," he possessed a "manly voice," "a pure tenor voice of fine quality and sufficient range and power," a "smooth and mellow voice without the typical Italian bleat," a "voice that is true, of fine quality and marvelous endurance." "Not a great tenor, but an eminently satisfactory one." Criticism was mainly of his physique ("a generous girth," "short and squat") and of his conventional operatic acting ("stout and slow in his movement"). Then the inevitable comparison: "All memories of Jean de Reszke are not effaced."[3]

Caruso's acceptance grew modestly but steadily in the next six weeks. In *Tosca,* the audience heard "an uncommonly beautiful voice," but his "common," "bourgeois" stage manner annoyed. In *Bohème* voice and manner fused: "musical instincts as perfect as his voice is luscious," "electrical surprises at every point." His success took a leap in January. *L'Elisir d'amore* was his first unqualified triumph: "a truly beautiful voice and style," "captivating, melting, old-fashioned rhetorical passion." Comedy released his natural high spirits. He lacked the de Reszkian appeal to the boxes, but he won the balconies—forever. Caruso was satisfied at season's end. "The critics—they were kind, except about my fat and my clothes."[4]

The next five years established Caruso as the most popular singer at the Metropolitan, as the best-known singer in America, as the most potent attraction at the box office, and as something beyond these things: a phenomenon of a different order. Recordings had much to do with it. They sold well and the Victor Company, for whom he recorded, vigorously promoted them, so that when he went on tour his name was already familiar. As a Chicago critic noted after his first appearance there, "He began his evening amid applause. He ended it amid applause. The audience welcomed him heartily. It acclaimed him in everything he did."[5]

In 1904–1905 Caruso sang in thirty performances in fourteen weeks. Fashionable audiences took him up, insisting that he sing in the Monday night subscription series. "The smart set, which is a very stupid set indeed," wrote W. J. Henderson, "dislikes anything so serious as the great tragedies of Wagner. So Mr. Conried was informed that he would not be permitted to give Wagner on Monday night." Instead, Conried gave them Caruso—on nine Monday nights. *La Gioconda* was revived for him, and the instant he appeared there was a tremendous ovation. ("I never saw the auditorium so white with diamonds," he commented.) Because he did not know it in French, Meyerbeer's *Les Huguenots* was given in Italian, as *Gli Ugonotti,* and he was "tonally superb." The next year, 1905–1906, he added two French operas, in French—*Carmen* and *Faust*. He sang Don Jose with "unexpected delicacy and finish," but *Faust* was "a flat and unredeemable failure." His acting was stiff, his costumes absurd, his accent "imported from a quarter where perfection does not prevail." No matter. The invariable request at the box office was, "Can you let me have seats for Caruso's next appearance?"

In the fall of 1906 began the battle against Oscar Hammerstein, in which Caruso and Puccini were the chief Metropolitan weapons. In 1907–1908 Caruso sang fifty-one times. But he couldn't sing every night. Then what? "The plain truth," one writer commented, was that "without Mr. Caruso it is difficult to draw a large audience at the Metropolitan just at present." Alfred Hertz, the Metropolitan's German conductor, denied that interest in Wagner was decreasing. "Rather do I find that the interest in Mr. Caruso is increasing. It is not a great interest in the Italian opera, but a great interest in Mr. Caruso that fills the Opera House. Go to the opera on Italian nights when that tenor is not singing, and you will find smaller audiences than on the German nights."

People wanted to hear *that* voice—the stentorian top notes, the vibrant richness, even the Caruso sob, the special throbbing. It was the voice of gold. There was no other like it. But was this so? Was it the voice or the name that audiences shouted about? A revealing incident took place in Chicago when the Metropolitan was on tour. In the popular double-bill, Andreas Dippel was singing in *Cavalleria rusticana*, Caruso in *I Pagliacci*. There was a capacity house, attracted by Caruso, not Dippel. The latter was not in good voice that night and was worried about the famous offstage serenade that opens the opera. So the audience was told that he was indisposed and prepared itself to make allowances, a familiar enough incident in opera. Meanwhile, Caruso suggested that he sing that one aria for Dippel—and he did, gloriously. The audience, however, heard what it expected to hear—an unknown Dippel replacement—and responded with mild applause. Caruso was neither hurt nor angered, recognizing that his name was as potent as his voice.[6]

By 1910 Caruso towered over the operatic scene as singer, name, personality. But he was identified with no artistic movement or school, had no aesthetic ambitions, took no initiatives as de Reszke had done in the 1890s, had no real concern with repertory, other than to be careful to avoid roles which did not suit his voice. He was unintellectual, never read, took no interest in politics, cared nothing for general discussions about art, didn't like social life beyond his circle of mostly Neapolitan friends. Caruso was saved from what could have been prima-donnaism of a most tremendous kind by his modest, pliant, amiable nature, his genuine desire to sing as well as he could. Conductors never complained about him. Gatti-Casazza was right to say that no matter how much you paid Caruso he always turned out to be the least expensive of singers. Bonci, McCormack, Slezak, to mention only Caruso's tenor contemporaries, did many things he could not do, but Caruso by this point had gone beyond musicianship and become unique.

Americans pictured him as a nice guy, with a common touch. He wasn't a foreign artist specializing in an exotic art so much as a kind of innocent, high-spirited, boyish, his disposition infectiously sunny. The caricatures he did of his contemporaries had an edge to them, but were not harsh: "They bite but never snarl." The disproportionate publicity given to his practical jokes was a way of removing the strangeness from opera. Photographs showed him distorting his mobile features, outrageously hamming it up. Visiting Atlanta with the Met on tour, "Caruso arrived in excellent spirits; he strolled from the train, a Scotch plaid hat covering one eye, a cigarette between his teeth, and an irrepressible grin on his face." He cast his spell on everyone around him. The Atlanta papers likened "the behavior of the visitors to that of happy schoolchildren out for a holiday." Even in his concert appearances, where everyone agreed Caruso seemed uncomfortable, stiff, he sometimes got a laugh from his audience by doing little dog-trot steps as he left the stage. And he was relentlessly upbeat. He loved America, found skyscrapers "extraordinary," President Teddy Roosevelt "great," American women "fine." A primo divo without temperament, he was demanding about his personal comfort—his fear of drafts, hotel rooms which, however grand, were never grand enough. He was very nervous before going onstage, played solitaire in his hotel suite, hardly talked, smoked cigarettes incessantly before and during performances. "Of course I am nervous. The artist who boasts he is never nervous is not an artist—he is a liar or a fool." In cities where he had been criticized—Naples, Barcelona, Havana, Budapest—he refused to sing again.[7]

He had another claim on the admiration of American audiences: his success. He surpassed Patti's accomplishments in making money. He began singing at the Metropolitan for $960 a performance, a fee that quickly rose to $1,500, then $2,000 and $2,500. The Metropolitan was prepared to pay him more, but Caruso felt that was enough as compared with colleagues with whom he sang regularly. Impresarios offered larger and larger sums. A Parisian appearance paid $4,000 and the Argentinians paid him $7,000 an appearance in the 1910s. In Havana, later, he got $10,000 and in Mexico in 1917 he received $15,000 for a single performance. He also made a fortune from his records. From 1904, when his recordings first went on sale, he averaged $115,000 a year, earning an estimated $1,825,000 between that year and 1920. In 1921, the last year he recorded, he made $400,000. In Europe, where he had recorded before coming to America, he made another $1,000,000 from records during his lifetime.

Enrico Caruso was the first widely popular male singer in American operatic history. Before him the greatest favorites had been women. The most admired men—Brignoli, Campanini, de Reszke—appealed to the operatically discriminating. Caruso's appeal spread beyond them, beyond the operatic or even the musical public. A major reason was the identification of him as a "manly" singer, associated with power. The single quality of his voice people most frequently talked about was its volume. When he wished to do so, it was said, he could hit a certain note which would shatter glass. That he was neither elegant nor refined added to this kind of appeal. The critic Richard Aldrich observed that the public often admired him in roles that connoisseurs thought least suited for him—Don Jose in *Carmen,* for example. The general audience "did not want a perfectly groomed, immaculate, refined French stylist; they wanted Caruso in any guise, the man with the robust, golden voice who sang with all his heart."[8]

The Central Park Zoo monkey house affair exposed the contrast between opera singers' onstage personalities and their offstage lives. The New York Herald, *like most other papers in the city, gave Caruso's trial front-page coverage.*

Approval of his masculine potency was attested to by the Central Park monkey house affair. On November 16, 1906, in the late afternoon, Caruso was arrested by a policeman in the Central Park Zoo for allegedly bothering a woman who had been standing alone in front of one of the monkey cages. She preferred charges against him, he was arraigned and held at the police station until Heinrich Conried rushed down and bailed him out. A stream of newspaper reports followed. Caruso denied having "annoyed" the woman, about whom there was an air of mystery, a suggestion that her character was not what it should be. When the case came to trial, she didn't appear in court. Nevertheless, the judge found Caruso guilty of disorderly conduct and fined him ten dollars. At this distance in time it is impossible to untangle things. Caruso may have made advances which embarrassed and distressed the woman. The quickness with which the press suspected her motives suggests masculine bias. On the other hand, the judge appears to have been prejudiced against Caruso. It is possible, too, that the woman and her lawyer were extortionists who had set him up.

In the days immediately after the incident, Caruso didn't appear in public. Late in the month, with trepidation on his part and sheer panic on that of Conried and the Metropolitan management, he appeared in *La Bohème.* When the curtain went up and the audience spotted him, there was a tremendous ovation. His first notes were trembling and uncertain, but he rapidly gained assurance. Backstage he was beside himself with relief. In a way, this wasn't surprising. Immensely popular artist, dubious woman, trivial incident. What did it amount to, after all, a harmless pinch or squeeze? Support for Caruso appeared throughout the country. The whole thing was quickly forgotten, though not by Caruso, who was infuriated by any mention of it as long as he lived. Men like him were to be forgiven much. His sexual impulses were part of his fun-loving persona, connected with these practical jokes and pranks. His sexuality, like his art, wasn't threatening.[9]

W h a t would the American public have made of Caruso's family life, had they known the truth about it? In the mid-1890s Caruso had fallen in love and lived with the soprano Ada Giachetti, who was married but separated from her husband. Giachetti bore Caruso two children. They lived together openly for over a decade. When Caruso came to America, Giachetti sometimes came with him in the early years. American newspapers delighted in describing the jovial and amusing family man, "happily married and comfortably settled, with his dark-eyed, beautiful wife, Ada, exquisitely dressed in her Parisian gown, often at his side." This was a reassuring picture—the Latin artist, powerful and passionate, contained by bourgeois respectability.

The Giachetti-Caruso relationship was turbulent, complex beyond superficial pieties. While Giachetti's husband lived, divorce was out of the question. Anyway, she did not want to settle down, raise Caruso's children, and be tied to domestic life. She wished to pursue her own career. She was also much more free-thinking and unconventional than Caruso. She didn't relish the idea of staying in Italy with the children, living in the villa Caruso had bought for them—as the Metropolitan preferred—while he spent six months a year in America, pulling the wool over the eyes of the prudish Yankees. She didn't disguise her infidelities. While Caruso was away, Giachetti lived with her chauffeur. Absence from her bedeviled Caruso's seemingly cloudless life. Her presence was equally tormenting. Giachetti came to America in 1908–1909 and their life together was a continuous turmoil, punctuated by screaming scenes in the hotel where they lived. All that season he was terribly depressed. His throat hurt constantly and he canceled appearances twenty-one times.

When Giachetti returned to Italy, she left him. In 1912 she sued Caruso in Italian court, charging him with slandering her, impeding her career, and stealing jewelry which belonged to her. The trial was a journalistic sensation in Italy, though hardly reported in America. The judge decided against Giachetti. After the trial, Caruso's suffering persisted. He was prone to fits of weeping, attacks of fever, violent headaches. He forced himself to sing, but his appearances took their toll. His German agent said: "Never would I have believed that a human being could absorb into his system such quantities of aspirin, pyramidol." And after all the jealousy and suffering, Caruso could not get Giachetti out of his mind. His friends believed that he *never* got over her, though he later married an American woman. Long after the trial, when Giachetti went to South America to sing and Caruso toured there, he saw her and they spent time together.[10]

T h e figure of the clown who plays and sings and amuses his audience even though his own heart is breaking is an old one. Canio, in *I Pagliacci* (*The Clowns*), sings, "Laugh, clown, laugh," pouring out his heartbreak while concealing his true feelings. It became Caruso's most famous role, the one he performed most often, seventy-six times in eighteen years, "Vesti la giubba" was his best-selling record and his most familiar photograph was as Canio, dressed in his clown's suit, beating his drum. Nevertheless, Caruso didn't identify personally with this or any other role. "The moment one adopts a favorite role he becomes a specialist and ceases to be an artist." So he said. His agent insisted that Caruso always pictured Ada Giachetti as Nedda in *I Pagliacci* and that he would have avoided singing Canio at all had he been able to do so. The enormous popular audience, however, was more interested in the artist than in his art, more curious about the actor offstage than on. People followed Caruso on the streets, gawked at him when he ate in restaurants, devoured newspaper accounts of his marriage to Dorothy Park Benjamin, of an "old" New York family, in August 1918. When their daughter Dorothy was born, the papers were filled with photographs of the proud papa smiling at the little babe. This attitude toward entertainers is characteristic of mass culture, of which Caruso was an early hero.

At the same time and despite all the attention, Caruso knew that he represented for millions of people, of all classes, the stereotype of the Italian singer–organ grinder. Once he took part in a Long Island charity affair, sitting in a booth, drawing caricatures at ten dollars each, the proceeds going to a local hospital. When he arrived to take his place, he found the booth "festooned with fringes of dry spaghetti." "I am sorry, madame," he said to a member of the entertainment committee. "I cannot draw unless you remove that spaghetti. Spaghetti is for the kitchen." He concealed his fury, but later told his wife, "They do not imagine such things will offend because many people think of Italians only like that. What surprises me is that such nice people make such mistake."[11]

The happy-go-lucky Italian peasant, bursting with song, a crude but common picture of the Italian singer, was a special version of the deeper American image of the artist as a child of nature. Genius was entirely a natural endowment, the product not of labor or study or artifice, but of natural instinct. Americans believed it of Jenny Lind, of Luisa Tetrazzini, and most profoundly of Caruso. "Enrico Caruso sings just as nature prepared him to sing. Art and study may have done something toward fashioning and developing the material given him," one commentator argued, "but nature itself 'placed' his voice and he sings accordingly." Caruso angrily dissented. "I am told that many people in America have the impression that my vocal ability is a kind of God-given gift, that it is something which has come to me without effort. This is so very absurd that I can hardly believe that sensible people would give it a moment's credence."[12] But sensible people did just that.

This image of Caruso is uncannily like that of another male culture hero of the time. He too was childlike and a "natural," possessed a great talent as well as an earthy desire for women and fun, spent his money and his gifts prodigally. He was a boorish character who drank, which contrasted with Caruso's delicacy of behavior. Both men were creatures of the press and of publicity, both made fabulous amounts of money and came to seem larger than life. Babe Ruth was the Caruso of baseball.

T h e r e was one other star at the Metropolitan whose career (from 1906 uninter-ruptedly until 1922) paralleled Caruso's, who sang often with him, rivaled him as a public favorite, and, the most American of the American singers of the time, excited a special kind of public adulation. Geraldine Farrar (1882–1967), of Melrose, Mas-sachusetts, was the daughter of a baseball player who had a fine singing voice, and of a mother who was also interested in music and fanatically dedicated to her daughter's success. As a child, Geraldine's voice was "like a rich cello." At twelve she imperso-nated Jenny Lind in a local festival, "quite free from affectation in her obvious happiness and ease in appearing upon a public stage." The first opera she saw was *Carmen,* with Emma Calvé, "the supreme and daring French woman never to be forgotten once heard." She studied with teachers in Boston and New York, sang for Lillian Nordica, whom she later called "an example for all time of talent, perseverance and courage," and for Nellie Melba, "miraculously endowed with the finest natural vocal equipment since Patti." Both urged her to go to Europe. A friend loaned the family the money. Father, mother, and daughter sailed from Boston: "Our purses were thin but our hopes were boundless." Nordica's introductions enabled them to settle in Berlin, where Geraldine studied with Lilli Lehmann.[13] Although entirely without operatic experience, she had a remarkable musical memory, could dispense with prompters and "sense orchestral cues almost before they were played." Her voice, thin at the top, was beautiful in the middle and was suited for lyrical roles. Her strengths were intelligence, a fresh, enchanting beauty, and a vivid stage presence.

On October 15, 1901, at age nineteen, Farrar made her Berlin operatic debut as Marguerite in Gounod's *Faust* (though in Germany in those days this French trivializ-ation of a German classic was always billed as *Margarethe*). "No meteor or dazzling comet but a steady star was born that night." Once launched, she sailed steadily on to other roles, by Puccini, Massenet, Mozart (Zerlina in *Don Giovanni*), and to other places—Munich, Salzburg, Stockholm, Monte Carlo, where she vividly remembered meeting the tenor with whom she was to sing in *La Bohème,* an "apparition that walked into the first rehearsal clad in shrieking checks, topped by a grey fedora, yellow gloves grasping a gold-headed cane." She and Caruso would meet again.

Stories about her poured across the ocean and were snapped up by American readers, but not because of her singing and acting. The German crown prince, Friedrich Wilhelm, had fallen madly in love with her, it was said. Glamor and romance! "Ridiculous gossip and shameful observations ripened into the screaming headlines of scandal and libelous affirmation," in her mother's view. Her father, incensed by one newspaper story and "determined to avenge his daughter in the old-fashioned American way," pursued the editor and knocked him down. *Was* the crown prince her lover? The American Women's Club of Berlin wrote to the press to deny it. When Farrar signed to sing at the Metropolitan, her name was already well known, though she had never sung a note professionally in America. She was engaged for November 26, 1906, the only Metropolitan opening in which Caruso did not take part. The opera was Gounod's *Roméo et Juliette.* Farrar was cordially received: a "beautiful vision," a voice of "exquisite quality in the middle register." But the publicity produced a backlash and "critical resistance to her was more than moderate." "Miss Farrar has yet thrown but a pebble into the vast sea of vocal art." Also, there were many other accomplished singers who had prior claims to many of the roles she wanted. Her first popular success (remember: Puccini didn't like it very much) came with the Metropolitan's first *Madama Butterfly,* in February 1906. Not especially keen on contemporary opera, Farrar nevertheless appeared in some significant Metropolitan premieres: the first American performance of Humperdinck's *The King's Children* (*Königskinder*) in 1910, Charpentier's *Julien,* the long-awaited sequel to *Louise,* in 1913, Puccini's *Sister Angelica* (*Suor Angelica*) in 1918. Leoncavallo's *Zazà* (1919) was a personal success, at the end of her career. Her most famous roles were in established favorites, each of which she gave a personal quality—*Tosca, Carmen, Manon,* Cherubino in *Le Nozze di Figaro,* "under the magical Mahler," "a well-nigh perfect tribute to Mozart."

Farrar's popularity was more personal than that of any other American singer who had preceded her. People identified with Geraldine Farrar as much as with her Carmen or Tosca. They admired her combative independence. She stood up to anyone—Conried, Gatti-Casazza, Toscanini. ("I have never seen Vesuvius in eruption, but probably no more inflammable combustion takes place in its venerable interior than in the person of this musical Napoleon, when the wild mood is upon him," she wrote.) During World War I, she entertained German colleagues and friends and spoke well of Germany, which gained her a good deal of hate mail, but also respect. She represented nonconformity, rebellion against authority. Her realistic acting reflected greater sexual frankness, heightened by her lithe physical appeal. Richard Strauss had tried to interest her in singing Salome, totally unsuited to her voice: "You, Farrar," he told her, "have such dramatic possibilities, can act and dance half-naked, so no one will care if you sing or not." As Zazà she played a music hall entertainer in love with a married man, who at the end goes back to a previous lover. In the first act Farrar dressed and undressed before the audience. Some people purported to be shocked. Her father refused to watch the first act at all. To many, however, the performance was in keeping with her honesty.

At the same time, the great diva who had perhaps had a romantic affair with a crown prince was possessed of a no-nonsense matter-of-factness. There was always something of the tomboy about Farrar. It isn't clear how attractive men really were to her. She was unsnobbish about new forms of popular culture, the first opera star to take cinema seriously. She made a dozen movies, most of them not versions of operas. In 1915 she went to Hollywood to film *Carmen.* The young and admiring Agnes de Mille watched her with fascination. Farrar arrived with great pomp, with her mother, her father, her French maid, her business manager, her hairdresser, and two lady companions, all at the studio's expense. "That was quite proper. If she had come in any lesser manner we would have been disappointed." And yet, offstage she was sparkling, unassuming. One evening, at Cecil B. de Mille's house, she entertained guests after dinner. "She took off her black pearl rings, large as robin's eggs, her diamond and pearl bracelets, and tossed them on top of the piano, then sat down and played like a man—music and song and laughter reverberating throughout the house." Everyone adored "our Gerry."[14]

Geraldine Farrar was the first opera singer to treat movies as a serious art form. In this still from Jesse L. Lasky's 1915 film version of Carmen, *she brandishes a dagger in the brawl with Frasquita. Library of Congress.*

Like Caruso, Farrar made a large number of recordings, the earliest dating from her Berlin years. A perceptive critic noted that her singing was "startlingly original," "full of verve and passion, yet very modern, with none of the swooping into notes so prevalent at the time." Farrar felt at ease with the new technique. Unlike Nordica, whose recordings were few and disappointing in quality, Farrar's give us a good idea of the voice her contemporaries heard. She was "America's first superstar: a world-renowned media figure."[15]

The most remarkable aspect of Farrar's popular appeal was the "Gerryflapper" phenomenon. The critic W. J. Henderson coined the term to describe the large, unorganized, but fiercely vocal and loyal admirers who followed her from performance to performance—groupies of the 1910s and 1920s. "What is a Gerryflapper?" Henderson asked—and answered: "Simply a girl about the flapper age who has created in her own half baked mind a goddess which she names Geraldine Farrar."[16] Men made fun, but the Gerryflappers were the most intense public response to a singer since Jenny Lind. Farrar's attraction had two sources for women. Even though the public knew nothing of one explosive sexual affair, with Toscanini, Farrar represented unconcealed sexuality. She married once, a much publicized union with a movie actor, Lou Tellegen. It ended in an acrimonious divorce. The second source was her defiance of the operatic establishment. It was men she was defying, formidable, all-powerful men. Other incidents from her career carried these same associations. In *Carmen,* in 1916, she slapped Caruso resoundingly in act 1, and the entire performance was filled with reckless physicality. Caruso was angry and threatened not to sing with her again, but they made it up. One critic called it "disillusioning vulgarity," and it has always been taken as another example of Farrar's desire for realism. But to the young women who adored her, it was a feminist slap, the diva fighting back. In their behavior at her performances, the Gerryflappers got their message across in many ways. They stood in line for hours for standing room. They weren't regular operagoers, let alone subscribers. They cheered their heroine, screamed their approval.

Farrar abruptly announced her retirement from opera at the end of the 1921–1922 season, saying that she had always planned to leave the stage at forty. When she appeared in *Faust* soon afterward, there was a great demonstration of affection for her. People wept and waved handkerchiefs. She spoke to them: "Children, this is no occasion for a funeral." In the following weeks she appeared as Louise, Manon, Tosca, Marguerite, Carmen, "each occasion more hysterical than the last." With familiar mean-spiritedness, the unforgiving Gatti-Casazza chose *Zazà* as Farrar's farewell opera. Though intended by the Metropolitan as a snub, it was an appropriate choice—entirely her own role, redolent of her nonconformity. April 22 marked the end, "one of the most sensational demonstrations ever put on at the Metropolitan," "bordering closely upon mob-hysteria." "The singular fervor of the Gerryflappers excelled all bounds." They hung banners from the boxes, let loose balloons in the auditorium. After act 2 they presented her with a crown and scepter. When it was over Farrar stepped before the curtain. "I don't want a tear in this house," she said, concluding proudly: "I am leaving this institution because I want to go." Backstage she put on an outfit made by the Gerryflappers, distributed costumes and props to them, and then she was escorted to a car and driven away through ranks of cheering adorers.[17]

By contrast, Caruso represented the past—for some, the worst of the past: vocalism for its own sake, everything that supposedly had been discarded with Patti and Melba, the Italian vocal machine running of its own accord and beginning, at last, to run down. There had always been criticism of Caruso's style: Bonci was more subtle, Slezak had greater dramatic power. Caruso, it was charged, pandered to the applause

When Farrar retired from the stage in 1922, her fans—dubbed "Gerryflappers" by the critic W. J. Henderson—carried her through the streets of New York. **Opera News / Metropolitan Opera Guild.**

of the vulgar who were excited by the high notes, by the lingering on final phrases, by the ever-present Caruso sob. A character in Ernest Hemingway's *A Farewell to Arms,* that bible of the disillusioned of the 1920s, dismissed him brutally: "Caruso bellows." Critics in Havana were savage: "CARUSO ON THE EDGE OF THE ABYSS." "Tremendous failure of the ex-divo." He had been vastly overpraised, so it was said, his reputation due to the power and money of the Metropolitan. There was resentment at his outrageous fees. And now that voice was in decline.[18]

Though he feigned indifference, Caruso was sensitive to such comments. His voice had darkened—he was forty in 1913—and it was fashionable to say, even among those favorably disposed to him, that his great period had ended. (Some said his great period had ended *before* he came to the Metropolitan.) Even though he still sang with that "complete abandonment to his part" which impressed the young German soprano Lotte Lehmann, there was no question that Caruso looked back wistfully to an earlier time (perhaps imaginary) when "my reputation did not run any risk if I sang a false note. And I sang for the sheer joy of singing, with untortured nerves, without a worry in the world." Now he saw himself as unavoidably locked in a deadly combat with the expectations of his audiences. "Each time I sing I feel that there is someone waiting to destroy me, and I must fight like a bull to hold my own."

It wasn't as the clown in *I Pagliacci* that he finally showed the world how he could fuse his voice and musical instincts in true dramatic impersonation. It was as Eléazar, in a revival of Halévy's old French opera *La Juive,* the tragic outsider, the victim of fate, that the tenor was lost in the role. "In face, figure and bearing he makes of this operatic Shylock an interpretation which will remain long in the memory of those who saw it." "He raised himself a good notch higher in artistic stature" and won the "respect and admiration of all who regard operatic creations as of more import in art than their interpreters." But, as one critic noted sadly, "few of the million devoted admirers of his voice care."[19]

W a r exploded across the European and American operatic worlds in August 1914. The formal position of the United States government was clear: strict neutrality. Neutrality "in thought and deed," Woodrow Wilson admonished his fellow citizens, advice they found difficult to follow since the general feeling was that the Germans were more to blame for the war than anyone else, a feeling the British and French deftly exploited. Musical institutions were especially vulnerable to such feelings, because Germans played so prominent a role in them. "Should we boycott the printers because Guttenberg, a German, invented printing?" asked Gatti-Casazza.[20] National rivalries had influenced opera throughout its history, but the consequences of war upon artists had been random. As war took on a more popular character, centering on the willingness or unwillingness of the people to fight, art—song, symbol, image—was increasingly enrolled by the state in strengthening the resolve of its people, weakening that of its enemies. By the early twentieth century, new military technology affected everyone, as the Metropolitan Opera realized. In January 1916, as part of the Gatti-Casazza regime's policy of prestige through world premieres, the Metropolitan presented *Scenes from Goya, or The Fancy Ladies in Love (Goyescas, o Las Majas enamoradas)* by Enrique Granados (1867–1916), the first Spanish opera ever performed there. (The libretto was translated by James Weldon Johnson.) The composer was present and enthusiastically greeted, his opera less so. In March he and his wife sailed for home on the steamer *Sussex,* which was torpedoed and sunk by a German submarine. Both were drowned. The *Sussex* affair was a crisis of American neutrality, resolved only when Germany accepted an ultimatum from Wilson. All through 1915 and 1916 the American public's mood was volatile. Unpredictable things ignited controversy. Summer concerts in New York, given under municipal auspices for a number of years, now provoked letters protesting the presence of foreign performers. "Why are these affairs always put in the hands of foreigners . . . who know nothing of our ideals and aspirations?" a typical one ran. The Chicago Opera staged its first complete *Ring* cycle in 1915. It was greeted with rapture. One year later, when the cycle was repeated, the city's German population stayed home, "probably because they feared being condemned as un-American."[21]

The declaration of war against Germany and its allies by the United States on April 6, 1917 was followed by two acts which affected musical entertainment. The Federal Fuel Administrator decreed that all theaters had to remain dark one night a week. And Congress levied a 10 percent tax on tickets for theater and concerts. The most important consequence of the formal declaration was its effect on public emotions. President Wilson insisted that the war was directed only against the German government, not against the German people, but the general public ignored Wilson's antiquated point of view and directed the full force of its wrath against German ideas and German culture.

The previous popularity of musical artists was no protection. Violinist Fritz Kreisler was refused permission to play in Pittsburgh, which set a high standard for patriotic zeal by banning *all* German music. Frederick Stock, Theodore Thomas's successor as conductor of the Chicago Symphony and a venerable figure in the city, though still a German citizen, was forced into retirement for two years. German names were removed from buildings and streets, and absurdity approached its apex when sauerkraut was renamed "liberty cabbage." Belligerency increased the greater the distance from the actual fighting. California state authorities, arguing that German folksongs in school music books might produce negative emotional response, removed them. Nothing equaled the fury directed at orchestras, the nineteenth-century takeover by German instrumentalists now meeting its nemesis. The most shameful story was the rage directed at the Boston Symphony's conductor, Karl Muck, actually a Swiss citizen but German-born and German in culture, because he did not wish to play "The Star-Spangled Banner" before each concert. "Why will people be so silly?" Muck asked. "Art is a thing by itself and not related to a particular nation or group." The naïveté of his view was soon demonstrated. Under the enemy alien proclamation issued by Wilson, police censored Muck's mail, searched his house, arrested him there, seized his papers and letters, charged him with being a danger to the peace and safety of the country, and turned him over to military authorities, who imprisoned him at Fort Oglethorpe, Georgia. He was joined by Ernst Kunwald, conductor of the Cincinnati Symphony, who had been charged with espionage. They were imprisoned for over a year, ample time to reflect on the blessings of law and order, before being deported to Germany in August 1919.[22]

The operatic repertory, and German singers, absorbed the patriotic heat. News of the United States' declaration of war came to the Metropolitan on Good Friday, during a performance of *Parsifal*. A prelude of things to come, Johanna Gadski, respected Wagnerian soprano and outspoken patriot, was encouraged to "retire" at the end of the season. In the fall, only a week before the season's opening, the Metropolitan announced that all German operas would be prohibited for the duration of the war, "lest Germany should make capital of their continued appearance to convince the German people that this nation was not heart and soul in the war." All the leading German singers—Carl Braun, Otto Goritz, Melanie Kurt, Margarete Ober, Johannes Sembach—were summarily dismissed.[23] The Chicago Opera abandoned its German season. This frenzy did *not* die down with the end of the war but, in the Red Scare of 1919–1921, was directed at a different target, with Lenin replacing the kaiser as the requisite bogeyman. Slowly, the German repertory was restored in American opera houses. Sauerkraut returned, as did German folksongs. The dismissed opera singers did not, nor did Karl Muck. The deepest effect of the wartime excesses was not felt immediately: the further discrediting of nationalism among young musicians everywhere.

T h e Metropolitan Opera's opening night in 1918 was November 11, Armistice Day; the opera, Saint-Saëns' *Samson et Dalila,* evidence of the genius of France triumphant over the arrogant Hun, with Caruso serving as proof of the re-establishment of the old operatic order. He was directly responsible for another thing—a star singer—the Metropolitan looked for to revive the good old days. (What it most needed was Arturo Toscanini, but that was not to be.) That star appeared in the person of a new American soprano, Rosa Ponselle. Born Rosa Ponzillo, in Meriden, Connecticut, in 1897, of immigrant Neapolitan parents, she had a little teaching but gained most of her knowledge of how to sing by appearing with her sister Carmella in local cinemas and in vaudeville. One night Caruso heard her, quickly recognized the full possibilities of her luscious voice, and urged Gatti-Casazza to engage her. Within a year, with Caruso's encouragement and support, and with extra teaching, this operatic fairy tale became a reality. Ponselle's first operatic performance was at the Metropolitan, at age twenty-one, singing alongside Caruso in a revival of Verdi's *La Forza del destino,* unheard in New York since 1882.

Opening night for the 1920–1921 season was *La Juive,* and "club land, automobiledom, and the mercantile realm" turned out in force. Unfortunately, Caruso was in very bad voice. He regained his form in the three following performances and then, on December 8, he "pulled a muscle" during a performance of *I Pagliacci,* which left him in considerable pain. Caruso had always been remarkably conscientious about appearing as scheduled, and he was all too aware of the Metropolitan's dependence on him, so he went ahead with a performance of *L'Elisir d'amore* scheduled for December 11 at the Brooklyn Academy of Music. Soon after he began singing that night, he started spitting up blood, but he refused to stop and made it through to the end only because people behind the scenes passed him handkerchiefs to soak up the blood. His condition was diagnosed as lumbago and, astoundingly, he was allowed to sing again on the 13th. "Happiness reigned supreme," even if common sense was

Amiable, unintellectual, a primo divo without temperament, Caruso was the first widely popular male opera singer in America. This sheet music cover attests to his image as a nice guy with a common touch.

absent, when he made it through *La Forza del destino.* He missed his next scheduled performance, but believed he was well enough to sing in *La Juive* on the 24th. He finished in agonizing pain and went home to bed. He never sang again.

This time his condition was diagnosed as pleurisy, and he was required to rest for several months. The anxious public was reassured that all would be well. "Enrico Caruso will without any doubt again take his glorious post at the Metropolitan," Gatti-Casazza said. In May he returned to Naples to recuperate. In July he became much worse. Two operations followed. Caruso died on August 2, 1921. A popular song attempted to find consolation: "They Wanted a Songbird in Heaven, So They Took Our Caruso Away."[24] Every imaginable aspect of his art and life and career was touched upon in the volumes of commentary in newspapers and magazines. One recurrent theme was that his career had somehow been cut short. Although Caruso was forty-eight and had been singing for thirty years, that feeling was understandable. The public had come to believe that Caruso's art and voice would go on forever, that he was immortal.

We come back to the Caruso recordings. Wasn't the public right? Alfred Kazin, literary critic and memoirist, as a young boy in New York, would crank up the old brown Victrola for his mother and father—Amelita Galli-Curci, John McCormack, and "the high point," Caruso singing from *La Juive*. He inspired in the Kazin parents "such helpless, intimidated adoration" that the boy came to think of his voice as the invocation of a god, giving pleasure far beyond music. Caruso, "that Italyener," seemed the echo of a pagan voice singing from the roof of the world, "rising higher and higher with each note, that voice, that *golden voice,* leaping its way from one trapeze to another, while the listeners sat hunched in wonder and adoration and fear." Would he make it? Could any human being find that last impossible rung?

And then, suddenly bounding back to earth again, there was Caruso before them, "the voice welling out of him with such brazen strength, such irresistible energy, that he left them gasping—a centaur just out of the woods, not quite human, with that enigmatic, almost contemptuous smile on his face. 'What a voice!' my father would say over and over, deeply shaken. 'What a voice! It's not human! Never was there a voice like it! Only the other day I was reading that when they opened him up after he died they found his vocal chords were absolutely unique!' Then, his face white with pleasure, with amazement, with wonder: 'Oh that Italyener! Oh that Italyener! What a power he has, that Italyener!'"[25]

act five

Technology, 1921–1950

And now you hear not only a Handel who, disfigured by radio, is, all the same, in this most ghastly of disguises still divine; you hear as well and you observe, a most admirable symbol of all life. When you listen to radio you are a witness to the everlasting war between idea and appearance, between time and eternity, between the human and the divine.

—*Hermann Hesse*

In a time like ours, when the genius of engineers has reached such undreamed of proportions, one can hear famous pieces of music as easily as one can buy a glass of beer. It only costs ten centimes, too, just like automatic weighing scales! Should we not fear this domestication of sound, this magic preserved in a disc that anyone can awaken at will? Will it not mean a diminution of the secret forces of art, which until now have been considered indestructible?

—*Claude Debussy*

Chicago and Samuel Insull

The stock market crash of October 1929 broke the interwar years into two pieces—the glamorous, prosperous 1920s and the grim, impoverished 1930s. Operatically, the two periods were the reverse: the dazzling surface prosperity of the 1920s concealed ominous operatic decline, while the hard times of the 1930s obscured emerging creativity and growth. The Metropolitan Opera dominated American opera in the 1920s more than ever before. The Chicago Opera surpassed the Metropolitan in many ways but couldn't compete with it in national prestige. Elsewhere, the operatic picture was gloomy. For the first time in a century the amount of opera available to the American public had decreased. There were fewer touring companies. Opera houses closed down. New Orleans was without a company. San Francisco opera languished. Boston and Philadelphia were operatic colonies of New York and Chicago.

How different the 1930s! Early in the decade the Chicago Opera declared bankruptcy. Even the mighty Metropolitan lurched toward collapse. Radio, sound film, and records threw thousands of musicians out of work. Music teachers were among the first to lose their jobs. In 1935, about two-thirds of unemployed artists were musicians and teachers of music.[1] And yet: under the rubble there was life. American opera developed an identity and style rooted in native traditions. Conservatories began to redeem the unfulfilled promise of those nineteenth-century academies of music. Thousands of European musicians crossed the Atlantic, not for pots of gold but for asylum. They would stay and enrich their new home. Radio and recordings created a new opera audience, unbounded by theater walls and old categories of social class. And, finally, America began national patronage of the arts.

C h i c a g o opera was the most interesting in America in the 1920s. With the opening of the Auditorium Building in 1889, the city reaffirmed the American axiom that it was easier to build an opera house than to found an opera company or create an operatic audience. Chicago depended on touring companies for its opera. The repertory it heard between 1889 and 1909—278 performances of seventy-nine different operas—was thoroughly conventional. There was nothing to suggest that the city might be favorable to innovation. As it had showed in 1885–1887, however, Chicago was capable of surprises. In 1909 visits by two opera companies had opposite consequences. The Boston Opera Company came for two weeks and encouraged those people who wanted a resident company, not merely "the tail of the Metropolitan kite," but one in which "ensemble and adequate performance must be the slogan instead of 'plenty of stars.'"[2] A month later, in blew the Metropolitan kite, stars blazing. Behind its visit lay a more complex story.

As so often, we cross the trail of the Manhattan Opera Company. Oscar Hammerstein had seriously considered expanding into Chicago, as he had into Philadelphia. To forestall this, and to protect Chicago as a Metropolitan Opera market, Otto Kahn helped create a company—the Chicago/Philadelphia Grand Opera Company—ostensibly independent but really under absentee control. The 1910 roster of sponsoring Chicagoans also included directors from the Metropolitan's board, most notably Otto Kahn, plus Philadelphians. The Chicago/Philadelphia Company and the Metropolitan agreed not to invade the other's territory and not to bid against each other for singers. The visit of the Metropolitan in the spring of 1910, therefore, was a triumphant display of the benefits of this kind of territorial market division. The Metropolitan had frequently antagonized the provinces by substituting second-line casts with little notice and no explanation. This time it proudly displayed its riches, bringing a double company, German and Italian, two sets of principal singers, two choruses, two orchestras, and the two chief conductors, Alfred Hertz and Arturo Toscanini.[3]

The story of the next half-decade was the transformation of this New York-Chicago-Philadelphia cartel into a genuinely Chicago enterprise, planting the seeds for the efflorescence of the 1920s. The seedbed was the Manhattan company, vanquished in New York, reborn on the shores of Lake Michigan. Cleofonte Campanini came as musical director, bringing with him Mary Garden, Maurice Renaud, Charles Dalmorès, his old production staff, the Manhattan's sets and costumes, musical scores and rights to French opera, which the Metropolitan had no intention of presenting. The sensation of the season was Garden's *Salome*. Over the next half-dozen years, Campanini proved himself as resourceful in spotting talent as Hammerstein had been: Maggie Teyte, Jeanne Gerville-Réache, Rosa Raisa, Conchita Supervia, a sensational coloratura soprano, Amelita Galli-Curci, and Titta Ruffo, one of the remarkable male voices of the twentieth century.

Not content with remarkable singers, Campanini slowly broadened the Chicago repertory with *Monna Vanna, Il Segreto di Susanna, I Gioielli della Madonna* (rehearsed twenty-seven times: "To be ready is to be right," Campanini declared). He conducted more Wagner than anyone had before in Chicago, until the war made that impossible, and established his characteristic high standards of ensemble. A remarkably imaginative novelty was his concert performance of Claudio Monteverdi's *Orfeo*. This long, long forgotten opera by opera's inventor demonstrated conclusively that "opera composition may have gained something of deftness in three hundred years but certainly little in actual musical beauty." Thus did Chicago begin to repay America's debt to the Florentine Camerata of three centuries before. Unfortunately, this was premature. The Auditorium was one-third filled for *Orfeo*. And at the same time Campanini commissioned a contemporary work by Sergei Prokofiev.[4]

These things were made possible, financially, by the most generous of individual American patrons of opera—the McCormicks. Harold Fowler McCormick was heir to a farm machinery fortune. His wife, née Edith Rockefeller, the youngest daughter of John D., reserved, quiet, imperious, achieved the American middle-class dream of true aristocratic confidence. Edith Rockefeller never bothered to explain or defend anything she did. For her, "democracy was only a word in the dictionary." Harold was her opposite in many ways, charming, affable, with a gallant manner, interested in oddities and innovations. They were married in 1895, settled in Chicago in 1897. They entertained in their Lake Shore Drive mansion in splendid state. So long as she wished to exercise it, Edith Rockefeller McCormick's cultural leadership was undisputed. How could it not be? Daughter of the richest man in the world, her personal fortune was at one time estimated at $40 million. She taught Chicago "how to wear and to own a dress suit," but not how to drink champagne. She was a fanatical "dry."

Both McCormicks adored opera. She hated hymns because her pious father had made her sing them so often as a girl. Her musical interests were wide-ranging. Her specialty was subsidizing aspiring composers, and her support for innumerable artists of all kinds was generous, private, unpublicized. Harold was enthusiastic. After opening night in 1910, he said: "Everybody's happy. We could not ask for more." But he *did* more. He bought up all the shares in the company held by non-Chicagoans. That was how Chicago became independent. Two things marred this glowing picture. In 1913, depressed by the death of a son, still on amicable terms with Harold although their marriage was clearly under strain, Edith went to Switzerland to seek spiritual healing and to study with Carl Jung. She stayed away for eight years, while Harold remained in Chicago and happily absorbed the annual opera deficits. The second event was Campanini's death of pneumonia in January 1919. Elaborate and moving funeral services were held in the Auditorium. The magnitude of Chicago's loss was disguised for a time by the surplus of energy and excitement that had been released, but the guiding and restraining hand necessary to control the formidable array of singers and to make the most of McCormick patronage was sorely missed. Campanini's immediate successors didn't satisfy, so an unusual choice of director was made in 1921.[5]

O r rather, of Directa, since it was Mary Garden who was chosen and who insisted upon being so titled. Her employers would have been well advised to learn what it was she most admired about Oscar Hammerstein: that he wanted "the finest or nothing at all. Money never meant a damn to him." Garden embarked on a spending season of formidable proportions. She brought singers—Maria Ivogün, Marguerite D'Alvarez—from anywhere for a single appearance. She spared no expense in achieving her artistic goals, but they seemed improvised from week to week. Some singers sang only once, some twice, some were paid for performances which didn't take place, as the Directa changed her mind. One patron ruefully reported that "in any week of the season the lobby company far outnumbered the singing company." As much Italian opera was given as French. German opera was brought back after its wartime banishment. The most interesting opera of the season was Russian, Campanini's commission, *The Love for Three Oranges* (*L'Amour des trois oranges*) by Prokofiev (1891–1953), who had been in America for several years, composing, playing the piano, conducting his modernist music. Boris Anisfeld's set made the work "brilliant as spectacle," and it was staged with great imagination, but the audiences, though attendance was good, were bemused. It was the standard complaint: Without tunes, what was the use of opera? There *were* tunes but the audience couldn't yet hear them.

There were other forms of excitement, backstage rows, clashes of personalities, all reported with exuberance in the newspapers. Garden never failed to make her side of things public. "Somebody is always running Miss Mary through a printing press," the *Chicago Tribune* commented. When Lucien Muratore, a French tenor, resigned in protest about something, Garden responded with a jingoist vigor that would have done "Big Bill" Thompson, the notorious Chicago mayor, proud: "Foreign dictation is a thing of the past. We are to have a little American dictation for a while and see how that will work out." It endeared Mary to the "Garden City." At a charity affair a demented man threw a gun at Garden's feet. When interviewed in jail, he said only: "She talks too much." The season ended in "magnificent smashing ruin," with a deficit of a million dollars. Garden rose above it all. "It was news to me. It may very well have happened, but I didn't know. I do know that we finished in the way Mr. McCormick wanted us to finish—in a blaze of glory. . . . If it cost a million dollars, I'm sure it was worth it." Although Mary Garden insisted she could have stayed on had she wished, and did stay on as a singer with the company, she resigned, in a "very gentlemanly manner," as Directa.[6]

Harold McCormick paid the bill. But for the last time. He transferred his patronage from the opera company to an opera singer, Gana Walska, a Polish soprano whose modest musical talents were compensated for by an irresistible appeal to men. The McCormicks separated in 1917. Harold and Gana began a protracted and exceedingly public love affair. The McCormicks divorced in 1921. The Chicago Opera had to look elsewhere for support.[7]

Enter Samuel Insull. The son of a preacher and a temperance worker, born in London in 1859, Insull came to America in 1881 to work with Thomas Edison. In 1892 he moved to Chicago and entered the electrical business. By 1907 he was head of Commonwealth Edison and in control of everything connected with electricity in the city, and much involved with all public utilities as well. He made a colossal fortune. Personally honest, he was willing to use the city's corrupt political machine for his own interests. He saw himself as a populist Prince of Electricity, serving the people, as well as himself, and felt contempt for those of inherited wealth, less able and ambitious than he, who had always looked down on "new" men. This attitude dominated his increasing involvement in the arts. For several years Insull had been president of the Chicago Opera's board of directors. With the McCormicks' withdrawal, he took control. The opera company was reconstituted as the Chicago Civic Opera and announced un-Gardenish policies: "We will spend *our own* money."

Under Insull, the box office played a greater role than before in determining repertory. Operas that didn't draw were "speedily packed away." Despite a fine production and performance, "*Parsifal* went into the discard. *Die Walküre* disappeared in the same manner." Garden's championing of new operas was cut back as well. Garden went to see Insull about this. As she entered his office, she noticed an

Samuel Insull, a populist businessman of conservative musical tastes, briefly put opera in Chicago on a new footing in the 1920s. His portrait appeared on the cover of Time *on Nov. 4, 1929.*

enormous painting of Adelina Patti hanging on the wall facing his desk. It had been years since Patti had stopped singing, and Garden asked, jokingly, why Insull didn't replace Patti with a portrait of *her*. He replied: "Miss Garden, I hate modern opera. I like the old things."

At the same time, Insull genuinely wished a radical reconstitution of the social basis of opera's support. He launched a high-powered drive to raise a five-year guarantee fund of half a million dollars for the company, not by looking for five hundred people who would subscribe a thousand dollars apiece, but by encouraging guarantors who would contribute five hundred dollars, one hundred, or less. (If only Boston, ten years before, had done the same thing!) By 1928 there were thirty-two hundred guarantors, of whom 80 percent paid a hundred dollars or less per year. Yet there were limits to how far Insull would go in attacking privilege. It was the ruling elite he hated, not the idea of plutocratic privilege. When Insull's son wanted to go east to college, Insull agreed that he could go anywhere he wished, except Harvard, because Harvard men had condescended to him when he was getting started in his early Chicago years. So his son went to Yale.

This stable financial support enabled the Chicago Civic Opera Association to sustain the high level of quality of its productions and to attract remarkable European singers. Insull had no quarrel with the star system and no discernible interest in American opera. What he wanted to see and hear were the standard classics he had heard in London as a young man. Chicago was as adept as ever at finding singers who established their American reputations there and not in New York: Toti Dal Monte, Tito Schipa, Mariano Stabile, Alexander Kipnis. There were notable productions of *Der Rosenkavalier, Don Giovanni,* Rimsky-Korsakov's *The Snow Maiden.* Garden did virtually all the Massenet there was to do, though by now it seemed mild fare. *Sapho,* "wild and wicked when new," now didn't raise a moral hair. And she was allowed an occasional foray into the contemporary. One of her sensational dramatic successes was in *Resurrection (Risurezzione)* by Franco Alfano (1876–1954), better known subsequently as the composer who completed the final scene of Puccini's *Turandot* when the composer died in 1924. She succeeded in making *Judith* by Arthur Honegger (1892–1955) dramatically effective, though its austere declamatory style resisted popularity. That was Garden's last important novelty. She retired in 1934, singing *Risurezzione* at the Opéra-Comique in Paris, where she had begun her amazing career.

Chicago's major claim to significance in the history of opera in America has received scant attention. Between 1910 and 1929 it became the first large-scale, *national* American opera company by virtue of its lengthy, sustained, geographically wide-ranging tours. It prided itself on its 216 appearances in New York, challenging the Metropolitan head-on. But its greatest impact was elsewhere. In those same years it presented 1,009 performances in sixty-two other cities. All regions of the country were visited. It was Chicago which brought at least one night or day of opera of a high caliber to Helena, Fort Wayne, Indianapolis, Joplin, Nashville and Rochester, to St. Joseph, Salt Lake City, San Diego, and Spokane. The touring repertory was standard, but novelties were sometimes included. What did Birmingham make of *Risurezzione?* Chattanooga of *Mefistofele? Time* magazine, in a cover story about Samuel Insull in 1929, noted that he and his opera company did things on "the largest scale," "all over the country," not just "a few big cultural capitals where Otto Kahn's Metropolitan goes, but country-wide expeditions." Performing opera is a complex act of indeterminable consequences and it is, along with its less exalted aspects, an act of faith. And Chicago kept that faith.[8]

I n December 1925, Insull revealed the "stupendous dream" that had been occupying him for some time: a new opera house. The "venerated" Auditorium was aging and obsolete (he said). Anyway, Chicago opera audiences had to free themselves from the elitist associations of the past. The slogan for the future would be, Opera for the people. The new order would "take the high hat out of grand opera." Furthermore, the new opera house would be part of a large commercial building, revenues from which would be used to ensure the opera company a stable income. "The more things change . . . ," the ghost of Ferdinand Peck muttered.

Insull, being Insull, went rapidly ahead. He already had the site, Madison Street and Wacker Drive. Chicago being Chicago, the opera house would be a skyscraper, symbolizing "the spirit of a community which is still youthful and not much hampered by traditions." No more copies of European palaces. Financing, planning, and construction took three and a half years. The architects, Graham, Anderson, Probst, and White, a Chicago firm, were not Sullivan and Adler, but they at least spared the city another *Tribune* Tower. "Modernistic," relentlessly vertical in its lines, the new building had seven hundred thousand square feet of floor space, with a forty-two-

Chicago's new Civic Opera House in 1929. A forty-two-story skyscraper that cost twenty million dollars, it was meant to symbolize "the spirit of a community which is still youthful and not much hampered by traditions." Library of Congress.

419

story central tower looking down on two symmetrical lower wings, the whole forming a square U. It cost twenty million dollars.

The opera house itself was an effort to combine modernism, democracy, and luxury. The lobby was faced with Roman marble. Large bronze doors opened onto the grand foyer, with an imposing staircase leading from there to the mezzanine foyer. The oak-paneled auditorium was narrow and deep, seating 3,472 people, 1,682 of them in the orchestra. There were thirty-one boxes, tucked away in the first tier behind and above the main floor, "like the mezzanine floor in a great motion picture palace," designed "for those who come to opera to look at the stage and not at each other." There was no individual ownership of boxes, which were rented for a three-year period, but, as the first historian of the opera house noted reassuringly, "in practice, boxes will probably be kept in certain families and handed down to on-coming generations, about as they are in the Metropolitan Opera House." Above the boxes were two more tiers with 800 seats in each. "As a further tribute to democracy the lavish furnishing and decorations of the main floor had been carried through to the upper tiers." The lighting system, controlled by one person, was capable of extraordinary effects, and the equipment, "dazzlingly up-to-date," which raised, lowered, and tilted the stage, elicited rhapsodic newspaper praise. The sound was inferior to that of the Auditorium, however.

The 20 Wacker Drive Corporation built, owned, and operated the building, bor-rowing $10 million from the Metropolitan Life Insurance Company at 5 percent interest. Stock was issued for the other $10 million: a hundred thousand shares were bought by the public and by the officers of the corporation. The Civic Opera paid rent of $180,000 a year, and though revenue from the office space, shops, and concessions was estimated at $2.5 million, interest on the loan, fixed operating expenses, and dividends on the stock, plus $300,000 to be applied each year to the retirement of the mortgage, meant that the company would be dependent for many years on public support. In twenty-five years, it was confidently believed, building and opera house would be clear. In the meantime, and for all Insull's populist protestations, the opera house was an autocracy and its future rested on his power and money.[9]

The last opera given at the Auditorium, *Roméo et Juliette,* was the one that had opened it. At the end the orchestra played "Home, Sweet Home," and a few people there might have recalled Adelina Patti forty years before. Many people hated leaving the Auditorium, because of its rich memories, because of its wonderful sound, because they despised Samuel Insull and his massive power. "People were forced into subscribing to the Opera Building." "It was held over their heads like a club. . . . They had to put a certain amount of money into it, otherwise Insull would withdraw his support."

Such sentiments proved to Insull that he was on the right track. They were the plaintive wail of people deprived of a privilege. Despite the sickening sycophancy which surrounded him, there is no doubt he was a kind of popular hero to many people: "the Babe Ruth, the Jack Dempsey, the Red Grange of the business world. The people—butchers, bakers, candlestick-makers who invested their all in his stocks—fairly idolized him, and even titans viewed him with awe. He measured up to

America's image of itself: a rich, powerful, self-made giant, ruthless in smashing enemies, generous and soft-hearted in dealing with the weak." Much would depend, obviously, on how the enterprise worked out. The effusions of Insull's admirers left no room for doubt. "Mr. Insull is the kind of dreamer whose dreams come true, a poet who does not write verse but accomplishes enormous and beautiful things for the betterment of his community and nation." An admirer boasted: "Practically nothing has been left to chance."[10] Nothing, that is, but the stock market.

Otto Kahn and the Metropolitan

Prosperous and complacent, the Metropolitan Opera of the 1920s had been shaped by Gatti-Casazza into a smooth-running, money-making opera-producing machine. "Everything proceeded with certainty and calm confidence." Contrary to the sedulously promoted notion that opera was a financial burden for its patrons, the Wall Street Opera House was a cheap and appreciating investment. A profit of $48,000 in 1922 inched up to $66,000 in 1924, fell back slightly the next two years and then surged to its peak, $142,000 in 1927 and $144,000 in 1928. The season expanded as well, stretching to twenty-four weeks of opera from early November until May. The number of operas performed increased to astounding numbers—forty different productions in 1922, forty-four in 1924, forty-nine in 1929.

Although Chicago increasingly snatched away many of the finest artists, the Metropolitan's parade of famous singers seemed endless. Of the women, Maria Jeritza dominated the decade. Her startlingly good looks and theatrical flair, "enthralling vitality," and "luminous intelligence" immediately made her the commanding diva. Her first appearance, in 1921, was in a contemporary opera, Erich Korngold's *The Dead City* (*Die tote Stadt*), and she "smiled, danced and sang" her way into the affections of her audiences, her voice "flooding the auditorium with glittering tone." Equally at home in Italian and German opera, she became famous in America as Tosca. She sang "Vissi d'arte" lying on the floor, "a vocal feat as difficult as it was effective," Deems Taylor wrote, and Gatti-Casazza remembered that when the aria ended, "the theatre broke out in a demonstration the equal of which I can scarcely recall." Thereafter, Toscas everywhere assumed prone positions. Elisabeth Rethberg, Lucrezia Bori, Margaret Matzenauer were among the other stellar women singers. Antonio Scotti, among the men, went on and on, celebrating his twenty-fifth consecutive season at the Metropolitan in 1924, an unequaled career of service that went back to a time *before* Caruso.

Caruso. No discussion of singers, particularly male singers and most especially tenors, escaped his shadow. The tenors who followed him at the Metropolitan—Beniamino Gigli, Giovanni Martinelli, Tito Schipa (at the end of the decade)—were remarkable singers. Each achieved fame and popularity. Yet it wasn't, somehow, enough. Caruso's death ended an era, although few explained what it was that was over. Busy scanning the horizon for the next Caruso, the public barely noticed two singers. Lauritz Melchior had begun as a baritone and was still converting himself into a tenor when he first sang at the Metropolitan in *Tannhäuser.* Recognizing that he needed more training, he returned to Europe for further study and didn't make his Metropolitan mark until his first *Tristan,* in 1929. Ezio Pinza appeared in a large number of small roles: in *Norma,* in a revival of Meyerbeer's *Le Prophète,* and, memorably, as Basilio in *Il Barbiere di Siviglia.* "What he did was what made the 'Golden Age' golden. He was an actor who could sing, a singer who could act."

Gatti-Casazza, as he had done in his "American" period in the 1910s, promoted new operas, but critics complained that he didn't sustain them once they were produced. This was because the function of the new operas was primarily social, not artistic. A new opera was a "novelty," produced to vary the routine and perhaps to divert the subscribers who, like Queen Victoria, were often *not* amused. So the novelty quickly disappeared.

The House of Puccini assembled its full resources for *Turandot* in 1926. Tulio Serafin conducted, Joseph Urban created gorgeous sets, Maria Jeritza sang the title role. It was popular on opening night and for the next four years, but the critics were hostile to its "bloated futility." It dropped from sight and sound for forty years. *Jenufa,* by Leoš Janáček (1854–1928), found its way to the Metropolitan in 1924. Again, Jeritza was in the lead. Some critics found it interesting. Those who didn't were enraged by its "dismal and repellent" story and its seemingly nonmelodic score, filled with "shrieks and shouts." After five performances that season, *Jenufa* was not given again. Richard Strauss's *The Egyptian Helen* (*Die ägyptische Helena*), yet again with Jeritza, first performed in 1928, pointed up the anomalous position of its composer in American operatic culture of the day. Although there was considerable respect for the opera's appealing music, it did nothing to dispel the by now established idea that Strauss's was "a wearied and aging muse," that no Strauss opera after *Der Rosenkavalier* was worth much. But how was any New York audience to make up its mind? The two Strauss operas following *Der Rosenkavalier, Ariadne auf Naxos* and *The Woman Without a Shadow* (*Die Frau ohne Schatten*), had never been given at the Metropolitan. The operas which preceded it, *Salome* and *Elektra,* were still banned there. For all New York knew, Richard Strauss was a one-opera composer.

Two revivals of older operas were directly attributable to the presence of a famous and suitable singing star—*Mefistofele* for Feodor Chaliapin and *Norma* for Rosa Ponselle. Two other revivals were enterprising, but not sustained: Weber's *Der Freischütz,* given during three seasons, and Mozart's *Così fan tutte,* performed for the first time ever in America in 1921, given four times that first year, three times in 1922, two times in 1923 and 1924, once in 1927, and then abandoned. The Metropolitan's treatment of Verdi was puzzling. The revival of *La Forza del destino,* for Caruso and Ponselle, was put aside. *Don Carlos* was done in two seasons, then forgotten. *Ernani* was revived, given three seasons, then dropped. *Forza* was done intermittently. *Falstaff* was restored to the repertory for three seasons, then dropped. *Otello* was not done at all for twenty-five years between 1912 and 1937. There were two notable exceptions to the Metropolitan's pattern of erratic start-and-stop. *Boris Godunov,* one of Toscanini's successes, outlasted him. Given first in 1912, it was repeated every year through 1928, time enough for an odd and difficult opera to establish itself perma-

423

nently. Equally creditable to Gatti-Casazza was his support for *Pelléas et Mélisande*. He personally disliked French opera, but when the Metropolitan finally got round to *Pelléas* in 1925, only twenty-two years after its Paris premiere, Gatti-Casazza persisted in keeping it on stage for the next decade.

Despite its profitability and prestige, there were serious problems at the "world's greatest opera house," as the Metropolitan modestly described itself. If such pretensions were a problem in themselves, at the very least they justified the application of high standards of performance. Judged by such, in Ernest Newman's view, "with its human material and its financial resources, the Metropolitan could be very much better than it is." The average performance was slipshod and getting worse. The orchestra was sloppy in execution, crude in sound. Joseph Urban's work for the company was always facile, often charming, but no longer challenging. The sets for the standard operas, in a house that lived on standard operas, were dilapidated. Gatti-Casazza was at his most cynical about such things. Were the sets for the *Ring* shabby? They only seemed so. "They are almost new, owing to the marvellous quality of pre-war German materials."

There was little performance discipline. Artur Bodanzky and Tulio Serafin, the principal German and Italian conductors, outstanding musicians, lacked the will to impose order. Or was it that they lacked management's support? Beniamino Gigli and Michael Bohnen, tenors both, didn't even pretend to aim at dramatic coherence. Bohnen wandered about the stage while others were singing or, when the whim moved him, left it altogether. Gigli voraciously craved applause, "like a picturesque beggar appealing for alms." Chaliapin was a law unto himself, always close to the line dividing inspiration from self-indulgence. At times, in *Boris Godunov*, "he may have been Boris to those interested only in Chaliapin. For those interested also in Moussorgsky, it was short measure." In his first appearance at the Metropolitan, Lauritz Melchior was introduced to its way of doing things. Not only was there *no* rehearsal, but he had not even spoken to the conductor before he sang.

Personalities played a role in this chaotic state of affairs, but the causes were also institutional. There was "a controlling element in the Metropolitan's seasons that the general public didn't know anything about." The number of operas performed—forty and more—was beyond the capacity of any opera house to do adequately. In 1919 the Metropolitan had signed a labor contract with its orchestra which, in return for improved wages, stipulated that the players could be required to perform eight times a week. To get its money's worth, the company did just that, scheduling eight, sometimes nine, weekly performances. The wear and tear on the players was immediate and destructive. The "best players in the world" (which the Metropolitan's were not) could not sustain quality in a week's work which, to give one specific example, might entail the following: a *Tristan* matinee on Friday; a triple-bill Friday night; matinee and evening performances of *Butterfly* and *Rigoletto* on Saturday; a Sunday evening concert; and then *Siegfried* on Monday night. This was mass-production, assembly-line, opera. In W. J. Henderson's words: "The faded works have been performed over and over again, most of the time with mediocre singers going through their roles like so many robots." The Metropolitan's contractual policy for singers had also been changed. Singers were hired on a half-season basis, to give the company greater flexibility for its scheduling needs, but also producing "vagrant comings and goings," the weakening of ensemble and discipline.

In November 1924, a correspondent wrote to the *New York Sun,* insisting that Henderson, its music critic, "did not tell the truth about the Metropolitan." Henderson responded by admitting the truth of the assertion. He was perfectly aware that the recent *Carmen* "was faulty from top to bottom," that *Parsifal* was "anaemic," that *Les Contes d'Hoffmann* was "feebly done." The critic who told the unvarnished truth about the Metropolitan "was as one decrying in the wilderness," Henderson glumly confessed. "The experience of years had taught that the Metropolitan is not deeply touched by newspaper criticism." It was barely to be judged by musical standards at all. It was the resort for "persons in search of relaxation." Furthermore, judged by its own standards, the Metropolitan was a rousing success. "The buffooneries of Mr. Bohnen are correct because they draw money. The dull and heavy-footed interpretations of one work after another, are correct because they draw money." Why bring up the idea of ensemble? "The dollars can be drawn without it."[1]

The Metropolitan Opera House had suited the social purposes that created it in 1883 and reached their apogee with the Diamond Horseshoe of about 1910. Half a century later, it was still owned by people, descendants of the founders, who shared their ancestors' values. But another opera audience had grown up, of musical people and of the intelligentsia, with no social standing or interest in it. That audience was contemptuous of the Metropolitan and increasingly estranged from opera. Opera and the new audience, many thoughtful observers felt, could only be joined again if a new kind of opera house was built and run on musical principles. The most interesting story at the Metropolitan in the 1920s was a battle about these issues, one fought behind the scenes. It was a story like and unlike Chicago's at the same time. In both, an individual of great wealth and influence wanted a new opera house. However, the relationship of these two individuals to the social structure of each city was very different. In Chicago, Samuel Insull, in terms of social background, was eligible for inclusion within the dominant elite, but was by temperament and inclination an outsider. Otto Kahn, in New York, was a classic insider in temperament and behavior, but an outsider in culture and background.

O t t o Herman Kahn (1867–1934) grew up in a Jewish merchant banking family in Germany, prosperous, comfortably settled in society, well connected in Jewish banking circles. Tutored privately at home, the scene of frequent musical recitals by local musicians, he substituted a passion for art for his ancestral Judaism. Kahn wrote years later: "Art was a talisman capable of accomplishing wonders far greater than Tamino's magic flute." When Otto was eleven, a banker friend of the family took him to the opera, where, "spellbound," he first heard Wagner's music, while his host slept through the performance. "The contempt which [he] felt for this insensibility colored his attitude toward philistinism for the rest of his life." At seventeen he was sent to work in a bank in Karlsruhe, then on to another in London, where he took up the theater and music, dressed dandyishly, adopted an unflappable worldly air, became a

British subject. In 1893 the banking firm of Speyer and Company offered him a place in its New York office. "America was a new adventure, a new day, a new world to inspect." It was also a shock. Banking was conducted in a different atmosphere from that of London. The titans of American finance were dour, unsmiling, suspicious of urbanity. No successful banker consorted with artists. The theater was worst of all. James Stillman of the National City Bank thought Kahn "a promising chap, if he will only forget that art nonsense."

He was disturbed by the joylessness of Wall Street. Bankers snoozing in their Metropolitan boxes brought back disturbing memories. Still, he was no dissident. Kahn understood that business always came first. Besides, he needed a fortune to do great things in the art world. He married prudently, the daughter of a prominent American Jewish banking family. Adept, tactful, exceptionally hard-working (he said that he never slept more than five hours a night all his adult life), blessed with a tenacious memory for detail, Kahn moved rapidly ahead as a securities banker, concentrating on railroad finance. He became a partner in one of the power-house Wall Street firms, Kuhn, Loeb, and in the next decade and a half he made a fortune of several million dollars.

In 1903 Jacob Schiff, senior partner of Kuhn, Loeb, was asked to become a member of the Metropolitan's board of directors. He declined, but recommended Kahn in his place. That year Heinrich Conried was chosen as the new musical director. Rumor quickly had it that Kahn supported him because, given Conried's ignorance of music and of opera, Kahn would have "a chance to superintend, direct and manage." Such influence or prescience within a year is unlikely. Kahn, however, undoubtedly began to gather variegated threads of power into his hands. He knew something about music and was tireless in doing favors. He bought up the shares of other stockholders, and in 1911 he was elected chairman of the board of directors, president of the board in 1918. When Oscar Hammerstein's competition became too much for Conried to deal with, Kahn played an instrumental role in picking Gatti-Casazza to succeed him. He and William Vanderbilt made the transition relatively easy by buying out Conried.

O. H. K.: those initials became a "cabalistic symbol" at the Metropolitan in the following decade. Opera House Kahn, people joked. Kahn's relationship with Gatti-Casazza must have been complex. The formal division of responsibility was clear enough—Gatti-Casazza dealt with the artists and repertory, Kahn represented the directors and their interests. In his memoirs, Gatti-Casazza claimed all credit for policy decisions, while Kahn's biographer insisted that many decisions were actually made by Kahn. Of course, the two spheres were never entirely separable. Gatti-Casazza had to some extent to deal with the public and the subscribers, and Kahn, who cultivated the press, gave shrewd advice about how to manage both those constituencies, whose customs, tribal relationships, and language Gatti-Casazza barely knew. (His broadcast farewell message in 1935 surprised many people because his accent was so thick that his words were almost incomprehensible.) They agreed about much, and certainly both shaped the axiomatic principle on which the Metropolitan was run: that whatever they wished to do was possible, provided always that it didn't cost the shareholders anything beyond their season boxes. Kahn certainly intervened in musical matters—about singers, repertory. "I have been urging French repertory on Gatti for years," Kahn wrote in 1918. Their partnership increasingly pivoted around the money that Kahn poured into the opera house. Kahn's money made things possible that the shareholders would otherwise have been troublesome about.[2]

In 1918 Kahn employed Ivy Lee, John D. Rockefeller's famous publicist, as his press agent. Celebrated for his discretion, Kahn *craved* publicity. In his gray gloves, gray spats, opera cape, silk hat, swinging a silver-headed cane, leading two dachshunds on a leash, he blossomed into a readily identifiable New York City character. His circle of friends went beyond ultrarespectable society. He played cards with Enrico Caruso's entourage, enjoying their "coarse" suppers heavy with garlic and olive oil, enlivened by common red wine, cigars, and bawdy stories. "We never doubted that he was happier with us than anywhere else." During boring stretches of certain operas, he rounded up newspapermen and took them to nearby vaudeville and burlesque houses for a few minutes of truant relaxation, returning for the final curtain. He spoke up in defense of jazz (one of his sons became a jazz musician), making a platitude sound like a ringing principle: "Good jazz beats out poor opera." He was a familiar figure at theatrical openings and even cultivated movie entertainers. In her first talking picture, Fanny Brice made him the subject of a song—"Is Something the Matter with Otto Kahn?"

> Is something the matter with Otto Kahn
> Or is something the matter with me?
> I wrote a note and told him what a star I would make.
> He sent it back and marked it "Opened by mistake."
> I'd even get fatter for Otto Kahn,
> As all prima donnas must be.
> I studied with Scotti, if you know what I mean.
> He said I had the finest diaphragm he had seen!
> And if my high C don't hand Otto a thrill,
> I think my tra-la-la will.

Looking over the guest list for a weekend at their country mansion, Mrs. Kahn fled to New York, telling her husband she would leave him alone with his "zoo."[3]

Time magazine, celebrating him in one of its cover stories—"America's Foremost Patron of the Arts"—rhapsodized about the varied aspects of his career, from "lowly clerk" in a U.S. bank to companion to the mighty. And now he had become "chief stockholder, President, guarantor and presiding intelligence" of the Metropolitan Opera: "Cosmopolite, Metropolite." More than a patron, he was a power.

> Some millionaires get warm beneath their collars
> When asked to pay assessments of ten dollars;
> They are not everywhere so keen as
> Our Otto Kahn to play the real Maecenas.

The *Time* story appeared in 1925, at a time when Kahn needed all the guile and authority he could command, for Maecenas had embarked on a campaign to build a new opera house.[4]

In 1925 Time *magazine described Otto Kahn as "America's foremost patron of the arts." Although his dream of building a new home for the Metropolitan Opera came to naught, his leadership and philanthropy left a lasting mark on the company.*

F r o m the day it opened, the Metropolitan Opera House had been an unsatisfactory place to produce opera. The catalogue of its inadequacies had been clear to Kahn by 1908, when Gatti-Casazza arrived, got his first look at it, and "complained volubly" about its defects. "You will be satisfied shortly," Kahn assured him. "In two or three years a new Metropolitan Opera House will be built." The achievements of the Toscanini years obscured the problems, the war years were an impossible time for a change. The prosperous 1920s seemed the right time to make the effort. By then, however, Kahn's objectives had changed and owed as much to social as to architectural considerations. The heart of the matter was the power of the share-owning boxholders, which had somehow to be reduced. If a new house was built, it had to be organized on different principles from the old—no private ownership and control. But how to get the existing phalanx of boxholders to agree to this? Obviously, Kahn had to build a coalition of boxholders who shared his views, and who had enough votes to carry through the change and enough determination to resist the inevitable pressure from their reluctant peers. He had spent two decades flattering, mollifying, cajoling the boxholders, buying them off with his money, and he understood that they arrived at decisions in ways subtler than vote counting. However powerful he seemed to journalists, he knew the limits of his power and influence, knew that he was not one of the boxholders' peers.

He was the Disraeli of New York operatic life, adroit, efficient, flamboyant. One of J. P. Morgan's partners had insisted that there was no anti-Semitism on Wall Street. "Anyone who could obtain Kuhn, Loeb's cooperation in a business transaction considered himself fortunate." But that was "downtown," where business was business. The Metropolitan opera was "uptown," where opera was *social* business. There anti-Semitism was pervasive. Jacob Schiff, American citizen since 1870, senior partner of Kuhn, Loeb, was denied an opera box of his own. He was a "lessee of Box 18, for certain performances." Even Kahn didn't have a box of his own. When he became chairman of the board in 1911, he had the director's box at his disposal. That came with the job, and the distinction was clear and important to those who cared. When he was finally offered a box of his own, the event was called "notable" by the New York press.

Kahn's admiration for Oscar Hammerstein—he went frequently to the Manhattan Opera House, liked the house and the repertory, appreciated Hammerstein's "Napoleonic magnificence"—was closely related to his own situation. The two men had much in common as Germans, Jews, musically trained immigrants; and Kahn must have envied, as well as admired, Hammerstein's independence, symbolized by that rickety kitchen chair in the wings from which Hammerstein watched every performance in his house. As a matter of personal style, Kahn would *not* have indulged himself in a kitchen chair in the wings. Drinking cheap wine with Caruso's friends was as far as he wished to go in that direction. But the end of the Manhattan-Metropolitan war revealed the extent of Kahn's respect for Hammerstein, and that it was kept secret revealed a lot too. The $1,250,000 with which Hammerstein was bought out came personally from Kahn, a "virtual gift to the old man with the top hat and cigar."[5]

In pursuit of the dream of a new Metropolitan Opera House, Otto Kahn's tactic was to work behind the scenes building his coalition while he launched a public campaign, utilizing his extensive press contacts. He guessed that the Metropolitan's rulers were susceptible to public pressure in the 1920s as they never had been in earlier years. He gave an interview in which he argued that "it is a solemn obligation of a semi-public institution such as the Metropolitan Opera to provide amply and generously for music lovers of small or modest means." Shareholders might well have been annoyed to read also that "the poor brought more zest and enthusiasm to the theatre than the rich," but what of the notion that their opera house was "semi-public"? After shareholders turned down an indirect suggestion in 1922 or 1923 that a new house be constructed, Kahn became more specific about his aims. The new house must "conform to that genuinely democratic sentiment which ought to be characteristic in all ways of America." Therefore, it must be large enough to accommodate the masses and (echoes of the New Theater debacle) be a plain, welcoming building. He campaigned vigorously to promote his cause and went so far as to address the Socialist League for Industrial Democracy. If his words failed to persuade sceptics, some of the boxholders believed he meant what he said. "Each liberal utterance widened the gap between Kahn and the conservative Metropolitan boxholders, some of whom believed he was a Socialist."[6]

In 1925, the period of his greatest notoriety and influence, he made a decisive step, calculated to move the issue clearly into the public realm and to increase the pressure on the shareholders. He bought a site for a new opera house, a large plot on Ninth Avenue, between West Fifty-sixth and Fifty-seventh streets, two blocks west of Carnegie Hall and Steinway Hall, in the heart of the music district, and negotiated a loan from the Metropolitan Life Insurance Company to allow construction to begin. The boxholders refused to go along. R. Fulton Cutting, on behalf of the Metropolitan Opera and Real Estate Company, issued a statement denying that the old building was antiquated or the site hopeless. "If it is desirable that the building should be replaced by one larger and more scientifically equipped, I presume the company of which Mr. Kahn is the chairman will undertake the project." In short, and for those who needed things spelled out: Otto Kahn could do as he wished, but the Metropolitan wasn't moving.[7]

These events provoked public mockery and mirth. "Museum pieces," the boxholders were called. The *New York World* published "The Social Primer":

> K is for Kahn who is doing his best
> To give ultra-exclusives a kick in the chest.
> He'd deny them the privilege, so 'twould appear
> Of ruling the roost from the gilded parterre.

Time magazine alluded to "feudal barons, clinging to their castles and patents of nobility. So the elect of Manhattan's social register cling to the boxes of the Metropolitan."[8]

By 1926 a substantial group, persuaded by Kahn's arguments or embarrassed by the ridicule, supported a compromise. A new opera house would be built. Joseph Urban and Benjamin Morris drew up plans for the new building, a model of which was displayed in Urban's studio. Kahn would sell the Metropolitan his new site for what it cost him and the sale of the old property would net the shareholders a nice profit. On the central issue, the old guard had its way. Boxholders would still constitute an ownership group and would have undisputed sway in their boxes on Monday nights and either Thursday evening or Saturday afternoons. "For other performances the boxes would be available on rental to a group approved by a 'box committee.'" In April 1927 the majority of Metropolitan stockholders agreed to turn in their stock and allow building to proceed. Those who didn't want the new house would be bought out. Sometime in the spring or summer, though, this compromise fell apart. An irreconcilable group, led by Fulton Cutting, Robert Goelet, and Mrs. Cornelius Vanderbilt III, overturned the decision. There was never any "official" explanation—that was not how things were done. Nor was there one climactic moment when Kahn was defeated. But defeated he was, unconditionally. By the end of 1928 he put his Ninth Avenue property on the market. The story of the new opera house was over.[9]

If Kahn was crushed by the defeat, he didn't show it. Fundamentally, he always operated by the insider's code: give as little as possible away. He remained as chairman of the board for a while. Anyway, the devastating effect of his failure fell on the Metropolitan's permanent staff, who bore the brunt of the old house's inefficiencies. It has been suggested that the relatively large number of new operas produced in the 1928–1929 season—by Strauss, Pizetti, Respighi—was a kind of consolation prize for Kahn and his supporters, "to give freshness to the old stage, if no new one was available." One of these operas was *Johnny Strikes up the Band* (*Jonny spielt auf*) by Ernst Krenek (1900–1991), performed in January 1919, a very modernistic jazz opera about an African American entertainer, most decidedly not the sort of thing the old guard enjoyed. "He is a coming man," Kahn said of the composer. And of the opera: "I consider it a very interesting new departure and some of the music is really beautiful." Its performance afforded an epilogue to the foregoing. At the opera's conclusion, a "voluble anti-Semite from the boxholding clique thundered down" on Kahn, shouting: "I think this is disgraceful. You ought to be ashamed of yourself." Kahn, who had known the man for twenty years, turned to his companions and imperturbably asked: "Who on earth is that?"[10]

After the Crash

In the fall of 1929, though the stock market had drifted downward from its summertime peak, optimism still prevailed. The economist Irving Fisher expected to see the market "a good deal higher than it is today within a few months," and *Time* magazine put Samuel Insull on its cover "as though to emphasize its faith in the New Era." October 21, however, was a very bad day, with hectic selling. The 24th, "Black Thursday," was worse, a day of disorder and confusion. A group of prominent bankers moved into the market, buying stocks and dispelling fear. Prices rebounded—until Monday, October 28, when the bottom fell out and terror stalked the Exchange. "The worst continued to worsen." Tuesday, October 29, was "the most devastating day in the history of the New York stock market." *Variety,* the entertainment newspaper, summarized things briskly in its headline on the 30th: "WALL STREET LAYS AN EGG."[1]

The unpleasantness of the previous week was apparently far from the minds of the audience which filled the Civic Opera House on the night of November 4, the dawning of Chicago's New Operatic Era. Insull had decreed that there was to be no speech making to mark the event, jewels and expensive clothes were as evident as ever, and *Aida,* the opening-night opera, reassured everyone that nothing had changed. Mascagni's *Iris, Roméo et Juliette, Tristan und Isolde, Il Trovatore,* and *Norma* followed in the first week. There was a splendid roster of singers—Alexander Kipnis, Frida Leider, Maria Olszewska, Rosa Raisa, Tito Schipa. Mary Garden sang Mélisande. The company's guarantee fund was a source of stability and, as Insull's business empire was seemingly unaffected by the crash, Chicago confidently embarked on a "gargantuan undertaking," an eleven-week tour of New England, the South, and Southwest. A year later, stock prices continued to fall, unemployment continued to rise, but there was no reduction in the length of the opera season. The broader base of Chicago's subscription support, as Insull had planned it, insulated the company from the losses suffered by the wealthy. As if to demonstrate its confidence, the 1930 season opened with a new opera, *Lorenzaccio,* by an obscure follower of Massenet named Ernest Moret, which rejected all melody in favor of dramatic recitative. It was not "a happy choice" and was quickly forgotten in the stream of that season's riches: *Fidelio,* one of the company's "artistic triumphs"; a powerful *Otello;* Raisa in *Norma,* "vocal display in its most heroic aspects"; Leider singing Wagner "with great nobility and dramatic force." And even more singers of unusual quality added to an already extraordinary roster—Salvatore Baccaloni,

Jennie Tourel, and two Americans, John Charles Thomas, baritone, whose Tonio in *I Pagliacci* occasioned an almost unequaled demonstration, and Paul Althouse, baritone turned tenor, singing "fluently, freely, feelingly" in Wagner. Most notably, Chicago introduced America to one of the preeminent singing artists of the first half of the century. Lotte Lehmann, already a celebrated presence in Europe, revealed a lovely voice, scrupulous diction, superb vocalization, and remarkable dramatic intelligence.

Claudio Muzio opened the 1931 season in *Tosca,* one of her hauntingly individual interpretations, with Vanni Marcoux as Scarpia. The new artistic director, Herbert Witherspoon of the Juilliard School of Music, the first American to occupy so important an operatic position, recognized that the crash had become a depression, planned to shorten future seasons, cut costs but maintained an imaginative repertory. In this spirit Chicago saw its first *Zauberflöte,* with sets and costumes that "struck a modern and fantastic note." But Witherspoon's plans collapsed along with the exhaustion of the guarantee fund. Long-suppressed resentment against Insull boiled up, "everyone in those pink velvet boxes, grimly looking at each other. They all just hated Insull, the people in the boxes. At that moment, they hated him more than ever. And then they found themselves slithering down the toboggan." Insull went down with them.[2]

Insulldämmerung. The twilight of the Titan was dreadful. "People are very hard on those who, having had power, lose it or are destroyed. Then anger at past arrogance is joined with contempt for present weakness."[3] Confident that he would weather the Depression, Insull expanded his interests and took on more debt to finance them. His holdings, profitable throughout 1930, began to drop in value in 1931 and, in a nightmare of collapsing values and pressure applied by rivals, Insull's companies were taken over by the banks. He resigned from all his directorships. His collapse took the Civic Opera with him. Abruptly, in January 1932, it closed its doors. Insull left for Athens. There were charges of fraud. He was extradited, indicted, tried—twice—and exonerated. He went to Paris and died there in July 1938. The other major figures in this remarkable chapter of American operatic history also departed. Edith McCormick's colossal fortune was greatly reduced and she was in failing health, though active on behalf of opera until her death in August 1932. Harold McCormick divorced Gana Walska in 1931 but maintained his musical interests. He took up whistling and gave concerts, accompanied by the Baroness Beatrice von Wenner on the harp.[4]

T h e Metropolitan Opera's opening night in 1929 was October 28, the catastrophic Monday when the market collapsed. The opera was Puccini's *Manon Lescaut,* with Lucrezia Bori, popular Spanish soprano. She had made her Metropolitan debut in it in 1911, and her reappearance struck a reminiscent chord, the past looking ever more golden in light of the disturbing present. "A sinister note was already sounding in the midst of all this brilliance; extraordinary things had been happening Downtown during the course of the afternoon and disquieting rumors were circulating among the parterre boxes." Revivals were the order of the season: *Don Giovanni,* performed for the first time in twenty-seven years, with beautiful singing by Rosa Ponselle and

Ezio Pinza: *La Fanciulla del West,* Jeritza and Martinelli much liked; *L'Elisir d'amore,* Pina an "oily, amusing Dulcamara." *Louise* was revived for Bori. It shocked no one and struck young people as "weak and dull." The retrospective note sounded, too, in the Metropolitan's two hundredth performance of *Faust.* The bookkeeping at season's end was reassuring. Otto Kahn announced that attendance was "slightly diminished," and for the first time in twenty years there was a deficit, $14,743—trivial, of course, but "a straw in the wind that soon became a gale." Unperturbed, the directors extended Gatti-Casazza's contract for two years.

The unsinkable Metropolitan was sailing, *Titanic*-like, into a sea of financial icebergs. Complacency was grounded on unswerving faith in Gatti-Casazza's managerial magic, in the Metropolitan's way of doing things, in the comfort of settled routine. Even more, it was based on the huge surplus the Metropolitan had built up in the previous decade. There was a million dollars in a reserve fund, surely enough to outlast any short-term economic downturn. The money had not been used, as many urged, for refurbishing the aging scenery, installing air-conditioning, as all Broadway theaters were doing, replacing the decrepit electrical system, or remodeling the gallery seating. (When someone reminded Gatti-Casazza that people upstairs could see only a portion of productions designed solely with the main floor and boxes in mind, he said: "Then let them come down.") More than deferred maintenance mocked such arrogance. The Depression undermined the social structure that made the old Metropolitan possible, and the next five years revealed the choice to be made: a different Metropolitan Opera or none at all.

The first stage in this process began in 1930—with the denial that anything had changed. After a "dull and stupefying" opening-night *Aida* had failed to produce any magic, a number of different things were tried: Mascagni's *Iris,* Musorgsky's *The Fair at Sorochintsy,* the world premiere of Deems Taylor's *Peter Ibbetson.* None proved attractive, though Maria Jeritza in Franz von Suppé's *Boccaccio* definitely did—except with some critics who, encased in the massive solemnity of grand opera, reeled back from the spectacle of Jeritza singing with verve and showing off her shapely legs.

One unanticipated event brought back a feeling of earlier, better Metropolitan days. Without fanfare, a French coloratura soprano, Lily Pons, made her debut on January 3, in *Lucia.* Gatti-Casazza hoped to spring a complete surprise on his audiences, but, though word-of-mouth excited interest ahead of time, no one was prepared for the sensation Pons produced. Her singing in the first and second acts was clear and finished and of a brilliance not heard since Galli-Curci. The mad scene, "disclosing all the necessary vocal gifts that that super-aria calls for," removed all doubt, and the audience applauded "as madly as it has for a blue moon." They went on applauding madly for her in *Rigoletto, Il Barbiere, Les Contes d'Hoffmann,* and *Mignon.* She was indeed "Mr. Gatti's little Christmas gift from a kind providence." Even Lily Pons wasn't enough to offset the effects of sharply declining attendance combined with boom-time expenditures. Subscriptions for the 1930 season had declined 5 percent, but when the time came to pay for seat renewals, the percentage was even larger. The cheap seats were often filled. Downstairs, stretches of empty seats became a common sight. The deficit for the 1930 season was a startling $322,231.

The Metropolitan sailed on much as before in 1931–1932. The season wasn't reduced in length, prices were not lowered. There was a 10 percent drop in subscriptions for the year, and Kahn announced his retirement from the board of directors, after twenty-eight years. The star performers still sang wonderfully: Ponselle in *La Traviata,* Jeritza in *Tannhäuser,* Bori and Martinelli in *La Bohème.* They constituted no answer to the mounting problems, nor did the operas revived for Pons—*La Sonnambula, Lakmé.* In a second foray into operetta, von Suppé's *Donna Juanita,* Jeritza interpolated some of the jokes in English and did an adagio dance. Critics wondered "just what this kind of show was doing in the Metropolitan." Gatti-Casazza's answer, which they ignored, was: to attract audiences. There was mounting criticism of the orchestra, "shockingly inferior," and of the other elements of production, which remained what they had been in Toscanini's day, while in other houses "standards moved ahead in gargantuan leaps." After two years as stage director, Ernest Lert resigned, characterizing Metropolitan productions as a "variety show." There were still forty productions a year, and yet, Lert charged, nineteen out of twenty didn't have a single rehearsal. By the beginning of 1932 there was no point in denying that a crisis loomed. "In three years we lost more than thirty percent of our subscribers," Gatti-Casazza wrote in his memoirs. "The wealthy classes . . . formed the bulk of subscribers who cancelled," while "the general public which purchased its admission from day to day, continued at about the same level." The deficit for 1931 was $497,213. Four fifths of the reserve fund had disappeared in two seasons.[5]

The second stage in the Metropolitan's transformation began in 1932, when Gatti-Casazza proposed a "voluntary" pay cut of 10 percent for all salaried employees. On behalf of the musicians, Union Local 802 immediately declared such a cut unacceptable. All the singers agreed to the reduction except Beniamino Gigli, the company's leading tenor. Gatti-Casazza accused Gigli of "lack of co-operation and espirit de corps." Self-righteousness was unbecoming in Gatti-Casazza. His salary, $30,000 per year, had been doubled in 1928, and two years later, after the crash, it was raised again to $67,000. It was $69,000 in 1931, $57,000 in 1932, reduced to $43,000 in 1933. Gigli insisted that all contracts were worthless, as the 10 percent pay cut concealed a far-reaching legal reorganization.

In the spring of 1932, the Metropolitan Opera Company ceased legally to exist, its place taken by the Metropolitan Opera Association, a nonprofit opera-producing body. The association was freed from all former contracts and obligations and didn't have to pay entertainment tax. Ownership of the building and direction of the association remained in the hands of the still intact Metropolitan Opera and Real Estate Company. This dual organization caused difficulty for the rest of the decade. The 1932–1933 season was reduced to sixteen weeks, and prices were lowered. Certain singers—"too old, too expensive, too independent"—were replaced, Gigli and Jeritza among them. The opening-night opera, Verdi's *Simon Boccanegra,* was not a conventional audience-pleaser and its leading singer, Lawrence Tibbett, was the first American, trained entirely in America, chosen for this honor. It marked Gatti-Casazza's twenty-fifth year as director. Toscanini was present, but not, unfortunately, in the pit. Kahn was absent. The audience was plentiful and its composition changing:

"Many unfamiliar faces in boxes and stalls." "Business suits, and even sweaters, were eventually to appear in parterre boxes of a Monday night." There was marked improvement in the quality of German opera, Wagner especially. With the Chicago company defunct, several outstanding singers came from there to New York. Frida Leider, Maria Olszewska, Lotte Lehmann joined Lauritz Melchior, now at the zenith of his long career, and stimulated to greater heights by the quality of the women singing opposite him. Artur Bodanzky, revitalized as conductor, led a complete *Ring* cycle, *Tristan und Isolde* received its hundredth Metropolitan performance, and *Elektra* was finally given, twenty-three years after its Munich premiere. All this recalled "the fabulous days before the war." Nevertheless, the box office figures at the end of the season were dismaying. The deficit was $339,901. Perhaps it was the Wagnerian mood which led many responsible people to talk of *Operdämmerung,* the twilight of opera.

If the Metropolitan was to survive, it would have to find a new basis of support. At the beginning of the 1933 season, the conductor Artur Bodanzky ruminated about what this might be. "I say it was the artists who saved this distinctly great American institution from going to the wall. The bankers and the backers—why, they quit!" There must be a plan to take opera out of the hands of the "wealthy few" and put it in the hands of the "appreciative public." For the next few years the Metropolitan directors, although they had no "plan," groped to find their way. Radio was perhaps the way to reach this larger audience. Gatti-Casazza made a public radio appeal for help, as did Geraldine Farrar. "Similar appeals were made during intermissions of every broadcast for the rest of the season." The response was amazing. Various Metropolitan directors and patrons pledged $150,000. "It stands as the only spontaneous contributions by the so-called 'backers' in a quarter of a century." The season was cut to fourteen weeks. In 1935 a top fee of one thousand dollars per performance was established for singers. A Committee for Saving the Metropolitan Opera was formed. Two opera performances were given free of charge by the artists, to raise money. There was a grand ball. The Carnegie Corporation gave $25,000. The Juilliard Music Foundation made contributions of $50,000 one year and $40,000 the next. None of this seemed enough. The deficit for 1933–1934 was $317,000, for 1934–1935, $230,000.

In the next five years, public contributions and private support of a new kind saved, and transformed, the Metropolitan. The turning point was 1935. Gatti-Casazza retired. The Metropolitan Opera Guild was organized, to stimulate subscription sales and support from the general public, and it quickly grew and served as a model for other such groups in other places, other years. And that year the Juilliard Music Foundation trustees, having given modest sums the previous two years, offered $250,000, provided certain conditions were met: foundation representation on the Metropolitan board of directors; no budget deficit; increased subscription sales; opportunities for American artists. Herbert D. Witherspoon, professor of music at the Juilliard School and director of the Chicago Opera its last year, was appointed Gatti-Casazza's replacement. (Witherspoon dropped dead of a heart attack after a few weeks on the job. He was replaced by the Canadian tenor Edward Johnson.)[6]

There were grave and continuing difficulties, the most serious of which was that public money saved an opera company the public had no voice in administering. The resolution of this, as always in the history of the Metropolitan, came about in a curious fashion. Internal disarray among the shareholders precipitated the third stage of the transformation of the old order.

By 1939 half the opera house boxes were held by the estates of the original investors, some of whom, in the words of the head of the boxholders' association, "refused to pay the assessment levied on their shares, and in spite of repeated requests have persisted in this refusal." One way out was to sell the shares of the delinquents to new members, but "the immemorial clannishness of the box-holders" made this impossible. Alternatively, the shareholders might have sold the building to the nonprofit Opera Association for a nominal sum, "to earn some measure of gratitude from the public that had paid the upkeep of their social setting for so long." Very few of the shareholders had by this time personally invested a penny in their shares, since these had come to them through inheritance. No such offer was made. Instead, the Opera Association, the opera-producing body, proposed to pay $1,970,000 for the building, the price of the original construction. A vote was held. Sixty-eight percent of the voting shareholders accepted this offer, a hairbreadth margin over the two-thirds required. A recalcitrant group refused to accept this as a final decision and filed suit in court to overturn it. Eventually the courts decided against them, the terms of the purchase being deemed equitable. One million dollars of the purchase price was raised by a public campaign. New York mayor Fiorello H. La Guardia was chairman of a committee of 175 people who raised just over the amount needed, including important contributions from foundations. Much about this arrangement remained unclear, but one thing was certain: When, on June 28, 1940, the Metropolitan Opera House passed into the hands of the Metropolitan Opera Association, it in some form belonged to the people of the State of New York.[7]

A n o t h e r institution, operatic touring, also changed with the times. The old touring company became a more orderly and businesslike enterprise, with regular schedules, guaranteed local support, more sophisticated publicity. In the 1930s, the most important of these companies was the San Carlo Opera Company, managed by a bumptious immigrant named Fortune Gallo. He learned music by playing with a local band in Torre Maggiore, not far from Naples, where he was born in 1878. When Fortune was seventeen his parents sent him to America. "Every corner of Italy, it seemed, was thick with news of the wealth of America. Musicians, good ones, were worth their weight in gold. Or nearly so." In New York City he worked as a messenger for Tammany Hall, played with a touring Italian band, booked entertainments for an Atlantic City impresario. He quickly picked up the American language, an interest in popular music, songs, and ragtime, and modern ways of publicity. In 1910 he was in San Francisco when the Lombardi Opera Company, an example of the old-style opera group, talented but feckless Bohemians who had survived a northward migration through central America, arrived in northern California, tattered and broke. Gallo reorganized and revived them, placed them in a popular amusement park in Oakland, generated news about their South American adventures, then took them on a tour of small California towns. His terms as promoter were a fixed salary and 25 percent of the profits. He liked the experience and decided to establish his own company and try out his new ideas.[8]

Fortune Gallo's San Carlo Opera Company gave its first performance in December 1910. He believed that an irresistible modernist spirit pervaded American culture—the modernism not of advanced European composers but of a "new musical beat," "a break with the traditional musical pattern of the past." People wanted "to tap their feet and move their bodies. They wanted to be part of the music instead of just being listeners." How did this relate to opera? It would have to be streamlined, theatrically convincing, reduced in scale. "Puccini, with his light, tuneful arias, has made it possible for more singers to take up opera as a career where they might have been scared off by all the heavy stuff in the years gone by." Opera in America would also

For four decades the San Carlo Opera Company purveyed opera at popular prices from coast to coast. It was led by a bumptious Italian immigrant named Fortune Gallo, shown here about 1920. Library of Congress.

have to turn to operas by American composers—not imitations of European forms, but something light, indigenous. "In the not too distant future we may be hearing operas penned by some of the songsmiths who are now turning out our popular tunes." Gallo wanted compact and colorful scenery, a youthful and vigorous-voiced chorus. After some false starts and precarious moments, he evolved the form the San Carlo would stick to for the next four decades.

The San Carlo went only to places where there had been thorough preliminary work and where there was a financial guarantee for the company. A great deal of time and effort was spent on publicity, and Gallo left the company for extended periods while he acted as advance man, coordinator of publicity, and managing director all rolled into one. When business had been drummed up ahead of time, the San Carlo stayed in one place for one or two or more weeks. And it operated out of a home base in New York, where it would offer several weeks of opera at cheap prices. Its prices were kept low everywhere—in the 1930s, $1.50 was the top.

The crucial element in Gallo's work was the advance visit to a city. He contacted heads of railroad companies and showed them how they might increase their revenue by distributing opera tickets in the surrounding areas. In the city itself he would do careful preparatory work to identify the "social leaders of the district and intimate—discreetly of course—that a visit to the opera would be the social event of the season." At the same time, he didn't want to put off the ordinary audience who had no social pretensions, so he emphasized the San Carlo's connection with fraternal organizations. Whenever possible, he put his company's visit under the sponsorship of the Elks, the Moose, the Shriners, the Rotary, and similar organizations. By the time he left a city, he would "have the whole town selling tickets and talking up my troupe."

In New York, the San Carlo was ancillary to the Metropolitan, but not subordinate to it. It attracted substantial audiences during the Metropolitan season. The New York base was a great advantage in recruiting singers, who were eager to perform there under whatever auspices, no doubt hoping to attract the Metropolitan's eye and ear. A more formal relationship with the Metropolitan also worked to Gallo's advantage. He sometimes recruited famous singers—Jeritza, Martinelli—to sing with his company, out of the Metropolitan's season, which added luster to his company's name and also served as a reminder to aspiring singers that they could move from the San Carlo to the big time. In New York his company performed for many years at the Manhattan Opera House, and Gallo emphasized that his company was part of the Hammerstein tradition. "The people who patronize it are neither snobs nor sophisticates," *Time* magazine wrote in the mid-1930s. And Gallo's ticket prices, one-third of the Metropolitan's, bore it out. However, his repertory was in no sense innovative, standard Italian and French operas and occasionally Wagner. In any event, he had invested in New York real estate and did so well that his regular income made his operatic ventures possible.[9]

In the 1930s the San Carlo did remarkably well, partly because its costs were so low—ordinary singers got eighty-five dollars per week. A typical tour was as follows: From New York to Toronto, then Detroit, Chicago, Milwaukee, Minneapolis, one month in Kansas City, brief stops through the South, then up the Pacific coast to

Vancouver and back to St. Louis, where the season ended. Gallo also gained considerable publicity by giving outdoor performances in the summer—lavish spectacles, at Sheepshead Bay Speedway in Brooklyn or at Jones Beach State Park. He sent a company to Havana. He gave many seats to charitable organizations to bring people to opera for the first time, because he was certain of its power. Having come once, those people would return. He produced operettas and musical comedies by Kern, Romberg, Gershwin, Strauss, Porter. He put on opera in the Orange Bowl. Indoors, he used the Center Theater in Rockefeller Center from 1936 to 1950.

Some things didn't work out as Gallo hoped. A number of important American singers got their start with the San Carlo, but most of the company's roster was foreign-born. Nor was American opera given by the San Carlo: Puccini and Verdi made up most of the repertory. It continued to attract people when sceptics insisted that radio and films would wipe out opera audiences. The San Carlo showed that radio and recordings increased the appetite for *seeing* opera on the stage. Gallo's cultivation of local interest groups also played an unforeseen role in the proliferation, after World War II, of local opera associations and societies. The San Carlo came to an end in 1950, but that wasn't the end of American operatic touring.

The growth of American musical conservatories in the interwar years provided continuity between the 1920s and 1930s and played a big role in America's operatic expansion after World War II. The first steps in establishing proper American musical instruction had been taken in the middle of the nineteenth century. In 1857, in the country's first notable act of musical philanthropy, the banker-merchant George Peabody founded the Baltimore Academy of Music. An imposing Gothic building was completed in 1866 and instruction began in 1868. It eventually came to be known as the Peabody Conservatory, and included an art gallery, library, and lecture hall. Its most important director was Asger Hamerik, a Danish composer and conductor, pupil of Berlioz, who led it in imaginative and energetic ways from 1871 to 1898. In keeping with its pedagogical traditions, Boston had two conservatories, the Boston Conservatory, created by the violinist and composer Julius Eichberg, and the New England Conservatory, established by Eben Tourjée, both dating from 1867. That same year, in Cincinnati, Clara Baur, a German pianist and singer who had emigrated to America in 1849, started the Cincinnati Conservatory of Music, which she directed until her death in 1912. In later years it merged with another Cincinnati institution, the College of Music, begun in 1878, Theodore Thomas first director. All these conservatories were patterned after European models, drew heavily on European teachers, and emphasized orchestral music. New York's chief contribution to the nineteenth-century conservatory movement dated from 1885, when Jeanette Meyers Thurber, daughter of a Danish immigrant violinist, with the support and money of her merchant husband, received a state charter for the National Conservatory of Music. In 1891 she got it incorporated by an act of Congress and vigorously lobbied for federal support, but none was forthcoming. Thurber brought Antonín Dvořák to America as director (1892–1895), but her most innovative idea was to provide financial aid for students regardless of race. For the first time, African Americans and Native Americans had one small door opened into mainstream musical life. For two decades the National Conservatory rivaled the ones in Baltimore, Boston, and Cincinnati, but after 1910 it declined.

The second wave of conservatory founding began in New York in 1916, when David Mannes and Clara Damrosch founded the Mannes College of Music. In 1917 the philanthropist Janet Schenck founded the Neighborhood Music School, which became the Manhattan School of Music, flourishing under John Brownlee and John Crosby. In 1920 came the Juilliard School of Music, the legacy of the textile fortune of Augustus Juilliard. Starting with a Graduate School of Music in 1924, the Juilliard took over the Institute of Musical Art founded by Frank Damrosch and established itself as one of the premier American institutions. In Rochester, New York, a previous music school also was absorbed by a new foundation. The Eastman School of Music, founded in 1917, based on a fortune made in photography, was the first American cultural center, with a professional school, a theater for performance, a cinema, and a recital hall under one roof. In 1922 the Rochester American Opera Company grew out of the Eastman's opera department and toured widely in the 1920s, giving opera in English. Philadelphia completed this era of institution building in 1924. Mary Louise Curtis Bok, heir to a publishing fortune, founded the Curtis Institute of Music. With a substantial endowment and astute direction, it became one of the leading American conservatories and was notable for offering tuition-free instruction to students from many other countries.[10]

In the midst of this founding of new institutions, an old one reappeared—Colorado's Central City Opera House. In the early years of the century it had been converted into a movie theater and then, in 1927, closed its doors. In 1931 the University of Denver acquired, restored, and reopened it under the aegis of the Central City Opera Association, the site of a summer music festival.

New places, new music. Leopold Stokowski and the Philadelphia Orchestra led the way in introducing new music to America. Only Serge Koussevitzky and the Boston Symphony compared with the Philadelphians in this respect. In the late 1920s and early 1930s, Stokowski led several concert performances of opera and occasionally some staged productions in conjunction with the Philadelphia Grand Opera Company and the Curtis. Modest Musorgsky's *Khovanshchina*, in English, in 1928, was a notable instance, but the high point of Stokowski's operatic endeavors was the first American performance, in March 1931, of *Wozzeck* by Alban Berg (1885–1935). It attracted attention throughout the European and American musical world. A special train left New York on the day of the performance, crowded with musicians, critics, composers (and Otto Kahn) "eager to hear the work which had been called the most striking musico-dramatic composition since *Pelléas et Mélisande*." In his score, "written without compromise," and formidably difficult, Berg had sounded a new note. Robert Edmond Jones designed the production, "in the spirit of the present day theatre, avoiding all that is conventional." Stokowski thought Jones's use of light and of darkness was masterful. *Wozzeck* was sung in English. Anne Roselle sang Marie, Ivan Ivantzoff, Wozzeck. The Philadelphia Orchestra played magnificently. Stokowski was praised for the "searching penetration" of his reading of the complex score. "He revealed himself as a supreme operatic conductor." And although many found

Berg's music repellent, there was praise for it as well. "In a day when what is new seems old and dated so quickly, *Wozzeck* promises to stand the test of time." In November, Stokowski repeated the performance in New York, where large numbers of musicians turned out to hear it. Lawrence Gilman, champion of modernism early in the century, found his faith rewarded. "The evening was one not soon to be forgotten. An original and distinguished work of art, extraordinarily moving and sincere, was placed before us in the fullness of its power, its pity, and its truth."[11] Berg, pleased by accounts of the performances, wrote friends to ask for mementos of the arrival of his music in the New World.

New places, new music—and new American singers. The most popular of the new American women was Grace Moore, Tennessee-born in 1901. She studied singing in New York, appeared in operetta and musical revues. Her good looks and charming voice gained her a vociferous following, and when she returned to America in 1928, after study in France, her Metropolitan debut produced great publicity. Moore survived the dangers of being pushed forward prematurely and subjected to hysterical adulation, and she steadily matured in her command of her art in the next twenty years. Much of her popularity outside the opera house was due to her appearance in three films. She died in an airplane crash in 1947. Gladys Swarthout, born in Missouri, studied in Chicago and in Italy and then joined the Chicago Civic Opera. She first appeared at the Metropolitan in 1929 in small roles and moved slowly toward her finest achievements in the 1930s, as Mignon and especially Carmen. Her artistry was undervalued because of her placid demeanor, and because her small voice was not suited to the Metropolitan's hugeness.

Remarkable male singers appeared. American women—Kellogg, Nordica, Eames, Farrar—had overshadowed the first generation of men. Charles Adams, a Boston tenor, had sung in Berlin and Vienna in the 1870s. He took the lead in the first American performance of Wagner's *Rienzi* and campaigned, as singer and teacher, on behalf of Wagnerian music drama. Better known as a Wagnerian was David Bispham, a Philadelphia baritone who began to sing when he was thirty. European study and success brought him to the Metropolitan, 1896 through 1903, where his appearances in *Die Meistersinger* and *Parsifal* were much admired. A fine actor and tireless proponent of opera in English, he was also a teacher and the author of a charming memoir, *A Quaker Singer's Recollections*. Riccardo Martin was born Hugh Whitefield, studied in Europe, and sang there with success. Returning to America, he performed in New Orleans and Boston, toured with the San Carlo Company, and spent eight seasons at the Metropolitan, 1907 to 1915. He had a tenor voice of great beauty and was an admirable actor, though he was unfortunately overshadowed, like all other tenors in these years, by Caruso.

In the 1930s a generation of men came of age artistically who had much of their training in America and found opportunities at home. Charles Kullman, a tenor from New Haven, went to Yale, the Juilliard School, Europe and back, making his Metropolitan debut in 1935. He sang there, in a wide range of roles, for twenty-five years. Paul Althouse, born Paul Shearer in Reading, Pennsylvania, was educated at Bucknell University, spent several years touring America, then went to Germany to retrain his voice as a Wagnerian heroic tenor, sang with Chicago and the Metropolitan, sharing roles with Lauritz Melchior and then becoming an influential teacher. John Charles Thomas, of Meyersdale, Virginia, sang in operetta for many years, then with the San Francisco and Chicago companies until the Metropolitan finally gave him a chance in 1934. His booming baritone voice made him a popular performer in radio as well.

The road to the Metropolitan for Lawrence Tibbett led from Bakersfield, California, via church singing and operetta performances. After making an unremarkable Metropolitan debut in 1923, he gave an electrifying performance in *Falstaff* in January 1925 which won him instant acclaim. He gradually gained control of his rich and vibrant voice and, though an erratic performer, became a singer of refinement and intelligence, succeeding Antonio Scotti as the leading baritone of the house. The range of his interpretations, as well as the span of his career, can be marked by his appearances in Ernst Krenek's *Jonny spielt auf* in 1928 and Benjamin Britten's *Peter Grimes* in 1947.[12]

The great voice of the 1930s, however, belonged neither to Tibbett nor to any of his contemporaries. All were overshadowed by a singer who, in the middle of the decade, made a debut that ranked with the most celebrated in American operatic history: Kirsten Flagstad.

The Nordic Winged Victory

Saturday afternoon, February 2, 1935, the Metropolitan Opera House, a performance of *Die Walküre*. The theater audience had been joined by perhaps a million or more people sitting at home, for this was a radio broadcast performance. An announcer named Milton Cross, who was slowly becoming familiar to radio listeners as the "voice of opera," efficiently explained the story of the first act and described the setting. The radio audience heard the applause greeting the appearance of the conductor, Artur Bodanzky, just as Cross concluded his introduction. The music began. The first few minutes were nothing out of the ordinary. Gradually this gave way to a sense of growing excitement, an unmistakable awareness, for radio and theater audience alike, that something remarkable was taking place onstage. The cause of the excitement was Sieglinde—or rather, for radio listeners, the voice of the woman singing Sieglinde, a "fresh, unworn and vigorous voice," a voice of "abundant power" and "full-throated richness," a thrilling and commanding voice, a voice such as had not been heard for many years at the Metropolitan and which, in later days, would evoke from old-timers a comparison with those long-departed days of the golden age of singing at the Metropolitan. The first act ended in a "storm of applause." The buzz of excited conversation rippled through the lobbies. Geraldine Farrar, the featured speaker on the first radio intermission program, and not a person easily impressed, in a "rare burst of enthusiasm" announced flatly that a "new star has been born." Kirsten Flagstad, in a time of depression, doleful spirits, and decline, had achieved one of those legendary operatic debuts which had somehow come to seem part of the vanished past. And the more people learned about her, the more remarkable her story seemed.[1]

S h e was born in Hamar, Norway, in 1895. Both her parents were professional musicians. They played in a local orchestra and her father eventually became a conductor of opera and operetta at the Central Theater in Oslo. Throughout her childhood, Kirsten was surrounded by music. Two brothers became professional musicians and a young sister a notable singer of operetta. At age ten, Kirsten first became familiar with Wagner's music. She was given a vocal score of *Lohengrin* and learned Elsa's role in its entirety. Yet there was nothing precocious about her progress. If anything, her parents held her back. She didn't begin vocal studies until she was sixteen, and then with excellent, patient teachers. She first sang in public in Eugène d'Albert's once popular opera *Tiefland*, followed by Robert Planquette's *The Chimes of Normandy,* and after that in many operettas.

The following years included marriage at twenty-four, an active career at the Opéra-Comique in Oslo, and the birth of a daughter, which led Flagstad to abandon the operatic stage for some time. Her mother talked her into singing again, and she found that her voice had doubled its former power. Resuming her operatic career, she sang in Oslo with first-rank guest artists such as Leo Slezak and Alexander Kipnis. In 1928 she became a member of the opera company in Gothenburg, Sweden. There, and in Norway, she sang a wide range of roles, in *Tosca, La Bohème, I Pagliacci, La Fanciulla del West, Carmen, Faust, Aida, Der Freischütz, Die Meistersinger,* with considerable success.

Only her marriage was unsuccessful. After divorcing her husband in 1929, she met Henry Johansen, a wealthy Norwegian industrialist, whom she married in 1930. Happy to give up the grinding life of opera-house appearances, she returned to Oslo to be a wife and mother and seems to have felt more contentment and peace than ever before—or after. But she wasn't left alone. In the spring of 1930 she and Johansen, on vacation in Vienna, heard *Tristan und Isolde* for the first time. In later years, she liked to admit that "she was so bored she could hardly stay awake." Norwegian theaters importuned her to return from retirement. She wavered, singing in Handel's *Rodelinda* in Gothenburg and in 1932 learning the role of Isolde in six weeks and singing it in Oslo with great success. Still, few outside of Norway and Sweden knew of her, and Flagstad made absolutely no effort to change the situation. Indeed, she didn't respond at all to inquiries from abroad. In 1929 Otto Kahn, on a Scandinavian trip, heard her as Tosca and instructed the Metropolitan's European talent agent to find out more. His inquiries roused no interest on Flagstad's part and nothing more came of it. She was approaching forty, after all, perhaps too late for an international career, even had she desired it. She had local success, security. That was enough for her.

Not for her worldly and ambitious husband, however. At his behest, she sang minor roles at Bayreuth in 1933 and in 1934 returned as Gutrune and Sieglinde. Once again, nothing seemed to follow. Meanwhile, Kipnis urged her merits on the Metropolitan, and in 1934 Flagstad agreed to go to Switzerland to audition for Gatti-Casazza and Bodanzky. In keeping with her consistently nondramatic life, the meeting produced no lightning. The Metropolitan men heard an attractive voice, but not a startling one. Still, Flagstad was an experienced singer, able and well trained. There were few first-rate Wagnerian sopranos around. Gatti-Casazza, playing it safe, signed her to a one-year contract, provided she went to Prague for a period of intensive coaching with George Szell.

There was no sense of great anticipation and virtually no publicity about her forthcoming American appearances. Flagstad was the most placid of women and ardent ambition, if she had ever felt it, had been left behind with her youth. She didn't arrive in New York until January 1935. Rehearsals went well but unremarkably. And then something happened, a premonitory flash of lightning. At the dress rehearsal, perhaps because the acoustics of the Metropolitan, notoriously cruel to smaller voices, emphasized the volume of Flagstad's, Bodanzky suddenly began to discern

Kirsten Flagstad as Sieglinde, in Die Walküre, *the role in which she made her American debut in 1935. She was a mainstay of the second golden age of Wagner at the Metropolitan.*

that there was far more than merely a talented soprano before him. He sent for "Mr. Gatti," gave his baton to an assistant and went out into the theater, ordering the scene to be done again, to absorb "the wonder of what he heard and saw on the stage."[2]

F l a g s t a d ' s brilliant beginning was followed by ampler and even more impressive achievements. "Triumph" was the appropriate word. Four days later she sang Isolde to Melchior's Tristan. "It is long since the music has been so well sung," wrote one critic, "a depth of feeling quite beautiful." And another described with delight "a young woman of royal dignity and grace, one of the rarest, perhaps the rarest of our time." The house was sold out, with standing-room tickets at a premium. This was the case every time she sang thereafter, "suggesting that it was not Metropolitan opera that was depressed, but merely the attractions it offered." Then came Brunnhilde in *Die Walküre,* Brunnhilde in *Götterdämmerung,* Elizabeth in *Tannhäuser,* Elsa in *Lohengrin,* and finally, in April, Kundry in *Parsifal.* Flagstad sang in Boston and Rochester, when the Metropolitan went on a short tour. She was a rich source of revenue for the company in its time of desperate need.[3]

The next five years saw her sing with virtually unremitting vocal splendor. Melchior rose to the challenge of an artist with vocal endowments comparable to his own. Bodanzky's conducting gained renewed vitality, and to Elisabeth Rethberg and Friedrich Schorr, splendid singers already on its roster, the Metropolitan added Lotte Lehmann, from Chicago. "The matchless intensity of Lehmann, her consummate underlining of dramatic detail, bring back pictures for every climax." Where, only a year or two before, things had slumped as badly as the economy, Wagnerian music drama now led the way, as the Metropolitan struggled to re-establish itself securely, but this time as a different kind of opera house, as one where art mattered more than money.

The Wagner audience of the late 1930s showed this clearly. In an atmosphere not unlike that exciting period between 1885 and 1890, its members had no connection with "society" of any kind, attended in large numbers, and showed a refreshing intensity and seriousness after years of bored and routine indifference. From Flagstad's debut until the outbreak of war, the house was crowded whenever she sang. The rising tide of Wagnerism in America seems ironic against the backdrop of Nazism. Vincent Sheean, a perceptive student of opera, believed that the surge of interest was almost entirely due to Flagstad: that "the audiences did not care a fig what Wagner had written: they wanted to hear this golden flood of tone over the massive orchestra," the thrill of her singing which "never frightened, alarmed or repelled; she was not in the very slightest degree demonic."

One other aspect of the Flagstad story is in some ways the most remarkable. Her Sieglinde, that first afternoon, she had sung the year before at Bayreuth. *Tristan und Isolde* she had sung in Oslo. But both Brunnhildes, in *Die Walküre* and *Götterdämmerung,* and Kundry in *Parsifal* were new to her. She had learned the roles in the few weeks preceding her appearance onstage. Things which other artists labored on for years Flagstad regarded as ordinary business. "She probably did not realize for some years that what she had done, with such miraculous suddenness, had never been done before."[4]

F l a g s t a d ' s triumph was not limited to the East. In the fall she went to San Francisco and was a central part of the great season there which catapulted the San Francisco Opera to a new level. She again made her debut in *Die Walküre,* with a superb cast that featured Melchior's "tremendous tenor" voice as Siegmund, the great musicianship of Rethberg's Sieglinde, and Schorr's Wotan of "towering dignity and godly power." The only "unknown quantity" among them, Flagstad dominated the scene. A brief report of this performance by Alfred Frankenstein, a San Francisco critic of sophistication and sensitivity, communicates the excited response to her dazzling voice and presence. Flagstad was "a figure of timeless majesty and classic grace," "noble, heroic lyricism made manifest in human form." Her interpretation was not "cold, impersonal classicism," but rather "a deep warm compassion suffused the accents of her voice," a "heroic flood of human feeling surged through" it. "Before such an artist the customary analysis of vocalism and gesture would be nothing short of impudent," and Frankenstein captured the essence of what he had heard and seen in a striking phrase. She was "a kind of living Nordic Winged Victory."[5]

Four Saints *and* Porgy and Bess

Between the two great wars, unaffected by boom or bust, American composers created distinctively American operas, at last. Graustarkian fantasy dominated the early 1920s. Rudolf Friml's *Rose-Marie* of 1924 incorporated some new elements—a murder, an unusual setting (the Canadian Rockies). Its librettists insisted that "the musical numbers . . . are such an integral part of the action that we do not think we should list them as separate numbers." But it was essentially the old formula for this kind of opera, one with some life left in it, as 557 Broadway performances showed. *The Student Prince of Heidelberg,* by Sigmund Romberg (1887–1951), also 1924, a love story about a waitress and a prince, pretended to no innovations whatever and totaled 608 performances before it set out on an endless round of visits to the theaters and schools of small-town America. Romberg, born in Hungary, was sent to Vienna to study engineering, but instead fell in love with the operettas of Strauss and Lehár. He came to America, decided to become a songwriter, and worked in one of Tin Pan Alley's musical factories, Americanizing post–*Merry Widow* European operettas for the New York market. One of these was *Maytime* (1917), the first expression of his brand of bittersweet sentiment; another, *Blossom Time* (1921), was based on Schubert melodies. In 1925 Friml struck gold again, in medieval France, with *The Vagabond King.* In 1926 Romberg countered with *The Desert Song,* a story of "burning dunes and lofty tunes."

Nevertheless, Graustark was dying. By 1928, Friml's *The Three Musketeers,* though a box office success, seemed inert—"I did greatly enjoy the first few years of Act I," wrote Alexander Woolcott. In the social realist atmosphere of the 1930s, Friml stopped composing. "When I write music for the theatre, I like books with charm to them," he said, "and charm suggests the old things . . . luscious melody, rousing choruses, and romantic passions." Romberg was prepared to innovate in story and subject matter. *May Wine,* of 1935, was about psychoanalysis and did away with the chorus line entirely. He emphasized a different element. "I don't care what the form is. But a melody is still a melody. Nothing succeeds like a popular tune, a romantic tune."[1]

The most important achievement of African American opera of this time was *Shuffle Along* (1921), by Eubie Blake (1883–1983) and Noble Sissle (1889–1975). The child of ex-slaves, Blake studied music in Baltimore, where he was born and grew up. In 1914 he formed a songwriting partnership with Sissle, who had been born in Indianapolis and had toured on the Chautauqua circuit. *Shuffle Along* was a contemporary story about urban politics. Its sharp satire was complemented by a romantic subplot presented without awkwardness. It was dramatically loose—it was billed as "a musical melange"—and contained two hit tunes, "Love Will Find a Way" and "I'm Just Wild about Harry." It ran for 594 performances and then embarked on a national tour of a year and a half. Another African American opera, *Dixie to Broadway,* of 1924, also played successfully to racially mixed audiences. Blake and Sissle combined again for *Chocolate Dandies* in 1924, and for *Shuffle Along of 1933.* The most influential aspect of these African American operas was their dancing, which infused all aspects of American dance. In more general terms, "the explosion of the black American musical style was to fan out in all directions beyond Broadway to permeate the spirit of the Jazz Age." African American musical drama was part of a larger artistic movement, the flowering in poetry, fiction, painting, and sociology as well as music, that goes by the name of the Harlem Renaissance.[2] It captured the imagination of composers, and the three most important operas of these two decades were deeply influenced by African American subjects, music, and performance.

Shuffle Along (1921) was a satire of urban politics by Eubie Blake and Noble Sissle. It ran for 594 performances in New York. Billy Rose Theater Collection, New York Public Library for the Performing Arts.

T h e first of these three operas was composed by Jerome Kern (1885–1945), a native of New York City. He wrote songs as a boy, studied piano and harmony at the New York College of Music, and then went to London, where work for a theatrical producer convinced him to try composing for the theater. His first complete score, *The Red Petticoat,* about a woman barber in the mining town of Lost River, Nevada, may well be the first musical comedy western. *The Girl from Utah* (1914) looked back to the transatlantic theme of Americans in Europe. In 1915 Kern joined with Guy Bolton, a young English librettist, to produce musical plays for the tiny Princess Theater (299 seats) in New York, whose management wanted innovative musical shows. "Everyone seems to be reforming the drama," a literary agent commented. The Bolton and Kern operas aimed at integrated music and story. Casts were small, sets simple, there was an orchestra of a dozen pieces. "The musical numbers should carry the action of the play and should be representative of the personalities of the characters who sing them," Bolton explained. "Song must be suited to the action and the mood of the play." *Very Good, Eddie* (1915) led Bolton and Kern to a triangular collaboration with Pelham Granville Wodehouse, the English novelist then living in America. Of *Oh, Boy!* (1917), a Boston critic said: "Every song and lyric contributed to the action. The humor was based on situation, not interjected by the comedians." Of *Leave It to Jane* (1917), one of the first musical comedies about college life, an observer wrote: "No longer is the heroine a lovely princess masquerading as the serving maid, and no more is the scene Ruritania or Monte Carlo." These operas made the "formulas of George M. Cohan seem crude and obvious." "They were the first real advancements in the development of a truly native theatre."[3]

Then the trio broke up. Kern turned to composing wonderful songs for lavish Broadway star-driven productions produced by Florenz Ziegfeld and starring Marilyn Miller. The story for one of these, *Sunny,* was by Otto Harbach and Oscar Hammerstein II, grandson of Oscar the First. Kern and Hammerstein decided to search for a story which would allow them to work toward the integrated music drama of the Bolton-Kern-Wodehouse works, but on a larger scale and dealing with a noncomic subject. They found what they were looking for in a novel by Edna Ferber, *Show Boat.* Theater people urged them not to do it. The story included two unhappy marriages, a heroine of mixed blood. Racial intermixing, then a fearful topic, hovered in the background. In addition, the lives of African Americans in the South were shown to be harsh and precarious. Hammerstein and Kern were undeterred. The dramatic possibilities of the story excited them. If Hammerstein's libretto now seems awkward and contrived, at the time it was audacious. Kern's score was his greatest, a treasure house of songs which have become classics of musical theater. Ziegfeld produced it, Joseph Urban designed the sets.

Show Boat opened on December 27, 1927, at the Ziegfeld Theater, with Charles Winninger as Cap'n Andy and Helen Morgan as Julie La Verne. The show was greeted with enormous enthusiasm and ran for 575 performances, toured the country for many months, returned to New York three years later for a revival, was eventually turned into a movie. Its importance in the evolution of American opera would be difficult to exaggerate. The first scene was revolutionary: there was no chorus of long-legged, sexually appealing women. Instead, African American dock workers lamented the drudgery of loading cotton bales, and the song which expressed this, "Ol' Man River," served as a unifying theme throughout. *Show Boat* combined elements from much of American musical theater that had preceded it, but "raised the musical to a new height of attainment." The story was cohesive, the songs created mood, revealed character, and advanced the plot. "It laid the foundation for *Porgy and Bess, South Pacific,* and other serious musical plays." Stark Young, the critic and novelist, sensed its long-term significance. "Some of its best numbers are so successful in their combination of the theatrical elements, music, acting, scene," he wrote, "as to suggest an opening for the development not of mere musical comedy, but of popular opera."[4]

Kern continued to explore the possibilities of lyrical music drama of a highly individual kind. As *Show Boat* proved, he was very much aware of the social context of theater. Nevertheless, as his art was neither satirical nor ideological, the 1930s were not a favorable time for him. *The Cat and the Fiddle* (1931) and *Music in the Air* (1932), were set in contemporary Europe, and in both the songs subtly moved the action forward, while retaining their unequaled lyrical quality. "Broadway has not heard lovelier music in all its life," a critic wrote of *The Cat and the Fiddle,* and another of *Music in the Air:* "so drenched in melody that [it] is an unfailing delight." *Very Warm for May* (1939), though a box-office failure, contained charming music and was based on an intelligent libretto by Hammerstein.[5] Kern spent the last decade and a half of his life largely in Hollywood, composing for films.

T h e Metropolitan Opera would not even consider allowing a popular opera such as *Show Boat* on its stage. Almost a decade had passed since it had produced a full-length American opera, so the Metropolitan decided to show what composers of "grand" opera were doing in a contemporary idiom. It looked for someone with a knowledge of theater and of the current musical scene, and it settled on Joseph Deems Taylor (1885–1966), an exact contemporary of Jerome Kern, like him a native of New York City. Taylor attended New York University, was largely self-taught as a composer, and devoted much of his life to musical journalism, as influential critic of various newspapers and as editor of *Musical America.* Taylor was an odd choice in one way since, for all his knowledge of the contemporary musical world, he had no theatrical experience. His orchestral pieces had made his reputation. Anyway, Otto Kahn commissioned an opera. "Mr. Deemus," as Gatti-Casazza called him, selected Edna St. Vincent Millay as his librettist, and went to work.

The result was *The King's Henchman,* which opened in the same year as *Show Boat,* 1927. Millay's libretto was rightly praised for its sensitive language and the Metropolitan production was handsome—designed by Joseph Urban, conducted by Tulio Serafin, with an excellent cast led by Lawrence Tibbett, Florence Easton, Edward Johnson. Audiences were pleased. "The press was benevolent," Gatti-Casazza recalled. "The first and last acts were good, the third not so strong." All told, *The King's Henchman* received fourteen Metropolitan performances over two years—more than any Mozart opera received there in the interwar decades! The chief complaint was the familiar one about American grand opera—derivativeness. This criticism was charmingly expressed by an Italian singer who, during a rehearsal of another American opera, held his hat reverently over his head. "Whatever are you doing?" he was asked. "Saluting the spirits of dead composers."

Taylor, Kahn, and the Metropolitan tried again. Taylor's adaptation of Gerald Du Maurier's novel *Peter Ibbetson* received its world premiere in February 1931. Once again the singers—Bori, Tibbett, Johnson—were fine, the Urban sets and the Serafin conducting were praised, and once again audiences heard no individual voice. The general response of "not so bad" to *The King's Henchman* became "not so good" for *Peter Ibbetson*.[6]

The next Metropolitan commission, *The Emperor Jones* by Louis Gruenberg (1884–1964), was a self-consciously "modernist" work, an adaptation of the Eugene O'Neill play. It was to have been given first in Berlin but was withdrawn. An American opera with an African American as central figure would not do in Nazi Germany. At the Metropolitan Jo Mielziner, a Broadway designer, conceived bold sets, but they were modified "by the conservative Metropolitan minds." It was unacceptable for an African American to sing the lead role, which was given instead to Tibbett. However, the production was notable for breaking the color line: Hemsley Winfield, an African American, danced the role of the Witch Doctor. The inescapable problem was Gruenberg's music, "monochromatic," "turbulent, sometimes frenetic." More damning was the observation that the incessant drumbeat, a famous feature of the play, was more effective than anything Gruenberg composed. New York was unreceptive. San Francisco was hostile—*The Emperor Jones* was booed there.

The last instance of Otto Kahn's influence on the Metropolitan was *Merry Mount* by Howard Hanson (1896–1981), adapted from a Nathaniel Hawthorne story. First given in February 1934, it was heard six times and then no more. The estimate of these operas by a music historian seems fair: "sincere but weak essays that had no connection with the American people, the native idioms, theater itself, or with any sense of contemporary style."[7] This was especially true by contrast with two operas which, performed in 1934 and 1935, met that historian's prescription: indigenous in idiom, highly theatrical, freshly contemporary. After decades of expectant waiting, American audiences confronted two works of musical genius, *Four Saints in Three Acts* and *Porgy and Bess*.

V i r g i l Thomson was born in Kansas City, Missouri, in 1896, his boyhood "centered on school and church, with lots of play and reading thrown in." And music. He learned to play the piano at five, the organ at twelve, and recalled "rolling on the floor in ecstasy at hearing for the first time in real string sound the repeated high F's of the *Cavalleria Rusticana* Intermezzo." One of his teachers, an opera fan, put Virgil through the piano score of *Faust,* the "limpidities of *Fra Diavolo,*" "the turgid stream of *Parsifal.*" He learned all the standard operatic overtures and, at summer band concerts, heard the "great operatic set-pieces" and was "ravished on weekly Wagner nights by the most luscious harmonic experience that exists." It was the intense but extraordinary limited experience of American small-town culture in the days before radio and recordings. Like Thea Kronborg in *The Song of the Lark,* who had heard no Beethoven until she went to Chicago, Virgil had not yet heard a symphony orchestra, string quartet, or an opera. And yet at fourteen he declared his vocation. "There was no use thinking I was not to be a musician . . . I was one already. . . . Music was my life and always would be." A teacher took him to Chicago, where they went to the opera every night at the Auditorium. "I acquired an admiration for Mary Garden's artistic powers." She introduced him to the French operatic repertory, inclining him toward things French. In 1919 a modest bequest from his grandmother enabled him to continue his musical studies at Harvard, and a fellowship allowed him to stay one year in France. He studied composition and organ with the celebrated Nadia Boulanger and met many of the more advanced French composers, above all Erik Satie. After completing his degree, he returned to Paris in 1925 and stayed there, with occasional trips back to America, until World War II.[8]

In the 1920s, Paris was the home of the avant-garde in the arts. Satie's music was "the test, almost, of any composer's being inside twentieth centuryness," a music of reserve, avoiding excess and public rhetoric, a way of speaking "as if nobody were there." Thomson also became familiar with Dada, "the stylish tone for advanced artists and for the art-minded," and its principles: "that all art is convention, that all conventions have equal value (or none) and that therefore an artist is free to work in (or invent, if he can) any convention whatsoever that may please him." He regarded Dada as a declaration of independence, for himself, from commerce, the academy, and tradition, congenial to his own American Protestant iconoclasm. All Americans, he wrote, were a little Dada-minded: "What else is our free wheeling humor, our nonsense, our pop art?" He established his own claims as a modernist, but of an indisputably American kind, with songs and choral and chamber music, odd but not outrageous.

The notorious modernist among American composers of the time, then living in Europe, was George Antheil, who, "with his cheerful lack of modesty," was "the literary mind's idea of a musical genius—bold, bumptious, and self-confident." Antheil was born in New Jersey in 1900, of German ancestry. Musically precocious, he studied composition in Philadelphia and New York, with Ernest Bloch, the Swissborn composer who had emigrated to America in 1916. Antheil's first symphony *Zingareska* (1920–1922), used jazz rhythms in its last movement and struck Americans who heard it as ferociously advanced. Antheil went to Europe in 1922 as a concert pianist, but concentrated on composition, in an antiromantic, propulsive, strident style, influenced by Stravinsky and seeking to unite jazz rhythms with machinelike effects. His piano pieces, *Airplane Sonata, Death of Machines, Jazz Sonata,* were championed by Joyce, Yeats, Satie, Picasso, and others, and Ezra Pound wrote a book about his music, *Antheil and the Treatise on Harmony.* Antheil's most shocking work was the *Ballet mécanique* of 1925, a percussive ensemble scored for sixteen pianolas to be coordinated with the showing of a film. When it was finally given, in Paris and later in New York, it produced the obligatory outraged response, "fist fights and contumely in the aisles." After that Antheil turned to opera. *Transatlantic,* a satire about an American presidential election, to a libretto of his own, was performed in Frankfurt in 1930. The staging was imaginative, the final act being performed on four platforms with quick cinema cuts from one to the other. Musically, it was "an almost nonstop barrage of tango yowls, syncopation, and flatted thirds . . . set so that the vocal line accented the wrong syllables of words." For half a century it remained the most celebrated American opera America had never heard or seen.

At Harvard, Thomson had read Gertrude Stein and had set one of her pieces, "Susie Asado," for piano and voice, but he had not, in his first two years in Paris, met her, preferring to wait until it could happen informally. When at last they met—Thomson went along with Antheil to 17 rue de Fleurus—he felt that Alice Toklas didn't care for him, "but Gertrude and I got on like Harvard men." Later, he showed her his setting of "Susie Asado," and her reply was inimitable: "I like its looks immensely and want to frame it and Miss Toklas who knows more than looks says the things in it please her a lot and when can I know a little other than its looks but I am completely satisfied with its looks."

Early in 1927 Thomson asked Stein to write an opera libretto for him. She agreed. He wanted something which would give him both male and female leading roles, with secondary parts, and with choruses. "I thought we should follow overtly the format of classical Italian opera, which carries on the commerce of the play in dry recitative, extending the emotional moments into arias and set-pieces." It was a return to the Florentine and Venetian origins of opera, to *opera seria,* with its mythological subjects, provided that mythology be defined broadly enough to include subjects other than the Scandinavian and Greek, and possibly to include political history and the lives of saints. Eventually, "our saints turned out to be Baroque and Spanish," a solution that "delighted Gertrude, for she loved Spain."

Stein began writing and kept Thomson informed as to how it was going. "Four saints in three acts. And others. Make it pastoral. In hills and gardens." She added a postscript: "The saints are still enjoying themselves." Stein offered the services of Picasso as stage designer, but Thomson declined, "preferring to remain, except for her, within my own age group." By July Stein had finished. In November Thomson began composing, working at the piano, improvising melody to fit the words. He wrote nothing down. When the first act improvised itself in the same way every time, he wrote it down. On Christmas night 1927, he performed act 1 for friends. Act 2 was completed by February, acts 3 and 4 by summer.

Thomson was centrally concerned with one aspect of the relationship of words and music that had troubled English and American composers for two and a half centuries—recitative. He hoped "to crack open, and solve for all time anything still waiting to be solved, which was almost everything, about English musical declamation." How best to convey the meaning of Stein's text in sung speech? "The meanings of Stein's texts were so absent or abstract or multiplied—which came to the same thing—that it was impossible for the composer to choose . . . meanings along the conventional lines of 'birdie babbling by the brook,' or 'heavy hangs my heart.'" Instead, he set the text for sound. The meaning would take care of itself. He didn't try to do "any of the things already done by the words." His music "merely explodes these into singing and gives them shape." Shape meant musical reinforcement, because Stein's poetry alone was amorphous. "I do not mean that her writing *lacks* music; I mean that it *likes* music. Much of it, in fact, lies closer to musical timings than to speech timings."

Music contained energy long since lost to language, an excitement created by the contest between two rhythmic patterns, one of lengths and one of stresses. Lengths alone were static, while repetition of stresses alone became hypnotic. Together, and contrasted, they created tension and release, the energy that makes music take flight. Music's forward thrust would give shape to the independent pacing of Stein's text, what we mean when we say that words and music make opera "moving." Music thrusts the words forward in time. Thomson anticipated the criticism that his orchestral accompaniment to Stein's words was backward-looking music for a forward-looking text. It didn't use dissonance, the contemporary idiom, Thomson answered that this view assumed "discord is advanced and harmoniousness old-fashioned. That is not true, just as its opposite is not." Stein's text created a powerful trajectory of "verbal volubility that would brook no braking." Dissonance generated "interval frictions and contrapuntal viscosities which would trip up my verbal speeds." Conventional modernism was a booby trap. Instead, he took from Protestant and Catholic liturgical vernacular the kind of chords that gave strength to a text, that "had for centuries borne the weight of long prayers and praises."[9]

Four Saints abounded in paradoxes and oddities, resisted all categories. The literal-minded were disconcerted because there weren't four saints. (There were at least thirty, and there were four acts, not three.) Thomson set every word of Stein's text to music, including the stage directions. The opera was set in Spain, but its musical references were Missouri Baptist. Modernism emphasized the introspective artist's personal vision, often nightmarish, while *Four Saints* was objective, dispassionate. Modernism was formidably complex. *Four Saints* was simple but radically eclectic. "European historical models, music's old masters, let me assure you, are not easy to escape from." Quoting hymn tunes and operetta, with two nonsaintly commentators, filled with fun and playfulness, *Four Saints* reached back to the minstrel show of the mid-nineteenth century, affronting the old idea of grand opera. It paid a price for such effrontery, being too popular to be intellectual, too noncommercial to be popular. No conductor took it up. No publisher showed any interest. No opera house would touch it. Its fate was summed up in its own statement: "along with the saints, we wait."[10]

Finally, a group called the Friends and Enemies of Modern Music produced it in May 1934 at the Hartford Athenaeum in Connecticut. If music and text puzzled, its production excited interest and considerable comment. It had extraordinary all-cellophane scenery designed by Florine Stettheimer, a contemporary American painter. Its choreographic movement was by Frederick Ashton and John Houseman. It was sung by an entirely African American cast, selected "purely for beauty of voice, clarity of enunciation, and fine carriage." It provoked sufficient controversy to bring it to Broadway, where it had a six-week run. "There were constant editorials, cartoons and jokes about it." Its audience was "a most knowing one—that included all our choicest spirits of modern verse, music and drama." In the fall it went to Chicago, to "Louis Sullivan's monumental opera house, still favorable to the sound of music and to voices." Gertrude Stein was there, in Harold McCormick's box. Still, no publisher offered to issue it. No lecture agent took up Thomson's services. "The praiseworthy American operas respond less to tradition and continuity than to the one moment—

A scene from the original production of Four Saints in Three Acts *(1934), with the all–African American cast and Florine Stettheimer's cellophane scenery. The first of the Virgil Thomson–Gertrude Stein collaborations drew on minstrel traditions as well as opera. John Herrick Jackson Music Library, Yale University.*

that they themselves create," an astute opera critic has written. And as one moves on to *Porgy and Bess,* his words are again wonderfully perceptive: "How unlike are the great American operas—unlike anything at all, including each other."[11]

G e o r g e Gershwin was born in 1898 in Brooklyn, of Russian immigrant parents. There were four children: Israel, called Isidore by the family and Ira by everyone else; Jacob, who became George; and a younger son and daughter. Ira was bookish, keen on the theater; George was restless, absorbed in neighborhood life. Music meant nothing to him, though he later recalled hearing bits which stirred him—rags, blues, spirituals, Anton Rubinstein's "Melody in F," Dvořák's "Humoresque." The family bought a piano for Ira, but George, who was twelve, took it over and the family arranged lessons for him. He was bored by formal instruction until a teacher named Goldfarb, a Hungarian immigrant, gained his attention by concentrating entirely on selections from operas, which he encouraged George to play in a wild way.

Soon music displaced everything else in George's life. In 1912 he went to the composer-pianist Charles Hambitzer, for whom he played the *William Tell* overture in the Goldfarb manner. "Listen," Hambitzer said, "let's hunt out the guy who taught you to play this way and shoot him—and not with an apple on his head either." Hambitzer, Wisconsin-born, had received excellent instruction from German teachers, taught at the Wisconsin Conservatory, and realized that the boy was "deadly serious." He gave him free lessons. As well, he gave him a precious mixture of encouragement and self-discipline, exercises and scales, a start in concerts. George heard prominent soloists, pasted the pictures of great composers and performers in a bookkeeper's ledger, often coming home to play from memory the melodies he had just heard. At fifteen he composed his first song. "He wants to go in for this modern stuff, jazz and what not," Hambitzer complained. "But I'm not going to let him for a while. I'll see that he gets a firm foundation in the standard music first." Gershwin dropped out of school and got a job as a song plugger in a Tin Pan Alley publishing house. Swept up in the excitement of ragtime, impressed by Jerome Kern's songs, he worked his way toward musical theater. At the same time, he continued his studies.

When Hambitzer died in 1918, Gershwin went to Edward Kilenyi, a Hungarian who had studied at Columbia University and with Pietro Mascagni in Rome. For the next five years Kilenyi led him through the analysis of music by Beethoven, Haydn, Debussy, Strauss. Kilenyi discerned that Gershwin's future lay in composition, that popular music was his idiom. "You will face the same difficulty all Americans do trying to have their works performed," he said. "It will bring you nearer your goal if you become a big success as a popular composer, for then conductors will come to you to ask for serious work." Many people didn't understand Gershwin's desire to work both sides of the street. In the Tin Pan Alley cubicle where he worked, his fellow songwriters heard him practicing Bach. "Are you studying to be a concert pianist, George?" "No, I'm studying to be a great popular-song composer."[12]

He left Tin Pan Alley in 1918, wrote "Swanee," a song popularized by Al Jolson, which sold more than two million records and one million copies of sheet music. Gershwin composed his first complete musical comedy score, *La La Lucille,* in 1919. He was on his way, with music for a series of revues, *George White's Scandals,* and then popular musical shows, *Lady, Be Good!* (1924), *Oh, Kay!* (1926), *Funny Face* (1927), *Girl Crazy* (1930), most of them in collaboration with his brother Ira as lyricist and librettist. Studded with engaging songs of a distinctive style, vigorous, very danceable, the shows made no attempt to break any new ground conceptually, but were star vehicles for popular performers—Gertrude Lawrence, Victor Moore, Fred and Adele Astaire.

In the 1920s Gershwin's innovative and ambitious music was nontheatrical. Two concerts launched him publicly as a composer, one a very famous event, the other less well known. In 1923 the soprano Eva Gauthier gave a recital in New York's Aeolian Hall, singing a wide range of songs, from Purcell and Bellini to Schoenberg, Bartók, and Milhaud, and including three by Gershwin, with the composer accompanying her in his music and, in Deems Taylor's words, "doing mysterious and fascinating and contrapuntal stunts with the accompaniment." With their "almost classically severe form, and subtle fascinating rhythms, the Gershwin songs stood up very well in their distinguished company." In Boston, where the concert was repeated, H. T. Parker praised the "cross-rhythms, pliant and out-springing counterpoint, sustained cadences" of his music. "Gershwin is the beginning of the age of sophisticated jazz." The following year Paul Whiteman, violinist and band leader, organized a concert showing the evolution of popular music, emphasizing but not limited to the work of American composers, and he invited Gershwin to contribute a piece in the jazz idiom. Gershwin agreed but, busy with theatrical projects, completed his work with little time to spare. It was a rhapsody for piano and jazz band and was orchestrated by Ferde Grofé, American composer, pianist, and arranger for the Whiteman band. Ira Gershwin had recently seen a show of paintings by James McNeill Whistler, the titles of whose works combined musical forms and colors. And so—*Rhapsody in Blue.*

Well publicized by Whiteman, the concert on February 12, 1924, was sold out and attracted many famous musicians. They heard a varied program—African American jazz, comedy selections, songs by Schoenberg, Kern, MacDowell, and, next to last, Gershwin's *Rhapsody.* The opening wail of the clarinet seized the attention of the audience, which never relaxed, and at the end there was an ovation for the composer. (He played it himself.) The critical response was, if anything, excessive, both for and against. "Far superior to Schoenberg, Milhaud, and the rest of the futuristic fellows." "Greater than Stravinsky's *The Rite of Spring.*" Or: "Empty passage work and meaningless repetition." "How trite and feeble and conventional the tunes are."[13] *Rhapsody in Blue* soon worked its way around the world. It made Gershwin famous. It made him rich. It inspired him to more ambitious efforts, to larger forms: a Concerto in F for piano and orchestra in 1925; a tone poem, *An American in Paris,* in 1928; a Second Rhapsody for piano and orchestra in 1931. His works were performed in Carnegie Hall and in Symphony Hall in Boston. Gershwin went no further in orchestral music. He again turned to the theater.

Strike Up the Band of 1927, libretto by George Kauffman and Morrie Ryskind, lyrics by Ira Gershwin, was "a rather good satirical attack on war, genuine propaganda at times, sung and danced on Broadway to standing room only." The musical numbers moved the story forward and commented on the characters. The title song set the mocking tone of the work, which achieved one hundred ninety-one performances. In 1931 came *Of Thee I Sing,* again libretto by Kauffman and Ryskind, lyrics by Ira Gershwin. This too was satirical, its subject American political institutions, particularly presidential campaigns, capturing the mediocrity of American political life in two absurd caricatures: John P. Wintergreen, candidate for president, and Alexander Throttlebottom, candidate for vice president. It was the Gershwins' tribute to Gilbert and Sullivan, and H. T. Parker acutely described it as "one of the drollest satirical operettas of all time." The entire production was built on music and it constituted an advance in terms of integration of music, words, and story over anything Gershwin had yet achieved. The last scenes were a "profusion of arias, choruses and recitatives." It was an enormous hit and, as evidence of how far popular American opera had come, *Of Thee I Sing* won the Pulitzer Prize for drama. However, as there was no prize for music; the award went to *Ira* Gershwin and to Kauffman and Ryskind. Gershwin was not included, since his music had supposedly not contributed to the actual story. Its sequel, *Let 'Em Eat Cake* (1933), with the same librettists and lyricist, was an even more impressive effort at musical and dramatic coherence. With Wintergreen and Throttlebottom in power, and the possibility of a dictatorship of the proletariat looming, the satire was grimmer, less amusing. The contemporary American scene was reflected in the musical score, "discordant, contrapuntal," offering no easy melodious relief. There was only one love song, and the chorus was used as a harsh commentary on events. *Let 'Em Eat Cake* was not a commercial success. Gershwin, though disappointed, was not disheartened, considering it his "claim to legitimacy" as a composer for the theater. For his next work he turned away from satire and, drawing on blues as well as jazz, created a folk opera that was the culmination of the movement of African American music and culture to a position of central importance in American musical theater.[14]

T h e r e had been an earlier attempt. In 1922 Gershwin wrote a one-act, half-hour blues opera, *Blue Monday,* a story about a triangular love affair which converts jealousy into murder. It was sung throughout, with recitative carrying the story forward. It was to be sung by whites in blackface because it was part of a popular lavish Broadway revue, *George White's Scandals,* made up of songs, comic sketches, and elaborate dance routines. Incongruous as it was in such a setting, audiences apparently responded favorably. Ferde Grofé, Paul Whiteman, and others liked it, but Broadway critics were fiercely dismissive: "The most dismal, stupid and incredible black-face sketch that has probably ever been perpetrated." *Blue Monday* was withdrawn from the *Scandals,* renamed *135th Street,* given in concert performance by Whiteman in 1925 and again in 1936 (and on television in 1953). Whatever its merits and demerits, it shows how deeply rooted was Gershwin's intuition that an African American subject should one day be the subject of an opera.[15]

In 1926 Gershwin read *Porgy* by Dubose Heyward and was excited by it. Heyward dramatized the novel in 1927, fortifying Gershwin's belief in its operatic possibilities, but he was too busy to do anything about his idea. In 1932 the Theater Guild suggested that Oscar Hammerstein and Jerome Kern do a musical treatment of the story, with Al Jolson in the title role. Heyward preferred to wait for Gershwin. In 1933 they signed a contract, Heyward doing the libretto for Gershwin's music, Ira Gershwin once again writing the lyrics. All through 1934 Gershwin worked steadily on the music, corresponding by mail with Heyward, later going to South Carolina, where Heyward lived and worked, to get a taste of the sea island atmosphere. Heyward recounted how, when he presented the brothers with text, "after their extraordinary fashion [they] would get at the piano, pound, wrangle, swear, burst into weird snatches of song, and eventually emerge with a polished lyric." By the end of the summer of 1934, the music was finished.

Gershwin decided on the title *Porgy and Bess* to avoid confusion between novel, play, and opera. Rouben Mamoulian, who had directed the play, directed the opera. Alexander Smallens conducted, Serge Soudekine did the sets. The assembling of the large and largely African American cast was complex. Hundreds of auditions were held. Todd Duncan, who had been teaching music at Howard University, was picked as Porgy, Anne Brown, with almost no singing experience, as Bess. John W. Bubbles, a tap dancer in vaudeville, who couldn't read music, was Sportin' Life. The chorus was under the direction of Eva Jessye, born in Coffeyville, Kansas, in 1895, the first African American woman to win international distinction as a choral director. She had studied with Will Marion Cook, found radio and Hollywood closed to African Americans, but auditioned with her choir for *Porgy.* "That's it, that's what I want," George Gershwin said when he heard them. The original opera lasted four and a half hours. Severe cuts were made, removing the recitatives, so that what audiences saw and heard for decades was not the opera Gershwin had imagined and created. Still, the Boston opening night was an unquestioned success, the audience shouting its praise at the end.[16]

Porgy and Bess opened in New York on October 10, 1935, amid great curiosity and excitement. The audience response was enthusiastic, but the response of the critics

James Rosamond Johnson as Frazier and Todd Duncan as Porgy in the 1935 production of Gershwin's Porgy and Bess. Virgil Thomson called it "crooked folklore and halfway opera, a strong but crippled work." John Herrick Jackson Music Library, Yale University.

was a cruel disappointment. The drama critics admired it, the music critics had many reservations. The center of the disagreement was whether *Porgy and Bess* was or wasn't an opera. Olin Downes: "The style is at one moment of opera and another of operetta or sheer Broadway entertainment." Samuel Chotzinoff: "As entertainment it is hybrid, fluctuating constantly between music drama, musical comedy, and operetta." Virgil Thomson: "It is crooked folklore and halfway opera, a strong but crippled work." Lawrence Gilman: "Listening to such sure-fire rubbish as the duet between Porgy and Bess, 'You Is My Woman Now' . . . you wonder how the composer could stoop to such easy and such needless conquests."[17]

Another point of contention was whether *Porgy and Bess* was authentically African American, which reminds us that its premiere was only a quarter of a century after that of *La Fanciulla del West*. The familiar literal bias of American culture shaped the discussion of this issue. Eva Jessye later characterized *Porgy and Bess* as "a masterful work. [Gershwin] was definitely gifted. . . . He studied a great deal, but I've been black longer than he has. I had a great deal of fun saying that. I was black all day and he wasn't. . . . But of course, his stuff sounds quite white." Of course, Gershwin wasn't African American. Neither was Verdi Egyptian nor Bizet Spanish. Gershwin never imagined or pretended his opera was African American. "I believe I have achieved an American flavor in the melodies," he said, "and I have tried to preserve the inflections of Negro speech in the sections corresponding to recitative." Nor was his opera a "folk opera," though many people called it that. "There is no borrowed Negro folk material but I have composed a number of original 'Spirituals.'" Others objected that the issue was not Gershwin's race but his supposed stereotypical view of African Americans, as in Paul Rosenfeld's complaint: "It would seem as if Gershwin knew chiefly stage Negroes." If so, the source of this problem lay primarily with Heyward's novel and libretto.

Porgy and Bess ran for 124 performances on Broadway, an extraordinary achievement by any operatic standards. Yet it was deemed a failure. It didn't make money on its three-month tour. Gershwin never wavered in thinking it his greatest work and "never quite ceased to wonder at the miracle he had been its composer." He vigorously defended the quality and popularity of the opera's songs. "I am not ashamed of writing songs at any time so long as they are good songs. I realized I was writing an opera for the theater and without songs it could be neither of the theater nor entertaining." But in the age of operatic modernism, with its disdain for mere song and for the popular, we can understand his rueful comment: "Songs are entirely within the operatic tradition."[18]

After *Porgy and Bess,* Gershwin composed no more for the theater. He went to Hollywood where, on July 11, 1937, he died of a brain tumor. He was not yet forty. An appropriate epitaph comes from the night of the Boston opening of *Porgy and Bess*. Eva Gauthier, the soprano with whom Gershwin had concertized over a decade earlier, gave him a copy of Monteverdi's *Orfeo* inscribed: "The first opera ever written to the composer of the latest opera."[19]

New Deal America in Peace and War

In 1933, to cope with catastrophic unemployment, the newly elected Roosevelt administration launched an unprecedented program of work relief—payment for labor as opposed to direct relief, the dole. It accepted two ideas that had important consequences for the arts in America: that in time of need artists were entitled to employment *as artists;* and that the arts were the legitimate concern of the federal government. When, in September 1935, the Works Progress Administration (WPA) created Federal Project Number One to create and supervise work relief programs in the graphic arts, theater, writing, and music, there began a New Deal for the arts.[1]

The Music Project covered a wide range of activities in addition to employing musicians for performance. Musical works were commissioned from American composers—George Antheil, William Schuman, David Diamond, Elliott Carter. A composers' forum, for the performance of new works, was established. There were radio broadcasts by WPA music groups, an extensive music education program in schools, the compilation of an index of American composers and their compositions from colonial times, and, in San Francisco, a multivolume history of the city's music.

The Music Project's first head, Nikolas Sokoloff, was born in Russia in 1886 and trained as a violinist, came to America at age thirteen, and was given a scholarship to the Yale University School of Music. He became a violinist with the Boston Symphony and, in 1920, the first conductor of the Cleveland Orchestra. Sokoloff believed the Music Project should emphasize performance. Between 1935 and 1939 the concert division, employing about seven thousand musicians, included twenty-eight symphony orchestras, ninety small orchestras, sixty-eight brass bands, fifty-five dance bands, fifteen chamber music groups, thirty-three opera and choral units, and one soloists' group. The project encouraged African American composers and sponsored performances of *Il Trovatore, Fra Diavolo,* and *Aida* by African American groups. None of the arts projects practiced racial segregation, which subjected them to intense criticism.

The opera aspect of the Music Project was limited by the fear that productions would prove too expensive. Anything beyond labor costs had to be raised by private subscription. To get around this, many operas were presented in concert form with a few rudimentary props and costumes. In this way English-language performances were given in New York, Los Angeles, Jacksonville, Buffalo, Cleveland, Omaha, Philadelphia, and San

Swing Mikado, *an African American version of the Gilbert and Sullivan operetta produced by the Federal Theater, was a hit in Chicago in 1935. Library of Congress.*

Francisco of *Carmen, The Bartered Bride, Samson et Dalila.* A chamber opera group presented *Abu Hassan* by Weber and *The Princess and the Pea* by Ernst Toch (1887–1964), an Austrian composer who had come to America in 1934. These played for three weeks, to capacity audiences, in New York and would have had more performances except for the difficulty in finding an adequate theater. Later the chamber group did a double-bill of Pergolesi's *The Maid as Mistress* (*La Serva padrona*) and a contemporary opera, Frederic Hart's *Romance of a Robot,* twenty-one times.

Some of the most interesting opera originated in the Theater Project. There was one big hit—the *Swing Mikado,* Gilbert and Sullivan done to African American rhythms by an all–African American cast. First performed in Chicago, it ran there for five months and was taken to New York in February 1939, where its audience was "comprised of the type of people that you never see in the Broadway theatres." Orson Welles, a member of the New York Federal Theater, first gained national attention by presenting an African American *Macbeth,* set in Haiti, with music by Virgil Thomson.[2]

The New Deal's relationship to American art went far beyond government sponsorship, important as that was. Artists, by and large, supported the New Deal, partly because they admired Franklin Roosevelt (though his interest in art was meager), more because the New Deal challenged the domination of American culture by business. Always conscious of their marginal position in America, artists now saw themselves as coming into their own. This explains why, for artists, the 1920s were affluent but despairing, the 1930s depressed but optimistic. "The Thirties were a time of fulfillment for musicians of my age," Thomson wrote, "because we were ready for that, and also because our country was ready for us."

The art of the 1930s, even if unassociated with New Deal politics and far from Washington, can rightly be called New Deal art. Two ideas united the political and artistic New Deals. The first was the return to the land as the source of fundamental value. Millions of people in their everyday lives saw depictions of an abundant nature in the post office murals of the painters of the Art Project; millions saw the result of the exploitation of nature in the photographs of the artists working for the Farm Resettlement Administration (FSA). The good earth was the subject of the regionalist painters, Grant Wood, John Steuart Curry, Thomas Hart Benton, a vision paralleled by the documentary films of Pare Lorentz (with music by Thomson), *The Plow That Broke the Plains* and *The River,* also sponsored by the FSA. Cherishing the land and the land's history inspired the oral and local histories undertaken by the WPA, the Rivers of America series that came from the Writing Project, and the ballets by Aaron Copland: *Billy the Kid* (1938), *Rodeo* (1942), *Appalachian Spring* (1944). New Deal art outlasted the political New Deal—witness that masterpiece about the sustaining land, Rodgers' and Hammerstein's *Oklahoma* of 1943. The second idea was the quest for social justice. This too was everywhere—in the WPA murals, in the work of Ben Shahn, in the dramatized news reports of the Theater Project's "Living Newspaper," in novels and in plays, such as Clifford Odets's *Waiting for Lefty* (1936). And it was found in opera too, in Marc Blitzstein's *The Cradle Will Rock.*

C h i l d of a prosperous Philadelphia banking family, advanced in its social views, conservative in its musical taste, Marc Blitzstein (1905–1964) was precocious: studying music at three, performing publicly as a pianist at five, composing at seven. He attended the University of Pennsylvania and the Curtis Institute of Music, then studied with Nadia Boulanger in Paris and Arnold Schoenberg in Berlin. From 1928 to 1935 he lived and worked as composer, performer, and critic in Europe, writing intellectual modernist music, some of it for the theater, influenced by the operas of Kurt Weill and Bertolt Brecht. The economic crisis and the advent of the New Deal awakened his interest in American events. "I don't think I want to stay here any more. I want to be working in my own country. There are things going on there I want to be a part of."[3] He returned to America.

In the spring of 1936, in a five-week period, Blitzstein wrote a "play with music," in ten scenes, about industrial violence in the steel industry. He called it *The Cradle Will Rock* and dedicated it to Brecht. Efforts to find a producer for the opera came to nothing until the spring of 1937, when John Houseman arranged for Blitzstein to play and sing the opera for a group of people, including Hallie Flanagan, director of the Federal Theater. Blitzstein "played, sang and acted with the hard hypnotic drive which came to be familiar to audiences. It took no wizardry to see that this was not just a play set to music, nor music illustrated by actors, but music and play equaling something new and better than either." The Federal Theater agreed to sponsor the opera, with Houseman producing and Orson Welles directing. Flanagan knew that this would produce a political storm, but calculated that, as the arts projects were under fire anyway, "there was no safety in prudence and no virtue in caution."[4]

The Cradle Will Rock was propaganda opera. It depicted the capitalist system, represented by the lord of Steel-town, Mr. Mister, who was challenged by the pro-

Marc Blitzstein's The Cradle Will Rock *served as a reminder of the political potency of opera. In 1937 it was given a hastily improvised production in New York, after the Federal Theater withdrew its sponsorship. Blitzstein (front row, center) was photographed rehearsing the cast. Library of Congress Federal Theater Project Collection at George Mason University Library, Fairfax, Virginia.*

letariat's hero, Larry Foreman. Its scenes were set in a court, on a street corner, in a church, drugstore, hotel lobby, faculty office, doctor's rooms. Its style combined realism, vaudeville, and formal declamation, with recitatives sung throughout, arias, patter songs, a strong blues under-rhythm. There was an elaborate Federal Theater production, orchestra of twenty-eight conducted by Alexander Smallens, cast of sixty, chorus of thirty-two, all African Americans, singers and dancers from the arts projects.

Even as it was being rehearsed for its June opening, *The Cradle Will Rock* was overtaken by actual events. The overtly political messages of much of the work of the arts projects produced a hostile response among anti–New Dealers, which precipitated fierce criticism from the other side. In the spring and summer of 1937 the efforts of the emergent Congress of Industrial Organizations to unionize the automobile and steel industries provoked a furious response from management and from much of the press. Sit-down strikes took place. Violence was common. Blitzstein's opera suddenly had significance beyond even the composer's imaginings. The Roosevelt administration, caught in the middle, tried to find some way to placate its enemies without losing its supporters. Just before the first performance, a government directive announced the postponement of any new work until July. Houseman and Welles refused to accept the postponement, believing it to be a cancellation in disguise. They held a dress rehearsal, open to the public. The arts administrators in Washington responded by closing the theater and canceling the opera. Blitzstein, Welles, and Houseman decided to present the opera in some form, no longer under the auspices of the Federal Theater. They announced a performance. But how and where? In closing the theater, the government had seized the sets, costumes, and props. The American Federation of Labor prohibited its union orchestra from performing, and members of Actors' Equity were forbidden to appear on any stage not sponsored by the WPA.

The night of the scheduled first performance, a crowd gathered outside the Federal Theater. An hour before curtain time, someone figured out what to do: move the opera. Another theater, twenty-one blocks uptown, was found and rented for the night, along with a piano. Welles appealed to the audience outside to follow those performers willing to defy the WPA edict and perhaps lose their jobs. Curtain time was set for 9 p.m. By bus, taxi, automobile, and on foot, several hundred people moved north, joined by others as word spread about what was happening. By nine o'clock the Venice Theater—an auspicious name for the production of an opera— was jammed. No one understood exactly what would come next, but the lights went down and the performance got under way.

Blitzstein sat at the piano and began speaking and singing all the roles. And then, as if by magic, many of the singers rose and took part, not "onstage," but in various places in the audience. People in their seats turned their heads as though at a tennis match, from front to back, from downstairs to the balcony, as the improvised spot-light tried to pick out and follow the singers and the chorus, grouped together in the front rows. Scene followed scene in an atmosphere of frantic excitement and defiance, until the final chorus, with Larry Foreman's shouted prediction of coming revolution:

> That's thunder, that's lightning,
> And it's going to surround you!
> No wonder those stormbirds
> Seem to circle around you. . . .
> Well, you can't climb down, and you can't sit still;
> That's a storm that's going to last until
> The final wind flows . . . and when the wind blows . . .
> The Cradle Will Rock!

"There was a second's silence," John Houseman recalled later, "and then all hell broke loose. It was past midnight before we could clear the theatre."[5]

The "runaway opera," the newspapers wrote the next day. Welles and Houseman and Blitzstein produced *The Cradle Will Rock* in the same "improvised" way for another two weeks, with little publicity but to mostly sold-out houses, and it was given at the end of the year in a concert performance. Though it rocked, the cradle did not fall. The steel companies were eventually unionized. There was no revolution. The nation moved away from Blitzstein's vision. But he had created an opera of enduring charm and reminded people of the political potency of opera.

T h e New Deal influenced the future of opera in America in other ways too. It was responsible for a vast program of civic building, roads and bridges, ballfields and parks. Throughout the land, the old opera house of the turn-of-the-century was replaced by a Public Works Administration auditorium, ranging from very modest affairs to the Music Hall in Kansas City, Missouri, an art deco building seating twenty-four hundred. These civic auditoriums, where countless people attended operas, drama, and concerts in the 1930s and 1940s, later became the focal point of the proliferation of civic opera associations in the 1960s. The New Deal didn't create this spirit of collective civic enterprise; it reawakened it. Civic building had preceded it, as in the municipal Kiel Auditorium and Opera House in St. Louis. In the center of the opera house proscenium arch there was a depiction of the city's namesake, Louis XIV, the Sun King, as patron of the arts in republican America. Earlier, in San Francisco, an unlikely conjunction of three factors stimulated civic enterprise: the earthquake of 1906, which left the city without an adequate opera theater; the First World War; and the incalculable appearance of an opera man of vision and energy. The war's consequences, for opera, took time to reveal themselves. Gaetano Merola made his presence felt immediately.

He was born in Naples in 1879, the son of a court violinist, attended the city's conservatory, where he studied piano and conducting, and at age twenty came to the United States. He worked for a year as an assistant conductor at the Metropolitan, then spent several years with the Henry Savage Opera Company, touring the East and Midwest, gaining experience as conductor and opera producer. He heard Luisa Tetrazzini in San Francisco and recommended her to Oscar Hammerstein, who promptly hired Merola as the Manhattan Opera Company's chorus director. He stayed with Hammerstein throughout the life of the company and then, as conductor, went with Hammerstein to London. After that, Merola returned to New York and became a leading operetta conductor, presiding at the premieres of *Naughty Marietta, The Firefly,* and *Maytime.*

He also worked for Fortune Gallo and the San Carlo Company. This meant yearly trips to San Francisco, "my other Italy." He decided to stay in the city, calculating that it was ready for an operatic revival. There was continuous talk about building an opera house, but Merola made a crucial decision. He reversed the usual American order: an opera company would precede the opera house. Merola also perceived that he could not live on the airy notion of the city's past allegiance to opera. He had to rebuild an audience as well as found a company. His first effort, in the summer of 1923, was to use the Stanford University football stadium for a season of open-air opera, *Carmen, I Pagliacci, Faust.* The season resulted in a deficit, but over thirty thousand people attended.

The next year Merola tried again, hoping to draw on small businessmen, white-collar workers, artists, as well as the rich. As one of his supporters said: "If we can't get seventy-five [people] to give $1,000 each, we'll get 750 to give $100, with a season ticket for each $50 contributed." Such support was forthcoming. Some people advanced money for singers' contracts, other were signatories for a bank loan. The cavernous Civic Auditorium was adapted to operatic needs. Props were borrowed. "That was my best rug in the center of the last scene," Mrs. X might exclaim. The first season was a success, and so was the next, Merola playing it safe with familiar operas, established star singers. He enrolled two thousand individuals and businesses as "founders." With costs kept carefully under control, the San Francisco Opera weathered the stock market crash and the onset of the Depression. Slowly Merola broadened the repertory: the first Wagner, *Tristan und Isolde,* was given in 1927, the year of the first *Turandot. Falstaff, Tannhäuser, La Fanciulla del West, Die Meistersinger* were added in the next few years. Meanwhile, Merola now waited for an opera house, which was about to be realized, the first municipally owned and municipally maintained opera house in America.[6]

Victory in World War I produced in many San Franciscans the desire to honor the men who had won it with something more enterprising than a statue or monument. Seizing on this idea, veterans organizations argued that the memorial should be a building for them. Others suggested that it include an opera house and art museum. A coalition eventually emerged in favor of a project embracing both those ideas. The fund-raising fervor of both constituencies was enlisted, land purchased, and two million dollars raised. Then there were legal difficulties, and the project foundered. After complicated negotiations, the project was split into two halves, veterans rooms and art museum in one building, opera house in another. Two lots across from the City Hall were made available. Both groups, veterans and opera lovers, realized that they must support both or all might be lost. Once more the project went ahead. A bond issue was proposed, and in 1927 the voters approved it. Arthur Brown and G. A. Landburgh, local architects, were selected. By October 1931, when the two cornerstones were laid, labor costs had dropped sharply. The final cost of the two buildings, $5,500,500, was less than the bond issue.

The result was two massive, matching Palladian-style buildings. The opera house seated thirty-two hundred with two tiers rising above the main floor and twenty-five boxes under the first tier and extending down each side of the auditorium. The interior was a subdued cream and brown, dominated by the proscenium arch, almost as high as it was wide, flanked by art deco Amazon-ridden horses and a ceiling-filling chandelier in the shape of a star. The most notable feature of the house was its handsomely proportioned, coffered-ceiling lobby. The War Memorial Opera House opened on October 15, 1932, with Claudia Muzio in *Tosca.* The first act was broadcast nationally. Lily Pons followed in *Lucia,* captivating San Franciscans with her technical command and charming personality. The most impressive musical achievement of the company's first decade was the 1935 production of the *Ring* in which Flagstad made her debut. No Mozart was given until *Le Nozze di Figaro* in 1936. The absence of first-line conductors was a problem which Merola made special (and successful) efforts to solve, attracting Fritz Reiner in 1936–1939 and Erich Leinsdorf in 1938–1941.[7]

The success of the handsome opera house posed a danger not readily discerned—that the old San Francisco tradition of a *musical* audience might be permanently supplanted by a *social* one. As Merola succeeded in attracting wealthy guarantors—from 1935 on, subscribers for orchestra, box, and grand tier seats had to pledge a certain amount of money in addition to the price of their tickets—the almost inevitable tendency was to play it safe in terms of repertory. San Francisco's plutocracy, with an opera house in which it could display itself to advantage, converted opening night into a much publicized event, harmless enough, no doubt, and the source of amusement for onlookers. But it played dissonantly with the prevailing mood of the decade. The company traveled to Los Angeles for the first time in 1937, beginning to fulfill its potential as a serious force for the spread of opera on the West Coast.

Mayor Fiorello La Guardia orchestrated municipal support for the arts and played a key role in the founding of the New York City Opera. Here he takes the podium for a radio broadcast. La Guardia and Wagner Archives, La Guardia Community College, City University of New York.

A decade later, but very much as a result of progressive politics and New Deal culture, New York City committed itself to civic opera. A crucial role was played by the city's irrepressible mayor, Fiorello H. La Guardia. Raised in a musical family—his father had been an accompanist for Adelina Patti—he had helped establish the city's High School of Music and Art and, in 1936, created a Municipal Arts Committee to make recommendations about the city's cultural situation. He was influenced as well by the success of the Federal Music Project in developing a large and enthusiastic audience for music of high quality and low cost.

The question of where an opera company could perform was temporarily resolved by the existence of the Mecca Temple, an Arabian Nights building (originally built by New York City Shriners) which contained a 2,692-seat auditorium, wide and shallow so that audiences were close to the well-equipped stage. Having failed as a paying proposition, it came into the hands of the city in lieu of delinquent taxes. Morton Baum, a shrewd and forceful lawyer interested in the arts, and Newbold Morris, a descendant of an old New York family, persuaded La Guardia that a private but nonprofit corporation be created which would run the Mecca Temple, with private citizens underwriting possible losses. In return, the city promised to lease the building for one dollar a year.[8] In March 1943, the City Center of Music and Drama was incorporated to book arts groups which would present entertainment at modest prices. When the city reneged on its promise and charged the City Center Corporation a substantial rent, it became apparent that the center could not operate only as a booking agent. If it wished to offer opera, the City Center would have to produce it.

So the City Center directors appointed László Hálasz (1905–) musical director. Hungarian born, trained in Budapest as a pianist, he studied under Bartók, Kodaly, and Dohnanyi, and began a conducting career in various European cities. In 1936 he joined the exodus of musicians streaming out of Europe and eventually found himself with the St. Louis Grand Opera Association. Hálasz emphasized the ideal of opera as the synthesis of all its elements, and he also wished to make it a popular art, even if it meant flouting orthodox opinion. His St. Louis production of *Il Barbiere di Siviglia*, for example, was called *Once over Lightly*. (He favored opera in English.) Hálasz's approach marked him as the right person for the City Center position, and he became available when St. Louis suspended operatic activities because of the war. Dynamic, tenacious, contentious, he threw himself passionately into his work. With surprising speed, City Center prepared for opening night—February 21, 1944. The roaring applause that greeted Hálasz's first appearance on the podium was both a tribute to him and a sign of recognition that a historic step had been taken in the history of opera in America: opera production as a civic enterprise.

''W h e n the cannons are heard, the muses are silent.'' City Center came to life in defiance of the old saying, but everywhere else the Second World War silenced the muses—resources and talent destroyed, careers interrupted. In America there were no boycotts of German or Italian opera, with the exception of *Madama Butterfly*, which was withdrawn after Pearl Harbor. The combination of a Japanese subject, an Italian composer, a deceiving American naval officer was thought to be too much for American audiences. The ban was trivial, however, compared with the shameful internment of Japanese American citizens in concentration camps. When the cannons are heard, reason goes into hiding.

Cutting the German and Italian operatic supply lines added urgency to the search for American singers. By October 1942, there were 51 native-born singers on the Metropolitan roster of 105, and Americans now had as much to fear from exploitation as from indifference. Some made careers of distinction—Nadine Conner, Margaret Harshaw, Patrice Munsell (pushed into a debut at seventeen, but a survivor), Jan Peerce, Eleanor Steber, Robert Weede. In 1944–1945, no singers of foreign birth were added to the Metropolitan rolls, and the American Guild of Musical Artists, flexing its new-found muscles, insisted that a ratio of three native-born singers for every foreign one be made permanent. The Metropolitan Opera orchestra, too, was rebuilt with able native players. Circumstances, not policy, had made the Metropolitan more of an American opera house than anyone would have predicted a decade earlier.

Among the new singers, Helen Traubel's career was the most remarkable, her path to operatic celebrity entirely American. She had never been to Europe and had no desire to go. "Stubborn, determined on her own way, unwilling to sing until she felt herself fully prepared, she made a career which bears no resemblance to any other."[10] She was born in St. Louis in 1899 and spent much of her life there, growing up in a German-speaking household in which there was a lot of music. She was taken to Chicago several times to hear opera, and later recalled the adoring crowds at the Metropolitan to hear Geraldine Farrar. She sang professionally at thirteen, married at nineteen, and was content to limit herself to the St. Louis area. In 1926 she sang the Liebestod from *Tristan und Isolde* with the St. Louis Symphony in New York. Gatti-Casazza offered her a trial at the Metropolitan, but Traubel declined. In 1937 she sang the leading role in the company's production of Walter Damrosch's *The Man without a Country*. But by that point the Metropolitan was indifferent, for it had both Flagstad and a lithe, dramatic, ringing-voiced Wagnerian soprano from Australia, Marjorie Lawrence. In any event, Traubel still felt unready for the Wagnerian repertory, yet refused to go to Europe to gain experience, though Farrar offered to subsidize her stay there.

Then things came together in a remarkable way. Traubel sang in a radio concert, along with Lauritz Melchior and Emmanuel List, accompanied by Dimitri Mitropoulos and the Minneapolis Symphony. That caused a stir. She sang with the New York Philharmonic-Symphony, John Barbirolli conducting, again broadcast—the Immolation Scene from *Götterdämmerung*. Traubel's soaring voice provoked storms of applause and demands that the Metropolitan open its doors to her. Edward Johnson offered her the role of Venus in *Tannhäuser*. Traubel refused. It was physically unsuitable for her, she believed, and vocally of no interest. She wished to sing Sieglinde in *Die Walküre,* the role in which Flagstad had made *her* first appearance. There was much internal opposition to Traubel, but at last the Metropolitan yielded to the growing popular clamor that she be given a chance to succeed Lillian Nordica. In December 1939, singing Sieglinde to Flagstad's Brunnhilde and Melchior's Siegfried, Traubel "left no doubt of her powers." Her Elizabeth in *Tannhäuser* was a "majestic vocal feat." Even so, she sang only twice at the Metropolitan in the 1940 season, three times the next. Abruptly, the war changed everything. Flagstad returned to Norway. It was Traubel's turn to ascend the heights.

T h e war had begun before fighting broke out. In the early 1930s the German and Italian governments began an assault upon artists, scientists, and intellectuals, producing the greatest migration of artists in the history of Europe, above all to the United States. Every art, every science, all the humanities were represented in this transatlantic movement. For American opera the most immediate consequence was the influx of conductors: Arturo Toscanini and Otto Klemperer (though neither would conduct opera in an opera house in America), Bruno Walter, Dimitri Mitropoulos, Erich Leinsdorf, Fritz Reiner, George Szell, Fritz Busch. Unlike their predecessors at the beginning of the century, whose task had been to impose order, this group had to save standards in danger of being forgotten. Walter, receiving "a hero's welcome at his appearance," nourished the growing Mozart revival and brought to the Metropolitan the most moving performance of Beethoven's *Fidelio* since that of his mentor, Gustav Mahler. Thomas Beecham conducted notable performances of the

French repertory—a *Manon* of style and elegance, and "the most eloquent *Louise*" New York had heard in decades. Szell made his debut with a dazzling performance of *Salome,* and followed that with an equally impressive *Boris Godunov.*[11]

Famous composers crossed the Atlantic: Igor Stravinsky, Arnold Schoenberg, Béla Bartók, Darius Milhaud, Paul Hindemith, Arthur Honegger, Bohuslav Martinů. Universities and colleges were enriched by their presence—Hindemith at Yale, Milhaud at Mills College, Krenek at Minnesota, Schoenberg at UCLA, and Toch at the University of Southern California. Their presence had incalculable importance in the stimulation it afforded to teaching and to scholarship, also in lending prestige to contemporary music. But they were more important for their impact on symphonic and chamber music than upon opera, with one exception.

Kurt Weill (1900–1950), the son of a cantor who composed music, was born in Dessau, Germany, studied composition in Berlin with Engelbert Humperdinck and Ferruccio Busoni, and soon made a reputation as the brightest theatrical composer of his generation. He wanted to compose in a popular style, on contemporary subjects, for a general audience, from a radical political point of view. In *Royal Palace* (1926), a jazz-inspired opera, Weill combined different musical idioms, defying the idea that music drama had to be in one unified style. He worked with talented librettists, most famously with Bertolt Brecht (1898–1956), creating a series of brilliant satirical operas bridging the gap between singspiel and grand opera: a modern version of *The Beggar's Opera* called *Die Dreigroschenoper* (1928; known in its American adaptation by Marc Blitzstein as *The Threepenny Opera*), *Happy End* (1929), *Aufsteig und Fall der Stadt Mahagonny* (*The Rise and Fall of the City of Mahagonny;* 1930). Although not performed in America for a number of years, their reputation spread among musicians and intellectuals. Weill and Brecht went their separate ways and came to America, where their paths diverged. Weill began working in the popular commercial theater, forging a style which combined European and American elements.

His first American opera, *Johnny Johnson* (1936), a fusion of music and antiwar satirical fancy, was well received critically—"The most effective of all satires of its class," said Robert Benchley—but its uncompromising point of view denied it popularity. *Knickerbocker Holiday* (1938) was also political satire, but in the seemingly innocuous form of a fable about seventeenth-century New Amsterdam. Maxwell Anderson's libretto used the figure of the tyrannical Pieter Stuyvesant to suggest current concerns about dictatorship. It ran for four months and contained one very popular number, "September Song." Weill's next works, *Lady in the Dark* (1941), lyrics by Ira Gershwin and Moss Hart, and *One Touch of Venus* (1943), story by S. J. Perelman, were both imaginative explorations of operatic forms. The first was a "musical play," as Weill termed it, about psychoanalysis, with spoken dialogue, built about three separate but related dream sequences which examined the heroine's psyche, all of the music being kept within the dreams. It was "a long step forward" toward a new musical dramatic form, in the opinion of the *New York Times*'s Brooks Atkinson. *One Touch of Venus* was less innovative, but was musically ingenious and had dances by Agnes de Mille.

In the post–World War II years (as we shall see later in our story), Weill went on inventively mingling European and American theatrical forms, a synthesis which provoked fierce criticism, some seeing his American work as an abandonment of his earlier radicalism, others as a futile effort to convert simple American musical theater to operatic purposes. But in the history of opera he is readily recognizable as one of its most adept internationalists.[12]

T h e European premiere of *Porgy and Bess* took place during the war, at the Royal Opera House in Copenhagen in March 1943, in a Danish translation, with a Danish cast. It was given twenty-two times to sold-out houses and its withdrawal, because of German pressure, only made its music more popular. Every time the Germans sent communiqués over Danish radio announcing news of their victories, the Danish underground interrupted them with a recording of "It Ain't Necessarily So."

America also brought death and destruction, American bombs raining down on many of Europe's opera houses: the San Carlo, La Scala, the Semper Opera House in Dresden, the Residenz in Munich. On March 11, 1945, American airplanes, returning from a different mission, gratuitously scattered incendiary bombs on Vienna, setting the Opera on fire. Citizens gathered to watch the great old house burn through the night. One month later, the European fighting was over, and with peace came renewal and rebuilding. "When the cannons are silent, the muses are heard."[13]

Milton Cross

Sporadically and erratically, wireless broadcasts had been taking place in America since the late nineteenth century. They were a combination of stunt and experiment. On January 13, 1910, for instance, a broadcast was made directly from the stage of the Metropolitan Opera House, where Enrico Caruso was singing in *I Pagliacci* and *Cavalleria rusticana.* A five-hundred-watt transmitter was installed on top of the opera house, two microphones on stage and in the wings. Despite considerable interference and the fading of the signals, listeners heard the great tenor's voice and the "ecstasy" it conveyed.

By 1921 a number of radio transmitting stations had been established. Music, sporting events, and election broadcasts furnished much of their early material. In Chicago the first broadcast wasn't politics or sports—it was Mary Garden. In November 1921, station KYW broadcast from the Auditorium Building, afternoons and evenings, six days a week. "The ears of the entire Midwest," according to one writer, "had been in the opera house all that winter." How many ears? Few enough. At the beginning there were perhaps thirteen hundred receivers in all Chicago. No radio sets were available for purchase in stores. Within months that changed dramatically. People were clamoring for radios, and assembling them became a round-the-clock operation. Soon, crude homemade aerials were sprouting on the roofs of houses and tenements throughout the city.[1]

The question of public or private ownership of radio broadcasting was still unsettled. Municipal ownership took hold in a few cities. In a number of states, public educational radio stations operated on university campuses. Secretary of Commerce Herbert Hoover dismissed the notion that radio broadcasting should be solely for commercial gain, insisting that it would be unfortunate if it came to be controlled by any "corporation, individual or combination." At the same time, he also believed that the final decision should be left to the play of market forces. Between 1922 and 1924 the market's response became crystal clear: commercial advertising demonstrated how lucrative the private ownership of the airwaves might be. Initially, radio advertising took the form of one program sponsored by one manufacturer. Then came advertising by more than one sponsor between programs, and finally, in an imaginative leap which has edified the American public ever since, advertising *during* programs. Well might a Utah businessman exult: "What has education contributed to radio? Not one thing. What has commercialism contributed? Everything—the life blood of the industry."[2]

Music—live music—dominated commercial radio in its first years. Even the commercials began to sing! The music played in the 1920s was conservatory music, teatime hotel music, orchestral versions of the "classics," with lots of opera excerpts included. In the 1930s radio stations played a greater variety of music, but the major commercial networks that emerged were woefully unwilling to assume the role of patrons of the arts. Their failure to sponsor works by American composers or to promote performances of their compositions contrasts scandalously with the enlightened role of the British Broadcasting Corporation and the state-run European networks in the same period. The best that American operatic or symphonic music could hope for was the emergence of a few scattered oases of program time: the *Walter Damrosch Music Appreciation Hour* during the week; Arturo Toscanini and the New York Philharmonic-Symphony on Sunday afternoons. Most enduringly, Saturday afternoon became opera time.

H o w that came about was closely associated with the life and career of Milton Cross

Mary Garden in Chicago radio station KYW, 1921: opera enters the age of mass culture. Library of Congress.

475

(1897–1975). A New Yorker with an attractive tenor voice, he studied composition and singing at the Damrosch Institute of Music, hoping to become a music teacher in the public schools. Dared by a friend, he tried out for a job as a ballad singer with a Newark, New Jersey, radio station—and got it. The station's manager, however, preferred Cross's speaking to his singing voice, and he became an announcer. It was as an announcer that he worked with the Chicago Civic Opera, which pioneered American opera broadcasting, and it was with that company that an accidental feat of improvisation gained him notoriety in radio circles. Having begun a broadcast of *Il Trovatore*, Cross was suddenly informed that the performance would be held up while Samuel Insull gave a report to the opera house audience on the company's financial condition. Insull droned on for half an hour, unheard by the radio audience while Cross ad-libbed, describing the opera house, the stage scenery, the preparations for a forthcoming tour, even explaining the plot of *Il Trovatore*, a notable achievement in itself.

In 1931 the National Broadcasting Company proposed to Gatti-Casazza that it broadcast a series of weekly performances from the Metropolitan. The proposal triggered the Metropolitan's formidable snobbery. When Chicago had broadcast the garden scene from *Faust* in 1927, a Metropolitan spokesman had sniffed that such a thing "was not opera." Furthermore, there were justifiable doubts about the quality of the sound reproduction. On the other hand, a great deal of money was involved. NBC was prepared to pay a hundred thousand dollars annually for the right to this noncommercially sponsored program. It would be impractical to worry excessively about vocal quality, and Gatti-Casazza was a surpassingly practical person. On Christmas Day 1931, an abridged version of Humperdinck's *Hänsel und Gretel* inaugurated Metropolitan Opera broadcasts. It was a clever choice. NBC had only one hour of nonsponsored time at its disposal, and the opera's charm came across quickly. (All subsequent broadcasts in the first season were one hour long.) Cross was chosen to introduce the opera. "I was the only one who knew anything about it," he said modestly and accurately. Since *Hänsel und Gretel* was sung in German, NBC decided that its primary task was to make the story comprehensible to its auditors, and that the music could not do this by itself. Therefore, the network selected Deems Taylor as opera "commentator." Cross introduced the program and then introduced Taylor, who talked about the opera before, after, and during the broadcast. Listeners protested vehemently. Taylor's intrusive commentary was dropped. NBC had stumbled on something that was attractive to opera lovers—a span of continuous, uninterrupted music.[3]

"This broadcast succeeded perfectly," Gatti-Casazza wrote, "and the entire public received it with great favor."[4] The first broadcast had gone out to about 190 stations. The following year the opera performances were given in their entirety. The audience steadily increased in size. On the first Saturday matinee performance of the Depression-shortened 1933–1934 season, the radio audience heard Ambroise Thomas's *Mignon*, and also its first commercial announcement—for the American Tobacco Company. For the next nine years the broadcasts were sponsored by various companies. In 1940 the Texaco Company took over and has maintained it ever since,

Milton Cross was the radio voice of the Metropolitan Opera for more than four decades. Here he is in the original sound booth used for the Saturday afternoon broadcasts. Metropolitan Opera Archives.

the longest continuous coast-to-coast commercial sponsorship of the same program in American radio history. Texaco was shrewdly restrained. Its commercials only mentioned its name, no more, and so it achieved a reputation for virtue.

T h e new radio audience was only half the story. There was also a recordings audience, with its own sensibility and history. Thomas Edison built the first phonograph in 1877, and a patent was issued to him in 1878. His instrument consisted of a metal cylinder, with a spiral groove in its surface, and two diaphragm-and-needle units, one for recording sound, the other for reproducing it. "Mary had a little lamb," Edison shouted into the mouthpiece, as he set the recording needle and turned a crank to set his instrument into motion. He then adjusted the reproducing needle, cranked again, and heard a recognizable reproduction of his voice. "I was never so taken aback in my life," he admitted later.

People did *not* immediately understand the potential of this crude mechanism. The Edison Speaking Phonograph Company promoted it as a curiosity. Five hundred machines were manufactured and taken on tour, amusing audiences by reproducing voices, barking dogs and crowing cocks, and coughs and sneezes so lifelike that doctors present "instinctively began to write prescriptions." There were also utopian hopes. Politicians would repeat their speeches to the phonograph, have it play their words back to them, and thus "prevent them from making rash or overheated or silly remarks." This has not happened.

From the first, the most popular part of the evening's entertainment was the reproduction of music. "The voices of [famous singers] will not die with them, but will remain as long as the metal in which they may be embodied will last," a contemporary wrote, thinking of Euphrosyne Parepa-Rosa and Therese Tietjens, both recently dead. Little was done, however, to follow up on the phonograph's talents as historian. Franz Liszt lived until 1886, Jenny Lind until 1887, yet no effort was made to record them, though an enterprising person, in 1889, recorded Johannes Brahms playing one of his *Hungarian Rhapsodies*. In 1887 Alexander Graham Bell and associates took up the phonograph, developed a more flexible needle, and covered the cylinder with wax. Flat discs replaced cylinders. Although Edison continued to think of the phonograph—the English called it the gramophone—as a machine for business, it flourished as a musical instrument.

In the 1890s people in many countries began making commercial musical recordings—short pieces, marches, polkas, waltzes, national anthems, and operatic selections. A ten-inch disc played for three minutes, a twelve-inch disc for four. Operatic arias happened to suit this limitation very well, and by 1900 most well-known arias had been recorded somewhere, by someone. Caruso's career coincided with this development. In 1902 Fred Gaisberg, an American in search of recording talent, recorded Caruso in a Milan hotel room, Caruso "dispatching ten arias as fast as Gaisberg could put wax blanks on his machine." Payment—one hundred pounds. These were the first really successful operatic records. Caruso's powerful voice, drowning the surface noise, was peculiarly attuned to the phonograph of the day and of the future. There were also voices from the past. Baroness Cederstrom, age sixty-two, made fourteen discs which were released in 1905 with terrific fanfare. Stores

Geraldine Farrar was one of many singers who made opera recordings an essential feature of middle-class American parlors. She posed beside a Victrola in 1915. Library of Congress.

festooned their windows with streamers: "Patti Is Singing Here Today." Her discs, with pink Patti labels, sold for six dollars each. (The Queen of Song had always been expensive!) A recording machine was taken to the Sistine Chapel, where the last living castrato, Alessandro Moreschi, bequeathed to the world "the eerie bleat of the male soprano."

In America, two companies, Victor and Columbia, dominated the market and, in the abiding spirit of the time, tried to monopolize it, pooling their patents, controlling production of phonographs. Victor outstripped Columbia by promoting an expensive "celebrity" series of discs which claimed the prestige associated with everything that was "best"—Steinway pianos, the Metropolitan Opera. Singers' discs were priced according to their eminence. By 1912 Victor's advertising budget was over $1.5 million. Along with leather-bound volumes of Dickens and Thackeray, piano transcriptions of Gilbert and Sullivan, Victor Red Seal records became a feature of the middle-class American parlor, "to be displayed with becoming pride to impressionable guests and relations." The Victor company reached where touring companies couldn't go, into individual homes. The *Victor Book of the Opera,* one of numerous books explaining the plots and stories of the operas, a 375-page volume, well illustrated, sold for seventy-five cents. What had been done by the piano was now taken over by the phonograph. "Across the land, in towns where opera companies had never set foot, a growing clientele for standard arias and ensembles was to be found patronizing Victor's ten thousand authorized dealers."

In the early 1920s the record business boomed. A hundred million discs were sold in 1921. Most of them were popular songs, but opera accounted for a substantial percentage. Alma Gluck's recording of "Carry Me Back to Old Virginny" was the first Red Seal disc to sell over a million copies, and John McCormack "crossed over" so successfully into recorded songs that he abandoned operatic performances entirely.

Electric recording, in the 1920s, enhanced the quality of recorded sound over that of the old acoustical process.

Radio and records were seen as deadly enemies. In the contest between them, radio had important advantages. Its sound was superior. Its programming was more varied. It was free. For a while, both prospered, but with the stock market crash and Depression, "the phonograph and record business withered as if frozen in full bloom by a bitter Arctic frost." In 1932 a total of six million records were sold in the United States, 6 percent of the sales in average years in the 1920s. "The phonograph belongs to the past and radio to the future." Red Seal records were relegated to the attic, the Victrola to the junkyard. As if to underline the ascendance of radio and the demise of the recording industry, in 1930 RCA Victor issued the last Caruso recording in its vaults and announced: "The book of Enrico Caruso's recordings is closed forever."[5]

Of course, the phonograph didn't disappear. Instead, in the 1930s, the character of its operatic audience changed. It attracted a smaller, more specialized following. The earlier emphasis on popular excerpts meant that the operatic repertory on records consisted of many versions of a relatively small number of songs. In Europe, an influential countermovement was directed against the "hit" operatic record, "a child of the times, begotten of the shallow and trivial, toward which a wide segment of the popular taste is oriented."[6] The recording of complete operas had dated from 1903, in Italy, but the operas had been cut and different singers were sometimes used for one recording. After World War I, first-rate orchestras, conductors, and singers began to take part in important interpretations—Leoncavallo conducting *I Pagliacci,* Siegfried Wagner at Bayreuth conducting large parts of the *Ring,* a French version of *Pelléas et Mélisande.*

The most significant development of the 1930s was the growth of "societies," whose members subscribed in advance for records not in the general catalogue. Most of these featured orchestral and chamber music, but the operatic achievements—the Glyndebourne Opera performances of Mozart operas, Thomas Beecham's *Die Zauberflöte, Der Rosenkavalier* with a celebrated cast of singers—were extraordinarily influential. All through the 1930s the United States lagged far behind these developments. American recording companies were as indifferent to serious operatic projects as were American radio networks. When the American record business did come back to life, around 1940, the emphasis was on orchestral music.

Everyone agreed that the radio and recordings audience was important, but whom did it consist of? Did listening encourage people to attend live performances? Speculation outstripped information. Record companies kept sales figures to themselves. Radio people were more inventive in dramatizing the size of their supposed audience. One afternoon Metropolitan opera broadcast, it was said, equaled three hundred sold-out opera house performances. The broadcasts that Milton Cross presided over were continually modified to fit the character of the audience as that character became clearer. They afford possible clues to a complex phenomenon.

The regularity of the broadcasts was an important part of their appeal. Saturday afternoon was a time for opera lovers to look forward to, and the presence of Cross, always there, in place, and on time, never missing a performance until the early

1970s, fused his personal identity with that of the performances. Cross was an introducer, explaining the plot of the stories simply, highlighting their drama. He didn't talk down or up, prided himself on the clarity of his diction, occasionally used an Italian or German or French phrase to sound an authentic note. In the first decade he prepared all his own material, but after 1940 scripts were written for him. The seeming informality was carefully studied. He prepared "ad-libbed" comments, brought notes with him. Opera, as he talked about it, never seemed formidable or off-putting, and yet, in his matter-of-fact way, he contrived to make what was forthcoming seem exciting. The orchestra tuning up in the background, the echoing sound of the opera house, the gradual hush descending on the house, the applause greeting the maestro as he came to the podium, the first notes of the overture—for tens of millions, over many years, that was opera. Everything was done to make this weekly event something special. "I don't know what is worn in an opera house today," an elderly woman wrote, "but on Saturdays I get my black velvet dress out of its box. And I dress my hair and put a fresh flower in a vase beside me. After all, I am to spend the afternoon with dukes and duchesses."[7] For many others, the excitement was entirely musical, allowing greater concentration, without the distractions and noise always present in the opera house. For some, it was better than being there.

At the same time, the Saturday afternoon broadcasts came to have a character and shape of their own. Famous singers of the past were interviewed between the acts. There was musical analysis, with examples played on the piano. Someone hit on the idea of the opera quiz, and this became the program's most popular feature. Education was mixed with entertainment. Singers soon wanted to take part in broadcast performances because they helped make their names familiar, and from that flowed recording contracts, concert performances. The broadcasts became as much a sign of a singer's importance as performing on opening night. Imagine what a Caruso radio audience might have numbered! It was radio which made the Metropolitan Opera into a national institution. Milton Cross became "Mr. Opera," but he remained subordinate to the opera, to the medium he presided over, unobtrusive, personally unremarkable, the ordinary leading to the extraordinary, "the single most important musical event in the country."[8]

a c t   s i x

Empire, 1950–

What on earth has given opera its prestige in western civilization, a prestige that has outlasted so many different fashions and ways of thought? Why are people prepared to sit silently for three hours listening to a performance of which they do not understand a word and of which they very seldom know the plot? Why do quite small towns all over Germany and Italy still devote a large portion of their budgets to this irrational entertainment? Partly, of course, because it is a display of skill, like a football match. But chiefly, I think, because it *is* irrational. "What is too silly to be said may be sung"—well, yes; but what is too subtle to be said, or too deeply felt, or too revealing or too mysterious—these things can also be sung and only sung. When, at the beginning of Mozart's *Don Giovanni,* the Don kills the Commendatore, and in one burst of glorious music the murderer, his mistress, his servant and the dying man all express their feelings, opera provides a real extension of human faculties.

—*Kenneth Clark*

c h a p t e r   f o r t y

The New Audience

The 1950s was the greatest period of growth in American operatic history. No one had foreseen this. The task of the 1930s and early 1940s had been survival. It was unclear whether prosperity or depression would follow the war. It took time to re-establish European connections, to mend the shattered operatic establishments there. Few anticipated the prolongation of the American wartime economy in the form of the Cold War. The half-decade of peace after 1945 gave few indications of any new underlying patterns. The most immediately noticeable change was the disappearance of many of the great names of the previous operatic generation—Lotte Lehmann, Alexander Kipnis, Lauritz Melchior, Helen Traubel, Ezio Pinza, Lily Pons. Some reappearances—Maria Jeritza singing in *Die Fledermaus* at the Metropolitan, Maggie Teyte in *Pelléas et Mélisande* at the New York City Opera—served to emphasize how distant seemed the days of Debussy and Garden and Gatti-Casazza, of Boston and Chicago opera. By contrast, Kirsten Flagstad's reappearance rekindled wartime memories. San Francisco, to its credit, welcomed her ecstatically, as did Los Angeles and, finally, New York. All three cities heard a voice only slightly modified by time. She didn't stay long and her departure, in 1952, occasioned Virgil Thomson's tribute: "unique among living vocal artists."[1]

Straddling past and present, in the 1940s Arturo Toscanini broke his long American operatic silence and reintroduced himself to Americans—in the radio studio, performances with the NBC Symphony Orchestra of *Fidelio* (1944), *La Bohème* (1946—the fiftieth anniversary of the world premiere he had conducted in Turin), *La Traviata* (1946), *Otello* (1947), *Aida* (1949), *Falstaff* (1950), and *Un Ballo in maschera* (1954). They were the most far-reaching, most publicized radio broadcasts (some were also televised) of the time, and after the last Toscanini confided: "This was my last opera performance. I began by hearing a performance of *Un Ballo in maschera* at age four, up in the gallery; and I've finished by conducting it at eighty-seven." He died, in New York, in January 1957.[2]

The Toscanini broadcasts were a bridge between the old order and the new. It was significant that they took place away from the opera house. Grand opera houses remained, and more would be built in America, but the transformation of American operatic culture did not take place in them. It was the consequence of social and class change, of economic affluence, of technological innovation. The virtual end of European emigration to the United States, between the world wars, meant that the children and grandchildren of those earlier emigrants no longer looked to opera as a way of maintaining ethnic identities. Instead, they sought to modify or efface their ties to the past. Opera was domesticated as an American form of entertainment. The end of legislated social segregation directed against African Americans reduced another barrier to joining the operatic audience. Even as the cost of opera rose, more people could afford it. Technology was ever more influential. In 1948 Columbia Records introduced the long-playing record. All this added up to a new operatic audience, though important vestiges of the old one lingered. It was more a musical audience, a theatrical audience. Change was incessant. In the 1960s and 1970s, films and television extended the recording and radio audience to an undreamed of size. Compact discs made LPs obsolete. A famous conductor calculated that he would have to conduct the same live program every day for the rest of his life, and then for a lifetime more, to equal the audience for *one* of his televised or filmed performances. "There has been an explosion in the appreciation of music," said Herbert von Karajan. "After the hate, destruction and death of two wars, people's values have changed. Things such as music have become more important to the world . . . and the people responsible for our recording technology—which allows music to be spread—they are the ones who should win the Nobel Prize for Peace."[3]

In America, the original operatic audience—the mixed audience—regained its ascendancy. Evening dress, the social uniform of an uneasy plutocracy trying to pass for a European aristocracy, went the way of the Diamond Horseshoe culture. Opening night, while still a chance to show off clothes and jewels, became a fancy-dress costume party. "The era of the old lady with the headache band and strings of pearls is over," said Beverly Sills. "Her money has passed to the next generation, probably much diluted. Instead of the senior partner in the law firm, we have the junior partner—someone who still has to worry about the baby sitter, the parking and the dinner when he considers the price of his ticket." Opera mattered less socially because other forms of entertainment surpassed it as occasions for ostentatious display, and because "society" virtually disappeared. Money, and money alone, became the measure of social standing, as was shown by the contemporary fate of that symbol of the old operatic and social order, the opera box. Opera boxes, their numbers and visibility reduced, survived the democratization of the American opera house, but as a symbol of privilege they simply changed their location. Taken up by popular culture, in baseball and football stadiums throughout the land, "luxury" boxes are the thing. Their cost—several hundred thousand dollars—and the facilities in them for self-indulgence make the old retiring room of the opera box a monastic cell by comparison. Cities strain their resources to build stadiums with boxes more splendid than those of their rivals. Everywhere, unabashed and unassailable, plutocracy rules.

Live performance and recordings, stimulating each other, were an important element in what historians of the future are likely to characterize as the most significant development of the last half of the twentieth century in operatic America—the vastly increased operatic repertory. American audiences awakened from the grand opera trance into which they had lapsed in the middle of the nineteenth century. First came, in the 1950s, the revival of the operas of Rossini, Bellini, and Donizetti, of Cherubini and Spontini, personified by the career of Maria Callas. This was soon followed by a more surprising development, the early music revival, including Baroque operas unperformed for two and three hundred years. As if by magic, Handel and Haydn, Gluck and Rameau, Cavalli and Lully, Vivaldi and Monteverdi awakened from centuries of sleep.

In Europe and England, the Baroque revival reached back to the first two decades of the twentieth century. The French reconsidered Lully and Gluck, and the English Purcell, Locke, and Blow. In Germany, it was the "Handel Renaissance" of the 1920s that had the greatest impact on musical culture everywhere, as German musicians, in the words of one of the movement's historians, "answered the German people's yearning for stability and, more importantly, a sense of national pride" in a period of increasing political disorder. The German influence touched America too, in the 1920s, in the person of Werner Josten, a German-born composer who taught at Smith College in Northampton, Massachusetts. There, between 1926 and 1931, Handel's *Giulio Cesare, Serse,* and *Rodelinda,* and Monteverdi's *L'Incoronazione di Poppea* and *Orfeo* were performed before responsive audiences. One critic celebrated the emergence of America's "own little Bayreuth at Northampton, with Monteverdi and Handel as substitutes for Wagner." Thus, in the post–World War II period the operatic past was transformed into an archive open to the new American operatic audience; it was a new opera house without walls. "It is like the Renaissance rediscovering the ancient classics and holding them fast by means of the printing press. It marks an epoch in Western intellectual history."[5]

A g a i n s t this background, only dimly discerned at the time, the major American opera companies reorganized themselves to plot their course in postwar America. The 1950s and 1960s were years of impressive growth and maturity in San Francisco. The operatic season was expanded in length and in the imagination and quality of productions. Gaetano Merola's thirty years of operatic service to the city ended with his death in 1953. He was succeeded by Kurt Herbert Adler (1905–1988), Viennese born, who had assisted Toscanini at Salzburg in 1936 and come to the United States in 1938. In 1943 Merola brought him to San Francisco as conductor, choral director, and chief deputy. He was a formidable figure, harsh and demanding, irascible and imperious. "It was one-man rule, the definitive artistic tyranny." Adler raged and bellowed, charmed and cajoled, changed San Francisco into one of the exciting operatic places in the country.[6] He introduced unfamiliar operas—Poulenc's *Dialogues of the Carmelites* (*Les Dialogues des Carmélites*), Strauss's *Die Frau ohne Schatten,* Britten's *A Midsummer Night's Dream,* Shostakovich's *Lady Macbeth of Mtsensk,* Janáček's *The Makropoulos Case,* and, in a greatly abbreviated version, Berlioz's *Les Troyens.*

Merola, to give his company a flavor of its own and to hold the interest of his subscribers, had early on brought promising singers from Europe. After the war he got the jump on everybody in America by introducing Tito Gobbi, Ferruccio Tagliavini, Elena Nikolaidi, Renata Tebaldi, and Mario del Monaco to his enthralled audiences. Adler continued the policy, with dazzling success, bringing, among others, Elisabeth Schwarzkopf, Birgit Nilsson, Margaret Price, Anja Silja, Ingvar Wixell, Geraint Evans, Leonie Rysanek, Boris Christoff. American singers—Mary Costa, Marilyn Horne, James McCracken, Thomas Stewart, Leontyne Price, Jess Thomas—

were given a chance. "I sort of grew up in San Francisco vocally and professionally," Price said. Serious efforts were made to cultivate young singers through a program of auditions and a spring season in which smaller-scale and innovative operas were performed away from the opera house. The regular season grew to two and then three months and the city expanded its civic sponsorship by means of a hotel tax.[7]

T h e New York City Opera survived the difficulties of its first years by defining its own identity, inviting the inevitable comparison with the Metropolitan by freshness of production and coherence of dramatic effect, if not in vocal splendor, and also by doing things the Metropolitan didn't do: operas by American composers and forgotten operas of the European repertory. *The Pirates of Penzance, Show Boat,* and *The Gypsy Baron* flouted sclerotic notions of what constituted opera, while *Eugene Onegin, Ariadne auf Naxos, L'Amour des trois oranges* rectified decades of neglect. There were operas thought too advanced for the Metropolitan audience—*Bluebeard's Castle* by Bartók, *Wozzeck,* Ravel's *The Spanish Hour* (*L'Heure espagnole*). Striking successes, surprising failures, novelties, turbulence, and growing pains marked the first decade. László Hálasz, dismissed in rancorous circumstances in 1952, was succeeded by Joseph Rosenstock, Erich Leinsdorf and, in 1957, Julius Rudel. He had been a member of the company since its inception, and his appointment was a notable event. He was the first native-born American to head a major American opera company. And a decade before any other American opera company consulted its racial conscience (if any), the City Opera had acted. On September 28, 1945, Todd Duncan, African American baritone, sang Tonio in *I Pagliacci.* Contemporary American composers got a hearing: William Grant Still's *Troubled Island*; David Tamkin's *The Dybbuk*; and three operas, *The Old Maid and the Thief, Amelia Goes to the Ball,* and *The Medium,* by a composer who captured the American public's fancy to an unrivaled extent, Gian Carlo Menotti.

In the early 1950s the City Opera encountered serious difficulties. The range of its activities outran its audience. Box office support fluctuated wildly from work to work. The revivals fared well, the new works less so. The audience of these years was not easy to characterize. If it didn't support new works or modernist revivals with any consistency, it also flagged in its support of the standard repertory. In that field, comparison with the Metropolitan was often perilous because famous names in famous operas was the Metropolitan's strong suit. Furthermore, though its municipal support was restricted, the City Opera was a stepchild when it came to finding private support. In the mid-1950s, City Center reorganized its finances and embarked on a brilliant decade. The city and state governments waived its annual rent. A first public fundraising drive was successful. Corporations began to contribute modest amounts, and philanthropic foundations, those new figures on the cultural scene, took an interest. In 1957 the Ford Foundation gave $105,000 (a very large sum it seemed then), specifically to sponsor a season of American operas the following year—not new works, but ones already performed in the past. As several decades of American operatic experience had shown, the greatest difficulty for American composers was not in getting an opera performed once or a few times in one season, but in having it taken up over a longer period, giving the work a chance to establish itself—or not—with audiences.

The spring season of 1958 saw performances of Douglas Moore's *The Ballad of Baby Doe,* Mark Bucci's *Tale for a Deaf Ear,* Kurt Weill's *Lost in the Stars,* Vittorio Giannini's *The Taming of the Shrew,* Carlisle Floyd's *Susannah,* Marc Blitzstein's *Regina,* a Menotti double-bill of *The Medium* and *The Old Maid and the Thief,* Still's *Troubled Island.* There was also one world premiere, *The Good Soldier Schweik* by Robert Kurka. There were thirty-five performances of ten operas, and though attendance was poor at many of them, the season was an artistic success and served as a means of helping to establish the City Opera as "the most American of opera companies." The next spring season was also devoted to the work of American composers, including *The Devil and Daniel Webster* by Moore, *Wuthering Heights* by Floyd, *The Triumph of Saint Joan* by Dello Joio, *Street Scene* by Weill. *The Cradle Will Rock* was revived in 1960, *Porgy and Bess* in 1962. Five of these operas toured nineteen cities east of the Mississippi. "I shall be surprised if musical history does not record that American opera, as a movement, had its beginning at the New York City Center in the spring seasons of 1958 and 1959," wrote an observer. As it also made its stage available to European operas of the recent past, especially the operas of Benjamin Britten, City Center took Hammerstein's place as a sponsor of contemporary opera.[8]

I n 1950 Edward Johnson retired as general manager of the Metropolitan Opera. Depression and war had made the Johnson years difficult, but they were not without their achievements—an impressive array of American singers, outstanding conductors, the restoration of Mozart to the repertory. On the debit side? House discipline was almost nonexistent, cast changes were frequent. Costumes and scenery had become shamefully shabby. "It is this very mixture of good and bad, positive and negative, backing and filling, make-shift and make-do that gave the Johnson period its characteristic tinge."

With the arrival of Rudolf Bing (1902–) the Metropolitan began one of its most exciting periods. He was born in Vienna, studied music there, worked in opera in Darmstadt and Berlin. In 1934 he went to Glyndebourne, England, where he became general manager in 1936. He helped found the Edinburgh Festival in 1946. At the Metropolitan, Bing's primary objectives were to establish administrative order and to restore the standard repertory by means of fresh and imaginative productions. He brought in directors from the Broadway theater and first-rank conductors. *Don Carlo,* the opening-night opera of his first season, had sets by Eugene Berman and direction by Margaret Webster. Strauss's *Die Fledermaus,* a great popular success, was conducted by Eugene Ormandy and directed by Garson Kanin. *Così fan tutte,* in English, directed by Alfred Lunt, finally restored that masterpiece to the Metropolitan repertory. *Don Giovanni,* a production "that might have delighted the eye as well as the ear of Mozart himself," was conducted by Karl Böhm, sets by Eugene Berman. Jean Morel conducted and Cyril Ritchard directed a captivating *La Périchole,* which proved that Offenbach and other comic operas were possible in a huge house when there was enough confidence and imagination behind them. Bing broke some old Metropolitan traditions: the annual performance of *Parsifal,* the weekly visit to Philadelphia. He made some highly publicized innovations: Marian Anderson the first African American to sing with the company, Thomas Schippers the first full-time American conductor. Bing was conventional in his personal tastes and ambitions, happily accepting the view that the Metropolitan audience was unshakably conservative. He gave only token support for American opera. The Metropolitan remained a Puccini house, 25 percent of its performances being devoted to his operas. There were as many *La Bohèmes* as all the Wagner operas combined.

Women singers dominated the Bing years. In the 1950s it was Maria Callas (briefly), Renata Tebaldi, and Zinka Milanov. In the 1960s, Leonie Rysanek, Joan Sutherland, and Birgit Nilsson. Sutherland compelled comparisons with the coloratura dazzlers of the past, while Nilsson's debut in December 1959 ranked with the great first appearances. Aptly, Irving Kolodin used Willa Cather's words in *The Song of the Lark* describing Thea Kronborg's triumph: "At last somebody with enough."

The second decade of Bing's tenure lacked the excitement of the first. The autocratic Bing was not well equipped to deal with the complex situations facing the Metropolitan in the 1960s. He fought with singers and with theatrical and musical unions. The remarkable level of attendance in terms of seats sold, 97 percent for one season and comparable levels for others, could not disguise the uneven level of performance. "Nothing at the Metropolitan is ever so bad that it cannot get worse," the company's historian wrote, a reality not obliterated by the company's huge budget, powerful publicity machinery, and fifty-dollar top price for tickets. In any event, the 1960s yielded the oldest of Metropolitan new stories—plans to build a new opera house, at last.[9]

I n the 1950s opera was reborn in Chicago. The sporadic efforts to revive it after the Insull collapse had come to nothing. The Auditorium Building, sadly dilapidated, was in continual danger of being demolished. Three people changed everything: Lawrence Kelly, a businessman, Nicola Rescigno, musician and vocal teacher, and Carol Fox, whose father's money underwrote the enterprise. The three formed the Lyric Theater of Chicago in 1952, their plan, a familiar one, to spot European singing talent that San Francisco overlooked or the Metropolitan ignored. To this they added two innovations: they reduced their costs by borrowing productions from other companies, and they revived the bel canto operas of the early nineteenth century. In 1954 the Lyric Opera put on a series of sensational performances at the Civic Opera House that "launched [it] into international orbit." Maria Callas made her American debut in *Norma,* and her performance exceeded all expectations. Her Violetta in *La Traviata* was an even more popular success, while her reception in *Lucia* was rapture encroaching on hysteria: "Question: WHICH IS MAD, THE CALLAS LUCIA OR HER FRENZIED PUBLIC?" asked the critic Claudia Cassidy. There were twenty-two curtain calls, the aisles full of men pushing as close to the stage as possible. "I am sure they wished for bouquets to throw, a carriage to pull through the streets," Cassidy wrote. "Myself, I wished they had had both."[10]

Callas sang again in Chicago the following year, as did Renata Tebaldi. The 1956 season included performances conducted by Dimitri Mitropoulos and George Solti. Critics derided the conventionality of the Chicago repertory. "La Scala West," they jeered. Then, too, there was another Chicago tradition—bickering between the partners. Fox emerged in control. "I was stronger than they were." Kelly and Rescigno went to Dallas to found the Dallas Civic Opera, an important part of the 1950s Texas opera boom.[11] The rejuvenation of opera in Chicago was also part of a civic renaissance marked, in the arts, by the justifiably proud acquisition of works by Picasso, Chagall, Miró, and Calder. Pride of place, however, went to the preservation of a local masterpiece. After World War II, the Auditorium Building became the home of Roosevelt University, which eventually undertook its restoration, made possible by the efforts of a group of civic-minded citizens. On October 3, 1967, the restored Auditorium was rededicated to the arts.

Marian Anderson

In a singing career that stretched over fifty years and covered the globe, Marian Anderson sang in only a half-dozen performances of opera. Even so, she played an important role in the history of opera in America. A major figure in the bringing together of African American and European American musical audiences, she bridged the gap between New Deal America of the 1930s and the new American operatic world of the 1950s, as two celebrated events in her career show.

She was born in Philadelphia, on February 17, 1902, the oldest of three daughters, and grew up in a poor, racially mixed neighborhood. Religion was the dominant force in her life. Her father was an officer in the Union Baptist Church, and at six Marian was enrolled in the church choir. There was a family piano but no money for a teacher, and she never imagined that she could play the piano until one day, delivering a basket of laundry for her mother, she heard one being played in a neighboring house. Marian peered inside the window and saw the pianist. "Her skin was dark, like mine. I realized that if she could, I could."[1]

By age eight her voice had begun to capture people's attention, and in the next few years she sang everywhere she could, in choirs, in school concerts, in the high school chorus. She sang whatever was set before her, but had "no thought about technique or style." She went to a concert by Roland Hayes, the African American baritone who with immense courage confronted the racial barriers set before him and carved out a concert career. He sang Italian and German and French songs, all a revelation to Anderson. "Even people with little understanding of music knew it was beautiful singing." Hayes heard her sing and recommended her to African American churches and colleges. "All this time I was singing from nature, so to speak, without any thought of how. . . . It slowly dawned on me that I had to have some training." She heard Ernestine Schumann-Heink, who "though she was no longer young, reached me most deeply," and Sigrid Onegin, who sang a song by Richard Strauss. "I had not heard music like that before and as soon as I could spare the money bought a copy." Giuseppe Boghetti, a former opera singer, took her on as a student and taught her a great deal about the use of her voice, which was now a rich contralto. He introduced her to *Aida.* "I realized then that I liked doing opera tremendously." But in the United States of the 1920s, there was no hope of that.[2]

In those years Marian Anderson learned the reality of racial attitudes in the United States. Friends suggested a private music school in Philadelphia, where she was told: "We don't take colored." "It was as if a cold, horrifying hand had been laid on me." Invitations to sing came from outside Philadelphia. On a trip to Savannah, Georgia, she and her mother were forced to sit in a dirty and smelly Jim Crow railroad car. Her religion helped her deal with all this—and her mother, who "was not one to cause a fuss or to argue."[3]

Slowly, her engagement with music turned into a career, but the way forward was clogged with difficulties. She applied to the Yale School of Music and was accepted. There was no money for tuition. She won a singing contest in Philadelphia which entitled her to take part in a concert in Lewisohn Stadium in New York in August 1925. The *New York Times* devoted four sentences to her: "Miss Anderson made an excellent impression. She is endowed by nature with a voice of unusual compass, color and dramatic capacity. The lower tones have a warm contralto quality, but the voice has the range and the resources of the mezzo-soprano. In passages of sustained melody the singer showed a feeling for melodic lines." There were other opportunities, other disappointments. It wasn't always possible to tell one from the other. She sang with the Hall Johnson Choir at Carnegie Hall and Arthur Judson, one of the most powerful musical managers of the time, offered to guide her, but he saw no future for her except one limited to African American audiences. A recital was arranged at Town Hall. The audience was tiny. She tried music that was too difficult for her. The newspaper notices were uncomplimentary: "Marian Anderson sang her Brahms as if by rote." She felt lost. "I did not want to see any music; I did not want to hear any; I did not want to make a career of it. The dream was over."[4]

She wasn't the only African American singer facing these barriers. Lillian Evans Tibbs, of Washington, D.C., sang with provincial French and Italian companies in the 1920s and 1930s under the name Lillian Evanti. Catherine Yarborough, of Wilmington, North Carolina, was the first African American to break through some of the barriers, appearing in *Aida* with the Salmaggi Opera Company of New York in July 1933. There was nothing else for her and so she went to the Théâtre La Monnaie in Brussels, where she sang, as Caterina Jarbobo, for four seasons. Anderson decided to go to Europe and told Judson, who was harshly dismissive. "If you go to Europe, it will only be to satisfy your vanity." Anderson replied with great spirit: "I will go, then, for that purpose."[5]

L i k e Nordica and Eames and Farrar and countless others, Marian Anderson mastered her art and came into her own as an artist in Europe. Unlike them, she did so in Scandinavia, giving a series of concerts in Oslo, Stockholm, Bergen, Helsinki. Newspapers described her as "looking very much like a chocolate bar," or compared her to "cafe au lait." She took no offense. "The comments had nothing to do with prejudice," she insisted. "They expressed a kind of wonder." People were kind, phoned her hotel, brought her flowers. The cold north was heated in its enthusiasm. Copenhagen was most responsive. "I felt as if I were among my own people and closest friends. People accepted you as an individual in your own right, judging you for your qualities as a human being and artist and for nothing else." She began to hope that "what I dared aspire to was not impossible." She stayed for two years.[6]

In 1933–1934 Anderson gave 112 concerts in the Scandinavian countries. There were weeks when she sang eight concerts in nine days, "something a singer should not do. But who can blame her if in those years she succumbed to the pleas of the people who first responded to her great gift?" In Finland she called on Jan Sibelius at home. He greeted her warmly, and after she sang one of his songs to a German text, he embraced her. "My roof is too low for you." Her reputation spread beyond Scandinavia. The great and famous began to pay her tribute. In Russia, the celebrated theatrical director Konstantin Stanislavsky brought her a bouquet of white lilacs and asked her to stay so that he could teach her the role of Carmen for a Moscow Art Theater production. She declined. In August 1935, Toscanini was conducting at the Salzburg Festival. Anderson was told that he might come to her recital. She hoped he would not. "I held him in such high esteem that I felt I could not possibly do anything of interest to him." He came and at the intermission appeared in her dressing room. "The sight of him caused my heart to leap and throb so violently that I did not hear a word he said." Bystanders told her what the maestro said: "A voice like yours is heard once in a hundred years."[7]

Marvelous as all this was, and though she would return again and again to Europe, she never doubted that she would go back to the United States. "I want to test myself as a serious artist in my own country." To make that test, she gained support more immediately helpful than the generous words of the famous. Sol Hurok, the greatest impresario of the next quarter-century, saw a notice that "an American contralto" was to sing at the Salle Gaveau in Paris. He went, expecting little. "I was shaken to my very shoes." He signed her to a contract and prepared to promote her across the Atlantic.[8]

"You won't be able to give her away," an experienced business colleague of Hurok's said. He was wrong, but the task was far from smooth sailing. Anderson's first American appearance was at Town Hall. The reviews were cautious for the most part, but Howard Taubman in the *New York Times* began his in ringing terms: "Marian Anderson has returned to her native land one of the great singers of our time," and ended: "It is time for her own country to honor her." Hurok had planned fifteen recitals for that first season, but by the time of the Town Hall concert only six had been booked. Recitals in Carnegie Hall followed in January and March. The other engagements were filled in. Back and forth Anderson moved across the ocean until the coming of the war. She sang at the White House, for the visiting king and queen of England, but outside of New York and Washington her appearance challenged deeply rooted sentiments. Was she going to appear with a white accompanist? (Yes.) "She'll be stoned," Hurok was warned. She made a tour of the South. It was noted that she held the hand of her accompanist when they took bows together. "She can't take a white man's hand—you must tell her we can't have that sort of thing here." "I warn you there will be a riot." She sang, and took her accompanist's hand, and there was no riot. But there was much meanness, many affronts. Everywhere. No hotel in midtown Manhattan would have her until the Algonquin welcomed her, as good a claim to fame, many would think, as the presence of its circle of wits.[9]

Inch by inch, there was change. It wasn't only Hurok's tact and perseverance and Anderson's steadfastness. The Depression had undermined many old habits. The New

Deal brought with it a different atmosphere and thereby earned the undying hatred of many. The walls did not come tumbling down. The recipient of honorary degrees, awarded civic honors, welcomed by European royalty, Marian Anderson often could not dine in restaurants or stay in hotels in the cities where audiences cheered her. Out of these contradictory tides there emerged the single event that made her famous throughout the nation, among millions who knew nothing of her art. On a stage incomparably grander than that of any opera house, history took a hand as impresario.

I n June 1938 Howard University asked Hurok to schedule a recital by Anderson for Washington, D.C., as part of her next year's concert tour. Early in 1939 Howard applied to the management of Constitution Hall, owned by the Daughters of the American Revolution (DAR) and the finest concert hall in the city, to reserve April 9 for the concert. The management replied, disingenuously, that the date was already booked, and when pressed about this, made it clear that it was not available for an Anderson recital on any date. Howard sought an alternative site, a high school auditorium, and the Washington school board refused the request. Kirsten Flagstad, Walter Damrosch, and others protested. In February, Eleanor Roosevelt resigned from the DAR, and in her newspaper column explained her reasons for doing so. The National Association for the Advancement of Colored People joined in the mounting clamor. Hurok then hit on the idea that converted a routine music recital into a major social and political event: he requested permission to use the Lincoln Memorial for an outdoor concert. Harold Ickes, secretary of the interior, readily agreed to the request. Anderson had been disturbed by "the weight of the Washington affair." "I did not want to talk, and I particularly did not want to say anything about the DAR." There was no escaping it. "My significance as an individual was small in the affair. I had become, whether I liked it or not, a symbol, representing my people." She knew what her decision had to be. "I said yes, but the yes did not come easily or quickly." As late as the night before, she phoned Hurok: "Must we go through with this?"[10]

April 9 was Easter Sunday. Anderson arrived in Washington by train and went to the home of a once famous Theodore Roosevelt Progressive, Gifford Pinchot, where she could change—"The Washington hotels would not take us." On a platform on the steps of the Lincoln Memorial, six microphones had been set up to carry her voice to a crowd estimated at seventy-five thousand, including congressmen, senators, cabinet secretaries, Supreme Court Justice Hugo Black. Her nerves almost failed her. "I could not talk. I even wondered whether I would be able to sing." But sing she did—"The Star-Spangled Banner," "America," "O mio Fernando" from Donizetti's *La Favorite,* Schubert's "Ave Maria," three African American spirituals. The murmur of the great crowd was converted, during her singing, into a tangible wave of affection which engulfed her. At the end, when the shouting would not die down, she said a few characteristic words. "I can't tell you what you have done for me today. I thank you from the bottom of my heart again and again." Who could say, for those there and for countless others elsewhere, heartened by her voice and by her presence, what Marian Anderson had done for *them?*[11]

An estimated seventy-five thousand people heard Marian Anderson sing at Washington's Lincoln Memorial in 1939. Mitchell Jamieson commemorated the concert in a mural for the new Interior Department building, entitled **An Incident in Contemporary American Life** *(1942). U.S. Department of the Interior, Washington, D.C. Photograph by David Allison.*

To commemorate the concert, a privately sponsored competition was held for a mural for the new Interior Department building. The winner was a Maryland painter, Mitchell Jamieson (1915–1976), whose work, in the "heroic tradition of Mexico's great proletarian muralists," Rivera, Orozco, and Siqueiros, captured both that moment and much of the spirit of the New Deal. In January 1943, Anderson was present for the formal dedication of the mural, the art of the singer and of the muralist testifying to "the dignity of the human spirit."[12] And that week she sang at a war relief concert—in Constitution Hall.

T h e second great symbolic event of Anderson's career took place in an opera house, a quarter of a century later. It, too, was something larger than herself. Her entire career had been shaped by the impossibility of singing in opera in the United States. Mary Cardwell Dawson (1894–1962), an intrepid organizer of an African American opera company, invited Anderson to take part, but she committed herself to a concert career instead. "I must say that I was not losing any sleep over the prospect of having an operaless career." Abruptly, the final door opened. At a party in New York, Rudolf

Marian Anderson singing "The Star-Spangl'd Banner" at the dedication of Jamieson's mural on Jan. 6, 1943. A dozen years later, Anderson became the first African American to sing at the Metropolitan Opera. Library of Congress.

Bing drew her aside. "Would you be interested in singing at the Metropolitan?" "I think I would." Bing proposed the role of Ulrica, the gypsy fortune-teller, in Verdi's *Un Ballo in maschera.* "Do you know it?" She knew *no* role in any opera, commenting with restrained irony: "I had never had a pressing need to learn operatic roles." A rehearsal was arranged with Dimitri Mitropoulos, who would conduct. "You don't know it thoroughly," he said to her. "When you know it, it will go." Hurok, Bing, and Mitropoulos conferred that day, and within forty-five minutes had worked out the arrangements. How easy it now seemed.[13]

Anderson's debut produced front-page newspaper publicity. ("The Metropolitan Opera board," Bing later wrote, "was not among the many organizations that sent congratulations when the news was announced.") The first performance would be January 7, 1955. Anderson went to work. The Metropolitan stage was familiar to her, as she had sung there in recitals over the years. But now there was the complexity of an operatic performance, costumes, learning to move on stage. Herbert Graff worked with her on acting: "Do the thing that seems natural to you." Hearing the voices of the others in the cast—Zinka Milanov, Richard Tucker, Leonard Warren—in rehearsal brought home the reality of what was to happen. "I felt incredibly alive, able to do any amount of extra tasks."[14]

At last, January 7. Anderson's family came up from Philadelphia and sat with Hurok in a center box. The house had sold out faster than for the season's opening night. People came from all over the country, customers for standing room lining up at 5:30 that morning. Some of these were African Americans, "a rare sight on the standees' queue." Reporters from the African American press came from everywhere. "It was a safe guess that no previous Metropolitan Opera performance had so many Negroes in the audience as last night's," and throughout the house were men and women "for whom Miss Anderson has been not only a singer but the voice of a people."[15] She later remembered the preparations for the performance as a blur, costume, makeup, warming up, members of the cast coming by to wish her luck.

When the curtain rose on the second scene to show Ulrica, a grim figure stirring her witch's brew, the audience broke into a tumultuous demonstration. "The crowd on stage regarded her with broken exclamations of awe and reverence." Mitropoulos stopped the orchestra and let the ovation expend itself. Anderson's voice trembled, wavered a little in pitch. "With all the experience I had behind me, I should have been firm and secure, but my emotions were too strong." As the act went on, her voice warmed and gained in sonority. Of course, she should have been singing with the voice of ten years before, or ten years before that, but "by her native sensibility, intelligence, and vocal art, Miss Anderson stamped herself in the memory and the lasting esteem of those who listened." Milanov was a magnificent Amelia and Mitropoulos unleashed a "torrent of orchestral tone that swept the voices and the drama itself forward on its crest." But the curtain calls were above all for her—outburst after outburst, people shouting, "Anderson! Anderson! Anderson!" hoping for a solo bow forbidden by the new rules of the Bing administration. Anderson and Milanov came out together, and when the soprano threw her arms around Anderson and kissed her on the cheek, there was another demonstration. "Men as well as women in the audience were dabbing at their eyes." On the night of the 11th, she again sang in *Un Ballo in maschera*, in Philadelphia, to an ovation such as the historic old Academy of Music had rarely heard. "Marian Anderson had come home in glory."[16]

A n d e r s o n ' s career paralleled that of another greatly gifted African American singer, close to her in age, from a deeply religious family and from the same section of the country—Paul Robeson (1898–1976). The differences between them, in ideas and in temperament, were more striking than the similarities—one of them bold, outspoken, the other shy, accommodating. Success came early to Paul Robeson, as an all-American football player at Rutgers University, law student at Columbia University, actor, singer. In all these spheres he encountered racial bigotry. Instead of turning the other cheek, like Anderson, Robeson spoke out. It was racial prejudice which led him to abandon law as a career, because he understood that "the highest prizes were from the start denied to me."[17] Endowed with a rich baritone voice and an impressive physique, Robeson turned to singing and acting. In the summer of 1921 he sang in a quartet in Eubie Blake's *Shuffle Along*. "That boy will bear watching," Blake said. From that modest start, Paul Robeson rocketed upward, to Eugene O'Neill's *The Emperor Jones* at the Provincetown Playhouse in 1922, O'Neill's *All God's Chillun Got Wings* on Broadway in 1924, the London production of *Show Boat*. By the end of the 1920s, while Anderson struggled in frustration and obscurity, Robeson was "in the front rank of African American artists, more universally applauded by white intellectuals than by blacks but recognized even by dissenting blacks as superbly gifted."

In the late 1920s Robeson began a career as a concert singer, following in the wake of the talented and intrepid Roland Hayes (1887–1977). Born in Georgia, the son of ex-slaves, Hayes early on showed unusual vocal talent. Hearing a Caruso record, he made up his mind to become an operatic singer. He came to New York and studied there for a number of years. Diminutive in size, with a light, clear tenor voice, he found his only chance in Europe. After overcoming initial hostility there, he returned to America and established himself as a concert singer, reaching white as well as black audiences; he pioneered the singing of African American spirituals on his programs.

Robeson's indebtedness to Hayes was direct. Hayes's accompanist, Lawrence Brown, transcribed spirituals for Robeson's use, and Robeson became the first African American artist to present an entire program of this music for American audiences. This earned him great acclaim, and he increasingly turned to the music of his African American heritage. It also allowed him an escape from the limited roles available to him on the spoken and singing stage—the O'Neill plays, *Porgy and Bess,* and *Show Boat* (in the mid-1930s he appeared in the Hollywood film of the latter)—always playing a black man. The European operatic repertory might have been a way out, but to try for a European career would have required years of study and financial sacrifice. At thirty years of age, there were too many risks. "I will not go into opera, where I would probably become one of hundreds of mediocre singers, but I will concentrate on negro music," he said. "I may sing a little opera in the morning but only in the bathroom." It was American opera's loss.

In the late 1930s and early 1940s, Anderson and Robeson matched each other in popularity and fame. After traveling to Russia and becoming passionately concerned with the Spanish Civil War, Robeson wholeheartedly and uncritically embraced communism and subordinated art to political aims, while Anderson, despite the Lincoln Memorial concert, steadfastly turned away from political involvement. After 1945, Anderson's career was in the ascendant. The fears generated by the Cold War made her attitude seem reassuring, while Robeson, staunchly upholding unpopular views, confronted public and governmental opposition and harassment. His popularity plummeted and he was transformed into a dangerous enemy. In 1955, unable to travel and sing abroad because the State Department refused him a passport, Robeson lapsed into a devastating psychological depression from which he emerged only near the end of his life. That year Anderson sang at the Metropolitan.

N u m e r o u s African American women followed Anderson onto the operatic stage in America, at the Metropolitan and elsewhere, for which Rudolf Bing deserves much credit. Mattiwilda Dobbs, who had sung in Europe, made her Metropolitan debut as Gilda in *Rigoletto* in November 1956, the first African American woman to perform in a romantic role with a white male singer. After her, with varying degrees of success, came Felicia Weathers, Gloria Davy, Reri Grist, and then, in the 1970s and 1980s, singers who have gained a commanding place in American opera—Grace Bumbry, Shirley Verrett, Leona Mitchell, Jessye Norman.

The great diva of the 1960s and 1970s was Leontyne Price. Born in Laurel, Mississippi, in 1927, she early on revealed musical inclinations which were encouraged by her family. She too faced obstacles, but the social world in which she grew up allowed her to be positive. "Being a human being, being in America, and being black, all three were the greatest things that could happen to you." She also acknowledged her predecessors. "My mother took me to see Marian Anderson. When I saw this wonderful woman come from the wings in this white satin dress, I knew instantly: one of these days, I'm going to come out of the wings. I won't know what color the dress is going to be but I'm going to be center stage, right there, where I saw her. The light dawned. It was a magic moment." She won a scholarship to the Juilliard School of Music. Virgil Thomson chose her for a Broadway revival of *Four Saints in Three Acts.* Then came a revival of *Porgy and Bess,* which toured the world for two years. Her great operatic breakthrough came in San Francisco, in the American premiere of Poulenc's *Les Dialogues des Carmélites,* and in *Aida,* which opened European doors: sensational appearances in Vienna, London, Salzburg. In January 1961, Price made her Metropolitan Opera debut in *Il Trovatore.* The following October—opening night of the 1961–1962 season—she was Minnie in the revival of *La Fanciulla del West.* She sang seven roles in her first season with the company. She was "a black diva that was going to hang on." "Marian had opened the door. I kept it from closing again." That debut at the Metropolitan she regarded as her proudest operatic achievement.[18]

The path for male African American singers has been more difficult. George Shirley, an African American tenor, singing at Santa Fe in 1965, daubed his face with pinkish cream and dusted it with light powder, fearing that racial prejudice might detract from his performance, since tenors are romantic leads and audiences "don't like the lover of a white girl to be a Negro, make-believe or not."[19] Whatever the kind

Leontyne Price as Massenet's Thaïs, about 1958. She and others kept the door that Anderson had opened from closing again. Jahant Collection, Music Division, Library of Congress.

of voice, male singers face special problems in America. Robert McFerrin, a bass, was the first African American to sing at the Metropolitan. Simon Estes, a fine bass-baritone, who has sung very well in Wagnerian roles, believes that many opportunities, especially recordings and television, are denied to African American men, and many people would agree with him. Estes' greatest popular success came as Porgy when, in 1985, the Metropolitan finally got around to *Porgy and Bess*.

chapter forty-two

New York Opera

The years between 1940 and 1960 saw the flowering of a distinctive form of American popular opera, New York opera. Touring companies took it abroad at the end of World War II. Recordings and radio carried its song where touring companies couldn't go. Everywhere it was recognized, in its propulsive energy, its brashness and naïveté and unshakable optimism, as indisputably American. But the style that made it nationally representative had its origins in a particular time and place. It was essentially New York, stamped with the mark of that city as surely as waltz opera was Vienna's and can-can opera belonged to Paris. Its composers were polyglot, like the city, some of them native New Yorkers, some from the hinterlands, some from Europe, their variety absorbed and fused into a distinctive style by the pressure of that extraordinary place. Nothing was more characteristic of New York opera than the insistence that it wasn't opera at all. "Opera" was European. These American dramas-by-means-of-music were something else. What to call them? *Operetta* or *comic opera* were terms too tied to the European past. *Musical comedy* had adherents, but best of all was *musical*. Americans felt comfortable with that—unpretentious, vague enough to include anything. Why not? An opera by any name sounds as sweet.

Looking back at the evolution, sporadic and indirect, of American popular opera from its ballad opera beginnings, we can see certain of its features revealing themselves over and over. Its scale was modest, its orchestra small, its music not complex. In time it achieved dramatic integration of words, songs, and story, but its songs, melodious and singable, stood out on their own. Its language was colloquial. Spoken dialogue moved the stories forward and a version of recitative, half sung and half spoken patter, was also used. Its principals were actors who sang more than singers who acted. The style of singing was less full-bodied than that of European opera, closer to popular crooning, less ardent and abandoned. Most of all, American popular opera was laconic, underplayed, operatic expression that was unoperatic.

New York opera came of age as America entered its new imperial age of worldwide economic and political ascendance. It became an item of cultural export, along with dance and painting and architecture as well as American mass culture, film and television. Its essential spirit and values, however, had been shaped in the decade before the war, in the affirmative national spirit of the 1930s, in the emergence of a racially mixed, culturally diverse, liberal culture. New York opera might also be called New Deal opera.

I t s great age began with *Pal Joey* of 1940, by Lorenz Hart (1895–1943) and Richard Rodgers (1902–1979). The son of German immigrants, Hart was a New York boy who immersed himself in the city's theater, then attended Columbia University. Rodgers was Long Island–born, his mother a pianist, his father a medical doctor who was also a singer. He began writing songs at age fourteen and also went to Columbia. In 1919 Rodgers and Hart collaborated on their first song. "Any Old Place with You" revealed the unorthodox Hart idiom—"I'll go to hell for ya—or Philadelphia!" During the 1920s, they worked together on *The Garrick Gaieties,* small-scale, off-Broadway revues, fresh, impudent, largely satirical. One of them included a lengthy attempt at jazz opera, another a lampoon of operettas. *Dearest Enemy,* a story about the American Revolution, challenged critics to find the proper term to describe it: "An operetta with more than a chance flavor of Gilbert and Sullivan"; "something very akin to a genuine comic opera"; "a baby grand opera." Odd rhymes, fetching tunes, offbeat rhythms characterized their work. *Peggy Ann,* of 1926, was a Freudian dream, with a prologue and epilogue, no opening chorus, no songs at all for the first fifteen minutes, the end performed in semidarkness. Despite these departures from convention, it achieved 333 performances. *Chee-Chee,* their most ambitious effort, a parody of Graustarkian romance, Hart thought of as "a new form of musical show," "the songs . . . a definite part of the progress of the piece, not extraneous interludes without rhyme or reason."[1]

The 1930s brought varied efforts. *Jumbo,* "a compound of opera, animal show, folk drama, harlequinade, carnival, circus, extravaganza and spectacle,"[2] contrasted with *On Your Toes* of 1936, a unified work, with dancing a central part of the action. George Balanchine, émigré choreographer recently arrived in America, created a memorable dance sequence, the "Slaughter on Tenth Avenue" ballet. *I'd Rather Be Right* (1937), a satire about contemporary politics, excited interest because George M. Cohan was cast in the leading role. He dismissed Rodgers and Hart's songs as "Gilbert and Sullivan," which was of course a great compliment, though not intended so by Cohan. *The Boys from Syracuse* (1938), one of Rodgers's most delightful scores, was an interesting adaptation of Shakespeare's *A Comedy of Errors.*

And so *Pal Joey.* Based on short stories by John O'Hara, it was an unsentimental depiction of a dancer who was a low-life heel surrounded by a world of stupidity, greed, and ordinary fallibility, a kind of night-club *Beggar's Opera,* "a song-and-dance production with living, three-dimensional figures, talking and behaving like human beings." Its depiction of moral sordidness distressed some. "Although it is expertly done," one critic asked querulously, "can you draw sweet water from a foul well?"[3] The answer, in musical theater if not hydrology, was a resounding Yes, as audiences affirmed. *Pal Joey* ran for 374 performances, proving that it was not too far in advance of its time to be appreciated. It did take time to appreciate its significance as a work which inaugurated a great period. Twelve years later, when it was revived and achieved 542 performances, critics compared it to Brecht and Weill's *Threepenny Opera* and used words like "classic" and "masterpiece" to describe it. By then it was enveloped in sentimental feeling because it was the last Rodgers and Hart opera. The year of Hart's death was the year of the emergence of a more famous collaboration, the words and music of Richard Rodgers and Oscar Hammerstein II. If *Pal Joey* represented a milestone in American opera, *Oklahoma* marked its full realization.

T h e audience in the St. James Theater on March 31, 1943 had no reason to anticipate anything momentous. The reports from Boston about *Away We Go!* were favorable but not enthusiastic. A change of title wasn't enough to alter expectations, so one of the most important premieres in American operatic history took place with empty seats in the theater. After the overture, the curtain rose on a relatively bare stage. Before the stylized representation of a farm scene of the early 1900s, a woman sat alone, dressed in the costume of the period, while offstage a baritone voice sang the opening song, "Oh, What a Beautiful Mornin'." Other memorable songs followed, as did a ballet sequence, choreographed by Agnes de Mille, through which the heroine projected her thoughts and feelings. A rousing chorus brought the curtain down to thunderous applause. *Oklahoma* was a success of the *Merry Widow* order. "People Will Say We're in Love" was played so often on the radio as to become synonymous in the national consciousness with the middle years of the war. The original cast recording sold 1.3 million copies. The 2,212 performances shattered every attendance record. As early as October 1943, the first touring company began what turned out to be a ten-and-a-half-year odyssey—sixty weeks in Chicago alone, visits and revisits to all the major cities, 153 cities all told plus 10 in Canada, reaching Berlin by 1951. There were three thousand tour performances in a decade.

Every two years Rodgers and Hammerstein produced another work which established the central canon of the popular American operatic repertory. *Carousel* (1945), a story of New England mill workers and fishermen, its leading male figure a shiftless failure, was even more unconventional in its musical and dramatic ambitions. Its "soliloquy," an attempt at extended recitative, presented a wide range of contrasting emotions and inner thoughts, and though the opera was thought by some to be "too tragic" for audiences of the time, it concluded with the chorus singing "You'll Never Walk Alone," a characteristic Rodgers and Hammerstein note of affirmation. *Allegro* (1949) carried the effort at innovation and dramatic coherence further still. An attempt (some thought a pretentious one) at "a large universal story," it recounted, with formal sets removed and with a modern Greek chorus commenting on the action, the life of a young doctor from birth to age thirty-five, music expanding the plot, few separate songs. Compared with its two predecessors, it was not a popular or commercial success.

South Pacific (1949) was not innovative in form. What was unusual was its combination of a conventional love story with a parallel one about mixed racial love, a powerful theme since *Show Boat.* Notable for its melodic score, 1,925 performances, and for winning the Pulitzer Prize for drama, *South Pacific* gained immense publicity too because of the presence of Ezio Pinza, crossing over from grand opera. *The King and I* (1951) was a melodious excursion into exotica, as was *Flower Drum Song.* Helen Traubel's move from the Metropolitan to *Pipe Dream* didn't recapitulate Pinza's success, while *The Sound of Music* (1959), "more in the style of a Romberg operetta than in the innovative style of their early years," enchanted audiences (as did the film). "It will be most admired by people who have always found Sir James M. Barrie pretty rough stuff," one critic sniffed caustically.[4] That was the end of the great collaboration. Oscar Hammerstein II died in 1960.

The Rodgers and Hammerstein operas deserve their central position in the popular opera repertory, as innumerable revivals have shown. Popular tunes were ingeniously embedded in a plausible dramatic context. Dance played an important role as a means of expression, and Hammerstein's lyrics were often a delight. The team also expanded the emotional bounds of popular opera by introducing serious subjects, though conflict was kept within careful bounds. Sentiment and fantasy played a larger role in the later operas, but in all of them the overriding qualities were optimism and faith in human nature. They might be seen as variations on a Rooseveltian theme: "The only thing we have to fear is fear itself." "What's wrong with sweetness and light? It's been around quite a while," Rodgers asked, and Hammerstein echoed his words: "There's nothing wrong with sentiment because the things we're sentimental about are the fundamental things in life." No one equaled the sureness with which they reflected values their audiences shared, or aspired to. No wonder Cole Porter, asked to identify the most important changes in American musical theater in the previous half-century, said simply: "Rodgers and Hammerstein."[5]

O t h e r composers and other works amplified the scope of New York opera. Different as they were from each other, all bore the stamp of the liberal culture of the period. Irving Berlin, after forty years of prolific success as a songwriter, challenged to do something more ambitious, wrote *Annie Get Your Gun* (1946), drawing on the *Oklahoma* vein of frontier innocence and high spirits. Frank Loesser's *Guys and Dolls* (1950), based on Damon Runyon stories, was urban culture treated as fable. This Manhattan *Beggar's Opera* underworld of gangsters and prostitutes was charmingly conceived as one in which sinners were redeemable and innocence lurked in the hardest of hearts. Its simple folk gained a remarkably moving dignity by expressing themselves through complex musical forms—a fugue for the description of a horse race, a grandly operatic duet. Innocence marked the translation of small-town America into New York opera in Meredith Willson's *The Music Man* of 1957. Born in Mason City, Iowa, Willson drew on autobiographical reminiscence. "Innocent, that was the adjective for Iowa. I didn't have to make anything up for *The Music Man*. All I had to do was remember."[6] Audiences heard a hymn of praise for the marching band and a catalogue of small-town popular musical forms—march, barbershop quartet, soft shoe.

There was nothing innocent in the work of Cole Porter, though his origins were in small-town Indiana of 1891. He grew up in affluent circumstances, went east to private schools and to Yale University, and emerged, like a character in a Scott Fitzgerald novel, as the personification of urbane worldliness. His airy nonchalance concealed a serious interest in his art. Living in Paris throughout the 1920s, he studied harmony and counterpoint with Vincent d'Indy. Back in America in the 1930s, his considerable number of commercial successes, *DuBarry Was a Lady, Panama Hattie, Mexican Hayride,* were a means of escape from the solemn social seriousness of the New Deal years. He became notorious for the sexual suggestiveness of his lyrics, for the risqué if not erotic combination of double meanings and insinuating rhythms. Some disapproved and regarded him as no more than a "genteel pornographer." Porter, too, responded, in the mid-1940s, to the Rodgers and Hammerstein challenge—"The librettos are much better and the scores are much closer to the librettos than they used to be"—and to Irving Berlin's example in *Annie Get Your Gun:* "His having so much music in *Annie* made me feel like trying a similar thing." Porter's contribution, in 1948, was *Kiss Me, Kate,* a treatment of Shakespeare's *The Taming of the Shrew,* an opera self-conscious about its place in the history of American musical theater, deft in playing itself off against other operatic forms, from a "show biz" rouser ("Another Op'nin, Another Show") to plaintive ballads and, in "Wunderbar," a parody of Viennese waltz-operetta.[7]

The work of another pair of collaborators, Frederick Loewe and Alan Jay Lerner, revealed the broad range of New York opera's subjects. Loewe, born in Berlin in 1904, the son of a popular operetta tenor, studied music under Ferruccio Busoni, left Germany in the 1920s to come to the United States, gave up writing music for a decade. Lerner decided on a musical career at an early age, went to Harvard, wrote songs for college shows and for Broadway. He and Loewe teamed up in 1942. *Brigadoon* (1947), a satirical political fable set in a Scottish village, was their first success. The California gold rush was the setting for *Paint Your Wagon* (1951), celebrating "the robustness and vitality and cockeyed courage that is so much a part of our American heritage." But their previous work (and everything else) paled into insignificance beside their American vision of Edwardian English as they converted George Bernard Shaw's *Pygmalion* into *My Fair Lady* in 1956. To a charming score, melodious and vigorous, and deft characterizations through music, they added an unfailing theatrical flair.[8]

In these years, the most musically complex New York music drama was composed by Kurt Weill, who, having adapted to the American idiom in the 1930s, composed two powerful works in the 1940s. *Street Scene* (1947), libretto by playwright Elmer Rice, lyrics by Langston Hughes, the African American poet, Weill thought his most successful "blending of drama and music, in which the singing continues naturally where the speaking stops, and the spoken word, as well as the dramatic action, is embedded in the overall musical structure." A cross section of life in a New York tenement, this urban verismo work had individual songs, duets, and dances which spilled over from street to tenement and back. *Lost in the Stars* (1949), based on Alan Paton's novel *Cry, the Beloved Country,* achieved 273 performances and entered the repertory of the New York City Opera. It "continued the history of black American folk opera, for Weill had so naturalized himself by then that the jazz of Johannesburg speaks of Hot Harlem as well as the lilt of American country ballads." Weill's death, in April·1950, only fifty years of age and his powers undiminished, was a great loss— how great Virgil Thomson, at least, understood at the time: "He was probably the most original single workman in the whole musical theater, internationally considered, during the last quarter century."[9]

The other musical cosmopolitan among New York composers was Leonard Bernstein (1918–1990). A native of Lawrence, Massachusetts, he went to Harvard and majored in music. Dimitri Mitropoulos and Serge Koussevitzky promoted his career, and he became the much publicized wonder-boy of American music, as conductor and pianist. And composer. He wrote the music for *Fancy Free,* a ballet by Jerome Robbins, about three sailors uninhibitedly exploring wartime New York City. Fresh

Urban verismo: the original New York production of Kurt Weill's Street Scene. John Herrick Jackson Music Library, Yale University.

and appealing, it also announced a primary Bernsteinian theme—the celebration of New York. "Perhaps only one not native to the city could capture it so well in music." Bernstein was emphatic. "This town still gets me. No wonder I keep composing about it. It's so dramatic and alive. New York! The amazing, confusing beauty of the place." The ballet became an opera in 1944, one of its songs, "New York, New York," the first of Bernstein's paeans to the Big Town. He returned to this subject in 1953, with *Wonderful Town,* set in the 1930s. The Depression decade, as Bernstein remembered it, was a time of excitement and promise. "The Thirties! My God, those were the years! The excitement that was around! The political awareness! F.D.R.! Fiorello! Real personalities. And the wonderful fashions! Glorious! And the songs! What beat!"[10] Dance was at the heart of *Wonderful Town,* with such numbers as "Conga" and "Swing." The songs tied the whole together, a theme from one being used as part of another, or as the introduction to something else.

With a libretto by Lillian Hellman and lyrics by the poet Richard Wilbur, *Candide,* of 1956, abounded with answers to that familiar American question, What is an opera? There were dances of all kinds—waltz, gavotte, mazurka, tango, schottische, an overture with Rossinian crescendo, parodies of the styles of other composers, a chorus of pilgrims, folksongs, a brilliant coloratura aria, "Glitter and Be Gay," and an eloquent finale. Too much? *Candide* failed to find favor. (A revised, reduced version in 1973 was better liked.) Bernstein's greatest popular success came in 1957. For years he had thought of composing a music drama, based on some sort of significant American social conflict, which would aim for greater depth of feeling without becoming "operatic." He found his subject in the Puerto Rican immigrants living on Manhattan's West Side. *West Side Story,* notable in itself, was remarkable also as an effort by New York opera to escape from its own rigidifying conventions, and it did so by means of a highly stylized realism and a passionate, agitated musical score.

In 1957 West Side Story *brought together the new faces of New York opera. Grouped around Hal Griffith are, from left to right: Steven Sondheim, Arthur Laurents, Hal Prince, Leonard Bernstein, and Jerome Robbins. Billy Rose Theater Collection, New York Public Library for the Performing Arts.*

The great days of New York opera ended around 1960. One might mark its end by the death of Oscar Hammerstein II that year, or by the relative failure of Lerner and Loewe's curiously Graustarkian *Camelot*. New York opera's energy and machine-tooled precision had floated on a sense of innocence and delight. After 1960, American culture furnished less delight. Urban life lost its appeal. New Deal liberalism slowly dissolved. The sordid exercise of imperial power in Vietnam made confidence in the future suspect. But the sources of decline, as well as of creativity, in an art form elude easy analysis.

I n the last third of the twentieth century, the operas of Stephen Sondheim stand out as works of great accomplishment and as indicators of the post–New York opera sensibility. Born in New York in 1930, Sondheim showed remarkable promise as a composer for the musical theater and became a protégé of Oscar Hammerstein's. "Where Kern got his practice writing interpolations and Rodgers and Hart wrote college shows, Sondheim won a splendid apprenticeship at the fount, writing four musicals in an informal course with the master."[11] He also ranged well beyond Broadway, studying music at Williams College and taking a course in composition with Milton Babbit. His first reputation came as a lyricist, for *West Side Story* and for Jules Styne's *Gypsy*. His first opera, *A Funny Thing Happened on the Way to the Forum* (1962), a resetting of Roman comedy in a contemporary idiom, amusing and inventive, did not suggest that a break with the prevailing tradition was forthcoming. *Anyone Can Whistle* (1964) pointed in a new direction. It was a social satire of withering bleakness, its music entirely integrated in the story. The next two decades continued the development of something very different, and it has taken time fully to understand the originality of *Company* (1970), *Follies* (1971), *A Little Night Music* (1973), *Pacific Overtures* (1976), *Sweeney Todd* (1979), and *Sunday in the Park with George* (1984).

The community of *Company* is that of the neurotic and estranged who make up contemporary America. The focus of Sondheim's dramatic world is not specifically urban; it is all of mass culture. Nor are the alienations enmeshing the opera's characters susceptible to political or social reform. In any event, music predominates. There are many extended sung scenes. *Sweeney Todd* is three-quarters musical exposition, and Sondheim has perfected a form of contemporary recitative. The musical structure is complex—arias, duets, ensembles, motifs that recur as a way to sustain narrative in plotless stories. Not surprisingly, Sondheim's operas have gained more respect than popularity. *Sweeney Todd* has been given by first-class opera companies, but most opera houses remain indifferent, in the traditional way, to his work, and Sondheim has vehemently insisted that his works are not operas, a form of musical theater that he regards as exhausted. But operas they are, and of an especially compelling and disturbing kind. Stephen Sondheim may someday be recognized as the first modernist of American popular opera.

The New Places

The story of opera in America has continually reflected the dynamic nature of American culture. In the last half of the twentieth century, this dynamism has been exemplified by the rise of the so-called regional opera companies—such as Kentucky Opera, Tulsa Opera, Opera Memphis, Lyric Opera of Kansas City, and San Jose Opera. Misleading as numbers can be, the statistics for regional opera are eye-opening: between 1962 and 1987, the number of companies with budgets exceeding one hundred thousand dollars grew from 27 to 154; attendance at operas given by these companies rose from 4.5 million to 13 million; opera performances increased from 4,000 to 13,000 per year.

In this context it is no surprise that five places which had been of no operatic consequence earlier rose to national prominence. As cities—opera aside—their histories had been diverse. Santa Fe (established in 1610) was as old as opera itself, while the rest had been nineteenth-century foundings, contemporary with gold rush San Francisco. Their gold rush came later, in the form of factories and railroads, oil and airplanes, aerospace and tourism. Each of the five cities pursued a different path toward operatic importance.

T h e most influential of the new places was Santa Fe, whose animating spirit was John O'Hea Crosby, born in 1926, in Bronxville, New York, son of a lawyer father and an English chemist-and-violinist mother, who started her son out on violin and piano. Suffering from asthma as a boy, he was sent west to school in Los Alamos, New Mexico. "It was then his love affair with the Southwest began."[1] After service in the Army during World War II, Crosby went to Yale University, studied composition with Paul Hindemith, and graduated in 1950 with a degree in music. That led him to Columbia University, where he studied conducting, gained experience in and around New York, went regularly to the Metropolitan to observe and listen to Fritz Reiner at work. Although he had never been particularly interested in opera, "it now became Crosby's obsession." He was animated by three seemingly unrelated things: love of country, a desire to reform operatic production, a sense of place. His patriotic pride—"Let us not permit our nation to be remembered only for its marketplaces for it will then soon be forgotten"—echoed the words of William Henry Fry a century earlier. In 1956, Crosby contrived to bring these three things together with the most imaginative enterprise of the operatically fermenting 1950s: he founded his own opera company—in Santa Fe.

"A harmonious blend of the arts of theatre and music" was the objective, in pursuit of which a small repertory company, with no stars, was formed and, taking advantage of the magnificent surroundings, there was built "the only out-door theater in America exclusively designed for opera," eventually expanded to seat 1,150. The most important aspect of the Santa Fe enterprise was its repertory. "Opera is a living art," Crosby said. "We think it important to present the new, the different, sometimes controversial." Each season a world premiere or an American premiere was given, along with the central repertory of Mozart, Strauss, Puccini, and Stravinsky. Santa Fe performed virtually all the Stravinsky operas, as well as five operas by Hans Werner Henze, received with varying degrees of puzzlement, outrage, and enthusiasm. Two productions—Luciano Berio's *Opera* (1970) and Krzysztof Penderecki's *The Devils of Loudon* (1969)—occasioned fierce controversy. Critical response to Santa Fe's efforts, if not to the operas, was favorable. *Time* magazine was jauntily upbeat: "Santa Fe has shelled out for opera as though it were investing in big-league baseball." The critic Harold Schonberg praised it for "diving in where the big companies had fastidiously picked up their skirts and circled away." Martin Bernheimer emphasized that Santa Fe was run "not by a businessman, nor a social dilettante, but by an honest-to-goodness musician."

The audience was created out of nothing. Seventy percent of the first year's audience had never heard opera before, but within a few years, as its reputation was established, the summer festival atmosphere and beautiful countryside attracted a cosmopolitan audience. Yet this audience was no more sympathetic to new operas than were others. After the first fifteen years, only three of its first-performance operas were given a second time. Crosby was undisturbed by this. It was an impresario's responsibility to present important works, popular or not. "If we miss out on these . . . we're not doing much about seeing to the continuity of opera. Everything is a link." The first decade and a half were far from trouble-free. Costs continually outstripped income. In 1967 the enterprise received a staggering blow. Fire, the opera house nemesis of previous centuries, proved still deadly. After the season's opening night, the opera house burned down. With impressive resilience, the season continued in a local gymnasium while plans were laid for immediate rebuilding, and a new opera house was ready for the 1968 season, its lines clean and soaring, open to the enchantment of the night.

Santa Fe opera became more conventional in some ways during its thirty-five years. Ticket prices rose steadily. It became less of a repertory company, with famous singers appearing occasionally. Foundation support was essential. The company would not have survived after the fire if the Ford Foundation hadn't made a $700,000 grant in 1972. But its imaginative productions and repertory have been retained. In the 1970s and 1980s it turned to Baroque opera, while maintaining its commitment to Mozart. Historically, its great achievement was its leadership in America in the reappreciation of the late operas of Richard Strauss. Every Strauss opera but two has been given, including American professional or stage premieres of *Capriccio, Daphne, Die Liebe der Danae* (*The Love of Danae*), *Intermezzo*. It is the most appropriate testimony to Crosby's vision that these works, supposedly the dry harvest of a spent creator, are now understood as the enchanting work of a fertile genius.

The Santa Fe Opera, founded in 1956, was in the vanguard of the burgeoning regional opera move-ment. Most of Strauss's operas have been performed in its open-air theater; this is the 1990 produc-tion of Ariadne auf Naxos. *Photograph by Hans Fahrmeyer. Copyright Santa Fe Opera.*

D a l l a s reversed the Santa Fe pattern, beginning with star singers and aiming for an immediate international reputation. This brilliant renaissance of the 1950s came after an earlier operatic history in no way distinguished from that of other small towns. Field's Opera House was built in 1873 and its first opera, *Martha,* followed two years later. In 1883 the Dallas Opera House opened with Gilbert and Sullivan's *Iolanthe.* It burned down in 1901. Another was built in 1904 and was the site of visits by the Metropolitan and Chicago companies for the next two decades. In the 1920s and 1930s, the San Carlo Company's appearances kept opera alive. The rebirth of Dallas opera took place in 1956, when Lawrence Kelly and Nicola Rescigno, pushed out of Chicago, established the Dallas Civic Opera. They surveyed the national situation carefully and chose Dallas because it was a rapidly growing technological and educational center, where a new kind of audience, informed by radio and recordings, would flourish. They began with a performance of Rossini's *L' Italiana in Algieri,* with Giulietta Simionato, and followed it with a Maria Callas concert, a taste of things to come. In 1957 "Callas in Dallas," their much publicized catchwords, took the form of Callas in Donizetti's *Anna Bolena,* to feverish applause. In 1958 they hit the jackpot: Callas in *La Traviata,* a production designed by Franco Zeffirelli, and a memorable revival of Cherubini's *Médée* (*Medea*): "a Callas vehicle full of Callas opportunities"—Callas standing, arms outstretched, eyes blazing. "We can thank her for one of the most electrifying last acts that may be encountered within a lifetime," wrote a Dallas critic. "The curtain calls lasted an eternity," shared by a soon-to-be-celebrated tenor, making his American debut, Jon Vickers.[2]

The legacy of such a beginning—"the summit by which everything the company achieved was measured for years to come"—was mixed: imaginative repertory, but also an emphasis on lavish productions, star singers. Although Callas left Dallas in a rage, never to return, other famous singers followed: Joan Sutherland in Handel's *Alcina,* not staged before in America; Elisabeth Schwarzkopf; American debuts by Montserrat Caballé, Gwyneth Jones, Teresa Berganza. Opera became fashionable and Dallas became an opera town. "It must have the performing arts to be the model of a modern, major metropolis."[3] Opera brought support for symphony and ballet with it. But by the 1960s troubles multiplied. Star-struck opera was especially vulnerable to changes in fashion. Costs rose as support lagged. By mid-season 1970, there wasn't money enough to raise the curtain. The Ford Foundation and the National Endowment for the Arts came to the rescue, and the handicap of not having a first-class opera house was ameliorated by rebuilding State Fair Music Hall.

In 1974 Kelly died. Rescigno led Dallas into a more stable but continually imaginative period, featuring Baroque opera—Monteverdi, Handel, Vivaldi. A spring season presented other unusual works. Artists went out to perform throughout the region. A network of supporting organizations was built up and an endowment fund established. Dallas began to reach a national audience by radio. Symbolic of its responsibility as a center for opera, the company commissioned and performed Dominick Argento's *The Aspern Papers* (based on the Henry James novella), shown widely on national public television.[4] The mid-1980s were a roller-coaster period of economic uncertainty. Rescigno resigned after thirty-three years of service. In addition, Dallas's eminence as an operatic center was challenged by Houston's spectacular emergence.

N i n e t e e n t h - c e n t u r y Houston depended on the familiar cast of operatic tourers, Emma Abbott, Emma Juch, the Wagnerian wave of the 1890s, the Metropolitan in 1901, sporadic local productions in the early twentieth century, the Chicago Opera in the 1920s. The visiting German Grand Opera Company did all four operas of the *Ring* in the 1930s. And, as always, there was the San Carlo. In 1901, Spindletop became the first great oil gusher in the territory. In the following years there was a lot more oil than opera. Even after World War II, the city's operatic life depended on visitors, such as Kirsten Flagstad singing the Immolation Scene from *Götterdämmerung:* "That matchless voice poured out like a force of nature; it cut through and rose over the orchestral sound and became a living, tangible thing." Nevertheless, such moments didn't obscure the truth: "Houston was a total operatic wasteland."

Walter Herbert (1902–1975) incorporated the Houston Grand Opera Association in 1955 and things began to change. European–born (and -trained), Herbert had promoted opera in New Orleans before coming to Houston. His initial efforts were exceedingly modest—short seasons of familiar operas. Attendance was fitful. About 1960 things began to pick up. New young singers—Cornell MacNiell, Sherrill Milnes, Beverly Sills—caught the city's attention. The move to the Jesse H. Jones Hall for the Performing Arts was an improvement. In the 1970s the petroleum industry boomed. The city's population soared, and among the people who migrated there were those, more cosmopolitan in their taste, for whom urban life was intolerable without the arts. "It is illustrative of this point that Joan Sutherland sang to small audiences . . . in the sixties. When she returned to Houston in the seventies . . . she sang to capacity and enthusiastic audiences." Herbert left Houston, and in 1972 David Gockley, age twenty-nine, was appointed general director. He had studied composition, conducting, and voice at Brown University and the New England Conservatory of Music, gained administrative experience at Santa Fe and at Lincoln Center. Gockley was determined to bring the large new potential audience to his theater, "to present more different kinds of opera to a broader, more varied and more discerning audience. . . . We want to combat the image of opera as a medium for only the wealthy and elite."[5]

Gockley sold opera by many contemporary means, from T-shirts to television. American singers were encouraged. A spring opera festival was given free of charge, an American series of opera in English at reduced prices. Coast-to-coast radio broadcasts gained listeners. The Houston Opera Studio, jointly sponsored by the opera company and the University of Houston, provided tuition and a stipend for young singers. The Texas Opera Theater, an educational affiliate with its own artists, staff, and repertory, traveled by bus to small towns.

Three notable Houston productions captured the attention of anyone interested in the American operatic past. In 1976, with Marilyn Horne in the title role, audiences heard Rossini's *Tancredi,* 151 years after the Garcías had introduced it to New York. Two other revivals were closer to home. *Porgy and Bess,* in the full original version, received a sumptuous production that was so successful that it returned to its original home, Broadway, was recorded and awarded a Tony award—all of this a big step toward the reclaiming of an American masterpiece. The other "revival," at the 1975 spring festival, was Scott Joplin's *Treemonisha.* Under the loving and imaginative care of Gunther Schuller, the production inevitably reignited the hoary old argument as to whether *Treemonisha, Porgy and Bess,* John Philip Sousa's *El Capitan* (revived in 1976 as a Houston bicentennial present to the country), or Weill's *Threepenny Opera* were "really" operas, and whether they ought to be given in opera houses. Audiences in Houston had no doubt, and *Treemonisha,* with a spectacular production and lively direction, worked its naive and charming spell and then went on a national tour, until it too went home to Broadway and then reached many more people by means of a recording. At last, at long, long last.

Seattle's early history bore out that familiar American operatic principle— opera houses but no opera. Squire's Opera House, built in 1879, was Seattle's first theater. Fry's Opera House followed in 1884. No opera was given in either. Touring company visits were infrequent. In 1914 the local Standard Grand Opera Company produced English-language performances of *Carmen* and *Faust,* and after a protracted intermission, Cecilia Schultz, "the Sol Hurok of the Pacific Northwest," and others founded the Northwest Grand Opera Company and brought in Glynn Ross to put on opera on a "one-at-a-time and couple-a-year basis." Ross, born in Omaha in 1914, trained in music, had an unusual career as an opera administrator in San Francisco, Los Angeles, and New Orleans and as the first American director of a major Italian opera house, the San Carlo in Naples. He wasn't disturbed by the meager Seattle beginnings. "The rest will come in time. First we must establish a need, an audience for opera." The Seattle World's Fair of 1962 was a catalyst for growth. "At least—and at last—Seattle had its opera menu, brief as it was."

Ross emphasized musical values. "Music is always supreme. Of what use are the most striking sets, costumes, lighting and special effects if the voices and the music are second-rate?"[6] The emphasis was on mainstream operas, with an occasional departure from the norm—Carlyle Floyd's *Of Mice and Men* in 1970, Thomas Pasatieri's *The Black Widow* in 1972. In time, the audience totaled fifty thousand, an Opera Guild was formed, programs reached out to schools. Ross unleashed the techniques of contemporary publicity and promotion: skywriting, placards proclaim-

Opera companies large and small became increasingly resourceful in marketing their productions. Glynn Ross, then artistic director of the Seattle Opera, strolled down the street with a Valkyrie to advertise the company's Ring *cycle in the 1970s.*

ing WITTCO (What Is This Thing Called Opera), cement mixers advocating "Get Mixed up with Opera," bumper stickers, "Opera Lives!" campaign buttons, signs on gasoline tankers ("Opera's a Gas!"). He also raised money, made connections with foundations, and soon could boast that Seattle had the largest per capita opera audience in America.

In 1975 he began his most audacious enterprise, a summer presentation of the complete *Ring*, in two versions, one in German, one in English. It seemed to many a wildly far-fetched idea, a complete reversal of the past history of Wagner in America, the opera most unsuited to any but the largest cities. Ross calculated on the cosmopolitanism of the contemporary operatic world, on the new audience. And people did come from all over. In 1983 Speight Jenkins, a Manhattan opera critic with no previous administrative experience, took over in Seattle. He kept the Wagner but introduced modernist productions in place of Ross's conventional ones. "We wanted to run the Shiite Wagnerians out of here," Jenkins said, and succeeded in provoking intense reaction from the "terminally polite" Seattle audiences.[7] The "radical" *Ring* of 1985–1986 attracted great notoriety. More impressive than publicity was the growth of the shoestring budgets of the early years to three million dollars in 1980 and eight million by the end of the decade. Half the opera's contributions came from people who gave less than a hundred dollars. Seattle described itself as the seventh-largest opera company in the United States—this a city which in the 1950s was described as not having "a trace of an operatic tradition."

St. Louis was a still different story. It had a substantial operatic history, dating from 1837, when a potpourri of tunes from Rossini operas was presented as *Cinderella*. "Cut out the music; it is tedious," someone in the audience shouted. The Seguins succeeded with *The Bohemian Girl* in the 1840s and 1850s, but "the fact is," insisted Sol Smith, the actor and theatrical impresario, "the people of St. Louis had very little taste for music in any form."[8] Smith was wrong. In the middle of the nineteenth century the city grew rapidly and developed a lively artistic and intellectual life, but a sober and conventional one. Local audiences were not easy to please. All the important touring companies of the era visited St. Louis—Louise Kellogg's, Max Maretzek's, Jeanette Thurber's American Opera Company, the Metropolitan Opera in 1889, in its German phase. St. Louis had a large German population, cultivated, prosperous, knowledgeable. There was a complete *Ring*. (Lilli Lehmann, singing all three Brunnhilde roles on successive evenings, formed a company all by herself.) It didn't draw well. A local observer warned that St. Louis "wanted hand-organ music, even yet. We are happiest with *Lohengrin, Trovatore, Carmen, Faust, Rigoletto, Lucia* and others like them."

Yet, a few years later, the Metropolitan, with Caruso, lost ten thousand dollars on a visit, tried again in 1910, and then didn't return for another thirty-six years. The Chicago company, St. Louis's supplier after 1911, tried operas which were unfamiliar, if not advanced, and succeeded—*Les Contes d'Hoffmann, Louise,* "the last word in operatic realism," *Salome.* That featured Mary Garden and promised scandal. A huge crowd was on hand, and so were the police, ready to drop the curtain if Garden "went too far." The curtain stayed up, and everyone agreed that Garden's acting "eclipsed anything of the kind seen on the local boards in many years, and her voice met all the demands Strauss put upon it."

The city was unpredictable in its taste. But the pattern of its opera was very predictable. St. Louis was content to be a consumer of opera and not a supplier. During World War I there was a local effort. The Municipal Opera Association presented outdoor productions in the publicly owned Municipal Theater, but this wasn't sustained. When the Depression finished off the Chicago Opera, St. Louis was at operatic ebb-tide. Then the huge Municipal Auditorium was built as a public works project, and there, at the end of the 1930s, László Hálasz headed a promising operatic enterprise which was brought to a halt by World War II. The real beginning of St. Louis opera dates from the incorporation of the Opera Theatre of St. Louis in 1968. (The first productions were not seen until 1976.) The company was modeled on Santa Fe, but sought its own mix of style and personnel to suit the city's character. It determined to build upon a local audience and support and had the advantage of both a first-class symphony orchestra and an intimate theater, the Loretto-Hilton Center of Webster University, seating 954, with a thrust stage and adequate technical facilities. There was a connection with England as well as Santa Fe. Richard Gaddes, the first director, was English and had worked as artistic administrator at Santa Fe. Colin Graham, who became associated with St. Louis in 1978, was also an Englishman, actor, singer, dancer, and composer, and author of two librettos for Benjamin Britten operas. Charles McKay, who succeeded Gaddes as director in 1985, grew up in Santa Fe, played in its orchestra, and conducted it.

Opera Theatre began with a summer program of ten performances and grew steadily in the next fifteen years until its season extended into the winter. There have been a number of notable St. Louis successes. A production of Britten's *Albert Herring* was filmed by the BBC, and it is estimated that fifty million people have seen it. Jonathan Miller made his American operatic debut as director of *Così fan tutte*. Sculptor Louise Nevelson did the sets and costumes for Gluck's *Orfeo ed Euridice* in 1984. St. Louis was the first American company to appear at the Edinburgh International Festival, presenting Delius's *Fennimore and Gerda* and Stephen Paulus's *The Postman Always Rings Twice*. To celebrate its tenth anniversary in 1985, it presented two world premieres, Minoru Miki's *Joruri* and Paulus's *The Woodlanders*. By turning its back on star singers, St. Louis kept ticket prices low. However, the smallness of its house and consequent modest ticket income meant that, though the company was playing to over 95 percent capacity by the mid-1980s, its earned income was also low. This deficit was the connecting link between the company and its local audience. Ninety-two percent of the money raised to cover the deficit came from the St. Louis area. Other agencies, city and state, contributed, but it was the citizens of St. Louis who assumed responsibility for their opera—a dramatic change from a past marked by capricious indifference.

N e w places: there is the enigma of Los Angeles. Its early operatic history was like that of other small American towns, except that Hollywood became the center of a form of entertainment more popularly glamorous than opera. Between 1937 and 1982, Los Angeles depended on the San Francisco and New York City companies for its opera. In the 1960s the city built the downtown Music Center, the Dorothy Chandler Pavilion being used for opera. This took place against the background of astonishing urban and suburban growth. One out of twelve Americans now lives in southern California. But the establishment of a local opera company has been inordinately delayed, and the city still lacks a suitable home for it. The nature of that company and its objectives have been bitterly contested. Should it be a local company emphasizing American singers? Should it offer an experimental repertory or superstar opera, on a lavish scale, with the inevitably traditional repertory? A good deal of the future of opera in America rides on the answer to these questions.

The Song of the Thrush

A great singing voice is a gift, arbitrary and inexplicable, from some providence. It is bestowed on artists who cherish it and on those who are ignorant of its nature, reckless in its use. The arbitrariness of its bestowal is paralleled by the possible arbitrariness of its withdrawal. Every day of their lives, singers sing in the awareness of their vulnerability to chance, a vulnerability that is often remorselessly public. And audiences respond to this situation in ambivalent ways. They are adulators and antagonists, throwing flowers one time, radishes the next. Because their art is a magic spell, singers are superstitious, employing charms and incantations to ward off ever-impending danger. Even so armed, however, they live in a state of chronic anxiety, the most famous and amply endowed vocally— Caruso, Anderson, Ponselle, Patti—as nervous as the rest. Many singers have thought of the voice as a thing apart, something with a will of its own, sometimes needing to be subdued as well as nurtured. Maria Callas believed that vocal troubles were always mental, not physical. "Only a happy bird can sing," she said. "It is not my voice which is sick, it is my nerves."[1]

This battle of wills—between the voice and its possessor—has produced moments of high drama. Of the numerous stories of singers confronting vocal rebellion on stage, two stand out as especially memorable. In Paris, Callas's voice broke on a high note. The house "fell into an uproar, half the audience booing, half cheering." Imperiously, Callas raised her hand, commanded silence, motioned to the conductor to start again and the second time sang without mishap. In the 1930s the great Wagnerian soprano Frida Leider was singing Brunnhilde in *Die Walküre* at the Metropolitan. Vincent Sheean described the scene. On her knees before Wotan, Leider was about to sing the phrase "Why so insulting?" ("War es so schmählich?"). She uttered the first two words and then a strange, small sound came out of her throat, but no notes followed. There had been a click, as if "the electrocution, the murder, of a great voice."

> Leider kept her head down and I saw her shake it in a kind of fury. Now the voice itself, the very sense of her existence, refused its divine grace and there she was, on her knees, with the ruin of a great career in plain view before her. I felt, or imagined I felt, the struggle of her will to conquer her body. Then she threw back her really grand head and looked out beyond all the three thousand of us to some utter truth beyond us, opened her mouth with confidence, it seemed to me, and by some power (I could see her throat quivering) the voice was given again.[2]

''*P e r f o r m a n c e* is a venture beyond the limits of life." Dramatic agony becomes musical ecstasy and the end of ecstasy is death, "reaching for the sky from which music first poured down like Apollo's sunlight." Opera proudly and boldly explores the irrational aspects of experience, among them the mysterious alliance between love and death. "Music is a song both of the senses and the spirit, and its genius for modulation and metamorphoses empowers it to represent a passage from one existence to the next."[3]

Walt Whitman, the greatest singer among American poets, pondered the connection between song and death. In the carnage of the Civil War, inspirited by the martyrdom of Lincoln, he conceived a magnificent threnody, "When Lilacs Last in the Dooryard Bloom'd," called by the English poet Algernon Swinburne "the most sweet and sonorous nocturne ever chanted in the church of the world." In it Whitman moved beyond the forms of Italian opera to an organic union of music and language in which the act of singing was the structure of the poem. As a counterpoint to the poem's two primary symbols, lilacs (perennial spring) and the evening star (the poet's love for Lincoln), Whitman introduced the song of the hermit thrush, the chant of death.

"Withdrawn to himself," the thrush sings because he must, and in singing seems to escape from death.

> *Song of the bleeding throat*
> *Death's outlet song of life (for well dear brother I know*
> *If thou wast not granted to sing thou would'st surely die)*

But the poet understands the true meaning of the thrush's song.

> *O singer bashful and tender, I hear your notes, I hear your call,*
> *I hear, I come presently, I understand you.*

The only escape from death is to embrace it. Song is "the carol of death."

A r m a n d Castlemary was a French bass who had first sung in the United States in the 1870s with the New Orleans French Company, and then with touring companies. On February 10, 1897, age sixty-three, he was singing the role of Sir Tristram Mikleford in Flotow's *Martha* at the Metropolitan. Near the end of the second act, Sir Tristram collapsed and the audience, thinking it a fine piece of acting, applauded heartily. Jean de Reszke, watching from the wings, realized what had happened and burst into tears as Castlemary was carried to his dressing room, where he was pronounced dead. A substitute took Castlemary's place, and the audience learned of his death only on leaving the opera house.[4]

Gustav Harold Lindau, born in Sweden in 1889, came to America as a boy and, when he revealed a promising voice, was sent to Italy for musical study. There he took the name of Aroldo Lindi. He returned to America and spent the next thirty years singing opera where and when he could. In the 1930s and 1940s he toured with the San Carlo Opera Company, and it was with them that on March 8, 1944, he was singing the role of Canio in *I Pagliacci,* the clown hiding his heartbreak at his wife's unfaithfulness. "Go hide with laughter thy tears and thy sorrow," Lindi sang and staggered toward the footlights. "Sing and be merry, playing thy part," he gasped, pitched forward and lay still. The audience clapped and yelled wildly, but Lindi could not hear the greatest ovation of his career.[5]

T h e r e were many reasons to look forward eagerly to the performance of Verdi's *La Forza del destino* at the Metropolitan Opera on the night of March 4, 1960. It marked the return, after a considerable absence, of Renata Tebaldi, the greatly admired Italian prima donna. Performing with her was a formidable cast of Americans—Richard Tucker, Leonard Warren, Jerome Hines—as well as the conductor, Thomas Schippers. When the curtain rose and the audience discovered Leonora (Tebaldi) on stage, they cheered for almost a minute. Her voice was "full, rich, and pliant as of old," "her pianissimos of pure velvet." Joined by Don Alvaro (Richard Tucker), she sang a fervent love duet. Born Reuben Ticker, in Brooklyn, Richard Tucker (1913–1975) sang on radio and in synagogues, went to the Metropolitan in 1945 and soon moved into the front rank of tenors. "He had few peers in the projection of Italianate passions, or in fervor, ease, evenness, and vocal security," and this night his voice and Tebaldi's soared together, producing a clamorous response from the audience. In the uproar no one would as yet have heard a different melody, Whitman's thrush chanting its "song of death."

> *Over the tree-tops I float thee a song,*
> *Over the rising and sinking waves, over the myriad fields and the*
> *Prairies wide,*
> *Over the dense-pack'd cities all and the teeming wharves and ways,*
> *I float this carol with joy, with joy to thee, O death.*

In the second act came the fateful confrontation denoted by the opera's title. Don Carlo (Warren) has been trying to find Don Alvaro, whom he blames for disgracing the family name. When the two meet, each is disguised, his identity unknown to the other. Alvaro saves Don Carlo from an attack by assassins, earning his gratitude, and when Alvaro is wounded, Carlo implores the surgeon to save his life; and the two sing one of Verdi's most famous duets, "In this solemn hour" ("Solenne in quest'ora"), pledging eternal friendship. Warren and Tucker outdid themselves for the enraptured audience. "A listener would have had to go back many years to recall a performance of comparable beauty." Thinking he is dying, Alvaro entrusts Carlo with a packet of letters and a portrait locket, and Carlo, in a magnificent dramatic monologue, "Fatal urn of my destiny" ("Urna fatale del mio destino"), betrays his friend's trust, looks through the letters and at the portrait, and realizes that his newfound friend is actually the man whom he has been pursuing. The claims of vengeance cannot be denied. Destiny is at hand. Concluding his monologue, Warren spread his arms out in what was with him a familiar gesture of triumph, as the audience roared its approval.

> *O liquid and free and tender!*
> *O wild and loose to my soul—O wondrous singer!*

These were the days and the moments that had marked the climax of Warren's career. He had now gained a commanding position on the American operatic stage and could fairly lay claim to the title of greatest baritone in the entire world of Italian opera, the greatest of American male singers, successor to Lawrence Tibbett. He had brought his huge voice entirely under control and had worked ceaselessly at refining his acting. Rudolf Bing spoke for many when he wrote of his admiration for Warren's seriousness of purpose and capacity for hard work. "Never an actor, he worked hard at everything he did, and invariably improved his dramatic performance from year to year. I honored him especially, perhaps, for the care he took of himself, not racing around to parties or to perform in far places, making sure he would be in the best possible condition for every performance." He was true to the gift that had been given him.

Only three nights before, Warren had brought his career full circle and scaled his greatest heights. He had sung the title role in a new Metropolitan production of Verdi's *Simon Boccanegra*. (Twenty-one years earlier he had made his Metropolitan debut in a small role in this opera.) The conductor Dimitri Mitropoulos had led an entirely American cast in a blazing performance, evidence of the depth of American singing talent and an appropriate backdrop for Warren's dominance of the stage. "It is one of the great baritone roles," a reviewer wrote the next day, "and last night it was entrusted to a great baritone. Leonard Warren made Boccanegra altogether his own, a vibrant, tragic, and mesmerizing portrayal."[6]

And so this night in *Forza*, the triumphs of the singer and of the character he was playing came together. The surgeon saves Don Alvaro's life and Don Carlo exults in the revenge that will soon be his. "He's saved, he's saved . . . O joy, O joy," he sang, and turned to leave the stage to meet the fate Verdi's opera had determined. And his own.

> *Dark mother always gliding near with soft feet,*
> *Have none chanted for thee a chant of fullest welcome?*
> *Then I chant it for thee, I glorify thee above all,*
> *I bring thee a song that when thou must indeed come, come unfalteringly.*

He was standing to the right of the stage, holding the locket portrait of Leonora, the clue to Don Alvaro's identity. Suddenly, the portrait slipped from Warren's hand, and an instant later he fell forward on his face. Roald Reitan rushed to his side, and Schippers motioned for the orchestra to stop. Reitan threw the conductor a desperate glance and the curtain came down. Richard Tucker, standing in the wings, rushed toward Warren's prostrate body, calling, "Lennie, Lennie!"

> *Come lovely and soothing death,*
> *Undulate around the world, serenely, arriving, arriving,*
> *In the day, in the night, to all, to each,*
> *Sooner or later delicate death!*

It was 9:55 p.m. when Leonard Warren fell to the stage. The house physician had rushed backstage and called for oxygen and an ambulance. Two staff attendants tried to breathe into Warren's mouth. Monsignor Edwin Broderick of St. Patrick's Cathedral, who had been sitting in a box with Mrs. Warren (Warren, born a Jew, had converted to Roman Catholicism), came backstage and administered the last rites of the church. The audience had waited—apprehensive, uncertain. At 10:30 Rudolf Bing came before the curtains. "This is one of the saddest nights in the history of the Metropolitan." Gasps of "No" from the auditorium, as Bing asked it to rise "in memory of one of our greatest performers," and then: "I am sure you will agree with me that it would not be possible to continue with the performance."[7]

> *Approach strong deliveress,*
> *When it is so, when thou has taken them I joyously sing the dead,*
> *Lost in the loving floating ocean of thee,*
> *Laved in the flood of thy bliss, O death.*

Three Operatic Monuments

The quarter-century after World War II marked the transformation of the old federal republic into a centralized imperial state of colossal wealth and power. Naturally, the nation wished to celebrate itself. Missiles and money, Coca-Cola and Levis didn't entirely erase the old American sense of cultural inferiority compared with Europe. Therefore, the arts were called into service. Musicians and dancers, painters and professors, writers and architects were sent abroad. Exchange programs, symposia, and fellowships spread the American achievement. *Porgy and Bess* and *Oklahoma* went everywhere. The New World of the old European imagination, devoid of art, was replaced by the Free World, where the arts flourished. At home, many American artists rubbed their eyes in disbelief. "Creative artists are always begging," Leontyne Price said, "but always being used when it's time to show us at our best."[1]

American cities also called upon the arts to express civic pride and, even more, civic renewal. Cultural centers of the arts would fill the void created as people left downtowns. They would be spatial centers, power centers, centers for bringing people together in a way that the old political civic center—the city hall, the court house, the jail—could not do. The cultural center wasn't brand new. A few examples dated from New Deal days. In the 1950s and 1960s the desire for a cultural center became a civic mania. By 1966, of ninety-three cities surveyed by two economists, fifty-four stated that a cultural center of some kind was already in operation, thirty-nine reported one in some stage of construction. Of smaller cities, eighty-two claimed to be planning such a center. For the arts to give coherence to civic life was a monumental task.

The building of cultural centers was part of the "culture boom" or "cultural explosion" of the 1960s. The new audience of the 1950s was purported to have spent 130 percent more on the arts than before World War II. Alvin Toffler's *The Culture Consumers* was the most enthusiastic and influential discussion of this phenomenon, but there were many other articles and radio and television shows about it. Toffler pictured people flocking to record stores and buying 17.5 million discs "of what not long ago was derisively termed 'long hair stuff.'" "Housewives have been buying classical LP's along with their frozen vegetables at nearby supermarkets." The purchasing power of the new culture consumer was eye-catching: more piano players than fishermen with licenses; as many painters as hunters; twice as many concert and recital goers as attendees at major league baseball games; more theatergoers than boaters, skiers, golfers, and skin divers combined."[2] With 120 million Americans attending art events annually and 50 million participating in some sort of art activity, "a major swing to 'conspicuous esthetics' was underway." The actual extent of consumer spending on the arts was the subject of considerable disagreement, but many forms of artistic expansion in the 1950s and 1960s were indisputable. Parallel to the growth of cultural centers was the formation of community and state arts councils. Eight of them were established between 1945 and 1950. By 1955 there were 15, 50 by 1960, 250 by 1965.

In 1966, two economists studied the problems confronting theater, opera, music, and dance. Their report, *Performing Arts—The Economic Dilemma*, presented a detailed picture, of a kind not previously available, of the present condition and future prospects of the performing arts in America.[3] Dismissing exaggerated claims of a "culture boom," the authors argued that expenditures on the arts, from the 1920s to the 1960s, had grown, but only modestly. Arts expenditures over those years had been remarkably constant. The arts audience (based on surveys handed out in theaters) was chiefly distinguished by education and professional training. Of the men attending, 55 percent had done postgraduate college work, while less than 3 percent had not graduated from high school. Of the women, 33 percent had done college or graduate work. It was a more male audience than expected—50 percent. Its median age was thirty-eight years. Students made up 15 percent, blue-collar workers 2 to 3 percent. The opera audience was the most varied. Arts audiences were largely made up of regular attenders, but opera attracted more occasional visitors than the others. Moreover, the percentage of blue-collar workers was higher: at the New York City Opera, it was estimated at 7 to 9 percent. Nevertheless, the authors concluded that "the 'common man' was an uncommon attender at professional entertainment in the performing arts."

The central concern of *Performing Arts—The Economic Dilemma*, as the title made clear, was its analysis of the financial situation of the arts in America in the 1960s in relation to technology and productivity. America's remarkable economic growth had been based on increased productivity. Output per man hour had steadily increased in the first three quarters of the twentieth century, doubling every thirty years or so. And in no sector of the economy had technology produced a greater change than in the arts. The phonograph had sharply reduced the cost of an hour's entertainment. Film produced even more striking results. To produce an opera for television took less than twice the man hours of a live performance, but it reached an audience of perhaps twenty million, as compared to the twenty-five hundred or so in the opera house. This represented an increase in productivity of 400,000 percent. However, the efficiency of live performance had changed very little over the centuries. "From an engineering point of view, live performance is technologically stagnant." Opera presented the extreme case. With constantly changing performances, different casts, high rehearsal costs, high fees commanded by stars (whose reputations were made by film and recordings), "the picture of opera's extreme financial burden is complete." The result was an "income gap" that the authors rightly predicted would increase in the future. Given the scale of the national economy, the income gap for the arts was a "minuscule fraction of the nation's wealth," but that was of little consolation to individual arts organizations struggling to survive as their costs went up while their performance income remained constant. The crux of the matter was labor. Opera was labor-intensive, and labor was the most rapidly increasing cost in the performing arts of the twentieth century. It hadn't always been so.

O p e r a was based on cheap labor. Opera companies had been run on the backs of its musicians, choristers, stagehands, and technicians. Those surpluses that Gatti-Casazza was so proud of at the Metropolitan were made possible by sweat-shop labor behind the curtain and in the pit. Impresarios believed that any effort by opera workers to organize to increase their pay must be relentlessly smashed. That pay was certainly low enough. At the end of the nineteenth century the Metropolitan paid orchestral players fifty dollars per week for seven or eight performances, choristers fifteen dollars. Four conductors drew a total of twenty thousand dollars for the year. The company's entire ballet corps collectively received half that amount. At this time, Caruso and Melba each made between two and three thousand dollars a performance, and also took part in strike-breaking.

At the Metropolitan Opera in 1905, the men's chorus, believing it had the support of the stagehands and orchestra, informed Heinrich Conried, at six o'clock on the afternoon of the season's opening night, that they would not perform unless their pay was increased and certain working conditions improved. When the curtain went up—the opera was *Faust,* with Caruso—the orchestra was in the pit and the stage-hands at work backstage. The conductor, Nahan Franko, the first American-born conductor at the Metropolitan, had spent the day editing out passages in the score for the chorus. (This performance was given without the Soldiers' Chorus.) The audience was divided in its sympathies. The boxholders staunchly supported management, but when Conried appeared onstage during the first intermission to explain his resistance to the choristers' demands, there were "howls of derision" from the standees. The next performance, *Tristan und Isolde,* went ahead as well, and the choristers then accepted Conried's compromise: salaries raised to twenty dollars a week, improved transportation to the opera house. In Chicago in 1916, the male chorus of the company, forty-three in all, struck just before the curtain for *Götterdämmerung.* Four members of the administrative staff sang in their place, and Cleofonte Campanini was prepared to perform operas without any chorus. After two days, the chorus capitulated.[4]

The inability of supporting artists and workers to gain assistance or to organize themselves was rooted in the history of music and labor in the United States. Throughout most of the nineteenth century, music was not thought of as a profession or a trade. Musical performers earned little respect from society. Baltimore and Chicago had musicians' unions as early as 1857, but these were primarily social organizations and didn't last long anyway. A trade union for musicians was organized in New York City in 1863, and in the following decade locals were formed in other eastern cities. A Philadelphia local took the initiative in forming a national organization, the National Musical Association, which grew to seventeen locals. It lasted only ten years. Musicians moved around too much to sustain organizations, and they lacked bargaining power. Even so, by 1885 enough unions of musicians had established themselves to allow for another effort at national organization, the National League of Musicians. It had fifteen locals in 1887, had grown to seventy-nine locals by 1896, with nine thousand members. Its growth, however, was undermined by a profound division as to its philosophy and principles of organization.

Were musicians professional artists or workers? Those who considered themselves workers called the others "silk hats" or "toppers," while the artist-professionals called their opponents "stove polishers" or "shoe makers." The American Federation of Labor (AFL), organized in 1881, regarded musicians as workers, though skilled craft workers, and organized its own national union of musicians in 1896, the American Federation of Musicians (AFM). The National League of Musicians scorned affiliation with them, describing them as "laborers in the field of music." Friction between the rival organizations lasted through the century. Eventually the AFM prevailed and, in the early years of the twentieth century, under the energetic but tactful leadership of its president, Joseph Nicholas Weber, it gained members and power. By 1905 it had members throughout the United States and Canada. Symphony orchestras were unionized, as were opera orchestras and stagehands, but there was no effort to enroll opera singers or instrumental virtuosos. The chief AFL activity affecting opera was the effort to exclude foreign musicians. Despite ferocious opposition by American capitalists and American courts, despite yellow-dog contracts, blacklists, lockouts and injunctions, violence and strikebreakers and all the other means routinely used to attack them, unions grew in strength.

In Chicago in the 1920s and 1930s, the AFM was led by the ruthless, intransigent James Caesar Petrillo (1892–1984), the son of an Italian immigrant, who left school after the fourth grade and played trumpet in the Hull House band. He rose to be head of the Chicago local, gaining control of theater orchestras, dance bands, symphony and opera orchestras, and he waged a determined campaign to gain his members a share of the enormous revenue from recorded music. For a period one of the most reviled men in American public life, Petrillo largely succeeded in his efforts for his union. At the same time a rival union, the American Guild of Musical Artists (AGMA), founded in 1933, recruited soloists and singing stars and became a powerful force as well.[5]

In the New Deal and post–World War II years, the days of the old operatic impresario, a law unto himself, hiring and firing at will, came to an end. She or he now worked within a sphere hedged about with restrictions, laws, regulations, a tangle of union jurisdictions. The opera house has become what it has always been in Europe, an interest of the state. The opening of the new Metropolitan Opera House was made possible, at the last moment, by the intervention of the United States secretary of labor, and few have been the opera companies that have not had seasons threatened, or shortened, and in some cases entirely canceled due to bitter labor disputes. The contemporary predilection for lavish productions has conflicted with rising labor costs, as has the expansion of the repertory by means of Baroque and bel canto operas; and this has worked against the production of new operas. The modest scale of regional opera company productions is one element in their leadership in this respect. Yet these difficulties and tensions should be balanced against the fact that higher wages for orchestral musicians have raised the level of orchestral performance, most notably in the case of the Metropolitan Opera, where James Levine has shaped a first-class ensemble. The impresario opera house builders have also disappeared; an opera house is now woven into the complex fabric of governmental, trade union, and corporate power.

L i n c o l n Center for the Performing Arts was conceived as the powerhouse of American culture: a symphony hall, theater, chamber music hall, park, library, music school, and two opera houses, on four city blocks. Its planners and builders were preoccupied with the worldwide importance of the project. New York, "the cultural capital of the world . . . deserves a monumental focus as criterion of free world music, art, theatre and dance." "We're building something that will be here for 500 years."[6]

Three coincidental events made Lincoln Center possible: the decision to build a new Metropolitan Opera House; the proposed demolition of Carnegie Hall, which meant a new home was required for the New York Philharmonic; and the Federal Housing Act of 1949, which provided money to cities for slum clearance and urban renewal. New York identified a seventeen-block area around Lincoln Square as an area suitable for clearance.

These three things might well have meant nothing in relation to each other except that John D. Rockefeller III, the one person with power and money and influence enough to bring order out of coincidences and possibilities, took up the idea that the Lincoln Square site might combine new housing with a center for various of the city's arts institutions. Rockefeller established an Exploratory Committee for a Musical Arts Center in 1955. The next year that group recommended the incorporation of a nonprofit organization, the Lincoln Center for the Performing Arts. By 1957 the Metropolitan Opera, the Philharmonic, and the Juilliard School of Music agreed to join Lincoln Center and to make it the site of their future homes. In 1958 Lincoln Center, with federal funds, purchased the Lincoln Square area from the city. This

A view of New York's Lincoln Center, the prototype of the late twentieth-century performing arts complex, showing the new Metropolitan Opera House on the left: a monument to corporate wealth. Photograph by Bob Serating.

required negotiations with Washington and Albany, in which the influence of John D. Rockefeller was of inestimable value. (It also helped that the governor of New York was his brother.) "He was adept at the delicate art of choosing the people to make a project move." There were 188 buildings to be demolished, 1,647 families to be relocated. Lawsuits were filed to prevent the project happening. Lincoln Center got its way in the courts, as elsewhere. The groundbreaking ceremonies on May 14, 1959, dramatized the power that had been marshaled. Much of the corporate and banking might of Wall Street was there, and President Dwight D. Eisenhower flew up from Washington.[7]

Lincoln Center was planned as a group of free-standing buildings in a setting of plazas and parks, accessible to the city life swirling about it. Although each building was designed by a different architect, unity was derived from similar modernistic arches and columns and from the use of the same light-colored limestone facing. Wallace K. Harrison (1895–1981), who had worked for the Rockefeller interests for thirty years and had been chief architect of the United Nations buildings, was chosen as overall supervisor and as architect for the Metropolitan Opera House.

An important addition to the original group of institutions comprising Lincoln Center was forced upon it by chance and political necessity. New York State was committed to the development of a World's Fair in 1964 in Queens and, with the support of Governor Nelson Rockefeller, the state legislature appropriated fifteen million dollars for a theater in Lincoln Center which would be the site of the fair's musical and theatrical programs and then be sold to New York City. This became the New York State Theater, the home, in 1965, of the New York City Opera and the New York City Ballet. Although it welcomed the New York City Ballet, the Metropolitan Opera bitterly opposed the City Opera. Politically, however, the people's theater was not easily denied a place in the people's culture center. When the presence of the City Opera became inevitable, the Metropolitan attempted to gain administrative control over it. The City Opera successfully resisted this effort.[8] Inadvertent though it was, placing two separate opera companies adjacent to each other was symbolically appropriate for this new operatic age.

Building costs soared. The original estimate for Lincoln Center, $75 million, rose to $102 million in 1960, $120 million by 1963. Philharmonic Hall cost 250 percent more than its first estimate, the Metropolitan Opera House and the Vivian Beaumont Theater 100 percent more. The New York State Theater was a bargain at only 50 percent more. When completed, Lincoln Center cost $184 million. City, state, and federal governments contributed some $40 million. The Ford Foundation gave $25 million, the Rockefeller Foundation and John D., personally, an equivalent amount. Half of the cost came from individuals and corporations.

Historically, the most important thing about Lincoln Center was that American business corporations were mobilized to finance it. "No one had ever gone to big business for big money to support the arts." A professional fundraising firm organized this corporate campaign, but the assistance of prominent corporate leaders was crucial. Clarence Francis, chairman of the board of General Foods, was designated manager. He knew that his request seemed odd to many corporate executives. "New

York City was just No-Man's-Land as far as its cultural reputation was concerned," Francis said. Corporate leaders saw the city as solely "a financial institution—it was profits, it was money, money, money. And this was wrong. The thing that fascinated me was that New York now could be made the cultural center of the world." John Rockefeller often went with Francis. "They went where the money was to be found. A company president would listen carefully, then say, 'John, you really *do* believe in this?' And Rockefeller would answer, 'Yes, I do believe in it. I believe it is important for our city. I believe it is important for our country. I believe it is important for the world.'"

The campaign began with a list of several hundred serious givers. This soon became a list of ten thousand names. "Someone was even put to work tracing genealogies to check if any member of a wealthy family had an obvious interest in the performing arts." The handful of fundraisers grew into a highly organized group of five thousand. Small contributors were welcomed, but Lincoln Center was a monument to corporate wealth. George Moore, the vice president of the First National City Bank and chairman of the center's Patron Committee, would never ask for less than $100,000. American arts sponsorship entered a new stage with the emergence of corporate patrons.[9]

T h e New York State Theater was the first of the two Lincoln Center opera houses to be completed, in 1964. Designed by Philip Johnson (1906–   ), the one-time boy wonder of architectural modernism, the theater's sober and rational exterior enclosed an elegant interior, suggesting eye-filling ceremonial pleasures, regal amusement from a European past. Above the functional entrance lobby, Johnson created a spectacular social space, the Grand Promenade, "a royal room of cream and gold," two hundred feet long, sixty feet wide, fifty feet high, running the entire width of the opera house, glass-fronted, with a gold-leaf ceiling and three tiers of gold-screened balconies looking down from the inside, "the baroque spirit domesticated by democracy." After such bravado, the 2,729-seat auditorium, a five-tiered, flattened horseshoe, somehow conveyed a sense of "quiet dialogue between amplitude and intimacy."[10] Its sight lines (the theater had initially been intended for ballet, not opera) were excellent, but its sound was poor.

And then there was, after decades of anticipation and disappointment, the new Metropolitan Opera House. But first the old house, "this interminably inconvenient, unquestionably difficult and unforgettable place," had to be vacated and destroyed. No possibility of saving it was allowed. On April 16, 1966, a stagefull of famous singers closed down the great old singers' house—Marian Anderson, Lotte Lehmann, Birgit Nilsson, "wearing in pride the gold wreath that had been presented to Christine Nilsson on the night the theater opened" in 1883. Soon enough the past dissolved into the excitement of opening the new house, heralded by unrestrained exaggeration as "the single biggest theatrical event in all human history": "the biggest house, the fanciest trappings, the highest budget, the most careful planning, the most talented artists, the hardest work, the loftiest hopes . . . nothing less than the cultural superevent of the cultural center of the culture capital of the civilized world." It was a costume party, with "hundreds of formally dressed tycoons, aristocrats, nabobs, bankers, moguls, diplomats, potentates, fashion plates, grand dames and other assorted Great Society over-achievers," who paid $250 for orchestra and box seats. It was also an affair of state. Three boxes had been converted into a state box, in which sat the wife of the President of the United States, the secretary of defense, the ambassador to the United Nations, and President Ferdinand E. Marcos of the Philippines and his wife, the tiara-topped Imelda.[11]

This excess overshadowed the evening's opera, the world premiere of *Anthony and Cleopatra* by the American composer Samuel Barber, conducted by Thomas Schippers, with an entirely American cast headed by Leontyne Price. In fact, "almost everything about the evening, artistically speaking, failed in total impact." The staging was drab, the set dismal, and Barber's score didn't please—neither traditional nor modern, lacking in ardor, big in sound, meager in melody. Anyway, what chance did the opera have compared with the opera house? Wallace Harrison aimed for grandeur. Five enormously tall, deeply recessed, glass-filled arches formed the front and conveyed grandness of scale, as did two large murals by Marc Chagall on either side of the lobby, in which the central double-staircase should have commanded attention, but didn't. That was claimed by two large white-marble slabs, on which were etched in gold the names of the contributors—143 individuals and families on the left, 73 corporations and foundations on the right—who had paid for the house. The enormous five-tiered auditorium seated 3,788, with twenty-nine boxes, rented according to "seniority," in the parterre and twelve in the grand tier. The orchestra pit was spacious, the proscenium arch commanding, sight lines unobstructed, and sound very good. To make up for the notorious insufficiencies of the old house, the new one prided itself on its mechanical and electrical marvels: turntables; elevators; raked, raised, and lowered stages; moving footlights and scenery; and a computerized lighting system.

It wasn't the Metropolitan of Wallace Harrison's dreams, however. He had conceived an innovative building, a structurally independent auditorium within an arcaded shell, but the Metropolitan board resisted it. "We couldn't have a modern house," Harrison said ruefully. "I finally got hammered down by the opera people." Inside, the board and patrons got what they wanted: the gilded trappings of tradition. Swags and tassels on the tops of the boxes, a gilded cheese-straw pattern around the proscenium. "The opera people wanted those," Harrison explained. The Metropolitan's ambitions were as conventional in the 1960s as they had been in the 1880s. The new opera house was "a monument manqué."[12]

T h e Pentagon of American cultural centers, the Kennedy Center for the Performing Arts in Washington was designed by Edward Durrell Stone (1902–1978), who "can be credited with the creation of a major post–World War II style—that of the classic pavilion, a simple rectangular box surrounded by a colonnaded porch on three or more sides."[13] An oblong 630 feet long, 300 feet wide, 100 feet (six stories) high, its interior plan was simple. A corridor, the Grand Foyer, running the length of the Potomac River side of the building, was cut at right angles by two corridors which divided the interior space into three auditoriums: the 2,200-seat, four-level Opera House; a 2,750-seat, rectangular Concert Hall; and the fan-shaped, 1,142-seat Eisenhower Theater for spoken drama. There were smaller theaters as well as restaurants and a library on the top level.

Even in a city where marble was used "like cotton wool," the Kennedy achieved "Washington superscale." The Grand Foyer was one of the biggest rooms in the world—600 feet long, 60 feet high, the length of three New York city blocks, of two end-to-end football fields. The two marble-walled, red-carpeted, and flag-draped corridors, the Hall of States and the Hall of Nations, which divided the Grand Foyer, were each 250 feet long and 60 feet high. Countries throughout the world paid tribute to the American hegemony by decorating it with chandeliers, marble, tapestries, curtains. As a "symbol of American artistic achievement before the nation and the world," it pleased the American public. "This is architectural populism," Ada Louise Huxtable wrote, "a genuine people's palace." Tourists admired its size, approved its splendor. "They are obviously loving it and perfectly at home."[14]

Created by the Cultural Center Act of 1958, which asserted that "cultural enrichment is a vital part of our nation's well being," the Kennedy Center was a semipublic, nonprofit organization, built on land donated by the federal government, governed by a board of trustees appointed by the President, who advised a general director. The center presented performances but didn't produce them, had no government subsidy, and, initially, wasn't even maintained by the government. The money to build it came from private sources and, as with the New York City Opera, contributors thought of it as a public enterprise and were reluctant to give. Fundraising began in 1962 and went very slowly. After a year of strenuous effort, $13 million had been raised of the $58 million needed. Ironically, President John Kennedy's assassination in 1963 probably ensured the project's completion. In 1964 the center was named for him, the one official Washington memorial in his honor. Lyndon Johnson broke ground for the Kennedy Center in December 1964, Congress appropriated the construction and maintenance funds. Private money came forward. Construction began in 1966 and

The John F. Kennedy Center for the Performing Arts in Washington: "architectural populism" on a colossal scale. Photograph by Jack Buxbaum.

the dedication took place in September 1971. The center's final cost was $70 million, of which $43 million was federal money ($20 million of that in long-term bonds for underground parking) and $27 million private donations. In addition, foreign nations contributed over $3 million.

In time the Kennedy Center greatly stimulated the performing arts in the city. The National Symphony moved into the concert hall. The New York City Opera made annual visits to the Opera House. The Washington Theater Guild sold fourteen thousand subscriptions for plays at the Eisenhower Theater. Gradually, the Center ceased being solely a real-estate operation and promoted its own works and companies. There were negative aspects. Renting the center was expensive. Ticket prices were high. A time came when foreign visitors could better afford it than the native population. Its first director, Roger Stevens, grumbled that the Kennedy Center "was not supposed to solve the sociological problems of the city of Washington," but the implied promise of cultural centers was that they *would* address urban problems, even if they alone couldn't solve them. However, in the case of the Kennedy Center in particular, Stevens had a point. It was intended to look beyond Washington, to symbolize a transformation more national than local, the sleepy southern town turned into Rome-on-the-Potomac.

B u i l t on three acres of city-donated land in the heart of downtown Houston, the Wortham Theater Center embodied the city's prosperity and ambition. Its Texas brick and red Finnish granite enclosed the George and Alice Brown Theater, the 2,176-seat Houston Opera House, and the Lillie and Roy Cullen Theater for spoken drama, dance, and more intimate opera. In May 1987, *Aida* inaugurated the Opera House, *Die Entführung aus dem Serail* the Cullen Theater. The Wortham Center represents the first postmodernist cultural center. Gone are the austerities of the International style. There is a delight in the theatrical about its eighty-eight-foot-high Romanesque entrance arch, a sense of grand processions and ceremony about the Pantheonlike grand foyer, twelve thousand square feet of prairie-sized space: "A herd of longhorns could roam there without feeling too hemmed in."

The intimate feeling of the Opera House was a calculated move in the direction of the opera house of the future, one spatially receptive to all kinds of cross-over opera. The chief production of the inaugural year, in October 1987, was John Adams's *Nixon in China.* Advanced in its sound and lighting and stage equipment, the Houston Opera House marked a return to the nineteenth-century horseshoe auditorium. A three-tiered orchestra pit, which can be raised to stage level to create a thrust stage, adapts opera to the prevailing fashion for abolishing the proscenium. The Opera House looks back in celebrating the return of the opera box as an uncompromising symbol of privilege. Founders' boxes form the lowest tier of the house. Curving around the theater, they jut out from the walls in the shape of frying pans, connected to the lobby by walkways called panhandles. The boxes, surrounded by the sound which pours all around, are good places to listen from, but they are no place for those wishing Venetian privacy; and those who can't stand the social heat are advised to get out of the frying pan.

Houston's postmodernist Wortham Theater Center, opened in 1989: a monument to entrepreneurial individualism. Photograph by Joe C. Aker. Houston Grand Opera Archives.

Fundraising began in 1977 but was soon overtaken, in the early 1980s, by the decline in Texas oil and real estate values. Yet the freshness and boldness of the theater's design survived that threat, as well as interventions and intrusions by patrons and contributors, the curse of building by compromise and committee. The architect, Eugene Aubry, counted twenty-one versions of his building. "Chewing through these got to be a popular local entertainment," he said. "A board member would come in and say, 'I like triangles.' Another would like arches." The original idea was scaled back, but Aubry's design essentially prevailed.[15]

The Wortham Center was a surprising chapter in the history of a city rich in surprises. Houston has outgrown its oil wildcatter's days to become as much a part of the age of the impersonal corporation and of bureaucracy as anyplace else. Yet Gus Wortham was an insurance salesman, George Brown an engineer, Roy Cullen an oil man. About the Wortham Center there remains something of the entrepreneurial individualism of the nineteenth century.

S p l e n d i d as these buildings are, a more significant national achievement was the National Foundation on the Arts and Humanities Act signed into law by President Lyndon Johnson on September 29, 1965. The National Endowment for the Arts, (NEA), created by this law, was the imaginative answer to the questions about public patronage which have recurred so frequently throughout these chapters. It was, appropriately, another instance of that mixture of public and private support that had gradually evolved in America, very different from the European system of central patronage and control. The NEA provided grants to individuals and institutions which were matched by individuals, corporations, and foundations. Opera companies were among the beneficiaries, the celebrated major companies but also the numerous smaller local and regional companies. Every aspect of American operatic culture was encouraged by the NEA: touring companies, programs for audience development, training for singers, television broadcasts, and films. In a national budget of hundreds of billions of dollars, the funding for the NEA was, and remains, exceedingly modest. But it has grown over the years: $10 million in 1967, when the NEA got underway; $29 million in 1972, when President Richard Nixon pointed proudly to the "outstanding record of accomplishment in advancing the artistic development of the nation"; $77 million by 1977; $143 million in 1982. In 1987 the total was $151 million, and the Endowment's Research Division noted that in both the previous years admission receipts for nonprofit performing arts events exceeded those for spectator sports.

The deeply rooted suspicion of art, characteristic of American culture for two centuries, produced a predictable reaction. Nourished by economic depression and by the recognition that votes can be gained by a populist attack on the "elitism" of art, opponents subjected the NEA to ferocious assault in the late 1980s and early 1990s. Familiar, too, was the deeply felt anxiety about the eroticism of art, this time directed not at opera but at photography and performance art of various kinds. At the same time, a quarter of a century of accomplishment touching the lives of all the members of the new American artistic audience produced vehement support for the NEA. Artists and other citizens rallied to support the idea that the arts, like education and business and science, were all equally necessary to the well-being of the community. Despite restrictions in the NEA's budget, even the threat of its destruction, there can be no going back to the ice age of national indifference.

Sarah Caldwell Presents

Behind the large audiences and huge dollar signs, opera in America in the 1970s and 1980s had been nagged by doubts about the future. One was the familiar problem of financial support. Equally familiar was the cry that "opera is dying," a death predicted almost since its birth. Was there a new reason for believing that an art so long and deeply embedded in people's affections and needs would disappear? Surely the issue was not the death of opera but its transformation. And that was not new. Opera has always been changing—and will continue to do so. Jazz opera, folk opera, electronic opera, rap opera—the possible forms and permutations are many. One particular form of opera and of opera production—grand opera in grand opera houses—may very well be insupportable in the twenty-first century, except in one or two houses distinguished as repositories of the great tradition of the first four hundred years. In the United States, the future may belong to small groups giving small-scale opera in small theaters and spaces. This has been happening for several decades.

T h e new operatic audience of the 1950s and 1960s was made up of at least four overlapping but different audiences. The first was in the major opera houses, listening to companies defined as "major" by the size of their budgets and their use of international singing stars. The second audience was that of the regional companies, emphasizing lively interpretations, offbeat repertories. This audience supported the Amato Opera and the Chamber Opera Theater of New York, Donald Pippin's Pocket Opera in San Francisco, Opera Ebony in Philadelphia, and many, many others. Their work refuted what Rudolf Bing said in 1958: "There is no opera in America worth speaking of outside New York City. . . . I see no desire of the public in this country to build opera from young companies."[1] This comment was less notable for its arrogance—that was Bing's stock-in-trade—than for its ignorance of opera outside New York.

A third audience was most concerned to build on local foundations, emphasized community effort, often through amateur performance. It was a "cross-over" audience in that it paid little attention to distinctions of genre; it placed operetta, musical comedy, and light opera alongside conventional European opera. It especially cared for American operas of the past. Something of this audience was represented by the Goodspeed Opera House in East Haddam, Connecticut, which, in its restored 1870s local glory, with its intimate, 398-seat auditorium, revived the popular

American works of the 1910s, 1920s, and 1930s, going back to Sousa's *El Capitan* or Cohan's *Little Johnny Jones*. It was the audience for outdoor summer performances and for civic light opera associations.

A fourth audience, nourished on rock, jazz, and non-Western music and on multimedia shows, found its home in colleges and universities. Indiana University represents this constituency at its grandest. Imaginative leadership paved the way from a first operatic production in 1948 to an opera theater program which attracted students from all over the world and the building of a Musical Arts Center unrivaled as a university facility. Over two hundred fully staged operas have been performed there, usually in English: Mozart, Verdi, Puccini, and also Kern, Sondheim, Rodgers. Indiana became widely celebrated for its operatic training and influence, but equally significant operatic growth took place in less well known places, where art hadn't previously flourished. The story of the North Carolina School of the Arts, founded in Winston-Salem in 1962, demonstrated that state and private support could work wonders. American colleges and universities contributed to opera in another important way. They became a haven for émigré composers and producers—Carl Ebert, Wolfgang Martin, Jan Popper, Vladimir Rosing, Hugo Strelitzer, Fritz Zweig—who introduced higher standards of performance.[2] It was the three audiences away from the large opera houses who were most receptive to new things. And it was the smaller performing groups who made the most audacious efforts. One of the most remarkable of these appeared in an unlikely place—Boston.

I n 1958, in one of the shabbiest acts in American operatic history, the Boston Opera House was demolished to make way for a parking lot. The anti-Brahmin and anti–high culture vengefulness in the determination to tear down the building was all too familiar in Boston culture. The city was left with no satisfactory place to hear opera and with no prospects of building one. A revival had begun in 1957, fostering "the dream of a new Boston opera company to replace the famous old one which had died with World War I." This new company, very different from the old, aimed to attract a new audience, emphasized an unusual repertory. It was the Opera Company of Boston, its inspiration Sarah Caldwell, Boston's "prima dynamo."[3]

Born in Maryville, Missouri, in 1924, Caldwell attended the University of Arkansas and won a scholarship to the New England Conservatory of Music to study violin. She arrived in Boston in 1943 with no clear idea of what she wanted to do in music. "All I knew was that somewhere in the world, maybe far away, there were great, great people who made great music."[4] Once she saw and heard opera at the conservatory, she fell in love with it, gave up the violin, and soon revealed a gift for conducting and directing it. At the Berkshire Music Center in 1947, she staged Vaughan Williams's *Riders to the Sea*. Later she studied with Boris Goldovsky. Born into a musical family in Moscow in 1908, Goldovsky attended the Moscow Conservatory and, after extensive experience as a performer, emigrated to the United States in 1930. His chief influence thereafter was as a director and popularizer of opera, at the New England Conservatory, the Curtis Institute, and with his own Goldovsky Opera Theater. He introduced Britten's *Peter Grimes* and *Albert Herring* and Mozart's *Idomeneo* to the American stage, and reached an even wider audience by his appearances on the Metropolitan Opera radio broadcasts. The title of one of his books summed up his approach— *Bringing Opera to Life.*

From 1952 to 1960 Caldwell was head of the Boston University opera workshop. She began to produce opera with lively ideas and little money. There were the usual ups and downs. In 1958 she produced, conducted, and directed Offenbach's "masterpiece of whimsey," *The Voyage to the Moon.* Encouraged by its success in Boston, she took it on tour. Although it lost twenty thousand dollars, Caldwell never doubted that the kind of audience she was trying to find had grown up around Boston since World War II—a large college population, educated middle-class professionals, intellectuals, and people in the arts and journalism, individuals of diverse backgrounds, for whom the old "social" associations of opera were repugnant or nonexistent. By 1959 she was ready for her first "season."

From the first, the Opera Company of Boston suffered from the absence of a proper place to perform. The season took the form of three or four operas, given two or three times. It moved from theater to theater, often old movie houses, dank, shabby, without orchestra pits or proper lighting equipment. An abandoned synagogue doubled as rehearsal hall and workshop. But the constant peregrinations, the improvised conditions, added a sense of adventure to the company's productions. Word got around. People came from far away to take part.

Caldwell generated the excitement and did everything else as well—selected and directed her cast, commissioned sets and costumes, supervised lighting, prepared the scores, rehearsed the orchestra, conducted. "Miss Caldwell is one of the great producers of the world," said Joan Sutherland. "One of the finest stage directors I've ever known," agreed László Hálasz. "She's a mad genius." That set the tone for much of the publicity about her—a mixture of admiration and derision. The easiest way to place her was as an opera-mad eccentric: wearing outlandish cloaks, carrying her comb, lipstick, keys, in a paper bag, sleeping in the theater. She sold her car, it was said, because she got tired of trying to remember where she had parked it. Perhaps most bizarre for an American, she admitted, "I'm afraid that I do not relate well to possessions."[5]

Closer to the truth was the observation that Caldwell possessed "the instincts of a riverboat gambler." She knew what she wanted to do and simplified the means to achieve it. She efficiently organized support—corporate sponsorship, an opera guild, a board of trustees that included proper Boston names. "I was fascinated with the idea of building a professional company at home." Her means were eclectic. When it suited her, she built productions around famous stars and absorbed them within *her* vision of the work. Or, without stars, "maybe a mixed bunch of enthusiasts playing in a gym, maybe a cast of seasoned pros assembled rather too late for detailed ensemble rehearsal," she would reveal "a born opera director's genius for ordering the resources at hand."

Many of her most notable achievements were operas the major companies mostly avoided: Schoenberg's *Moses und Aron,* Prokofiev's *War and Peace,* Roger Sessions's *Montezuma,* the first Rossini *Semiramide* in half a century, Rameau's *Hippolyte et*

Aricie. She took a special interest in Berlioz, *Les Troyens* and *Benvenuto Cellini.* There was nothing bizarre in her productions, no gimmicks, no outlandish effects. "Nothing in the way of eccentricity and everything in the way of bringing to light all the musical and dramatic subtleties that a score contains," observed Winthrop Sargeant. Andrew Porter compared her to the English director Peter Brook. "There is the same fiercely accelerating intensity of concentration . . . the same gift for disconcerting last-minute improvisations that suddenly refine the expression of a long-held, long-pondered ideal."[6]

Ironically, her reputation as a producer overshadowed her conducting. She was the first woman to conduct opera at the Metropolitan, and Houston and Santa Fe invited her as well. But she was not the first important American woman conductor. Antonia Brico, who was born in the Netherlands and came to the United States as a child, had an impressive conducting career. She conducted WPA orchestras during the 1930s, organized her own all-woman orchestra, was the first woman to conduct the New York Philharmonic, and, though denied operatic conducting opportunities, worked as an opera coach. Ethel Leginska, born in England and trained in Germany, had a brilliant career as a pianist and took up conducting in the 1920s in the United States, but she was given no chance to perform opera in America, though she conducted in European opera houses. After World War II more and more women went into opera orchestras and into conducting. Judith Somogi was the first woman to conduct at the New York City Opera, and Eve Queller organized and conducts the Opera Orchestra of New York. Opera brought out the best in Sarah Caldwell. She pursued the great dream, musical and dramatic unity, and though sometimes the result was a "crashing bore," "once in a while, when everything is just right, there is a moment of magic," she mused. "People can live on moments of magic."[7]

T h e small opera companies were crucial to American operatic composers who, while influenced by New York opera's theatrical flair and popular audience, didn't work in its style. These composers aimed for great musical complexity and dramatic seriousness—their subjects were often tragic—while ignoring the traditional distinctions between kinds of opera. The large opera houses were closed to their work.

Of all of these composers, Gian Carlo Menotti succeeded in reaching the largest popular audience. He belonged to the venerable tradition of the internationalist composer for whom nationality was an ambiguous category. Born in Cadegliano, Italy, in 1911, he attended the Milan Conservatory and in 1928 was sent to study at the Curtis Institute of Music in Philadelphia. *Amelia Goes to the Ball* (1937), a one-act comic opera, was his first success. It opened at the New Amsterdam Theater in New York, Fritz Reiner conducting, gained favor, and was transferred to the Metropolitan Opera, the only Menotti opera ever to be performed there, as *Amelia al ballo.* It received three performances in 1937 and was done again in 1938. From the first, Menotti had a larger audience in mind, and in 1939 he composed *The Old Maid and the Thief,* tuneful and well received, as a radio opera, commissioned by NBC.

The 1940s and 1950s were the most fruitful period of a prolific career. *The Medium,* a two-act tragedy about spiritualism, marked an advance in power as well as in musical technique, while retaining identifiable melodies. It opened in a Broadway theater, where it ran for eight months in 1946. As a curtain raiser, Menotti composed a one-act comedy, *The Telephone,* popular in its own right. Menotti directed a film version of *The Medium,* and in 1955 the State Department promoted a European tour of the two operas. His first full-length opera, *The Consul,* a Kafkaesque vision of a Cold War police state, opened in Philadelphia in 1950, ran for eight months in New York, and was then taken up by small opera companies throughout the country. It won the Pulitzer Prize and the New York Drama Critics Circle Award, was translated into a dozen languages, and performed in twenty countries. *Amahl and the Night Visitors,* the first opera written for television, commissioned by NBC and first presented on Christmas Eve 1951, was designed to be given by amateur groups, and it has achieved its aim. In 1969 alone, it was given 444 times by semiprofessional and amateur companies. *The Saint of Bleecker Street* (1954), a drama set in contemporary New York, also swept the major prizes. In the ensuing decades Menotti did not recapture the combination of melodic flow and dramatic power of these operas. But he, and they, have retained a large and loyal audience.

Folk opera proved the most successful operatic style in these years, gaining the stage of some of the major opera houses. Douglas Moore (1893–1969) was its leading proponent. He began writing songs when he was a boy, studied at Yale with Horatio Parker, in Paris with Vincent d'Indy and Nadia Boulanger. From the mid-1920s he taught at Barnard College and Columbia University, where he exercised considerable influence on American professional musical life. He wrote a good deal of music for the theater, three film scores, a ballet, an orchestral suite on P. T. Barnum, and a symphonic poem on *Moby Dick. The Headless Horseman* (1936), based on the Washington Irving story, was a high school opera, *The Emperor's New Clothes* (1948) a children's opera, and *Puss in Boots* (1950) a children's operetta.

His first important success came early on, with *The Devil and Daniel Webster* (1939), subtitled "a folk opera," which quickly became a favorite with operatic groups throughout the country. Moore's dramatic skill was evident in his "keen timing and musical characterization, accurate colloquial prosody and dominating vocal line." His interest in American literary texts manifested itself again in 1951 with *Giants in the Earth,* O. E. Rölvaag's grim novel of Scandinavian immigrants in the Dakotas. The opera won the Pulitzer Prize in 1951. Critical praise, popular favor, prizes, and awards all came to Moore's greatest work, *The Ballad of Baby Doe* (1958). The story of Horace Tabor, who struck it rich as a silver miner in Colorado, charmingly and vigorously evoked the atmosphere of the late nineteenth century with its sentimental ballads, popular waltzes, and dance-hall tunes. "All seem familiar, as if they had arisen from the attic pile of once popular sheet music."⁸ With wonderful appropriateness, *Baby Doe*'s world premiere took place in the restored grey-granite Central City Opera House.

Sadly and surprisingly, *The Tender Land* (1954) by that master of the folk idiom, Aaron Copland, was flat and uninspired, but there was an overflow of impish vitality and humor in the second opera by Virgil Thomson. In the spring of 1945, Moore commissioned Thomson to write an opera to be produced in 1947 at Columbia University. Thomson traveled to France to visit Gertrude Stein. (Unknown to anyone, she was suffering from the cancer which would kill her within fifteen months.) She agreed to write the libretto for Thomson's opera, to be set in a period of his choosing. He chose "the fifty glorious and tragic" years between 1820 and 1870, when "great issues were debated in great language." To this Stein added "feminism as her central theme and Susan B. Anthony as her heroine," and the opera became *The Mother of Us All*. Disdaining mere chronology, Stein brought John Adams, Lillian Russell, Susan B. Anthony, Ulysses S. Grant, and others together, not to talk—"The dialogue is a reflection of personality rather than a vehicle for advancing a plot"—but "simply to say what is most on their minds, turning the text into a bright confusion of inconsistencies, each clear and reasonable in itself." The libretto, completed in March 1946, was Stein's last written work. She died in July.[9]

Thomson wanted simply to communicate with his audience by means of the "evocation of 19th century America," "its gospel hymns and cocky marches, its sentimental ballads, waltzes, darn-fool ditties and intoned sermons." *The Mother of Us All* was "a memory book, a souvenir of all those sounds and kinds of tunes that were once the music of rural America." John Cage, most influential of modernist American composers, considered the opera a fascinating achievement in recollection: "Everything Americans feel about life and death, male and female, poverty and riches, war and peace, blacks and whites, activity and loitering" was in it. "Much of the music has a familiar ring because it evokes familiar things," Cage wrote. "Everyone thinks he remembers the tunes, but no one knows what they are." It is original. "Yes," as Susan B. says in another connection, "it is wonderful."[10]

Columbia University was the site of the world premiere on May 9, 1947, a production supervised in all details by Thomson, with professional singers in the major roles, Columbia students in the rest. "The stage was beautiful for sight and sound, though not to be compared to my Negroes-and-cellophane *Four Saints*." Everybody up-to-date (and others too) came to hear it, and the reviewers were pleased.[11] It was taken up by American universities—Case Western Reserve, Harvard, Denver, UCLA. The Santa Fe Opera performed it in 1976.

A third path to popularity is represented by the work of two contemporaries, Philip Glass and John Adams. Born in Baltimore in 1937, Glass studied music as a child, then at the University of Chicago and the Juilliard School. Interested in the exotic and in the eclectic mixing of forms and influences, and an internationalist, he studied with Ravi Shankar in Paris. Back in the United States, he formed the Philip Glass Ensemble, which performed on a variety of instruments (flute, electric organ, saxophone, electric synthesizer) and in many different locales (art galleries, night clubs, museums), and toured in Europe. In 1975 Glass turned to opera, with exhilarating results. There eventually emerged a series of works, connected thematically, about "historical figures who changed the course of world events through the wisdom and strength of their inner vision": *Einstein on the Beach,* a collaboration with the mixed-media artist Robert Wilson, first performed in Europe in 1976; *Satyagraha,* commissioned by the city of Rotterdam and given by the Netherlands Opera for the first time in 1980, about Gandhi's nonviolent activities in South Africa; *Akhnaten,* the story of the Egyptian pharaoh martyred for his monotheism, in 1984 in Stuttgart; and *The*

Voyage, commissioned by the Metropolitan Opera to commemorate the Columbus quincentenary in 1992. Glass's work first became popular in Europe and was, for some time, better known there than in America. But the Houston, San Francisco, and New York City operas have taken these pieces up, and he has become well enough known to attract large audiences to hear his works and to sell recordings to a cross-over audience.

John Adams was born in Worcester, Massachusetts, in 1947, studied clarinet with his father, then went to Harvard, where he studied composition and conducting. He taught at the San Francisco Conservatory of Music from 1972 to 1982, composed in a variety of forms, combining jazz and gospel and electronic music. Conventionally categorized as "minimalist," orchestral works such as *Harmonium* and *Shaker Loops* transcended the repetitive structure of that genre, revealing a lyrical quality accessible to a general audience. Adams's first opera, *Nixon in China,* in collaboration with Alice Goodman and Peter Sellars, commissioned by the Houston Grand Opera, the Kennedy Center, and the Brooklyn Academy of Music, and first performed in Houston in 1987, the most discussed American opera for half a century, established him as a composer of international reputation and made clear a distinctive style, highly dramatic, melodious, elegant. That opera and the one that followed, *The Death of Klinghoffer,* in addition to their musical and dramatic merits, have by their choice of contemporary subjects, some of their characters still living, created an exciting sense of immediacy, unique in American operatic history.

D e s p i t e the work of Joseph Urban, Norman Bel Geddes, Boris Aronson, Donald Oenslager, and others, American operatic production remained traditional in empha-

John Adams turned to contemporary subject matter for Nixon in China, *produced in 1987 by the Houston Grand Opera. Photograph copyright 1987 by Jim Caldwell.*

sizing historical accuracy. The first challenge to this came after World War II, the Appia-inspired reforms of Wieland Wagner at Bayreuth—the stage stripped bare, illusion created by the union of lighting and music. It took a little time to subdue the natives, but this second Wagnerian conquest eventually swept all before it. Everywhere on darkened American stages Wagnerian singers, dressed in timeless shrouds, trooped up and down ramps and platforms and dodged in and out of pools of light. The non-Wagnerian repertory saw few innovations. The most admired productions were those of Franco Zeffirelli, most notable for their lavishness and for the huge numbers of people on stage, and for the director's determination to keep those people moving. "The only sin in the theater is to bore," Zeffirelli said. "In opera you have to give everyone motion because so much of the time nothing happens. Singers only want to sing."[13] In a Zeffirelli production, something was always happening. But none of it was disconcerting. It was reassuring. It was very "grand" opera.

More explicit sexuality was now allowed on stage. As late as the 1950s, at the Metropolitan, the Marschallin in *Der Rosenkavlier* was not shown in bed in the first act, and every effort was made *not* to suggest what had been going on with Octavian. Within a few years, she was in bed and, in some opera houses, Octavian was with her. "We will yet see a topless Aida," one director said. There have been a virtually nude Manon, Salome, and Thais. In the bacchanal scene of a San Francisco Opera production of Boito's *Mefistofele,* Adam and Eve cheerfully simulated copulation, to the apparent indignation of no one. Films and television ended the days when opera was more sexually provocative than other forms of theater.

The great development of the 1970s and 1980s was the much debated rise to predominance of the operatic director. As recently as the early twentieth century, operatic directors were of no consequence. Their names didn't even appear on the programs. Innovative scene designers, Roller in Vienna or Urban in Boston, shaped a production to a considerable extent but ultimately deferred to the conductor, who, if anyone, was responsible for the production's controlling conception. No more. "Nowadays, the director is regarded as a kind of artistic god." The hallmark of director's opera was "the split between musical tradition and dramatic innovation," beginning with a complete break with the original historical setting of the opera: *Così fan tutte* set in a diner, *Carmen* in the Spanish Civil War, Handel's *Orlando* at Cape Canaveral, and so on. Was this classic work in modern dress? Shakespeare had been done that way for decades. The discontent with conventional opera, manifested by the director's supremacy, went deeper than that. In this view, the problem was the operatic texts, "monuments to human stupidity," in Peter Brook's words. For some, the problem was deeper than the shallowness of the story. Music was the enemy of drama, music drama a contradiction in terms. "The spoken text can be sped up or slowed down but the sung text is given and unalterable."[14]

At last America produced an operatic revolutionary of its own. Peter Sellars's provocative Mozart productions at the PepsiCo Summerfare Festival, at Purchase, New York, in the 1980s went far enough along such lines to disturb and infuriate many. What Sellars said he was doing does not suggest the "deconstruction" of the musical-dramatic link. Of his *Don Giovanni,* set in an urban, grimy, crack-and-fast-foot neighborhood, he commented: "It seemed more important to me to convey these people's private fates than their inter-relationships; their personal programs for damnation or salvation are what is resonant."[15] Of course Sellars, or others, may go further in challenging the union of words and music that the Florentine Camerata set out to create four hundred years ago.

W. H. Auden, with a poet's intuition, spotted the trend years ago. To commemorate Mozart's two hundredth birthday, in 1956, he wrote a "Metalogue to *The Magic Flute*":

> A work that lasts two hundred years is tough,
> And operas, God knows, must stand enough:
> What greatness made, small vanities abuse.
> What must they not endure? The Diva whose
> Fioriture and climactic note
> The silly old composer never wrote,
> Conductor X, that overrated bore
> Who alters tempi and who cuts the score,
> Director Y who with ingenious wit
> Places his wretched singers in the pit
> While dancers mime their roles, Z the designer
> Who sets the whole thing on an ocean liner,
> The girls in shorts, the men in yachting caps;
> Yet Genius triumphs over all mishaps. . . .[16]

One genuinely new element in operatic production was "supertitles"—the projection, on a screen above the stage, of a translation simultaneously with the singing and acting. First seen at the Canadian Opera of Toronto, supertitles have gained wide (though not unanimous) acceptance throughout the United States. They made an immense difference to audiences, who now understood what was going on, listened attentively to recitatives, and laughed at comic situations and jokes. Supertitles have already affected the overblown style of operatic acting, necessary to explain by mime what was incomprehensible to audiences. More subdued and subtle acting may be the new order of the operatic night. Some critics insisted that supertitles distracted audiences, kept them from really *listening* to the music. Beverly Sills, who introduced them at the New York City Opera, disagreed.[17] The most notable holdout has been the Metropolitan Opera.

A s so often in this story, we come back to the Metropolitan Opera, the glory and despair of American operatic history. Once it was believed that the Metropolitan was synonymous with opera in America. While never true, that attitude testified to the Metropolitan's prestige and power. In the contemporary American opera world, such a view is meaningless. Under James Levine, artistic direction is in the hands of a musician born and trained in America, and the opera house orchestra has achieved the highest level of proficiency in its history. The Metropolitan remains the largest, the richest, the most famous of American companies. Furthermore, the contemporary company has gone a considerable way toward modifying the image of the arrogant Metropolitan of earlier decades. It has been forthcoming with advice to regional opera companies as they have struggled to establish themselves. The Metropolitan Opera Guild has supported such efforts, and its magazine, the widely read *Opera News,* has a policy of promoting regional companies. The Central Opera Service, sponsored by the Guild, has become an invaluable clearinghouse of statistics and information. And the Metropolitan's broadcasts, radio and television, reach a large audience. Saturday afternoon remains uniquely a Metropolitan time of day for opera lovers.

History. In the post–World War II era, the Metropolitan has at last evolved its identity—as the great national museum of opera, as the repository of the traditional operatic repertory, the standard operas given at a high level of performance and authenticity. Rudolf Bing put it with his usual forthrightness. "We are entrusted with the works it has taken 300 years of genius to create. It's not fair to the Met's public to test new composers on them. I don't believe in undiscovered genius or undiscovered great works."[18] In practice, the Metropolitan's definition of masterpieces has been narrow. It has had little to do with opera before Mozart or after Puccini. It was, and remains, primarily the home of nineteenth-century opera. Its historical function is an important one, wholeheartedly supported by its subscribers and numerous others. It is America's National Gallery of Opera. Ironically, the Metropolitan's connection to its own history has been broken. The links to that not-so-golden age have been severed. Its stage is not the one on which Caruso and Nordica, Flagstad and de Reszke, Warren and Ponselle sang. As it conserves and perpetuates the traditions of the past, the Metropolitan sacrifices a good deal. It isn't likely that the future of American opera will be much shaped there.

Chicago and San Francisco, too, have faced choices. Since their brilliant periods in the 1950s and 1960s, both companies have struggled to find their way. Will it be by reviving forgotten operas from the past? Or by being hospitable to contemporary operas? Their subscribers and supporters, like the Metropolitan's, are conservative and sceptical of such departures. But it may well be, in the words of Chicago's director, that "the company which finds the answer and introduces successful works, playing La Scala to our next Verdi or Puccini, will certainly be the nation's leading operatic light and make history."

Mozart in America

The best measure of the maturity of an operatic culture is its response to the operas of Mozart. The evolution of a knowledgeable and discriminating audience in America in the last half of the twentieth century is, therefore, an instructive chapter in the history of American musical taste. As well, the story of Mozart in America affords us an illuminating perspective by which to reconsider important aspects of American operatic history, and it also suggests what may be important issues in the twenty-first century.

Mozart's operas were introduced to the English-speaking world in two London seasons, in 1811 and 1812. Two decades after his death, his was still "new" music, and like new music then and later, audiences had difficulty in understanding it because it was dense and complex. "It leaves me out of breath," a critic said of the music London first heard. The passage of time changed that view, replacing it with one that endured for a long time. Whereas the operas of other composers provoked great fluctuations of admiration and denigration, the common response to Mozart's operas was steady: they were always respected, often neglected, never in fashion, never entirely out of it. A majority was always charmed by the lovely tunes but found nothing dramatically compelling in the operas, while for a steadfast minority they represented an accomplishment of a simply incomparable order. Could Mozart ever be the true possession of a general audience? Nowhere was this question more provocative than in the democratic culture of the United States.

"Society," aristocratic or middle-class, never took up Mozart's operas. In those first London seasons, the boxes at the King's Theatre were often vacant. In St. Petersburg in the 1840s, Pauline Viardot-García noted the response of Russian aristocrats to *Don Giovanni* as "dry, pale, meagre, and inducing, if not boredom, at least impatience."[1] In America, in the decades which followed, when an opera opening night was a major social occasion, a Mozart opera was a very unlikely choice. Impresarios avoided them because, for all their seeming musical simplicity, each required several accomplished singers who could also act; they required ensemble, not individual stars, and a lot of rehearsal. Always it was other musicians, especially other composers—Haydn and Schubert, Chopin and Brahms, Tchaikovsky and Mahler—who expressed almost boundless admiration for Mozart. When Pauline Viardot-García bought the manuscript copy of *Don Giovanni,* Rossini came to see it, "went down on his knees and kissed the page which had been written by his adored Mozart's own hand and exclaimed: "It's God himself."[2]

T h e Park Theatre was the first American home for Mozart operas. They were performed in English and gave every indication of becoming part of ordinary American musical theatrical culture, treated with the carefree lack of inhibition of the time. Mrs. Holman and Mr. Pearman and other members of the resident Park company did *Le Nozze di Figaro* on May 10, 1824. Then, and for many years, it was assumed that *Figaro* (and the other operas) required "adaptations," changing the stories, dropping much of Mozart's music and adding that of other composers. Sometimes *Figaro,* an opera of four hours' length, was cut so much that it could be given as part of a double-bill! Even such drastic reduction couldn't keep *Figaro* down, and occasionally very good English singers were assembled to meet its challenge. In January 1828, Charles Horn, Mrs. Austin, and Mr. Pearman combined, and some of the glory came through. In March 1839, an all-star English cast, Anne Seguin, Jane Shireff, Arthur Seguin, attracted an audience which "crowded the National Theater to the very street doors," and *Figaro* was repeated several times.[3]

It was at the Park, in 1833, in English and with local artists, that New York first heard *Die Zauberflöte.* So elaborate were the preparations that the theater was closed for a week before the first performance. It was Charles Horn's "adaptation," and though the music was simplified, the singers from the resident company did "only the remotest justice to the music." But it proved popular and was performed several times. A more complete *Zauberflöte* took place in Philadelphia in 1841, sponsored by the Musical Fund Society, conducted by the American Benjamin Cross, who led an immense orchestra of sixty-four. People came from as far away as New York and Boston, and the *National Gazette* insisted, overoptimistically, that after "such an example of operatic excellence, mediocrity will no longer answer." In 1844 a group of actors at the Olympic Theater in New York did *Figaro,* music "selected and arranged by a Mr. Woolf." A popular actress, Mary Taylor, made a success of *Figaro* in 1847, and Burton's Theatre performed it in 1848.[4]

In retrospect, the appearance of the Garcías performing Mozart in Italian inaugurated a gradual movement of Mozart away from the realm of the popular. This was not an inevitable development. In the late 1840s at the Astor Place Opera House, Max Maretzek put on *Don Giovanni* and won "support from all classes," "people of all professions and every description. . . . Fourteen consecutive evenings was it played to crowded houses. . . . Nor was this the first time that Mozart's matchless masterpiece has saved some poor devil of a Manager from ruin." It also led Maretzek to attempt to explain the music's special qualities: "It is music which asks us for no description, music which literally needs no analysis from the critic, music which demands only a feeling heart to understand its marvellously individual character, music which at once seizes upon the hearer's soul and steeps it in a distinctive joy, music which. . . ." But, Maretzek added, "to write a critical disquisition upon Mozart's miraculous musical genius would be a gratuitous insolence."[5]

I n the 1850s, the discovery of Mozart's operas and their adoption by the English-language popular operatic audience gave way to the next phase. Increasing dissatisfaction with the limited vocal skill of the English-language companies, the building of large and lavish opera houses, the appearance of European singers of fabulous abilities—all propelled Mozart away from the popular operatic repertory of the commercial theaters and into the Italian-language European repertory. Theater orchestras often played wildly, and acting was sometimes close to vulgar caricature, "the barbaric foolery wherein we think we delight and which we honor and applaud as opera or 'lyric drama.' "[6]

The Mozart story of the 1850s unfolds in the wonderful diary of George Templeton Strong (1820–1875), New York music lover and lawyer. His initial response to Mozart's music, based on orchestral music, had been cool: "I've heard very little of his that I could get up any enthusiasm for." But this soon turned to fervent admiration, and Strong and others soon experienced Mozart for the first time on the stage. In 1858 he heard his first performance of *Le Nozze di Figaro,* which, "though so famous and so brilliant, has been unheard and unknown in New York except in a mutilated and mangled English version twenty-five years ago." His verdict: "Music beyond my expectations, which were high." A week later he went again, and returned home to his diary "still tingling and nervous from undergoing that most intense and exquisite music." That same year he experienced *Don Giovanni,* but found it "a little disappointing on the stage, because its music is too exalted for the barbaric foolery wherein we think we delight and which we honor and applaud as opera or 'lyric drama.' " Its "glorious melodies are degraded and their effect impaired by their accompaniment of idiotic puppet-show behind the foot-lights," like "a choir of angels accompanying a troupe of monkeys and dancing bears." *Die Zauberflöte,* in 1859, made Strong despair at the discrepancy between heavenly music and earthbound production. A second visit produced surprise—"It finds more favor with opera-goers than I thought possible"—and a third exaltation: "Grammar must be enriched with a new double extra super-superlative degree of comparison before I can do justice to Mozart."[7]

This was not the common view, however. Out of occasional comments and incidental references of the time, a different picture emerges. Mozart's music was "very pretty," but, compared with Verdi and Bellini, "undramatic and unimpassioned." The problem was that "the absence of square melody, and the predominance of orchestral detail over the voice part, prevent the auditor from concentrating his attention where it belongs, namely, on the singer." Furthermore, "the music, being very easy, may be rendered without effort or skill." In an age of ardent romanticism, Mozart's music seemed to lack passion. George Strong recognized that "his work is so simple and true that it seems easy," and later in the century George Bernard Shaw explained the situation: "You cannot 'make an effect' with Mozart, or work your audience up by playing on their hysterical susceptibilities."[8]

An equally serious limitation was the bewildering mixture in the stories of the operas of seriousness and farce, of high-minded sentiment and buffoonery. *Die Zauberflöte* was the worst offender. "As to the plot, human language is unable to express its idiocy." Even Strong mocked the pretentiousness of its ideas "about Truth and Virtue (always with a big T. or V.)." The charge against *Le Nozze di Figaro* was not absurdity but triviality. "Why must I listen to a comedy of vulgar intrigue," one observer wrote, "couched in childish semi-idiotic language, because to it is wedded music in which three or four charming melodies seem only like oases in a dreary waste?" "What a plot indeed," lamented John Sullivan Dwight, "for a nature so sincere as Mozart!" Out of Beaumarchais' "sceptical and sneering comedy," Da Ponte had presented Mozart with a story that was entirely "miserable intrigues and tricks, in which every one of the eight or ten characters in intriguing against every other almost; a mesh of complicated love relations, in which each lover forfeits any interest you once begin to take in him, by showing himself insincere, jealous and at the same time false." It was a picture "of the prose side of life," and in the time of Wagner and Verdi, opera was poetic myth. Only *Don Giovanni* escaped these censures. It was universally regarded, throughout the nineteenth century, as the supreme Mozartian masterpiece. It had a quality of "the supernatural," of "the sublimest grandeur."[9]

The consequence of the inability of the nineteenth century to understand the range and depth of Mozart's music dramas was the radical narrowing of the Mozartian operatic canon. *Idomeneo* and *La Clemenza di Tito* were never performed in the United States in that century or in the first half of the twentieth. It is rare to find even a reference to them in the journals or the handbooks of opera of the time. *Die Entführung aus dem Serail* had been given in New York in the 1860s by German companies for German audiences. The charge of triviality removed it from the repertory for decades. Most astonishing was the fate of *Così fan tutte*. Frivolous, or worse, a story about erotic sexuality and a disenchanted view of marriage, it was seen and heard nowhere. Mozart-blindness was not just American. Europe had its own geographic and cultural boundary beyond which Mozart didn't travel. When Arturo Toscanini conducted *Die Zauberflöte* in Milan in 1923, it was the first time that opera had been there in 117 years. The first Italian production of *Die Entführung* took place in 1935. That these two were Mozart's German operas perhaps contributed to Italian indifference. Furthermore, comic opera was, everywhere, contrary to the spirit of the age. The serious and sober middle class disdained it, confusing solemnity with seriousness. The greatest comic-opera master of the period, Offenbach, was not thought to be a serious composer.

Mozart labored under an additional handicap in America: his art was thought to be unmanly. Charles Ives thought his music "too sweet, too pretty, too easy on the ears." He confessed that when other boys, during school vacations, were working or riding or playing baseball, "I felt all wrong to stay in and play the piano." "Hasn't music always been an emasculated art?" Ives asked, and added: "Mozart helped too much" in that emasculation.[10] The lack of manly potency in Mozart's art was connected with the belief that he was some kind of ethereal being who had strayed into this world from another realm. In the middle of the century, an American visitor to the then remote town of Salzburg visited the Mozart house, the home of the "gentle, affectionate, disinterested and gifted creature" who "learned everything almost instinctively," "as if he had just caught from the celestial spheres some of those immortal melodies." "In recalling [Mozart's] history he seems hardly a man—rather a divine impersonation of art—an embodied tone, or foundation of tones—whose life was not upon earth, but amid the etherealities of the creative sphere."[11]

As though that weren't enough, Americans thought of Mozart as hopelessly old-fashioned: "an obsolete, bewigged old pedant." Overmatched in power and force by the colossal mythic dramas of Wagner, the music of the future, Mozart's was the music of the past. After all, his operas were the oldest in the American repertory. One writer identified the weaknesses of *Don Giovanni*. "It lacks cohesion and the concentrated and limited interest arising from the development of a single motive. The action scatters, and the interest of the audience with it. The curtain falls often in perfect silence, and probably during the last thirty or forty years there have been a large number of persons who thought, at the end of every representation, this work is becoming antiquated, and will soon disappear." An anonymous writer had attended *Le Nozze di Figaro* and found "the much vaunted music decidedly dull." The verdict of the marketplace would emphatically endorse his own, he believed, if it were given a chance to express itself. "Were *The Marriage of Figaro* to be offered to the public as the work of any modern composer it would have an uninterrupted run of one night." Mozart's operas were now of only historical interest. "His grander operas were a great advance on anything that had preceded them. His music, however, has served its purpose and its day has passed away, just as the days of stage coaches and sailing packets have. . . . Why must the critics and tradition lovers cling to this antiquated music simply because it is by Mozart?" Such was the law of progress. Verdi and Gounod and Wagner too, in their turn, would be superseded by new and better forms of art. "The world at large will recognise that art as well as the material sciences progresses, and does not retrograde."[12]

The last quarter of the nineteenth century seemed to bear out predictions of Mozart's impending disappearance as an operatic composer. Touring companies rarely performed the operas. Only the Metropolitan Opera of the 1890s offered encouragement to Mozart lovers. In 1893–1894, for the first time at that opera house, two Mozart operas, *Don Giovanni* and *Figaro,* were given in the same season. In 1899–1900, a third, *Die Zauberflöte,* was added and all three were performed in the same season. (For years the Metropolitan performed it only in Italian, as *Il Flauto magico.*) This wasn't part of any Mozart revival. Rather, it had to do with the efficient use of resources. The notorious need for several first-class vocalists in these operas coincided with the Metropolitan's strength—"all-star casts." The consequences of this approach were harmful. With mediocre conducting, shabby productions, the operas emerged as compendiums of famous tunes, not as musical dramas. They were concert performances in costume.

W o r s e followed. The first forty years of the twentieth century marked the lowest point in the performance of Mozart in America. Gustav Mahler's presence in New York between 1907 and 1909 might have sparked a revival, as it had in Europe, but two years was too short a time. The advent of Gatti-Casazza and Toscanini made things worse. Toscanini rarely conducted any Mozart, and the Mahler productions were shelved. Even the presence of a generation of superlative Mozartians did not help. The leading historian of the Metropolitan once mordantly proposed a group of singers for *Don Giovanni,* all available at the time—Scotti, De Luca, McCormack, Farrar, Easton, Hempel—who constituted the best cast *never* to perform it in New York. Caruso sang in *Don Giovanni* at Covent Garden, with considerable critical success, but not at the Metropolitan. Most shocking of all, McCormack, one of the superlative Mozart singers of the century, never sang a note of Mozart on the Metropolitan stage.

The Manhattan Opera Company, home of modernist opera, virtually excluded Mozart. In Chicago, between 1910 and 1929, *Don Giovanni* was performed eight times, *Figaro* five, compared with the fifty to sixty performances in those years of *Aida, La Bohème, Rigoletto.* This neglect reinforced the view that contemporary popularity was a certain sign of vulgarity: "Of course Mozart is too beautiful to be appreciated by those who like *Tosca* or *Cavalleria Rusticana.*"[13]

Between 1910 and 1940, the Metropolitan specialized in neglecting Mozart, as a few statistics will show. *Don Giovanni* was not performed there between 1907 and 1929. *Die Zauberflöte,* performed a few times in the first decade of the century, was steadily and intelligently performed between 1912 and 1916 and then, inexplicably, was not given again until five performances in 1926, after which there were no more until 1941. However, the treatment of *Figaro* wins the prize. After scattered performances in the first years of the century, and six Mahler performances in 1908, it was not given again until three performances in 1916, two in 1917. And then not a single performance for twenty-two years. Between 1900 and 1940, the Metropolitan gave 99 performances of the three Mozart operas. In those same forty years, Metropolitan audiences heard *La Bohème* 225 times.

Europe, by contrast, had embarked on a genuine reconsideration of Mozart's stage music—Mahler in Vienna, Thomas Beecham in England. Mozart scholarship cleared away a century's accumulation of legend and misunderstanding. "Mozart was a major problem in those days," wrote Virgil Thomson, "and restudying his works, forging a new style for playing them which would be convincing to a music world longing to hear them rendered with a grandeur appropriate to their proportions, had replaced the Bach problem of thirty years before." The most direct influence on Americans came from Glyndebourne, England, where the productions led by Fritz Busch and directed by Carl Ebert, and with the American-born soprano Ina Souez singing brilliantly, were a revelation for an entire generation. The festival's influence spread by means of recordings. The Salzburg Festival also played a role in adding prestige to the reconsideration of Mozart. There, Vincent Sheean heard someone complain that a concert contained "too much Mozart," which led him to reflect: "I doubt if that precise combination of words ever hit my ears before Salzburg. 'Too much' we never had; 'too little' was what we had known."[14]

The prevailing darkness of the 1920s and 1930s was lightened by a few glimmers of hope. On March 24, 1922, 132 years after Vienna first heard it, New York witnessed the first American production of *Così fan tutte.* The *New York Times* critic Richard Aldrich warned possible attenders that "a public that is used to expecting the more sweeping and vivid effects of modern music drama" might have difficulty in discerning "the beauty of this fragile 'opera buffa.'" Furthermore, Aldrich lamented the "unutterable stupidity" of *Così*'s libretto, "pure farce and at times burlesque, silly if examined in the light of pure reason." But, he added, "of course it is not to be considered from the point of view of realism." For all the opera's faults, Aldrich concluded, "Mozart's music has touched it with fascination," seemed "wholly delightful." After this beginning, something might have developed, but *Così* was struck down by the Metropolitan curse of distracted inattention, forgotten for another quarter of a century.

Any Mozart revival in America encountered a formidable difficulty: the absence of a tradition of Mozartian singing. When Chicago revived *Figaro* in the 1920s, attention was focused on its "modernistic" production, "stylized rococo carried to the point of madness," when the real accomplishment was a "suave, unsentimentalized, flashing, stimulating" sense of style by a magnificent cast—Marcoux, Raisa, Mason, Schipa, Kipnis.[15] Unfortunately, the Depression ended Chicago's efforts. The stylistic problems emerged when the Metropolitan got around to *Don Giovanni* in 1929. The cast, Gigli, Rethberg, Ponselle, Fleischer, and Pinza, was talented, but any idea of a unified style was "for the future rather than for the present." Pinza, who would one day be an accomplished Don, had not yet found "the elegance, the grace, the adroitness, the magnetic charm" of late years, but Ponselle and Schipa sang marvelously and the "shape of future Giovannis began to be apparent."[16]

T h e American revival got under way in 1940. It wasn't the result of any one event, performance, or person, but of a gradual and persistent growth, for audiences and performers, in understanding what Mozart's operas contained. The Metropolitan Opera's role in the revival was the most positive achievement of the Edward Johnson years. Between 1940 and 1950, the company gave more Mozart performances than in its previous fifty-seven years. John Brownlee was "the shining deed" of the 1940 *Figaro,* displaying the style he had shaped at Glyndebourne. In 1941 there was an English-language *Zauberflöte,* in the lively translation of Ruth and Thomas Martin, directed by Bruno Walter, who, along with Fritz Busch and George Szell, polished interpretations and nourished the immature but hardy plant. With the rapid spread of opera beyond New York in the postwar years, no one opera house could claim individual leadership. The New York City Opera put on *Così* in 1949 with an all-American cast, Phyllis Curtin, Frances Bible, Judith Raskin, John Alexander, John Reardon, and James Pease, "one of the most admirable productions in the company's career." An English-language *Così* at the Metropolitan in 1951 was a spectacular success, did much to restore it permanently to the Mozart canon. San Francisco's performances in 1956, with Elisabeth Schwarzkopf and American singers, were memorable for their elegant style.

Everywhere now, throughout the country, it was taken as a matter of course that companies, small and large, amateur and professional would include at least one Mozart opera in their season, and the Mozart repertory expanded to include the full range of his achievement. *Idomeneo* was first given in America in the 1960s, *La Clemenza di Tito* in the 1970s. New York didn't see *Idomeneo* until 1975, when the City Opera performed it; the Metropolitan not until 1982, when Jean-Pierre Ponelle's production "almost made up for past sins of omission." The level of singing rose as the

The Metropolitan Opera's production of Le Nozze di Figaro *in 1940 helped set the Mozart revival in motion. The cast included Bidu Sayao and Ezio Pinza (shown here), as well as John Brownlee.* Opera News / Metropolitan Opera Guild.

repertory expanded. A fair-minded observer asserted that the sense of ensemble in Mozart demonstrated by American singers was "on a higher level of ease and ingrained knowledge" than ever before "and can be taken as a given rather than as something that has to be painstakingly taught to a cast in rehearsal."[17]

The most interesting development of the 1980s was the reconsideration of Mozart's operas as drama. Mozart had become of interest to the theatrical avant-garde, a development of great interest for all of American operatic culture. The old order had been turned upside down. Now, dramatic considerations took precedence over musical ones, as in the explorations of Peter Sellars and others. These excited some, infuriated others; but whatever else, they were a recognition of the perpetual richness of Mozart's art. In a culture saturated with visual images, like America's, preoccupation with theatrical values is predictable. Producer's opera is likely to dominate the early years of the twenty-first century as much as it has the last years of the twentieth. Anyway, as Andrew Porter remarked about a production of *Don Giovanni,* "the illusion that there can be an ideal, 'complete' Mozart performance fades. . . . There is no 'whole truth' about *Don Giovanni*; no pattern or scheme fits more than a part of it. Contraries coexist . . . in this work (rich as life itself)."[18]

A s rich as life itself. And as inexhaustible. The past fifty years have been a Mozart half-century in America, his operas firmly established as an indispensable part of the repertory, American singers emerging as their sensitive and stylish interpreters. What was it American audiences have sought? The celebration of the bicentenary of Mozart's death in 1991, while it ranged from the search for rarities—St. Louis's *Mitridate, rè di Ponto* (*Mithridates, King of Pontus*), San Francisco's *Lucio Silla*—to Lincoln Center's performance of all eight hundred known compositions, was essen-

*Peter Sellars's uncon-
ventional Mozart pro-
ductions of the 1980s
turned the old order up-
side down. This is* Così
fan tutte *at the PepsiCo
Summerfare festival in
1986. Photograph by
Peter Krupenye.*

tially the culmination of the yearning for other values: balance and restraint in a time
of blatant excess; order contrasted with a culture of disorder; purity and perfection in
an art world of gross materialism. Most of all, perhaps, in a world racked for so long
by national rivalries, audiences sought, beyond musical harmony, the vision of
human concord. It was transcendence, reconciliation that Rossini had perceived
many years before when, in 1867, near the end of his life, he talked of Mozart to a
German visitor. Mozart had combined German harmony with Italian melody, Rossini
observed, the magic of Italian song with German inwardness. "This man rises above
both nations." Was it true, Rossini asked his visitor, that German audiences had begun
to forget Mozart in their admiration for Wagner? Whatever the answer, the "old
gentleman," undisturbed in his Mozartean faith, voiced sentiments shared by millions
of Americans today: "If Mozart is no longer regarded as the beautiful and the lofty,
then we old ones, who still are left over, can be entirely happy to quit this earth. But
one thing I know for certain, Mozart and his audiences will meet again in Paradise!"[19]

Maria Callas

Cecelia Sophia Anna Maria Kalogeropoulos was born in New York in 1923. How she came to be born there, and named as she was, reveals a good deal about her family. Her father was a pharmacist in Maligala, Greece, her mother the daughter of a soldier with a fine voice but no musical training. The marriage of George Kalogeropoulos and Evangelia Demetriadis was bitterly unhappy. There were two children, first a daughter, then a son, whose death from typhoid added to the parents' misery. To escape from this hopeless situation, George sold his house and pharmacy and prepared to emigrate to America, not telling his wife until the day before they were to sail. When they arrived in New York in August 1923, Evangelia was five months pregnant. The much longed-for son turned out to be another daughter, whose name the parents could not agree on. As a compromise, the girl was given *all* the names they had argued about.

Evangelia, who had dreamed of a stage career, transferred her ambitions to her daughters—tall, slender, beautiful Jackie and tall, fat, homely Maria. "Prompted by memories of her father's glorious singing," Evangelia filled their apartment with operatic gramophone music. George disliked it and thought money spent on records extravagant, but even when the crash of 1929 reduced the family's income, Evangelia insisted that Maria be given music lessons. Maria borrowed records from the New York Public Library and spent hours at home listening to them.

Maria's voice attracted attention, winning prizes in radio talent contests. She reflected bitterly on this years later. "There should be a law against that kind of thing. . . . They shouldn't deprive a child of its childhood!" Home life was stern. "My daughters never looked at dolls but they read, and at night they would play the piano until eleven o'clock, when I would send them to bed." Maria was fiercely competitive. "Convinced that when others came forward, she herself went back, she fancied herself locked in combat with the world." One Saturday afternoon, listening to a Metropolitan Opera radio broadcast featuring the new sensation, Lily Pons, Maria insisted that Pons was singing off-key. Those listening with her disagreed. After all, Pons was a star. "I don't care if she is a star," shouted Maria. "She sings off-key. Just wait and see, one day I'm going to be a star myself, a bigger star than her." It was a cheerless and friendless time for her, and she cherished the applause she gained at twelve and thirteen when she sang in school performances of *The Mikado* and *H.M.S. Pinafore*. That was soon eclipsed by a greater excitement. Evangelia decided that she must take Maria back to Greece where, free of George's objections, Maria would get proper instruction and have a better chance to make a singing career than in the crowded American field. In 1937, mother and daughters returned to Greece.

Not quite fourteen, she was admitted to the National Conservatory of Music in Athens, with a scholarship. Maria worked with fanatical intensity. "Her earnestness was oppressive," one of her conservatory contemporaries said later. Maria agreed. "I work: therefore I am. What do you do if you do not work?" At sixteen there came into her life Elvira de Hidalgo, a Spanish soprano who had sung throughout the world (briefly at the Metropolitan), who discerned promise in a voice capable of "violent cascades of sound, full of drama and emotion." Five years of strenuous study followed. De Hidalgo taught Maria how to move and stand onstage and loaned her the scores of the unfashionable, almost forgotten operatic repertory of the first half of the nineteenth century, of tragic queens and priestesses. Maria memorized the scores, "her mind full of runs, roulades, trills, cadenzas—the whole panoply of *bel canto* embellishments."

That was a great deal, but de Hidalgo stimulated something more: the dramatic sense and vocal technique to bring those old operas to life again. Bel canto was not an end in itself but a means of dramatic expression perfectly suited to the operas created in its style. The vocal technique required was formidable. It was widely believed that singers no longer were capable of mastering it, even had they wished to do so. Maria's voice had remarkable range and power, was uneven in the joining of its registers, and not sensuously beguiling, though extraordinarily distinctive in its coloring. Criticisms of it, then and later, were reminiscent of those leveled against Mary Garden's, and, like Garden, Maria developed several voices, each one adapted to the music and the role she was dramatically expressing. Maria thought of her voice as a thing apart, "almost a semi-hostile, intractable force outside herself." That was how she spoke of it: " 'The voice was answering tonight,' or 'the voice was not obeying tonight.' "[1]

In November 1940, Maria made her professional debut, "applauded, praised, appreciated," at the Athens National Lyric Theater in von Suppé's *Boccaccio* and was enrolled as a permanent member of the company just as Italy declared war on Greece. In April 1941, Germany invaded Greece and, despite heroic resistance, overran all opposition. There were hardships, but the war and occupation didn't much affect Maria's development. She was lucky to spend these years in Athens. Maria's mother, from whom she now became increasingly estranged, had been right in the gamble she took in 1937 in returning to Greece; for the young woman had opportunities to sing and mature that she would never have had in America. By 1945, Maria was ready for broader experiences. De Hidalgo urged her to go to Italy but, independent now of everyone, including her teacher, she decided to return to the United States. That was a mistake. Her Athenian reputation meant little in New York, and she was soon frustrated and depressed. Then came a dazzling opportunity. Edward Johnson, general manager of the Metropolitan, heard her sing and offered her two roles for the following season—Leonora in *Fidelio,* in English, and Cio-Cio-San in *Madama Butterfly.* Surprisingly, Maria turned down Johnson's offer. She didn't want to sing in English and, as her weight had ballooned to 180 pounds, she would be ridiculous as Butterfly.

Then came the break she needed, and wanted. Giovanni Zenatello offered her a chance to sing at the Verona Festival in Italy, of which he was artistic director. Maria returned to Europe, but under a new name. In America the family had adopted an Americanized version of Kalogeropoulos. This had been abandoned when in Greece, but was now taken up again in New York. So it was that Italy and then the world knew her as Maria Callas.

I n the next two years, despite difficulties, problems, disappointments, Maria Callas became internationally famous. At Verona, she fell into the hands of Tulio Serafin, the greatest Italian operatic conductor of the mid-twentieth century. "As soon as I heard her sing," he recalled, "I recognized an exceptional voice. A few notes were still uncertainly placed but I immediately knew that here was a future great singer." Under his baton, *La Gioconda,* in the summer of 1947, was a success. Venice proposed *Tristan und Isolde.* Callas didn't know the role. Serafin was untroubled: "One month of study and hard work is all you need."[2] Her Isolde was an unqualified success, as were *Turandot* and Leonora in Verdi's *La Forza del destino.*

At the end of 1948 came a chance to move to newer ground, toward which de Hidalgo had pointed her a decade before: her first *Norma.* There was a special intensity in Callas's absorption with Norma, a role she identified with and sang more than any other—ninety times in eight countries. She struggled to find the correct rhythms for the recitative, to convey the proper force and emphasis for the words, for she understood that, far from being an outmoded curiosity, *Norma* contained great dramatic power. The result was what Stendhal discerned in the performances of the creator of the role, Giuditta Pasta, in the 1830s: "an instantaneous hypnotic effect upon the soul of the spectator."

Next Callas went to Venice to sing Brunnhilde in *Die Walküre.* Meanwhile, the soprano who was to sing in a revival of Bellini's *I Puritani* fell ill. Serafin persuaded Callas to take her place, though she didn't know the role, and didn't even know the story. In between *Die Walküre* on Wednesday, Friday, and Sunday evenings, she was learning and practicing *I Puritani.* She sang it the following Tuesday. Callas made mistakes and had to be fed lines by the prompter, but she and Bellini and *I Puritani* were stunning. Franco Zeffirelli was there: "What she did in Venice was really incredible. You need to be familiar with opera to realize the size of her achievement that night."[3] As old buffers invoked the sacred name of Lilli Lehmann, Callas rocketed across the Italian operatic sky: *Turandot* in Naples, *Parsifal* in Rome.

She became the most famous singer of the 1950s, sweeping conquests onstage, turbulent scenes offstage. She fought with impresarios, photographers. In a time when it was a truism that the days of great divas had passed, Callas reigned as a queen of singing drama. But the diva wasn't the woman who had come from America. "I was a heavy, uncomfortable woman finding it difficult to move around." She lost eighty pounds, became lithe, moved with attenuated, tigerish grace, sculpted the "physique she needed for characters—for expressiveness not elegance. A fat face, she thought, couldn't register tension or cruelty or rage." Arturo Toscanini asked: "How did you make yourself so beautiful?" At twenty-three she married (like Malibran) a businessman twice her age. With Giovanni Meneghini she shared an identity of in-

Temperamental and ambitious, Maria Callas was one of the great singing actresses of modern times. In 1958 the Dallas Opera revived Cherubini's Médée for her. "She bit on words, she chewed them, she spat them," wrote one observer. Dallas Opera.

terests—her career. Theirs was a life based on "Spartan domestic economy, rigorous self-discipline and hard work."[4] For a decade, her ambition, will power, passion for self-improvement were focused on her art. Nothing interfered with it. This offended many people, and, as she could also be ungrateful and spiteful, her belief that she was fated always to quarrel with her friends became a self-fulfilling prophecy.

Callas's importance in the history of opera was based on two things. The first was the bel canto revival. Many people were involved in it, but Callas more than anyone else dramatized and popularized it. She gained force by narrowing her focus. Her early fame was based on her spectacularly wide repertory, but with a sure instinct for the work in which she could best express her individual gifts, she abandoned much: no more Wagner, no Mozart, no French opera, nothing contemporary. Although she made an important contribution to the revival of eighteenth-century opera by singing in Gluck's *Alceste* and *Iphigénie en Tauride* and in Haydn's *Orfeo ed Euridice,* she didn't move back beyond that toward Baroque opera. She sang Verdi and Puccini, though not many roles. The two that most attracted her, as they had every fine singing actress (and many who weren't), were Violetta in *La Traviata* and Tosca. This last was the role which gained her the most intense public interest. Nevertheless, what finally mattered most was her concentration on the first forty years of the nineteenth century, where she gave life to Rossini's *Armida,* Bellini's *Norma* and *I Puritani,* Donizetti's *Anna Bolena,* Spontini's *La Vestale,* Cherubini's *Médée,* and others.

How Callas sang—how she sang and acted—was her other claim to significance. Although the perfect fusion of action and music *is* opera, it is an ideal rarely achieved, and each operatic age achieves it in different ways. Callas put her stamp on the mid-twentieth century's version. What was most remarkable about her idea of musical drama was the extreme to which she carried it. As Elisabeth Schwarzkopf noted: "Callas had an absolute contempt for merely beautiful singing." Her acting (like Malibran's) was marked by extraordinary intensity in achieving dramatic effects at the expense of vocal beauty. Callas put it clearly. "After all, some of the texts we have to sing are not distinctive poetry. I know that to convey the dramatic effect to the audience and to myself I must produce sounds that are not beautiful. I don't mind if they are ugly as long as they are true."[5]

Seeing and hearing Callas's first *Norma* at the Metropolitan, Irving Kolodin was disconcerted at the obtuse reaction of some of the critics. "The uncommon talent sought in vain for the uncommon appraisal that was its due." Uncommon was Callas's conception of opera as "something seen whole and consecutive from beginning to end," the concentrated attempt to achieve "a single overpowering purpose: realization of everything that Bellini's genius had poured into his sorely tried heroine." Victor Gollancz, the English publisher, wrote of Callas's Norma: "I thought, in a sort of ecstasy, 'Here at last it is again! Yes, she's in the great tradition.'" Victor de Sabata, eminent Italian conductor, wished "the public could understand how deeply and utterly musical Callas is." Leonard Bernstein: "Callas? She was pure electricity." She also avoided the trap this repertory always presented to singers, that had turned later generations against it—the temptation to overdo ornamentation. She handled it with exquisite taste.[6]

Observers recalled unforgettable moments. In Chicago, Callas's Violetta, a fragile, feverish young woman, not a worldly courtesan, concluded with a death scene of wrenching pathos. Dallas never forgot her Medea, sprawling prone on the stage, face twisted with rage, hands rigid with fury. "Her voice keens and shrills, then plummets into chesty growling menace." "She bit on words, she chewed them, she spat them." As Milan's Medea, wearing a blood-red cloak, she sang while lying head-downward across a huge staircase, "tormenting the text into meaning." And in New York's *Tosca,* there was the supreme moment when she saw the knife with which she would kill Scarpia. "Callas alone persuaded the viewer that she had not discovered the knife— the knife discovered her in that moment of extremity and need. And she used it as this Tosca had to use it, in a lightning swift lunge, thrust, and shuddering rejection of her own act." The stunned New York audience "knew why Callas was Callas."[7]

Callas suggested the elemental, the mythic. For the directors Luchino Visconti and Franco Zeffirelli, she was the "black goddess," who assaulted rational self-control through the sensuality of music. "Visconti called her 'a monstrous phenomenon. Almost a sickness.'" For the critic Peter Conrad, Callas symbolized what opera might ideally be. "Like everyone else, I was converted to opera by Callas." He was converted first by her speech, not her song, by her realization of what Verdi meant when he spoke of "the word which becomes musical when it becomes dramatic, when it turns into the emotion it had previously merely named." Wallace Stevens's poem captures the archetypal image.

> She was the single artificer of the world
> In which she sang. And when she sang, the sea,
> Whatever self it had, became the self
> That was her song, for she was the maker. Then we,
> As we beheld her striding there alone,
> Knew that there never was world for her
> Except the one she sang and, singing, made.[8]

''N o t even Callas owned or exhausted the roles she sang." The bel canto revival became an international movement, and many other singers followed Callas's example and pushed on beyond it—Monserrat Caballé, Renata Scotto, Giulietta Simionato, Joan Sutherland. Just as Patti and Grisi appeared together once in the 1860s, there was one joint appearance of Callas and Sutherland, also at Covent Garden, a performance of *Norma* in 1952 in which Sutherland had a small role: "an awesome moment," in Marilyn Horne's words, "this crossing of Callas and Sutherland." By the late 1960s Sutherland reigned alone in bel canto opera as "La Stupenda," a very different reign, a very different style, essentially vocal. In America, of the many singers who were "A.C."—"After Callas"—two stand out, Beverly Sills and Marilyn Horne.[9]

Both singers came to bel canto indirectly, by means of that other operatic revival, Baroque opera. Sills began in Brooklyn, where she was born Belle Silverman in 1929, studied music at the Manhattan High School of Music and Art, sang in many operas in many cities until, in 1955, she began a long association with the New York City Opera. Stardom came to her in a 242-year-old opera, Handel's *Giulio Cesare*. But there had always been in her mind a different example. "Callas showed the world that . . . *bel canto* works were tremendous dramatic vehicles, true masterpieces of character development." Sills's great contribution came in the 1970s, in Donizetti's Elizabethan trilogy, *Roberto Devereux, Maria Stuarda (Mary Stuart)*, and *Anna Bolena,* unsung in America for a century and a quarter. She was the first modern-day soprano to sing all three queens.

Horne's road to bel canto was also indirect, from Bradford, Pennsylvania, where she was born in 1934, to the University of Southern California, where she studied music. Her voice, remarkable for range and richness, attracted notice, but opportunities for performance were still scarce. So Horne went to Germany to gain experience. Her breakthrough came in Berg's *Wozzeck,* in San Francisco in 1960, after which she committed herself to mezzo-soprano roles, always mindful of Callas's example. "Alas, I never saw Callas perform, but I became very familiar with her recordings." Horne became famous for her apparently effortless mastery of Baroque singing; she sang in *Rinaldo,* the first Handel opera ever performed at the Metropolitan, but equally she sang in Bellini and Rossini operas, and it is in the latter that she has made her greatest mark—*Le Siège de Corinthe, Semiramide,* and, repaying a long-standing American operatic debt, *Tancredi,* singing Malibran's famous role in the Fenice Opera House in Venice.

Ironically, Callas's own career had taken a very different and astonishing turn. In 1958 she fell in love with the immensely wealthy Aristotle Onassis and left her husband to live with him. This affair made her name known to tens of millions of people who knew nothing of her as an opera singer. Even more read about her when, in the mid-1960s, Onassis left her to marry Jacqueline Kennedy. In these years Callas's voice, or her nerves, disintegrated, or she lost the desire to sing. She made films, went on a long concert tour. And then it was over. In the 1970s she lived a reclusive life, rarely leaving her Paris residence. (Visitors to her apartment noted that the solitary operatic memento in it was a portrait of a singer.) It is surprising to realize that Callas's international singing career lasted only a dozen years.

''*Shriveled*, shrunken, isolated," Maria Callas died of a heart attack on September 16, 1977, in her bedroom, a quiet end to a tumultuous life, a life lived in art and for art, art of such intensity that it threatened to consume life, and then, love supplanting art, love of such intensity that it devoured art. When art and love were both lost, she was left with a shadow life, of desolating emptiness, of dissolving memories, clamorous audiences fading, spiteful critics fading, intransigent impresarios fading, everything fading, fading, a life, as our story also ends, merging with the lives of the operatic immortals who preceded her, differing from each, similar to each: Mary Garden's command of the stage; Lillian Nordica's iron will; Adelina Patti's journey to Europe and to fame; and, at last and always, that first great diva of America, impassioned in her art, impulsive in her challenge to social conventions, whose portrait was nearby Callas at the end, her sister in song, in spirit, in name: Maria Malibran.

Notes

At the head of chapters, and occasionally within them, I list sources I have used, even if not quoted from directly. After the first full citation, books and articles are identified by author and abbreviated title. The place of publication is New York City unless otherwise indicated. I have drawn on three sources so often it would be unwieldy to cite them chapter after chapter. Instead, I list them here to make clear my indebtedness: H. Wiley Hitchcock and Stanley Sadie, eds., *The New Grove Dictionary of American Music*, 4 vols. (1986); Harold Rosenthal and John Warrack, eds., *The Concise Oxford Dictionary of Opera* (2d ed., 1979); and Stanley Sadie, ed., *The New Grove Dictionary of Music and Musicians*, 20 vols. (1980).

Act One. Origins

Epigraphs: Rossini, *Il Barbiere di Siviglia*, act 1, scene 1. Stendhal, *Life of Rossini* trans. Richard N. Coe (1957), 15.

Chapter 1. The Garcías at the Park

Jo Cowell, *Thirty Years Passed among the Players in England and America* (1844). April Fitzlyon, *The Libertine Librettist: A Biography of Mozart's Librettist, Lorenzo Da Ponte* (1957). April Fitzlyon, *The Price of Genius: A Life of Pauline Viardot* (1964). John W. Francis *Old New York; or, Reminiscences of the Past Sixty Years* (1865). Henry E. Krehbiel, *Chapters of Opera* (1908). Julian Mates, *The American Musical Stage Before 1800* (1962). Molly Nelson, "The First Italian Opera Season in New York City: 1825–1826" (Ph.D. diss., University of North Carolina, 1976). George C. D. Odell, *Annals of the New York Stage* (1927–1949). Oscar G. Sonneck, *Early Concert-Life in America, 1731–1800* (1907). Herbert Weinstock, *Rossini: A Biography* (1968). James Grant Wilson, *The Life and Letters of Fitz-Greene Halleck* (1869).

1 *New-York Evening Post*, Nov. 30, 1825. Francis Rogers, "America's First Grand Opera Season," *Musical Quarterly* 1, no. 1 (January 1915), 93–94.

2 "Pauline Viardot-Garcia to Julius Rietz (Letters of Friendship)," *Musical Quarterly* 1, no. 4 (October 1915), 526. Sterling Mackinlay, *Garcia the Centenarian and His Times* (1908), 95–96. Arthur Pougin, *Marie Malibran: Histoire d'une cantatrice* (Paris, 1911), 18–19.

3 Stendhal, *The Charterhouse of Parma*, trans. C. K. Scott Moncrieff (1954), 128, 444.

4 Francis, *Old New York*, 259–60.

5 Cowell, *Thirty Years*, 60–61. Fitzlyon, *Libertine Librettist*, 261–62. Mates, *Musical Stage*, 105–18. Nelson, "First Opera Season," 123–32.

6 Odell, *Annals*, 3:183. *New-York Review and Atheneum Magazine*, December 1825, 78–83.

7 *New-York Evening Post*, Nov. 30, 1825.

8 Ibid. Walt Whitman, "The Opera," in *New York Dissected: A Sheaf of Recently Discovered Newspaper Articles by the Author of Leaves of Grass* (1936), 22.

9 *New-York Evening Post*, Dec. 6, 1825. Lately Thomas, *Sam Ward: "King of the Lobby"* (Boston, 1965), 16. Don C. Seitz, *The James Gordon Bennetts, Father and Son* (Indianapolis, 1928), 20.

10 Allan Nevins and Milton Thomas, eds., *The Diary of George Templeton Strong* (1952), 4:458.

11 *New-York Evening Post,* Dec. 6 and 18, 1825. *The United States Literary Gazette,* March 1, 1826, 414–22. *New-York Review and Atheneum Magazine,* Feb. 26, 1826, 230–35.

12 *New-York Evening Post,* Jan. 11, 1826. *New York American,* Jan. 3, 1826. George Derwent, *Rossini and Some Forgotten Nightingales* (London, 1934), 85–86. *New-York Evening Post,* Feb. 4, 1826. Odell, *Annals,* 3:190. When Charles Gounod was twelve, he was taken to hear Malibran as Desdemona. "The performance made such a deep impression on him that it influenced his decision to devote his life to music." Malibran, in later years, sometimes sang the part of Otello. Fitzlyon, *Price,* 89.

13 *New-York Evening Post,* Feb. 9, 1826. *Musical Quarterly* 1, no. 1 (January 1915), 99. *The New-York Mirror and Ladies' Literary Gazette,* Jan. 28, 1826, 215, and March 4, 1826, 255.

14 *New-York Mirror and Ladies' Literary Gazette,* Jan. 28, 1826, 215; Feb. 25, 1826, 239; and March 18, 1826, 271. *New-York Evening Post,* May 1, 1826.

15 *New-York Mirror and Ladies' Literary Gazette,* May 13, 1826, 335. *New-York Evening Post,* May 23, 1826. *American Quarterly,* January 1915, 100.

16 *New-York Evening Post,* July 19 and Aug. 12, 1826. *New York American,* June 1, 1826.

17 Ibid., Aug. 12, 1826. W. S. B. Matthews, ed., *A Hundred Years of Music in America* (Chicago, 1889), 50. Blanche Muldrow, "The American Theater as Seen by British Travellers, 1790–1860" (Ph.D. diss., University of Wisconsin, 1953), 90.

18 *New-York Mirror and Ladies' Literary Gazette,* Jan. 21, 1826, 207; April 8, 1826, 295; and July 22, 1826, 415.

Chapter 2. England and Italy

Wallace Brockway and Herbert Weinstock, *The World of Opera* (1963). Peter Conrad, *A Song of Love and Death: The Meaning of Opera* (1987). Edward Dent, *Opera* (1949). Cecil Forsyth, *Music and Nationalism* (London, 1911). Donald J. Grout, *A Short History of Opera* (3d ed., 1988). Joseph Kerman, *Opera as Drama* (rev. ed., 1988). Herbert Lindenberger, *Opera: The Extravagant Art* (1984). Robin May, *Opera* (1977). Leslie Orrey, *A Concise History of Opera* (1972). Paul Robinson, *Opera and Ideas: From Mozart to Strauss* (1986).

1 Robert Donington, *The Rise of Opera* (London and Boston, 1981), 89. On England: Roger Fiske, *English Theatre Music in the Eighteenth Century* (1973). E. D. Mackerness, *A Social History of English Music* (London, 1964). Eric Walter White, *A History of English Opera* (1983). Percy M. Young, *A History of British Music* (1967).

2 White, *English Opera,* 70. On Lully: James R. Anthony, *French Baroque Music: From Beaujoyeulx to Rameau* (London, 1973). Robert Isherwood, *Music in the Service of the King: France in the Seventeenth Century* (Ithaca, 1973).

3 Anthony, *French Baroque Music,* 45.

4 Isherwood, *Music,* 189, 389.

5 White, *English Opera,* 104.

6 On Handel: Winton Dean, *Handel and the Opera Seria* (1969). Winton Dean and John Merrill Knapp, *Handel's Operas, 1704–1726* (1987). Reinhard Strohm, *Essays on Handel and Italian Opera* (1985).

7 Edmond M. Gagey, *Ballad Opera* (1937).

8 Henry E. Krehbiel, *Chapters of Opera* (1908) and *More Chapters of Opera* (1919). Irving Lowens, *Music and Musicians in Early America* (1964). Julian Mates, *The American Musical Stage Before 1800* (1962). Hugh F. Rankin, *The Theater in Colonial America* (Chapel Hill, 1960). Kenneth Silverman, *A Cultural History of the American Revolution: Painting, Music, Literature and Theatre in the Colonies and the United States from the Treaty of Paris to the Inauguration of George Washington* (1976). Oscar G. T. Sonneck, *Early Opera in America* (1915).

9 William Byrd, *Another Secret Diary of William Byrd, 1739–1741,* ed. M. H. Woodfin (Richmond, Va., 1942), 334.

10 Rankin, *Theater,* 50–51.

11 E. E. Hipsher, *American Opera and Its Composers* (Philadelphia, 1927), 22.

12 Henry Mayer, *A Son of Thunder: Patrick Henry and the American Republic* (1986), 25.

13 Silverman, *Cultural History,* 92–93.

14 Ibid., 271, 371.

15 Ibid., 365.

16 Theodore Fenner, *Leigh Hunt and Opera Criticism: The "Examiner" Years, 1808–1821* (University Press of Kansas, 1972), 28.

Chapter 3. New Orleans

Liliane Crété, *Daily Life in Louisiana, 1815–1830* (Baton Rouge, 1981). Lucille Gafford, "A History of the St. Charles Theatre in New Orleans, 1835–1843" (Ph.D. diss., University of Chicago, 1930). Howard Mumford Jones, *America and French Culture, 1750–1848* (Chapel Hill, 1927). John S. Kendall, *The Golden Age of the New Orleans Theater* (Baton Rouge, 1952). Grace King, *New Orleans: The Place and the People* (1968). Henry A. Kmen, *Music in New Orleans: The Formative Years, 1791–1841* (Baton Rouge, 1966). Robert Tallant, *The Romantic New Orleanians* (1950).

1 Blanche Muldrow, "The American Theater as Seen by British Travellers, 1790–1860" (Ph.D. diss., University of Wisconsin, 1953), 90.

2 Kmen, *Music in New Orleans,* 56–92.

3 Kendall, *Golden Age,* throughout. Tallant, *Romantic New Orleanians,* 194–200. Kmen, *Music in New Orleans,* 92–111. *New York Morning Courier,* Aug. 11 and Sept. 17, 1828.

4 Kmen, *Music in New Orleans,* 119.

5 *New-York Mirror,* July 21, 1827. *The Albion,* July 21 and Aug. 11, 1827. *New-York Evening Post,* Aug. 15, 1827.

6 *National Gazette,* Oct. 15, 1827, and Sept. 15, 1829.

7 Kmen, *Music in New Orleans,* 115.

8 *National Gazette,* Sept. 12, 1829.

9 *New York Courier and Enquirer,* Feb. 18, 1834. Noah M. Ludlow, *Dramatic Life as I Found It: A Record of Personal Experience* (St. Louis, 1880), 237–38.

10 Crété, *Daily Life in Louisiana,* 202–35. John W. Ward, *Andrew Jackson: Symbol for an Age* (1955), 13–15.

11 *New Orleans Bee,* March 7, 1836.

12 *New Orleans Weekly Picayune,* June 16, 1839.

13 *New Orleans Bee (L'Abeille),* June 15, 1839.

Chapter 4. Buildings and Audiences

Robert Donington, *The Rise of Opera* (London and Boston, 1981). Michael Forsyth, *Buildings for Music: The Architect, the Musician, and the Listener from the Seventeenth Century to the Present Day* (Cambridge, Mass., 1985). Robert Isherwood, *Music in the Service of the King: France in the Seventeenth Century* (Ithaca, 1973). Simon Towneley Worsthorne, *Venetian Opera in the Seventeenth Century* (Oxford, 1954).

1 Stanley T. Lewis, "The New York Theatre: Its Background and Architectural Development: 1750–1853" (Ph.D. diss., Ohio State University, 1953), 129.

2 Donington, *Rise of Opera,* 40.

3 Worsthorne, *Venetian Opera,* 3, 29–30.

4 Ibid., 12.

5 Robin May, *Opera* (London, 1977), 13. Leslie Orrey, *A Concise History of Opera* (1972), 2–4.

6   Worsthorne, *Venetian Opera,* 11–12.

7   Walter Pater, "The School of Giorgione," *The Renaissance: Studies in Art and Poetry,* ed. Donald Hill (Berkeley, 1980), 119.

8   Alfred Einstein, "The German Opera," *Mozart: His Character—His Work* (1946), chap. 23, throughout. Bauman, *North German Opera,* throughout.

9   James R. Anthony, *French Baroque Music: From Beaujoyeulx to Rameau* (London, 1973), 19. *Dwight's Journal of Music,* Feb. 29, 1868, 193–94.

10 Isherwood, *Music in the Service of the King,* 182.

11 Ibid., 39.

12 Henry Wikoff, *The Reminiscences of an Idler* (1880), 199.

13 J. H. Plumb, *The First Four Georges* (London, 1956), 14.

14 Kenneth Clark, *Civilization: A Personal View* (1969), 218.

15 Eric Walter White, *The Rise of English Opera* (1951), 47–50. Angus Heriot, *The Castrati* (London, 1956), throughout.

16 Samuel Johnson in "The Life of Hughes," *The Lives of the English Poets,* 3 vols., ed. G. B. Hill (1967), 2:159–66. Eric Walter White, *A History of English Opera* (1983), 167.

17 George Saunders, *A Treatise on Theatres* (London, 1790), 33, 34.

18 Ibid., 27.

19 Forsyth, *Buildings for Music,* 100.

Chapter 5. Philadelphia

W. G. Armstrong, *A Record of the Opera in Philadelphia* (Philadelphia, 1884). Nathaniel Burt, *The Perennial Philadelphians* (Boston, 1963). John Curtis, "History of Opera in Philadelphia," 2 vols. (unpublished typescript, Pennsylvania Historical Society). Robert A. Gerson, *Music in Philadelphia* (Philadelphia, 1940). Reese D. James, *Old Drury of Philadelphia: A History of the Philadelphia Stage, 1800–1835* (Philadelphia, 1935). Lillian B. Miller, *Patrons and Patriotism: The Encouragement of the Fine Arts in the United States, 1790–1860* (Chicago, 1966). George B. Tatum, *Penn's Great Town* (Philadelphia, 1961). Russell F. Weigley, *Philadelphia: A 300-Year History* (1982). Theodore B. White et al., *Philadelphia Architecture in the Nineteenth Century* (Philadelphia, 1953).

1   William Dunlap, playwright and theater historian, as quoted in Oscar G. Sonneck, *Early Opera in America* (1915), 132.

2   Washington Irving, *Salmagundi* (1807–1808), in *The Complete Works of Washington Irving* (Boston, 1977), 6:186.

3   Blanche Muldrow, "The American Theater as Seen by British Travellers, 1790–1860" (Ph.D. diss., University of Wisconsin, 1953), 114.

4   Richard Grant White, "Opera in New York," *Century Magazine,* April 1882, 871–73.

5   Van Wyck Brooks, *The World of Washington Irving* (1944), 10–11. Fanny Kemble quoted in Muldrow, "British Travellers," 233. Frances Trollope, *The Domestic Manners of the Americans* (1832), 271.

6   *National Gazette,* Oct. 4 and 20, 1827.

7   Ibid., Oct. 2, 1827. For New York City's response to the success of the French in Philadelphia, see *The Albion,* Oct. 27, 1833.

8   *National Gazette,* Sept. 29 and Oct. 6, 1827, and Sept. 11, 1833.

9   Ibid., Sept. 8, 1829. *New-York Mirror,* July 22, 1826.

10 *National Gazette,* Oct. 3, 1829.

11 Max Maretzek, *Crotchets and Quavers, or Revelations of an Opera Manager in America* (1855), 69–73.

12 The marquis de Chastellux, as quoted in Dixon Wecter, *The Saga of American Society* (1970), 77. Ferdinand Bayard, *Voyage dans L'intérieur des Etats-Unis* (1797), commented: "The inhabitants of Philadelphia, like all the citizens of the United States, are classified by their fortunes" (ibid., 74).

13 Muldrow, "British Travellers," 139. "The visitors to the theatre are entirely unrestrained; the

gentlemen keep on their hats in the boxes, and in the pit they make themselves in every respect comfortable" (Bernard, duke of Saxe-Weimar Eisenach, *Travels through North America during the Years 1825 and 1826* [Philadelphia, 1828], 133).

14 Henry Wikoff, *The Reminiscences of an Idler* (1880), 188. Allison Delarue, *The Chevalier Henry Wikoff, Impresario* (Princeton, 1968), 20.

15 Wikoff, *Reminiscences,* 113. *Morning Courier and New York Enquirer,* June 17, 1833. *New-York Mirror and Ladies' Literary Gazette,* April 1, 1826.

16 James, *Old Drury,* 179.

17 *The Albion,* Feb. 10 and Aug. 11, 1827. Joseph Norton Ireland, *Records of the New York Stage, from 1750 to 1860* (1866–1867), 1:528. Theodore Shank, "The Bowery Theater, 1826–1836," 2 vols. (Ph.D. diss., Stanford University, 1956), 1:162–63.

18 *New-York Mirror,* Oct. 15, 1831.

19 Muldrow, "British Travellers," 142.

20 Thomas Hamilton, *Men and Manners in America* (Philadelphia, 1833), 198.

21 A. Koch and W. Peden, eds., *Selected Writings of John and John Quincy Adams* (1946), 66.

22 Trollope, *Domestic Manners,* 348–49.

23 Lorenzo Da Ponte, *An Incredible Story But a True One: A History of the Italian Opera Company Brought to America by Giacomo Montresor in August of the Year 1832* (1833), 7.

24 Oliver Larkin, *Art and Life in America* (1949), 150.

25 Talbot Hamlin, *Benjamin Henry Latrobe* (1955), 166–67, 189–90.

Chapter 6. Three American Theaters

John Curtis, "History of Opera in Philadelphia" (unpublished typescript, Pennsylvania Historical Society). McDonald W. Held, "A History of Stage Lighting in the United States in the Nineteenth Century" (Ph.D. diss., Northwestern University, 1955). Reese D. James, *Old Drury of Philadelphia: A History of the Philadelphia Stage, 1800–1835* (Philadelphia, 1935). Henry Kmen, *Music in New Orleans: The Formative Years, 1791–1841* (Baton Rouge, 1966). Stanley T. Lewis, "The New York Theatre: Its Background and Architectural Development, 1750–1853" (Ph.D. diss., Ohio State University, 1953). Theodore Shank, "The Bowery Theatre, 1826–1836" (Ph.D. diss., Stanford University, 1956). Kenneth Silverman, *A Cultural History of the American Revolution* (1976). William B. Wood, *Personal Recollections of the Stage, Embracing Notices of Actors, and Auditors, during a Period of Forty Years* (Philadelphia, 1855).

1 Silverman, *Cultural History,* 351.

2 John Esten Cooke, *The Virginia Comedians* (1855), 46–47.

3 Washington Irving, *Letters of Jonathan Oldstyle, Gent.,* in *The Works of Washington Irving,* 12 vols. (1881), 8:20.

4 James, *Old Drury,* 19, 11.

5 Wood, *Recollections,* 341.

6 Ibid., 341–42.

7 Ibid., 341. The observer was the marquis de Chastellux, as quoted in Dixon Wecter, *The Saga of American Society* (1970), 74.

8 Frances Trollope, *The Domestic Manners of the Americans* (1832), 339.

9 Shank, "The Bowery Theatre," 244–45.

10 *Morning Courier and New York Enquirer,* June 17, 1843.

11 Shank, "Bowery Theatre," 380–82.

12 Ibid., 458.

13 Lucille Gafford, "A History of the St. Charles Theatre in New Orleans, 1835–1843" (Ph.D. diss., University of Chicago, 1930), 32.

14 Blanche Muldrow, "The American Theater as Seen by British Travellers, 1790–1860" (Ph.D. diss., University of Wisconsin, 1953), 142.

15 Henry Wikoff, *The Reminiscences of an Idler* (1880), 188–89.

Chapter 7. A Columbia Professor

Memoirs of Lorenzo Da Ponte, trans. Elizabeth Abbott, ed. Arthur Livingston (Philadelphia, 1929). Lorenzo Da Ponte, *An Incredible Story But a True One: A History of the Italian Opera Company Brought to America by Giacomo Montresor in August of the Year 1832* (*Storia incredibile ma vera, della compagnia dell' opera italiana, condotta da Giacomo Montresor in America, in Agosto dell' anno 1832;* 1833) and *A Squib to Make You Laugh* (*Frottola per far ridere;* 1835). April Fitzlyon, *The Libertine Librettist: A Biography of Mozart's Librettist, Lorenzo da Ponte* (1957). Sheila Hodges, *Lorenzo Da Ponte: The Life and Times of Mozart's Librettist* (London, 1985). Henry Edward Krehbiel, *Chapters of Opera* (1908). Allan Nevins, ed., *The Diary of Philip Hone, 1828–1851* (enlarged edition, 1936). Joseph Louis Russo, *Lorenzo Da Ponte, Poet and Adventurer* (1922). Sam Ward, *Sketch on the Life of Lorenzo Da Ponte* (1842).

1 W. H. Auden, *Secondary Worlds* (1984), 78–79.

2 Da Ponte, *Incredible Story,* 7–8.

3 Ibid., 5, 9–10, 19.

4 Ibid., 20, 8, 12.

5 *Diary of Philip Hone,* 71.

6 Da Ponte, *Incredible Story,* 11.

7 George C. D. Odell, *Annals of the New York Stage* (1927–1949), 3:644. *Morning Courier and New York Enquirer,* Dec. 10, 1832.

8 Da Ponte, *Incredible Story,* 50.

9 Richard Grant White, "Opera in New York," *Century Magazine,* March 1882, 702. *Diary of Philip Hone,* 103–04.

10 White, "Opera in New York," 703. *New York Mirror,* Nov. 30 and Dec. 7, 14, and 28, 1833.

11 *Morning Courier and New York Enquirer,* Feb. 4, 1834.

12 Ibid., Jan. 13 and 17, 1834, Feb. 4, 12, and March 12, 1834.

13 Da Ponte, *Squib,* 22.

14 *Morning Courier and New York Enquirer,* Feb. 4, 1834. Blanche Muldrow, "The American Theater as Seen by British Travellers, 1770–1860" (Ph.D. diss., University of Wisconsin, 1953), 252. *Diary of Philip Hone,* 183.

15 White, "Opera in New York," 703.

16 Thomas Love Peacock, *Crotchet Castle,* in *The Novels of Thomas Love Peacock* (London and New York, n.d.), 436. Henry James, *Hawthorne* (London, 1879), 3.

17 *New-York Mirror,* Oct. 27, 1832; see also Nov. 3, 1832.

18 Da Ponte, *Squib,* 3.

19 John Francis, *Old New York; or, Reminiscences of the Past Sixty Years* (1865), 264–69. Ward, *Sketch,* throughout. A monument to Da Ponte has been erected, at last: a group of admirers put up a marker in the Calvary Cemetery in Queens. *New York Times,* Oct. 21, 1987.

20 Henry E. Krehbiel, "Da Ponte in New York," *New York Tribune,* Aug. 28, 1887. Alfred Einstein, *Mozart* (London, 1971), 487.

Interlude: Maria Malibran

Howard Bushnell, *Maria Malibran* (1979). H. Sutherland Edwards, *The Prima Donna* (London, 1888). April Fitzlyon, *Maria Malibran: A Diva of the Romantic Age* (1987). April Fitzlyon, *The Price of Genius: A Life of Pauline Viardot* (1964). M. Sterling Mackinlay, *Garcia the Centenarian and His Times*

(Edinburgh, 1908). Henry Myers, *The Signorina* (1956). Arthur Pougin, *Maria Malibran: The Story of a Great Singer* (London, 1911).

1   "Pauline Viardot-Garcia to Julius Rietz (Letters of Friendship)," *Musical Quarterly* 1 no. 3 (July 1915), 350–80.

2   Joan Bulman, *Jenny Lind* (London, 1956), 37–43. Mrs. Raymond Maude, *The Life of Jenny Lind* (London, 1926), 15–18. Jenny Lind was better treated than other García pupils: "Although I consider he was the finest teacher of his day, I must say he was at times quite violent with his pupils. It was nothing for him to fling a book at an unsuspecting head during a lesson." Henry J. Wood, *My Life of Music* (London, 1938), 29–30.

3   T. J. Walsh, *Second Empire Opera* (1981), 111–14. Fitzlyon, *Price of Genius,* 464.

4   Mackinlay, *Garcia,* 80.

5   Ibid., 81.

6   Theodore Shank, "The Bowery Theatre, 1826–1836" (Ph.D. diss., Stanford University, 1956), 154–57.

7   Shank, "Bowery Theatre," 158–60. George C. D. Odell, *Annals of the New York Stage* (1927–1949), 3:329–31. *The Albion,* Oct. 20, 1827.

8   Fitzlyon, *Malibran,* 32. Edwards, *Prima Donna,* 249.

9   Bushnell, *Malibran,* 128.

10 Ibid., 137. George Derwent, *Rossini and Some Forgotten Nightingales* (London, 1934), 130.

11 Herbert Weinstock, *Rossini: A Biography* (1968), 50. John W. Francis, *Old New York; or, Reminiscences of the Past Sixty Years* (1865), 258–59.

Act Two. Expansion

Epigraphs: Walt Whitman, *Leaves of Grass,* "Song of Myself," no. 26. William T. Upton, *William Henry Fry: American Journalist and Composer-Critic* (1954), 138. Max Maretzek, *Crotchets and Quavers, or Revelations of an Opera Manager in America* (1855), 75.

Chapter 8. The Bohemian Girl

Charles Lamb Kenney, *A Memoir of Michael William Balfe* (London, 1875). George C. D. Odell, *Annals of the New York Stage* (1927–1949). Eric Walter White, *A History of English Opera* (London, 1983).

1   Odell, *Annals,* 4:298.

2   *Morning Courier and New York Enquirer,* April 15, 1834.

3   Odell, *Annals,* 4:343.

4   Ibid., 4:446.

5   *Knickerbocker Magazine,* January 1845, 79–81. *New York Herald,* Dec. 13, 1844. Odell, *Annals,* 5:92–93.

6   *New York Herald,* Dec. 7, 1844. John Curtis, "A History of Opera in Philadelphia," 2 vols. (unpublished typescript at the Pennsylvania Historical Society), 1:324. By 1854 one newspaper complained of the "wearisome prettiness" of *The Bohemian Girl. New-York Evening Post,* Oct. 20, 1854.

7   *New York Herald,* Dec. 1, 1844.

8   T. J. Walsh, *Second Empire Opera* (London, 1981), 262. White, *English Opera,* 260–94.

9   Kenney, *Memoir,* 185–86.

10 Ibid., 200.

11 Artemus Ward, *In Washington* (1863).

12 Curtis, "Opera in Philadelphia," 1:324.

13 Max Maretzek, *Crotchets and Quavers, or Revelations of an Opera Manager in America* (1855), 11. Julian Budden, *Verdi* (London, 1986), 122.

Chapter 9. William Fry and the American Muse

W. G. Armstrong, *A Record of the Opera in Philadelphia* (Philadelphia, 1884). John Curtis, "History of Opera in Philadelphia," 2 vols. (unpublished typescript, Pennsylvania Historical Society). Robert Gerson, *Music in Philadelphia* (Philadelphia, 1940). Thomas Goodwin, *Sketches and Impressions, Musical, Theatrical and Social (1799–1885),* ed. R. O. Mason (1887). Delmer Dalzell Rogers, "Nineteenth-Century Music in New York City as Reflected in the Career of George Frederick Bristow" (Ph.D. diss., University of Michigan, 1967). Robert C. Toll, *Blacking Up: The Minstrel Show in Nineteenth-Century America* (1974). William T. Upton, *William Henry Fry: American Journalist and Composer-Critic* (1954).

1 Upton, *Fry,* 4–29.
2 Ibid., 42–43, 327–29. Gerson, *Music in Philadelphia,* 73–77. Curtis, "Opera in Philadelphia," 1:326–36.
3 Irving Lowens, *Music and Musicians in Early America* (1964), 220. Upton, *Fry,* 42.
4 *Dwight's Journal of Music,* Nov. 19, 1870, 349.
5 Upton, *Fry,* 36.
6 Ibid., 137.
7 Gerson, *Music in Philadelphia,* 73–75. Upton, *Fry,* 177. *Putnam's Monthly Magazine,* January 1853, 119; February 1853, 237; March 1853, 350–51. Lowens, *Music and Musicians,* 216–19. *Harper's New Monthly Magazine,* January 1853, 271.
8 *Putnam's Monthly Magazine,* November 1855, 560. Rogers, "Nineteenth-Century Music in New York," 107–11, 164–66. *Dwight's Journal of Music,* Nov. 19, 1870, 349. Goodwin, *Sketches and Impressions,* 288–89. Waldemar Rieck, "When Bristow's 'Rip' Was Sung at Niblo's Garden," *Musical America,* Dec. 5, 1925, 19.
9 Upton, *Fry,* 330.
10 Oliver Larkin, *Samuel F. B. Morse and American Democratic Art* (1954), 104. Upton, *Fry,* 330. *Dwight's Journal of Music,* Jan. 15, 1870, 173.
11 Toll, *Blacking Up,* 50.
12 Gilbert Chase, *America's Music: From the Pilgrims to the Present,* rev. ed. (Urbana and Chicago, 1987), 257.
13 H. Wiley Hitchcock, *The Phonograph and Our Musical Life* (Brooklyn, 1980), 62.
14 *Dwight's Journal of Music,* May 28, 1864, 243–44. Henry E. Krehbiel, *Chapters of Opera* (1908), 49.
15 Richard Grant White, "Opera in New York," *Century Magazine,* May 1882, 31–43.

Chapter 10. Gold Rush

Ronald L. Davis, *A History of Opera in the American West* (Englewood Cliffs, 1965). Kenneth Dorst, "A Descriptive Investigation of the Theatrical Structures Built by Thomas Maguire in the Far West" (Ph.D. diss., University of Denver, 1966). William Charles Miller, "An Historical Study of Theatrical Entertainment in Virginia City, Nevada, or Bonanza and Boresca Theatres on the Comstock, 1860–1875" (Ph.D. diss., University of Southern California, 1947). Lois Foster Rodecape, "Tom Maguire, Napoleon of the Stage," *California Historical Society Quarterly* 20 (1941):289–314; 21 (1942):39–74, 141–82, 239–75. Howard Swann, *Music in the Southwest, 1825–1950* (San Marino, Calif., 1952). Works Progress Administration, *History of Music in San Francisco,* 7 vols. (San Francisco, 1939).

1 WPA, *History of Music in San Francisco,* vol. 3, "The Letters of Miska Hauser," 22.
2 Jack Chen, *The Chinese of America: From the Beginnings to the Present* (1981), 60–61. Lois Rodecape, "Celestial Drama in the Golden Hills," *California Historical Society Quarterly* 1944, 97–116. Charles Nordhoff, *California: For Health, Pleasure, and Residence* (1872), 63, 86–88.
3 Ibid., vol. 1, "The Gold Rush Era," 120–37.
4 Rodecape, "Tom Maguire," 20:289–314.

5   Ibid., 21:39–74.

6   Dorst, "Theatrical Structures," 120.

7   Rodecape, "Tom Maguire," 21:141–82.

8   Ibid. Craig Timberlake, *The Bishop of Broadway: The Life and Work of David Belasco* (1954), 107.

9   Allan Nevins, *The Ordeal of the Union* (195), 2:536. Blanche Muldrow, "The American Theater as Seen by British Travellers, 1790–1860" (Ph.D. diss., University of Wisconsin, 1953), 318.

10 Lately Thomas, *Sam Ward: "King of the Lobby"* (Boston, 1965), 192. Louis Moreau Gottschalk, *Notes of a Pianist,* ed. J. Behren (1964), 309. Page Smith, *A People's History of the United States* (1976–1987), 4:247.

Chapter 11. New Orleans and Havana

W. G. Armstrong, *A Record of the Opera in Philadelphia* (Philadelphia, 1884). Gilbert Chase, *A Guide to the Music of Latin America* (rev. ed. 1962). George C. D. Odell, *Annals of the New York Stage* (1927–1949). Robert Sevenson, *A Guide to Caribbean Music History* (Lima, 1975).

1   *Morning Courier and New York Enquirer,* May 19, 20, 22, 25, 29, 1843; June 1, 2, 3, 7, 12, 16, 19, 23, 29, 1843; July 3, 7, 8, 10, 19, 20, 21, 28, 1843; Sept. 6, 9, 11, 1843.

2   Odell, *Annals,* 5:103–05, 158.

3   A study of the Havana company and of its influence on opera in the United States is much needed. There is material of interest in Armstrong, *Opera in Philadelphia,* 305–17, 372–77.

4   *Morning Courier and New York Enquirer,* Sept. 15, 19, 21, 1843, and Oct. 2, 3, 1843. Odell, *Annals,* 4:694–95. Richard Grant White, "Opera in New York," *Century Magazine,* May 1882, 31–43.

5   Odell, *Annals,* 5:266, 301. *Morning Courier and New York Enquirer,* April 17, 1847. *New York Herald,* April 14, 16, 1847, and June 17, 20, 22, 28, 29, 1847. Luigi Arditi, *My Reminiscences* (1896), 5–9. White, "Opera in New York."

6   Odell, *Annals,* 5:563–66, 575–76. *The Albion,* April 13 and May 4, 1850.

7   Odell, *Annals,* 5:563–64. White, "Opera in New York."

8   Armstrong, *Opera in Philadelphia,* 73–75.

9   Ibid., 70, 56.

Chapter 12. The Song of the Nightingale

P. T. Barnum, *Struggles and Triumphs, or Sixty Years Recollections* (Buffalo, 1872). Joan Bullman, *Jenny Lind: A Biography* (1956). Mrs. Raymond Maude, *The Life of Jenny Lind, Briefly Told by Her Daughter* (London, 1926). W. Porter Ware and Thaddeus C. Lockard, Jr., *P. T. Barnum Presents Jenny Lind: The American Tour of the Swedish Nightingale* (Baton Rouge, 1980).

1   Allan Nevins and Milton Thomas, eds., *The Diary of George Templeton Strong* (1952), 2:17–18.

2   Max Maretzek, *Crotchets and Quavers, or Revelations of an Opera Manager in America* (1855), 121–22. Barnum, *Struggles and Triumphs,* 106. Ware and Lockard, *Barnum Presents,* throughout. There were single concerts in Madison, Memphis, Natchez, Pittsburgh, Providence, Richmond, and Wheeling; two concerts apiece in Charleston, Nashville, and Washington, D.C.; three apiece in Louisville and Havana; four in Baltimore; five apiece in Cincinnati and St. Louis.

3   Maretzek, *Crotchets and Quavers,* 121–22. Barnum, *Struggles and Triumphs,* 106.

4   L. de Hegermann-Lindencrone, *In the Courts of Memory, 1858–1875* (1912), 86.

5   Louis Moreau Gottschalk, *Notes of a Pianist,* ed. J. Behren (1974), 46.

6   George P. Upton, *Musical Memories: My Recollections of Celebrities of the Half Century, 1850–1900* (Chicago, 1908), 25. Bullman, *Jenny Lind,* 67, 162.

7   Ware and Lockard, *Barnum Presents,* 4–5.

8   Ibid., 29.

9   Nevins and Thomas, *Diary,* 2:47. *New York Home Journal,* Sept. 28, 1850.

10 Ware and Lockard, *Barnum Presents,* 118.
11 Ibid., 127–28.
12 William T. Upton, *William Henry Fry: American Journalist and Composer-Critic* (1954), 116.
13 Gottschalk, *Notes of a Pianist,* 48.
14 Upton, *Musical Memories,* 19.
15 *Boston Semi-Weekly Advertiser,* Sept. 25, 1850.
16 Hegermann-Lindencrone, *In the Courts of Memory,* 65.
17 *New York Home Journal,* April 19, 1851.
18 Upton, *Musical Memories,* 24.
19 *Harper's Monthly Magazine,* May 1852, 844 and June 1852, 127. *New York Home Journal,* April 26, 1852.
20 Bullman, *Jenny Lind,* epigraph.

Chapter 13. Mario and Three Divas

Luigi Arditi, *My Reminiscences* (1896). Elizabeth Forbes, *Mario and Grisi* (London, 1985). Cecilia Maria de Candida Pearce, *The Romance of a Great Singer: A Memoir of Mario* (London, 1910). Arthur Pugin, *Marietta Alboni* (Paris, 1912). Frank Russell, *Queen of Song* (1964).

1 Max Maretzek, *Crotchets and Quavers, or Revelations of an Opera Manager in America* (1855), 65, 184. Herman Klein, *The Reign of Patti* (London, 1920), 381.
2 Pugin, *Marietta Alboni,* 28.
3 Ibid., 146–47.
4 Richard Grant White, "Opera in New York," *Century Magazine,* May 1882, 38. *New York Herald,* June 24, 1852.
5 White, "Opera in New York," 38. Walt Whitman emphasized Alboni's wide appeal: "All persons appreciated Alboni—the common crowd quite as well as the connoisseurs"—and remembered the upper tier of the Broadway Theatre on the nights of her performance, "packed full of New York young men, mechanics, 'roughs,' etc. entirely oblivious of all except Alboni" (Robert D. Faner, *Walt Whitman and Opera* [Philadelphia, 1951], 59).
6 Russell, *Queen of Song,* 97.
7 Lately Thomas, *Sam Ward: "King of the Lobby"* (Boston, 1965), 474.
8 Russell, *Queen of Song,* 235. *Dwight's Journal of Music,* April 23, 1853, 21–22.
9 *Putnam's Monthly Magazine,* January 1853, 117–18; March 1853, 348–50; May 1853, 588–91.
10 *Putnam's Monthly Magazine,* May 1853, 589. *Harper's Monthly Magazine,* November 1852, 843.
11 George C. D. Odell, *Annals of the New York Stage* (1927–1949), 6:240–42. White, "Opera in New York," 42. *Putnam's Monthly Magazine,* March 1853, 349.
12 Arditi, *My Reminiscences,* 18–20. White, "Opera in New York," 39.
13 Two American singers heard Alboni at the very end of her career. "Her contralto voice had a volume, sonority and flexibility which I have never heard since. Many of her auditors actually wept" (Minnie Hauk, *Memories of a Singer* [1925], 50). "She had a wonderful range, the most perfectly even scale possible and great finish. At well over sixty, and absolutely weighted down with fat, she had complete command of her voice and could do with it as she willed" (Emma Eames, *Some Memories and Reflections* [1927], 71–72).
14 Pugin, *Marietta Alboni,* 147. White, "Opera in New York," 38.
15 Flora Fairfield [Louisa May Alcott], "The Rival Prima Donnas," Boston *Saturday Evening Gazette,* Nov. 11, 1854.
16 Forbes, *Mario and Grisi,* 46–130.
17 *New-York Evening Post,* Aug. 21 and Sept. 5, 6, 12, and 26, 1854.
18 *New-York Evening Post,* Sept. 12, Oct. 5, and Dec. 29, 1854.

19 Ibid., Sept. 6 and 26, Oct. 5, and Dec. 29, 1854. Forbes, *Mario and Grisi,* 131–34.

20 *New-York Evening Post,* Oct. 7, 1854. *New York Morning Courier,* Oct. 4, 1854.

21 *New-York Evening Post,* Sept. 5, 1854.

Chapter 14. Boston

Michael Broyles, *The European Diary of Lowell Mason* (Ann Arbor, 1991) and *"Music of the Highest Class": Elitism and Populism in Antebellum Boston* (New Haven, 1992). Walter L. Fertig, "John Sullivan Dwight: Transcendentalist and Literary Amateur of Music" (Ph.D. diss., University of Maryland, 1952). H. Earle Johnson, *Musical Interludes in Boston, 1795–1830* (1943). John Dayton Lind, "Music in 'The Nation': 1875–1935" (Ph.D. diss., University of Montana, 1970). Joseph A. Mussulman, "Music in the Literary Magazines: 1870–1900" (Ph.D. diss., Syracuse University, 1966). Paul Eric Paige, "Musical Organizations in Boston: 1830–1850" (Ph.D. diss., Boston University, 1967). Frederick L. Ritter, *Music in America* (1883). Oscar G. Sonneck, *Early Opera in America* (1915).

1 Sonneck, *Early Opera,* 157–60.

2 Ritter, *Music in America,* 243.

3 Ibid., 252–53.

4 Ibid., 259.

5 *Dwight's Journal of Music,* Nov. 20, 1869, 138–39.

6 Fertig, "John Sullivan Dwight," 160.

7 Ibid., 162. Theodore Parker, Boston Transcendentalist minister and abolitionist, said of one of Dwight's essays on *Don Giovanni:* "To think of a man's being able to make all that out of an opera! It is more than an analytical criticism; it is a work of art!" William Foster Apthorp, "John Sullivan Dwight," in *Musicians and Music-Lovers and Other Essays* (1894), 277–86.

8 Betty E. Chmaj, "Fry versus Dwight: American Music's Debate over Nationality," *American Music* 3, no. 1 (Spring 1985), 63ff.

Chapter 15. Gardens and Academies

John Curtis, "History of Opera in Philadelphia" (unpublished typescript, Pennsylvania Historical Society). Susan Stockbridge Day, "Productions at Niblo's Garden Theatre, 1862–1868, during the Management of William Wheatley" (Ph.D. diss., University of Oregon, 1972). James V. Kavenaugh, "Three American Opera Houses: The Boston Theatre, The New York Academy of Music, The Philadelphia American Academy of Music" (Ph.D. diss., University of Delaware, 1967). Stanley T. Lewis, "The New York Theatre: Its Background and Architectural Development, 1750–1853" (Ph.D. diss., Ohio State University, 1953). John Francis Marion, *Within These Walls: A History of the Academy of Music in Philadelphia* (Philadelphia, 1984). Eugene Tompkins, *The History of the Boston Theatre, 1854–1901* (Boston, 1908). Nicholas B. Wainwright, ed., *A Philadelphia Perspective: The Diary of Sidney George Fisher, Covering the Years 1834–1871* (Philadelphia, 1967).

1 Thomas Goodwin, *Sketches and Impressions, Musical, Theatrical, and Social (1799–1885)* (1887), 275–91. Richard Grant White, "Opera in New York," *Century Magazine,* April 1882, 867. *Morning Courier and New York Enquirer,* June 13, 1829, and June 18, 1830. *New York Times,* Aug. 12, 1878.

2 Lewis, "New York Theatre," 165–88. Walt Whitman, "Plays and Operas Too," in *Specimen Days* (Boston, 1971), 10–11.

3 George C. D. Odell, *Annals of the New York Stage* (1927–1949), 5:150–53, 399.

4 White, "Opera in New York," 874. Frederic L. Ritter, *Music in America* (1883), 307–08. Odell, *Annals,* 5:50. Lewis, "New York Theatre," 312–14.

5 Max Maretzek, *Crotchets and Quavers, or Revelations of an Opera Manager in America* (1855), 14–15. White, "Opera in New York," 879–81. Lewis, "New York Theatre," 323–27.

6   Meade Minnigerode, *Fabulous Forties, 1840–1850: A Presentation of Private Life* (1924), 187–203. Richard Moody, *The Astor Place Riot* (Bloomington, Ind., 1958), 127–75. On the relationship of the riots to American theatrical and sporting culture, see John Dizikes, *Sportsmen and Gamesmen* (Boston, 1981), 214–17.

7   *New York Herald,* Nov. 28, 1844.

8   Maretzek, *Crotchets and Quavers,* 57–59.

9   Alan Nevins, ed., *The Diary of Philip Hone, 1828–1851* (enlarged ed., 1936), 837. Maretzek, *Crotchets and Quavers,* 15. White, "Opera in New York," 880.

10 *Putnam's Monthly Magazine,* July 1853, 112–13.

11 Marion, *Within These Walls,* 15, 17–18, 20, 24–27, 30, 46–47, 67. Kavenaugh, "Three American Opera Houses," 52–72. George B. Tatum, *Penn's Great Town* (Philadelphia, 1961), 94–95. Curtis, "Opera in Philadelphia," 540–41. Louis Moreau Gottschalk, *Notes of a Pianist,* ed. J. Behren (1964), 73. Wainwright, *Philadelphia Perspective,* 268.

12 Kavenaugh, "Three American Opera Houses," 24.

13 Ibid., 28–51. *Putnam's Monthly Magazine,* November 1854: 567–68.

14 *Putnam's Monthly Magazine,* June 1853: 699–700.

15 Gottschalk, *Notes of a Pianist,* 234.

Chapter 16. A Letter from Max Maretzek

Vera Brodsky Lawrence, *Strong on Music: The New York Music Scene in the Days of George Templeton Strong, 1836–1875* (1988). Laurence M. Lerner, "The Rise of the Impresario: Bernard Ullman and the Transformation of Musical Culture in Nineteenth-Century America" (Ph.D. diss., University of Wisconsin, 1970). Max Maretzek, *Crotchets and Quavers, or Revelations of an Opera Manager in America* (1855) and *Sharps and Flats* (1890).

1   Maretzek, *Crotchets and Quavers,* 11–59.

2   Ibid., 119–28.

3   *Putnam's Monthly Magazine,* April 1853, 471.

4   *New-York Evening Post,* Feb. 20 and 24, 1855. *Putnam's Monthly Magazine,* May 1855, 559.

5   *New York Herald,* May 1, 3, 7, and 8, 1855. *New-York Evening Post,* May 3, 1855. William T. Upton, *William Henry Fry: American Journalist and Composer-Critic* (1954), 269.

6   *New York Herald,* Dec. 3, 4, and 8, 1856. *New York Times,* Dec. 4, 8, 1856, and April 12, 1859.

7   *New York Times,* Dec. 4, 1856. *New York Herald,* Dec. 4, 1856. John Curtis, "History of Opera in Philadelphia" (unpublished typescript, Pennsylvania Historical Society), 1:550–51.

8   *Putnam's Monthly Magazine,* January 1857, 110–11. Louis Moreau Gottschalk, *Notes of a Pianist,* ed. J. Behren (1964), 29.

9   Clara Louise Kellogg, *Memoirs of an American Prima Donna* (1913), 36. *Dwight's Journal of Music,* Oct. 2, 1858, 234 and Feb. 23, 1861, 383–84.

10 Walt Whitman, "Beat! Beat! Drums!" Drum-Taps, *Leaves of Grass.*

11 Frederic Louis Ritter, *Music in America* (1883), 349–50, 374–75.

12 *Dwight's Journal of Music,* March 2, 1861, 387–88.

13 George C. D. Odell, *Annals of the New York Stage* (1927–1949), 8:582–83. Upton, *Fry,* 268.

14 Allan Nevins and Milton Thomas, eds., *The Diary of George Templeton Strong,* 4 vols. (1952), 3:384. Odell, *Annals,* 7:583. Fry's review appeared in *Dwight's Journal of Music,* January 1864, 171–73. Luigi Arditi, *My Reminiscences* (1896), 105–09. T. J. Walsh *Second Empire Opera: The Théâtre Lyrique, Paris, 1851–1870* (1981), 140.

15 Richard Grant White, "Opera in New York," *Century Magazine,* May 1882, 31–43.

16 *Dwight's Journal of Music,* Oct. 22, 1870, 333.

17 Maretzek, *Crotchets and Quavers,* 194, 111.

Chapter 17. Sweet Adeline

Luigi Arditi, *My Reminiscences* (1896). Herman Klein, *The Reign of Patti* (1920).
1   Klein, *Reign of Patti,* 11–13.
2   Arditi, *Reminiscences,* 70. Richard Grant White, "Opera in New York," *Century Magazine,* June 1882, 204–05.
3   George C. D. Odell, *Annals of the New York Stage* (1927–1949), 6:181–82. Klein, *Reign of Patti,* 24–25.
4   *The Albion,* May 8, 1852. Odell, *Annals,* 6:415. Robert A. Gerson, *Music in Philadelphia* (Philadelphia, 1940), 68. George P. Upton, *Musical Memories: My Recollection of Celebrities of the Half Century, 1850–1900* (Chicago, 1908), 38. Emilio J. Pasarell, "El Centenario de los conciertos de Adelina Patti y Luis Moreau Gottschalk en Puerto Rico," Revista del Instituto de Cultura Puertorriquena 2 (January–March 1959), 52–55. John Curtis, "History of Opera in Philadelphia" (unpublished typescript, Pennsylvania Historical Society), 1:474–76.
5   Upton, *Musical Memories,* 38.
6   Ibid., 39–40.
7   *New York Times,* Nov. 25, 1859. *New York Times,* Nov. 28, 1859. Clara Louise Kellogg, *Memoirs of an American Prima Donna* (1913), 15. John Francis Marion, *Within These Walls: A History of the Academy of Music in Philadelphia* (Philadelphia, 1984), 55–56. Richard Aldrich, "Adelina Patti in America," in *Musical Discourse* (1928), 242–65.
8   Aldrich, *Musical Discourse,* 243. *New York Herald,* Dec. 3, 1859.

Interlude: Walt Whitman

Gay Wilson Allen, *The Solitary Singer: A Critical Biography of Walt Whitman* (1955). Thomas Brasher, *Whitman as Editor of the "Brooklyn Eagle"* (Detroit, 1970). Robert D. Faner, *Walt Whitman and Opera* (Philadelphia, 1951). Clifton J. Furness, *Walt Whitman's Workshop* (1964). Emory Holloway, ed., *The Uncollected Poetry and Prose of Walt Whitman* (Garden City, 1921). Raymond A. Schroth, *"The Eagle" and Brooklyn: A Community Newspaper, 1841–1955* (1974). Horace Traubel, *With Walt Whitman in Camden,* 3 vols. (1906–1914). Walt Whitman, *New York Dissected: A Sheaf of Previously Undiscovered Newspaper Articles,* ed. Emory Holloway and Ralph Adimari (1936).
1   John Townsend Trowbridge, "Reminiscences of Walt Whitman," *Atlantic Monthly,* February 1902, 163–75.
2   Brasher, *Whitman as Editor,* 42.
3   Holloway, "Art-Singing and Heart-Singing," in *Uncollected Poetry and Prose,* 1:104–06.
4   Faner, *Whitman and Opera,* 43.
5   Whitman, "The Opera," *New York Dissected,* 20.
6   Faner, *Whitman and Opera,* 84.
7   "Proud Music of the Storm," Autumn Rivulets, *Leaves of Grass.*
8   "Out of the Cradle Endlessly Rocking," Sea-Drift, *Leaves of Grass.*
9   "Proud Music of the Storm."
10 Faner, *Whitman and Opera,* 65, 91.
11 "I Hear America Singing," Inscriptions, *Leaves of Grass.*
12 Faner, *Whitman and Opera,* 3. Traubel, *With Walt Whitman in Camden,* 2:173.

Act Three. Monopoly

Epigraph: Edith Wharton, *The Age of Innocence,* 3–5.

Chapter 18. Erie, Eros, and Offenbach

Rudolph Aronson, *Theatrical and Musical Memoirs* (1913). Gerald Boardman, *American Operetta, from "H.M.S. Pinafore" to "Sweeney Todd"* (1981). Alexander Faris, *Jacques Offenbach* (1980). Robert H. Fuller, *Jubilee Jim: The Life of Colonel James Fisk, Jr.* (1928). Donald R. Henry, "The American Theatre as Viewed by Nineteenth-Century British Travellers, 1860–1900" (Ph.D. diss., University of Wisconsin, 1964). Henri Kowalski, *A travers l'Amérique: Impressions d'un musicien* (Paris, 1872). Siegfried Kracauer, *Orpheus in Paris: Offenbach and the Paris of His Time* (1938). Karl Kraus, *Offenbach-Renaissance* (Vienna, 1927). Lander MacClintock, ed. and trans., *Orpheus in America: Offenbach's Diary of His Journey to the New World* (Bloomington, Ind., 1957). James Oliver Morgan, "French Comic Opera in New York, 1855–1890" (Ph.D. thesis, University of Illinois, 1959). Frederic L. Ritter, *Music in America* (1883). W. A. Swanberg, *Jim Fisk: The Career of an Improbable Rascal* (1959). Dixon Wecter, *The Saga of American Society* (1970).

1 Gore Vidal, *Lincoln* (1988), 231.
2 Ritter, *Music in America,* 352–53. Wecter, *Saga,* 108–56, 196–251.
3 Faris, *Offenbach,* 17–50. Morgan, "French Comic Opera," 38–48. William Foster Apthorp, *Musicians and Music-Lovers and Other Essays* (1894), 187. In 1881 Richard Wagner wrote to the conductor Felix Mottl: "Look at Offenbach. He writes like the divine Mozart." Faris, *Offenbach,* 27.
4 *The Spirit of the Times,* Oct. 5, 1867. *New York Herald,* Sept. 25 and Oct. 29, 1867. Boardman, *American Operetta,* 10–12.
5 *New York Times,* July 13, 1868. *The Spirit of the Times,* Jan. 29, 1870.
6 *Frank Leslie's Illustrated Weekly,* Oct. 26, 1867: 83. *New York Tribune,* March 27, 1868. *The Spirit of the Times,* Oct. 24, 1868. *Dwight's Journal of Music,* Jan. 18, 1868, 174–75; May 23, 247–48; Aug. 1, 288; Sept. 12, 308–09; Sept. 26, 317–18; Nov. 7, 346; and Feb. 13, 1869, 399. Ritter, *Music in America,* 353. Morgan, "French Comic Opera" has many such quotations.
7 Swanberg, *Jim Fisk,* 11–21, 22–27, 122–41. See also Clifford Browder, *The Money Game in Old New York: Daniel Drew and His Times* (1986).
8 Swanberg, *Jim Fisk,* 184–85.
9 Ibid., 170–71.
10 MacClintock, *Orpheus in America,* 35, 129. This is the most recent version of Offenbach's diary, *Notes d'un musicien en voyage.*
11 Faris, *Offenbach,* 174–82.
12 MacClintock, *Orpheus in America,* 69–73.
13 Morgan, "French Comic Opera," chap. 7.
14 Russell B. Nye, *The Unembarrassed Muse: The Popular Arts in America* (1970), 1–7. William L. Crosten, *French Grand Opera: An Art and a Business* (1948), 1–7, 70–132.

Chapter 19. Gilbert and Sullivan

Rudolph Aronson, *Theatrical and Musical Memoirs* (1913). Gerald Boardman, *American Operetta: From "H.M.S. Pinafore" to "Sweeney Todd"* (1981). Arthur Jacobs, *Arthur Sullivan: A Victorian Musician* (1984). John Bush Jones, ed., *W. S. Gilbert: A Century of Scholarship and Commentary* (1970). Hesketh Pearson, *Gilbert and Sullivan: A Biography* (London, 1935). Cecil Smith, *Musical Comedy in America* (1950).

1 Pearson, *Gilbert and Sullivan,* 17–44, 58–89.
2 Jacobs, *Sullivan,* 1–74. *New York Times,* Nov. 17, 1875.
3 Jacobs, *Sullivan,* 125–33. George P. Upton, *Musical Memories: My Recollections of the Half Century, 1850–1900* (Chicago, 1908), 148–50. *New York Times,* Jan. 16, 1879, and Jan. 1, 1880. *Harper's New Monthly Magazine,* November 1879, 947. *San Francisco Chronicle,* May 21, 1978. One American paper commented ruefully: "At present there are forty-two companies playing *Pinafore* about the

country. Companies formed after six p.m. yesterday are not included." Pearson, *Gilbert and Sullivan*, 115. Boardman, *American Operetta*, 25.

4   Boardman, *American Operetta*, 36. Oscar Wilde went to a performance of *Patience* in New York in which the actor who played Bunthorne was made up to resemble him. This led Wilde to comment: "This is one of the compliments that mediocrity pays to those who are not mediocre." Richard Ellmann, *Oscar Wilde* (1987), 160–61.

5   Aronson, *Memoirs*, 99.

6   Isaac Goldberg, ed., *New and Original Extravaganzas* (Boston, 1931), xvii.

7   *Harper's New Monthly Magazine*, May 1879, 932–33.

8   *Harper's New Monthly Magazine*, April 1879, 777–79.

9   Pearson, *Gilbert and Sullivan*, 114.

10   Boardman, *American Operetta*, 46–50.

11   Aronson, *Memoirs*, 111–12. Boardman, *American Operetta*, 29–31.

12   Boardman, *American Operetta*, 23.

13   Cecil Smith, *Musical Comedy*, 87–88.

14   All quotations in this section are from James D. Hart, *The Popular Book: A History of America's Literary Taste* (1950), 180–200.

Chapter 20. The Building of the Metropolitan Opera House

John Briggs, *Requiem for a Yellow Brick Brewery* (Boston, 1969). John Frederick Cone, *First Rival of the Metropolitan Opera* (1983). Paul E. Eisler, *The Metropolitan Opera: The First Twenty-five Years, 1883–1908* (1984). Irving Kolodin, *The Story of the Metropolitan Opera, 1883–1950* (1953). James H. Mapleson, *The Mapleson Memoirs, 1848–1888,* 2 vols. (London, 1888). Martin Mayer, *The Met* (1982). Dixon Wecter, *The Saga of American Society* (1970).

1   Lilli Lehmann, *My Path through Life* (1914), 340.

2   Cone, *First Rival*, 1–22.

3   Eisler, *Metropolitan Opera*, 1–12. Briggs, *Requiem*, 3–10. Kolodin, *Story of the Metropolitan*, 3–5.

4   Briggs, *Requiem*, 11–17. Eisler, *Metropolitan Opera*, 12–19. Kolodin, *Story of the Metropolitan*, 5–6. Louis de Coppet Bergh, Cady's chief assistant, came from a musical family and had studied architecture in Stuttgart. His sister, a musician, had studied in Italy and provided her brother with pictures of European opera houses and also gave him suggestions about the antechambers to the boxes, patterned after those at La Scala. Eisler, *Metropolitan Opera*, 17.

5   Mapleson, *Memoirs*, 2:10–13. Cone, *First Rival*, 23–31. Kolodin, *Story of the Metropolitan*, 6–8. Briggs, *Requiem*, 21–30. Eisler, *Metropolitan Opera*, 21–43. *New York Times*, Oct. 13, 14, 15, 1883.

6   Cone, *First Rival*, 40–53. Briggs, *Requiem*, 30–32. Eisler, *Metropolitan Opera*, 43–53. John Rosselli, *The Opera Industry in Italy from Cimarosa to Verdi: The Role of the Impresario* (Cambridge, 1984), 77–79. *New York Times*, Feb. 16, 1884.

7   *New York Times*, Feb. 14, 16, 1884.

8   Eisler, *Metropolitan Opera*, 58.

9   *New York Times*, Feb. 16, 1884.

10   Eisler, *Metropolitan Opera*, 57, 60–64.

Chapter 21. The Queen of Song

H. Sutherland Edwards, *The Prima Donna* (London, 1888). Herman Klein, *The Reign of Patti* (London, 1920). James H. Mapleson, *The Mapleson Memoirs, 1848–1888* (London, 1888).

1   George P. Upton, *Musical Memories: My Recollections of Celebrities of the Half Century, 1850–1900* (Chicago, 1908), 38.

2   Klein, *Reign of Patti,* 64.

3   Edwards, *Prima Donna,* 2:104.

4   "No Gilda of recent years has dulled our keen remembrance of Bosio. . . . For the first time she has now been efficiently replaced. Mme. Patti's singing was simply faultless; and the reedy quality of her voice renders it still more susceptible of expression than that of Bosio." *Dwight's Journal of Music,* Aug. 14, 1869, 85; repr. from *The Atheneum* (London), July 24, 1869.

5   Luigi Arditi, *My Reminiscences* (1896), 243–45. Edwards, *Prima Donna,* 2:92–93. Klein, *Reign of Patti,* 208.

6   Mapleson, *Memoirs,* 2:50–69. Henry E. Krehbiel, *Chapters of Opera* (1908), 72–74.

7   Edwards, *Prima Donna,* 2:87.

8   *New York Times,* Feb. 28 and March 3, 1881.

9   Mapleson, *Memoirs,* 2:1–7. In Boston, *Semiramide,* with Sofia Scalchi, was "exceptionally brilliant," and drew the largest receipts in the city's operatic history, $12,000. Years later, a historian of the New York theater remembered *Semiramide* as "an ineffaceable joy. . . . The memory of it is a benediction . . . the most exquisite singing ever heard by any person now living." George C. D. Odell, *Annals of the New York Stage* (1927–1949), 5:132.

10 John Frederick Cone, *First Rival of the Metropolitan Opera* (1983), 23–39, 40–50. Consuelo Vanderbilt Balsan, *The Glitter and the Gold* (1952), 12.

11 Mapleson, *Memoirs,* 2:23–24.

12 Clara Louise Kellogg, *Memoirs of an American Prima Donna* (1913), 130.

13 Herbert Weinstock, *Rossini* (1968), 276–77.

14 George Bernard Shaw, *Shaw's Music* (1981), ed. Dan H. Laurence, 3:222–24.

15 Giulio Gatti-Casazza, *Memories of Opera* (1940), 194–95. Vincent Sheean, *Orpheus at Eighty* (1958), 3, 331. Verdi, asked to name his three favorite prima donnas, replied: "First, Adelina; second, Adelina; third, Adelina!" Klein, *Reign of Patti,* 379. Eduard Hanslick, the leading Viennese critic of the last half of the nineteenth century: "In Adelina Patti I have learned to know a musical organization perfect beyond all others—I may, indeed, say: a musical genius." Hanslick, *Vienna's Golden Years of Music, 1850–1900,* edited and translated by Henry Pleasants (1950), 188.

16 Klein, *Reign of Patti,* 373.

Chapter 22. Leopold Damrosch and the Triumph of Wagner

John Briggs, *Requiem for a Yellow Brick Brewery* (Boston, 1969). Paul E. Eisler, *The Metropolitan Opera: The First Twenty-five Years, 1883–1908* (1984). H. Earle Johnson, *First Performances* (Detroit, 1979). Irving Kolodin, *The Story of the Metropolitan Opera, 1883–1950* (1953). Henry Edward Krehbiel, *Chapters of Opera* (1908). David C. Large and William Weber, eds., *Wagnerism in European Culture and Politics* (Ithaca, 1984). Fritz A. H. Leuchs, *The Early German Theatre in New York, 1840–1872* (1928). George C. D. Odell, *Annals of the New York Stage* (1927–1949). Frederic L. Ritter, *Music in America* (1883). L. R. Walz, "Opera in Cincinnati: The Years before the Zoo, 1801–1920" (Ph.D. diss., University of Cincinnati, 1983).

1   Leuchs, *Early German Theatre,* 18. See also Maurer Maurer, "The Professor of Music in Colonial America," *Musical Quarterly* 36 (1950), 520.

2   Odell, *Annals,* 4:393–96. Albert Bernhardt Faust, *The German Element in the United States,* 2 vols. (1927), 2:82. In 1846 a New Yorker of German descent wrote to a Leipzig musical paper describing the current state of American musical affairs. "A German opera, but a German one only would be very sure to keep its own here, but neither a French nor an Italian one, especially since the American people prefer German music to the French and Italian tinkling sounds. If five or six able male singers, and several pretty and agreeable female singers, led by an efficient conductor, were to come over, they would, no doubt, win success. To be sure, there must be nothing objectionable as to their

character, otherwise the Germans would desert them, and they would then be ruined." Ritter, *Music in America,* 278–79.

3 Louis Moreau Gottschalk, *Notes of a Pianist,* ed. J. Behren (1964), 127. In 1842, the first year of the New York Philharmonic's existence, 42 percent of its personnel was German. This rose to 79 percent by 1855, 97 percent by 1892. Every conductor of the Philharmonic from 1852 to 1902 was German or Austrian by birth and training.

4 George P. Upton, *William Henry Fry* (1954), 264. Odell, *Annals,* 7:516–17.

5 H. E. Johnson, "The Germania Musical Society," *Musical Quarterly* 39 (1953), 75.

6 Beethoven's first and second symphonies, first performed in New York and in Boston in the 1820s, reached St. Louis and Chicago in the 1840s and 1850s. His third, fifth, and sixth symphonies, introduced in eastern cities in the 1840s, reached the Middle West in the 1850s and 1860s. Even after first complete performances, however, it was still common for single movements to be given on programs. Beethoven's Ninth Symphony, first performed in New York in 1846 and in Boston in 1853, was first given as a complete work in Chicago in 1870, in Philadelphia in 1874, in Milwaukee in 1878, in Pittsburgh in 1889.

7 *Dwight's Journal of Music,* May 21, 1870: 246–47. Thomas Goodwin, *Sketches and Impressions, Musical, Theatrical, and Social (1799–1885)* (1887), 199. "It is the historian's business to put forth the claims of the real originator of modern music in New York; and Bergmann labored notably in that direction. He, however, is already forgotten by those who have gained most by his plucky labors, done at a time when comparatively few of the New York musical public were able to appreciate their importance." Ritter, *Music in America,* 464–65.

8 Johnson, *First Performances,* 376. *The New-York Albion,* April 22, 1855. Ritter, *Music in America,* 375.

9 *Putnam's Magazine,* June 1853, 699–700.

10 Bryan Magee, *Aspects of Wagner* (1978), 14.

11 *Harper's New Monthly Magazine,* October 1873, 774.

12 Theodore Thomas, *A Musical Autobiography* (1905), ed. George P. Upton (1964), 3. *Harper's New Monthly Magazine,* July 1882, 306–08 and May 1883, 954–55.

13 *Dwight's Journal of Music,* Dec. 14, 1872, 351.

14 Leopold Damrosch, in his four reports (Aug. 13, 18, 19, and 23, 1876), conveyed the excitement of the time and place. "Envy, malice, and ignorance must give way before so mighty a creation. . . . It is a pleasant thing to see the great master, who has conquered the world, still restlessly at work, and by no means the smallest testimonial of his greatness is the unanimous goal of all the executants to execute worthily their share of the duty." *New York Sun,* Aug. 18, 1876. Walter Damrosch, *My Musical Life* (1923), 13–15.

15 Ritter, *Music in America,* 370–71. *New York Times,* Aug. 17 and Nov. 18, 20, 25, 27, 1884; Jan. 8, 18, 24, 25, 29, 1885. Eisler, *Metropolitan Opera,* 80–89.

16 *New York Times,* Jan. 29 and 31, 1885.

17 *New York Times,* Feb. 16 and 18, 1885. John F. Cone, *First Rival of the Metropolitan Opera* (1983), 147–51.

18 *New York Times,* Jan. 5 and Dec. 2, 1886; Nov. 10, 1887; Jan. 26, 1888. *New York Tribune,* Jan. 5 and Nov. 10, 1886. Henry Adams, *The Education of Henry Adams* (Boston), 404–5. Sidney Homer, *My Wife and I* (1939), 25–26.

19 Kolodin, *Story of the Metropolitan,* 100–101. Briggs, *Requiem,* 36–37.

20 *New York Times,* Feb. 2, 1890. Kolodin, *Story of the Metropolitan,* 56.

21 *New York Times,* Jan. 10, 1891. Kolodin, *Story of the Metropolitan,* 112–16. Eisler, *Metropolitan Opera,* 147, 149–50, 160–63. H. Krehbiel, *Chapters of Opera* (1908), 206–7.

22 "And now, with the supremacy of Bismarck on the one hand and Wagnerism on the other, with men's ideals all reversed, dawns the critical moment for music." *Autobiography of Anton Rubinstein* (Boston, 1890), 119–20. "It would be presumptuous to call ourselves as yet a musical people, in the full sense,

for instance, that the Germans are, or that the Italians were." *Dwight's Journal of Music,* Nov. 9, 1867, 135.

23 William James Homer and Lloyd Goodrich, *Albert Pinkham Ryder: Painter of Dreams* (1989), 162.

Chapter 23. Chicago

Ronald L. Davis, *Opera in Chicago* (1966). Emmett Dedmon, *Fabulous Chicago* (rev. ed., 1981). Karleton Hackett, *The Beginning of Grand Opera in Chicago, 1850–1859* (Chicago, 1913). Edward C. Moore, *Forty Years of Opera in Chicago* (1930). Bessie Louise Pierce, *A History of Chicago* (1947), vol. 3, *The Rise of the Modern City, 1871–1893.* Louis Sullivan, *Autobiography of an Idea* (1924). George P. Upton, *Musical Memories: My Recollections of Celebrities of the Half Century, 1850–1900* (Chicago, 1908). Edward Wagenknecht, *Chicago* (1954).

1 Hackett, *Beginning of Grand Opera,* 1–23. Thomas J. Riley, *A Study of the higher Life of Chicago* (Chicago, 1905), 103. Upton, *Musical Memories,* 225–30. Davis, *Opera in Chicago,* 17–31. When his theater caught fire, Rice stepped to the front of the stage and shouted, "Sit Down! Sit Down! Do you think I would permit a fire to occur in my theater?" Dedmon, *Fabulous Chicago,* 86–87.

2 McAllister quoted in John Szarkowski, *The Idea of Louis Sullivan* (Minneapolis, 1956), 42.

3 Wagenknecht, *Chicago,* 129. Dedmon, *Fabulous Chicago,* 93–94.

4 Paul Bourget, *Outre-mer: Impressions of America* (1896), 117–18. Chicago looked to Paris for its clothes, furniture, art. "In Chicago we don't buy Renoirs. We inherit them from our grandmothers." Aline Saarinen, *The Proud Possessors: The Lives, Times and Tastes of Some Adventurous American Art Collectors* (1958), 13–21.

5 *Chicago Tribune,* March 1, 2, 6, 8, 11, 13, 15, 1885.

6 Ibid., March 29, 30, April 4, 5, 6, 7, 8, 9, 10, 11, 12, 14, 15, 16, 17, 18, 19, 1885.

7 Ibid., April 19, 1885.

8 On Sullivan and Adler: William Connely, *Louis Sullivan as He Lived: The Shaping of American Architecture* (1960). William H. Jordy, *American Buildings and Their Architects* (1972), vol. 4, *Progressive and Academic Ideals at the Turn of the Twentieth Century.* David Lowe, *Lost Chicago* (1975). Hugh Morrison, *Louis Sullivan: Prophet of Modern Architecture* (1935). Sherman Paul, *Louis Sullivan: An Architect in American Thought* (1962). Szarkowski, *Louis Sullivan.* Robert Twombly, *Louis Sullivan: His Life and Work* (1986). John Zukowsky, ed., *Chicago Architecture, 1871–1922: Birth of a Metropolis* (Munich, 1987).

9 Morrison, *Sullivan,* 23–51. Connely, *Sullivan as He Lived,* 23–79. Twombly, *Sullivan,* 1–102, 163–68, 172–73. Sullivan insisted that Ferdinand Peck named it the Auditorium Building—"nobody knows just why. Anyway it sounded better than 'Grand Opera House.'" Sullivan, *Autobiography,* 293–94.

10 *Chicago Daily Inter-Ocean,* Sept. 10, 1889. Twombly, *Sullivan,* 193–94.

11 Moore, *Forty Years of Opera,* 62–63. Morrison, *Sullivan,* 108–9. Connely, *Sullivan as He Lived,* 121–22. *Chicago Tribune,* Dec. 10, 11, 12, 1889.

12 Jordy, *Progressive and Academic,* 162–63. Paul, *Louis Sullivan,* 1–3. Twombly, *Sullivan,* 193–94. Sullivan, *Autobiography,* 292–94.

13 Connely, *Sullivan as He Lived,* 128–31. Jordy, *Progressive and Academic,* 160–64. Sullivan, *Autobiography,* 208–09.

Chapter 24. On Tour

L. W. Connolly, ed., *Theatrical Touring and Founding in North America* (Westport, Conn., 1982). Quaintance Eaton, *Opera Caravan: Adventures of the Metropolitan on Tour, 1883–1956* (1957). Alice Henson Ernst, *Trouping in the Oregon Country: A History of Frontier Theatre* (Portland, 1961). Louis

Moreau Gottschalk, *Notes of a Pianist,* ed. J. Behren (1964). W. Stanley Hoole, *The Ante-Belleum Charleston Theatre* (University of Alabama Press, 1966). Clara Louise Kellogg, *Memoirs of an American Prima Donna* (1913). James H. Mapleson, *The Mapleson Memoirs, 1848–1888* (London, 1888). Sadie E. Martin, *The Life and Professional Career of Emma Abbott* (Minneapolis, 1891).

1 Gottschalk, *Notes of a Pianist,* 251.
2 *New York Herald,* Dec. 3, 1856.
3 Gottschalk, *Notes of a Pianist,* 251. Vincent Sheean, *First and Last Love* (1956), 32–33.
4 Sidney Homer, *My Wife and I* (1939), 146.
5 Bruce Carl Jacobsen, "A Historical Study of the Bozeman, Montana, Opera House" (Ph.D. diss., University of Minnesota, 1969), 50.
6 Gottschalk, *Notes of a Pianist,* 231. Sol Smith, *Theatrical Management in the West and South for Thirty Years* (1868), 238.
7 *New York Times,* May 3, 1855.
8 All quotations in this section are from Hoole, *Ante-Bellum Charleston,* 3–50.
9 Clara Louise Kellogg, *Memoirs,* 227, 234, 254–75.
10 *The Spirit of the Times,* June 8, 1872.
11 All quotations in this section, unless otherwise noted, are from Martin, *Emma Abbot.*
12 The disparaging remarks, written under the name J. Travis Quigg, appeared in the *American Musician.* Quoted by Martin, *Emma Abbot,* 171.
13 Martin, *Emma Abbot,* 119.

Chapter 25. Local Glories

I wish to thank the fifty state historical societies for responding so very helpfully to my letter of inquiry about opera houses. I have also depended a good deal on the National Register of Historic Places Inventory, especially the nomination forms.

Byrne D. Blackwood, "The Theatres of J. B. McElfratrick and Sons, Architects, 1885–1922" (Ph.D. diss., University of Kansas, 1966). Ned Donahoe, "Theatres in Central Illinois, 1850–1900" (Ph.D. diss., University of Illinois, 1953). Benjamin P. Draper, "Colorado Theatres, 1859–1969" (Ph.D. diss., University of Denver, 1969). Jesse W. Gern, "Colorado Mountain Theatre: History of Theatre at Central City, 1859–1885" (Ph.D. diss., Ohio State University, 1960). Shirley M. Harrison, "The Grand Opera House (Third Varieties Theatre) of New Orleans, Louisiana, 1871–1906: A History and Analysis" (Ph.D. diss., Louisiana State University, 1965). Sadie F. E. Head, "A Historical Study of the Tulane and Crescent Theatres of New Orleans, Louisiana, 1897–1937" (Ph.D. diss., Louisiana State University, 1963). Jerry Henderson, "A History of the Ryman Auditorium in Nashville, Tennessee: 1891–1920" (Ph.D. diss., Louisiana State University, 1962). Grant M. Herbstruth, "Benedict Debar and the Grand Opera House in St. Louis, Missouri, from 1855 to 1879" (Ph.D. diss., Iowa State University, 1954). William E. Hezlep, "A History of the Detroit Opera House, 1898–1931" (Ph.D. diss., Wayne State University, 1973). Bruce Jacobsen, "A Historical Study of the Bozeman, Montana, Opera House" (Ph.D. diss., University of Minnesota, 1969). Richard K. Knaub, "The History of English's Opera House and the English Theatre [Indianapolis]" (Ph.D. diss., Indiana University, 1962). William C. Miller, "An Historical Study of Theatrical Entertainment in Virginia City, Nevada, or Bonanza and Borasca Theatres on the Comstock (1860–1875)" (Ph.D. diss., University of Southern California, 1947). Donald T. Shanower, "A Comparative and Descriptive Study of Three Opera Houses in Southern Michigan, 1880–1900" (Ph.D. diss., University of Michigan, 1959). Richard M. Tutor, "A History of the Detroit Opera House, 1869–1897" (Ph.D. diss., Wayne State University, 1972).

1 Edward N. Waters, *Victor Herbert: A Life in Music* (1955), 203. Theodore Dreiser, *The "Genius"* (1915).

2 Centennial Historical Committee, *Cheyenne: The Magic City of the Plains* (1967), 88–90.

3 National Register of Historic Places Inventory, Nomination Form, Bismarck, North Dakota.

4 National Register of Historic Places Inventory, Nomination Form, Rushville, Illinois. Also Jerrilee Cain-Tyson, *Illinois Opera House: A Time of Glory* (Western Illinois University, n.d.). *Mobile Daily Register,* Dec. 19, 1890.

5 "Finnish Hall and Opera House," Red Lodge, Mon., Inventory Form, Montana Historical Society. National Register of Historic Place Inventory, Nomination Form, Rockford, Ill. Jack Chen, "American Chinese Opera, Chinese American Reality," *East Wind,* Spring–Summer 1986, 15–16.

6 Madison, Dakota, *Leader,* Oct. 10 and 22, 1969. National Register of Historic Places Inventory, Nomination Form, Galva, Ill.

7 *Mobile Daily Register,* Dec. 19, 1890. Bruce E. Mahan, "At the Opera House," *The Palimpsest* 5, no. 11 (November 1924), 408–23. Edith Harper Ekdale, "The Grand Opera House" (Burlington, Iowa), *The Palimpsest* 28, no. 6 (June 1947), 184–92. "An Iowa County Seat," *The Iowa Journal of History and Politics,* October 1940, 346–55.

8 Toni Young, *The Grand Experience: A History of the Grand Opera House* (Wilmington, Del., 1976). Virginia E. Lewis, *Russell Smith: Romantic Realist* (Pittsburgh, 1956), 1–20.

9 *Harper's New Monthly Magazine,* November 1867, 804–05. Kentucky Historical Society information sheets, 54, 64–65. *Daily Corinthian* (Mississippi), Dec. 15, 1971.

10 *Wisconsin State Gazetteer,* 1888–1889, 1891–1892, 1901–1902, 1911–1912. Kevin L. Graves and Robert L. Seymour, "A Study of Ten Existing Opera Houses in the State of Kansas," manuscript, May 1973, Kansas State Historical Society.

11 *Santa Cruz Sentinel,* Dec. 2, 1984.

12 Jacobsen, "Bozeman Opera House," 119–20. John S. McCornick, *Salt Lake City: The Gathering Place* (Woodland Hills, Calif., 1980), 28–29.

13 All quotations in this section are taken from Gern, "Colorado Mountain Theatre," 1:147–61.

14 Kenneth Clark, *Civilization: A Personal View* (1969), 242. Louis Moreau Gottschalk, *Notes of a Pianist,* ed. J. Behren (1964), 31.

15 Willa Cather, *The Troll Garden* (1904; rept. 1981), 49.

16 Willa Cather, *The Song of the Lark* (1915). All quotations are from the revised shortened version done by Cather in 1932. See also E. K. Brown, *Willa Cather: A Critical Biography* (1953). Cather modeled Thea Kronborg on the great Norwegian-American Wagnerian soprano Olive Fremstad (1871–1951). On Fremstad, see Mary W. Cushing, *The Rainbow Bridge* (1954).

17 Mildred R. Bennett, *The World of Willa Cather* (1951), 152–53.

Chapter 26. End of the Century

On the Metropolitan Opera: Eugene Bonner, *The Club in the Opera House: The Story of the Metropolitan Opera Club* (Princeton, 1949). John Briggs, *Requiem for a Yellow Brick Brewery* (Boston, 1969). Paul Eisler, *The Metropolitan Opera: The First Twenty-five Years* (1984). John Hetherington, *Melba* (1967). Henry James, *The American Scene* (1907). Irving Kolodin, *The Story of the Metropolitan Opera, 1883–1950* (1953). Clara Leiser, *Jean de Reszke and the Great Days of Opera* (1934). Martin Mayer, *The Met* (1982). Dixon Wecter, *The Saga of American Society* (1970). John K. Winkler, *Morgan the Magnificent* (1930).

On the French Opera House: Joseph Gabriel de Baroncelli-Javon, *Opéra Français de la Nouvelle-Orléans: Souvenir Album, Saison 1913–1914* (New Orleans, 1914). Ronald L. Davis, *A History of Opera in the American West* (Englewood Cliffs, 1965). Joy J. Jackson, *New Orleans in the Gilded Age: Politics and Urban Progress, 1880–1896* (Baton Rouge, 1969). John S. Kendall, *The Golden Age of the New Orleans Theater* (Baton Rouge, 1952). Grace King, *New Orleans: The Place and the People* (1895, repr. 1968). Harry Brunswick Loeb, *The Opera in New Orleans: A Historical Sketch from the Earliest*

Days through Season 1914–1915, Publications of the Louisiana Historical Society, vol. 9 (1917). Robert Tallant, *The Romantic New Orleanians* (1950).

1 Stephen Steinberg, archivist, San Francisco War Memorial Opera House exhibit "Music-Mad San Francisco: The Tivoli Opera House, 1875–1913" (1986), press release. Also *San Francisco Examiner,* "Review," Oct. 12, 1986.

2 San Francisco Archives for the Performing Arts, annual programs in "Tivoli" file folder. *San Francisco Examiner,* Oct. 19, 26, 1924. The young Gertrude Stein, living in Oakland in the 1880s, learned about opera at the Tivoli. "The next thing was the opera the twenty-five cent opera of San Francisco. . . . As a matter of fact I gradually saw more of the opera because I saw it quite frequently." Gertrude Stein, *Lectures in America* (Boston, 1935), 113.

3 Kolodin, *Story of the Metropolitan,* 58.

4 Ibid., 59.

5 As quoted in ibid., 60.

6 *American Mercury,* December 1932, 508, 510. Walter Damrosch, *My Musical Life* (1923), 94–95.

7 Bonner, *Club,* 12–13.

8 Elizabeth Drexel Lehr, *"King Lehr" and the Gilded Age* (London, 1935), 139. Kolodin, *Story of the Metropolitan,* 24. Harvey O'Connor, *The Astors* (1941), 198–200.

9 Bonner, *Club,* 30–35, 52.

10 Kolodin, *Story of the Metropolitan,* 130.

11 Ibid., 140–41. *New York Times,* April 28, 1894, and Feb. 22, 1896.

12 Kolodin, *Story of the Metropolitan,* 151.

13 Ibid., 146.

14 David Bispham, *A Quaker Singer's Recollections* (1920), 245.

15 Wecter, *Saga,* xiv–xv. *American Mercury,* December 1932, 510.

16 Briggs, *Requiem,* 8.

17 Kolodin, *Story of the Metropolitan,* 68.

18 Edward N. Waters, *Victor Herbert: A Life in Music* (1955), 10.

19 Henry James, *The American Scene* (1907), 164–65.

20 J. H. Plumb, *The First Four Georges* (London, 1966), 34–36. Sidney Homer, *My Wife and I* (1939), 116.

21 Eisler, *Metropolitan Opera,* 310.

22 *New Orleans Daily Picayune,* Feb. 27, 1854.

23 Tallant, *Romantic New Orleanians,* 211–12.

24 On Paul Morphy, see John Dizikes, *Sportsmen and Gamesmen* (Boston, 1981), 159–91.

25 Edward C. Moore, *Forty Years of Opera in Chicago* (1930), 36.

26 Jackson, *New Orleans in the Gilded Age,* 258–82. Loeb, *Opera in New Orleans,* 11–13.

27 Tallant, *Romantic New Orleanians,* 308.

Interlude: Lillian Nordica

1 Clara Louise Kellogg, *Memoirs of an American Prima Donna* (1913), 11.

2 Ira Glackens, *Yankee Diva: Lillian Nordica and The Golden Days of Opera* (1963). All quotations are from this book unless otherwise indicated.

3 Irving Kolodin, *The Story of the Metropolitan Opera, 1883–1950* (1953), 91.

4 George Bernard Shaw, *Shaw's Music,* ed. Dan H. Laurence (1981), 3:274–77, 282–83.

5 H. T. Parker, *Boston Evening Transcript,* Nov. 9, 1909. Of a performance of *Faust,* in which Nordica sang, age 52, Parker wrote: "She has if anything, ripened in imagination, in consequent penetration of her characters and grasp upon them. What she learned from her experience with Wagner's personages, she has now applied to others." *Boston Evening Transcript,* Dec. 6, 1910.

6 Ibid., May 1, 5, 10, 11, 1913.

Act Four. Modernism

Epigraphs: Friedrich Nietzsche, *The Case of Wagner,* trans. Walter Kaufmann (1967), 156. Claude Debussy, *Debussy on Music,* edited by François Lesure, translated by Richard Langham-Smith (1977), 74.

Chapter 27. The Wagnerian Aftermath

Some late nineteenth- and early twentieth-century American books on musical modernism: Arthur Elson, *Modern Composers of Europe* (1905); *A Critical History of Opera* (1901). Henry T. Finck, *Wagner and His Works* (1893); *Massenet and His Operas* (1910); *Richard Strauss: The Man and His Works* (Boston, 1917). Lawrence Gilman, *Phases of Modern Music* (1904); *Debussy's "Pelléas et Mélisande": A Guide to the Opera* (1907); *Edward MacDowell: A Study* (1909); *Aspects of Modern Opera* (1908); *Nature in Music and Other Studies in the Tone Poetry of Today* (1914); *Wagner's Operas* (1937). William J. Henderson, *Preludes and Studies: Musical Themes of the Day* (1892); *Richard Wagner: His Life and Dramas* (1901); *The Art of the Singer* (1906). James G. Huneker, *Bedouins* (1920); *Franz Liszt* (1911); *Melomaniacs* (1920); *Mezzotints in Modern Music* (1912); *Overtones* (1909); *Unicorns* (1917); *Variations* (1922).

1 Gilman, *Aspects of Modern Opera,* 3–30. Norman Del Mar, *Richard Strauss: A Critical Commentary on His Life and Works,* vol. 1 (1962), 118. Mosco Carner, *Puccini: A Critical Biography* (1959), 159.

2 *Boston Evening Transcript,* Jan. 1, 1912. Parker continued, "It is time to revive *The Flying Dutchman* in America, for a whole operatic generation knows it not."

3 Edward Maiserl, *Charles T. Griffes,* rev. ed. (1984), 49. Gilbert Chase, *America's Music: From the Pilgrims to the Present,* 3d ed. (Urbana, 1987), 379.

4 Elise K. Kirk, *Music at the White House* (Urbana, 1986), 176. Nietzsche is quoted in Carl E. Schorske, "The Quest for the Grail: Wagner and Morris," in Kurt H. Wolff and Barrington Moore, Jr., *The Critical Spirit* (Boston, 1967), 216–32. George Bernard Shaw, *Shaw's Music* (1981), 2:300. Henry Adams, *The Education of Henry Adams* (Boston, 1918), 404–06. Mark Twain, "At the Shrine of St. Wagner," in Charles Neider, ed., *The Complete Essays of Mark Twain* (1963), 59–70.

    An estimate of Wagner's music by Charles Ives: "Wagner seems less and less to measure up to the substance and reality of Cesar Franck, Brahms, d'Indy, or even Elgar (with all his tiresomeness); the wholesomeness, manliness, humility and deep spiritual, possibly religious, feeling of these men seems missing." Ives remembered his father returning from a performance of *Siegfried* and saying with a look of surprise that "somehow or other he felt ashamed of enjoying the music as he did for beneath it all he was conscious of an undercurrent of make-believe—the bravery was make-believe, the love was make-believe, the passion, the virtue, all make-believe." When Charles was 25, he listened to Wagner with enthusiasm, but by the time he was middle-aged "this music had become cloying, the melodies threadbare—a sense of something commonplace, yes, of make-believe came." Henry and Sidney Cowell, *Charles Ives and His Music* (1955), 87–88.

5 *New York Times,* May 17, 1898.

6 Finck, *Richard Strauss,* 38, 52–53, 62. *Musical America,* Feb. 5, 1910: 1.

7 Edward L. Bernays, *Biography of an Idea: Memoirs of Public Relations Counsel Edward L. Bernays* (1965), 107, 128. Mary Garden and Louis Biancoli, *Mary Garden's Story* (1951), 216–17. George Marek, *Puccini* (1951), 169. *New York Times,* Feb. 5, 1901; Oct. 17, 1902; Nov. 13, 1906.

8 Irving Kolodin, *The Story of the Metropolitan Opera, 1883–1950* (1953), 211–14. Edward C. Moore, *Forty Years of Opera in Chicago* (1930), 82.

9 Garden, *Mary Garden's Story,* 215. Moore, *Forty Years,* 82.

10 *Boston Evening Transcript,* March 29, 1910.

11 Gilman, *Aspects of Modern Opera,* 143–44.

12 *New York Times,* May 17, 1898. Also: Dec. 27, 1900.

13 Gilman, *Aspects of Modern Opera,* 45–48.

14 Ibid., 41–45.

15 On Farrar's Violetta compared with Frieda Hempel's, see the *Boston Evening Transcript,* Dec. 2, 1909, and March 1, 1913. As Basilio, Chaliapin spat on the floor and wore a dirty cassock, which he used to wipe his nose. In Boito's *Mefistofele,* Chaliapin appeared nude from the waist up. For his unhappiness with American audiences, see Chaliapin's autobiography *Man and Mask* (London, 1932) and Victor Borovsky, *Chaliapin: A Critical Biography* (1988).

16 Kolodin, *Story of the Metropolitan,* 278. *New York Times,* Dec. 3, 1912.

17 Even *Lucia* barely survived. "The simple truth is that public taste has outgrown the *Lucia* sort of opera. There is no dramatic vitality in the music and the public has come to demand such life as a prime necessity in an operatic score." *New York Times,* April 27, 1894.

Chapter 28. Oscar and Goliath

John Frederick Cone, *Oscar Hammerstein's Manhattan Opera Company* (Norman, Okla., 1966). John Curtis, "A History of Opera in Philadelphia" (unpublished typescript, Pennsylvania Historical Society). Henry Edward Krehbiel, *Chapters of Opera* (1908). Vincent Sheean, *Oscar Hammerstein I: The Life and Exploits of an Impresario* (1956).

1 Sheean, *Oscar Hammerstein,* 3–47.

2 Cone, *Manhattan Opera Company,* 10.

3 Sheean, *Oscar Hammerstein,* 73.

4 Nellie Melba, *Melodies and Memories* (London, 1925), 243–44.

5 *New York Daily Tribune,* Dec. 4, 1906.

6 H. E. Krehbiel, *Chapters of Opera* (1908), 367.

7 Cone, *Manhattan Opera Company,* 98–99. John Hetherington, *Melba* (1967), 151–57.

8 Edward N. Waters, *Victor Herbert* (1955), 370. *Musical America,* July 24, 1909: 3.

9 Mary Garden and Louis Biancoli, *Mary Garden's Story* (1951), 62–63.

10 *New York Herald,* Dec. 1, 1907. *Boston Evening Transcript,* Dec. 3, 1912.

11 *New York Times,* Nov. 10, 1907. *Musical America,* Nov. 30, 1907, 1. Cone, *Manhattan Opera Company,* 139.

12 Irving Kolodin, *The Story of the Metropolitan Opera, 1883–1950* (1953), 222. Luisa Tettrazzini, *My Life of Song* (Philadelphia, 1922), 235–41. Cone, *Manhattan Opera Company,* 144–48.

13 Cone, *Manhattan Opera Company,* 152–57. "*Pelléas and Mélisande* has this peculiar distinction among operas. It carries out most clearly and most completely the union of the music to the drama. The [listener] is not looking upon drama . . . he is not thinking upon poetry; he is not listening to music. He is experiencing a vague harmony of all three." *Boston Evening Transcript,* Jan. 15, 1912.

14 *New-York Evening Post,* Nov. 5, 1907.

15 Sheean, *Oscar Hammerstein,* 248–52, 261–62, 274–75.

16 Edward C. Moore, *Forty Years of Opera in Chicago* (1930), 69–76. *New York Daily Tribune,* Jan. 29, 1909. *New York World,* Jan. 29, 1909.

17 *Philadelphia Public Ledger,* Feb. 9, 1909. *Philadelphia Evening Bulletin,* Feb. 11, 1909. Curtis, "Opera in Philadelphia," 2:575–76.

18 *Musical America,* April 10, 1909, 1. Lily McCormack, *I Hear You Calling Me* (Milwaukee, 1949), 55–61.

19 Cone, *Manhattan Opera Company,* 264–68. Henry T. Finck, *Richard Strauss: The Man and His Works* (1917), 245. *New York Sun,* Feb. 1, 1910. On *Elektra* in Boston: *Boston Evening Transcript,* March 29, 1910.

20 Sheean, *Oscar Hammerstein,* 252–54. Cone, *Manhattan Opera Company,* 32, 274–84. Near the end of the 1907–1908 season, Hammerstein told Mary Garden he was going to put on *Salome* next season.

"But isn't it risky?" she asked. "I'm not worried. I'm free to do what I like. I don't have a board of directors." Garden, *Mary Garden's Story,* 123. Carl Van Vechten recorded some of Hammerstein's most revealing comments. "The tobacco business is prose. Opera is poetry. It's more fun to make Melba sing than to make cigars." On *La Traviata:* "He felt there was more sentiment and beauty in the last act of Verdi's opera than in all of Wagner." On Mary Garden: "She does not know how great she is. She knows she is greater than any of the others, but she does not know how much greater." Carl Van Vechten, "Oscar Hammerstein: An Epitaph," in *In the Garret* (1920), 237–59.

Chapter 29. Whiskey per tutti

Giuseppe Adami, ed., *Letters of Giacomo Puccini,* rev. ed. (London, 1974). Mosco Carner, *Puccini: A Critical Biography* (1959). George R. Marek, *Puccini: A Biography* (1951). Charles Osborne, *The Complete Operas of Puccini: A Critical Guide* (London, 1951). Craig Timberlake, *David Belasco: The Bishop of Broadway* (1954). William Winter, *Life of David Belasco* (1918).

1 *New York Daily Tribune,* Dec. 11, 1910. Marek, *Puccini,* 262.
2 Lise-Lane Marker, *David Belasco: Naturalism in the American Theatre* (Princeton, 1975), 139. Winter, *Life of Belasco,* 2:197–208.
3 Carner, *Puccini,* 150.
4 Marek, *Puccini,* 239–41. Carner, *Puccini,* 150.
5 Carner, *Puccini,* 151–54, 176–78. Adami, *Letters of Puccini,* 180–92.
6 *New York Daily Tribune,* Dec. 11, 1910. Adami, *Letters of Puccini,* 193–94.
7 Marek, *Puccini,* 262–69.
8 Timberlake, *David Belasco,* 290. Marek, *Puccini,* 262.
9 Marek, *Puccini,* 265–69. Toscanini said: "There are new things in the music, above all, exquisite new timbres, tones and colors—in the instrumentation. It has more vigor, more variety, more masculinity, than the orchestration of Puccini's earlier operas. It is more complex. In one word, it is more modern." *Boston Evening Transcript,* Nov. 10, 1910.
10 *New York Daily Tribune,* Dec. 18, 1910. *New York Sun,* Dec. 11, 1910. *Boston Evening Transcript,* Dec. 15, 1910.
11 Eugene Bonner, *The Club in the Opera House* (Princeton, 1949), 58. Timberlake, *David Belasco,* 294. Americans were "amused at the operatic miners who wore pistols on the wrong side of their belts, they rejoiced at the 'allo' and 'Eep, eep, urra.'" Edward C. Moore, *Forty Years of Opera in Chicago* (1930), 82.

Chapter 30. Virtuoso Conductors

Oliver Daniel, *Stokowski: A Counterpoint of Views* (1982). Christopher Dyment, *Felix Weingartner: Recollections and Recordings* (London, 1976). David Ewen, *The Man with the Baton: The Story of Conductors and Their Orchestras* (1936). Giulio Gatti-Casazza, *Memories of Opera* (1940). Norman Lebrecht, *Mahler Remembered* (1988). Harold C. Schonberg, *The Great Conductors* (1967).

1 Irving Kolodin, *The Story of the Metropolitan Opera, 1883–1950* (1953), 217–18. Mary Garden and Louis Biancoli, *Mary Garden's Story* (1951), 169.
2 John Frederick Cone, *Oscar Hammerstein's Manhattan Opera Company* (Norman, Okla., 1966), 97.
3 Schonberg, *Great Conductors,* 223–35. Ewen, *Man with the Baton,* 122–26. Heinrich Kralik, *The Vienna Opera* (Vienna, 1963), 64–70.
4 Schonberg, *Great Conductors,* 223. *Musical America,* Nov. 10, 1932, 7. Alma Mahler, *Memories and Letters,* 3d ed. (1975), 135–36. Knud Martner, ed., *Selected Letters of Gustav Mahler* (1979), 301.
5 Martner, *Selected Letters,* 309, 311. Kolodin, *Story of the Metropolitan,* 216. Kralik, *Vienna Opera,* 69.
6 *New York Sun,* March 13, 1909. Alma Mahler, *Memories and Letters,* 3d ed. (1975), 131. Kolodin, *Story of the Metropolitan,* 224, 234–35, 248.

7   *Musical America,* Nov. 10, 1932, 7, 29.

8   On Toscanini: Joseph Horowitz, *Understanding Toscanini* (1987). Harvey Sachs, *Toscanini* (Philadelphia, 1978). Howard Taubman, *The Maestro: The Life of Arturo Toscanini* (1951). Also: Schonberg, *Great Conductors,* and Ewen, *Man with the Baton.*

9   Sachs, *Toscanini,* 104–05, 120. Kolodin, *Story of the Metropolitan,* 274–75. H. T. Parker on Toscanini's *Tristan* in Boston: "Proof that the Wagner of *Tristan* at least is universal and not Teutonic; that quite as high standards and high ideals for the performance of his music dramas prevail on Latin and cosmopolitan stages as on the German; and that the merit of them, in its conductors, singing-actors or scene-painters, depends upon individual intelligence, imagination and executive power, and not upon Teutonic extraction." *Boston Evening Transcript,* Jan. 11, 1910.

10   Kolodin, *Story of the Metropolitan,* 297–96. Sachs, *Toscanini,* 126–31.

11   Sachs, *Toscanini,* 128. *Boston Evening Transcript,* Sept. 30, 1915. Kolodin, *Story of the Metropolitan,* 295–98. Taubman, *Maestro,* 133.

12   Schonberg, *Great Conductors,* 236.

13   Ibid., 236. Ewen, *Man with the Baton,* 162–63. Quaintance Eaton, *The Boston Opera Company* (1965), 153.

14   Eaton, *Boston Opera,* 153.

15   *Boston Evening Transcript,* Jan. 29, 1914.

16   Gilbert Chase, *America's Music,* 3d ed. (Urbana, 1987), 329.

Chapter 31. Boston Renaissance

On Boston: Cleveland Amory, *The Proper Bostonians* (1947). E. Digby Baltzell, *Puritan Boston and Quaker Philadelphia: Two Protestant Ethics and the Spirit of Class Authority and Leadership* (1979). Van Wyck Brooks, *New England: Indian Summer, 1865–1915* (1940). Joseph Edgar Chamberlin, *The Boston Transcript: A History of Its First Hundred Years* (Boston, 1930). Quaintance Eaton, *The Boston Opera Company* (1965). Martin Green, *The Problem of Boston: Some Readings in Cultural History* (1966). M. A. DeWolfe Howe, *A Great Private Citizen: Henry Lee Higginson* (Boston, 1920). H. Earle Johnson, *Symphony Hall, Boston* (Boston, 1950). George B. Oliver, "Changing Pattern of Spectacle on the New York Stage (1850–1890)" (Ph.D. diss., Pennsylvania State University, 1956). Dennis P. Ryan, *Beyond the Ballot Box: A Social History of the Boston Irish* (Rutherford, N.J., 1983). William V. Shannon, *The American Irish* (1963). Ronald Story, *The Forging of an Aristocracy: Harvard and the Boston Upper Class, 1800–1870* (Middletown, Conn., 1980). Stephan Thernstrom, *The Other Bostonians: Poverty and Progress in the American Metropolis, 1880–1970* (Cambridge, 1973). Sam Bass Warner, *Province of Reason* (Cambridge, 1984).

1   Brooks, *New England,* 330. Thernstrom, *Other Bostonians,* 9–28. Johnson, *Symphony Hall,* v. L. E. Tourjée, *For God and Music: The Life Story of Eben Tourjée* (Los Angeles, 1960).

2   Green, *Problem of Boston,* 102–06.

3   Brooks, *New England,* 409.

4   Green, *Problem of Boston,* 110–11.

5   Howe, *Private Citizen,* 1–40. Green, *Problem of Boston,* 108–13. Johnson, *Symphony Hall,* 6–9.

6   Eaton, *Boston Opera,* 41. For an opposing view: *Boston Evening Transcript,* Nov. 3 and 8, 1909.

7   Eaton, *Boston Opera,* 15–20. *Musical America,* Dec. 5, 1908, 1; Sept. 18, 1909, 20 and Dec. 27, 1909, 30. *New York Times,* Aug. 2, 1916.

8   Eaton, *Boston Opera,* 21–29, 7–10. *Musical America,* Sept. 18, 1909, 20.

9   *Musical America,* Sept. 18, 1909, 20.

10   Eaton, *Boston Opera,* 40–41, 44. *Boston Evening Transcript,* Nov. 9, 1909.

11   Eaton, *Boston Opera,* 48, 52.

12   *Boston Evening Transcript,* Nov. 3, 1910. Eaton, *Boston Opera,* 83, 87.

13   *Boston Evening Transcript,* Nov. 4, 8, 12, 15 and Dec. 5, 15, 16, 19, 1910; Jan. 4, 5, 7, 1911.

14 Ibid., Nov. 21 and 26, 1910.

15 Eaton, *Boston Opera,* 135.

16 *Boston Evening Transcript,* Jan. 8, 9 and Feb. 15, 18, 21, 24, 1912.

17 Ibid., Jan. 30 and Feb. 1, 3, 11, 1913.

18 Eaton, *Boston Opera,* 187–90. "That," said McCormack, "was my Big Moment." Lily McCormack, *I Hear You Calling Me* (Milwaukee, 1949), 61.

19 *Boston Evening Transcript,* Dec. 13, 1910.

20 Peter Loeffler, *Adolphe Appia: Staging Wagnerian Drama* (Basel and Boston, 1982), 9–35. *Boston Evening Transcript,* Jan. 7, 1911.

21 Eaton, *Boston Opera,* 211–20. *Boston Evening Transcript,* Dec. 19, 1912, and Jan. 18, 1913.

22 *Boston Evening Transcript,* Nov. 26, 1912. "Well, the audience that can't enjoy Offenbach's music has the blood of a fish; the musician who cannot respect it is lacking in knowledge and understanding of his own art. Let us repeat now without flippancy. Offenbach is the Mozart of operetta." *Boston Evening Transcript,* Jan. 1, 1914.

23 Ibid., Nov. 25, 1913; Jan. 24 and Feb. 24, 1914.

24 Ibid., March 14 and 28; May 7, 12, 28; and June 6 and 16, 1914. Eaton, *Boston Opera,* 253.

25 *Boston Evening Transcript,* Dec. 6, 1913. Eaton, *Boston Opera,* 173–76.

26 *Boston Evening Transcript,* Dec. 6, 1913; Jan. 24, Feb. 24, and March 14 and 28, 1914. Emerson is quoted in Eaton, *Boston Opera,* 80–81.

Chapter 32. The American Muse Again

Gerald Boardman, *American Musical Theatre: A Chronicle* (1978) and *American Operetta: From "H.M.S. Pinafore" to "Sweeney Todd"* (1981). Stanley Green, *The World of Musical Comedy,* rev. ed. (1968). Edward E. Hipsher, *American Opera and Its Composers* (Philadelphia, 1927). Julian Mates, *America's Musical Stage* (Westport, Conn., 1985). MacDonald Smith Moore, "Yankee Blues: Musical Culture and American Identity" (Ph.D. diss., New York University, 1980). Cecil Smith, *Musical Comedy in America* (1950). Judith Tick, "Towards a History of American Women Composers before 1870" (Ph.D. diss., City University of New York, 1979). Edward N. Waters, *Victor Herbert: A Life in Music* (1955).

1 *New York Times,* Oct. 20, 1907. Boardman, *American Operetta,* 74–87. *Musical America,* Oct. 26, 1907: 21. Green, *World of Musical Comedy,* 63. When Rudolf Aronson heard *The Merry Widow* in Berlin, he predicted that it would be a great success in the United States, but a prominent American theater manager to whom Aronson wrote about it disagreed, saying that he didn't want any more "Dutch operas!" Rudolf Aronson, *Theatrical and Musical Memoirs* (1913), 222–23.

2 Boardman, *American Operetta,* 78. Smith, *Musical Comedy,* 154.

3 Boardman, *American Operetta,* 87.

4 Waters, *Victor Herbert,* 3–25, 72–134, 135–91.

5 Ibid., 257–363. Smith, *Musical Comedy,* 175–77. Green, *World,* 37–41.

6 Green, *World,* 25–35. Smith, *Musical Comedy,* 147–52. *Musical America,* Oct. 26, 1907, 1. Stephen M. Vallillo, "George M. Cohan's 'Little Johnny Jones,'" in Glenn Loney, ed., *Musical Theater in America* (Westport, Conn., 1984), 233–42.

7 Mary Jane Matz, *The Many Lives of Otto Kahn* (1963), 68–77. Smith, *Musical Comedy,* 143. *New York Sun,* Nov. 20, 1909.

8 Waters, *Victor Herbert,* 368–69. Boardman, *American Operetta,* 48–50. *Musical America,* July 24, 1909, 3.

9 Matz, *Many Lives,* 55–67. Giulio Gatti-Casazza, *Memories of the Opera* (1941), 237.

10 Irving Kolodin, *The Story of the Metropolitan Opera, 1883–1950* (1953), 252–53. Gatti-Casazza, *Memories,* 237.

11 Kolodin, *Story of the Metropolitan,* 268–69. Gatti-Casazza, *Memories,* 237–38. George W. Chadwick, *Horatio Parker* (New Haven, 1921), 18–21. Sidney Homer, *My Wife and I* (1939), 217.

12 Walter Damrosch, *My Musical Life* (1923), 114–16, 149–52. Kolodin, *Story of the Metropolitan,* 276. Gatti-Casazza, *Memories,* 238–39. *Boston Evening Transcript,* Feb. 28, 1913.

13 Hipsher, *American Opera,* 234–37. Kolodin, *Story of the Metropolitan,* 334.

14 Gatti-Casazza, *Memories,* 240: "Cadman revealed himself a composer of unmistakable lyric gifts. He wrote well for the voice. He had a fluent style, but his libretto was weak, and he was not experienced in the theatre." Harold Briggs, "Indians!" *Opera News,* June 1976, 23–24, 51. Kolodin, *Story of the Metropolitan,* 319. Other Native American operas of the time: Mary Carr Moore, *Narcissa,* 1912; William F. Hanson, *The Sun Dance,* 1913, and *Tam-Man-Nacup,* 1928; Charles Sanford Skilton, *The Sun Bridge,* 1930; Alberto Bimboni, *Winona,* 1926; Arthur Nevin, *Poia,* 1910. Cadman, and all other contemporary composers who drew on Native American materials, were indebted to the labors of Arthur Farwell (1872–1952), editor and composer, who founded the Wa-Wan Press in 1901 and the Wa-Wan Society in 1907, for "the advancement of the work of American composers."

15 Waters, *Victor Herbert,* 367–400. Edward C. Moore, *Forty Years of Opera in Chicago* (1930), 95–98. Mary Garden and Louis Biancoli, *Mary Garden's Story* (1951), 236–39. Kolodin, *Story of the Metropolitan,* 262–63.

Chapter 33. Treemonisha

Coleridge A. Braithwaite, "A Survey of the Lives and Creative Activities of Some Negro Composers" (Doctor of Education diss., Columbia University, 1952). Gilbert Chase, *America's Music: From the Pilgrims to the Present,* 3d ed. (Urbana, 1987). Ronald L. Davis, *History of Music in American Life* (Huntington, N.Y., 1980). Nathan I. Huggins, *Harlem Renaissance* (1971). Glenn Loney, ed., *Musical Theatre in America* (Westport, Conn., 1984). Thomas L. Riis, "Black Musical Theatre in New York, 1890–1915" (Ph.D. diss., University of Michigan, 1981).

1 Chase, *America's Music,* 213–20.

2 Riis, "Black Musical Theatre," 1–5.

3 William T. Upton, *William Henry Fry: American Journalist and Composer-Critic* (1954), 35–36, 44.

4 Russell Sanjek, *American Popular Music and Its Business: The First Four Hundred Years* (1988), 2:219.

5 Riis, "Black Musical Theatre," 13–19, 40–41.

6 Willia Daughtry, "Sissieretta Jones: A Study of the Negro's Contribution to Nineteenth-Century American Concert and Theatrical Life," Ph.D. diss., Syracuse University, 1968. Riis, "Black Musical Theatre," 265–70.

7 Riis, "Black Musical Theatre," 51–92.

8 Ibid., 150–51, 169–93, 232–43.

9 Helen Armstead-Johnson, "Themes and Values in Afro-American Librettos and Book Musicals, 1898–1930," in Loney, *Musical Theatre,* 133–41. Riis, "Black Musical Theatre," 242–43.

10 Lynne Emery, "Black Dance and the American Musical Theatre to 1930," in Loney, *Musical Theatre,* 301–07. Riis, "Black Musical Theatre," 302–19.

11 Chase, *America's Music,* 415–19. Davis, *Music in American Life,* vol. 2, *The Gilded Years, 1865–1920,* 214–18.

12 Chase, *America's Music,* 545–46.

13 Sanjek, *American Popular Music,* 2:302.

Interlude: Enrico Caruso and Geraldine Farrar

Howard Greenfeld, *Caruso* (1983). Stanley Jackson, *Caruso* (1972). Michael Scott, *The Great Caruso* (1988). T. R. Ybarra, *Caruso: The Man of Naples and the Voice of Gold* (1953). On World War I:

Bernays, *Biography of an Idea.* John A. Hawgood, *The Tragedy of German-America: The Germans in the United States of America during the Nineteenth Century—and After* (1940). Barbara L. Tischler, *An American Music: The Search for an American Musical Identity* (1986).

1 Jackson, *Caruso,* 14.
2 Greenfeld, *Caruso,* 73.
3 Jackson, *Caruso,* 107. Greenfeld, *Caruso,* 86–87. Kolodin, *The Story of the Metropolitan Opera, 1883–1950* (1953), 185–86.
4 Kolodin, *Story of the Metropolitan,* 186–87. Greenfeld, *Caruso,* 92.
5 Greenfeld, *Caruso,* 101.
6 Kolodin, *Story of the Metropolitan,* 191–94, 198–99. Greenfeld, *Caruso,* 101–02, 107. *New York Times,* April 13, 1908.
7 Ybarra, *Caruso,* 116, 267. Greenfeld, *Caruso,* 110–111, 176.
8 Greenfeld, *Caruso,* 109.
9 Scott, *Caruso,* 93–96. Jackson, *Caruso,* 149–53.
10 Greenfeld, *Caruso,* 110. Ybarra, *Caruso,* 195–96.
11 Ybarra, *Caruso,* 215, 86–187. Edward Bernays wrote: "His glamor affected me as it did others. I was talking to the sun god and the sun god by his light obliterated his surroundings. When we walked down Broadway together people forgot themselves and their interests for the moment and focused their attention on him. And the strange part was that everyone took this attitude for granted; it appeared the natural thing to do. I wondered why I too felt this way. In this case, I recognized I was letting the public's reaction to Caruso affect my own attitudes. This is how people feel toward movie stars." Edward Bernays, *Biography of an Idea* (1965), 198.
12 Greenfeld, *Caruso,* 235.
13 The quotations in this section, except where indicated otherwise, are from Geraldine Farrar, *Such Sweet Compulsion* (1938), 3–30, 35, 42, 44, 69, 47–51, 87, 121. See also Elizabeth Nash, *Always First Class: The Career of Geraldine Farrar* (Washington, D.C., 1982).
14 Agnes De Mille, *Dance to the Piper* (1952), 19–22. *New York Times,* Feb. 28, 1982.
15 *New York Times,* Feb. 28, 1982.
16 *New York Sun,* Nov. 20, 1920.
17 Kolodin, *Story of the Metropolitan,* 305, 333, 356–57. Eugene Bonner, *The Club in the Opera House* (Princeton, 1970), 62.
18 Ernest Hemingway, *A Farewell to Arms* (1929), 9. Greenfeld, *Caruso,* 235.
19 Greenfeld, *Caruso,* 232–33. See also *Boston Evening Transcript,* March 19, 1913. In 1901 Toscanini said of Caruso: "By God, if this tenor continues to sing like this, he'll have the whole world talking about him!" A few years later, when he heard Caruso at the Metropolitan: "Yes, you make much money—but no! no! NO!" Harvey Sachs, *Toscanini* (1978), 77.
20 Hawgood, *Tragedy,* 287–308. Tischler, *American Music,* 68–91. Giulio Gatti-Casazza, *Memories of Opera* (1941), 178–84.
21 Kolodin, *Story of the Metropolitan,* 302–03. Edward C. Moore, *Forty Years of Opera in Chicago* (1930).
22 Tischler, *American Music,* 72–91. H. Earle Johnson, *Symphony Hall, Boston* (Boston, 1950), 74–80. Theodore Roosevelt added prophecy to hysteria: "If the Boston Symphony Orchestra will not play 'The Star-Spangled Banner,' it ought to be made to shut up. If Dr. Muck will not play it, he ought not to be at large in this country." Tischler, *American Music,* 79.
23 Kolodin, *Story of the Metropolitan,* 313–16. Gatti-Casazza, *Memories,* 178–84. One of the dismissed singers sued for damages. The Metropolitan Opera attorneys cited "intense hatred of the United States" by the singers as justification for breaking their contracts. The courts upheld the Metropolitan.
24 Kolodin, *Story of the Metropolitan,* 338–40, 346–47, 350–51.
25 Alfred Kazin, *A Walker in the City* (1951), 63–64.

Act Five. Technology

Epigraphs: Hermann Hesse, *Steppenwolf,* trans. Basil Creighton (1963), 240. Claude Debussy, *Debussy on Music,* edited François Lesure, translated by Richard Langham Smith (1977), 288.

Chapter 34. Chicago and Samuel Insull

Clarence J. Bulliet, *How Grand Opera Came to Chicago* (Chicago, n.d.). Ronald L. Davis, *Opera in Chicago: A Social and Cultural History, 1850–1965* (1966). Mary Garden and Louis Biancoli, *Mary Garden's Story* (1951). Forrest McDonald, *Insull* (Chicago, 1962). Edward C. Moore, *Forty Years of Opera in Chicago* (1930). Edward Wagenknecht, *Chicago* (Norman, 1964).

1 William F. McDonald, *Federal Relief Administration and the Arts* (Columbus, Ohio, 1969), 84–85.
2 *Boston Evening Transcript,* Feb. 10, 1910. Moore, *Forty Years,* 1–44. Davis, *Opera in Chicago,* 52–75.
3 Bulliet, *Grand Opera,* 1–17. Irving Kolodin, *The Story of the Metropolitan Opera, 1883–1950* (1953), 253. Moore, *Forty Years,* 48, 52–53.
4 Moore, *Forty Years,* 93–94, 106–07, 113, 117–22, 151, 155–56. Davis, *Opera in Chicago,* 78–126. Wagenknecht, *Chicago,* 153–56. Vincent Sheean, *First and Last Love* (1956), 36–48. Wolf-Ferrari's *Il Segreto di Susanna* produced moral outrage of a special kind. Suzanne's secret was that she smoked cigarettes. The sight of her brazenly smoking on stage was appalling to some. One woman said: "Horrible. Horrible. One after another. I saw her with my own eyes. It is enough to turn one forever against grand opera. An artful embellishment of a pernicious vice which should receive the stamp of disapproval from every true American woman." Emmett Dedmon, *Fabulous Chicago,* rev. ed. (1981), 308.
5 Dedmon, *Fabulous Chicago,* 301–02. Bulliet, *Grand Opera,* 28–46. Garden, *Mary Garden's Story,* 169–71. Sheean, *First and Last Love,* 36–51.
6 Garden, *Mary Garden's Story,* 238, 100–101. Moore, *Forty Years,* 240–41. Dedmon, *Fabulous Chicago,* 310.
7 Dedmon, *Fabulous Chicago,* 310.
8 McDonald, *Insull,* 242–43. Moore, *Forty Years,* 240–59. Garden, *Mary Garden's Story,* 245. Davis, *Opera in Chicago,* 127–78.
9 McDonald, *Insull,* 242–45. Wagenknecht, *Chicago,* 155. Moore, *Forty Years,* 305. Garden, *Mary Garden's Story,* 246–47. *Time,* Nov. 4, 1929. *New York Times,* Nov. 3, 1929.
10 Studs Terkel, *Hard Times* (1970), 192. McDonald, *Insull,* 237, 280–85. Moore, *Forty Years,* 341–42.

Chapter 35. Otto Kahn and the Metropolitan

Stephen Birmingham, *Our Crowd* (1967). John Briggs, *Requiem for a Yellow Brick Brewery* (Boston, 1969). Giulio Gatti-Casazza, *Memories of the Opera* (1940). Irving Kolodin, *The Story of the Metropolitan Opera, 1883–1950* (1953). Mary Jane Matz, *The Many Lives of Otto Kahn* (1963).

1 Kolodin, *Story of the Metropolitan,* 350–410. Gatti-Casazza, *Memories,* 215. A performance of *La Bohème,* of "almost unbelievable crudity," "rarely rising above the third rate," suggested that the Metropolitan's view was that "heavy opera needed to be produced but a light opera could be left to produce itself." *New-York Evening Post,* Nov. 5, 1925.
2 Matz, *Many Lives,* 6–43, 55–67.
3 Ibid., 233–34.
4 *Time,* Nov. 2, 1925, 19–24. Matz, *Many Lives,* 83.
5 Birmingham, *Our Crowd,* 330–40. Matz, *Many Lives,* 91.
6 Matz, *Many Lives,* 231.
7 Kolodin, *Story of the Metropolitan,* 21–22.
8 Matz, *Many Lives,* 101. *Time,* Nov. 2, 1925, 19–24.

9 Kolodin, *Story of the Metropolitan*, 23. Robert Goelet, *The Old Order Changeth* (1940), 48–49. Matz, *Many Lives*, 97–102.

10 Matz, *Many Lives*, 87.

Chapter 36. After the Crash

John Briggs, *Requiem for a Yellow Brick Brewery* (Boston, 1969). John Kenneth Galbraith, *The Great Crash* (Boston, 1955). Irving Kolodin, *The Story of the Metropolitan Opera, 1883–1950* (1953). Forrest McDonald, *Insull* (Chicago, 1962).

1 Galbraith, *Great Crash*, 98, 99, 106–30.

2 *Musical America*, Nov. 10, 1930, 3–4, and Nov. 25, 3, 44, and Nov. 10, 1931, 3–4. Studs Terkel, *Hard Times* (1970), 193.

3 Galbraith, *Great Crash*, 120.

4 McDonald, *Insull*, 305–39. *New York Times*, May 18 and Aug. 26 and 27, 1932.

5 Eugene Bonner, *The Club in the Opera House* (Princeton, 1949), 67. Kolodin, *Story of the Metropolitan*, 410–30. Briggs, *Requiem*, 205–12. *Musical America*, Jan. 10, 1931. Giulio Gatti-Casazza, *Memories of the Opera* (1940), 118–19, 313.

6 Kolodin, *Story of the Metropolitan*, 431–56. Bonner, *Club*, 67. Briggs, *Requiem*, 233–41, 253–59. Irving Kolodin, "In Memoriam: Gatti-Casazza," *American Mercury*, May 1935, 33–40.

7 Kolodin, *Story of the Metropolitan*, 398. Briggs, *Requiem*, 151–69.

8 Fortune Gallo, *Lucky Rooster: The Autobiography of an Impresario* (1967).

9 *Time*, Oct. 7, 1935. *Musical America*, Nov. 10, 1932. Gallo said that Enrico Caruso once told him: "This America of yours is a great country populated by many peoples. They love their popular songs. In the larger cities they may hear opera. But in the smaller towns they have only the records we make for their phonographs. That is wrong. Destiny some day will appoint someone to bring opera to them. Whoever it will be will have my prayers and the prayers of everyone who loves opera." *Lucky Rooster*, 112.

10 Edward John Fitzpatrick, Jr., "The Music Conservatory in America" (Doctor of Musical Arts diss., Boston University, 1963). L. E. Tourjée, *For God and Music: The Life Story of Eben Tourjée* (Los Angeles, 1960).

11 *Musical America*, March 25, 1931, 3, 13. Oliver Daniel, *Stokowsky: A Counterpoint of Views* (1982), 260–66.

12 David Bispham, *A Quaker Singer's Recollections* (1921). Oscar Thompson, *The American Singer* (1937). Lawrence Tibbett, *The Glory Road* (1933). Grace Moore, *You're Only Human Once* (1944). Gladys Swarthout, *Come Soon, Tomorrow* (1945).

Chapter 37. The Nordic Winged Victory

Edwin McArthur, *Flagstad: A Personal Memoir* (1965). Vincent Sheean, *First and Last Love* (1956).

1 *New York Times*, Feb. 3, 1935. John Briggs, *Requiem for a Yellow Brick Brewery* (Boston, 1969), 242–50. Irving Kolodin, *The Story of the Metropolitan Opera, 1883–1950* (1953), 446–47. McArthur, *Flagstad*, 7–8. Sheean, *First and Last Love*, 115–16.

2 McArthur, *Flagstad*, 3–9

3 *New York Times*, Feb. 7 and 16, and April 18, 1935. Kolodin, *Story of the Metropolitan*, 447–48.

4 Vincent Sheean, *First and Last Love*, 115–23.

5 *San Francisco Chronicle*, Nov. 5, 1935. When Flagstad made her debut in Vienna in 1936, Felix Weingartner was the conductor. He said of her: "She is the only Wagnerian singer I have conducted who sings absolutely flawlessly." Christopher Dyment, *Felix Weingartner: Recollections and Recordings* (London, 1976), 56.

Chapter 38. Four Saints *and* Porgy and Bess

Merle Armitage, *George Gershwin: Man and Legend* (1958). Gerald Boardman, *American Operetta: From "H.M.S. Pinafore" to "Sweeney Todd"* (1981). Gilbert Chase, *America's Music,* 3d ed. (Urbana, 1975). Lehman Engel, *The American Musical Theater,* rev. ed. (1975). David Ewen, *A Journey to Greatness: The Life and Music of George Gershwin* (1956). Isaac Goldberg, *George Gershwin: A Study in American Music* (1958). Stanley Green, *The World of Musical Comedy* (1960). Kathleen Hoover and John Cage, *Virgil Thomson* (1959). Edward Jablonski and Lawrence D. Stewart, *The Gershwin Years* (1958). Julian Mates, *America's Musical Stage* (Westport, Conn., 1985). Wilfrid Mellers, *Music in a New Found Land,* rev. ed. (1987). Ethan Mordden, *Opera in the Twentieth Century: Sacred, Profane, Godot* (1978). Cecil Smith, *Musical Comedy in America* (1950). Virgil Thomson, *Virgil Thomson* (1966).

1 Smith, *Musical Comedy,* 239–43. Green, *World,* 37–47, 49–61. Boardman, *American Operetta,* 107–28.
2 Chase, *America's Music,* 334–35, 376–77. Smith, *Musical Comedy,* 234–35. Nathan Irvin Huggins, *Harlem Renaissance* (1971).
3 Green, *World,* 63–83. Smith, *Musical Comedy,* 207–08, 210–16.
4 Smith, *Musical Comedy,* 274–76. Boardman, *American Operetta,* 134–36.
5 Green, *World,* 79–83.
6 Giulio Gatti-Casazza, *Memories of Opera* (1941), 242–44. Mary Jane Matz, *The Many Lives of Otto Kahn* (1963), 94–95, 226–27. Irving Kolodin, *The Story of the Metropolitan Opera, 1883–1950* (1953), 419–20.
7 Kolodin, *Story of the Metropolitan,* 435, 441–42.
8 Thomson, *Virgil Thomson,* 3–72. Hoover and Cage, *Virgil Thomson,* 13–49.
9 Thomson, *Virgil Thomson,* 73–83. Hoover and Cage, *Virgil Thomson,* 50–79. Noel Stock, *The Life of Ezra Pound,* rev. ed. (San Francisco, 1982), 252–56, 263–67, 288–89. See also Thomson, *Music with Words* (New Haven, 1989).
10 Thomson, *Virgil Thomson,* 89–107. Hoover and Cage, *Virgil Thomson,* 80–84.
11 Chase, *America's Music,* 549–50. Mordden, *Opera,* 303–04. Thomson, *Virgil Thomson,* 236–47. *New York Times,* Feb. 21, 1934. Hoover and Cage, *Virgil Thomson,* 156–58. Virgil Thomson, "Words and Music," *New York Review of Books,* April 13, 1989, 43. Donna Graves, "'In Spite of Alien Temperature and Alien Insistence': Emily Dickinson and Florine Stettheimer," *Woman's Art Journal,* Fall 1982–Winter 1983, 21–27. Parker Tyler, *Florine Stettheimer: A Life in Art* (1963).
12 Ewen, *Journey,* 29–37, 38–50, 59–63.
13 Jablonski and Stewart, *Gershwin Years,* 76–79, 81–87. Ewen, *Journey,* 96–98, 103–14. Goldberg, *Gershwin,* 142–63.
14 Green, *World,* 119–23.
15 Ibid., 113–14.
16 Ewen, *Journey,* 251–68. Jablonski and Stewart, *Gershwin Years,* 177–215. *New York Times,* July 21, 1935. Brian Lanker, *I Dream a World* (1989), 20.
17 Ewen, *Journey,* 268–69. Green, *World,* 125–27. *Time,* Oct. 21, 1935, 48.
18 *New York Times,* Oct. 20, 1935. Ewen, *Journey,* 267, 269.
19 Ewen, *Journey,* 267. "An objective evaluation of *Porgy and Bess* was made difficult not only by the operatic expectations it aroused but also by the drastic cuts of the initial production and the several productions that followed, thus obscuring some of the operatic features while emphasizing the 'Broadway' aspect. It is a curious fact, indicative of the eccentricities in America operatic history, that *Porgy and Bess* had to wait until the 1970s before it was produced in its complete form—not only as 'a real American opera' but also as a *real* opera. There is an analogy between *Treemonisha,* which arose like the phoenix from the ashes of oblivion, and *Porgy and Bess,* which suddenly appeared in its full dramatic stature some four decades after its initial production." Chase, *America's Music,* 547.

Chapter 39. New Deal America in Peace and War

Arthur Bloomfield, *The San Francisco Opera, 1923–1961* (1961). Ronald L. Davis, *A History of Opera in the American West* (Englewood Cliffs, N.J., 1965). Hallie Flanagan, *Arena* (1940). Donald Fleming and Bernard Bailyn, eds., *The Intellectual Migration: Europe and America, 1930–1960* (Cambridge, Mass., 1969). John Houseman, *Run-Through: A Memoir* (1972). William F. McDonald, *Federal Relief Administration and the Arts* (Columbus, Ohio, 1969). Richard D. McKinzie, *The New Deal for Artists* (Princeton, 1973). Francis V. O'Connor, ed., *Art for the Millions: Essays from the 1930s by Artists and Administrators of the WPA Federal Art Project* (Greenwich, Conn., 1973). Grace Overmeyer, *Government and the Arts* (1939). Ralph Purcell, *Government and Art* (Washington, D.C., 1956). Arthur M. Schlesinger, Jr., *The Age of Roosevelt,* 3 vols. (Boston, 1956–), vol. 3, *The Politics of Upheaval* (1960). Martin Sokol, *The New York City Opera: An American Adventure* (1981). Barbara L. Tischler, *An American Music* (1986).

1 Schlesinger, *Politics,* 343–61. McDonald, *Federal Relief,* 66–83, 116–33.
2 McDonald, *Federal Relief,* 584–46. Virgil Thomson, *Virgil Thomson* (1967), 248–68.
3 Houseman, *Run-Through,* 245. See also Eric A. Gordon, *Mark the Music: The Life and Work of Marc Blitzstein* (1989).
4 Flanagan, *Arena,* 201–06. Houseman, *Run-Through,* 247.
5 Houseman, *Run-Through,* 249–79.
6 Bloomfield, *San Francisco Opera,* 1–42.
7 Bloomfield, *San Francisco Opera,* 43–46, 48–64. *Musical America,* Oct. 25, 1932, 5.
8 Sokol, *New York City Opera,* 1–46, 50–56.
9 Kolodin, *The Story of the Metropolitan Opera, 1883–1950* (1953), 495–96.
10 Helen Traubel, *St. Louis Woman* (1959), ix, 14–23, 59, 66–70, 88–105, 112, 131.
11 Fleming and Bailyn, eds., *Intellectual Migration,* 3–10. Kolodin, *Story of the Metropolitan,* 501, 516–17.
12 Stanley Green, *The World of Musical Comedy,* rev. ed. (1968), 251–57. Matthew Scott, "Weill in America: The Problem of Revival," in Kim H. Kowalke, ed., *A New Orpheus: Essays on Kurt Weil* (New Haven, 1986).
13 Truman Capote, *The Muses Are Heard* (1956).

Interlude: Milton Cross

Erik Barnouw, *A History of Broadcasting in the United States,* 2 vols. (1966), vol. 1, *A Tower in Babel.* Roland Gelatt, *The Fabulous Phonograph, 1877–1977,* rev. ed. (1977).

1 Barnouw, *Broadcasting,* 1:27, 88.
2 Ibid., 178–79, 283.
3 *Music Trade Review,* July 1950, 26–27. A. J. Elias, "Mister Opera," *Etude,* December 1955, 18. Milton Cross, "More Than Meets the Ear: The Met Broadcasts," *Theatre Arts,* January 1957, 68–69. "This Is 'Mr. Opera,'" *Opera News,* Feb. 23, 1959, 14–15. Milton Cross, "My View Has Changed," *Opera,* Dec. 23, 1961, 6. *New York Times,* Jan. 4, 1975.
4 Giulio Gatti-Casazza, *Memories of Opera* (1940), 304.
5 All the quotations in this section are from Gelatt, *Fabulous Phonograph,* 21, 30, 32, 115, 118–21, 148–49, 194, 219–28, 252.
6 Ibid., 175.
7 *Stereo Review,* January 1973, 59–65.
8 Ibid., 65.

Act Six. Empire

Epigraph: Kenneth Clark, *Civilization* (1969), 243.

Chapter 40. The New Audience

Arthur Bloomfield, *The San Francisco Opera, 1923–1961* (1961). Irving Kolodin, *The Metropolitan Opera, 1883–1966* (1967). Martin L. Sokol, *The New York City Opera: An American Adventure* (1981).

1 Garry O'Connor, *The Pursuit of Perfection: A Life of Maggie Teyte* (London, 1979), 200–201. *New York Herald Tribune,* March 5, 1952.

2 Harvey Sachs, *Toscanini* (1978), 306. Joseph Horowitz, *Understanding Toscanini* (1987), 283–306.

3 *New York Times,* Oct. 22, 1982.

4 *New York Times,* July 6, 1984.

5 Harry Haskell, *The Early Music Revival: A History* (London, 1988), 131–52. Roland Gelatt, *The Fabulous Phonograph, 1877–1977,* rev. ed. (1977), 301.

6 Bloomfield, *San Francisco Opera,* 77–119. Robert Commanday in the *San Francisco Chronicle,* Feb. 9, 1988.

7 *San Francisco Chronicle,* Feb. 9, 1988. Cobbett Steinberg, "The San Francisco Hotel Tax Fund: Twenty-five Years of Innovative Arts Funding, 1961–1986," *Encore* 3 (Spring 1986), 4–61.

8 All quotations in this section are from Sokol, *New York City Opera,* 57–147, 162. See also Andrew H. Drummond, *American Opera Librettos* (Metuchen, N.J., 1973); H. E. Johnson, *Opera on American Subjects* (1964); and C. Northouse, *Twentieth-Century Opera in England and the United States* (Boston, 1976).

9 All quotations in this section come from Kolodin, *Metropolitan Opera,* 493–97, 595, 602, 619–20, 710.

10 *New York Times,* July 23, 1981. Arianna Stassinopoulos, *Maria Callas: The Woman behind the Legend* (1981), 112–14.

11 *New York Times,* July 23 and Aug. 2, 1981. *Chicago Tribune,* July 22, 1981.

Chapter 41. Marian Anderson

Marian Anderson, *My Lord, What a Morning* (1956). Martin Duberman, *Paul Robeson* (1988). Sol Hurok, *Impresario: A Memoir* (1946). Hugh Lee Lyon, *Leontyne Price: Highlights of a Prima Donna* (1973). Paul Robeson, *Here I Stand* (Boston, 1958). Kosti Vehanen, *Marian Anderson: A Portrait* (1941).

1 Anderson, *My Lord,* 38–39, 11.

2 Ibid., 14, 29, 35, 48–53, 56–57.

3 Ibid., 37–45.

4 *New York Times,* Aug. 27, 1925. Anderson, *My Lord,* 73–74.

5 Anderson, *My Lord,* 117.

6 Vehanen, *Marian Anderson,* 15–23. Anderson, *My Lord,* 144–45.

7 Hurok, *Impresario,* 244, 240. Vehanen, *Marian Anderson,* 25–31, 127–31. Anderson, *My Lord,* 148–49, 155, 157–58.

8 Hurok, *Impresario,* 237–40.

9 Anderson, *My Lord,* 170. Hurok, *Impresario,* 242–43, 251–52.

10 Peggy Anderson, *The Daughters: An Unconventional Look at America's Fan Club—the DAR* (1974). Margaret Gibbs, *The DAR* (1969). Anderson, *My Lord,* 188–90.

11 Anderson, *My Lord,* 190–93.

12 David W. Look and Carole L. Perrault, *The Interior Building: Its Architecture and Its Art,* Preservation Case Studies (Washington, D.C., 1986), 113–14. *Washington Post,* Jan. 10, 1943.

13 Anderson, *My Lord,* 293–94.

14 Rudolf Bing, *5,000 Nights at the Opera* (1972), 228. Anderson, *My Lord,* 301.

15 *New York Times,* Jan. 8, 1955.

16 Anderson, *My Lord,* 302–03. *New York Times,* Jan. 8, 1955. John Francis Marion, *Within These Walls* (Philadelphia, 1984), 260–61.

17 The Paul Robeson quotations are from Duberman, *Paul Robeson,* 55, 67, 111.
18 Brian Lanker, *I Dream a World: Portraits of Black Women Who Changed America* (1989), 44.
19 Eleanor Scott, *The First Twenty Years of the Santa Fe Opera* (Santa Fe, 1976), 70.

Chapter 42. New York Opera

Leonard Bernstein, *The Joy of Music* (1959). Gerald Boardman, *American Operetta: From "H.M.S. Pinafore" to "Sweeney Todd"* (1981). Stanley Green, *The World of Musical Comedy: The Story of the American Musical Stage as Told Through the Careers of Its Foremost Composers and Lyricists,* rev. ed. (1968). Abe Laufe, *Broadway's Greatest Musicals* (1969). Julian Mates, *America's Musical Stage: Two Hundred Years of Musical Theater* (Westport, Conn., 1985). Ethan Mordden, *Broadway Babies: The People Who Made the American Musical* (1983). Cecil Smith, *Musical Comedy in America* (1950).

1 Green, *World,* 142, 151. *New York Times, Theatre* magazine, and *New York Herald Tribune,* as quoted in Green, *World,* 148.
2 Smith, *Musical Comedy,* 302.
3 Wolcott Gibbs was the critic who liked it, Brooks Atkinson the one who didn't. Quoted in Green, *World,* 161. Smith, *Musical Comedy,* 306–08.
4 Green, *World,* 276, 283–85. Smith, *Musical Comedy,* 346–47. Mordden, *Broadway Babies,* 138–46.
5 Green, *World,* 285–86. Mordden, *Broadway Babies,* 133–36. Smith, *Musical Comedy,* 343–45. Gerald Boardman devotes a chapter to *Oklahoma* as the exemplar of the musical play as folk operetta or people's opera. See *American Operetta,* 149–54.
6 Green, *World,* 343.
7 "Cole Porter . . . appears never to have been simple, never artless." Smith, *Musical Comedy,* 308. Green, *World,* 182, 197.
8 On *Paint Your Wagon,* see Green, *World,* 301. Boardman, *American Operetta,* 176.
9 Green, *World,* 257–59. Ethan Mordden, *Opera in the Twentieth Century: Sacred, Profane, Godot* (1978), 320–21. Mordden, *Broadway Babies,* 125–28. *New York Herald Tribune,* April 9, 1950.
10 Green, *World,* 292, 295.
11 Mordden, *Broadway Babies,* 185–96. Boardman, *American Operetta,* 174–75. Mates, *America's Musical Stage,* 198–200.

Chapter 43. The New Places

William G. B. Carson, *St. Louis Goes to the Opera, 1837–1941* (St. Louis, 1946). Robert I. Giesberg, *Houston Grand Opera: A History* (Houston, 1981). Harry Haskell, *The Early Music Revival: A History* (London, 1988). Eleanor Scott, *The First Twenty Years of the Santa Fe Opera* (Santa Fe, 1976). Gary Jack Weisenthal, "An Anatomy of Regional Opera: A Study of American Opera, Its Development, Practice, and Place in the Community" (M.A. diss., University of Louisville, 1980).

1 The quotations in this section are from Scott, *Santa Fe Opera,* 27, 5, 8, 73, 51, 11, 32, 13, 73–74, 53, 128, 81.
2 *Dallas Times Herald,* "Opera Coast to Coast," undated clipping supplied by Dallas Opera.
3 *Dallas Morning News,* Jan. 7, 1990.
4 *Dallas Times Herald,* Jan. 14, 1990.
5 The quotations in this section are from Giesberg, *Houston Grand Opera,* 5–6, 14, 15, 23, 24, 26.
6 "1983–1984 Season," Seattle Opera program, n.p.
7 *New York Times,* Aug. 20, 1989.
8 Sol Smith quoted in Carson, *St. Louis,* 1. Other quotations in this section are from ibid., 9, 11, 25, 28, 32.

Chapter 44. The Song of the Thrush

1 Arianna Stassinopoulos, *Maria Callas: The Woman behind the Legend* (1981), 205.
2 Stassinopoulos, *Callas,* 248–49. Vincent Sheean, *First and Last Love* (1956), 100–101.
3 Peter Conrad, *A Song of Love and Death: The Meaning of Opera* (1987), 357, 360, 20.
4 Irving Kolodin, *The Story of the Metropolitan Opera, 1883–1950* (1953), 143.
5 Fortune Gallo, *Lucky Rooster: The Autobiography of an Impresario* (1967), 282.
6 *New York Tribune,* March 2, 1960.
7 *New York Herald Tribune,* March 5, 1960. This prize-winning account was by Sanche de Gramont. *New York Times,* March 5, 1960. Irving Kolodin, *Story of the Metropolitan,* 634–37. Rudolf Bing, *5,000 Nights at the Opera* (1972), 262–63.

Chapter 45. Three Operatic Monuments

William J. Baumol and William G. Bowen, *Performing Arts—The Economic Dilemma: A Study of Problems Common to Theater, Opera, Music and Dance* (1966). Milton Goldin, *The Music Merchants* (1969). Rosanne Martorella, *The Sociology of Opera* (1982). Bruce McConachie and Daniel Friedman, *Theatre for Working-Class Audiences in the United States, 1830–1980* (Westport, Conn., 1985). Jack Poggi, *Theater in America: The Impact of Economic Forces, 1870–1967* (Ithaca, 1968). Russell Sanjek, *American Popular Music and Its Business: The First Four Hundred Years* (1988). Jay R. S. Teran, "The New York Opera Audience, 1825–1974" (Ph.D. diss., New York University, 1974). Alvin Toffler, *The Culture Consumers* (1964).

1 Brian Lanker, *I Dream a World: Portraits of Black Women Who Changed America* (1989), 44.
2 Toffler, *Culture Consumers,* 16–23.
3 The quotations in this section are from Baumol and Bowen, *Performing Arts,* 43–69, 164, 153.
4 Irving Kolodin, *The Story of the Metropolitan Opera, 1883–1950* (1953), 196–99. Edward C. Moore, *Forty Years of Opera in Chicago* (1930), 160–63.
5 Quotations in this section are from Robert D. Leiter, *The Musicians and Petrillo* (1953), 9–53.
6 On Lincoln Center, see Ralph G. Martin, *Lincoln Center for the Performing Arts* (1971); Edgar B. Young, *Lincoln Center: The Building of an Institution* (1981); and Martin L. Sokol, *The New York City Opera: An American Adventure* (1981). Sokol, *City Opera,* 167. Martin, *Lincoln Center,* 18.
7 Young, *Lincoln Center,* 35–48. Martin, *Lincoln Center,* 14. *New York Times,* May 15, 1959.
8 Sokol, *City Opera,* 166–73.
9 Martin, *Lincoln Center,* 18–19.
10 *New York Times,* May 23, 1964. Martin, *Lincoln Center,* 55, 61.
11 *Life,* Sept. 30, 1966, 30–42. *New York Times,* Sept. 17, 1966.
12 *New York Times,* Sept. 17, 1966. Martin, *Lincoln Center,* 12.
13 David Gebhard, "Edward Durrell Stone." *Britannica Encyclopedia of American Art,* 542–43.
14 *New York Times,* Sept. 6–7, 1971. "Capital Glitter," *Opera News,* September 1971, pp. 9–11.
15 "Can Do," *Opera News,* October 1987, pp. 12–16. *New York Times,* May 8 and 11, 1987.
16 Annual Reports, National Endowment for the Arts, 1967, 1972, 1977, 1982, and 1987 (Government Printing Office, Washington, D.C.).

Chapter 46. Sarah Caldwell Presents

Leslie Banner, *A Passionate Preference: The Story of the North Carolina School of the Arts* (Winston-Salem, 1987). Gary J. Weisenthal, "An Anatomy of Regional Opera: A Study of American Opera, Its Development, Practice, and Place in the Community (M.A. thesis, University of Louisville, 1980).
1 "Directory of Opera Companies and Workshops in the United States and Canada," Central Opera

Service *Bulletin* 14, no. 2 (December 1971). Compare the list of opera companies and workshops put out by the Central Opera Service in August 1966 and March 1979. Eleanor Scott, *The First Twenty Years of the Santa Fe Opera* (Santa Fe, 1976), 19.

2 *Opera Now!* (Bloomington, Ind., n.d.). Banner, *Passionate Preference.* Peter Stansky, "Peter Grimes, Jan Popper, and Stanford," in Stanford Historical Society, *Sandstone and Tile* 12, nos. 2–3 (Winter–Spring 1988), 8–11.

3 Quaintance Eaton, "Renaissance Woman," *Opera News,* April 18, 1964, 26–29.

4 "She Puts the Oomph in the Opera," *Life,* March 5, 1965, 77–85.

5 Ibid., 77–78.

6 *Opera News,* April 18, 1964, 28–29. Winthrop Sargeant, *New Yorker,* Oct. 14, 1967, 154. Andrew Porter, *New Yorker,* Jan. 6, 1975, 61–63.

7 Winthrop Sargeant, *New Yorker,* Oct. 14, 1967, 154. *Life,* March 5, 1965, 78.

8 Jack Beeson and H. Wiley Hitchcock, "Douglas Moore," *The New Grove Dictionary of American Music,* 3:266–67. Virgil Thomson, *American Music since 1910* (1970), 161–62.

9 Kathleen Hoover and John Cage, *Virgil Thomson: His Life and Music* (1959), 105–07.

10 Ibid., 201–03.

11 Virgil Thomson, *Virgil Thomson* (1966), 385.

12 Gregory Sandow and Pamela Bristah, "Philip Glass," *The New Grove Dictionary of American Music,* 2:228–29.

13 Ralph G. Martin, *Lincoln Center for the Performing Arts* (1971), 132.

14 Martin, *Lincoln Center,* 66. Peter Conrad, "Drama against Music," in *A Song of Love and Death: The Meaning of Opera* (1987), 278–91.

15 *Observer* (London), Nov. 19, 1989.

16 W. H. Auden, "Metalogue to *The Magic Flute,*" in *Homage to Clio* (1960), 71–72.

17 Beverly Sills and Lawrence Linderman, *Beverly: An Autobiography* (1987), 315, 331–34, 339.

18 Patrick J. Smith, *A Year at the Met* (1983), 150–57, 211–15.

Chapter 47. Mozart in America

1 April Fitzlyon, *The Price of Genius: A Life of Pauline Viardot* (1964), 152–53.

2 Lord Derwent, *Rossini and Some Forgotten Nightingales* (1934), 27.

3 George C. D. Odell, *Annals of the New York Stage* (1927–49), 4:299.

4 Ibid., 3:621.

5 Max Maretzek, *Crotchets and Quavers, or Revelations of an Opera Manager in America* (1855), 98–99.

6 George Templeton Strong, *The Diary of George Templeton Strong* (1952), 7:421.

7 Ibid., 2:421–23, 470–71.

8 *Strong, Diary,* 2:471. George Bernard Shaw, *Shaw's Music* (1981), 2:482.

9 Odell, *Annals,* 7:158. *Dwight's Journal of Music,* June 4, 1870, 249–50 (a reprint of a Dwight article which first appeared in 1858).

10 Henry and Sidney Cowell, *Charles Ives and His Music* (1955), 23, 37. Chopin's failing was the same. "Most of Chopin is pretty soft, but you did not mind it in him so much, because one naturally thinks of him with a skirt on him, but one which he made himself" (p. 89).

11 *Putnam's Monthly Magazine,* May 1855, 510–15.

12 *Harper's New Monthly Magazine,* May 1881, 945. Robert D. Faner, *Walt Whitman and Opera* (Philadelphia, 1951), 52. *Dwight's Journal of Music,* March 5, 1870, 212, and June 4, 1870, 249.

13 Strong, *Diary,* 4:38. Odell, *Annals,* 4:64.

14 Alma Mahler, *Gustav Mahler: Memories and Letters* (Seattle, 1975), 22. Virgil Thomson, *Virgil Thomson* (1966), 307. Vincent Sheean, *First and Last Love* (1956), 223–24.

15 Edward C. Moore, *Forty Years of Opera in Chicago* (1930), 432. *New York Times,* March 25, 1922.

16 Irving Kolodin, *The Story of the Metropolitan Opera, 1883–1950* (1953), 432.

17 *New York Times,* Feb. 8, 1989.

18 Andrew Porter, *Financial Times* (London), July 15, 1965.

19 Herbert Weinstock, *Rossini: A Biography* (1968), 347.

Finale. Maria Callas

George Jellinek, *Callas: Portrait of a Prima Donna* (1960). Pierre-Jean Rémy, *Maria Callas: A Tribute* (1978). Adriana Stassinopoulos, *Maria Callas: The Woman behind the Legend* (1981).

1 Stassinopoulos, *Callas,* 6, 10, 13, 17, 18, 19, 21, 22, 24, 25.

2 Ibid., 52, 55.

3 Ibid., 63.

4 Ibid., 97–98, 101, 115. Elisabeth Schwarzkopf, *On and off the Record: A Memoir of Walter Legge* (1982), 203.

5 Schwarzkopf, *On and off the Record,* 199.

6 Irving Kolodin, *The Metropolitan Opera, 1883–1966* (1967), 576. Victor Gollancz, *Journey towards Music: A Memoir* (1965), 24–25. Schwarzkopf, *On and off the Record,* 194, 199.

7 On *Medea,* see Peter Conrad, *A Song of Love and Death: The Meaning of Opera* (1987), 320–21. Stassinopoulos, *Callas,* 106. On *Tosca,* see Kolodin, *Metropolitan Opera,* 719–20.

8 Wallace Stevens, "The Idea of Order at Key West."

9 Conrad, *Song,* 330. Marilyn Horne, *Marilyn Horne: My Life* (1983), 134.

10 Beverly Sills and Lawrence Linderman, *Beverly: An Autobiography* (1987), 1.

11 Sills and Linderman, *Beverly,* 54–55, 60.

12 Horne, *Marilyn Horne,* 132.

Index

Page numbers in **boldface** refer to illustrations.

Abbey, Henry, 219–22, 289
Abbott, Emma, 264–68, 273, 513
Academy of Music. *See under* New York: Opera
  houses; Philadelphia
Adam, Adolphe, 91, 261
Adams, Charles R., 301, 442
Adams, Henry, 243, 312
Adams, John, 533, 542
Adler, Dankmar, 251–54
Adler, Kurt Herbert, 587–88
African Americans: musical theater of, 105–08,
  386–94, 448–49, **205**; as performers, 383–
  86, 451, 455, 459–63, 492–501, **465**; restric-
  tions on, in musical life, 26, 165, 261, 294,
  383, 440, 452, 498–99
African Grove. *See under* New York: Opera
  houses
Alboni, Marietta, 139–45, 156, 179, 186–88,
  224, 280
Alcott, Louisa May, 145
Alda, Frances, 379–81
Aldrich, Richard, 370, 551
Alexander, John, 552
Alfano, Franco, 418
Althouse, Paul, 381, 433, 442–43
Alvary, Max, 242
Amato, Pasquale, 340, 379
Amato Opera, 536
American Opera Company, 238, 263, 516
Anderson, Marian, 492–99, 530
Angrisani, Felix, 5, 9, 11
Anschutz, Karl, 233
Antheil, George, 453–54
Antognini, Cirillo, 123
Appia, Adolphe, 365–66
Arditi, Luigi, 122, 140, 175, 179, 219
Argento, Dominick, 513
Arne, Thomas, 100; *Love in a Village,* 20, 23, 47,
  85
Arnold, Samuel, 47
Aronson, Rudolph, 208–11
Astor Place Opera House. *See under* New York:
  Opera houses
Auber, Daniel, 28, 30, 50, 53, 111, 120–21,
  142, 159, 166, 261

Aubry, Eugene, 534
Auden, W. H., 72, 544
Audiences: associated with court life in Europe,
  33–34, 38–40; challenge to court monopoly,
  35–37, 40–42; immigrants in, 8, 25–27, 32,
  158–59, 231–33, 239–44, 321–22, 357–58,
  361, 456; influence of radio and recordings in
  expanding, 474–81, 485–87, 536–37; pru-
  dishness, 53–54, 131–34, 192, 313–16; social diversity, 50–53, 65–70, 109–15, 155–
  65, 174–75, 208–09, 269–79, 281–83, 321–
  27, 361–63, 418–21; women in, 50–52,
  131–38, 172–73, 266–68, 285–86, 362–63,
  404–05. *See also under* Opera houses
Auditorium. *See under* Chicago
Audran, Edmond, 199, 272, 283

Baccaloni, Salvatore, 433
Balfe, Michael William, 267; *The Bohemian Girl,*
  93–97, 111, 159, 193, 247, 261, 266, 274–
  76, 569*n*6
Ballad opera: adopted by American composers,
  21–22, 46–48, 373–74; disdain for, 26–30,
  97, 100–103, 377–80; origins, 17; trans-
  formed into American idiom, 93–97, 202–
  07, 502–07
Baltimore, 18, 46, 63; Peabody Conservatory of
  Music, 440
Barber, Samuel, 531
Barilli-Patti, Caterina, 178, 185
Barnum, Phineas Taylor, 126–38, 147–48, 168,
  170–71, 184
Bartók, Béla, 472, 488
Barton, Andrew (pseud?): *The Disappointment,*
  21, 22
Beardstown, Ill., Opera House, 280
Beecham, Thomas, 471, 480, 551
Beethoven, Ludwig van, 153, 234; *Fidelio,* 50,
  92, 101, 233, 239, 241, 250, 283, 350, 556
Beggar's Opera, The, 17–23, 30, 66, 503
Belasco, David, 115, 339–44, 365
Bellini, Vincenzo, 74, 77, 125, 146, 159, 171,
  261, 325, 557; *Norma,* 31–32, 99–101, 112,
  117–18, 127, 144–45, 147, 160, 169, 178,
  186, 247, 283, 320, 490, 558–59; *La Sonnam-
  bula,* 88, 91, 101, 109, 111, 117, 140, 181,
  186, 220, 247, 250, 265–66, 320, **182**